Thi book is

CONCISE COLLEGE TEXTS

"A" LEVEL LAW

Other Books in This Series

AUSTRALIA
LBC Information Services
Sydney

CANADA AND USA
Carswell
Toronto

NEW ZEALAND
Brooker's
Auckland

SINGAPORE AND MALAYSIA
Thomson Information (S.E. Asia)
Singapore

CONCISE COLLEGE TEXTS

"A" LEVEL LAW

FOURTH EDITION

The Late BRIAN HOGAN, LL.B.
of Gray's Inn, Barrister,
Professor of Common Law, University of Leeds

PETER SEAGO, J.P., LL.M.
Senior Lecturer in Law,
University of Leeds

GEOFFREY BENNETT, M.A.
of the Inner Temple, Barrister,
Professor of Law, University of Notre Dame

LONDON
SWEET & MAXWELL
1996

Published in 1996 by
Sweet & Maxwell Ltd of
100 Avenue Road,
London
Computerset by P.B. Computer Typesetting,
Pickering, N. Yorks
Printed in England by Clays Ltd, St Ives plc

A CIP catalogue record for this book
is available from the British Library

ISBN 0421 548800

Preface

Our colleague, Brian Hogan, had just finished working on his part of this fourth edition when he became ill and, following a short illness, died in February. He will be remembered for many qualities. As co-author of Smith and Hogan's Criminal Law and a former Editor of the Criminal Law Review he was undoubtedly one of the leading criminal lawyers of his time. He was also a very fine teacher who thrived on the challenge of explaining complex points of law to all manner of audiences and this is what originally attracted him towards producing a book for A Level Law students. Perhaps most of all he will be remembered as an extremely kind and humorous person; meetings at which he was present were rarely dull.

Once again in the four years that have elapsed since the last edition there have been many developments particularly in the Criminal Law area decisions of the House of Lords have necessitated the re-writing of the sections on provocation as a defence to murder, gross negligence, manslaughter and involuntary intoxication. Additionally there have been important new decisions on automatism and the use of force in public and private defence. Students of Criminal Law should make every effort to read the consultation papers produced by the Law Commission during this period on a variety of topics. Not only do they point the way to possible future reforms of the criminal law, they also provide an excellent statement of the current position. We have made reference to these throughout the text, but the confines of space prevent any full discussion of them.

Whilst developments in the law of contract have been less dramatic few pages have escaped some revision. Account has been taken of recent legislation such as the Sale and Supply of Goods Act 1994 and the potentially very significant impact on consumers and suppliers alike of the Unfair Terms in Consumer Contracts Regulations 1994. In the area of case law revision of the topic of undue influence has been necessitated by recent decisions of the House of Lords and the Court of Appeal.

In the English Legal System section new materials include the Report of the Royal Commission on Criminal Justice (1993) and the transfer under the Criminal Appeals Act 1995 to an independent body of the Home Secretary's power to refer cases to the Court of Appeal. In the area of statutory interpretation *Pepper v. Hart* is a major new decision by the House of Lords.

We are indebted to Nick Taylor for his assistance with the English Legal System section and to our publishers for their help in the preparation of this edition.

We have attempted to state the law as it was on June 1st 1996.

Peter Seago   Geoffrey Bennett

The Publishers would like to take this opportunity to express their sadness at the death of Brian Hogan, and to extend their condolences to his family. His extraordinary contribution to legal education over the past 40 years is well known and has been acknowledged by his colleagues above. Sweet & Maxwell would like to express their particular gratitude for his 30 year association with the company and for his contribution to various publications during that period.

Addendum

Law Reform (Year and a Day Rule) Act 1996

Until the Law Reform (Year and a Day Rule) Act 1996 came into effect it was an essential element of all offences involving the causing of death and of suicide that the death should have occurred within a year and a day of the last act of the accused alleged to have caused the death. Thus in Dyson (1908) (below page 9) the failure of the prosecution to establish this element of the *actus reus* meant that his conviction for manslaughter had to be quashed. In earlier days medical science would have been unable in many cases to substantiate the allegation that the accused's act had caused the death of the victim and so an irrebuttable presumption that a death which occurred after a year and a day was not caused by the accused provided a rough and ready test of causation (see below page 199). The advances of medical science make such a presumption unneccessary and evidence may be able to establish that the cause of death was an injury inflicted, for example, two years previously. However, until the passing of the present Act of Parliament such medical evidence would have to yield to the year and a day presumption. The presumption is now abolished, but the following points should be noted:

(a) In *Dyson* the case would now be decided differently, but the principle that the prosecution must prove all the elements of the *actus reus* and mens rea of the offence or fail, still holds good.

(b) The Act provides that in proceedings against a person for a fatal offence (murder, manslaughter, infanticide, or any other offence of which one of the elements is causing a person's death, or the offence of aiding, abetting, counselling or procuring a person's suicide) the proceedings must be instituted by or with the consent of the Attorney-General where:

(i) the injury alleged to have caused the death was sustained more than three years before the death occurred, or

(ii) the person has previously been convicted of an offence committed in circumstances alleged to be connected with the death.

(c) This note must also be read in conjunction with the passages on pages 236, 345 and 348.

Contents

Part Two: Criminal Law

Introduction

Table of Cases

xxiv   TABLE OF CASES

Table of Statutes

Part One

The Legal System

Chapter 1

Legal Concepts and Legal Reasoning

In this chapter an attempt is made to explain in outline how law works, how lawyers approach problems and how the courts resolve them. Issues raised in this chapter will be taken up in more detail in later chapters; the idea here is to give the essential flavour of law. One of the aims of this chapter is to assist a student who is minded to study law at "A" level to decide whether law is likely to interest him and whether he feels confident to study it.

Suppose B returns from holiday to find that during his absence an unsolicited parcel containing a book has been delivered to his home. With the parcel is a letter from the Ace Book Company offering to sell the book for £25 and the letter concludes, "If we hear no more from you in 14 days we will consider that you have bought the book." The 14 days elapsed while B was on holiday. Is B bound to pay for the book?

B knows no law but his instinctive feeling will surely be that he is not bound to pay; B will think it unfair if a bargain can be foisted on him against his will. However, B subsequently receives several aggressive demands for payment and thinks it wise to seek legal advice; after all B has read somewhere that the law can be a bit assinine at times. So B consults C, a solicitor. Before C gives legal advice he will first of all wish to get the facts as clear as he can. He will want to know whether the book was really unsolicited and did not arrive as the result of B responding to some advertisement, or because B was a member of a book club operated by the Ace Book Company. If B appeared to look young enough, C would also ask his age because if B is under 18 he is in law a minor and is accordingly in a privileged position under the law which regulates contracts. Of course, C cannot definitely establish the facts at this stage. No doubt B is telling the truth as he sees it but it may be that the Ace

3

Book Company takes another view of the facts. Hopefully the Ace Book Company will accept B's version of the facts; if they do not, it may be that after some argument through correspondence the parties can agree what the facts were. If there is still no agreement, it may be necessary to take the matter to court where it will be for the judge, after hearing evidence, to decide what the facts were.

Most cases involve disputes about the facts rather than the law. Once the facts are determined the law, that is, the legal consequences following from those facts, is *usually* clear. A major area of civil litigation these days arises from road accidents. It must not be thought that this is owing to any great uncertainty in the law. The law is well settled and relatively straightforward; if the plaintiff (the party bringing the action) establishes that the defendant drove his car negligently (that is failed to measure up to the standards of the reasonably competent driver) and as a result caused injury to the plaintiff then the plaintiff is entitled to compensation. The difficulty of such cases usually lies in the facts. What the court has to determine is whether the lights were red when the defendant crossed them, or whether his brakes were properly maintained, or whether he failed to signal his intentions and so on. Once the facts are established there is normally no difficulty in applying the law. The same is true of criminal cases. The difficulty in a shoplifting case is much more likely to concern the facts (for instance, whether X deliberately or absent-mindedly took the tin of salmon) than a complex issue in the law of theft.

Notice, incidentally, that in a civil case it is for the plaintiff to establish the facts and for the prosecutor in a criminal prosecution. The plaintiff and the prosecutor normally bear what is called the burden of proof. In a civil case the plaintiff has to establish his case on what is called the balance of probabilities, that is that his version of the facts is more likely to be true than the defendant's version. In effect the plaintiff has to make the running. In a criminal case it is the prosecutor who has to make the running but it is not enough for him to prove his case on balance of probabilities. A criminal conviction is a serious matter so the standard required of the prosecutor is that he must prove the accused's guilt so convincingly that there can be no serious doubt about it. Today, judges tell juries to convict only if they feel sure that the accused is guilty; this may be generous to the accused but a criminal conviction is so serious a matter that a very high standard of proof is required.

In a civil action against a motorist the plaintiff succeeds if he establishes that it was probable that the motorist went through the lights at red. But if on these same facts the motorist is charged with careless driving it is not enough to establish that it was probable that he went through the red light. It is quite possible to form the view that an event probably happened while retaining a real doubt whether it did happen, and in that event a man cannot be convicted of crime. Take a case which was decided in 1966 when the accused was charged with murdering a woman by strangulation. The accused admitted that he had gone to bed with the woman and claimed that he must have strangled her in his sleep. Had this been so the accused was entitled to an acquittal either on the ground of automatism or insanity. The doctors who gave evidence said they had never come across a case where a man had in his sleep strangled another. Nevertheless the jury acquitted. From the medical evidence it may have appeared probable that the accused had deliberately strangled her but the jury was still left with a real doubt, probably because while the doctors knew of no such cases they could not rule them out as a possibility. It may seem strange but a jury in a criminal case must acquit a man whom they think to be probably guilty if they think there is a real possibility that he may be innocent. But had the woman's dependants brought a civil action for compensation it seems clear that the evidence which was insufficient to establish the accused's guilt on the criminal charge would have been enough to establish his civil liability.

In the practice of law the establishment of the facts is of paramount importance. The law student because he is studying the law and therefore concentrating his attention on cases which raise legal issues, may get the impression that every dispute raises an issue that requires litigation to resolve it. This is far from being the case; only a fraction of disputes ever reach the courts and, as we have seen, most of these are likely to turn on disputes of fact rather than law. Even so there are still areas of doubt and difficulty in the law and there is a vast body of law to be learned.

To go back to B's case with the Ace Book Company. C, the solicitor, can assure B that, on the facts as B has presented them, B has nothing to worry about. The law in this instance (as most often it does) accords with common sense for it is only fair that B's silence in response to an offer of which he was entirely unaware should not constitute an acceptance of the offer. But if C is asked why he has formed the opinion he has, he will not reply that it is because it is the "common sense" or "fair" result. C knows that he must have legal authority for his statement to be found in a statute or a decision of the courts. In this instance his authority would be the (to lawyers) well-known case of *Felthouse v. Bindley* decided in 1862.

What happened in that case was that John Felthouse was about to sell his farming stock by auction, and Paul Felthouse, John's uncle, was anxious to buy a horse forming part of the stock. A misunderstanding arose over the price, John thinking he had sold the horse for 30 guineas, Paul thinking he had bought it for £30. So Paul wrote to John offering to split the difference and said, "If I hear no more about him, I consider the horse mine at £30.15s." John did not reply but he was clearly satisfied with the offer because he told the auctioneer, Bindley, to withdraw the horse from the sale. Unfortunately, Bindley forgot this instruction and sold the horse. Paul sued Bindley claiming that at the time of the auction the horse had already been sold to him by John so that Bindley had sold Paul's horse.

It was held by the court that Paul's claim against Bindley failed because there was no concluded contract between himself and John before the auction took place. One judge, Willes J., said that while it was clear that John intended to accept his uncle's offer, "he had not communicated such his intention to his uncle, or done anything to bind himself."

The case of *Felthouse v. Bindley* is not exactly the same as B's case with the Ace Book Company but C must be right in saying that if the court held there was no concluded bargain on the facts of *Felthouse v. Bindley* it necessarily follows that there was no concluded bargain between the Ace Book Company and B. Indeed, B's case is clearer than *Felthouse v. Bindley* because B never had any intention of accepting the offer of the book and was entirely unaware of the offer until he returned from holiday.

In advising B, C would also take account of the Unsolicited Goods and Services Acts 1971 and 1975. This legislation was intended to deal with the mischief of "inertia selling," that is of foisting unsolicited goods on another and purporting to treat the other's inaction as an acceptance. It is now a criminal offence for a person (including a company) who, not having reasonable cause to believe there is a right to payment, makes a demand for payment for what he knows are unsolicited goods. The Ace Book Company may have committed an offence under this section but not necessarily so. It may be, for instance, that D played a practical joke on B by responding to an advertisement by the company in B's name.

In such a case the company might in good faith believe that the goods were solicited by B, and hence would not be guilty of an offence. The Acts also specify a procedure whereby the recipient may, if the goods are not collected within six months or after notice by the recipient, treat the goods as an unconditional gift to him. No doubt C would consider whether in the circumstances B may avail himself of this procedure. But the Acts do not in any way modify the law of contract. C will consider separately (i) B's contractual position; and (ii) any rights which B may have under the Act.

What the lawyer does, then, when presented with a problem is to consider the relevant legal rules to be found in the statutes and the decisions of the courts. He cannot rely on his own (or even abstract) notions of fairness and justice as guides for these would be much too uncertain and it is fundamentally important that the rules which regulate our social and business life should, so far as possible, be known and applied in a predictable way. Hence the lawyer's respect for precedent, that is he seeks to solve problems consistently with earlier cases which are similar to the case in hand. Moreover, as we shall see in more detail later, lower courts are bound by the decisions of higher courts so that certainty and predictability of result can be maximised. Obviously it would not do if lawyers had in every instance to advise their clients to take their cases to court to see what the judges thought was a "fair" result.

Sometimes, however, the lawyer does have to tell his client that the law is uncertain and that it will be necessary to take the matter to court in order to resolve it. We are never likely to reach the stage where the law is so developed and comprehensive that it provides an instant solution to every problem that arises; life is too complex for that. What we hope for is that the law is sufficiently comprehensive and developed to solve most disputes without undue difficulty, but at least some cases are bound to arise where even judges in appellate courts can differ as to the proper result.

The problem B presented to C was for C an easy one. But we can pose more difficult problems. Suppose that the insurance policy on B's motor cycle expired on April 30. On April 29, B received from his insurers a cover note valid for 15 days. B intends to renew his policy but, being pressed for money, he decides that he will make payment on May 14, just before the cover note expires. In the meantime B takes his cycle on the road; on May 10, he is stopped by a policeman and is subsequently charged with driving without insurance. This is a criminal prosecution and not an action for breach of contract but the law of contract is relevant because if B had a valid contract of insurance on May 10, he has a defence to the charge.

Felthouse v. Bindley is again in point. The prosecution will point out that the cover note was an offer to renew the insurance but was an offer B had not accepted by May 10. Like John Bindley, B intended to accept the offer but had done nothing to communicate his acceptance nor done anything to bind himself.

As it happens, while this particular problem has never been *decided* by any court, it has in fact been *considered* by Lord Parker C.J. in *Taylor v. Allen* (1965). In the doctrine of precedent, courts are bound only by what other courts decide is the law applicable to the decision (called the *ratio decidendi*) and not by the opinions (called *obiter dicta*) which judges might express on issues which do not fall to be determined in that case. Such opinions can be persuasive and the opinion expressed, as it was in this case, by the Lord Chief Justice is bound to carry a lot of weight. Lord Parker said that it might be said in such a case as this that the motor-cyclist had accepted the offer by conduct (*i.e.* by taking his cycle on the road) in reliance on the offer made and without any formal communication. Lord Parker was aware that *in general* silence in response to an offer cannot be taken as an acceptance but was no doubt thinking that there was no reason why, if it suits him, the offeror should not dispense with communication.

What Lord Parker was prepared to do, it seems, was to *distinguish Felthouse v. Bindley*. He was not questioning the actual decision in that case, merely saying that the motor-cyclist's case was sufficiently different to permit an exception to the general rule that silence is not acceptance. If Lord Parker is right, the question arises as to what the result would have been in *Felthouse v. Bindley* if John had sued his uncle Paul for the purchase price of the horse. Suppose that John's instructions for the withdrawal of the horse had been complied with but the following day, and before John had communicated with Paul, Paul had written to say he was no longer interested in the horse. Would Lord Parker have been inclined to say that there was a contract because (a) Paul dispensed with the need for John to communicate his acceptance; and (b) in reliance on that John withdrew the horse from an auction at which it might otherwise have been sold? It is worth noting that in *Felthouse v. Bindley* itself one judge, Keating J., said that while he agreed that Paul failed in his action against Bindley, "Had the question arisen between the uncle and the nephew, then probably there would have been some difficulty."

Some writers (writers do not make, though they may influence, the law) have therefore questioned whether *Felthouse v. Bindley* was correctly decided. These writers are not questioning the principle that *in general* silence cannot constitute acceptance (and all of them would certainly agree that the Ace Book Company cannot treat B's silence as an acceptance) but they are saying that if the offeror chooses to dispense with acceptance *and* the offeree acts in reliance on what the offeror says, then the offeror ought to be bound. It is of course open to higher courts (the Court of Appeal or the House of Lords) to overrule *Felthouse v. Bindley*. The case has stood for over 100 years but that does not mean it cannot be overruled if it is thought to be wrong.

It seems that Paul Felthouse's lawyers were not entirely happy with the decision because they advised an appeal. While the appellate court affirmed the view of the trial court, there was next to no argument on this issue because it was held that Paul failed on another ground, namely, there was not sufficient written evidence to satisfy the Statute of Frauds 1677. At that time (this is no longer the law) the statute required that any contract for the sale of goods of £10 and upwards should be in writing and there was no sufficient writing in this case. So it might be said that Paul lost his case on a "technical" point which had nothing to do with the real merits of the case.

Cases can be lost and won on so-called technical points which, to the layman at least, seem to have nothing to do with the justice of the case. A dramatic example is provided by *Dyson* (1908). Dyson was charged with the manslaughter of his baby daughter who had died in March 1908 following brutal assaults by Dyson in November 1906 and December 1907. The judge had directed the jury that Dyson might be convicted of manslaughter if satisfied that death was caused by the assault in 1906 or accelerated by the assault in 1907 and the jury found Dyson guilty. This seems a sensible verdict and, you may think, the sentence of ten years' penal servitude was fully deserved. But it so happens that before anyone can be convicted of homicide (whether murder or manslaughter) it must be proved that death occurred within a year and a day of the injury causing death. This "somewhat recondite rule of law", as Lord Alverstone C.J. called it in *Dyson* became part of the law of homicide for arcane reasons and it may be that Parliament, following recommendations of the Law Commission, may soon abolish it. However, it is still a rule of law and it therefore followed that the trial judge had misdirected the jury in telling them that they could convict on the basis of the 1906 injuries which occurred 15 months before the death. Dyson's conviction was accordingly quashed. To some this might appear unjust because Dyson had unquestionably killed his daughter in circumstances where condign punishment was called for. But to the lawyer any other result is unthinkable. The rule requires death to occur within one year and one day of the injury, and while it stands the courts must apply it. That is what justice according to the law requires. In such circumstances it may be that the defendant can be convicted of some other offence (Dyson was convicted of common assault in respect of the two attacks on his child) but it also happens that some defendants escape scot free on a "technical" point even though their conduct would be regarded by all as reprehensible.

It must not be thought from these examples that the law is concerned only with technicalities, with notions of fairness and justice taking a back seat. Parliament seeks to enact fair laws which will command the respect of thinking people and the courts seek to apply the laws sensibly in order to produce fair results. But lawyers must act within the framework of the rules, must seek to apply the rules in a predictable and not capricious way. It must not be thought, however, that laws can be applied like mathematical formulae in order to produce the "right" result. Sometimes a court will express its unhappiness at, or even its distaste for, a decision which it feels constrained to reach. *Sullivan* (1983) provides a striking example. The defendant, a man of blameless reputation, attacked a friend during an epileptic seizure, unaware that he was attacking him and entirely unable to control his actions. At his trial it was argued that he ought to be acquitted because his conduct was involuntary and, as a general rule, no one is criminally liable for conduct he cannot control. The trial judge accepted that his conduct was involuntary but ruled that it arose from a "disease of the mind" within the rules laid down in *M'Naghten's Case* (1843) and accordingly the proper verdict, though it would be one of acquittal, was not guilty by reason of insanity. The defendant promptly changed his plea to guilty because he, very sensibly, preferred to receive a defined punishment (he was placed on probation for three years subject to submitting himself to medical treatment) there and then for a crime which he had not committed rather than an acquittal which would then have been followed (the law has subsequently been modified) by an indefinite period of incarceration in a secure hospital. The ruling of the trial judge was upheld by the Court of Appeal and the House of Lords. In the latter, Lord Diplock said that while it was natural to feel reluctant to attach the label insanity to sufferers from epilepsy, and sympathise though he did with the defendant, the authorities (see further, below, p. 287) constrained him to reach that decision. The remedy lay with Parliament; it was not for the courts to alter the established law.

Just as the law does not always produce the "right" answer, nor does it always produce only one answer. Frequently more than one solution is possible and lawyers (whether judges or practitioners, teachers or students) may differ sharply as to which solution correctly expresses the law.

Consider the case of *Morgan* (1976). A number of men charged with rape claimed that they believed that the victim had consented when as a matter of fact she had not. The trial judge, three Lords Justices of Appeal in the Court of Appeal and two Law Lords in the House of Lords took the view that an honest belief in the victim's consent was not a defence unless that belief was based on reasonable grounds. But three of the Law Lords held that an honest belief in the victim's consent was a defence even if it was an unreasonable belief. These three judges, since they constituted a 3–2 majority in the House of Lords which is the highest court, established the law though if judicial heads were to be counted there was a 6–3 majority the other way. All nine judges, however, were considering the same authorities and using the same techniques of reasoning but this happened to be a case where either view of the law was tenable.

The interest of the case does not end there. *Morgan* provoked such a storm of controversy (some critics thought it amounted to a rapist's charter) that the Government set up an Advisory Group to consider whether any changes in the law of rape were desirable. The approach of the Advisory Group was entirely different to the approach of the courts. Courts have to decide what the law *is* and in so deciding are confined to a consideration of legally relevant authorities. In deciding what the law *ought to be* the group's inquiry was much more wide ranging. The group issued a public invitation and received opinions from, among many others, the Association of Police Surgeons, the Mothers Union and the British Broadcasting Corporation. In the result the group recommended that the law relating to consent as a defence to a charge of rape should remain as the three Law Lords had stated it so that an honest, even though unreasonable, belief in the consent of the victim should be a defence. In no sense was the group deciding that the three were "right" while the view expressed by the six was "wrong." For all we know the members of the Advisory Group may have been privately of the opinion that, in view of the authorities, the opinion of the six was the preferable view. But the group was not sitting as a sort of further court of appeal to decide whether the decision of the House of Lords was in law the correct one. They were deciding, in the light of all the evidence presented to them, what would be the best rule to operate for the future.

Courts cannot possibly approach their task by soliciting views from members of the public on what the law ought to be. The judges are aware that the proper application of law can sometimes produce an injustice. Nor can the judges resolve issues of law by applying their own, or even generally accepted, standards of fairness. Justice can only be dispensed according to law. It has to be said, however, that some judges are bolder in their approach to authorities than others and are more willing to remould the law to achieve what they see as being a fair result. But even the boldest judge seeks to work within the framework; he may be able to recast the rules but he cannot, as it were, destroy the mould and start again. The advantage of the bold approach is that the law can be better adapted, as the judge sees it, to modern conditions. A startling example of that was the decision of the House of Lords in R. v. R. (1991) to abolish, an anachronistic and offensive in present-day society, the long-standing rule that a husband could not be guilty of the rape of his wife. The disadvantage is that the outcome of cases becomes less predictable so that the lawyer is that much less certain in advising his client. The law student will have to decide for himself whether he prefers the conservative or the progressive approach to the development of law but he can only make an informed choice in the matter after much study of the subject.

Chapter 2

Institutions of the English Legal System

1. The Constitution in Outline

Britain has no written constitution which neatly defines the respective spheres of the Crown, Parliament, the Executive (the Government), and the Judiciary. Historically there has been adjustment and readjustment. The Crown, once firmly holding the reigns of government, is now largely confined to a titular role and ceremonial duties. Parliament, once little more than a sounding board, is now the supreme legislative body; once dominated by the Lords, it is now dominated by the Commons. The Judiciary who once developed large areas of the law of their own initiative and once even asserted, though never established, the supremacy of the common law now accept the supremacy of Parliament. And Parliament itself is in practice dominated by the Government which formulates the policy of the day and can in large measure ensure the legislation to implement it. Nor is the end of change in sight. There have long been moves to abolish the House of Lords, or to severely truncate its powers, or to replace it with a differently constituted chamber. There are moves also, perhaps prompted by the fear of an all-powerful Commons, to introduce an entrenched Bill of Rights, which would ensure that certain fundamental rights could not be readily abrogated by Parliament.

Some political theorists have argued for a rigid separation of powers between the legislature, the executive and the judiciary. The idea is that no one branch ought to be paramount and that liberty is best ensured by a system where each arm acts as a check on the others. Such a system is most nearly maintained in the United States. The President may propose legislation to Congress but it is Congress which has the power of disposal. While Congress has the exclusive law-making power, the courts, who have to a degree assumed the power which the English courts once hankered after, may invalidate legislation on the ground that it is contrary to their written constitution—the fundamental law.

We have no such rigid separation but it has to be said that our constitution works tolerably well and, if the absence of violent revolutionary change is taken as the measure, has in the past adapted itself to change with less trouble than many constitutions elsewhere. It may be asked what is meant by saying that our constitution "works" and an answer to that can only be given in relation to the values which people seek to preserve. At the risk of oversimplification it may be said that our constitution, at the public level, seeks to ensure freedom of political action so that by free and fair elections we may have the Government of our choice; and, at the private level, to ensure equality of treatment before the law and freedom from arbitrary action by the authorities of the state. To most of us these appear to be values which are worth having and preserving.

Just how does the constitution guarantee these and other rights? Parliament is supreme and there are only theoretical limits on its law-making power. It may be, for instance, that Parliament could not pass a law binding its successor not to repeal that law. But Parliament can pass a law to continue its own life notwithstanding that the Parliament Act 1911 states that five years shall be the maximum duration of a Parliament. Parliament could pass a law which would retrospectively make illegal that which was legal when it was performed. Parliament could pass a law authorising arbitrary action by the police. Thus, in theory, a Government commanding a majority in Parliament could almost overnight establish a police state. However, and quite apart from practical restraints on actions which might provoke a constitutional crisis or even violent reaction, there are constraints imposed by constitutional conventions and by respect for the rule of law.

Moreover our membership of the European Community involves a cession of paramountcy at least in some respects, and they are respects of vital importance to our economic well-being, to institutions of the European Community (see further, below, p. 163). So some of our "sovereignty" (the power to act independently of any other body) has been given up. Strong and strident voices have been raised against any further concession but continued membership of the European Community seems likely to involve, however reluctantly, further concessions. In addition our subscription to the

European Convention on Human Rights (see below, p. 175), though the Convention does not have, as directives of the European Commission and decisions of the European Court do, direct effect in English law, it is nevertheless the case that our law must be brought into conformity with decisions of the European Court of Human Rights made under the Convention. Complete sovereignty no longer resides in Parliament—if it ever did.

(1) Constitutional Conventions

In its essential respects our constitution is governed by conventions. These conventions are not rules of law which must be followed but they are practices which are normally regarded as obligatory; only in exigent circumstances may they be modified or ignored. Thus the Crown in which great legal powers are vested might, for example, dismiss and appoint Governments, prorogue Parliament, or refuse the Royal Assent to Bills passed by Parliament. By convention, however, the Crown accepts the advice of his or her Ministers in these and many other constitutional matters. In turn the Government is a slave to convention. By convention a Government which cannot command a majority in the Commons may advise the Crown to dissolve Parliament and call an election; alternatively the Crown may, following soundings taken from Party leaders, nominate someone who can form a Government which will command a majority. There is no law which requires Ministers of the Government to be Members of either House of Parliament but it is a conventional requirement that they be so in order that Ministers can answer in Parliament for the conduct of their Ministries.

The advantage of conventions is that they provide a flexibility not given by rules of law. It might be countered that Parliament may just as easily alter a law as a convention, and perhaps the only adequate counter to that is that we have found it preferable to maintain the constitution more by convention than by law. Take the law, just noted, which limits the life of a Parliament to five years. There is no law which says that Parliament cannot repeal this law but there is a convention that this is not done, and in ordinary circumstances no Government would seek to prolong its life for this would provoke a constitutional crisis. In ordinary circumstances, note. During both World Wars Parliaments were continued beyond five years and, for obvious reasons, no constitutional crisis was caused.

In theoretical terms the difference between convention and law is slight. Conventions are regarded as binding in all but highly exceptional circumstances. Law, of course, binds even in the exceptional circumstances. Nevertheless when exceptional circumstances do arise people just as readily accept a change in the law as they accept a modification of the conventional practice.

(2) The Rule of Law

The rule of law means something more than rule in accordance with the law. The most terrifying dictatorship can rule in accordance with law by enacting laws to give effect to its policies, however inhuman these may be. The rule of law in the sense it is used here really involves certain presuppositions about law itself. The nature and extent of these presuppositions is open to argument but most would agree that the rule of law requires that all power and authority in the state be derived from law, and the notion of equality before the law.

In a dictatorship judges might be understandably reluctant to question the legal basis upon which the dictator and his designates act. In a parliamentary democracy there is no such reluctance. The ministerial powers, however widely phrased, are generally subject to review by the courts and if a Minister has acted *ultra vires* (beyond the powers of) his authority, his action is invalid even if done in complete good faith and in accordance with the public interest. If the police effect an arrest or search premises without the legal powers to do so, the arrest or search is illegal and it will not help the police to show that their action was reasonable or that it was done in good faith.

Equality before the law requires that like should be treated as like. We accordingly accept that differences of sex, religion and race are not proper factors to be taken into account when it comes to questions of political rights, criminal liability or job eligibility. But equality is a slippery concept. Only in this century have women secured political parity. Our forebears, incidentally, probably did not see the denial of the vote to women as a breach of the principle of equality; they did not see women in this respect as "like" to men. We accept that for many purposes the young may be treated more favourably in law than those of mature judgment but the age at which equality of treatment is accorded is for most purposes 18 and not 21 as it was only a few years ago. So our notions of equality change but we accept that arbitrary (unreasoned) exceptions to equality of treatment before the law are intolerable.

If past practice is a guide, it is safe to assume that Parliaments approach their affairs with an awareness of, and acceptance of, the rule of law. Parliamentarians may not have identical definitions of the rule of law but there would be substantial accord on legal accountability and equality. In Germany in 1935 an Act was passed stating that persons should be punished if their acts were "deserving of punishment according to fundamental conceptions of a penal law and sound popular feeling." This Act was unquestionably a law and the judges were bound to apply it. Even in the exigent circumstances of war it is inconceivable that any British Parliament would find such a law even remotely acceptable. That Parliament has the power to pass such a law is clear; but legislation so vague and oppressive in its terms would be thought to violate the rule of law which informs our thinking about law.

The point about the British constitution is that the limitations within which it is operated are largely self-imposed. With the doctrine of parliamentary supremacy the potential for abuse is great but the traditions to which we subscribe have ensured that Parliament, or Governments rather, do not often abuse their power. An active opposition and a free Press make abuse, if not impossible, at least difficult. The cynic might say, as the man who jumped off a skyscraper was heard to say as he passed the twentieth floor, "It's been all right so far." Some have accordingly argued for a Bill of Rights which would set out and guarantee certain basic rights and freedoms (cf. the European Convention on Human Rights, below, p. 175) but Parliament has not been persuaded of the need for such a Bill.

2. The Common Law

"Common law" has several meanings. When asked what it means a lawyer is most likely to reply that it refers to the law as developed by the judges since the Norman Conquest. When William I established himself he did not seek to impose on the English an entirely new system of law. There was no very developed Norman law which he could impose and, in any case, the imposition overnight of an entirely new system of law could only have caused legal and administrative chaos.

So William was content to endorse the Saxon laws subject to such changes necessary to secure his own position. The Normans were great administrators (Domesday Book bears witness to that) and they set out to centralise and regularise the government of the country. While local courts and local laws continued to flourish, the central government appointed its own judges (*justiciars*) to look after its own interests. A principal interest of the Crown was to secure its own revenues so it is no accident that the Court of Exchequer was the first to emerge as a distinct court. As the Crown's interest became more pervasive the central courts expanded at the expense of local ones, an expansion accelerated by their superior procedures and remedies.

The common law gradually came to mean exactly what the expression conveys: a law common to England and Wales. In the early development of that law custom (briefly, a usage acquiring such force as to become obligatory) played an important and fruitful part but progressively the decisions of the courts (the precedents established by the cases) supplanted custom. "The scope of custom," observed Professor C. K. Allen, "diminishes as the formulation of legal rules becomes more explicit and as more elaborate machinery is set up for the making and administering of law." It is, however, still possible, under rather stringent conditions, to establish a local custom which constitutes an exception to the general common law, such as a right of way or a right of fishermen to dry their nets on another's property.

So in developing the law the judges made use of customary law, both Saxon and Norman, adapting these to the needs of a developing society. In so doing the lawyers used the technique of developing the law by reference to judicial decisions; arguing the case in hand by reference to decisions in similar cases after the fashion outlined in Chapter 1. Much of our law was developed in this way with relatively little legislative interference until the nineteenth century. So long as the pace of social change was slow, as it was until the Industrial Revolution, the judges could adapt the law to that change. Once the pace of change quickens the development of the law solely by judicial decision cannot keep abreast. Legislation becomes increasingly necessary, for legislation can do overnight what may take the courts years to accomplish. Although substantial parts of our law are still to be found in the decisions of the courts, most of our law is now to be found in statutes.

But this has not entailed the demise of the common law; much of it has been little more than restated in statutory form and the common law technique—that of arguing deductively from like cases—continues to govern our legal reasoning.

Many statutes, for example the Sale of Goods Act 1979 or the Theft Acts 1968 and 1978 can only be understood through the veil of the decisions made under them. Indeed, it is a rare case involving the interpretation of a statute, even a statute on some novel subject-matter, where counsel cannot cite some precedent aimed at persuading the court to adopt the interpretation favoured by counsel. It is in this sense—that of a technique of reasoning—that the common law remains pervasive. The English lawyer who goes to Australia, or Trinidad and Tobago, or to most states of the U.S.A. may find differences in the content of the criminal and civil law but he or she will find the technique of argument wholly familiar.

This is not to claim any inherent superiority for the common law. Students tend to like the common law because the principles and the details are informed by stories, some sad, some funny, many banal. But now our membership of the European Community means that we must be prepared to look at other approaches to law. We have already embarked on a common law of the European Community in the important fields of commerce and human rights (see Chapter 5). Quite how far we shall—or should—go in the direction of integration, political and legal, is now a matter of acute political controversy, but the modern student of law who ignores this new dimension does so at his or her peril.

3. Equity

As we saw in Chapter 1, judges are not free to decide cases on the basis of fairness but only on the basis of the established laws. Sometimes the proper application of the law can lead to an unfair or harsh result. In such cases the judge may draw the matter to the attention of law reform agencies with a view to legislative change of the law. In the formative era of the common law there were no such law reform agencies. Litigants who were dissatisfied with the outcome of litigation took to petitioning the Crown, as the fount of all justice, to redress their grievances. The Crown, in turn, assigned such petitions to the Lord Chancellor. It is sometimes said that this was because the Chancellor, invariably an ecclesiastic in early times, was the keeper of the King's conscience and thus peculiarly well qualified to determine issues of right and justice. The real reason may have been more practical. The Chancellor would inevitably be familiar with the law; he was in fact intimately connected with its early development, and was a legal adviser to the King's Council (the *Curia Regis*). Moreover he had a secretariat (the Chancery, later to become the Court of Chancery) which had the all-important administrative machinery to deal with such petitions.

Suppose, for instance, that A had agreed to sell land to B but had reneged on his promise. In the common law courts B could get damages (compensation in money) for the breach of contract but B might find damages less than adequate; what B wanted was the land itself and he could see no reason why A should not be kept to the terms of his promise. To us it may seem strange that the common law courts failed to respond by ordering A to convey the land but they did so fail and it was the Chancellor who intervened to give B a decree of specific performance (see below, p. 622). Similarly if A built a wall which interfered with the light to B's house, what B required was not monetary compensation but an order to take down the wall; the Chancellor was prepared to give that order—the injunction. The common law for all its innovation and flexibility became rigid and unresponsive to the needs of certain situations; the Chancellor was not so inhibited and could act on the conscience of the parties, ordaining what he thought to be fair (equitable) in the particular case. But what is "fair"? One Chancellor might take one view, his successor another. Hence the seventeenth century jibe that equity varied with the length of the Chancellor's foot.

Inevitably there was conflict between the Court of Chancery and the courts of common law since the Chancellor was recognising rights and granting remedies not accorded at common law. Moreover the Chancellor made the claim, true but for that reason no less galling to common lawyers, that he dispensed a superior justice; and, worst of all, he was even prepared to issue an injunction—the so-called common injunction—to restrain the litigant from enforcing his legal rights if it was against "conscience" to do so. In 1530 Sir Thomas More (the first layman to become Lord Chancellor), learning of the grumblings of the common law judges against the issue of common injunctions, invited them to dine with him. He there defended the justice of his decisions and the judges were forced to confess that in like cases they would have done likewise. More even invited the judges to apply equitable principles to obviate the need for the common injunction but this they declined to do. The separate administration of law and equity continued much to the inconvenience of the litigant who could be involved in the burdensome and expensive task of going to the common law courts to establish the right and then going to Chancery to get the appropriate remedy.

In the end, though the end was a long time in coming, the supremacy of equity was acknowledged in the ruling, first made by James I but subsequently endorsed in the Judicature Act 1873, that where rules of equity and law conflict, equity prevails. By that same Act the common law courts and the Court of Chancery were united in the Supreme Court of Judicature and henceforth *all* judges were enjoined to apply both law and equity in the resolution of cases. And by this time equity no longer merited the old jibe; Chancellors such as Ellesmere, Nottingham, Hardwicke and Eldon systematised the rules of equity so that equity became as predictable and rigid as the common law. Chancellors had always claimed that equity was to supplement, not supplant, the common law; by the nineteenth century that claim was a reality. Courts now administer the law and that law includes both common law and equity; law and equity have at last been fused. Nevertheless, the distinction between law and equity remains important for more than merely historical reasons, and equitable remedies (because they have their basis in conscience) may still be denied a party even though his right to damages at common law is unimpaired.

This is not to suggest that the law (the rules of common law and equity) has reached a stage where it is incapable of improvement, nor to say that the proper application of the law is now incapable of producing a harsh or unfair result. But it is true to say that most judges, faced with a case in which the application of the law produces what appears to be an unfair result, will content themselves by drawing attention to the apparent injustice in the expectation that Parliament, after appropriate inquiry and consultation, will put the matter to rights. Some judges, however, are bolder and will not wait on legislative reform so that even in recent years there have been some striking judicial innovations, an example of which is provided by equitable estoppel.

4. The Courts

The courts exercising civil and criminal jurisdiction may be diagrammatically shown as on page 23.

While this diagram conveys the essential structure of the courts, it is both inaccurate and incomplete. It is inaccurate in suggesting a precise distinction between civil and criminal jurisdiction. While the jurisdiction of the High Court is primarily civil, the Queen's Bench Division exercises an important supervisory jurisdiction in criminal cases (see below, p. 63); and while the jurisdiction of the Crown Court is primarily criminal, it has some civil jurisdiction such as licensing appeals from the magistrates' courts. It is incomplete in that it does not show the Court of Justice of the European Communities. While this court is not part of the English legal system it has jurisdiction in matters of Community law and its decisions take effect here (see below, p. 170). Nor are tribunals (see below, p. 52) part of the recognised court system, though the collective jurisdiction of these is immense.

In fact the court system cannot be precisely categorised. It is common to refer to courts exercising appellate jurisdiction and courts exercising original (trial) jurisdiction but it has to be recognised that some courts (the High Court, the Crown Court) exercise both. Another distinction is between superior courts (House of Lords, Court of Appeal, High Court, Crown Court) whose jurisdiction is unlimited, and inferior courts (county courts, magistrates' courts) whose jurisdiction is limited to a particular geographical area or by the seriousness of the offence in criminal proceedings. One test of an inferior court is whether it is subject to the prerogative orders (see below) of the High Court but the Crown Court is recognised as a superior court although it is so subject when exercising its appellate jurisdiction.

So classification has only a limited value. The court structure, after all, is not one which has been modelled and imposed by logicians. It has evolved over a long period and has been frequently adapted to meet changing situations where convenience often requires solutions that do not make for neat categorisation.

5. The Personnel of the Law

In this chapter an account is given of the personnel of the legal system and their functions, ranging from the foot-soldiers of the law (barristers and solicitors) to the highest judicial office, that of Lord Chancellor.

COURTS EXERCISING CIVIL JURISIDICTION	COURTS EXERCISING CRIMINAL JURISIDICTION

HOUSE OF LORDS

COURT OF APPEAL

Civil Division	Criminal Division

HIGH COURT OF JUSTICE

Chancery Division	Family Division	Queen's Bench Division

CROWN COURT

COUNTY COURTS

MAGISTRATES' COURTS

Over the centuries the legal professions have proved to be conservative ones; professions which have built up monopolies which they have jealously guarded. But in this regard fundamental reforms have been introduced by the Courts and Legal Services Act (hereafter C.L.S.A.) 1990.

But first something about the professions of barrister and solicitor. In the popular mind, the distinction between barristers and solicitors is that the former are concerned with advocacy in court while the latter are concerned with legal work out of court. This is not quite the case. Barristers are primarily concerned with advocacy, but they are not confined to advocacy and may devote a deal of their time to giving expert opinions on legal matters. Nor are solicitors exclusively concerned with out-of-court work for they have long had a right of audience in magistrates' courts, county courts and, in some instances, the Crown Court.

This division of the legal profession is a curious one and is unknown even in many Commonwealth countries which might have been expected to adopt the English professional model along with their adoption of the common law. The education of both barristers and solicitors has common features. Both will normally complete the academic stage of their legal education by obtaining a law degree, though a law degree is not the only way to complete the academic stage. Both undergo a vocational stage though here the differences are more marked. The barrister takes the Bar Examination under the aegis of the Inns of Court School of Law while the solicitor takes the Solicitors' Final Examination under the aegis of the Law Society and in these courses and examinations the emphasis differs to take account of their different roles. Both must complete a period of apprenticeship; pupillage in the case of barristers served under a pupil master (an experienced barrister), and articles in the case of solicitors served under an experienced solicitor. Here, at this "practical" stage, the difference is perhaps most marked since the day-to-day work of the barrister is quite different to the office routine of the solicitor.

The difference, however, is one of function rather than purpose. It is the purpose of both to ensure that the citizen has available sound professional services and advice to enable him to order his business and social life. When a citizen consults a lawyer it is more likely to prevent matters going wrong (e.g. he wishes to form a company, or to organise his business affairs to attract the minimum of tax, or to make a will) than because matters have gone wrong (e.g. he is threatened with civil or criminal proceedings). Only exceptionally will the citizen require the specialist services of the barrister, hence practising barristers number some 7,000 as against some 65,000 solicitors. But even a distinction between the "specialist" barrister and the "generalist" solicitor can be misleading; many barristers, particularly in their early years at the Bar, may take whatever cases come their way, and many solicitors, especially those in large firms—which accounts for the majority of them, anyway—may specialise in a particular area of law.

That the fusion of the two professions is *possible* is demonstrated by experience in similar common law jurisdictions elsewhere. Whether it is *desirable* is another matter. The acid tests must be whether fusion would secure for the citizen an improved standard of legal services or whether it would significantly reduce their cost. The Royal Commission on Legal Services (1979) took the view that the public interest was best served by retaining the existing division, and that legal services would not be improved, nor costs significantly lowered, by fusion. The Commission was, however, inclined to think that there should be a common education for barristers and solicitors so that entrants to the legal profession could make the decision as to which branch of the profession they should join after the completion of their apprenticeship and not, as now, at the outset of their professional careers.

Both professions established monopolies which were jealously guarded over the centuries. Barristers, who may of course appear in all courts, enjoyed a monopoly of the right of audience (the right to present a case on behalf of another) in the High Court, the Court of Appeal and the House of Lords; solicitors enjoyed a right of audience only in the magistrates' courts, the county courts and, where the Lord Chancellor might so exceptionally direct, the Crown Court. In addition barristers enjoyed a monopoly on appointments to virtually all professional judicial appointments.

Solicitors, too, enjoyed their monopolies. These included the right to conduct litigation, that is to commence proceedings in the courts and to perform functions ancillary thereto, the right to prepare papers for probate work, and the right to conduct conveyancing. These were often the mainstays of the solicitor's income.

But now, and principally as a result of the C.L.S.A., the goalposts have been moved. So far as the provision of legal services is concerned the Act is informed by the principle set out in section 17(1):

"The general objective ... is the development of legal services in England and Wales (and in particular the development of advocacy, litigation, conveyancing and probate services) by making provision for new or better ways of providing such services and a wider choice of persons providing them, while maintaining the proper and efficient administration of justice."

The Act stops short of fusing the two professions, nor does it impose a common system of education and training. What it does is to end monopolies enjoyed by the professions by opening up each profession to competition by the other, *and* by opening up both professions to competition by other persons or bodies. The principal changes may be summarised as follows.

Advocacy and rights of audience. While practising barristers and solicitors retain their existing rights of audience, a right of audience *in any designated court or courts*, may be granted to suitably qualified persons, even persons without legal qualifications. This does not mean that a right of audience is available to any Tom, Dick or Harry because the qualifications required by the Act are stringent. Moreover, the application must be supported by the Lord Chancellor's Advisory Committee and, given a positive recommendation by the Advisory Committee, this in turn must be approved by the designated judges (*viz* the Lord Chief Justice, the Master of the Rolls, the President of the Family Division and the Vice-Chancellor of the Chancery Division). The course to admission is a formidable one.

Rights of audience do not have to be granted on an all-or-nothing basis. At the extreme a "Supreme Court qualification", entitling the holder to appear in all proceedings in the Supreme Court may be given, while, at the other extreme, a 'magistrates' courts qualification' only may be conferred Moreover, a 'general qualification' may be given, authorizing the holder to appear only in certain classes of proceedings.

Following the Act, the Law Society, inevitably, sought wider rights of audience for practising solicitors and limited rights of audience for employed solicitors (*i.e.* persons qualified as solicitors employed other than in practice in law firms). The Advisory Committee and the designated judges approved the application in relation to practising solicitors, and the way is now open to practising solicitors to have their individual applications considered by the Higher Courts Qualifications Casework Committee; but the application in respect of employed solicitors was deferred.

The Director of Public Prosecutions also sought for employed barristers in the Crown Prosecution Service the same rights of audience as are enjoyed by practising barristers but the Advisory Committee rejected this proposal.

The Bar has viewed these developments with alarm but its worries appear to be unfounded. The number of practising solicitors seeking right of audience appears to be small (a few hundred so far) and although rights of audience may be granted to non-lawyers (*e.g.* chartered accountants, patent agents) their numbers are likely to be much smaller still and any right of audience granted may be restricted to particular courts or particular classes of case.

Conducting litigation. The Act ends the monopoly of solicitors to start and conduct litigation on behalf of another. Solicitors do of course retain their existing right to conduct litigation but litigation may now be conducted by a person approved by an "appropriate body" (an 'appropriate body' being the Law Society or any other body so designated on the recommendation of the Lord Chancellor, a recommendation which must be approved by the designated judges, by Order in Council).

Conveyancing. The monopoly which solicitors enjoyed in relation to conveyancing was ended by the Administration of Justice Act 1985. This enables persons other than solicitors (most obviously employees of building societies and banks who have the necessary skills) to become licensed conveyancers. The C.L.S.A. sets up the Authorised Conveyancing Practitioners Board to oversee the provision of conveyancing services by practitioners.

Judicial appointments. This matter is more conveniently taken up below.

The Legal Services Ombudsman. The C.L.S.A. establishes a Legal Services Ombudsman whose functions, broadly stated, are to oversee the provision of legal services and to investigate complaints.

(1) Magistrates

There are some 30,000 lay magistrates in England and Wales and some idea of their importance may be gleaned from the simple fact that over 95 per cent. of criminal cases begin and end in magistrates' courts.

Lay magistrates, along with stipendiary magistrates may fairly be said to provide the backbone of the criminal justice system. In qualitative terms their jurisdiction relates only to minor offences, but in quantitative terms they deal with some two million defendants a year (apart from their other functions) and it is imperative that they deal both efficiently and fairly with them.

The magistrates' courts are administered by magistrates' courts committees and their administration was given a face-lift (showing a smile on the faces of some but a grimace on the faces of others) by the Police and Magistrates' Courts Act 1994. Shortly stated this Act aims to improve efficiency (or to get better value for money which is not always the same thing) by (i) encouraging the amalgamation of magistrates' courts committees (composed largely but not necessarily exclusively of magistrates selected for their administrative abilities and reflecting a fair balance of political affiliations, sex and age) to form larger administrative units; (ii) the appointment of a justices' chief executive (who does not need to be legally qualified) to each committee (the relationship of the magistrates' courts committee to the justices' chief executive may be likened to that of a board of management which determines the policy and the managing director who implements that policy); and (iii) the introduction of an inspectorate to oversee the efficiency of the service provided by magistrates' courts.

The heavy reliance which our system has on laymen in the administration of justice may appear odd and the reasons for it are historical and practical. The historical reason (really a practical one at the time) was that in the fourteenth century, and probably in response to what was perceived as a crime wave, it was decided to accord judicial powers to lay justices of the peace because there were not enough professional lawyers available. The practical reason for their continuance remains the same. To replace 30,000 unpaid lay magistrates with stipendiary magistrates would cost a fortune. And, it may be added, both the lay magistracy and the jury system give laymen the opportunity to participate in the administration of justice on the ground floor. That may be no bad thing.

Justices of the Peace are appointed in the name of the Crown under the hand of the Lord Chancellor or, in Lancashire, by the Chancellor of the Duchy of Lancaster. Since nearly 2,000 appointments are made each year it is clear that the Lord Chancellor cannot have sufficient knowledge of individual applicants to enable him to select the most suitable candidates. At one time the power to nominate candidates for magistracy—effectively the power to appoint—was largely in the hands of the Lord Lieutenant of the county who might, and frequently did, appoint persons of his own political persuasion. That system was changed by the Royal Commission on Justices of the Peace (1910) whose recommendation for a system of local advisory committees, more broadly representative so as to avoid political influence, was accepted. Members of the local advisory committees are appointed by the Lord Chancellor.

Their names, once shrouded in secrecy to avoid lobbying, are now made available to the public along with the name of the committee's secretary. Members of the public are invited to nominate themselves or others, and advertisements to apply for magisterial office even appear on buses. Application is easy; the road to appointment is, rightly enough, rigorous. It is, however, open to all.

The only qualification laid down by law (Justices of the Peace Act 1979, s.7) for appointment, and the Lord Chancellor may dispense with this if it is in the public interest to do so, is that the justice must reside within 15 miles of the area for which he is to act. Beyond that there are guidelines, which may be altered from time to time, laid down by the Lord Chancellor. The present guidelines state that a person will not be appointed who is aged over 60 (in practice it is unusual to appoint a person over 55—a guideline which an increasingly ageing but active society may call into question), nor will a person convicted of certain offences (minor motoring offences would not disqualify but an offence involving violence or moral turpitude would do so) be appointed, nor an undischarged bankrupt, nor a member of the armed forces, a police officer or traffic warden, or any person whose work is incompatible with the duties of a magistrate. On the positive side what is being sought is a person who has, or appears to have, the judicial qualities of detachment, impartiality and good sense. In practice few people are disqualified under the guidelines and many more applicants are qualified than there are places to fill.

In addition there is an important practical consideration which is that candidates must be able to sit for an average of thirty-five sittings per year for which the holder receives only out-of-pocket expenses. This may be easy enough for the self-employed and those in occupations where flexible working arrangements can be made. It is more difficult, of course, for the nine-till-five worker. While employers are required to give an employee who is appointed a magistrate reasonable time off work, not all employers can pay wages for the time taken off. To meet this difficulty provision has been made for a loss-of-earnings allowance but this is not overly generous and an employee who takes up the appointment against the wishes of his employer may find his promotion prospects jeopardised. The outcome is that wage-earners are proportionately under-represented on the bench which is still predominantly drawn from the professional classes.

In a related connection, Lord Gardiner, then Lord Chancellor, in 1966 caused something of a stir by directing local committees *not* to disregard the political affiliations of candidates. This may seem surprising but what Lord Gardiner sought, and properly sought, to do was to ensure that the magistracy was truly representative of all sections of society and all shades of opinion within it. What we do not want is a middle-aged, middle-class, male-dominated magistracy, all with similar social and political values.

No knowledge of law, still less legal qualification, is required but is equally not a bar to appointment. Nevertheless it would hardly do to leave magistrates in blissful ignorance of at least a rudimentary knowledge of the legal system, the principles of criminal law, evidence and procedure and notwithstanding that they will have available to them the advice of a clerk. Perhaps more especially they need to know something of judicial technique and the conduct of cases in court. Much can be learned from experience but the learning process can be accelerated by instruction. Consequently newly-appointed magistrates are required to attend courses of instruction to acquaint them with the essentials of the relevant law and procedure and to inform them of judicial technique and the principles of sentencing, and magistrates appointed since 1980 are required to attend refresher courses.

The commitment of the Lord Chancellor's Department to the training and retraining of magistrates is now clear. Although instruction is not compulsory for magistrates appointed before 1980, the expectation is that such magistrates will attend and a recent ruling that only magistrates who have attended such courses will be permitted after 1994 to take the chair in court will act as a powerful incentive.

In practice it appears that training problems are more logistical than financial. New legislation, and there is much of that affecting the jurisdiction of magistrates, may require many hours of instruction to absorb. This means that magistrates must give up a deal of their time at weekends or during evenings to attend courses. The obligations for magistrates are thus not inconsiderable and are increasing, and the magistrate of the twentieth century may well envy his nineteenth century counterpart. Though the lay magistrate is appointed without reference to his knowledge, which may be non-existent, of law, procedure and sentencing, it is now demanded that he or she becomes, at the very least, a gifted amateur.

In court the magistrates will have the services of a court clerk, to whom they may turn for advice on law and procedure. In each magistrates' courts area there is a clerk to the justices for which office the usual qualification is a five-year magistrates' courts qualification. He or she cannot of course attend at every court so there are accordingly powers to appoint additional clerks to the justices and to appoint assistant clerks. In practice a courts area will have only one "clerk to the justices" and will appoint deputy clerks who will be similarly qualified and assistants, called court clerks, for whom a professional qualification is not a requirement.

The clerk's role is an important one but it is the ancillary role of adviser. The responsibility for determining the facts and the law lies exclusively with the magistrates and the clerk must not usurp, nor *appear* to usurp, their functions. That appearance may arise when the magistrates, having retired to consider their decision, call in the clerk for advice. Depending on the circumstances, this may give rise to a suspicion that the clerk is taking part in the decision. Certainly the clerk must not retire with the magistrates as a matter of course but wait to be asked. When asked he may advise the magistrates privately on matters of law and matters of mixed law and fact but, whenever it is practicable to do so, the magistrates should return to the bench so that such advice can be given in open court. When exercising their legal functions, clerks are not subject to any directions from the magistrates' courts committee, or the justices' chief executive, or any other person.

A magistrate must normally retire at 70 but may be moved to the supplemental list (*i.e.* compulsorily retired) if by reason of age or infirmity he cannot discharge his judicial functions or if he neglects to do so. He may also be removed by the Lord Chancellor for misbehaviour which is not defined. A minor motoring offence would not be grounds for removal, an offence involving dishonesty certainly would be.

A note on judicial appointments

Until the Courts Act 1971 practising barristers held a virtual monopoly on salaried judicial appointments subject only to two exceptions. One was that solicitors could become stipendiary magistrates. The other (strange though it may seem) was that there were, and still are, no formal qualifications required of a person appointed Lord Chancellor.

The first significant inroad on the Bar's monopoly came with the Courts Act 1971, which provided that solicitors should be eligible for appointment as recorders. Since recorders were, in turn, eligible for appointment as circuit judges solicitors could, and did, become circuit judges but solicitors could progress no further up the judicial ladder.

The Courts and Legal Services Act 1990 goes much, much, further. As has been shown rights of audience, once the monopoly of barristers and solicitors (and of barristers only in the High Court and above) may now be accorded to suitably qualified persons and a person may be so qualified alhough she or he has no formal legal qualifications.

Eligibility for judicial appointment is accordingly expressed in the C.L.S.A. mainly, though not exclusively, in terms of holding the appropriate qualification to a right of audience for a prescribed period. So, for example, a person may be appointed a stipendiary magistrate if he or she has held for seven years a "general qualification" (*i.e.* a right of audience in relation to any class of proceedings in any part of the Supreme Court, or to all proceedings in county courts or magistrates' courts) while for appointment to the High Court a person requires to have held for ten years a 'High Court qualification' (*i.e.* a right of audience in relation to all proceedings in the High Court).

The way is thus open for a person without any formal legal qualifications to become a Lord of Appeal in Ordinary. Readers of this book may live to see that day but it is unlikely in the extreme that the writers of it will do so.

(2) Stipendiary Magistrates

A person who has a seven-year general qualification is eligible for appointment as a stipendiary magistrate. The office carries a salary (hence "stipendiary" for lay magistrates are unpaid) and is full-time. The number of stipendiaries who can be appointed at any one time is limited to 60 in the Inner London area (which until 1964 was served almost exclusively by stipendiaries) and up to 40 elsewhere. In the past stipendiaries have often been appointed in response to local dissatisfaction with the lay magistracy. There is no demand for the general replacement of lay magistrates by professional

from the judges of the High Court and on appointment they are created life peers. There are presently 12 of whom two are normally appointed from similarly qualified Scottish lawyers—the House of Lords being the final court of appeal from Scottish courts in civil matters.

(8) The Lord Chancellor

The Lord Chancellor holds the highest judicial office and is also Speaker of the House of Lords where (unlike his Commons counterpart) he is the Government's principal spokesman. He is a Minister of the Crown and usually a Cabinet Minister. The judicial duties are considerable. We have seen that he recommends most judicial appointments and is consulted in all others. He is the *ex officio* head of the Chancery Division, President of the Court of Appeal (though he rarely sits in either), and presides over judicial sittings in the House of Lords and Privy Council. The increasing burdens of the office have been such that for a period after the Second World War Lord Chancellors sat only infrequently on appeals but recent Chancellors have somehow managed to reverse the trend.

Oddly enough there are no formal qualifications for the office, any doubt whether a Roman Catholic could become Lord Chancellor being removed by statute in 1974. He is now invariably a lawyer and in the nature of things a lawyer of considerable experience and standing; not infrequently he will have served the Government as a law officer (Attorney-General or Solicitor-General).

(9) Lord Chief Justice

The Lord Chief Justice is next in judicial rank to the Lord Chancellor. The appointment is made on the recommendation of the Prime Minister after consultation with the Lord Chancellor. A person qualified for appointment as Lord Justice of Appeal, or who is a judge of the Court of Appeal, is qualified for appointment as Lord Chief Justice.

The Lord Chief Justice is, in the absence of the Lord Chancellor, President of the High Court; he is also President of the Queen's Bench Division and presides over the Criminal Division of the Court of Appeal. In practice the Lord Chief Justice is to be found in one of two appellate courts, the Court of Appeal or the Queen's Bench Divisional Court. Sometimes he sits as a trial judge, but this is now much less common than it was.

(10) Master of the Rolls

The appointment of, and qualification for, this office and for the offices of President of the Family Division and the Vice-Chancellor are as for the Lord Chief Justice after whom the Master of the Rolls next ranks. He presides in the Civil Division of the Court of Appeal.

So far as the development of law is concerned, the Lord Chief Justice and the Master of the Rolls occupy key positions. Although the House of Lords is the final appellate court the number of civil appeals heard by the House in an average year is about 50 while it is nearer 1,000 in the Civil Division of the Court of Appeal; the comparable figures for criminal cases are of the order of 12 and 2,000, leaving out of account appeals against sentence only. Figures can be deceptive, but it can be appreciated that in practical terms the influence of the Court of Appeal outweighs that of the House of Lords. In the Court of Appeal the Lord Chief Justice and the Master of the Rolls are the dominant figures—hence their importance in the legal system.

(11) President of the Family Division

He is responsible for the organisation and management of his division, sits in the division and is also an *ex officio* member of the Court of Appeal.

(12) The Vice-Chancellor

As we have seen, the Lord Chancellor is the President of the Chancery Division, but he now rarely sits in that court; he may, and ordinarily he does, appoint a Vice-Chancellor who is responsible to him for the organisation and management of the business of the division. The Vice-Chancellor and the President of the Family Division are appointed on the recommendation of the Prime Minister.

(13) The Appointment of Judges

It will have become clear that the Lord Chancellor enjoys enormous patronage in the appointment of judges. Most are appointed on his recommendation and even in the case of the very senior appointments made on the recommendation of the Prime Minister he is consulted and his view is likely to be decisive though, in turn, the Lord Chancellor will have consulted other senior judges.

The appointment of judges is now much more systematic than was once the case. The Lord Chancellor is assisted by the Judicial Appointments Group which is composed of senior members of his office and has the function of ensuring that the Lord Chancellor has all the information and advice to discharge his responsibilities. The Group will interview applicants or possible candidates for appointment and will consult with judges and senior members of the profession. So when the then Lord Chancellor, Lord Hailsham, admitted that he kept files on barristers (and perhaps files will in future be kept on all persons who have a Supreme Court or High Court qualification, whether barristers or not) no sinister motive can be attributed to him. The Lord Chancellor needs to know as much as he can about the suitability of candidates for judicial appointment. Appointments to any permanent judicial post will ordinarily be made only after the candidate has proved himself by experience in a part-time capacity.

Take a typical case. A person who is appropriately qualified wishes to become a judge. The first step is normally to seek appointment as an assistant recorder. All may apply but application is less necessary in the case of those in respect of whom files are kept. The candidate is interviewed, references may be taken up and soundings made. The candidate must commit himself to sitting for at least 20 days a year and if considered suitable he will be appointed for a fixed term but he may not sit until he has fulfilled the training requirements which presently involve a residential course of three-and-a-half days' duration and seven days sitting with a Circuit judge.

After a period, on average three years, the assistant recorder will be considered for appointment as Recorder and, if he merits it having regard to the judicial ability he has displayed as assistant, he will also be so appointed or otherwise stood down. The Recorder so appointed may then normally expect his recordership to be renewed for periods of three years at a time unless his performance is unsatisfactory.

The next step is Circuit judge. The formal qualifications are set out above but in practice a candidate will normally be expected to prove himself by satisfactory performance as assistant recorder and Recorder. The average "apprenticeship" to be served before becoming a Circuit judge appears to be of the order of six years and this ought to be enough to ensure that the Circuit judge is appropriately qualified for his duties.

The next step is the High Court, the qualifications for which are given above. Since Circuit judges of two years' standing are eligible for appointment to the High Court it might therefore be that the normal progression would be from recorder to Circuit judge to High Court judge, but this is far from being the case. Until the C.L.S.A. 1990 such progression was possible for Circuit judges who were barristers, but it was very rare. Since the C.L.S.A. all Circuit judges, however qualified, are eligible and the indications are that progression from Circuit judge to High Court judge will now be less rare.

But the great bulk of appointments to the High court is made directly from persons holding the alternative 10-year High Court qualification. Although this qualification may be held by persons other than practising barristers, the reality, at least for the time being, is that most appointments to the High Court will be made from the ranks of practising barristers, for the most part Q.C.s, who have proved to be outstanding. Such persons would normally have some judicial experience since most will have served as deputy High Court judges.

But we are experiencing the first stirrings of a wind of change. Lord Mackay L.C. has introduced the advertising of judicial appointments though only below the rank of High Court judge. He is committed to an equal opportunities policy which seeks to address the issue that certain groups (women, ethnic minorities) are underrepresented in the judicial ranks. Some would wish him to go much further. There have been suggestions, from within and without the legal profession, for a more broadly based selection system, but successive Lord Chancellors, although gradually opening up the system of appointment to professional and public scrutiny, have kept the reins of power firmly in their own hands.

(14) The Attorney-General

The Attorney-General is the principal legal adviser to the Crown (the Government) and is invariably a Member of Parliament and of the Government. The Government may require legal advice on a wide range of problems but perhaps especially on issues of constitutional law and international law, and the Attorney is expected to advise the Commons on legal issues. The Attorney exercises a large measure of control over criminal proceedings; prosecutions for certain offences (*e.g.* under the Official Secrets Act 1911) cannot be commenced without his consent, and by entering a *nolle prosequi* (be unwilling to proceed with) he may terminate any prosecution which has been commenced on indictment. By tradition he represents, though in an impartial manner, the interests of the Crown in the courts; accordingly he conducts certain cases (*e.g.* prosecutions for treason or for serious breaches of the Official Secrets Act) where the Crown has a special interest, or cases (*e.g.* certain prosecutions for murder) where the "public interest" appears to require it.

(15) The Solicitor-General

The foregoing brief review of the Attorney-General's duties indicates that he has a burdensome office. The Solicitor-General (who, like the Attorney, will normally be both a Member of Parliament and of the Government) assists the Attorney in the discharge of these duties, and may deputise for the Attorney during his absence or a vacancy in the office.

(16) Director of Public Prosecutions

The office of Director of Public Prosecutions was established in 1879 because of the widespread abuse of the system of private prosecution. Under the superintendence of the Attorney-General he was to conduct certain prosecutions and was to advise chief officers of police in the conduct of proceedings. In practice the Director conducted a relatively small percentage of prosecutions and most prosecutions (leaving aside those conducted by public agencies such as customs and excise) were conducted by the police. The position was radically altered by the Prosecution of Offences Act 1985 which set up a Crown Prosecution Service and redefined the powers of the Director. The functions and operation of the Crown Prosecution Service are described in the next section.

The Director, who must have a 10-year general qualification, is appointed by the Home Secretary.

6. The Courts: Composition and Jurisdiction

(1) Magistrates' Courts

For most purposes a magistrates' court must be composed of two justices (a stipendiary has the powers of two lay justices) though normally the Bench will be composed of three. A single lay justice has very limited powers (*e.g.* issue of summonses or warrants of arrest) but a single justice may determine whether a person is to be tried summarily or on indictment.

(a) Criminal jurisdiction

Some offences are so serious (*e.g.* treason, murder, manslaughter) that they can be tried *only* on indictment (hence they are known as indictable offences) at the Crown Court before a judge and jury; and some offences are so minor (*e.g.* many traffic offences such as driving without due care, speeding) that they can be tried *only* summarily (hence summary offences) by the magistrates. But there is an intermediate type of offence where the seriousness turns upon the circumstances (*e.g.* theft may involve property valued at only a few pence to property worth many thousands of pounds) and these offences may be tried either summarily or on indictment (hence they are known as offences triable either way).

The criminal jurisdiction of magistrates extends to the trial of summary offences and to offences triable either way which are suitable for summary trial, and they also have functions in relation to committing an accused for trial on indictment. These matters are more conveniently dealt with in the context of Chapter 4 (see below, p. 110).

(b) Civil jurisdiction

The magistrates' courts have odds and ends of civil jurisdiction including such matters as enforcing demands for the council charge and investigations into shipping casualties. The most important, and homogeneous, aspect of civil jurisdiction relates to domestic proceedings. This jurisdiction is extensive (extending to such matters as maintenance orders in favour of either spouse or their children, exclusion of either spouse from the matrimonial home for the protection of the other spouse and children, contact and residence orders, adoption orders, affiliation orders) but is generally subject to financial limits. This has led to the criticism that there is a secondary system of domestic courts for the poor; the better off using the county courts and High Court which are staffed by professional and highly qualified judges. To meet this criticism it is now provided that magistrates sitting in domestic cases must be drawn from a panel of specially qualified magistrates and that of the three magistrates comprising the bench at least one must be a man and one a woman.

(c) *Administrative functions*

Apart from the foregoing, magistrates also perform administrative, or quasi-judicial, functions. The best known of these is liquor licensing which probably found its way into the hands of the magistrates because of the close connection between drunkenness and breaches of the peace.

(2) County Courts

County courts are concerned exclusively with civil work and their jurisdiction is entirely statutory. Set up in 1846 to replace with a uniform system an uneven provision of local courts, their purpose was to provide a cheap process for minor civil claims. They are sometimes regarded as courts for the recovery of small debts but this is an entirely misleading index of their importance which has been recently enhanced by the Courts and Legal Services Act (C.L.S.A.) 1990 following a lengthy review of the civil justice system.

Broadly the jurisdiction of the county court is similar to that of the High Court with its jurisdiction constrained by reference to a financial limit—"the county court limit"—which limit is subject to adjustment. A further limitation relates to the remedies available to a judge of the county court. The effect of the changes introduced by the C.L.S.A. is greatly to enlarge the powers of the county court. All remedies are made available to them with limited exceptions such as that they cannot issue a prerogative order nor a so-called *Anton Piller* order which enables a plaintiff to enter the defendant's premises to seize documents. In addition the C.L.S.A. makes the arrangements for the transfer of cases between the county court and the High Court much more flexible. The aim is to redistribute business between these courts to provide a more efficient and speedy service for litigants. The outcome will inevitably involve a significant shift of business from the High Court to the county courts.

Take proceedings in contract and tort. Subject to specified exceptions, county court jurisdiction will be concurrent with the High Court. Claims involving less than £50,000 *must* be commenced in the county court while claims for more than £50,000 *may* be commenced in the High Court. Either court may then transfer a case to the other having regard to such facts as (a) the amount claimed; (b) whether the action is otherwise important and in particular whether it raises issues of general importance to persons who are not parties to the action; (c) the complexity of the facts, legal issues, remedies or procedures involved; and (d) whether transfer is likely to result in a more speedy trial except that a case may not be transferred on this ground alone.

An index of the significance of these changes can be seen by considering the extension of the jurisdiction of the district judge. The district judge (formerly the registrar of the county court and so restyled by the C.L.S.A., and who must hold a seven-year general qualification) attends to the administration of the county court but additionally has jurisdiction to try claims not exceeding £5,000 which sum was formerly the limit for Circuit judges and Recorders. Where a claim is for less than £1,000 it will be automatically referred to small claims arbitration. The arbitrator is a district judge (or a deputy or assistant). The litigants will ordinarily present their cases in person so the proceedings are informal; new rules have been introduced to make these proceedings as "user-friendly" as possible. It is perhaps these small claims arbitrations which come nearest to meeting what was the initial aim behind the setting up of the county courts: to provide a cheap process for minor civil claims.

(3) The High Court

The High Court was established by the Judicature Acts 1873–75 to overcome with a single court the problems caused by separate courts with differing procedures, and in particular the separate administration of equity and law. All judges of the High Court accordingly have the same jurisdiction and the same powers. For administrative reasons, however, and to take account of the nature of the work and the expertise of the judges, the court is made up of various divisions which are now the Chancery, Family, and Queen's Bench divisions. But note that administrative changes do not affect the authority of decisions; for example, the authority of *Felthouse v. Bindley* (discussed in Chapter 1) is unaffected by the fact that it was decided by a court, the Court of Common Pleas, which in name has long since ceased to exist.

(a) *Chancery division*

This division deals with those matters (such as the administration of estates, trusts, mortgages, actions for specific performance and injunctions) which were formerly dealt with by the Court of Chancery together with certain other business (such as revenue and company matters) which have been assigned to it.

(b) *Family division*

The business of this division extends to all defended matrimonial causes, to proceedings concerning wardship, adoption and guardianship of minors, and to the settlement of property disputes between spouses.

Since the magistrates' courts and county courts also have jurisdiction in family matters, matrimonial business is shared by three courts and this, it has been argued, leads to an unevenness in the handling of matrimonial causes. Proposals have therefore been made for a unified family court which would not only standardise the legal approach but which would also integrate the social services involved in domestic matters. These proposals enjoy wide support but the cost involved has so far ruled them out of serious practical consideration.

(c) *Queen's Bench division*

The business of this division extends to all civil matters (mainly actions in contract and tort) not falling within the purview of the other divisions. Within the division there is a court, designated the Commercial Court, to deal specifically with commercial matters; and a court, designated the Admiralty Court, dealing with shipping matters. Obviously judges are assigned to these courts who have a special expertise in commercial or admiralty law just as judges are assigned to the divisions of the High Court itself.

(d) *Appellate jurisdiction of the High Court*

Although the principal appellate courts are the Court of Appeal and the House of Lords, the High Court also has an important, if limited, appellate jurisdiction. All three divisions may constitute courts, somewhat confusingly called Divisional Courts, where the quorum (*i.e.* number of judges required to be present) is usually two puisne judges but, for some minor matters, may be constituted by a single judge. Thus, for example, the Chancery Divisional Court hears appeals from the county courts in bankruptcy matters; the Family Divisional Court hears appeals from the magistrates' courts in matrimonial matters; and the Queen's Bench Divisional Court hears appeals from certain tribunals.

The Queen's Bench Divisional Court also exercises an important supervisory jurisdiction. The court may issue orders of mandamus (*e.g.* to require a person to carry out a public duty imposed by law), certiorari (*e.g.* requiring an inferior court to transfer a case to the High Court for speedy trial), prohibition (*e.g.* requiring an inferior court to desist from hearing an action in which it has no jurisdiction), and habeas corpus (*e.g.* requiring someone who holds another in custody to show cause that the imprisonment is lawful). Another very important aspect of this supervisory jurisdiction is where on a case stated (which is explained below, p. 62) the court advises magistrates' courts on issues of criminal law.

(4) The Crown Court

Following a Royal Commission Report in 1969, the Crown Court was established by the Courts Act 1971 to replace the former courts of assize and quarter sessions whose jurisdiction was essentially local, with a single court (though of course it sits in many different places) having jurisdiction throughout England and Wales. The essential idea of the Royal Commission was to improve administrative efficiency to expedite the trial of criminal cases, to replace a ramshackle system by one that was efficiently run and monitored. When the court sits in the City of London it is known as the Central Criminal Court (popularly, the Old Bailey) and while the titles of Recorder of London and Common Serjeant are retained the persons holding such offices are Circuit judges. The jurisdiction is mainly, though not entirely, criminal; it has exclusive jurisdiction over trials on indictment, hears appeals from magistrates' courts and deals with committals for sentence.

The jurisdiction and powers of the Crown Court may be exercised by any High Court judge, any Circuit judge or Recorder; or any of the former sitting with justices of the peace. Where there is an appeal to the Crown Court from a decision of the magistrates or a committal for sentence by them, at least two and not more than four justices *must* sit with the judge or Recorder; in such cases the justices have an equal say in the decision but in the event of the court being equally divided the judge or Recorder has a casting vote.

Cases coming before the Crown Court vary enormously in seriousness and complexity. Offences are accordingly classified mainly according to their gravity so that the most serious offences are usually reserved to High Court judges while the least serious may be assigned to a Recorder with provision made for interchangeability. Court centres are also ranked according to the type of business from first tier centres which provide for all Crown Court business together with High Court civil work to third tier centres which provide only for offences triable either way. The responsibility of the administration for the new legal system lies in each circuit (of which there are six) and the circuit administrator. Each circuit administrator works under the aegis of, and in collaboration with, the presiding judges. Two presiding judges from the High Court are appointed for each circuit and a Lord Justice of Appeal is appointed as the senior presiding judge. Their functions, nowhere precisely defined, appear to be to ensure "quality control," to ensure that judges within the circuit are appropriately assigned to cases, and to monitor the performance of judges and the administrative arrangements for the circuit.

(5) The Court of Appeal

Another effect of the rationalisation of the courts system introduced by the Judicature Acts 1873–75 was the replacement of the Court of Appeal in Chancery and the Court of Exchequer Chamber by a single Court of Appeal to deal with civil appeals. There was not at this time a similar court for the hearing of appeals in criminal cases (though judges could reserve points of criminal law for consideration by the Court for Crown Cases Reserved) and it was not until the Criminal Appeal Act 1907 established the Court of Criminal Appeal that a general right of appeal was accorded in criminal cases. The Court of Criminal Appeal functioned as a separate court until it was abolished by the Criminal Appeal Act 1966 and its jurisdiction transferred to the Court of Appeal. There is now a single court with civil and criminal divisions.

The *ex officio* membership of the Court of Appeal comprises the Lord Chancellor, former Lord Chancellors, Lords of Appeal in Ordinary, the Lord Chief Justice, the Master of the Rolls and the President of the Family Division but of these only the Lord Chief Justice and the Master of the Rolls, who preside in their respective divisions, sit regularly. Lords Justices of Appeal are ordinary members of the court. The Lord Chancellor may request any ex-Lord Justice or ex-High Court judge to sit in the court and may require any High Court judge to do so.

Certain minor matters apart, three judges are required to make a quorum. Where a case is considered to be one of great importance it is not uncommon for the court to be composed of five judges; such courts are referred to as full courts but a full court has no more authority and power than a court of three members.

(a) *The civil division*

A court in the civil division will normally consist of either the Master of the Rolls sitting with two Lords Justices, or three Lords Justices. The jurisdiction of the court extends to all appeals from the High Court, appeals from the county courts in common law and equity matters, and appeals from many tribunals.

(b) *The criminal division*

The Lord Chief Justice, after consultation with the Master of the Rolls, may require judges of the Queen's Bench Division to sit as judges in the criminal division; in practice he regularly does so and a court in the criminal division is normally composed of the Lord Chief Justice sitting with two puisne judges, or a Lord Justice of Appeal sitting with two puisne judges. The reason for this is the day-to-day familiarity which the judges of the Queen's Bench have with criminal cases; they can provide a particular expertise perhaps especially in relation to sentencing.   In this connection the Royal Commission on Criminal Justice (1993) noted that in practice only 5 per cent of the work in the Crown Court was done by High Court judges while 67 per cent was done by Circuit judges. The Commission therefore recommended that Circuit judges (obviously senior judges with considerable experience of criminal cases) should be eligible to sit in the Criminal Division of the Court of Appeal with the qualifications that a Circuit judge should not sit to determine an appeal against a conviction before, or a sentence imposed by, a High Court judge; nor be able to exercise the functions exercisable by a single judge of the court. These recommendations were implemented by the Criminal Justice & Public Order Act 1994. The jurisdiction of the court almost entirely concerns appeals following trial on indictment in the Crown Court.

(6) The House of Lords

By the Appellate Jurisdiction Act 1876 an appeal may not be determined by the House of Lords unless at least three (in practice it is normally five) of the following are present: the Lord Chancellor, the Lords of Appeal in Ordinary, and peers who have held high judicial office (*e.g.* ex-Lord Chancellors). Strictly, all members of the House may vote on an appeal but by convention do not do so.

The House of Lords has both original and appellate jurisdiction. The original jurisdiction, not of much practical importance, extends to contested claims to peerages, and, in theory, it is still open for the Commons to impeach any person before the Lords. The appellate jurisdiction extends in civil cases to appeals from the Court of Appeal and (by what is known as the "leap-frog" appeal described below, p. 68) from the High Court; and in criminal matters from the Court of Appeal and the Divisional Court of the Queen's Bench Division. The House of Lords is also the final court of appeal for Northern Ireland and, except for criminal matters, for Scotland.

(7) The Privy Council

The composition of the Judicial Committee is similar to that of the House of Lords when hearing appeals, and as in the House five members usually sit though the quorum is three. The bulk of its work is done by the Lords of Appeal in Ordinary and the Lord Chancellor frequently sits, but it is not uncommon for a member of the Privy Council who holds a designated judicial office in specified Commonwealth countries to sit as a member of the court.

The Judicial Committee has jurisdiction to hear appeals from British Colonies and Protectorates and from independent Commonwealth countries though the latter have increasingly availed themselves of their right to exclude appeals to the Privy Council. Its jurisdiction also extends to appeals from the Admiralty Court of the Queen's Bench Division in prize cases (which concern the ownership of vessels captured during hostilities), certain appeals from ecclesiastical courts, and certain appeals from the disciplinary committee of the General Medical Council.

(8) Tribunals, Inquiries and Administrative Law

Administrative law has been defined (de Smith, *Constitutional and Administrative Law* (6th ed.), p. 533) as concerning—

> "the day-to-day administration of the country at central and local level and putting into practice constitutionally decided policies. Administrative law regulates that process. It relates to the organisation, composition, functions

and procedures of public authorities and special statutory tribunals, their impact on the citizen and the legal restraints and liabilities to which they are subject. It controls the making of subordinate legislation by public authorities."

It will be appreciated, therefore, that any comprehensive treatment of the subject would be of enormous dimensions so that what follows here is only the barest outline.

We might begin by supposing that the Government has decided to build an additional airport to serve London. Legislation will be required to empower the appropriate Minister to decide on the best site, to authorise him to acquire land compulsorily, to authorise him to engage contractors and so on. These are not matters which can be decided by the courts for they involve issues of policy entirely unsuitable for resolution by judges. No doubt the residents of north London would prefer the airport to be sited in south London while those in the south would prefer it to be the north, but their differences of view could not be satisfactorily resolved by a court.

On the other hand, members of the public will demand a forum where their views can be aired, where they can argue about the suitability of particular sites, about the effect on the environment, even about the consequences for wildlife. People whose property is compulsorily purchased will want a forum where they can challenge the Minister's decision or his assessment of the value of their property. The contractors need to be assured that, in the event of a dispute with the Minister, their complaints will be impartially determined. In theory the Government might by legislation empower the Minister to site the airport without regard to the interests of the public and to acquire land compulsorily without compensation. But in practice this is unthinkable. Most likely the legislation would provide for public inquiries as to the siting of the airport where, although the final decision would remain with the Minister, this would be after individual or collective representations of members of the public have been heard. The legislation would also likely provide that disputes as to the valuation of compulsorily acquired property would be settled by the Lands Tribunal while contractual claims could be left to be settled in the ordinary way by the courts.

Thus the critical decision—the location of the airport with all its social, economic and environmental consequences—is an administrative one. Important decisions relating to compensation are made by a tribunal rather than a court because it is felt that a specialist tribunal is better equipped for this task than a court. It would be possible to set up a specialist tribunal to deal with contractual claims but these can be left to resolution in the courts which are well able to deal with them.

The pattern may be repeated at local government level where the local authority must make decisions about new roads or new housing developments. Or a local authority may be concerned with the licensing of taxi-cab operators; on the face of it a purely administrative matter but it can be appreciated that the grant or withholding of a licence can vitally affect the livelihood of particular people.

The Government may also decide that certain matters are best adjudicated by a specialist tribunal rather than by the ordinary courts. In fact Governments have increasingly resorted to tribunals, especially in relation to the administration of the welfare state, as a means, not only of providing specialist expertise, but also in the interests of cost-effectiveness and expedition. So great has been the proliferation of such tribunals that the man in the street is much more likely to have some dispute resolved by a tribunal than by a court.

Tribunals are not all of the same pattern. At the one extreme is the high-powered tribunal of inquiry (such as the inquiry conducted by the Lord Chief Justice into the events of "Bloody Sunday" in Northern Ireland in 1972, or the inquiry conducted by Lord Scarman into the Brixton riots of 1981) where the judge has power to subpoena (*i.e.* compel the attendance of) witnesses and require the production of documents. At the other extreme a householder may be seeking planning permission for a garage or a porch. Some tribunals may be set up to deal with a particular issue, some may be established on a permanent basis; some may have an exclusively legally qualified membership, some may have lay membership. It may be helpful to consider the composition and jurisdiction of just two such tribunals though it must not be thought that all tribunals follow the pattern shown by these.

(a) *Criminal Injuries Compensation Board*

It will be appreciated that where X is deliberately injured by Y, X is usually entitled to claim compensation from Y; such a claim may be brought, depending upon the amount claimed, either in the county court or in the High Court or may be sought by way of a compensation order in criminal proceedings. Whether it is worth X bringing such a claim will depend on the means of Y and Y may be of such limited means (a "man of straw") that X's right to compensation is worthless, or it may be that X's assailant is never identified.

To deal with this sort of problem a scheme—the Criminal Injuries Compensation Scheme—was introduced in 1964 under which victims of crimes of violence who have suffered personal injuries may claim compensation from public funds. To eliminate minor claims the minimum award, first fixed at £50, has been progressively raised and now stands at £1,000. In the first year of operation the compensation paid totalled some £400,000; by 1994 the amount was in excess of £165M. Compensation is calculated by reference to what the applicant would have received in a civil action less certain deductions for such things as social security payments or payments under a compensation order. Most awards are for sums less than £10,000 but awards in excess of £500,000 have been made.

The scheme extends not only to injuries sustained as a result of a crime of violence but also to injuries sustained in the apprehension of offenders and "to an offence of trespass on a railway." This last looks odd but it is to deal with cases, formerly not within the scheme since there was no crime of violence (see *R. v. Criminal Injuries Board, ex p. Warner and others* [1986] 2 All E.R. 478, C.A.), where train drivers suffered trauma where, perforce, they killed or injured suicides or would-be suicides (of which there are some 400 each year) on railway lines. The scheme extends to domestic violence provided the parties no longer live together and a sum, presently £5,000, is payable to a woman who conceives as a result of rape and decides to keep the child.

A person sustaining personal injuries, or his family in the event of his death, may claim compensation. The application is in the first instance considered by one member of the Board (all of whom are legally qualified) who normally makes the decision on the basis of the papers submitted to him, but if an applicant is dissatisfied with the decision of the single member it may be referred to a panel of two members which may then conduct a hearing at which the applicant and witnesses may be heard and examined. The Board now deals with over 70,000 applications a year; a considerable backlog of cases has built up but recent improvements in staffing and administration have been made with a view to relieving delays.

The Board has a discretion whether to award compensation or to make a reduced award, and any payment made is *ex gratia*. In the exercise of its discretion the Board will have regard to such factors as whether the applicant unreasonably failed promptly to inform the police of the incident, whether the applicant failed to cooperate in proceedings against the offender, whether the applicant caused or contributed to the injuries sustained, and whether the person causing the injuries might benefit from the award (*e.g.* where a wife continues to live with her husband following his assault on her).

There is no appeal against decisions of the Board on questions of fact or of mixed fact and law. It is, however, open to an applicant to apply to the High Court to quash the decision of the Board where it is alleged to be wrong in law. This may be illustrated by *R. v. Criminal Injuries Compensation Board, ex p. Thompstone* (1983) and *R. v. Criminal Injuries Compensation Board, ex p. R.J.C. (An Infant)* (1978). In deciding whether to make an award the Board is enjoined to have regard to the applicant's "character and way of life." In the former case the High Court acknowledged that the Board had been given the widest possible discretion and held that the Board properly refused compensation to an applicant who had numerous convictions for offences of violence and dishonesty even though there was no connection between his character and the particular assault in respect of which he claimed compensation. But in the latter certiorari was granted where the Board ruled it would not give compensation to any member of a gang injured in a gang fight; such a decision was not an exercise of discretion but a decision never to exercise their discretion in a particular class of case. The Board had gone too far in laying down a general rule which precluded the exercise of any discretion in particular cases.

It is possible to make criticisms of the scheme: in particular there is no provision for economic loss caused by crime. Essentially the scheme is viewed by Governments, not from the viewpoint of what ought to be made available, but from the point of view of resource allocation; as a matter of what can be afforded and how best to distribute what can be afforded. But the scheme is expeditious and cheap and nearly all claims are settled by a single member to the satisfaction of the applicant. The pluses of the scheme outweigh the minuses.

There are provisions in the Criminal Justice Act 1988 to place the scheme on a statutory footing. The Act provides for a right to compensation and a right of appeal, on law alone, to the High Court and, with leave, to the Court of Appeal. These provisions have not yet been brought into force but in *R. v. Secretary of State for the Home Department, ex parte Fire Brigades Union & others* [1995] 1 All E.R. 888, C.A., were nevertheless held to have an important side effect. The Government, with a view to halving the cost of criminal injuries compensation by the year 2000, proposed to replace the present basis of assessing compensation on common law principles by a flat-rate tariff related to the type of injuries inflicted. It was held that while the provisions of the 1988 Act remained unrepealed, albeit not yet m force, it was not open to the Government, other than by securing the repeal of those provisions, to introduce a compensation scheme wholly at variance with those provisions.

(b) *Industrial tribunals*

No one of sense needs to be reminded of the cardinal importance of maintaining good industrial relations and the consequent importance of ensuring that employees are treated with fairness and dignity. What the lawmakers have to do is to ensure a fair balance between the interests of the employer and those of the employee. While there can be no question of paramountcy for either, it would be right to say that successive Governments in this century have sought to redress in favour of the employee a balance which formerly very much favoured the employer. In recent years there has been legislation aimed at protecting the employee against discrimination, against unfair dismissal, and against the consequences of redundancy. It would, of course, have been possible for this law to have been administered by the courts but instead the task has been assigned to tribunals. Tribunals have the advantages of informality, low costs and expedition not matched by the courts. Moreover, such tribunals may be staffed by members having a particular knowledge of, and expertise in, the area of law which they administer.

Hence industrial tribunals were established in 1964 at first with a limited, but now a growing, jurisdiction. The tribunal is constituted by three members, a legally qualified chairman with two lay members who are appointed after consultation with organisations of employers and employees but in no sense do the persons appointed represent these organisations. The lay members have an equal voice with the chairman and decisions are by majority.

Appeal lies to the Employment Appeal Tribunal (E.A.T.) which is composed of a High Court judge sitting with two lay members. The lay members are again appointed after consultation with organisations of employers and employees but once appointed they are independent members and decisions are by majority. Appeal lies on questions of law under a variety of enactments and, in some cases, on questions of fact or law. It appears that appeals are made against the decisions of industrial tribunals in about 4 per cent. of the cases heard; it is also worth noting that only exceptionally are the decisions of the E.A.T. not unanimous, and that on occasion the judicial member has found himself in the minority.

Other than on a question of fact appeal lies from the E.A.T. to the Court of Appeal and thence to the House of Lords.

Overall the system has worked well enough though not without its stresses. Increasingly parties are legally represented but, and since legal aid is not available for these proceedings, the employer is much more likely than the employee to be legally represented. Proceedings, meant to be informal and user-friendly, have become increasingly formalised and are now not unlike those of a county court. The body of law is considerable and complex; long gone are the days when students referred to Employment Law as "Contract and Tort in a boiler-suit".

Indeed, it may not be unfairly said of tribunals generally that that while they have proved to be cheaper and more expeditious than courts they have increasingly succumbed to what may be called the vice of legalism. "For legalism," as the Lord Chancellor, Lord Mackay, has observed, "is the enemy of efficiency and user-friendliness as well as cost-effectiveness—whether within the judicial system or outside it." So the thoughts of some, including Lord Mackay, have turned to alternative dispute resolution (A.D.R.) as a means of resolving some disputes, say, resolution of disputes between husband and wife on the breakdown of their marriage as to custody of children or the division of property, disputes between neighbours concerning nuisances, disputes over package holidays. Such disputes might be quickly and cheaply resolved if the parties voluntarily agree (there can be no question of compulsion) to accept binding arbitration. A.D.R. looks attractive. Proceedings could be informal, user-friendly, cheap and expeditious. But the parties to A.D.R. proceedings can hardly be denied the services of a lawyer to present their cases. Nor can such proceedings be exempt from judicial review so it may turn out to be a case of two steps forward and two steps back. A.D.R. may operate "outside" the courts system but will inevitably be subject to judicial control. Once lawyers involve themselves in A.D.R., as inevitably they will, then legalism may well reappear. The neophytes who read this book need to address this problem. Unlimited legal aid might be an answer but the country can no more afford unlimited legal aid than it can provide unlimited aid for any other social service that it provides. So what is the answer? How do we provide cheap and expeditious justice for all?

(c) *The supervision of administrative action and tribunals*

As we have seen, administrative action is essential if the airports, the roads, the hospitals, the schools and a thousand things besides which are necessary to the functioning of modern society are to be provided within a reasonable timescale. But decisions about these matters may vitally affect the interest of any of us. We are all in favour of roads and hospitals until our private interests are affected. While roads and hospitals cannot be built without adversely affecting someone's interests, we need a system which ensures a measure of fairness for all. Similarly with tribunals. We can see the need for specialist tribunals, with their advantage of expertise, expedition and informality, but we need to be assured that their decisions, like those of the courts, are subject to correction by appeal. In fact many tribunals are substantially indistinguishable from courts. Decisions of industrial tribunals, as has been shown, are subject to review by the Employment Appeal Tribunal from which appeal lies to the Court of Appeal and the House of Lords. But we have also seen that in the case of the Criminal Injuries Compensation Board there is as yet no such constituted system of appeal while the system for social welfare has a two-tier system of appeals within its own administrative framework. These instances show that tribunals have not been created in pursuance of a master plan but in response to the expanding needs of a complex society. Not surprisingly, the solution adopted for one sort of problem may differ markedly from that adopted for another. The acid test is whether tribunals "work."

To ensure that they do, and independently of judicial control which will be examined below, the Tribunals and Inquiries Act 1958 (the governing statute is now the Tribunals & Inquiries Act 1992) set up a Council on Tribunals whose function it is to keep under review the constitution and workings of some 60 specified tribunals. The Council, which consists of up to 15 members appointed by the Lord Chancellor, works part-time and has no power directly to interfere with the decisions or the workings of tribunals. Nevertheless, the reviews which it conducts and the reports which it produces have proved invaluable in securing what are considered to be the essentials of administrative justice, namely, openness, fairness and impartiality.

Nor have the courts been prepared to play a spectator's role. They have of course recognised the need for administrative action, but the courts may intervene to quash administrative decisions under a process known as judicial review. Judicial review is no easy subject matter to explain and has been described by authoritative commentators as "a very difficult area of law to chart" and "an extremely complicated subject with intricate ramifications". It is also a growth area of the law (applications for judicial review quadrupled in the decade 1980–90) as the courts—at first tentatively but progressively with increasing boldness—have examined the actions taken by persons and bodies in authority (primarily, but no means exclusively, by government ministers or agencies as well as administrative tribunals) where those actions have unfairly or improperly adversely affected individuals in the exercise of their rights, interest or legitimate expectations.

What the courts exercising their powers of judicial review will not do is to substitute their views of what should be done for those of the decision-maker. What the courts will do is to quash a decision which has been reached improperly because, for example, the decision-maker has acted *ultra vires* (outside the powers accorded), or has given account to irrelevant factors or has left out of account relevant factors, or has exhibited bias, or has taken a wrong view of the relevant law. While the quashing of a decision leaves it open to the decision-maker, on a reconsideration that is not flawed by impropriety, to reach the same decision, the effect of quashing a decision is often to oblige the decision maker to revise the decision.

Consider *Secretary of State for Education and Science v. Metropolitan Borough of Tameside* (1976). In 1975 a local education authority (at this time Labour-controlled) submitted proposals to the Secretary for introducing a system of comprehensive education which would have given admission to schools without reference to ability and which would have resulted in the abolition of five grammar schools. The Secretary approved these proposals but before implementation a local election resulted in control of the education authority passing to the Conservatives. They decided to modify these proposals by retaining the grammar schools but their proposals to the Secretary were rejected by him on the grounds that the authority was acting unreasonably, and he required them to implement the original proposals. It was held by the House of Lords that even though the Secretary might legitimately take the view that the subsequent proposals were misguided and wrong, there were no grounds on which he could find them to be unreasonable because, given the expected willingness of the teachers to co-operate with the revised plan, there was nothing to suggest that it could not operate satisfactorily. The consequence of quashing the Secretary's decision was effectively to reverse it because the Secretary had no other objections to allege and the new proposals were accordingly implemented.

What *Tameside* appears to show is that the concept of "reasonableness" does not mean that only one course of action can be the reasonable one. There may, in a given situation, be two or three or more courses of action which may fairly be regarded as reasonable. The view adopted by the Minister in *Tameside* may have been entirely reasonable and even preferable to that of the local authority, but the Minister had powers to overturn the local authority's proposed course of action only if that proposed course of action was outside the bounds of what was reasonable. Here the course proposed was not an unreasonable one.

Another example is provided by *R. v. Secretary of State for the Home Department, ex parte Bentley* [1993] 4 All E.R. 442, D.C. Derek Bentley had been convicted in 1952 of murder, then a capital offence, and sentenced to death. Notwithstanding the jury's recommendation to mercy, which was supported in the advice given him by his principal officers in the Home Department and having regard also to the fact that Bentley was close to being feebleminded, the Home Secretary of the day declined to recommend the commutation of the death penalty to life imprisonment and Bentley was hanged. Bentley's sister campaigned thereafter for a free pardon for her brother but this was refused in 1992 by the then Home Secretary who, while expressing his disquiet by his predecessor's decision not to commute the death penalty, stated that he could not substitute his own judgment for that of his predecessor because it had been "the long established policy of successive Home Secretaries that a Free Pardon in relation to a conviction for an indictable offence should be granted only if the moral as well as technical innocence of the convicted person can be established".

Ms Bentley sought judicial review of this decision. The court, holding that it had jurisdiction to review the exercise of the royal prerogative of mercy by the Home Secretary, held that the Home Secretary's decision in 1992 not to grant a posthumous pardon was flawed because he had failed to consider the grant of a conditional posthumous pardon which it was open to him to consider and which, while recognising that Bentley was properly convicted of murder, would acknowledge that the Home Secretary in 1952 had been wrong in not recognising that Bentley's sentence should have been commuted from hanging to life imprisonment.

In the light of this decision, the Home Secretary might have reconsidered his decision and have reached the same decision taking account of the factors that had led the court to quash his decision. But he was really obliged to reach the conclusion which the court had indicated, *i.e.* that Bentley should be given a conditional pardon and this subsequently followed.

Consulting authorities on judicial review as to what would have been the outcome of an application by Bentley in 1952, following the refusal of the Home Secretary to commute the capital sentence, the authors have found that such an application in 1992 would have been greeted by the courts with nothing short of incredulity. Such has been the development of judicial review in the forty or so years that have passed since then.

It is not the function of the courts to decide which is the best course to adopt, to decide between competing views. The courts would then have to enter the political arena and this they are not equipped to do. In *Nottinghamshire County Council v. Secretary of State for the Environment* ([1986] 1 All E.R. 199, H.L.) and *Hammersmith & Fulham London Borough Council v. Secretary of State for the Environment* ([1990] 3 All E.R. 589, H.L.) the courts were concerned with the powers of the Minister to control local expenditure by, in the former case, reducing the level of rate support from central funds, and, in the latter, by "charge capping" (*i.e.* fixing the maximum community charge that could be levied). In both cases the complaining local authorities alleged that the exercise of the powers operated unevenly but the House of Lords refused to interfere. In a way these cases were the obverse of *Tameside*. This time it was for the local authorities to show that the Minister had acted unreasonably and this they could not do simply by showing that the Minister's decision operated to their disadvantage or that there were other, even preferable, alternatives. The courts would not, and could not, make political decisions, preferring one policy decision to another.

The courts may only interfere, according to Lord Diplock, where the decision is illegal (as where there is no warrant for it in the statutory powers conferred); or that it is irrational (it is a decision that cannot reasonably be supported); or where there has been some procedural impropriety (a failure to exercise the power as required by the relevant legislation or in accordance with the requirements of natural justice).

In the *Tameside* case it was held that the Minister had acted *ultra vires* (outside the powers). It will be appreciated that an authority given by statute to do one thing may carry with it powers to do that which is implicit in carrying out that authority, but that it cannot carry powers to do something else. To take an obvious, if far-fetched, example, a Minister who was by legislation authorised to build an additional airport for London would be restrained from using these powers to build a motorway between Leeds and Manchester. A good example is provided by *Bromley L.B.C. v. Greater London Council* (1982). The G.L.C. was by statute under a duty to provide "integrated, efficient and economic transport facilities" for London and was empowered to perform its function with due regard to "efficiency, economy and safety of operation." The G.L.C., having decided that it was in the best interests of the service to reduce fares, did so by 25 per cent. This increased the operating deficit and in order to balance the books the G.L.C. issued a supplementary rate demand to all London boroughs. This demand was successfully challenged by Bromley L.B.C., the House of Lords holding that although the G.L.C. had a wide discretion in the management of transport services it was nevertheless obliged to run them on ordinary business principles. The G.L.C. thus acted *ultra vires* in reducing fares by an arbitrary amount without regard to the ordinary business principle that the service should pay for itself by self-generated income.

Where standards of "fairness" have not been observed the courts have shown an increasing willingness to intervene, even where the relevant legislation has purported to exclude review by the courts. In *Anisminic v. The Foreign Compensation Commission* (1969) Lord Reid said that if a statute provided that a certain order could be made by a person holding specified qualifications and further provided that such an order could not be questioned in a court of law, an order which was alleged to be a forgery or to have been made by a person not possessing the specified qualifications would nonetheless be open to review by the courts. Thus in the *Anisminic* case itself a statutory provision saying "The determination by the Commission of any application made to them under this Act shall not be called in question in any court of law" did not prevent the House of Lords from reviewing the Commission's declaration when it appeared that in making the determination the Commission had taken into account a factor which it had no right to take into account. "Determination" meant a real determination properly arrived at and did not extend to a purported determination which had been arrived at improperly.

(d) *Conclusions*

In this brief review we have seen that administrative action is necessary and that while decisions on matters of national and local policy are rightly not matters for courts to determine, the courts are ever ready to intervene where there has been an infringement of rights protected by public law, or of a right under private law if an infringement of public law is involved in order to ensure that the procedures followed are essentially fair. Even where Parliament purports to oust the jurisdiction of the courts, the courts show an increasing willingness (even ingenuity) to review decisions arrived at by procedures which do not comply with the essential standards of fairness which the courts would require of their own procedures.

(e) *The Parliamentary Commissioner for Administration and Health Service Commissioner (Ombudsman)*

English courts and tribunals do not provide a remedy for all wrongs and every grievance. There are of course extra-legal avenues for airing grievances (*e.g.* letters to the Press, programmes on television and radio, complaints to local councillors or Members of Parliament) which not infrequently lead to a remedy, and these extra-legal avenues should not be discounted. Nevertheless they have their limitations, perhaps especially so when the citizen is dealing with the powerful bureaucracy of the state. For the citizen there may be no redress in the courts and extra-legal procedures may have failed to penetrate the secrecy with which bureaucrats, almost by instinct it seems, shroud their actions from public scrutiny. To meet this sort of case the Parliamentary Commissioner Act 1967 established the office of Parliamentary Commissioner for Administration (popularly called the Ombudsman following the innovation of the office in Denmark) to investigate complaints by citizens who claim to have suffered injustice as a result of "maladministration" at the hands of Government Departments.

The P.C.A. is appointed by the Crown on the advice of the Prime Minister and holds office until 65. There are no professional qualifications for the office; the office has been held by lawyers and also by ex-civil servants whose familiarity with administration may be both an advantage and a disadvantage. The P.C.A. cannot act of his own initiative, nor directly on a complaint by a member of the public; he can act only on a written complaint made on behalf of the complainant by a Member of Parliament. Thereafter the P.C.A. conducts his inquiry in private but he has the necessary powers to penetrate official secretiveness. He has no powers to alter decisions nor to compel redress of any maladministration he finds to be proved and is confined merely to publishing a report of his findings.

The results have not been spectacular and have led to the accusation that the P.C.A. is an Ombudsmouse. On the other hand, and given that our civil servants, though wedded to secrecy, do prize integrity and efficiency, it is not surprising that maladministration is more frequently found not proved than proved (about 20 per cent. of complaints prove successful), and that when proved rarely establishes alarming shortcomings. What is more surprising is that his findings have sometimes been hotly contested by the Minister on behalf of the Department to which they apply, and the *ex gratia* payment which he has recommended only grudgingly given. In the end, though, the P.C.A. has provided a means of redress where other avenues have been closed. He has, for example, persuaded the Inland Revenue (which, along with the Department of Social Security has been a frequent subject of complaint) to modify or forgo tax demands which, though legal, are oppressive or would cause hardship; and in the Sachsenhausen Case (1967) he found maladministration on the part of the Foreign Office in dealing with claims for compensation by former prisoners-of-war.

The Commissioner's duties were enlarged in 1973 to embrace complaints concerning maladministration in the Health Service involving an alleged failure in a service or a failure to provide a service but not complaints for which the complainant has another avenue of redress, for example, not for alleged professional negligence in respect of which a claim must be pursued in the courts. Where the complainant has a relevant complaint it may be made directly to the Commissioner and does not require referral from any other person or body.

In 1974 the Local Government Act established a Commission for Local Administration in England which provides for Local Ombudsmen to consider complaints about maladministration in local authorities in much the same way as the P.C.A. does with central government. The Local Commissioners cannot directly handle complaints which must be ordinarily referred to them by a local councillor on behalf of the complainant. Like the P.C.A. they cannot directly interfere with decisions but are confined to making reports which are concerned not with the merits of particular decisions but the way in which they are arrived at. Most complaints relate to planning and housing matters and only a minority of complaints result in a finding of maladministration. As with central government so in local government the report and recommendations of the Local Commissioners are not always greeted with unqualified acceptance by the local authority. In such a case Local Commissioners may issue a second report which, especially if given Press coverage, will be even more persuasive. In the end, though, the Local Commissioners cannot enforce their recommendations on a local authority which is prepared to dig in its heels. This is, however, the exception and normally local authorities comply with the recommendations of the Local Commissioners.

Mention may also be made of the Legal Services Ombudsman, an office created by the Courts and Legal Services Act 1990. Some perceived dissatisfaction with the way in which the professions dealt with complaints about legal services led the Lord Chancellor in 1989 to appoint the Lay Observer to examine the treatment of complaints. The office of Legal Services Ombudsman, which replaces the Lay Observer, is much enhanced, has a permanent staff and is independent of the Government and the professions.

7. The Courts: Appeals

(1) Criminal Cases

As we have seen a person charged with crime may be tried summarily in a magistrates' court or be tried on indictment in the Crown Court and the system of appeals differs accordingly.

(a) *Appeal following summary conviction*

A person convicted in a magistrates' court (*e.g.* of careless driving, shoplifting, assault) may appeal to the Crown Court as of right (i) against any sentence imposed if he pleaded guilty; and (ii) against conviction and/or sentence if he pleaded not guilty. In the Crown Court the appeal will normally be heard by a Circuit judge sitting with two to four magistrates (other, of course, than magistrates concerned in the trial) and each member has an equal vote except that if the court is equally divided the Circuit judge has a second or casting vote.

The appeal is by way of rehearing. In effect it is a retrial with the prosecution and the defence calling witnesses and adducing evidence even though not called or adduced at the trial. The Crown Court may, if it decides to convict, impose any sentence which the magistrates' court *might* have imposed on that charge so that the defendant may have imposed on him a sentence more severe than that imposed by the magistrates.

(b) *Appeal by way of case stated*

Quite independently of the foregoing right of appeal to the Crown Court, it is additionally open to the defendant *or to the prosecutor* to request the magistrates' court, or the Crown Court when hearing an appeal from the magistrates' court, to state a case for the opinion of the Divisional Court of the Queen's Bench Division on the grounds that the decision is wrong in point of law or is in excess of jurisdiction. It is necessary for the stated case to identify the point of law so it is necessary for the magistrates or the Crown Court to provide a statement of the facts which is agreed to by the parties, and the question of law sought to be resolved. Typically a stated case involves a case where the facts are not in dispute but the issue is whether those facts disclose an offence. For example, in *Fagan* (1969) it was common ground that the defendant had while parking his car inadvertently driven on to a police officer's foot but, having been told by the officer of this, he deliberately left his car there for a few moments before switching on his engine and releasing the officer. These facts raised a nice question of law as to whether the defendant had assaulted the officer (see below, p. 370) and hence a case was stated to resolve the legal issue.

On a case stated a further appeal is possible from the Divisional Court to the House of Lords provided that the Divisional Court (i) certifies that a point of law of public importance is involved; and (ii) that either the Divisional Court or the House of Lords gives leave to appeal (see below, p. 66). Thus a case which is tried in a magistrates' court may end in the House of Lords and may involve three, or even four if it goes to the Crown Court, separate hearings. But such cases are highly exceptional. In practice appeals from the decision of magistrates (both to the Crown Court, or by way of case stated) are taken in less than 0.5 per cent. of cases. This may seem a surprising statistic but it has to be remembered that the vast majority charged before magistrates plead guilty; and of those others who may feel aggrieved by a verdict of guilty, many would rather avoid the possible expense, publicity and embarrasment which may be involved in an appeal.

(c) *Judicial review*

Judicial review (see above, p. 53) is also available to challenge decisions in the magistrates' courts. Obviously judicial review is available where the magistrates have acted outside their jurisdiction or where the proceedings have been conducted unfairly. A novel instance of review is provided by *R. v. Bolton Magistrates' Court, ex p. Scally and others* [1990] *The Times*, October 4.

The defendants had inevitably pleaded guilty to driving with an excessive blood-alcohol concentration when scientific evidence showed excessive alcohol. It subsequently appeared that the samples may have been inaccurately high because the skin-cleaning swabs themselves contained the same concentration of alcohol as beer. The defendants could not appeal to the Crown Court since they had pleaded guilty; nor could they appeal by way of case stated since no point of law was involved. The Home Secretary had indicated that he was not minded to grant a pardon but in any event a free pardon would have done no more than relieve them from the penalty; the conviction would remain and, in the event of a subsequent conviction for the same offence, they would face a mandatory three-year driving ban.

Quashing the convictions the court said that though there was no suggestion of deliberate impropriety, the manner in which the case was conducted effectively deprived the defendants of their defence and was analogous to a conviction secured by fraud, collusion or perjury.

(d) *Appeal following conviction on indictment*

A person so convicted may appeal to the Court of Appeal (i) as of right on a point of law alone; and (ii) with leave of the Court of Appeal on a question of fact alone or of mixed law and fact. Unless the sentence is one fixed by law (*e.g.* the mandatory life sentence on conviction for murder) the defendant may, with leave, appeal against the sentence. On such an appeal, the Court of Appeal cannot impose a more severe sentence than that imposed by the Crown Court though, as we have seen, the Crown Court on an appeal from a magistrates' court can impose a sentence more severe than that imposed by the magistrates. The Crown cannot appeal against sentence. However, and because of public disquiet at the imposition of sentences in some cases which have been thought to be too lenient, there are provisions in the Criminal Justice Act 1988 which enable the Attorney-General, if it appears to him that a sentence is too lenient or the judge has erred in law as to his powers of sentencing, to refer the case to the Court of Appeal, with its leave, which may quash the sentence and pass such sentence as is appropriate.

A person convicted on indictment may apply to the Home Secretary to have his case referred to the Court of Appeal, and the Home Secretary may so refer a case without any application. In practice such references are made in cases which continue to excite public disquiet long after the trial has taken place; the Home Secretary may refer a case notwithstanding that it is outside, even by years, of the normal time limits for bringing an appeal, or there has already been an unsuccessful appeal, or notwithstanding that the defendant has since died. Following public criticism of the Home Secretary's role in this process such powers of referral are to be excised in the future by the Criminal Cases Review Commission, an independent body to be established under the Criminal Appeals Act 1995.

The Court of Appeal may allow an appeal against conviction if the conviction is unsafe or unsatisfactory (e.g. where the verdict cannot be supported by the proved facts); if there is a wrong decision on a question of law (e.g. a misdirection on the burden of proof); or a material irregularity in the trial (e.g. improper disclosure of the defendant's previous convictions). An appeal against sentence will be allowed only where the sentence is wrong in principle or manifestly severe; the court will not interfere merely because it might have passed a different sentence.

The procedure in the Criminal Division of the Court of Appeal when hearing an appeal is quite different to that of the Crown Court hearing an appeal against the decision of the magistrates where, as we have seen, there is a complete rehearing of the case. Broadly, it may be said, the court is concerned only with the record of the trial; whether it was properly conducted, whether evidence was rightly admitted, whether the judge properly directed the jury on issues of law. The jury's decision to convict the defendant will be set aside only if it is unsafe or unsatisfactory and this is a power which is sparingly exercised. The court may admit new evidence but this is done only where (i) it appears that the evidence is likely to be credible and would have been admitted at the trial; and (ii) there is a reasonable explanation for the failure to adduce it. This is again a power sparingly exercised and in this case, apart from other powers which the court has, it may order a retrial. The Criminal Justice Act 1988 considerably enlarges the powers of the Court of Appeal to order a new trial but it remains a power which the Court of Appeal only exceptionally exercises.

Though the Court of Appeal finds there are grounds for allowing an appeal, it may dismiss the appeal if it is satisfied that no miscarriage of justice has occurred. To apply this provision—something which the court finds difficult—it has to be satisfied that notwithstanding the error at the trial, no reasonable jury would have failed to convict the defendant. An example is provided by *Whybrow* (1951) where, notwithstanding the trial judge's misdirection on the mental element required on a charge of attempted murder, the court upheld the conviction because on the evidence in the case, there could be no doubt but that Whybrow intended to kill.

(e) *Appeal following an acquittal*

In general the prosecutor cannot appeal against the acquittal of the defendant even though the weight of evidence in the case clearly points to the defendant's guilt. One exception to this we have already noted; while the prosecutor cannot appeal to the Crown Court against the acquittal of the defendant by the magistrates, he may ask the magistrates (or the Crown Court following an appeal by the defendant), and though the conclusion of either is to acquit on the facts as found, to state a case for the Queen's Bench Divisional Court.

A further exception, though of a limited nature, was introduced by the Criminal Justice Act 1972. Notwithstanding an acquittal in a trial on indictment, the Attorney-General may now refer any point of law which has arisen in the case for the opinion of the Court of Appeal. The purpose of this power is to enable the Court of Appeal to review a potentially false ruling before it gains too wide a circulation in trial courts. Strictly, it is not an appeal because though the defendant may be represented thereat, he is not identified and his acquittal remains unaffected even if the point of law is decided against him. A good example is provided by *Att.-*

Gen.'s Reference (No. 1 of 1975) (1975) where the trial judge ruled that the defendant, who had caused X to consume alcohol by telling him that it was a non-alcoholic fruit punch, did not "aid, abet, counsel or procure" X to drive over the limit because there was no shared intention between the defendant and X. The case was referred to the Court of Appeal which held that the judge was wrong so to rule; the defendant had by his conduct procured X so to drive. Thus the Court of Appeal was able, in effect, to nip in the bud a ruling which, if followed, would have resulted in unjustified acquittals.

Curiously, there is one case where the defendant may appeal against his own acquittal. This occurs when the defendant has been found not guilty by reason of insanity. This verdict, though one of acquittal, may involve indefinite detention in a secure hospital so it is not really so curious that the defendant may seek to avoid this effect of his acquittal, and a right to appeal against it was introduced by the Criminal Appeal Act 1968. Somewhat similarly the 1968 Act provides that the defendant may appeal against a verdict that he is unfit to plead. Such a verdict denies the defendant a trial and may involve indefinite detention in a secure hospital; it is accordingly thought right that he should be allowed to appeal against such a verdict though it involves no decision about his guilt.

(f) *Appeal to the House of Lords*

An appeal lies either from the Court of Appeal or from the Queen's Bench Divisional Court to the House of Lords. Such an appeal lies only where (i) either the Court of Appeal or the Divisional Court has certified that a point of law of general public importance is involved; *and* (ii) either of those courts or the House of Lords gives leave to appeal. There can be no appeal against a refusal to certify a point of law under (i) but in the event that a point is certified while leave to appeal is refused (which may be done where the Court of Appeal or the Divisional Court is confident of the correctness of its decision) a party may ask the Appeals Committee of the House of Lords for leave to appeal.

In a sense all points of criminal law, since they involve the liberty of the subject, are of public importance but the point must be one of *general* public importance and in practice less than 10 cases a year reach the House of Lords. In dealing with an appeal the House has powers substantially similar to those of the Court of Appeal.

(2) Civil Cases

Depending on the nature of the subject-matter and the amount involved, civil actions may be commenced in the magistrates' courts, the county courts or the High Court.

(a) *Actions commenced in magistrates' courts*

As we have seen (above, p. 40) magistrates' courts have limited, but significant, civil jurisdiction, particularly in relation to domestic proceedings. In general appeal lies to the High Court (and it is also possible for the magistrates to state a case under the procedure outlined at p. 62, above) and in domestic matters appeals are usually determined by a Divisional Court of the Family Division. From the High Court appeal lies, with leave, to the Court of Appeal and the House of Lords. In some minor civil matters and in affiliation proceedings, appeal lies to the Crown Court.

(b) *Actions commenced in the county courts*

While the general rule is that an appeal lies to the Court of Appeal on matters of law and fact, there are exceptions where leave (either of the county court or the Court of Appeal) is required. The Court of Appeal considers the case on the basis of the notes made by the trial judge or other sufficient evidence of the proceedings, and it may affirm, vary, or reverse the judgment of the county court. Appeal lies from the Court of Appeal to the House of Lords with leave of either court.

(c) *Actions commenced in the High Court*

In general appeal lies as of right to the Court of Appeal. Nearly all actions in the High Court are tried by a judge (*i.e.* the judge finds the facts as well as determining all issues of law) but some civil cases (though now less than 1 per cent. of cases in the High Court) are tried by judge and jury where issues of fact are the province of the jury. The Court of Appeal is very reluctant to disturb a jury verdict and will do so only where there is no evidence which can reasonably support their verdict, or where an award of damages is obviously excessive. The Court of Appeal is less unwilling to intervene where the trial is by judge alone; since the trial judge has the advantage of observing the demeanour of witnesses giving their evidence, the Court of Appeal will hardly ever question his findings about their veracity and reliability as witnesses but is much more willing to differ from the trial judge on the inferences to be drawn from primary facts.

(d) *Appeal to the House of Lords*

Appeal lies from the Court of Appeal to the House of Lords with the leave of either court. While the appeal may concern matters of fact or law, appeals to the House of Lords are nearly always concerned with important issues of law.

In certain circumstances it is possible to appeal to the House of Lords direct from the High Court, thus avoiding the additional expense of a hearing in the Court of Appeal. This procedure (colloquially known as the leap-frog appeal) was introduced by the Administration of Justice Act 1969 and enables a judge to grant a certificate for leave to appeal to the House of Lords if a point of law of general public importance is involved which relates to the construction of any statute or is one in respect of which the judge is bound by a previous decision of the Court of Appeal or the House of Lords. All the parties must consent to the grant of the certificate and the House of Lords must give leave to appeal. The use of this procedure is exceptional; typically it is used in revenue cases where a particular decision has taxation implications of general application.

In dealing with appeals, the powers of the House of Lords are similar to those of the Court of Appeal.

Chapter 3

Sources of Law and the Doctrine of Precedent

Anyone might be forgiven for thinking that a book about law would begin with a definition, or at least a description, of what law is. This book began with an introduction to legal reasoning and then described the institutions and workings of the English legal system but has not so far attempted to define law. One reason for this may simply be tradition; this being the traditional way in which lawyers approach their subject. But another and more compelling reason is that lawyers find it extraordinarily hard to define what is law. They can tell you, as we saw in Chapter 1, how lawyers approach problems and they can tell you as we saw in Chapter 2, who administers the law and how it is administered. Nevertheless, they find it impossible even after hundreds of years of thought, to come up with a definition of law that all accept as authoritative. The question: "what is law?" still awaits an answer.

Hence most books of this kind examine the *sources* of law; they are more concerned with where the law is to be found than with what it is. Such books will describe, as the primary sources of law, legislation and precedents (*i.e.* the decisions of the courts) and, as secondary sources of law, such things as custom, textbooks, or even something as vague as the principles of right reason.

Suppose we begin with legislation, with Acts of Parliament. A moment's reflection tells us that an Act of Parliament is not a *source* of law: *it is law*. The decisions of the courts might be said to be rather different. It is not every word of a judgment, which may comprise many thousands of words, that is law. Only such words as constitute the reason for the decision (the *ratio decidendi*) are law; the rest, though it is all part of the process of reasoning, is strictly surplusage (*obiter dicta*). So a judgment might be said to be a source of law because we search through it to find what legal proposition the case established, just as we looked through *Felthouse v. Bindley* (above, p. 6) to discover for what legal proposition it was an authority. We do not look through a statute to discover which parts of it are authority for a legal proposition because the whole of a statute is law. But a *ratio* (*i.e.* the legal proposition which is determined in a case) is no more a *source* of law than a provision in a statute; the source of both is the process by which we identify these as rules of law.

It may be helpful to compare statute and cases with the writers of textbooks. Some writers on law (*e.g.* Coke, Hawkins, Lindley) have achieved such eminence that their opinions on law are frequently cited as authorities on law. But such opinions, however eminent the author, are persuasive only and are not themselves law; they become law only when adopted by a judge as the reason for his decision in a case. Though the judge who adopts the opinion of the writer may never aspire to the intellectual eminence of the writer, it is the judge, and not the writer, who declares the law of the land.

1. Legislation

Legislation is a primary source of law. It takes precedence over the common law and earlier legislation is subject to amendment and repeal by later legislation. Before 1972 it may fairly have been said that legislation was the supreme law but membership of the European Community has modified Parliamentary supremacy. The law of the Community is given direct effect in the United Kingdom (below, p. 169) and to the extent that there is a conflict between Community and English law, whether statutory or case law, it is the former which has primacy. The United Kingdom might by political decision implemented by legislation withdraw from the Community and to that extent Parliament remains sovereign. But membership of the Community involves some, and a progressively increasing, erosion of sovereignty. The change is a profound one but it still leaves Parliament as the primary source of English law, and courts must defer to Parliament's will as expressed in legislation. Legislation, as we have seen (above, p. 14), is the supreme law in that by legislation all law, including previous legislation, can be altered. Courts must give effect to the sovereign will of Parliament as expressed in its statutes. Judges may be critical of Acts of Parliament, they may even in their judgments suggest ways in which they might be improved, but it is not open to them to decline to apply them because they are thought to be unconscionable or to give them meanings which they cannot reasonably bear.

It may be helpful (for often it is) to begin at the beginning. Legislation originates in an idea (it may be that of the Government, or of the Law Commission, or a private individual) to regulate some aspect of human activity by reforming existing law or by creating new law. The project may be a large one (as reforming the law relating to trade unions or codifying the law of theft) or it may be modest (as by making the wearing of crash helmets by motor cyclists compulsory). Obviously the government of the day will be best placed for getting its ideas onto the statute book and very little Parliamentary time is allocated to proposals of law reform agencies and private members' bills; but, leaving that aside, the bill has to be drafted in a form which leaves the least doubt (it is probably impossible to draft a bill in terms which leave no doubt) about its meaning. One Prime Minister (Mr. Harold MacMillan) trying to explain the difficulties to the House of Commons (no easy task) pointed out that the apparently simple statement—A met B and he raised his hat—was capable of four interpretations. Drafting legislation is an art calling for very exceptional skills and most bills are drafted, or redrafted where they have been drafted by others, by Parliamentary Counsel. But, however skilled Parliamentary Counsel may be, as soon as they begin to use the English language (and it would make no difference whatever language they chose) problems of interpretation inevitably arise.

During their passage through Parliament bills are amended. Sometimes in haste and under pressure. Sometimes a particular form of language is accepted as a compromise, meaning one thing to one faction and something different to another. Even if the main objectives of the legislation are clear, resolution of shades of meaning must be left to the courts. So no statute can escape the process of interpretation by the courts. We might take a very simple example. Under section 9 of the Theft Act 1968 burglary is defined as entering a "building" as a trespasser with various intents, most commonly the intent to steal. The word "building," like most words in the English language, is capable of a number of meanings. Most people would not call a boat or a caravan a building and, realising this, Parliament specified in the Act that the reference to "building" should apply to an inhabited vehicle or vessel—the entry of a thief into your dwelling is no less serious because you happen to live in a boat or caravan. Otherwise Parliament did not attempt a comprehensive definition of "building" so it is for the courts to decide whether a person is guilty of burglary where he enters a telephone kiosk to steal the contents of the meter, or enters a park bandstand to steal a trombone, or enters a container taken off its chassis and used to store goods. Parliament might have specifically provided for these cases just as it has specifically provided for inhabited vehicles and vessels. So Parliament might have resolved a possible problem of interpretation by including, or excluding, telephone kiosks and bandstands. But there are certain difficulties. One is that it is in practice impossible to anticipate all cases in which there might be an argument as to whether a particular structure is a building. The other is that if, say, telephone kiosks and bandstands were to be included in the definition, further definitional problems arise as to what is a telephone kiosk or what constitutes a bandstand.

Hence the process of interpretation is inevitable. And that process becomes more complicated with the complexity of the subject matter. It may be assumed that only occasionally will the definition of "building" trouble the courts for in 999 cases out of 1000 it will be as clear as can be that a particular structure is or is not a building. But other cases are less straightforwad. Consider *London & North Eastern Railway Co. v. Berriman* (1946) (*Casebook*, Chap. 1). Mrs. Berriman sued the L.N.E.R. Co., claiming damages for an alleged breach of statutory duty resulting in the death of her husband. By statute railway companies were bound to provide a look-out man whenever a railwayman was engaged on "repairing or relaying" the permanent way, but no look-out man had been provided for Berriman whose job it was to top-up the oil-boxes which lubricated the points on the line. In the result Berriman was killed by an approaching train of which he had no warning as he was attending to his work. In enacting this legislation, as must be clear, Parliament had it in mind to protect by the provision of a look-out man any railwayman whose work made it impossible always to be on the look-out for his own safety and thus 'intended" to protect Berriman. But Mrs. Berriman lost her case; the House of Lords holding by a majority of three to two that while Berriman was engaged in *maintaining* the line, he was not engaged in *repairing* or *relaying*. Maintenance was not the same activity as repairing.

We might of course argue forever about *Berriman's Case*—the decision after all caused an acute difference of opinion among the judges. Some of us might take the view that "repair" is not the same function as "maintenance"; we do not say we have repaired a car because we have kept the oil topped-up. Some of us might say that Parliament really intended to protect the railwayman who could not look out for himself and thus an extended definition of "repairing" ought to have been taken. What must be clear, though, is that the judges in *Berriman's Case* were not taking sides in the sense of being in or out of sympathy with Mrs. Berriman but their function was to apply the law as they found it, *not* to guess at how Parliament would have provided for this situation had Parliament thought about it.

It happens that sometimes (it must not be thought that this is a matter of daily occurrence) the courts give to a statute a meaning which it was never intended to bear by the legislature. This sometimes leads to the accusation that the courts are usurping the functions of Parliament or flouting the will of the people; an accusation which was made, for example, following the decision of the Court of Appeal and the House of Lords disallowing the subsidising of transport fares by the G.L.C. *Bromley L.B.C. v. Greater London Council* (1982). It would be idle to pretend that in such cases the courts are always "right" and their critics always "wrong." What is clear is that, even among lawyers, legitimate differences of opinion may exist as to whether a telephone kiosk is a building for the purpose of the law of burglary, whether maintenance is embraced by repairing, or to what extent a statute permits the subsidising of fares at the expense of the ratepayer.

We might begin by examining traditional approaches to statutory interpretation before turning to a relative newcomer to statutory interpretation in the so-called "purposive" approach.

"In determining the meaning of any words or phrase in a statute," said Lord Reid in *Pinner v. Everett* (1969), "the first question to ask always is what is the natural and ordinary meaning of that word or phrase in its context in the statute." This—the so-called literal rule—is the starting point of all judicial interpretation though its application does not mean that all judges end with the same view.

Even so the application of the literal rule does not result in frequent conflict between Parliament and the courts. Language is not so imprecise, and the art of draftmanship so amateur, that experienced draftsmen (Parliamentary Counsel) cannot ensure that in most cases the words say what they mean. But with the increasing complexity of subject-matter (taxation provides the most extreme example) it is impossible for draftsmen to ensure that the words used always mean what they were intended to mean. In this matter it must not be thought that the courts are completely unhelpful, that they will hold to the literal meaning however absurd the result. In *Pinner v. Everett* (1969) Lord Reid went on to say, "It is only when that [*i.e.* the literal] meaning leads to some result which cannot reasonably be supposed to have been the intention of the legislature that it is possible to look for some other possible meaning of the word or phrase."

At first sight this may seem a somewhat grudging exception to the literal rule but it is hallowed by lawyers as the "golden" rule. A good illustration is provided by *Allen* (1872). Allen had been indicted for bigamy under section 57 of the Offences against the Person Act 1861 which provides that "whosoever being married shall marry again" during the lifetime of the former spouse shall be guilty of bigamy. It was proved that Allen had married W1 and had then "married" W2 while W1 was still alive but Allen took the point that he could not "marry again" W2 because such a marriage was necessarily invalid since it was bigamous and thus he had not "married" again! Had Allen's literal view of the statute been taken, it would have meant that no one could ever be convicted of bigamy; the court held that such an interpretation made an absurdity of the statute and that the words "shall marry again" must be read to mean "shall go through a ceremony of marriage" even though that ceremony could not produce a valid marriage. Another example is provided by *Adler v. George* (1964) (*Casebook*, Chap. 1). George had entered on a prohibited place where he obstructed a member of H.M. Forces. He was charged under section 3 of the Official Secrets Act 1920 which provides that no person shall "in the vicinity of" a prohibited place obstruct any member of H.M. Forces. His argument that he was not "in the vicinity of" a prohibited place because he was *in* the prohibited place was rejected; the court held that the expression must be read to mean "*in or* in the vicinity of" because it would be absurd to suppose that Parliament intended to proscribe such conduct outside but not inside the prohibited place.

But it must not be thought that the so-called golden rule is used by the courts to resolve ambiguities and doubts in favour of the meaning intended by Parliament, however the intention is to be determined. The rule is used only exceptionally and only where the application of the literal rule would render the statute virtually nugatory. That the intention of Parliament is largely defeated, that Parliament will be put to the trouble of passing amending legislation are not in themselves sufficient reasons for applying the golden rule. Take *Fisher v. Bell* (1961) (*Casebook*, Chap. 1) for instance. Following a number of incidents in which flick-knives had been used to cause injuries, Parliament decided to proscribe them. In the Restriction of Offensive Weapons Act 1959 it was made an offence to "sell or offer for sale" any flick-knife. The defendant had flick-knives in his shop-window and he was charged with offering these for sale. It was held that "offers for sale" must be given its ordinary contractual meaning (see below, p. 163) and that his was not an offer for sale but a mere invitation to treat so it followed that the defendant had committed no offence. Nothing could be clearer than that Parliament intended to proscribe the defendant's conduct but the wrong words had been used to proscribe it. Parliament was thus put to the trouble of passing amending legislation in 1961. It is, therefore, a nice question of judgment whether a result is so absurd that it cannot reasonably be supposed to have been the intention of the legislature.

In *Pinner v. Everett* (1969) Lord Reid spoke of interpreting words or phrases in their context in the statute. It is obviously important to have regard to the context of the statute as a whole. Consequently it was held by the House of Lords in *Beswick v. Beswick* (1967) that sections in the Law of Property Act 1925 which literally might have entitled a stranger to *any* contract to enforce its provisions must be confined to contracts affecting real property. No word or phrase can be read in a vacuum. It must at least be read in the context of the statute as a whole, and the statute itself must be read in the context of its time—in its contemporary historical and social setting. This received expression in the sixteenth century when in *Heydon's Case* (1584) (*Casebook*, Chap. 1) the judges decided that it was proper to look beyond the four corners of the Act itself. They said it was permissible to consider: (i) what was the common law before the Act; (ii) what was the defect for which the common law did not provide a remedy; (iii) what remedy Parliament had resolved on to cure the defect; and (iv) what was the true reason for the remedy.

This has come to be known as the "mischief" rule and its precise status is open to doubt. On a conservative view (and this must be the least for which the rule allows) a judge is entitled to have regard to the history of the statute. All events, including Acts of Parliament, have a context, historical, social and political; and the judge, unless he abjures books, newspapers, radio and television, can hardly be unaware of, and can hardly be uninfluenced by, this context. Judges do not try to work against Parliament and society but with them and the framework of their law is fashioned by their experience. At the other extreme the mischief rule might accord to the judge the prerogative of carrying out Parliament's intention however imperfectly this might have been expressed in the words used—an idea that was expressed in *Heydon's Case* itself.

In the latter sense the mischief rule has been rarely used. Not surprisingly it was used in this sense by Lord Denning when in *Magor & St. Mellons v. Newport Corporation* (1950) (*Casebook*, Chap. 1) he said that it was the function of courts to find out the intention of Parliament and Ministers and that this was best done by filling in the gaps and making sense of legislation than by opening it up to destructive analysis. But in this same case Lord Denning was taken to task by the House of Lords (1951) where his approach was described as a "naked usurpation of the legislative function under the thin guise of interpretation."

The mischief rule, then, cannot be used to carry out the *spirit* of the law when the *letter* of the law cannot reasonably bear the meaning which will carry out its spirit. Judges apply the law but do not make it; and though the line between the two can be a fine one, it is a line which must be observed.

Thus the mischief rule was not used in *Fisher v. Bell* (see above, p. 75) though it must have been clear that the court's interpretation of "offers for sale" rendered the enforcement of the statute almost impossible. Placing flick-knives in a shop window was clearly within the "mischief" which Parliament intended to proscribe but the words used failed to express this. On the other hand the mischief rule was used in *Smith v. Hughes* (1960) (*Casebook*, Chap. 1) when a prostitute maintained that she was not soliciting "in a street or public place" contrary to the Street Offences Act 1959 when, sitting in her own house, she solicited men through the window. She herself was not *in* the street when the soliciting took place but Lord Parker C.J. said regard should be had to the mischief at which the Act was aimed. The purpose of the Act was to enable people to walk the streets without being solicited and they were just as much solicited though the source of the solicitation came from private premises.

Some years ago the Law Commission examined the interpretation of statutes (Law Comm. Working Paper No. 14, 1967) and while it had "little hesitation in suggesting this is a field not suitable for codification" nevertheless discerned in contemporary judicial attitudes to interpretation "a tendency to an undue degree of literalism" and, among other cases, singled out *London & North Eastern Railway Co. v. Berriman* (above, p. 72) as an example of extreme literalism.

To remedy this the Commission proposed a more liberal use of internal aids, and of external aids such as the reports of official bodies leading to the legislation and explanatory material accompanying the bill during its passage through Parliament and the courts do seem to be making increasing use of pre-parliamentary material (*e.g.* the reports of official bodies such as the law reform agencies) as an aid to interpretation.

The Commission also recommended the adoption of a "purposive" approach to the interpretation of statutes, by which they meant that "a construction which would promote the general legislative purpose underlying the provision in question is to be preferred to a construction which would not." Since then the so-called purposive approach has found not a little favour in the courts. An example is provided by *Coltman v. Bibby Tankers Ltd* (1987) (*Casebook*, Chap. 1). At common law an employer was not liable to an employee who was injured by reason of a defect in equipment supplied by a manufacturer provided the employee had taken reasonable care to select a reputable manufacturer. This was felt to be unfair to the employee because the manufacturer might by the time of the injury become insolvent or no longer be in business. So a statute was passed providing that where an employee suffered death or injury in consequence of a defect in equipment provided by his employer, the injury or death was deemed to be owing to the employer's negligence.

The plaintiffs in *Coltman* were the personal representatives of a man who lost his life when the ship on which he worked capsized owing to a defect in the ship's hull. The question was whether the ship was "equipment" for the purpose of the statute. That question would have been answered with an unequivocal Yes, but for the fact that the statute defined "equipment" as "any plant and machinery, vehicle, aircraft and clothing." The Court of Appeal held that a ship was not equipment because "equipment" in the context of the statute denoted something ancillary and could not extend to the workplace, in this case the ship itself. The House of Lords reversed the Court of Appeal, holding that "equipment" did not necessarily mean something ancillary; it could properly be said, for instance, that a fleet is equipped with battleships and destroyers. But why, as counsel for the employers had asked, did the draftsman go out of his way to include vehicles and aircraft and yet leave out ships? The House declined to speculate on the reasons for the draftsman's omission. What appeared to be decisive to Lord Oliver, with whom three of their Lordships expressed agreement, was the purpose of the legislation and this appeared from the long title to make the employer liable to the employee for injury attributable to "any defect in equipment provided by the employer for the purposes of the employer's business."

It is difficult to avoid the conclusion that the purposive approach would have led to a different result in Berriman because the purpose of the statute in that case was to provide a look-out for employees engaged in duties which precluded them from looking out for themselves. But it must not be thought that the purposive approach gives the judge a free hand to carry out the legislator's purpose. However clear the legislative purpose is the judge cannot give to words and phrases meanings which they will not reasonably bear. Moreover, as May L.J. has observed, while it may be legitimate to use the purposive approach to hold that a statutory provision does apply to a given situation even though it does not apply on a strict literal interpretation, it would not be legitimate to adopt the purposive approach to preclude the application of a statute to a situation to which, on a purely literal interpretation, it would apply.

The Law Commission Working in Working Paper No. 14 also canvassed the advantages and disadvantages of allowing references to Parliamentary debates but made no firm recommendations on the matter. Until 1993 the courts adamantly took the view that no reference could be made to Parliamentary debates for the purpose of elucidating the meaning of statutes but in *Pepper v. Hart* [1993] 1 All E.R. 42 the House of Lords, having express regard to the adoption of the purposive approach which has now been adopted to ascertain the true intent of Parliament, decided to relax the exclusionary rule to permit reference to debates where (i) the provision is ambiguous or obscure or where the literal meaning leads to an absurdity; and (ii) the statement regarding its interpretation is given by a minister or other promoter of the Bill; and (iii) the statement made clearly resolves the ambiguity or obscurity.

Given the lengthy and firm adherence to the exclusionary rule this was an unexpected step but a justified one. Why, as a judge once asked, should we look into a crystal ball when we can read the book? It may be that statutory interpretation is moving closer to the principles spelled out in *Heydon's Case* and that the views expressed by Lord Denning in *Magor & St*

Mellons v. Newport Corporation would not now receive so severe a reprimand.

2. Case Law

(1) The Doctrine of Precedent

There is no positive provision of English Law which requires a judge to give reasons for his decision; it would suffice for the judge merely to conclude that he finds the plaintiff's case not proved, or that he finds it proved and assesses the damages at a specified sum. Nowadays judges always give reasons for their decisions though they may be very shortly stated (the early volumes of the Criminal Appeal Reports abound with cases where the judgment is expressed in two or three lines) or may be stated at great length (the judgment in *Tito v. Waddell (No. 2)* (1977) extends to nearly 200 pages and is prefaced by a table of contents).

Usually a judgment contains: (a) a statement of facts; (b) a review of the authorities applicable to those facts; and (c) the reason which is given for the decision (*ratio decidendi*) in the case. Some judges may even insert headings in their judgment which can be of considerable assistance to the reader, especially the student, in digesting the case. A very good example is provided by the judgment of Lord Denning in *Broome v. Cassell & Co. Ltd* (1971) a libel action arising from the German attack on the British convoy PQ17 taking supplies to Russia in 1942. Lord Denning's judgment (though it did not escape severe criticism in the House of Lords) sets out the facts with dramatic force, identifies and examines the issues with great clarity, and ends with a conclusion identifying the *ratio* of the judgment.

It is of the first importance to identify the *ratio* in a case for while a court may be bound to follow the *ratio* of a previous decision, it is not bound to follow other propositions of law asserted in that decision (*obiter dicta*) which do not form part of the reason for the decision. Sometimes it is an easy matter to find the *ratio*, as where in a single judgment the court shortly and clearly disposes of the point at issue. But the fact that there is a single judgment does not mean that the determination of the *ratio* is necessarily straightforward. Take the case of *Smith* (1960) which was concerned with the mental element required on a charge of murder and in which a single judgment was given by the House of Lords. There was acute controversy as to what was the *ratio* of this case; so much so that in *Hyam v. D.P.P.* (1974) Lord Hailsham L.C., having admitted that *Smith* had given rise to a "series of wholly irreconcilable interpretations" declined to overrule it because "it is difficult to know exactly what one is overruling."

Where more than one judgment is given in a case each judgment may give a different ratio; one judge may reach the same conclusion as another but for quite different reasons. Consider *Hyam v. D.P.P.* (above, and see below, p. 347) which, like *Smith*, was concerned with the mental element required on a charge of murder. The trial judge had directed the jury that Mrs. Hyam could be convicted of murder not only if she intended to kill or cause serious bodily harm to the deceased but also if she had foreseen that death or grievous bodily harm was "highly probable." In the House of Lords, where Mrs. Hyam's conviction for murder was affirmed by a majority of three to two, the affirming judges gave different reasons for their decision. Viscount Dilhorne contented himself with approving the direction of the trial judge that foresight of high probability sufficed. Lord Cross went further; he thought that "highly" should be deleted from "highly probable" so that foresight of a probability was enough. Lord Hailsham L.C., thought that the criterion of "high probability" was too vague for juries to apply; he thought that the test should be whether the accused intended to create a "serious risk" of death or serious bodily harm. It is not entirely clear what Lord Hailsham meant by this; arguably any risk of death is a serious risk even if it does not amount to a probability.

In *Moloney* (1985) (*Casebook*, Chap. 6), however, the House of Lords concluded that *Hyam* had misstated the law and was not to be followed. Murder, it was held, was a crime of intention only; either an intention to kill or cause serious bodily harm. But what did "intention" mean? Lord Bridge thought that in the ordinary run of case there would be no need to re-define or amplify its meaning to the jury. Where it was necessary to do so the jury should be told that a death was intended where (a) it was a natural consequence of what the defendant did; and (b) that the defendant foresaw it as being a natural consequence. In giving this definition Lord Bridge went beyond what was strictly necessary to decide *Moloney*. It was therefore *obiter* but it was followed by the trial judge (judges do not lightly disregard the considered statements of appellate judges even if they are *obiter*) in *Hancock and Shankland* (1986) (*Casebook*, Chap. 6) and two defendants were convicted of murder. Quashing these convictions and substituting convictions for manslaughter the Court of Appeal said that Lord Bridge had incorrectly defined intention but since what he had said was *obiter* they were free not to follow it. Not surprisingly this case went to the House of Lords no doubt with a view to securing an authoritative definition of intention (obviously an important matter in the criminal law) and this Lord Scarman proceeded to do. But this again was unnecessary because all that was required to decide the case was to say, as Lord Scarman did, that Lord Bridge's definition was too wide and not to provide an alternative direction. Perhaps this is just as well since many commentators are not at all clear as to what Lord Scarman meant.

Those who have attempted to formulate a test for determining the *ratio* of a case are generally agreed that the ratio must be a proposition of law which is *necessary* to the decision reached. One writer (Professor Goodhart) rightly reminds us that the first step must be to determine the facts treated by the judge as *material*, for his judgment relates only to the material facts. But determining what facts are material can be difficult. While judges normally include in their judgments a statement of the facts, only by a consideration of the judgment as a whole is it possible to determine which facts the judge considered material. In the great case of *Donoghue v. Stevenson* (1932) the plaintiff suffered gastroenteritis when, having consumed half the contents of an opaque bottle of ginger-beer purchased by a friend, she discovered a decomposed snail in the remaining half. It was held by the House of Lords that even where there is no contractual relationship between a manufacturer and a consumer, the manufacturer owes a duty to the consumer to take reasonable care that his product will not injure the consumer when that product is sold in such a form that there is no reasonable possibility of intermediate examination by the consumer (see below, p. 655). Here we can see that while opacity of the bottle was considered to be a material fact, for it was this that denied the plaintiff the opportunity to inspect the contents before consumption, it was not material that the product was ginger-beer for the case must have been decided in the same way had the contents been whisky or water. Nor was it a material fact that the product was sold in a bottle, nor that it was a food. The material facts were simply that a manufactured article had been used by a person whom the manufacturers could reasonably foresee would use it, that the consumer could not reasonably be expected to spot its defects and had suffered damage as a result of its use.

Donoghue v. Stevenson is entitled to be called a "great" case because its mundane facts resulted in the declaration of a principle capable of being applied to a vast field of commercial activity. But extensive though the principle is, it may fairly be asked whether it extends beyond manufactured *chattels*. Does it, for example, extend to houses which because of negligence in building cause harm to someone not in a contractual relationship with the builder? Does it extend to negligent statements which cause someone, again not in contractual relationship with the maker, to suffer economic loss? In fact the courts have made the negligent makers of both houses and statements liable for resulting loss but this has been by analogy with the *Donoghue v. Stevenson* principle, not because the *ratio* of that case necessarily *requires* that result.

Courts may use *material* differences of fact to distinguish a decision which could otherwise bind them. As we have seen, *Donoghue v. Stevenson* could not be distinguished on the grounds that the product was whisky or water but it could fairly be distinguished on the grounds that it is applicable only to manufactured chattels. Another example may be taken from the law of contract. Ordinarily an acceptance of an offer must be communicated to the offeror before a contract comes into existence but in the nineteenth century the courts modified this rule in connection with acceptance *by post* which were held to create a contract from the time of posting even though the posted acceptance might be delayed or even never reach the offeror. In *Entores Ltd v. Miles Far East Corporation* (1955) (*Casebook*, p. 407) the court had to decide whether the postal acceptance rule applied where a Telex machine was used. The postal rule for acceptance was held inapplicable because when the Telex is used communication is virtually instantaneous; it was thus to be likened to the case where the parties were in direct oral communication and was thus distinguishable from cases applying the postal rules of acceptance. This view was confirmed by the House of Lords in *Brinkibon Ltd v. Stahag Stahl* ((1982) and must now inevitably apply to acceptances sent by fax or e-mail. This discussion will have served to show that the determination of the *ratio* of a particular case may often prove a difficult task. Yet the process of determining the *ratio* is one in which lawyers (including law students) are *constantly* involved. No two cases are ever exactly alike and the lawyer's art is to determine whether the cases are sufficiently alike so that the principle for which the one is authority applies to the other, or whether the cases are sufficiently unalike so that a different solution may be sought.

(2) Law Reports

Obviously any system of precedent is inoperable unless there is an adequate and reliable system for reporting the cases that are to be used as precedents. Law reporting has always been in private hands. Even the *Law Reports*, which have been produced by the Incorporated Council of Law Reporting since 1865, are privately published reports and are neither published nor supported by any organ of the state. They may be said to enjoy a privileged status in that the reports appearing in them are revised by the judges themselves which explain of course why they appear later than other series of law reports. Sometimes there will be a marked difference between a judgment as it appears in the *Law Reports* and in other series not because the judge has been misreported in the other series but because he has modified his judgment as delivered in court. Strictly the precedent is the judgment as delivered in court and subsequent interpretations or deletions should be ignored but the judicial tendency has been to accept the *Law Reports* version.

Modern law reporting is of high quality and lawyers are well served by both generalised and specialised series of reports. In addition LEXIS, which is a computerised legal data retrieval service of astonishing capacity and capability, contains many unreported (strictly such cases are reported but do not appear in any published series) cases and by pressing certain keys it is possible to produce a shoal of cases of varying degrees of relevance to the point at issue. While any report vouched for by a barrister in court when judgment was given has in the past been the only criterion for the admission of a report, this proved too much for the courts and in *Roberts Petroleum Ltd v. Kenny Ltd* (1983) the House of Lords said that leave would only be given for the citation of unreported decisions of the Court of Appeal (Civil Division) on counsel's assurance that the case contained a principle of law not to be found in reported decisions which was binding on the Court of Appeal.

Before 1865, and this was why the Incorporated Council of Law Reporting was set up, law reports varied in quality and their coverage could be patchy. Over the centuries, (law reporting began with the Year Books in the thirteenth century) standards of law reporting have varied from the very good to the very bad. So bad that some judges refused to allow the reports of certain reporters to be cited before them. In *Indian Oil Corporation v. Greenstone Shipping S.A.* (1987)

Staughton J. considered a case decided in 1594 to be of little authority since the report came from a "mangled and ill-translated edition." But the quality of others are undoubted and, unless overruled or overtaken by statutory change, may still be cited as precedents. In *Rondel v. Worsely* (1966), which was concerned with whether a barrister could be sued for negligence, Lawton J. considered certain reports in the Year Books going back as far as 1430. In one of them the learned judge found an observation of Paston J. indicating that a barrister was liable for the negligent conduct of a case. Lawton J. declined to follow it but not because he had any doubts of the accuracy of the report. In *Reid v. MPC* (1973) Lord Denning M.R. preferred the views of Coke to Blackstone because Coke's were based on "good precedents," *i.e.* reliably reported cases.

3. Custom

In the judicial oath a judge promises to do right according to the "laws and usages of this realm." Usage, or custom, was of cardinal importance in the formation of the common law. Mediaeval judges did not, as it were, pluck laws from the air; they had regard to what was the actual practice of people and the extent to which these practices were regarded as obligatory. But once a custom received judicial recognition by incorporation as the *ratio* of a decision, lawyers thereafter looked to that case as the relevant authority, not to the antecedent custom. Over the course of centuries customs were, in effect, made the subject of a take-over bid by the courts so that custom has ceased to be a creative source of law.

On the other hand it is still possible to rely on a local, as opposed to a general custom even though it constitutes a derogation from the common law. Such customs must meet stringent tests. They must have existed since time immemorial (strictly 1189 but in practice such period as the memory of man does not run to the contrary), they must be reasonable and certain, they must be regarded as obligatory, and they must not be against any statutory provision. Thus an alleged custom that at a particular place a pound of butter should weigh 18 ounces was rejected because statute had provided that a pound should weigh 16 ounces everywhere. And in a nineteenth century case the courts rejected a parson's claim to a customary right to a fee of 13 shillings on the celebration of a marriage because 13 shillings would have been a wholly exorbitant fee in the Middle Ages. But courts have accepted rights based on custom to use common land for the playing of sports, to dry fishing nets on private property, and to establish rights of way.

4. Textbooks

When a lawyer needs to inform himself on some aspect of law he will usually turn in the first place, not to the statutes and cases themselves, but to a text where the law will be set out in a convenient and accessible form. The work may be an article in a review, a monograph or a multi-volume encyclopedia and its authority will turn upon the reputation its author or editor has acquired for it. When lawyers consult such works they know that they do not contain the law but contain the *opinions* of their authors, based upon their interpretation of the relevant statutes and cases, as to what the law is believed to be. The persuasiveness of such opinions varies according to the standing of their authors. In *Shivpuri* (1986) the House of Lords was persuaded to reverse a previous decision of its own largely owing to arguments advanced by Professor Glanville Williams in an article written in the Cambridge Law Journal. But the opinions expressed by writers can become law only by virtue of their adoption by a court as part of the *ratio* of a decision. Judges vary in the attention and deference they pay to textbook writers, but the citation of such "sources" of law before courts is now a commonplace and reference to them in judgments is far from uncommon.

5. The Operation of the Doctrine of Precedent

Since so much of our daily lives is regulated by law it is obvious that law must usually be certain and predictable. The man in the street does not as a matter of course see his daily routine as being regulated by law but this is in fact the case.

So soon as he takes his car on the road a whole host of laws govern his activity, and by the average day's end he has concluded not less than a dozen contracts all of which have legal obligations for himself and the other party. The man in the street usually only consciously adverts to law when things go wrong; when, for example, he is involved in a collision with another motorist or when the goods he buys do not measure up to the standards he expects of them. When such unfortunate events occur it would be intolerable if the invariable advice of his lawyer was that he would have to have his dispute tried by a judge and that there was no means of predicting what the outcome might be.

In practice the law achieves such a high degree of certainty that only a small proportion of disputes ever go to trial, and most of these concern the facts rather than the law. Given a particular set of facts, a lawyer can usually, having regard to the authorities, state with confidence what the legal outcome will be. Hence the broad justification for the system of precedent whereby lower courts are bound to follow the decisions of higher courts and whereby like cases must be decided alike. This doctrine of *stare decisis* (keep to what has been decided) is fundamental to our legal system. Of course our system does not achieve complete certainty of result and can probably never do so; we are light years away from a legal system that has an obvious answer to every legal problem that can possibly present itself.

(1) The House of Lords

Decisions of the House of Lords bind all lower courts. In *London Street Tramways v. L.C.C.* (1898) (*Casebook*, Chap. 2) the House went further and stated that the House of Lords itself was bound by its own previous decisions. Even if the earlier decision was now thought to be wrong it would be followed. At this time the House put the highest value on certainty and predictability of result and said it was for Parliament to remedy any erroneous decision by legislation.

There are, however, certain exceptions. First (strictly not an exception) the House of Lords is bound not to follow a previous decision which cannot stand with subsequent legislation. Second, the House is not bound to follow a decision given *per incuriam* (through carelessness), that is where that decision was made in ignorance of a relevant statutory provision or of a relevant prior decision of the House of Lords. In fact no clear instance of either form of carelessness has yet arisen. Third, where "public policy" is an element in a decision (as it is in connection with contracts in restraint of trade, below, p. 579) a decision with reference to the public policy of one age does not bind the House when considering the public policy of a later age.

The attitude to precedent expressed in *London Street Tramways v. L.C.C.* governed the practice of the House of Lords for nearly 70 years but in 1966 the House issued a statement ([1966] 3 All E.R. 77) (*Casebook*, Chap. 2) saying that while the House acknowledged the importance of certainty in the law and would *normally* follow its own previous decisions, it would depart from a previous decision "when it appears right to do so."

What this statement immediately reveals is that rules concerning the operation of precedent are rules of *practice* and not rules of law; the House of Lords changed from the practice adopted in *London Street Tramways v. L.C.C.* and is free to make further changes in its practice. What has become clear since is that the House will overrule previous decisions only exceptionally and, regrettably, it is not always clear whether it has done so. Only rarely is there an unequivocal statement that the earlier decision was wrong; often, it seems, the House prefers to consign earlier decisions to a sort of legal limbo rather than subject them to the fire. It is not enough that the earlier decision was reached only by a narrow majority, that the House might now have taken a different view (especially where the earlier decision relates to a matter of statutory interpretation), or even that the decision is considered wrong. Before the House will overrule itself there must be some very good reason, such as that the earlier decision is productive of clear injustice or that it seriously hampers the development of the law. Nevertheless the introduction of the new practice has been generally welcomed; Parliament cannot always respond rapidly to remedying what are now seen as bad decisions and it is as well that the House should be able to put matters to rights when there is a clear and pressing need to do so.

When a prior case is overruled, whether by the House of Lords or by some other court, it should be noted that the usual effect of the overruling is not to change the law but to state what the law has always been. Suppose, for example, that the case of *A v. B* in 1900 decided that a certain form of words would create a certain kind of interest, say a life estate in land. If in *C v. D* in 1990 the decision in *A v. B* is overruled the effect is that the *A v. B* form of words was *never* effective to create that interest, not that it is ineffective from 1990. The effect of overruling *A v. B* is thus retrospective. Now it may be that between 1900 and 1992 many lawyers, relying on the correctness of *A v. B*, have used that form of words to create a life interest. Because of this effect of overruling their Lordships said in their statement in 1966 that they would bear in mind the danger of disturbing retrospectively the basis on which contracts, settlements of property and fiscal arrangements had been entered into. One advantage of legislative change as opposed to judicial overruling is that the law can be changed *prospectively* thus avoiding any retrospective effect.

This is the *usual* consequence when the House of Lords (or the Court of Appeal, for that matter) overrules a previous decision. In *R. v. R.* [1991] 4 All E.R. 481 the House of Lords took the step of holding, *not* that previous case law had been wrongly decided, but that the law applied in the cases was no longer operative law. It had long been accepted law, largely owing to an opinion expressed by Hale in his influential treatise *History of the Pleas of the Crown* (1736), that a husband could not be guilty of the rape of his wife. In *R. v. R.* the House of Lords held, *not* that Hale had misstated the law and that the courts had been in error in accepting his opinion, but that the rule, which once was the law, no longer formed part of the law because it was unacceptable in a modern society which recognised the equality of husband and wife that a wife should submit to sexual intercourse by the husband secured by force.

With the actual ruling in *R. v. R.* few but revanchist male chauvinists would disagree. Before the case was heard the Law Commission had proposed to abolish the exemption and its proposal had met with almost universal approval. But the means by which the House of Lords anticipated the Law Commission's proposals and changed the law are questionable.

The power to change existing law had been thought to be confined to Parliament and in *changing* the law, as opposed to ruling that the law had been based on an error, it rather looks like a "naked usurpation of the legislative function" which the House had forthrightly condemned in *Magor & St Mellons v. Newport Corporation*.

The House was subsequently invited in *D.P.P. v. C.* [1995] 2 All E.R. 43 to abolish the presumption of innocence which exists where a child over 10 and under 14 is charged with crime and which requires the prosecution to prove not only that the child acted with *mens rea* but additionally to prove that the child knew that his/her act was seriously wrong. The House declined to do so. It held that while Parliament should review the law because the presumption gave rise to anomalies and absurdities, it was not open to the House to change the law. So why should the House have intervened to change the law in *R. v. R.* but not in *D.P.P. v. C.*? The House instanced a number of considerations which would be given account in deciding whether judicial legislation was justified. These included: (i) whether a clear consensus of opinion favoured change (the House felt that, while it was clear that the consensus of opinion no longer supported marital immunity in rape there was no such consensus regarding the presumption in favour of infants); (ii) whether Parliament had legislated on the subject matter without questioning the existing law; (iii) whether the matter was purely legal or involved issues of social policy; (iv) whether intervention would involve setting aside an accepted doctrine; and (v) whether a change in the law would produce finality or certainty.

Readers may judge for themselves how far these criteria were met in *R. v. R.* but not in *D.P.P. v. C.* What is clear is that we have moved into an uncharted sea. There is no indication in *R. v. R.* that the newly acquired power to change the law is confined to the criminal law. The power must, however, be confined to judge-law and cannot apply to legislation. It would not be open, for example, for the courts to hold that, contrary to the Wills Act 1837, which requires two witnesses to a will, that one will do (but what would the outcome be if the courts were to take this step?).

We may be in for an interesting time. Until the 19th century the judges were the principal makers of the law with little legislative interference although legislative supremacy was always acknowledged. In the 19th and into the 20th century the enormous growth in legislation made the judicial role more interpretative than creative. But with the growth of judicial review the courts have increasingly questioned the use of powers conferred by Parliament, and have now assumed, in relation to the common law, the power of judicial legislation. The law at the end of the day, is what the judges say it to be. So who is to be the master?

One last point in connection with the House of Lords is the extent to which inferior courts are entitled to avail themselves of the exceptions available to the House and not to follow its decisions. May the Court of Appeal or a High Court judge decline to follow a decision of the House because: (i) it has been overruled by statute; (ii) it was given *per incuriam*; (iii) that public policy has changed; or (iv) the case is one where the House might overrule a previous decision of its own? It is clear that in (i) an inferior court must prefer the subsequent

legislation to the earlier decision, and it is equally clear that in
(iv) it would not be open to an inferior court, in effect, to
second-guess the House of Lords. So far as (ii) is concerned
the House of Lords has decided (*Broome v. Cassell* (1972)) that
it is for it to determine whether one of its decisions was given
per incuriam and the Court of Appeal 1971 was forthrightly
admonished for declining to follow a decision of the House
(in *Rookes v. Barnard* (1964)) where, in the view of the Court of
Appeal, (a view not shared by the House of Lords), that
decision was given *per incuriam*.

In *Broome v. Cassell, Rookes v. Barnard* was said to have been
decided *per incuriam* because the House had failed to consider
certain previous *decisions*; a different view might have been
taken if the ground for the decision being *per incuriam* had
been that a statutory provision had been overlooked. As to
(iii) there appears to be no binding authority but it would
seem that lower courts must judge "public policy" in its
contemporary context and would be free not to follow
decisions of the House of Lords reached in a social or
economic context that is no longer apropos.

(2) The Court of Appeal (Civil Division)

The decisions of the Court of Appeal bind all inferior
courts, including Divisional Courts. As has been seen, the
Court of Appeal is bound, subject to certain limited
exceptions, to follow decisions of the House of Lords. What is
still not entirely settled is how far the Court of Appeal is
bound by its own decisions.

The starting point is provided by *Young v. Bristol Aeroplane
Co.* (1944) (*Casebook*, Chap. 2). Here the Court of Appeal
decided that it was bound by its own decisions and that for
this purpose a "full" court (there were five members in the
instant case) had no greater powers than any division of the
court properly constituted (normally three). The court then
went on to spell out three exceptions.

The first is that where there are two conflicting decisions of
the Court of Appeal, the court is entitled to choose between
them, thus impliedly overruling the one not followed.
Apparently the Court of Appeal does not consider itself
bound to prefer the earlier decision on the ground that the
latter is *per incuriam* and this introduces an element of
uncertainty in that a lawyer cannot advise his client which of
the two decisions will be preferred.

The second is that the Court of Appeal is bound *not* to
follow a previous decision of its own which cannot stand

with, even if not expressly overruled by, a *subsequent* decision of the House of Lords. Where it is alleged that a Court of Appeal decision (*C v. D*) cannot stand with an earlier decision (*A v. B*) of the House of Lords, the Court of Appeal should follow *C v. D* at least if *A v. B* was considered by the Court of Appeal in *C v. D*. If *A v. B* was not considered in *C v. D* it may be that the case would be considered under the third exception.

The third exception is where a decision of the Court of Appeal was given *per incuriam*. In *Young* the court gave the example of a decision reached in ignorance of a statutory provision but it also extends to the example just given where the prior House of Lords decision in *A v. B* was not considered by the Court of Appeal in *C v. D*.

This was the position in the Court of Appeal until Lord Denning assumed office as Master of the Rolls. During his tenure (1962–82) he frequently expressed his dislike for the principle of *Young's* case and took the view that the Court of Appeal should be free, as the House of Lords had made itself free, to overrule prior decisions which were now seen to be wrong.

Viewed as a matter of principle it can be appreciated that there are arguments either way. If the Court of Appeal is so free it adds to the uncertainty and makes it much more difficult for the lawyer to predict the outcome of litigation. Moreover the Court of Appeal while following its own decision can always indicate where it believes a decision to be erroneous, thus leaving it to the House of Lords to deliver the coup de grâce to the bad decision. But this ignores the fact that relatively few cases go to the House of Lords (it has been said that only the very poor and the very rich can afford to take a case there) so that if the Court of Appeal cannot overrule a decision thought to be wrong that decision may remain authoritative for many years.

Matters came to a head in *Davis v. Johnson* (1979) (*Casebook*, Chap. 2) where in a full court of five members, three expressed the view that earlier decisions could be overruled while two held that overruling was permissible only where the exception in *Young's* case applied. Of the three, Lord Denning M.R. thought that an earlier decision could always be overruled if it was thought to be wrong but the other two judges expressed the power more narrowly. Shaw L.J. thought the power should be exercised only in cases involving an element of "emergency"; he was prepared to exercise it in the instant case because the subject-matter (Domestic Violence and Matrimonial Proceedings Act 1976) concerned the exclusion from the domestic premises of a partner who was doing physical violence to the other. On the other hand, said Shaw L.J., the public interest would suffer no mortal blow if, say, a decision on a financial or commercial matter was allowed to stand even if thought to be wrong.

The House of Lords while approving the decision in *Davis v. Johnson* on the merits, was unanimously and strongly of the view that the Court of Appeal should adhere to its previous decisions subject only to the limited exceptions given in *Young's* case. The advice of the House of Lords was given in no uncertain terms. "In my opinion," said Lord Diplock, "the House should take this occasion to reaffirm expressly and unequivocally that the rule laid down in *Young* as to *stare decisis* is still binding in the Court of Appeal."

With the retirement of Lord Denning it might have been expected that the Court of Appeal would return to the "orthodoxy" of *Young's* case but the court still appears to be unwilling to be straightjacketed by the *Young* exceptions. In *Williams v. Fawcett* (1985) (*Casebook*, Chap. 2) the court said it would not follow a previous decision where (a) the growth of the error in the cases could be clearly discerned; (b) the liberty of the subject was involved (in the instant case the defendant was at risk of committal to prison for contempt); and (c) the case was of such a nature that it was unlikely to reach the House of Lords where the error could be corrected. The Court of Appeal admitted a possible further exception, though the court thought it was not strictly inconsistent with *Young's* case, in *Rickards v. Rickards* (1989) (*Casebook*, p. 39) where it indicated that it would overrule previous decisions of its own (a) which involved a wrongful rejection of its own jurisdiction to hear an appeal; and (b) where the House of Lords would have no opportunity to hear an appeal on the issue. The exceptions expressed in these cases are carefully articulated and fall well short of a claim to overrule previous decisions simply because they are thought to be wrongly decided; they nevertheless indicate that *Young's* case has not said the last word on the operation of precedent in the Civil Division of the Court of Appeal.

(3) The Court of Appeal (Criminal Division)

In their statement in 1966 the House of Lords said that in adopting its new policy on precedent it would have regard to "the especial need for certainty as to the criminal law." This contrasts oddly with the practice of the Criminal Division of the Court of Appeal (following the practice of its predecessor the Court of Criminal Appeal) which has adopted a more flexible policy than that adopted in *Young's* case. Thus in *Gould* (1968) (*Casebook*, Chap. 2) Diplock L.J. said that if the court was satisfied that the law had been misunderstood or misapplied in an earlier decision, the court was entitled to depart from it even if it could not be brought within any of the exceptions in *Young's* case if the liberty of the subject is involved. In other words it will follow a decision though thought to be wrong, if that decision favours the defendant's case but not where following that decision would result in keeping the defendant in confinement. In this regard a decision of a full court of five members has no more power than any properly constituted division of the court; in *Gould* a court of three members overruled a decision given by a court of five members.

(4) Divisional Courts

Divisional Courts of the High Court exercise appellate jurisdiction in both civil and criminal matters. In the exercise of civil jurisdiction it is accepted that a Divisional Court is bound by its own previous decisions subject to the exceptions in *Young's* case: *Huddersfield Police Authority v. Watson* (1947) (*Casebook*, Chap. 2). It is similarly accepted (*Younghusband v. Luftig* (1949)) that a Divisional Court is bound by its own decisions in criminal cases subject to the *Young* exceptions. In relation to criminal cases it has never expressly claimed the more flexible policy which has been adopted by the Criminal Division of the Court of Appeal, but nor has it expressly disclaimed that policy.

In *R. v. Greater Manchester Coroner, ex p. Tal* (1984), however, it was pointed out that the *Watson* and *Younghusband* principles applied only where the Divisional Court was sitting as an appellate court and had no application where the court was exercising its supervisory jurisdiction, as under the prerogative orders or by way of judicial review. There is, said Robert Goff L.J., no court known as the Divisional Court; it is simply a court constituted for the transaction of the business of the High Court. It followed that just as a judge of the High Court was not bound by a decision of another judge of the High Court (see next section) so a Divisional Court of the High Court was not bound to follow the decision of another division if it was convinced that the other division was wrong. Nor was Robert Goff L.J. entirely convinced that *Watson* might not need reconsideration in the light of the House of Lords' Practice Statement.

A Divisional Court is of course bound by decisions of the House of Lords. In the exercise of civil jurisdiction it is bound by decisions of the Civil Division of the Court of Appeal, and in the exercise of criminal jurisdiction by the Criminal Division. In the (unlikely) event of conflicting decisions of the civil and criminal divisions of the Court of Appeal, a Divisional Court would presumably follow the decision of the division of the Court of Appeal in which it was exercising jurisdiction.

(5) The High Court

While judges of the High Court are bound by the decisions of all superior courts, they are not bound by each other's decisions. Lord Goddard C.J. no doubt correctly stated the practice when in *Watson's* case (above) he said that a judge of first instance would, unless he was convinced that the judgment of a fellow judge was wrong, follow it as a matter of comity. No doubt inferior judges (circuit judges and magistrates) would feel even more constrained to follow the judgments of High Court judges but there exists no direction that they are formally bound to do so.

Chapter 4

The Legal System in Operation

From time to time all of us are involved in disputes which raise issues of law as well as of fact. Neighbours may dispute the boundary which separates their properties, a purchaser may allege that a washing-machine is faulty, a motorist may claim that his car has been damaged by the carelessness of another and so on. Such disputes involve issues of civil law but at least some of us will also come into contact with the criminal law which is much more likely to be in connection with our operation of a motor vehicle than with any other activity.

1. Civil Actions

So far as disputes concerning civil law are concerned, experience shows that only a very small fraction of these ever come before a court for resolution, and it can be confidently asserted that the vast majority are resolved without either party even seeking professional legal advice. Most disputes are settled without any overt reference to law, the parties reaching a settlement which strikes them as "fair"; the dispute concerning the faulty washing-machine will most likely be resolved though neither party has a working knowledge of the Sale of Goods Act 1979, or has even heard of its existence. The parties know that it is in their best interests to reach a speedy and acceptable settlement without recourse to lawyers and the courts because of the expense that will be incurred and, just as important, the time and worry involved. Even if the dispute is pressed to the point of taking legal advice, the solicitor will be of the same mind. He will always seek to obtain an acceptable settlement for his client long before he talks of issuing a writ.

(1) Costs

What it will cost to take a case to court depends upon such factors as its complexity, the time taken by the trial and the number and eminence of the lawyers involved. The average cost to the plaintiff of an action in the High Court is about £7,000 in London and about £2,000 in the provinces; in the county court the average is about £1,500. In particular proceedings, in a protracted libel action for example, the costs may be spectacularly in excess of these figures. It is to be noted that in the county courts the plaintiff's costs are usually equivalent to the damages recovered while in the High Court the costs are usually equivalent to one quarter of the damages recovered.

These figures relate to the costs incurred by one party. The other party, or parties, will incur similar costs and it has to be noted that an unsuccessful party (whether plaintiff or defendant) must usually pay the costs of the successful party; in general costs follow the event or, if you like, winner takes all. But even the winner's victory may be pyrrhic for the defendant may not have the means to pay the damages or meet the costs.

Hence it is no light decision to take a dispute to court. Up to a point it is possible to insure against legal costs. The motorist's insurance policy will ordinarily cover costs as well as damages, and the policies commonly taken out by the householder will normally indemnify the householder in respect of legal liability arising from use of the premises. Professional people, such as doctors, accountants and lawyers, will insure against the risk of malpractice actions. In fact policies are available from insurance companies which will cover the bringing or defending of a variety of claims up to a specified amount. In a consultation paper on legal aid issued by the Lord Chancellor's Department in 1991, one of the options that is canvassed is compulsory legal expenses insurance; such a system has been introduced in other countries and appears to work well.

So there will be some cases where a party need have no financial worries about the consequences of litigation. We have also seen how a wide range of disputes are now handled by tribunals which are much less expensive than courts. An unrepresented claimant before a tribunal will usually incur no costs even if his claim is unsuccessful. In an industrial tribunal, for example, an order for costs will be made against a party only where the proceedings have been instituted frivolously, vexatiously or otherwise unreasonably. On the other hand, if a party to such proceedings does engage professional legal representation this will have to be paid for and legal aid is not usually available in respect of proceedings before tribunals.

Nonetheless, there remain many cases where the claimant faces the daunting expense of litigation. A client or a patient may allege that he has suffered damage as the result of the negligent advice of a solicitor or a doctor and this negligence is denied. Win or lose the professional man will normally be insured but loss to the claimant will mean that he must bear the costs and these might even prove ruinous.

There is not only the matter of cost. The civil justice system is beset by procedural complexity leading to inordinate delays in the conduct of litigation and, of course, to escalating costs. Years may pass, and frequently do, between the accrual of a cause of action and its ultimate disposition by the courts.

Asked to review the matter, Lord Woolf has produced some radical proposals. Essentially he proposes that the management of cases should be in the hands of the judges and not in the hands of the lawyers. It would be for the judge to decide on the appropriate procedure for a case, set a realistic timetable for its resolution and to ensure that the procedure and the timetable are complied with. The judges would, in effect, become case managers directing cases down three tracks: (i) small claims arbitration in the county court for all claims of £3,000 or less (this is one proposal that has been implemented); (ii) a "fast track" procedure for all personal injury claims and for civil claims not exceeding £10,000; and a 'multi-track' (*i.e.* the case may be assigned, as appropriate, to the county court or the High Court) for claims in excess of £10,000.

These proposals (and there are many ancillary proposals to expedite proceedings) will inevitably place a heavy administrative burden on the judges and the judiciary which, according to the present Lord Chief Justice and the Master of the Rolls, is even presently undermanned. Lord Woolf recognises that his proposals, if implemented, will be costly in the short term but will pay dividends in the longer term. The Government has been non-committal. Governments tend not to be all that interested in the longer term. For in the longer term, as John Maynard Keynes profoundly observed, we are all dead.

(2) Legal Aid and Advice

For the person of poor, or even modest means, legal advice and assistance would be out of reach but for the provision of legal aid. Legal aid was first introduced for criminal cases in 1903 but really came of age with the growth of the welfare state after the Second World War. The principal statute is the Legal Aid Act 1988 which is supplemented by extensive regulations made thereunder.

It will be appreciated that in the provision of legal aid there are competing interests. Yes, it is desirable that the citizen should not be denied his rights owing to lack of means. "Legal rights," as Ole Hansen has observed, "are worthless unless they can be enforced." But this cannot be done at the expense of the lawyer who, like any other professional man, is entitled to fair recompense for his services. And there is the interest of the taxpayer as well. We sometimes regard the Government as paymaster and blame the Government for putting too little (it is never too much) into this or that social service—and legal aid is a social service. But the Government can only distribute what it receives in revenues; governments may slice the cake in different proportions but to enlarge the cake usually involves raising taxes. In the decade 1985–95 the cost of the scheme has risen from some £330 million to some £1.1 billion—an increase far in excess of the rate of inflation. The present Lord Chancellor, Lord MacKay, evidently seeks to put a brake on this exponential growth in expenditure and, as a corollary, to get the best value for this considerable outlay.

The expressed purpose of the Legal Aid Act 1988 is "to establish a framework for the provision ... of advice, assistance and representation which is publicly funded with a view to helping persons who might otherwise be unable to obtain advice, assistance or representation on account of their means." To this end the Act establishes the Legal Aid Board, an independent body of 11 to 17 members (two of which must be solicitors and two of which must be barristers) to administer the scheme. Legal aid in civil cases is largely administered by the Board while legal aid in criminal cases is largely administered by the courts though the Board does administer the Duty Solicitor Schemes. The Act is largely an enabling Act, leaving such crucial matters as eligibility for aid and the remuneration of barristers and solicitors to be fixed by regulation.

Legal assistance is available in three ways: (a) legal aid and advice in the so-called Green Form Scheme; (b) assistance by way of representation known as ABWOR; and (c) legal aid for proceedings in the courts.

Under (a) any eligible person may obtain free or subsidised out of court legal advice and assistance up to a specified limit (the limit is expressed in terms of the cost of two hours' worth of work for the most cases or three hours' worth of work in the case of matrimonial proceedings). That advice, subject to limited exceptions, may relate to any question of English law. Eligibility is determined by reference to the applicant's disposable income and disposable capital. Disposable income is the income left to the applicant after making deductions for such matters as taxes, rent or mortgage payments, maintenance of spouse and children, travelling expenses. Disposable capital refers essentially to savings and assets but excludes the value of the applicant's sole or main dwelling, the furniture and effects of same and tools of trade. Once the relevant calculation has been made a person with a disposable income of less than (at the time of writing) £72 per week *and* a disposable capital, in the case of a single person with no dependents, not exceeding (presently) £1,000 has nothing to pay under the Green Form Scheme; but a person with income or capital exceeding these limits is not entitled to any assistance under the scheme. The scheme is administratively simple and does not require the approval of the board unless the advisor seeks to exceed the prescribed limits.

ABWOR allows for representation in certain cases (mainly, domestic proceedings in magistrates' courts, applications to mental health review tribunals, and disciplinary proceedings before prison visitors) for which aid under (a) is not available. Administratively it is an extension of the Green Form Scheme except that the prior approval of the Board is required. The same *principles* govern eligibility except that (i) the qualifying amounts of disposable income and disposable capital are higher; and (ii) the applicant may be required to make a contribution depending on how far, for example, his disposable weekly income exceeds that (presently £64) under which he makes no contribution and that at which (presently £156) over which he is ineligible for legal aid.

As to (c) legal aid is available for most (there are exceptions such as defamation actions and undefended divorces) types of civil actions (as to criminal cases) but not for most types of tribunals. The principles governing eligibility are those outlined in (b) above with differences as to the lower limits (below which the applicant is qualified for full legal aid) and upper limits (above which the applicant is disqualified from receiving legal aid at all). To give a *rough* idea: The typical law student at university making his way solely on his grant and bank loans is most likely to fall below the relevant thresholds in (a), (b) and (c) and will make a nil contribution to legal aid. A junior law teacher would not normally qualify under the Green Form Scheme but, after the appropriate deductions have been made, may qualify for some aid under ABWOR or for civil legal aid. A senior lecturer, reader or professor of law can expect nothing. Unless, perhaps, he has been unduly profligate. In computing disposable capital we have seen that the value of the main residence is discounted. Suppose professor X has put all his money into his house. It is worth £500,000 and on top of that it is festooned with effects worth another £500,000. X, however, has no savings to speak of—he has spent pretty well everything on his house. Professor Y lives in a modest semi worth £50,000 but has saved £500,000 which he holds in a bank account. X, assuming his disposable income falls below the prescribed limits, may qualify for legal aid. Y will not. Is this right?

But there is, in addition to this means test, a merits test as well to ensure that public money is not wasted in worthless causes. The applicant must show "reasonable grounds for taking, defending or being a party to the action," and an application may be refused aid if it is unreasonable that he should be granted representation or where it is more appropriate that he should be given assistance by way of representation under ABWOR.

The levels of remuneration are fixed by the Lord Chancellor. It will surprise no one to learn that these have been a source of much tension leading in 1986 to proceedings, subsequently settled, brought by both branches of the profession against the Lord Chancellor for judicial review. Earlier legislation enshrined "the principle of allowing fair remuneration according to the work actually and reasonably done." This principle finds no place in the 1988 Act and while Lord MacKay L.C., has said that he would continue to have regard to this principle he added, somewhat archly, that "fairness is necessarily a vague and subjective concept."

In practice the levels of remuneration are on the low side compared with the privately funded sector. There has been a flight, most especially of the High Street firms, from legally aided work and such work is profitable only to firms which gear themselves for it and if legally aided work is remunerated on an unreasonably low scale these firms can always vote with their feet.

While most legally aided work is undertaken by lawyers it is to be noticed that the 1988 Act empowers the Board to make alternative arrangements for advice and assistance. The Government's view is that lawyers are not always best equipped to give advice and that in some areas, such as welfare law, lay agencies are as well or better equipped to deal with the matter. The Act also introduced provisions for the franchising of legal aid work. The idea here is that the Board will franchise specified categories of legal aid work to solicitors' firms and other agencies where the Board is assured of an accessible and quality legal aid service giving best value for money. So far over 1,000 firms and other organisations have been franchised and it is expected that this figure will rise to over 3,000 in the near future. Legal aid work is not restricted to franchisees but franchisees may exercise certain powers otherwise exercisable only by the Board and it may be that, working hand-in-glove with the Board, franchisees will provide a better service at less cost.

An alternative to legal aid for civil cases is provided by the conditional fee arrangement for which provision is made by the Act. This means, in effect, that the lawyer takes on the case on a no-win-no-fee basis. Such arrangements have long been common in the USA where the lawyer is permitted to conduct litigation in return, if the case is won, for an agreed percentage of the damages awarded. The scheme which has been introduced under the Act does not permit the lawyer to do so in return for a percentage of any damages recovered, but does permit to charge an uplift on his fees up to a 100% maximum (*i.e.* up to double his usual fee) which the lawyer will recover should the action be successful. The scheme is by no means uncontroversial. It has been pointed out that it may enable the unscrupulous lawyer to take on "cast-iron" cases while charging fees that may seriously bite into the client's award of damages.

But the fundamental problem of resource allocation—just how much money can the taxpayer contribute to this social service—has not been blown away. What is clear is that legal aid cannot continue to be 'demand-led' and accordingly to grow exponentially at the expense of the taxpayer. A simple solution, from the point of view of the taxpayer, if not the litigant, might be to cap the legal aid budget: so much but no more; a solution which the present Lord Chancellor has not abandoned. Another might be to set up a national legal aid service, permitting the service to do the best it can within an allocated budget. Resources are finite and we can have only what the taxpayer can afford. And bear in mind that those who pay the most tax are the least likely to be the recipients of legal aid.

(3) Course of Proceedings and Trial

Whether a civil action is to be commenced in a county court or the High Court normally depends, as has been shown, partly on the amount involved and partly on factors which make more appropriate for trial in the one court or the other. In this section what is described is the procedure governing actions in the High Court; it needs to be noted, however, that while the procedure governing county court actions is broadly comparable, there are some significant differences.

(a) *Proceedings before trial*

Civil procedure is governed by Rules of the Supreme Court. These, together with explanation and comment can be found in a publication called *The Supreme Court Practice* (the "White Book") and a notion of the size and complexity of the subject can be deduced from the fact that the White Book runs to some 2,000 pages. The comparable work for the county courts (the "Green Book") also runs to some 2,000 pages. The description which follows here is accordingly only the barest outline.

The purpose of rules of procedure is to ensure that the case comes to court with the issue or issues clearly defined, with what is agreed or what is disputed clearly delineated so that the trial can be conducted as expeditiously and efficiently as possible. The proceedings between the issue of the writ and the commencement of the action are called *interlocutory proceedings*. Obviously difficulties and disputes will arise in connection with the rules of procedure themselves; guidance and rulings on these are given by officers called *Masters* in London and *District Judges* elsewhere.

One thing that law students tend to forget is that clients in real life do not appear with their problem set out in the form of an examination question on contract. The client may not even know what remedy he wants let alone what branch of substantive law is involved. Assume, for instance that P (the plaintiff) tells his solicitor that he has suffered a substantial loss as a result, as P sees it, of D's (the defendant's) failure to deliver goods which were promised. From the facts given him by P, the solicitor will want to satisfy himself (if only provisionally at this stage) that P has a cause of action. He will thus consider whether there was a completed contract between P and D, whether there has been an actionable breach of that contract, and what remedies are available. He will also note when the cause of action arose because there are limitation periods (*i.e.* the period from the accrual of the cause of action within which the writ must be issued) which must be observed. These are now contained in the Limitation Act 1980.

When a dispute arises few people think in terms of litigation. A common complaint concerns goods alleged to be defective and here it is usually the buyer (or perhaps a friend or perhaps someone from the Citizens' Advice Bureau acting on the buyer's behalf) who attempts, usually with success, to reach a settlement on terms acceptable to both parties. Another common dispute arises in the event of an accident involving motor vehicles with each motorist blaming the other and neither wishing to lose the no-claims bonus. Here it will often be the insurers of the motorists involved who will negotiate a settlement.

A dispute will usually have reached an impasse before either side resorts to a solicitor. Even so, the solicitor will not be thinking of litigation at this stage. He will also seek, in the interests of his client, to negotiate with the other party, or the solicitor representing the other party, an acceptable settlement.

The law encourages such settlements. Neither party may have got exactly what he or she wants; either party may have got more, or less of course, had the matter been litigated. But both have got at least half a loaf and the other half might have been swallowed up in the costs of litigation. The law also recognises that in the process of reaching a settlement, a compromise, either or both of the parties, or the agent acting in their behalf, may make concessions that would not be made in litigation. The solicitor will make this clear by overtly conducting negotiations on a "without prejudice" basis which means that what is said or written in the negotiations cannot be used in any subsequent litigation. But there is no requirement that the negotiations be overtly labelled without prejudice; if the negotiations were implicitly conducted with a view to reaching a settlement they will be inadmissible in any subsequent proceedings. On the other hand, if one of the parties alleges that the without prejudice negotiations have resulted in an agreement to settle the action, the court may look at the correspondence to see whether such an agreement has been reached.

But if a settlement cannot be reached because of irreconcilable view concerning the facts, or differences of opinion on the applicable law, then P has to decide whether to withdraw from the field or to embark on litigation. An easy decision for P to make if he is fully legally aided, or where P is a government department or a High Street Bank; a much more difficult decision if P has to put his own money up front.

Actions in the High Court may be commenced by *writ*, *originating summons*, *petition*, or *originating motion*, each signalling the adoption of a particular procedure for the business in question. Proceedings are, however, most commonly commenced by writ and the Civil Justice Review, 1988, recommended that all proceedings should be commenced by a single form of writ, endorsed where necessary to a special procedure.

To issue the writ the plaintiff takes two copies to the Central Office in London or a local district registry. One copy is signed by the plaintiff or his solicitor, sealed, stamped and filed at court. The second copy is sealed and returned to the plaintiff. For purposes of limitation periods the action is now commenced. The plaintiff must either include in the writ his statement of claim (see below) or a brief statement of the nature of the claim and the remedy sought.

Once the writ has been issued it remains valid for service for a period of four months, except where leave to serve out of the jurisdiction is required. There are various methods which would constitute satisfactory service but the most normal would be to ensure that a copy is placed in the hands of the defendant or the defendant's solicitors. Once the defendant has received his copy of the writ he has 14 days within which to acknowledge service. If the defendant does not acknowledge service or indicates that he does not intend to fight the action then the plaintiff may proceed to obtain judgment in default of acknowledgment.

Assuming that the defendant intends to contest the action and that he has acknowledged service, the next stage is for the solicitors for both sides to get the action into a suitable form for trial. This is done through the *pleadings* and allied procedures. At this stage the plaintiff submits his *statement of claim* (if he has not already included this in his writ). The statement of claim is a formal document in which the plaintiff outlines the facts upon which his claim is based, together with the remedy he is seeking. Just as the plaintiff may proceed to obtain judgment if the defendant does not acknowledge service, so too the defendant may apply to have the plaintiff's action dismissed for want of prosecution if his statement of claim is not lodged within 14 days of the defendant's acknowledgment. Indeed these remedies are available to the parties at various stages of the proceedings as a penalty for undue delay. In practice the specified periods for the service of documents are often extended by mutual agreement where this suits the convenience of the parties.

Once the defendant has received the statement of claim, he must reply in a document known as the *defence*. The defendant must (except for damages alleged which are presumed to be denied) deny or refuse to admit all the allegations in the statement of claim which he intends to contest, otherwise he will be taken to have admitted them. The plaintiff may issue a *reply* to the defence but this is not normally necessary since he is presumed to deny any allegations in the defence. Even at this stage there may remain ambiguities and uncertainties in the allegations of the parties. In order to resolve these either party may apply to the other for further and better particulars. Since the aim of the pleadings is to clarify the issues, it is important that each party should know, as precisely as possible, the case he has to meet.

Occasionally the defendant may include a *counterclaim* or *set-off* in his defence. A counterclaim is a cross action independent of the plaintiff's action, but which may conveniently be tried at the same time; here the plaintiff will be the defendant to the counterclaim and the counterclaim is then, in effect, governed by the same procedural requirements as govern the original claim. A set-off is confined to money claims, and is a claim by the defendant to set-off against the plaintiff's claim a sum of money owed by the plaintiff to the defendant and arising directly from the plaintiff's claim.

The defence (or sometimes the reply) is normally the last of the formal documents and at this stage the pleadings are said to close. At any stage either the writ or the pleadings may be amended. Sometimes this may be done without the court's leave if it is before the pleadings have closed, but otherwise, and whenever a substantial change is to be made, leave of the master will be required. It is possible that the pleadings do not give one side enough information upon which to answer the claims and in this event he may, through the agency of a master, be able to compel the other side to provide further and better particulars. Answers to such questions are then attached to and become part of the pleadings.

It is quite conceivable, especially in commercial cases, that much will depend upon the construction of various documents that have passed between the parties. Within 14 days of the close of pleadings both sides must send to the other a list of documents he has which relate to the action. The rules provide that each side must indicate in one list those documents which he has in his possession and does not object to producing for inspection; a second list comprising those documents which he does object to producing and the reason for the objection (*e.g.* privileged document); and finally a list showing those documents which he no longer possesses. The master may make an order for *discovery of documents* if he feels that either side has not made a full disclosure or if he rejects the reason for objection to disclosure. A failure to make discovery may be punished by the master ordering the plaintiff's action to be dismissed or striking out the defendant's defence.

A further procedure which is available to enable the clarification of the issues with consequent savings in costs concerns *admissions* and *interrogatories*. Interrogatories are written questions which may be served by one party on the other with the leave of the master. They must be answered in a sworn document (affidavit). They are to enable the parties fairly to dispose of the issues or to save costs. The answers, for example, may enable the plaintiff to work out on what basis the action will be defended, and so enable him to concentrate on the contested issues. The answers do not form part of the pleadings, though they may be used at the trial. Either side can serve a notice to admit facts and this will enable the issue that has been admitted to be dropped from the trial and thus time and therefore expense will be saved.

Within one month of the close of the pleadings the plaintiff must take out a *summons for directions*. The idea behind this part of the proceedings is for the master to hold, in effect, a pre-trial review to see that all the cards are on the table and that as many non-contentious issues as possible have been eliminated so that the issues for trial are clearly articulated in order to ensure the "just, expeditious and economical" disposal of the case. In practice directions tended to follow a similar pattern and, to expedite further the disposal of the case, automatic directions are gradually being introduced although it remains open to the parties to seek additional or alternative directions.

Occasionally it may be possible to move for what is known as summary judgment under Order 14. Briefly this procedure may be used where the defendant is thought to have no answer to the plaintiff's claims. It cannot be used in actions for defamation or malicious prosecution, false imprisonment or actions based on an allegation of fraud. Where the defendant can show that he has a defence which ought to be tried or that there is a good reason for there to be a trial, the master will give him leave to defend and will then give the parties directions for the future conduct of the action. Otherwise the master will award judgment for the plaintiff which will be final if the damages are liquidated (*e.g.* it is an action concerning a dishonoured cheque where the amount of money in question is not disputed) or interlocutory if the damages are unliquidated; in the latter case the actual amount of the damages will be settled by trial.

The issue of a writ in no sense commits the parties to a trial of the action and at any stage (even during the trial itself) the parties may reach a settlement. At various stages the parties may take stock of the position to decide whether it is worth pressing the matter to litigation. In this connection the defendant may decide that he will meet part of the plaintiff's claim but not the whole of it. If the plaintiff finds this offer unsatisfactory, the defendant may make *payment into court* of that sum. If in the subsequent action the plaintiff recovers no more than the sum paid in then the plaintiff, though he is successful in the action, can recover costs only up to the time of the payment into court and will ordinarily be ordered to pay the defendant's costs incurred thereafter.

(b) *The trial of the action*

A civil action is normally heard by a single judge who determines the facts of the case as well as resolving any issues of law. Strictly, trial by jury is available for a wide range of civil actions since the judge has a discretion to direct jury trial; in practice the discretion is almost invariably exercised to exclude jury trial. For most kinds of civil actions the courts take the view that jury trial is unsuitable: trial by judge alone is said to produce a predictability and uniformity of result which would not be achieved by jury trial. Another important factor, most especially in personal injury claims, is that the assessment and award of damages is best left in the experienced hands of a judge rather than to the instinctive reaction of a jury which has no detailed experience in the matter.

There are, however, some cases where there is a right to jury trial and these include defamation actions, false imprisonment and cases involving an allegation of fraud. The right is not absolute in these cases because if the action is likely to involve issues unsuitable for jury trial (such as an extensive examination of documents or scientific issues) trial by judge alone may be directed. The decline in jury trial for civil actions has been a remarkable one; less than 150 years ago nearly all civil cases were tried by jury, now less than 1 per cent. are so tried. In those cases where jury trial is directed, eligibility for jury service, summonsing and empanelling is the same as in criminal cases tried on indictment.

A civil action is normally opened by the plaintiff who adduces evidence, which may be real (for instance, the goods alleged to be defective) or testimonial. Witnesses (including the plaintiff) may be called who will be examined by counsel for the plaintiff, and may be cross-examined by counsel for the defendant and then re-examined by the plaintiff's counsel. The plaintiff also normally carries the burden of proof which is usually expressed by saying that he must establish his case on the balance of probabilities. This means that the plaintiff must satisfy the judge (or, exceptionally, the jury) not that his allegations are necessarily true, but that they are *more likely* to be true than the defendant's allegations. The burden on a plaintiff in a civil action is thus less exacting than the burden on a prosecutor in a criminal case. Sometimes, an obvious example is where a counterclaim is involved, the defendant carries the burden of proof on an issue or issues and in such a case it is for the defendant to establish that his allegations are more likely to be true.

At the close of the plaintiff's case the defendant may submit that he has no case to answer, that is that the plaintiff has failed to adduce evidence on which the judge (or jury) could find for the plaintiff. Where this submission is made in a trial by judge alone, the judge will not rule on it unless the defence elects to call no evidence. The purpose of this election is, in effect, to prevent the defendant from having two bites on the cherry; it is not right that the judge should rule on the evidence (for that is the effect of a no case submission) until all the evidence is in. Where a civil action is tried by jury the judge has a discretion as to whether he will put the defendant to his election before passing on the submission. In a criminal trial the accused is not put to his election in this way.

If no submission is made then the defendant proceeds to adduce his evidence and his witnesses are subject to examination, cross-examination and re-examination. At the close of the case the judge, if he is hearing the case alone, will announce his decision. Normally he will rehearse the evidence and state which facts he finds to be proved, apply the relevant law to those facts and make a determination in favour of the plaintiff or the defendant; if he finds in favour of the plaintiff he will order the appropriate remedy together with making an order for costs. If the case has been tried with a jury then the judge will sum-up the case bearing in mind that while he gives any relevant directions as to law, the finding of the facts lies within the province of the jury.

While in broad outline the course of a civil action is similar to that of a criminal prosecution, there are important differences. Apart from those already noted in this section, three further distinctions may be mentioned. One results from the elaborate system of pleadings which governs civil, but not criminal, cases. By the time a civil action comes to trial each side will know a great deal of the other's case and the issues in the case will have been delineated. In a criminal prosecution this is far from being the case. In a summary trial the defendant may know no more than the details of the charge and equally the prosecutor may know nothing of the defendant's case. In a trial on indictment, the defendant will know something of the prosecution's case from the evidence tendered by the prosecutor in the committal proceedings but this does not prevent the prosecutor from tendering additional evidence at the trial. If, however, the prosecutor does wish to adduce additional evidence at the trial he must send a copy of the additional evidence to the defendant and to the court. The defendant will then know the essentials of the case he has to meet, but for his part he is not similarly obliged (other than that he must give notice of the essential details of an alibi if he proposes to rely on one) to give notice of his defence to the prosecutor. But, it may be noticed in passing, recent changes in the law affecting the accused's right of silence may make it hazardous for the accused to rely at the trial on a defence not previously disclosed which the accused might reasonably have been expected to disclose when questioned by the police or to refuse to give evidence regarding that defence.

A second distinction relates to the law of evidence. In criminal cases hearsay evidence is in general excluded. This means, in substance, that the actual witness of an event or the actual maker of a statement must be produced to prove this event or statement; it is not possible for someone who was informed by the actual witness or maker to relate what he was told was seen or said. There are several reasons for the rule against hearsay, one being that as A repeats what he has seen to B, and B to C, and C to D, the more unreliable the account becomes. But we commonly treat hearsay as having at least some reliability and for civil, but not criminal cases, first hand hearsay (that is, what A said to B) is generally admissible if proper notice has been served. If the trial is, as usually it will be, by judge alone, the judge, by reason of his experience, will know what weight to attach to a hearsay statement.

A third difference concerns the defendant as witness. In a criminal case the defendant cannot be compelled to testify whereas in a civil case he has no such privilege.

2. Criminal Proceedings

Traditionally in this country it has been open to any citizen to investigate crime and to bring a prosecution in respect of it. In practice both have been for the most part left to those who have the expertise and resources necessary to do so, namely the police for crime in general and other public agencies who will deal with particular categories of offences such as offences relating to the revenue, to customs and excise, to factories, to weights and measures and so on. While our law recognises no distinction between public and private prosecutions (all prosecutions are brought by a citizen standing forth on behalf of the Crown) and all prosecutions are governed by the same rules, it is, nevertheless, convenient to distinguish between public (*i.e.* official) and private (*i.e.* non-official) prosecutions. Private prosecutions, in this sense, are dwarfed by public prosecutions but cannot be dismissed as unimportant. More than the occasional cause célèbre has resulted from private prosecution and more than once successful private prosecutions must have embarrassed the officials who themselves had declined to initiate proceedings.

So far as the police are concerned their position was profoundly affected by the Prosecution of Offences Act 1985. The Act leaves unaffected prosecutions by private individuals and by official, non-police, agencies though the D.P.P. continues to be able to control all such prosecutions by his power under section 6 of the Act to take over criminal proceedings at any stage. But the power which the police had to conduct criminal proceedings is abolished. For long enough the criticism was made that those who were concerned with the investigation of crime should not be concerned with its prosecution and this was accepted by the Royal Commission on Criminal Procedure (1981) which recommended accordingly.

The Act established the Crown Prosecution Service (C.P.S.) headed by the D.P.P. His functions, which he discharges under the superintendence of the Attorney General, include:

(i) the duty to take over the conduct of all criminal proceedings (minor exceptions may be specified) instituted on behalf of a police force;

(ii) the duty of conducting criminal proceedings of such importance or difficulty that make it appropriate for him to conduct them;

(iii) the duty to give advice to police forces on such matters concerning criminal offences as he considers appropriate; and

(iv) to discharge such other functions as may be assigned to him from time to time by the Attorney General.

The national prosecution service which the D.P.P. heads has 31 C.P.S. areas each headed by a Chief Crown Prosecutor and each with a staff of Crown prosecutors.

"The C.P.S.," according to its strategy statement, "is committed to providing a high quality, independent prosecution service, working in the interests of justice." No one doubts the commitment of the service to this aim but there have been teething problems arising from a number of factors. One was that the C.P.S. was, at least initially, underfunded. While there is no public service which would claim to be overfunded and all can be improved by additional funding, it seems clear that the C.P.S. fared worse than other public services in being *initially* underfunded. It got off to a bad start.

Allied to this it may be that too much was attempted too soon. The service needed to attract some 2,000 legally qualified staff together with supporting staff. This was bound to prove difficult. In the market for lawyers the private sector generally pays more than the public sector. The service was promised "an attractive career structure" but the salaries initially offered—the position was much improved in 1990— proved less attractive. The service is also exclusively concerned with criminal work and not all lawyers find that fascinating. Moreover, barristers and solicitors employed by the C.P.S. can conduct cases, for the most part, only in the magistrates' courts and this is resented by lawyers in the service. As we have seen, wider rights of audience have so far been denied to the Service.

There has been the problem, again a resource problem, of acquiring suitable premises and appropriately equipping them. With the benefit of hindsight it may have been better for these to have been situated close by principal police stations to facilitate and foster a close working relationship between the service and the police.

This leads on to another problem. There is no doubt that some police officers, most obviously senior ones, resented the establishment of the C.P.S. It took away from them a very considerable power and few enjoy being stripped of power. But it might be noted that though the police no longer control who gets *prosecuted* they do decide who gets *charged*; the police may still decide not to charge or to caution in the alternative.

The C.P.S. has not been unaware of its problems. In particular the Service has set up national and regional liaison committees to improve the cooperation of the Service not only with the police but with other interested bodies such as magistrates, clerks to the justices and other professional bodies. When the Service now decides not to prosecute or to discontinue a prosecution it will, whenever possible, consult with the police beforehand to explain its reasons for so doing.

The principal aim of the Service is to provide independent and consistent decision-making in the conduct of prosecutions: "the firm, fair and effective prosecution of offenders." A laudable aim. It cannot be right that in similar circumstances a decision is taken in Bristol to prosecute X while a decision is made in Birmingham not to prosecute Y; nor that X, in similar circumstances, should be charged with a more serious offence while Y is prosecuted for a less serious offence. To secure uniformity the Service has promulgated a *Code for Crown Prosecutors* advising prosecutors in deciding whether to prosecute and of the "public interest" criterion to be taken into account in a decision not to prosecute. Of course this cannot ensure that Crown Prosecutors always get their sums right, but it does ensure that they are using the same arithmetic.

How far the Service has been a success ("success" is presumably measured in terms of improvement in fairness and efficiency on the replaced system of police prosecution) is difficult to say. The Service has been something of a whipping boy in the media but this has usually involved criticisms of particular decisions and provides no real evidence that the Service is failing to achieve its overall objectives. Most commentators are of the view that an independent prosecution service (*i.e.* independent of the police) is an imperative and that we are now on the right path. A minority took the view (and some still take it) that it was unlikely to achieve any significant improvement on the former system and was likely to prove very much more costly. These critics claim that the Service has already become over-bureaucratised, responding to problems by creating cumbersome procedures to deal with them. We shall see, but the Service does not yet appear to be clearly out of the wood.

(1) Police Powers: General

The substantial responsibility for the prevention and investigation of crime remains, of course, with the police. For this purpose the constable (all police officers are constables regardless of their rank within the force) is accorded more extensive powers than those accorded the ordinary citizen, and in the exercise of those powers he is answerable to the law. In the conduct of his office the constable may be subject to the orders of his superiors. A senior officer may, for example, direct his subordinates as to where and when they are to patrol but he cannot lawfully order them not to enforce particular laws or not to enforce the law against particular individuals. A constable cannot defend unlawful conduct by a plea of superior orders.

Unlike the citizen, a constable has a legal duty to enforce the law and if, without lawful authority or reasonable excuse, he fails to do so he is guilty of an offence. This does not mean that a constable must necessarily prosecute for every infraction that comes to his notice. Life would become intolerable for both the citizen and the constable if the latter did not occasionally turn a blind eye or issue a friendly caution. But in 1978 a constable was fined on a charge of misconduct as a police officer where he deliberately refrained from intervening in a brawl outside a club when from the cries and screams it was clear that someone was being done a serious injury (*Dytham* (1979)). The court said that his failure to act in this situation, where life itself was at risk, was such as to injure the public interest and to call for condemnation and punishment.

When a crime has been committed, indeed when any event has occurred, any person is at liberty to ask questions of participants or witnesses, and any participant or witness is equally at liberty to refuse to answer any such questions. In practice the police usually secure the co-operation of witnesses and, contrary to the image fostered in detective fiction, most crime is uncovered by information volunteered by members of the public. The informant thus plays a central role in the detection and prosecution of crime. Most of us are informants at one time or another, perhaps reporting a theft or burglary or volunteering evidence concerning a road traffic accident.

Socially we draw a distinction between the *informant* who volunteers his information disinterestedly except for an interest in the proper enforcement of the law, and the *informer* who trades his information for some advantage to himself which may be financial or otherwise. To take the matter a stage further, the informer may affect to join the participants in their criminal enterprise only to inform on them, or may even (and at this stage he is referred to as an *agent provocateur*) incite or instigate crime by others.

These are muddy waters. In dealing with terrorist organisations bent on the destruction of life, few would question the propriety of undercover police infiltration for the purpose of securing the conviction and punishment of the terrorists. But what of the inspector who orders a drink after hours with a view to entrapping the friendly publican? Or the woman police officer who affects to be pregnant to secure evidence against an alleged back-street abortionist? Or the agent who has "laid-on" a robbery so that his principals may be caught red-handed?

The courts have ruled unequivocally that "entrapment" is not a defence to the perpetrators. On the other hand the courts have recognised that law enforcement should not overstep the mark. This mark is ill-defined and it may be that the mark for offences of terrorism is not the same as it is for offences of shoplifting, but the courts are strongly inclined to reduce an otherwise appropriate sentence where it appears that the participants might or would not have committed the offence but for instigation by an agent. The Law Commission considered this matter (Law Comm. No. 83) and proposed that it should be made an offence positively to instigate, incite or persuade another to commit an offence but no action has been taken on this recommendation.

Another general problem concerns the interception of communications. Clearly eavesdropping is lawful; if X on a bus relates to Y in a loud voice his part in a murder, he has only himself to blame if a police officer sitting behind him hears all. In one case (*Maqsud Ali* (1965)) the police placed two men suspected of murder in a room which contained a concealed microphone and the court allowed the taped recording, tantamount to a confession, to be given in evidence. Evidence of crime taken by video-recorders is increasingly used in the enforcement of the law.

This leads to a consideration of telephone tapping and the interception of mail. Traditionally it has been assumed that the Crown (the power came to be exercised by the Secretary of State under a warrant issued by him) may lawfully intercept letters and this power was extended to telegrams and then to telephone communications. By convention warrants to intercept communications were issued only exceptionally in cases of serious crime where other methods of obtaining evidence had been tried and failed.

The legality of this practice was challenged in *Malone v. Commissioner of Metropolitan Police* (1979) where Malone's telephone had been tapped pursuant to a warrant and in connection with offences of handling stolen property. Megarry V.-C. held that Malone's action failed because there was no positive law against tapping, no property right of Malone's had been invaded, and English law did not recognise any right of privacy. Malone, however, pursued the matter to the European Court alleging a breach of Article 8 of the European Convention on Human Rights which provides that everyone has "the right to respect for his private and family life, his home and his correspondence." Article 8, goes on to provide that there shall be no interference with this right "except such as in accordance with law and is necessary in a democratic society . . . for the prevention of disorder or crime. . . . " The court declared Malone's application admissible on the grounds that English procedures relating to interception failed to satisfy Article 8.

The outcome was that Parliament placed the law on a statutory footing in the Interception of Communications Act 1985. The Act makes it an offence for any person, other than as authorised by the Act, to intercept a communication in course of transmission by post or by means of a public telecommunication system. The Secretary of State, however, is authorised to issue a warrant for interception in specified cases (where he considers it necessary in the interests of national security, preventing or detecting serious crime, or of safeguarding economic well-being) subject to requirements as to form, extent and duration. The Act further sets up a Tribunal to which any person who believes his communications have been intercepted may complain and if the Tribunal finds that there has been a contravention of the Act it shall, *inter alia*, make a report to the Prime Minister, and may order the destruction of the intercepted material or may make an order for compensation.

Finally, the Act provides for the appointment of a person who has held high judicial office as a Commissioner whose function it is to keep under review the carrying out by the Secretary of State of his functions under the Act and to report thereon to the Prime Minister and to Parliament.

It has been pointed out that everyone is at liberty to refuse to answer questions whoever poses the questions. If a man has nothing to hide, however, he is normally more than willing to answer questions whether put by the police, the press or his next-door neighbour.

But if a man is, *or is thought to be,* a participant in events that might show him in a discreditable light (most obviously a crime) then he would be best advised to stay silent at least until he receives professional legal advice. Our law long recognised this right of silence *and* additionally took the view that usually no adverse inferences could be drawn from an accused's refusal to answer questions. Hence no deduction of guilt could be drawn from an accused's silence in response to police questions or from his refusal to give evidence in court.

But in this matter the law has been radically altered by the Criminal Justice & Public Order Act 1994. This provides, in sections 34–38, that:

(i) If, after caution, an accused when questioned by the police fails to mention facts on which he subsequently relies in his defence and which he might reasonably have been expected to mention at the time of questioning, the court in determining whether there is a case to answer or the court or jury in determining whether the accused is guilty of the offence charged, may draw such inferences from the failure as appear proper (section 34).

(ii) If the accused when arrested (a) is found to have any object, mark or substance about him which gives rise to a reasonable suspicion that he participated in the crime; or (b) is found at the place or about the time of the crime in circumstances giving rise to a reasonable suspicion that he participated in the crime, and the accused fails or refuses to proffer an explanation for the object, *etc.,* or his presence, the court in determining whether there is a case to answer or the court or jury in determining whether the accused is guilty of the offence charged, may draw such inferences from the failure or refusal as appear proper (section 36).

(iii) Where the accused, without good cause, declines to give evidence or, having been sworn, declines to answer questions, the court or jury, in determining whether the accused is guilty of the offence, may draw such inferences from the failure to give evidence or to answer questions as appear proper (section 35).

It is still the law, however, that an accused cannot be compelled to answer questions or give evidence and section

38 provides a small safeguard for the accused in that it cannot be held that he has a case to answer or be found guilty of the offence charged solely on an inference drawn from his failure to answer questions or give evidence.

The foregoing provisions mark a substantial change in the accused's position. The Criminal Law Revision Committee, in its Eleventh Report published in 1972, had proposed, substantially, the changes now implemented on the grounds that it flew in the face of common sense not to allow a court or a jury to draw appropriate inferences from an accused's failure to proffer an explanation for his conduct in circumstances where he might reasonably be expected to do so. Take a simple example though no doubt practice will throw up much more difficult ones. Suppose D is arrested on suspicion of burglary in Leeds on the night of May 4. Under questioning D declines to give any account of his whereabouts on the night of May 4 and only later claims that he spent that night in Leicester. His failure to mention his alibi at the time of questioning when he might reasonably have been expected to mention it would ordinarily lead to adverse inference being drawn about its truth. Ordinarily it may be that D can offer a reasonable explanation for his failure to mention it at the time. He might have spent that night in Leicester with his mistress whom he did not wish to involve and, still less, to let it become known to his wife where he was.

When these proposals were first made by the C.L.R.C. in 1972 they ran into a storm of criticism and were promptly put into cold storage by the Government. But the climate has changed and some twenty years later they have been found acceptable to Parliament. One reason for that is that provisions in the Police & Criminal Evidence Act 1984 (discussed below) have seen a substantial improvement in a suspect's rights, not least in access to legal advice.

(2) Police Powers: Interrogation

A confession is not admissible against a defendant unless it is proved that it was not obtained by oppression or as a consequence of anything done or said which might render any confession unreliable. Not only is the rack proscribed but also a confession obtained by a promise of bail or other favourable treatment may be equally inadmissible.

But if this is the law, the reality is somewhat different. Few can resist the urge to communicate with a fellow human being even if he happens to be a police officer whose interest lies in securing evidence, most especially a confession, about a crime which the suspect is thought to have committed. The contest of wits may not be an equal one. The suspect (unless he is an old hand) is in foreign territory, his movements are controlled and he is dependent on his captors for his means of existence. He may have been stripped, for reasons of evidence or security, of possessions which are important to his dignity. The police officer, on the other hand, is entirely familiar with the environment and has all the trappings of control and authority.

It is probably the case that no interrogation is entirely "fair" as any errant schoolboy brought before his headmaster will testify. The headmaster brings the pupil to *his* office, unfamiliar territory to the pupil, and will subtly use the trappings of his office to erode the boy's confidence. The headmaster who needs to resort to beatings or threats or inducements to obtain damaging admissions cannot have read any worthwhile books on his trade in the last half century.

It is at this point that the Police and Criminal Evidence Act 1984 contains a comprehensive restatement of the law which aims to regularise the conduct of interrogation and in some respects to revise it. What is presently obscure or opaque is governed by comprehensive provisions in the Act and further supplemented by Codes of Practice which contain provisions governing detention in police custody and interrogation much more detailed than was formerly the case.

It remains the law that other than by authority of law (almost invariably following arrest) no one can be compelled to go to a police station and, still less, can he be compelled to give evidence against himself. It is still not uncommon to hear or read following a report of crime that a man is at a certain police station "helping the police with their inquiries." It is of course open to suspects voluntarily to attend a police station and to submit to questioning but such public-spiritedness in suspects is very much the exception. A suspect can be lawfully detained only following a lawful arrest; there is still no obligation on him to help the police, although, as we have seen, his failure during police questioning to proffer explanations which he might reasonably have been expected to make at the time of questioning may result in adverse inferences being drawn as to his guilt. There is no obligation on him to help and the police have no power to detain him for questioning. If a person is held against his will, that is, it is made clear to him that he is not a free agent, he is unlawfully detained unless he has been given a valid ground for his detention. It is true that the Act refers in Part IV to "detention" while in Part III it refers to "arrest" but "detention" here is simply a convenient way of referring to that period during which the suspect is constrained to be in police custody; the assumption always is that it has been preceded by a valid arrest and that the detention is in right of the arrest.

While the provisions in the Act are extensive it may be that they can be fairly summarised under three heads: (a) the timescale; (b) administrative supervision; and (c) detainee's rights.

(a) *The timescale* (see Figure 1)

For convenience Figure 1 assumes the suspect arrives at a police station on the dot of midnight but at whatever time he arrives the timescale for subsequent action remains the same.

Little needs to be said of the suspect who is (i) promptly released without being charged (though he may be bailed to return to the station at some specified later stage in which case his further detention is governed by the timescale); or who is (ii) promptly charged and promptly released with or without bail; or (iii) promptly charged and kept in custody except to note that in this case the custody officer must review the situation and may yet release the suspect with or without bail.

The real problem concerns the suspect who is neither released nor charged but is kept in detention so that further inquiries (including questioning of the suspect) may be made. In his case the really critical stages are Stage 5 at which he can be further detained only on the authorisation of a superintendent; Stage 6 after which he can be detained only if, after a hearing at which the suspect is entitled to be legally represented, a magistrates' court issues a warrant (or successive warrants) of further detention; and Stage 7 at which he must be charged or released.

The timetable must be adhered to strictly. A superintendent cannot authorise continued detention after the expiry of 24 hours and a court to which application is made for a warrant of further detention must dismiss the application if it is made after the expiry of 36 hours if it appears it could reasonably have been made within 36 hours.

(b) *Administrative supervision*

A general feature of the Act is the provision for what might be called administrative supervision which has resulted in a considerable increase in paperwork as the police are required

Figure 1

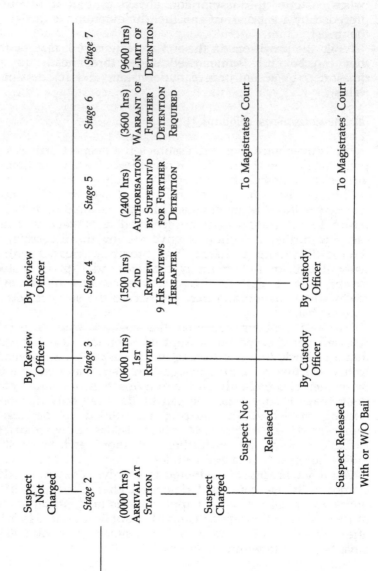

to log their actions and to record their reasons therefore. Some might regard this as, at best, a useless imposition, or, at worst, a brake on efficiency, but the idea seems to be—certainly a good one in principle—that the police are obliged to think carefully about what they are doing and to closely consider the justification for doing it. Allied to that the review officer or the custody officer as the case may be, provides an element of impartial supervision of the suspect's case. He may not be entirely impartial since he himself will be a police officer but he must be an officer who is not himself involved in investigating the case against the suspect. Detention, or continued detention thus has to be justified by the officers conducting the inquiry to their superiors.

(c) *Detainee's rights*

The detainee has two rights. One concerns his right to have someone informed of his arrest and the place where he is held. This was first introduced by section 62 of the Criminal Law Act 1977 and is enlarged and improved upon by section 56 of the Police and Criminal Evidence Act. Delay in according this right is now permissible *only* where (i) a serious arrestable offence has been committed ("serious arrestable offence" has an extensive definition in section 116 but may broadly be said to extend to an arrestable offence, as to which see below, p. 123, the commission of which has led, or is likely to lead, to serious harm to the state, the person, or to cause substantial financial gain or loss); and (ii) a superintendent is satisfied that one of the conditions in section 56(5) is met (broadly these refer to cases where disclosure would impede the course of justice as by alerting associates or preventing the recovery of property); and (iii) in any event the right of notification cannot be delayed for more than 36 hours. Moreover the suspect must be told the reason for any denial of his right and this must be recorded.

The other concerns access to a solicitor. Formerly this was governed by administrative directions but now appears for the first time in statutory form in section 58 of the Act. This provision closely follows section 56 in that it may be delayed only for the same reasons and for the same time.

Under both section 56 and section 58 it appears that the initiative—"if he so requests"—must come from the suspect but the Codes of Practice make it clear that the suspect must be informed of these rights as soon as practicable (even if the police are minded to deny him their immediate exercise) and in the case of legal advice the suspect who does not wish to avail himself of it must sign a waiver clause to that effect. One further point in this connection concerns the practicality of access. All very well if the suspect is Mr. Big who has prompt access to a solicitor at all hours, not so good for Widow Twanky who has never fallen foul of the law before. But there is now a publicly financed duty solicitor scheme which ensures that ordinarily a suspect will have access to legal advice at a police station.

It will be a rare case where the police may properly deny the suspect access to legal advice; in effect it can be lawfully denied only where the police have reasonable grounds for suspecting that the adviser will intentionally or inadvertently pervert the course of justice by informing confederates or hindering the acquisition of evidence. There is a quasi-exception to this. Where the suspect nominates a solicitor who cannot be contacted, or is contacted but cannot attend for some time, and the suspect declines the services of the duty solicitor or no duty solicitor is available, questioning may be commenced at once if there is an immediate risk of harm to persons or serious loss of or damage to property. A person entitled to consult a solicitor is further entitled to have the solicitor present during the interrogation though the solicitor may be excluded if his conduct is such as to prevent the proper questioning of the suspect. Less infrequently the police may properly deny the right to have someone informed of the arrest but this will be the exception rather than the rule.

What effect the Act and the Codes of Practice have had on the actual conduct of interrogations still remains to be finally evaluated. Compared with the prior law the suspect's position has been significantly improved. He will be informed of his rights under sections 56 and 58 and will normally be able to exercise them should he choose to do so. He is also afforded a copy of the Codes of Practice which inform him, in simple language of the ground rules governing detention in general and interrogation in particular. He may have a solicitor present. He must be cautioned, which means that he must be told of his right to remain silent while being reminded of the potential dangers of remaining silent, not only on arrest but also before any period of questioning commences. He will be given access to the custody record which is, in effect, a diary logging the events of his detention.

In addition to the foregoing, the Act provides for the tape-recording of interviews and this has now been widely introduced and is in general use for indictable offences. The tape provides not only a completely accurate record of what was said but also a means of checking on its conduct. If, at his trial, the defendant wishes to challenge the summary of his statement, his confession, submitted in written form by the police, he has access to the tapes.

It would be fair to say that the police were not enthusiastic about the reforms introduced by the Act and the Codes, most especially the tape-recording of interviews which were seen as cramping their style. Subsequent studies have shown these fears to be unfounded. There is no evidence that interrogation is hampered by tape-recording. There is some evidence that they give rise to more guilty pleas because allegations of "verballing" (*i.e.* putting words into the suspect's mouth) can be checked against the tape. The Crown Prosecution Service favours them. There is no evidence that the police are avoiding them and much that they now favour them. There are additional costs but these have not proved to be unduly burdensome.

The advantage in interrogation still lies with the interrogator. Perhaps inevitably so. He is the professional operating on home ground. He is well informed and well prepared. It is the interrogator who determines the agenda, sets the pace and calls the shots. The Act and the Codes ensure, as far as may be, compliance with the rules of the game but the seeded player usually comes out on top.

(3) Police Powers: Arrest

While the Police and Criminal Evidence Act restates and revises much of the law relating to arrest, it does not provide a code in the sense of providing a comprehensive and exclusive statement of the law. For example, the common law power to arrest for breach of the peace remains unaffected by the Act. Though the Act constitutes the most extensive review of arrest it will still be necessary in some particulars to resort to the common law.

The Royal Commission identified two principal defects in the existing system. One was its complexity, particularly in relation to statutory powers of arrest for there were many dozen such powers differently expressed in many statutes. The other was the issue of underreach and overreach in that sometimes powers of arrest were not available where they were obviously required and sometimes accorded where they were not required. The Commission proposed, broadly, that the power of arrest should be available only where it was necessary for the proper enforcement of the law. Thus, for example, it would be available to deal with bank robbers but not to deal with an elderly shoplifter who fully co-operates with the authorities. The Commission's proposals in this regard were not fully accepted and powers of arrest may be summarised as follows.

(a) *Arrest for arrestable offences*

The general powers of arrest formerly found in section 2 of the Criminal Law Act 1967 are re-enacted by section 24 of the Police and Criminal Evidence Act 1984. The section authorises any person, whether a constable or not, to arrest without warrant: (i) anyone who is, or who is reasonably believed to be, in the act of committing an arrestable offence; and (ii) where an arrestable offence has been committed, anyone who has, or is reasonably believed to have been, guilty of the offence.

The section then confers further powers on constables who may additionally arrest a person; (iii) where there are reasonable grounds for believing that he has committed an arrestable offence; and (iv) where a person is, or is reasonably believed to be, about to commit an arrestable offence. Moreover, a constable, but not a private citizen, is authorised to enter (if needs be by force) any place where the suspect is or is reasonably believed to be for the purpose of effecting an arrest.

So the powers of a constable are somewhat more extensive than those of a private citizen. Under (iv) a constable has a prophylactic power; he may arrest a man whom he reasonably believes to be about to throw a brick through a shop window while the citizen must wait until the window is broken. The additional power conferred on a constable under (iii) may be simply illustrated. Suppose a bookshop manager sees a shopper behaving in a way that reasonably leads the manager to believe that the shopper has taken a copy of Hogan, Seago and Bennett's *"A" Level Law* from the shelves and secreted it in his coat. In fact the shopper had been bent on stealing this priceless work but, guessing that he was being observed, had changed his mind. The manager follows the shopper into the street where he arrests him. In these circumstances the manager is not protected by the section because *no arrestable offence has in fact been committed* and is thus liable to pay damages for the unlawful arrest (false imprisonment). Had the manager communicated his reasonable suspicions to a passing constable and had the constable effected the arrest then neither would be liable; the manager because he has not made the arrest, and the constable because he is protected by (iii), (see *Walters v. W. H. Smith* (1914)).

Had the manager arrested the shopper at the very shelf where the manager reasonably believed he was stealing then the manager would have been protected by (i) which protects the manager even if the theft has not been committed so long as he reasonably believes the shopper to be *in the act of committing*. But once the shopper has left the premises he can no longer be said to be in the act of committing the theft.

It may seem odd that a citizen may be liable for an unlawful arrest even though he has acted reasonably on the available evidence. Not surprisingly the so-called "citizen's arrest" is very much the exception; it is usually possible, and certainly safer, to leave these matters to the police.

An arrestable offence is defined as any offence for which a person over 21 may be sentenced to five years' imprisonment but the Act goes on to include certain other offences as attracting the power of summary arrest even though they do not carry five years' imprisonment. These include going equipped for stealing (Theft Act 1968, s.25), taking vehicles without consent (Theft Act 1968, s.12) and indecent assault on a female (Sexual Offences Act 1956, s.14). Such offences are brought within the definition of arrestable offences because of the apprehended difficulties of enforcement if the power is not available. The significance of including any offence in the category of arrestable offences is that the power of arrest exists even though the "necessity" principles which are required by the next category are not met. Hence, for example, the elderly shoplifter may be arrested even though he co-operates fully with the police and an arrest is not "necessary" to secure compliance with the law.

(b) *General arrest powers under section 25 of the 1984 Act*

Somewhat paradoxically section 25 is concerned with powers of arrest for non-arrestable offences. The idea is simple enough. If certain conduct is made a crime (be it failing to sign a driving licence, or dropping litter, or taking the eggs of a protected bird) then the police must be given the necessary powers to enforce that law effectively and that means that every offence must have the ultimate long-stop of arrest if only for the purpose of identifying the suspect.

At a stroke section 25 effects a considerable simplification. The constable is no longer burdened with having to memorise over 100 statutory powers of arrest, and the citizen is not threatened with the risk of arrest provided he is co-operative and gives his name and address, and presents no further danger to himself or others.

(i) *The Identification Requirements.* A constable may arrest for *any* offence if he has reasonable grounds for suspecting (a) that the suspect's name is unknown to him and cannot be readily ascertained; (b) that the name furnished is not the suspect's real name; or (c) that the suspect has failed to furnish a satisfactory address. The ordinary run of case will present no difficulty since people ordinarily carry adequate evidence of identity (driving licence, credit cards). But it must not be supposed that people are required to carry and furnish means of identity; the constable must have reasonable grounds for suspecting that the name furnished is not the real name of the suspect and a mere failure on the suspect's part to provide confirmatory evidence would not constitute reasonable grounds. It will often prove possible for the police to confirm a name and address by contacting headquarters on their radios.

(ii) *The Preventive Requirements.* Under section 25 the police are also accorded powers of arrest for *any* offence where there are reasonable grounds for suspecting that an offence has been, or is being, committed and there are also reasonable grounds for believing that arrest is necessary to prevent the suspect causing physical harm to himself or another, suffering physical injury to himself, causing loss of or damage to property, committing an offence against public decency, or causing an unlawful obstruction of the highway.

Typically these powers might be used where the suspect has committed an offence involving drunkenness (drunk in a public place, for example) and his arrest is necessary because he cannot safely convey himself, or a child accompanying him, across the road; or of a "flasher" who has been causing alarm and annoyance to passing women by exposing himself.

(c) *Other statutory powers of arrest*

It might be thought in view of the foregoing powers that there was no need for any additional statutory powers of arrest but section 26 preserves some statutory powers of arrest which are set out in Schedule 2. The rationale of these offences appears to be that there are some cases where, though the offence is not an arrestable offence and there is no difficulty in identifying the suspect an arrest must be made if the law is to be properly enforced. Thus, for example, a deserter from the armed forces may be arrested and returned to the relevant authority even though his identity is not in question; though his identity is not in question his whereabouts very shortly will be unless he is arrested. With the exception of the preserved statutory powers of arrest all other statutory powers of arrest accorded to constables are abolished.

(d) Arrest for breach of the peace

The power of a constable at common law to arrest for a breach of the peace committed in his presence remains unaffected by the Act. To a suggestion during debate in Parliament that this power should be put on a statutory basis, the Government replied that this would be unacceptable because the common law basis of the power provides the police with a degree of flexibility, particularly when responding to situations requiring urgent intervention, which is not readily susceptible to precise statutory formulation. A breach of the peace is conduct which involves, or threatens, violence to the person or significant harm to property. Fighting in the street provides a common occasion for the exercise of the power and here the constable does not have to pass on the merits; he may properly arrest all the combatants though it turns out that one or more of them was acting in lawful self-defence. Faced with a breach of the peace, the constable's duty is to preserve it, not to hold an inquiry into the merits of the participants.

(e) Arrest for fingerprinting

By section 27 of the Act the police are empowered to require a person convicted of a recordable offence (*i.e.* any offence which the Home Secretary designates by statutory instrument to be recorded in police records) who has not at any time been in police detention to present himself for fingerprinting and if he does not he may be arrested.

(f) Arrest under warrant

Apart from powers of arrest without warrant, an arrest may also be effected under warrant. Warrants of arrest are usually issued by a magistrate after hearing evidence on oath and may be issued for both arrestable and non-arrestable offences. A warrant may be executed anywhere within the jurisdiction and reciprocal arrangements exist with Scotland, Northern Ireland and the Irish Republic. A constable who in good faith executes a warrant according to its terms incurs no liability to the suspect even though the warrant proves to be unlawful.

The officer need not have the warrant in his possession but the suspect must be shown it as soon as practicable.

(g) *General requirements of a valid arrest*

(i) *Reasonable Grounds.* All powers of arrest are conditioned by the requirement that reasonable grounds must exist for the suspicion on which the arrest is based. Reasonable cause cannot be defined in the abstract and has to be related to the circumstances of the case. Clearly a constable is not required to have an open-and-shut case against the suspect because it is his *suspicion* that he must justify, not prove that the suspect committed the offence. It will often be the case that it is only after further inquiries have been made following the arrest that sufficient evidence emerges on which to charge the suspect. But deprivation of liberty is a serious matter and can be justified only where good grounds exist for the suspicion. This requires, at the least, that the officer be open-minded and that he makes such inquiries as are practicable in the circumstances. The officer may act on information provided by third parties if it has every appearance of being reliable and leads to a reasonable inference of the suspect's guilt. It would, for example, be reasonable for the officer to rely on a report given him by a store-detective whom the officer knows to be experienced and reliable, but not on an anonymous tip-off given hurriedly over the telephone. One exception, of little practical importance, to the requirement for reasonable cause is where an arrest is effected of one who has in fact committed or is in the act of committing an arrestable offence; here an arrest is lawful though the person effecting the arrest has no reasonable grounds for his belief.

(ii) *Notification of Grounds of Arrest.* An arrest is lawful only if the suspect is given a *valid* reason for it. The suspect is entitled to know why he is being deprived of his liberty so that he can meet the case against him. In *Christie v. Leachinsky* (1947) police found Leachinsky in possession of stolen cloth and arrested him under the Liverpool Corporation Act 1921 on a charge of unlawful possession. This Act did confer a power of arrest for unlawful possession but only when the identity of the suspect was unknown and Leachinsky was well known to the officers concerned. It was held by the House of Lords that a suspect is entitled to know the valid ground for his arrest and since Leachinsky was given no such valid ground he was entitled to damages. It appears in this case that the police might have had reasonable grounds for suspecting that Leachinsky had received the cloth knowing it to be stolen and might have validly arrested him under the then Larceny Act 1916 which conferred an arrest power whether the suspect's identity was or was not known. But an arrest cannot be justified by showing that a power did exist if only the police had remembered it; and still less by showing that the suspect had committed some other arrestable offence.

In *Christie v. Leachinsky* it was said that the party arresting need not use technical language so long as the suspect knows for what he is arrested. The police are well advised to use unmistakable language, *e.g.* "I arrest you for stealing this watch/murdering your mother-in-law." But, and so long as the import is clear to the suspect, it would do to say "You're nicked laddie for lifting this watch/doing away with your dear old mother-in-law."

Section 28 of the Police and Criminal Evidence Act continues the requirement that the suspect be informed of the ground of his arrest unless it is not reasonably practicable by reason of the suspect having escaped from arrest before the information could be given. This marks another departure from the former law which did not require the suspect to be informed of the ground of the arrest where it is patently obvious why he is being arrested.

(iii) *Use of Force.* Section 3 of the Criminal Law Act 1967 which permits the use of such force as is reasonable in the prevention of crime and in the arrest of offenders continues in force. In addition section 117 of the Police and Criminal Evidence Act states that where any provision of the Act confers a power on a constable, not being a power which may be exercised only with the consent of some person other than a constable, the constable may use reasonable force, if necessary, in the exercise of the power. What is reasonable, of course, depends on the circumstances. While necessity must always exist for the use of the force, force is not justified simply because it is necessary if it is not also reasonable. If the only way to bring a fleeing shoplifter to justice is to gun him down this might be necessary but would not be reasonable and he will have to be allowed to go free.

(h) *Arrest for questioning*

The police have no power to arrest for questioning as such. An arrest would be unlawful if the officer gave as his reason: I am arresting you because I wish to question you in connection with the theft of Hogan, Seago & Bennett's *A Level Law* from the British Museum. On the other hand, if the officer has reasonable ground for suspecting that S has committed this awful crime, he may properly arrest S giving as his grounds his suspicion that S has stolen the book. The arrest in the latter case is not rendered unlawful by the fact that the officer, who has enough evidence to justify his reasonable suspicion but not enough evidence to justify a charge, hopes to obtain the evidence to justify a charge by questioning S, that is by securing a confession from S by questioning him. An arrest is lawful if there are reasonable grounds for the arrest and the arrest is no less lawful because the officer knows that additional evidence (such as forensic evidence relating to fingerprints, or the evidence of witnesses identifying S, or the admissions of S himself obtained by interrogation) will be required before S can be charged: *Holgate-Mohammed v. Duke* [1984] 1 All E.R. 1054, H.L.

(4) Police Powers: Search and Seizure

Just as the Police and Criminal Evidence Act rationalises and simplifies the former law relating to powers of arrest, so too it rationalises and simplifies powers of search and seizure. The new powers may be summarised as follows.

(a) *Search for stolen or prohibited articles*

Where a constable has reasonable grounds for suspecting that when in a public place a person has, or a vehicle contains, stolen goods or prohibited articles (articles are prohibited if they are made or adapted, or intended by the possessor, for causing injury or for use in connection with burglary, theft, deception or taking motor vehicles) he may detain that person or vehicle for the purpose of a search.

It has often been maintained that constables exercising powers of search do so on flimsy grounds, following no more than a hunch. To counter this possibility the Act by section 3 introduces the safeguard of requiring the constable to record, at the time or as soon as practicable, the object of the search and his grounds for making it, and the suspect is entitled to have a copy of this record. As has been indicated, the requirement for records and reasons is general to the scheme of the Act and may turn out to constitute a brake on precipitate and unthinking police action.

(b) *Road checks*

It has apparently long been the practice of the police to conduct checks on vehicles leaving a particular area where it is known that a crime has been committed and when there is reason to think that a suspect may be apprehended. Obviously this involved stopping and searching the vehicles of many innocent persons and the Royal Commission, considering that the practice was of doubtful validity, proposed that it should be put on a statutory basis. Accordingly section 3 provides that an officer not below the rank of superintendent may authorise a road check where there are reasonable grounds for believing that a serious arrestable offence has been, or will be, committed, that the suspect is still in, or is about to enter, the area in order that vehicles may be checked with a view to ascertaining whether the suspect or a witness is in any such vehicle. Once again records must be kept and reasons recorded.

(c) *Stop and search in anticipation of violence*

Experience showed that the powers detailed in (a) and (b) above were not entirely adequate to curb the possession of offensive weapons. Take the case, for example, of animals' rights demonstrations, which all too often erupt into violence, mostly directed at the police who are trying to keep the peace. The police have no power to conduct speculative searches for offensive weapons and only exceptionally would they have reasonable grounds for believing that a person has, or that a vehicle contains, offensive weapons.

Section 60 of the Criminal Justice & Public Order Act 1994 accordingly introduced a more extensive power of stop and search. Where a police officer of the rank of superintendent or above (or an inspector in an emergency) reasonably believes that incidents involving serious violence may take place in his area and that it is expedient to do so to prevent their occurrence, he may give an authorisation to stop and search both persons and vehicles for dangerous instruments or offensive weapons for a period normally up to 24 hours. While the authorisation cannot properly be given unless there are reasonable grounds, thereafter the police may conduct speculative searches of persons and vehicles.

(d) *Entry and search of premises under warrant*

Under the former law justices had certain specific powers to issue search warrants but no general powers to issue warrants to search for evidence of crime. The Act provides, by section 8, that justices may issue a search warrant where there are reasonable grounds for suspecting that a serious arrestable offence has been committed and that there is likely to be on the premises material of substantial evidential value. The Act, however, makes provision for "excluded material" (for example, personal records and journalistic material) which can be seized only after application to a circuit judge.

(e) *Entry for purpose of arrest, etc.*

While there is no general power to enter premises for the purpose of arresting a person in respect of whom a power of arrest exists, section 17 confers on constables in uniform a power, where reasonable grounds exist, to enter and search premises for the purpose of arresting a person:

  (i)   in respect of whom a warrant of arrest has been issued;
  (ii) who is suspected of having committed an arrestable offence;
  (iii) who is suspected of having committed certain public order offences; or
  (iv) who is unlawfully at large.

In addition the section confers upon uniformed constables:

  (v)   the power to enter premises for the purpose of saving life or preventing serious damage to property. This last power may be exercised though there is no suggestion of criminal conduct; a police officer might, for example, enter premises where a fire has accidentally started to preserve the safety of the occupants.

(f) *Entry and search after arrest*

It may happen that the police arrest a suspect for, say, theft, not at his own premises but in some other place. Nevertheless, they may have reasonable grounds for suspecting that a search of his premises will reveal evidence relating to that offence or to a similar offence, for example handling. A search in such circumstances must ordinarily be authorised, under section 18 of the Act, by an officer not below the rank of inspector but can be authorised by a constable of lower rank provided it is necessary for the effective investigation of the offence (where, for example, the constable has grounds for believing that the evidence may be removed or destroyed if he does not act promptly) and is notified as soon as practicable to an officer not below the rank of inspector.

(g) Search upon arrest

Where a person is arrested he may by section 32 of the Act be searched where there are reasonable grounds for believing that the suspect may present a danger to himself or others, that he has anything that might assist him to escape, or anything that might be evidence relating to an offence. The constable may "frisk" the suspect but he cannot require him to remove any of his clothing in public other than an outer coat, jacket and gloves.

(h) Search upon detention

If the suspect is to be detained at a police station the custody officer must record everything which the suspect has with him when arrested and may seize anything which he believes may be used to cause physical injury or damage property, or to interfere with evidence or to effect an escape; and anything which he reasonably believes may constitute evidence: section 54. The custody officer may seize anything falling within these categories but must tell the suspect the reason for the seizure; otherwise clothing and personal effects may not be seized. A suspect may co-operate in this procedure but if he does not he may be searched against his will though this must be done by an officer of the same sex as the suspect.

The power of search (which is referred to as the inventory search) under this section was extended by section 147 of the Criminal Justice Act 1988. Section 54 was thought to authorise only a once-and-for-all search at the outset of detention in a police station. Section 54 is amended to authorise subsequent searches of a person in custody at a police station and the search of a person in police detention otherwise than at a police station for the purpose of ascertaining whether he has with him anything falling within the proscribed categories. They may, therefore, search a prisoner following a court appearance.

(i) Intimate searches

An officer of at least the rank of superintendent may authorise an intimate search (*i.e.* a search of the body orifices) where he has reasonable grounds for believing that the suspect has concealed on him anything with which he may do injury or a Class A drug. This form of search is governed by stringent conditions as to place, manner of search and documentation but may be conducted against the will of the suspect.

An officer of at least the rank of superintendent may also authorise where a person is suspected of involvement in a recordable offence, again subject to strict conditions as to manner and documentation, the taking of an intimate sample (*i.e.* a sample of blood, semen or any other tissue fluid, urine, pubic hair, or a swab taken from a body orifice or a detail impression but only where the suspect consents in writing. Without the suspect's consent no intimate sample may be taken but if the suspect refuses without good cause then a court or a jury may draw such inferences from that refusal as appear proper.

Non-intimate samples (*e.g.* a sample of hair other than pubic hair, a sample taken from under the fingernails) may also be taken with the written consent of the suspect but in this case they may be taken without his consent if the taking is authorised by an officer of at least the rank of superintendent who has reasonable cause to believe that the sample will tend to confirm or disprove the suspect's involvement in a recordable offence. Once again, of course, there are strict conditions as to manner and documentation.

(j) *Search in general*

Even this brief survey will indicate that the Police and Criminal Evidence Act accords extensive powers of search of persons, premises and vehicles. They are certainly more extensive than the former powers (*e.g.* in permitting the issue of search warrants to search premises where there are reasonable grounds for suspecting that evidence relating to a recordable offence may be discovered) but in some instances (*e.g.* intimate searches) it is difficult to say how far the new powers may differ from the old in the absence of rulings by the courts. The minus may be that the Act has extended powers of search while the plus is that it has also clarified them so that the police and the citizen know more precisely what is permitted and what is not. While the provisions of the Act, especially in relation to documentation may appear to be prolix, the particular powers of search are exhaustively (save for the power to enter premises to prevent a breach of the peace when the common law is preserved) defined and, of course, the provisions as to documentation are intended as a check on arbitrary action since at every relevant stage reasons have to be given and recorded for action taken.

(5) Police Powers: Illegally Obtained Evidence

Except as authorised by law any arrest, search, seizure or interrogation is unlawful. Frequently the illegality will give rise to civil remedy or even a criminal prosecution. Thus if the suspect is not informed of the grounds of his arrest he may sue for false imprisonment; if an intimate search is made without the appropriate assents he may sue for assault; if there is an unauthorised search of his premises he may sue for trespass, and so on. But the risk of civil proceedings, which will only be pursued where the plaintiff has access to the necessary resources and is sufficiently determined, is at best a fitful safeguard.

Moreover breaches of the Act or of the Codes of Practice do not necessarily afford rights of redress on the suspect. If, for example, the suspect is improperly denied his rights to have someone informed of the arrest or to consult with a solicitor, it does not appear that he has any civil redress. So far as the Codes of Practice are concerned, it is specifically provided (s.67(10)) that a breach of the Codes shall not of itself render a police officer liable to criminal or civil proceedings. It is, however, provided (s.67(8)) that a police officer shall be liable to disciplinary proceedings for failure to comply with any provision of a Code. Though the effectiveness of this sanction must be largely in the hands of the police themselves, it may be assumed that it carries some potency.

A final sanction is the possibility that evidence obtained in breach of the Act or of the Codes may be rendered inadmissible with the attendant risk that the prosecution will fail.

There is no general rule of English law that requires the exclusion of evidence merely because it has been illegally obtained. At common law the judge has a discretion to exclude such evidence but the "discretion" is narrowly viewed and such evidence is to be admitted unless its prejudicial effect outweighs its probative value: *R. v. Sang* [1979] 2 All E.R. 1222, H.L. Thus, for example, evidence secured as the result of an illegal search of the defendant or his premises would ordinarily be admissible.

The Act contains a number of provisions bearing on this matter. Section 82(3) acknowledges, in broad terms, the discretion of a court to exclude evidence. Section 76 deals with the admissibility of confessions. Section 78 is more broadly based and states that a court "may refuse to allow evidence on which the prosecution proposes to apply if it appears to the court that, having regard to all the circumstances, including the circumstances in which the evidence was obtained, the admission of the evidence would have such an adverse effect on the fairness of the proceedings that the court ought not to admit it."

An explanation of the genesis of section 78 may be helpful. When the Police & Criminal Evidence Bill was before the House of Lords, an amendment was moved, the substantial effect of which would have been to render inadmissible illegally obtained evidence. The Government did not wish to go this far but felt it had to give some ground. The outcome was section 78—a compromise measure which seemed to satisfy most, perhaps because no one was quite sure of its effect.

These provisions, as the courts have subsequently acknowledged, overlap and particular evidence might be excluded under all three provisions. But it would seem convenient to deal with the exclusion of confessional evidence under section 76 and the exclusion of other evidence under section 78.

(a) *The operation of section 76*

A confession (a confession includes any admission made by the defendant whether orally or in writing) is regarded as cogent evidence of guilt. It is admissible provided it is voluntary and if its admission is in question it is for the prosecution to prove beyond reasonable doubt that it was so made. Section 76(2) provides that a court "shall not" allow a confession to be given in evidence if it has been, or may have been, obtained:

> "(a) by oppression of the person who made it; or (b) in consequence of anything said or done which was likely, in the circumstances existing at the time, to render unreliable any confession which might be made by him in consequence thereof."

The court thus has no discretion where section 76 applies. The court may be utterly convinced of the truth of the confession but must not allow it to be admitted if it was obtained as aforesaid.

Section 76(8) contains a partial definition of oppression: it "includes torture, inhuman or degrading treatment and the use or threat of violence." Obviously a confession obtained by the rack or thumbscrew stands excluded but conduct may be oppressive though there is no hint of violence. Some, even much, guidance on what is oppressive conduct can be inferred from the Codes of Practice. These contain, in effect, a code of good practice governing questioning. The suspect, exigent circumstances apart, must be questioned at reasonable hours and for periods of no more than two hours at a time in a room that is adequately lit and ventilated; that he is to be given adequate food and rest; that he is not to be questioned if he requires medical treatment or is intoxicated; and so on. Any breach of the Code, more especially if it is deliberate, is improper but whether it becomes oppression depends upon the seriousness and number of breaches. A confession is unlikely to be rendered inadmissible because the interview room was stuffy, or because the interrogator unnecessarily ran a few minutes over two hours. Conduct becomes oppressive, said Sachs J. in *R. v. Priestley* (1967) 51 Cr.App.R. 1, C.A., when it "tends to sap, and has sapped, that free will which must exist before a confession is voluntary." He added that what was oppression in the case of a child, invalid or old person or somebody inexperienced in the ways of the world may not be oppression in the case of a tough character who is an experienced man of the world. In *R. v. Fielding* [1987] 2 All E.R. 65, Lord Lane C.J. referred with approval to the O.E.D. definition of oppression as the "exercise of authority or power in a burdensome, harsh or wrongful manner; unjust or cruel treatment of subjects and inferiors." He added that it was difficult to think of a case of oppression which did not involve impropriety. An example is provided by *Paris, Abdullahi & Mille* (1993) 97 Cr.App.R. 99, C.A. M's conviction for murder was quashed where his confession had been obtained, in effect, by browbeating. Though during questioning M (and the court considered it relevant that M was on the borderline of mental handicap) had denied involvement over 300 times, he was shouted at by the police and told that questioning would continue until the police "got it right", *sc.* secured a confession. Clearly in such cases the tape-recording of police questioning is invaluable in detecting the nuances of oppression in a way which subsequent oral and written testimony of the questioning would not be.

Section 76(2)(b) might apply where the police offer to take no action against other members of the suspect's family, or say that they will not oppose bail if the suspect will admit his guilt. It is not enough that a confession is made after something is done or said unless what was done or said was likely to render the confession unreliable. It is rather lame to say it depends on all the circumstances but it does depend on all the circumstances.

It needs to be noted that the exclusion of a confession does not render inadmissible any facts discovered as a result of the confession or, where relevant, to show that the defendant speaks or writes in a particular way. But such evidence might fall foul of section 78.

(b) *The operation of section 78*

Notwithstanding the apparent opacity of section 78 it is clear that the courts have not adopted a cavilling or narrow approach to it. Quite the contrary and again it is compliance, or rather non-compliance, with the provisions of the Act and the Codes that has become the dominant factor. Even if a confession is admissible under section 76 it will be inadmissible under section 78 if it has been secured by serious breaches of the Codes. Thus confessions will normally be excluded if the defendant was not cautioned: *Okafar* [1994] 3 All E.R. 741, C.A.; or was improperly denied access to legal advice: *Samuel* [1988] 2 All E.R. 135, C.A. provided the defendant has been in some way prejudiced by the failure or denial. In *R. v. Mason* [1987] 3 All E.R. 481, C.A., a confession was held to have been wrongly admitted when it was made following a false statement made to him and his solicitor that they had evidence directly linking the defendant with the crime. Time and again the courts have emphasised the importance of strict adherence to the Codes and that they will not tolerate cynical and systematic breaches of them: *R. v. Keenan* [1989] 3 All E.R. 598, C.A.

On the other hand the courts found no breach of section 78 where the police, in order to trap thieves, set up a jeweller's shop staffed by two undercover police officers who pretended to be shady jewellers willing to buy stolen property: *Christou* [1992] 4 All E.R. 559, C.A.; and where the police left what were apparently cartons of cigarettes in an open and unattended van: *Williams* [1994] 98 Cr.App.R. 209, C.A. *Khan* [1994] 4 All E.R. 426, C.A., goes further. There the police, with a view to securing evidence against a suspected heroin dealer, surreptitiously placed a bug to the exterior of K's property and thereby obtained damning evidence. Notwithstanding that the placing of the bug was a trespass to K's property, the evidence was admitted. In all three cases the defendants had been tricked into providing evidence against themselves but the admission of the evidence did not affect the fairness of the criminal proceedings; in no way had they been persuaded, still less coerced into doing or saying what they did.

To exclude evidence under section 78 the court has to make a value judgment. Having regard to the circumstances in which the evidence was obtained would it have *such* an adverse effect on the *fairness* of the proceedings that the court ought not to admit it? The starting point will usually involve an examination of the propriety of the conduct of the police (but note that the section applies generally and is not confined to evidence obtained by the police) and this examination will hinge on a consideration of the number and gravity of breaches of the Codes. In evaluating the seriousness of the breach or breaches it cannot matter that the police have acted honestly or mistakenly if it or they affect the fairness of the proceedings, but deliberate and cynical breaches will weigh more heavily against the admission of the evidence. The court will also have regard to the causitive effect of the breach or breaches. Has the defendant in fact been disadvantaged in the preparation, presentation and conduct of his defence?

(6) Bail

Where a person is charged with a criminal offence it is obvious that there will normally be a delay before the prosecution will be ready to proceed with trial. What, therefore, happens to the accused in the meantime? There are various possibilities. At one extreme it may be necessary to keep the accused in custody pending the verdict; at the other it will suffice simply to give him a date on which he is to present himself before the magistrates' court. In between these two extremes are cases in which the accused is remanded on bail which may be unconditional or conditional.

In practice, and because most crimes are minor, criminal proceedings are usually commenced by summons and the defendant never even sets foot inside a police station. Most offences are dealt with by the police taking particulars on the spot and warning the defendant that he may be prosecuted. Some time later, if the Crown Prosecution Service decides to prosecute, the defendant will receive a summons through the post. No coercion is used other than the command to appear in court at an appointed time. Facing a charge of careless driving or operating a television receiver without a licence the defendant is not likely to skip the country. If, though, the defendant fails to appear in court a warrant of arrest may be issued.

(a) *Bail in general*

The principal Act is the Bail Act 1976 (*Casebook*, Part 1, 3.7) but there are other statutory provisions, particularly in the Police & Criminal Evidence Act 1984, the Criminal Justice Act 1988, the Bail (Amendment) Act 1993 and the Criminal Justice and Public Order Act 1994.

The Bail Act governs the grant of bail in "criminal proceedings" which are defined, in effect, as the period from the time when the arrest is made until a custodial sentence becomes operative. The defendant may accordingly be granted bail where he has been given a custodial sentence where he has been given leave to appeal and pending the outcome of the appeal. Obviously this would be done only exceptionally but it might be done where the defendant has been given a short custodial sentence which he would serve out before the appeal is heard; a successful appeal would be small comfort to a defendant who has already served the sentence.

(b) *Bail by the courts: general*

Where the defendant appears before a court (it will usually be a magistrates' court) in connection with proceedings for an offence, section 4 of the Bail Act assumes a general entitlement to bail. Section 4 states that the defendant "shall" be granted bail except as is provided in Schedule 1 to the Act. Schedule 1 then distinguishes between imprisonable and non-imprisonable offences.

It will be appreciated that it is only in highly exceptional cases that a defendant charged with a non-imprisonable offence may be refused bail but bail may be exceptionally so refused where, for example, he has previously absconded and the court believes he would again fail to surrender to custody, or where a remand in custody is necessary for his own protection.

Where the defendant is charged with (or has been convicted of) an imprisonable offence, a key factor is whether a custodial sentence is likely. If Widow Twankey is charged with shoplifting goods to the value of a few pounds then, since a custodial sentence is out of the question, only in exceptional circumstances would unconditional bail be refused. But if the defendant is charged with a serious offence for which a custodial sentence is likely then bail is less readily granted. Only in one case is bail ruled out altogether. The Criminal Justice and Public Order Act 1994, s.25, provides that a person charged with murder (or attempt), manslaughter, or rape (or attempt) shall not be granted bail if that person has previously been convicted of any such offence.

Part 1 of Schedule 1 of the Bail Act, as amended by the Criminal Justice and Public Order Act 1994, states that, in relation to imprisonable offences, bail "need not be granted if the court is satisfied there are substantial grounds for believing" that the defendant, if released on bail (whether unconditionally or conditionally) would (i) fail to surrender; or (ii) commit an offence while on bail; or (iii) interfere with the course of justice; or (iv) is charged with an indictable offence or an offence triable either way and was on bail at the time of the offence; or (v) other conditions specified in the schedule are met.

In determining whether these conditions are met the court may have regard to any relevant evidence but in particular they may have regard to:

(i) the seriousness of the offence and the probable means of dealing with it (a Widow Twankey, charged with shoplifting, has little incentive to abscond while someone facing the likelihood of a lengthy custodial sentence has every incentive to do so);

(ii) the character, antecedents, associations and community ties of the defendant (the better the character and the stronger the ties the less likely is the risk of absconding);

(iii) the strength of the evidence against him (a somewhat puzzling requirement since the court is not at this stage trying the case but it may be relevant that the defendant has confessed to or has denied the charge);

(iv) any other relevant matters.

(c) *Bail by the courts: the bail decision—unconditional and conditional bail*

What happens in practice is that the prosecutor informs the court that bail is not opposed or that it is opposed. If the prosecutor does not object to bail then bail is routinely granted though in certain cases (see below, p. 143) the court must give reasons for the grant of bail even if it is unopposed.

If the prosecutor opposes bail then the court has a serious decision to make. The defendant is not on trial, and much less has he been convicted, but if the bail decision goes against him he will lose his liberty even though he will not be subject to the regime of those serving a custodial sentence. It is accordingly proper that the presumption should always be in favour of bail. So if the court is *not satisfied* that there are *substantial grounds* for believing that the conditions specified in the schedule above are met it *must* grant unconditional bail.

If the court is satisfied that there are substantial grounds for believing that one or more of the conditions is met the court must go on to consider whether to remand in custody or to release on conditional bail. The Act does not say what conditions may be imposed except that provision is made for bail with sureties (*infra*). What the Act does specify is the *purposes* for which conditions may be imposed. Section 3 details these as such requirements as may be necessary to ensure that the defendant:

(i)   surrenders to custody;
(ii)   does not commit further offences while on bail;
(iii) does not interfere with witnesses or otherwise obstruct the course of justice; or
(iv)   makes himself available for a report to be made to assist the court in dealing with the offence. A condition imposed for any other purpose is invalid.

The sorts of conditions imposed include a requirement that the defendant reside at a particular place, or be at a certain place during certain hours (a curfew), or report to a police station at certain times, or surrender a passport, or any other appropriate condition—in one case a hoaxer was required not to use the telephone.

Alternatively or additionally the court may require sureties which, very simply, is money put up front to secure the surrender of the defendant. No surety may be demanded of the defendant himself unless it appears that he may leave the country (for, say, business reasons or a holiday) before the time appointed for surrender. Where a surety is required of another the court has to decide whether the surety is suitable and the amount of the recognizance. In determining whether the surety is so suitable regard will be had to the surety's financial resources and his relationship to the defendant. Commonly sureties are provided by relations, friends or employers. There is no minimum or maximum. It may be just a few pounds or it may be millions; the record appears to be the £3.5M required in respect of the chairman of Polly Peck

International who was charged with offences of dishonesty following the collapse of the company in 1990. Nevertheless, he subsequently absconded.

A surety is a guarantor of the defendant's surrender and is liable to forfeit his recognizance unless he is entirely free from blame for the defendant's failure to surrender.

(d) *Bail by the courts: reasons for refusing or granting bail*

If the court refuses bail it must give reasons because the defendant may wish to reapply for bail or to appeal against the refusal and accordingly needs to know the reasons for the refusal.

If the court grants bail it does not ordinarily have to give reasons but an exception is introduced by the Criminal Justice Act 1988, s.153 which amends the Bail Act to require the court to give reasons where the defendant is charged with murder (or attempt), manslaughter, or rape (or attempt). The reason for this was the disquiet that had been caused in cases where defendants charged with these offences had killed or raped while released on bail. In these cases, as we have seen, bail cannot be granted if the defendant has a previous conviction for any such offence.

(e) *Bail by the courts: reapplications and appeals*

Following a refusal of bail the defendant may apply to the High Court on grounds of fact or law. This is a relatively expensive procedure for which legal aid is rarely given. A better course is for the defendant to appeal to the Crown Court if he has been denied bail by the magistrates; this is less expensive and the defendant may qualify for legal aid. But in practice the most common way of challenging a refusal of bail is by reapplication for bail. At the bail hearing the magistrates ordinarily have power only to remand the defendant in custody for a period not exceeding eight days. This means that the defendant may appear every week and renew his application for bail. The broad effect of the present law is:

(i) to allow the defendant to renew his application whenever there has been a genuine change in the circumstances affecting his entitlement to bail;

(ii) to discourage defendants from reapplying where there has been no relevant change of circumstances; and

(iii)   to allow defendants who know there is no hope of bail to be reremanded without having to appear in court.

The prosecution, although it may oppose an application, or reapplication, for bail has no general right of appeal against a decision to grant bail. Where bail is granted, however, the prosecution has open to it two courses of action:

(i) The Bail Act, as amended by section 30 of the Criminal Justice and Public Order Act 1994, provides that where a defendant, who has been charged with an indictable offence or an offence triable either way, has been granted bail, the prosecution may apply for the decision to be reconsidered with a view to (a) varying the conditions of bail; (b) imposing conditions where bail was granted unconditionally; or (c) to withhold bail. But an application for reconsideration may be made only where the prosecution has information which was not available when the decision was taken.

(ii) The Bail (Amendment) Act 1993 gives the prosecution a limited right of appeal where a magistrates' court has granted bail. The reason for this legislation was the police surmise, subsequently shown by research to be well-founded, that many persons (it turned out to be about half) given bail on charges of stealing or taking motor vehicles or of burglary, committed further and similar offences whilst on bail. The Act accordingly provides that, where the defendant is charged with an offence punishable by imprisonment for five years or with vehicle taking and is granted bail, the prosecution may appeal to a judge of the Crown Court though only if the prosecution made representations at the original hearing that bail should not be granted and the representations were made before it was granted.

(f) *Bail by the police*

In some, even many, situations it is imperative that the police should be empowered to grant bail. Take two examples. The first is where Widow Twankey is arrested on Saturday morning on a charge of shoplifting. By midday inquiries have been completed and she is charged. She cannot be brought before a court before Monday morning and since a custodial sentence is out of the question it would be clearly unreasonable for her to be imprisoned until Monday. In such a case the police may grant bail.

A second case is where the defendant is arrested on suspicion of assault following a brawl in a public house. Fists were flying and it will not be clear who was to blame until further inquiries, perhaps taking a day or more, have been made. In this sort of situation the police are empowered to bail the defendant to return to the police station at a specified later date.

Police bail is largely regulated by the Police and Criminal Evidence Act 1984 and the Criminal Justice and Public Order Act 1994. Under section 38 of the former the police (through the custody officer) may admit to bail pending appearance in court. But the police could only admit a person to unconditional bail and this meant that in some cases the police would refuse bail where conditional bail might have been granted. Sections 27 and 28 of the latter Act accordingly provide the police with powers to grant conditional bail on grounds and in terms similar to those available to courts.

A person arrested other than for a serious arrestable offence must be charged or released within 24 hours of the commencement of detention, and in the case of a serious offence for not more than 96 hours. The system of administrative supervision provided by the Act is designed to ensure that the police act expeditiously and that, whenever appropriate, for the release of the defendant on bail.

(g) *The operation of bail*

As has been pointed out, most criminal proceedings are commenced by summons and the question of bail does not arise. Where bail applications need to be made it appears that of those who are granted bail 97 per cent. surrender to bail while only 3 per cent. fail to surrender. At first sight these figures are highly satisfactory. It would be unrealistic to expect the courts to get it right every time and a 97 per cent. "success rate" looks very good.

But there is another side to the coin. A major factor in the grant or refusal of bail is whether it is unlikely or likely that the defendant will receive a custodial sentence. Here the "success rate" appears to be not so good because studies show that of those refused bail and subsequently tried in magistrates' courts while some 55 per cent. receive custodial sentences, some 30 per cent. do not, and some 15 per cent. are acquitted. Of those refused bail and tried in the Crown Court, some 20 per cent. receive non-custodial sentences and some 10 per cent. are acquitted. But these figures also require explanation. A court may decline to impose a custodial sentence which otherwise it would have given but for the fact that the defendant has been in custody on remand.

Up to a point it is swings and roundabouts. If the courts (most especially the magistrates' courts) bailed no one who failed to meet the requirements under the Bail Act to an unqualified right to bail then failures to surrender would be reduced almost to vanishing point. If such a policy were pursued, the price to be paid would be that many more of those remanded in custody would not receive a custodial sentence or would be acquitted. Some, most obviously the relatives of someone killed by a person released on bail or the victim of a rape by such a person, might consider the price worth paying.

In the bail decision there is an inevitable element of risk taking. On the one hand we do not wish to incarcerate those who have not been convicted of crime; on the other we may fairly wish to incarcerate those charged with crime who, as the evidence suggests, may, say, commit further crimes whilst on bail or may interfere with the course of justice by intimidating witnesses. The Bail Act 1976 may be said to have been in favour of bail, whether unconditional or conditional. Subsequent amendments to that Act, prompted by cases where people released on bail have committed serious crimes, have been more restrictive, although the provisions in the Criminal Justice & Public Order Act 1994 may make bail by the police more readily available. Those making the decision to grant or withhold bail have to make an educated guess on the available evidence; sometimes they may get it wrong.

Electronic tagging, which assumes a simple and inexpensive device attached to the person granted bail and which will allow the police to monitor his movements to ascertain whether he is complying with restriction on his movements imposed as a condition of bail, would help to fine-tune supervision of those on bail but thus far the experiments have less than a complete success. It may seem surprising that technology allows us the successful monitoring of the movements of thousands of aircraft by the day but has not yet developed sufficiently for to be sure that Bill Sykes is or is not at his place of abode at 2 o'clock on a Saturday night.

(8) Legal Aid and Advice

As with legal aid and advice in civil cases, legal aid and advice in criminal cases is governed by the Legal Aid Act 1988 and regulations made thereunder and reference should be made to the general discussion of legal aid. Legal aid and advice in criminal proceedings is available broadly in two situations, in respect of pre-trial matters and in respect of the trial itself.

As to the former, legal advice is available under the "green form" scheme in the same way as in civil cases. Thus a person of poor means charged with an offence, say shoplifting or careless driving, may be given advice about the relevant law and the conduct of his defence. In addition there is the duty solicitor scheme. This scheme is managed by the Duty Solicitor Committee and its Regional Committees, the Duty Solicitor Committee being appointed by, and subject to the guidance and direction of, the Legal Aid Board. Essentially what happens is that the Duty Solicitor Committees approve appropriately qualified solicitors (or their representatives who may include trainee solicitors or solicitors' clerks who have appropriate experience and training) to give advice at police stations, or at courts, in relation to legal aid and bail applications. This scheme stops short of representation at the trial of the issue but is not subject to any means test and the cost is supported by the legal aid fund irrespective of the means of the suspect or accused.

Where representation at trial is sought the defendant applies to the "appropriate authority." For the time being the appropriate authority is the courts but in due course it is envisaged that the Legal Aid Board will become the appropriate authority. The initial application will usually be made to the magistrates' court (although an application may ordinarily be made to any court before which the defendant appears) where it will be processed by the clerk to the justices. While the clerk has authority to grant legal aid, only the magistrates have authority to refuse it.

As with civil legal aid there is a merits test and a means test. As to the merits test legal aid *must* be granted in certain cases, such as where the defendant is charged with murder, or where the prosecution appeals, or applies for leave to appeal, to the House of Lords, or where the defendant is brought before the court in pursuance of a remand in custody and may again be remanded in custody. Legal aid *may* be granted if:

(i)   the offence is such that, if proved, it will lead to loss of liberty or loss of livelihood or serious damage to reputation;

(ii) the case involves a substantial question of law;

(iii) the defendant may be unable to follow the pro-
        ceedings because of disability or inadequate com-
        mand of English;
(iv)   the nature of the case involves the tracing and
        interviewing of witnesses or expert cross-examina-
        tion of witnesses for the prosecution; or
(v)   it is in the interests of someone other than the
        defendant that the defendant be represented.

It follows from these criteria that legal aid will only rarely
be granted where the offence is triable only summarily, and
experience shows that it is only exceptionally granted in the
case of an offence triable either way where summary trial is
adopted. Where, however, the offence is tried on indictment
it will only be rarely that one of the stated criteria (most
obviously the risk of a custodial sentence) is not met.

But whether legal aid is mandatory or discretionary, the
grant of legal aid in criminal cases, as in civil cases, is subject
to a means test so that a defendant may, according to his
financial resources, may have to meet part, or even the
whole, of the costs of the defence. In practice it appears that
where the defendant meets the merits test for legal aid it is
only exceptionally that the defendant is required to make a
contribution to the costs of the proceedings.

(9) Plea Bargaining

Most people who are charged with a criminal offence plead
guilty, and in magistrates' courts an overwhelming majority
does so. Strictly, every defendant could plead not guilty and
put the prosecution to the trouble of proving its case. Were
this to be done by all defendants the results would be
catastrophic so far as the administration of criminal justice is
concerned. There is an old aphorism that delay defeats justice;
if all defendants pleaded not guilty delay would become
endemic and the administration of justice would be at least
seriously impeded and might even grind to a halt.

It could be said, therefore, that the state has an interest in
having the majority of defendants plead guilty. This is not to
suggest that there is a deliberate policy aimed at curtailing not
guilty pleas. Of those who plead guilty, most do so because
they face an open-and-shut case where there is little point in
prolonging the agony and where no steps have been taken by
the prosecution to induce a guilty plea. Even in these cases
the defendant knows, or will be so informed by his attorney,
that he will get a lesser sentence by pleading guilty. If the

tariff (*i.e.* the usual penalty for the offence) for a particular offence is "x," the practice is to give "x−y" where the defendant pleads guilty. The defendant is, in effect, rewarded for saving time and money and, perhaps, possible embarrassment and even humiliation of witnesses.

But then there are cases where some form of persuasion is brought to bear to secure the defendant's agreement to a guilty plea. This process is called plea bargaining, but it is important to note that the initiative for a plea bargain might be taken just as readily by the defence as by the prosecution. Bargains take many forms but may be reduced to two types: bargains as to plea and bargains as to sentence. An example of the former might be where X is charged with the serious offence of causing grievous bodily harm with intent and also with the less serious offence of malicious wounding; the prosecution and the defence may agree that in return for the accused pleading guilty to the less serious charge, the prosecution will drop the serious charge. An example of the latter might be provided by a charge of indecent assault on a very young child; in return for a plea of guilty, thus sparing the victim and his family the embarrassment of a trial, it might be indicated to the accused that he will receive a sentence lighter than he would have received on conviction after trial.

There is a difference between bargaining as to plea and bargaining as to sentence. The former can be done without the participation of the judge. A judge (or magistrates) normally accept bargains as to plea. Though it is open to the judge to insist that the prosecution proceeds with the more serious charge, this is done only exceptionally; in the case of Peter Sutcliffe (the so-called Yorkshire Ripper), for example, the judge insisted that the charge of murder be proceeded with though the Attorney-General had indicated that the prosecution was willing to accept a plea of guilty to manslaughter on the grounds of diminished responsibility.

A bargain as to sentence, on the other hand, necessarily requires the participation of the judge. It is, of course, perfectly proper for an accused's counsel to tell him that the likelihood is that he will get a lighter sentence if he pleads guilty but the circumstances in which the judge should enter into such a bargain are severely, if uncertainly, prescribed. Appellate courts have indicated that it is only in the most exceptional cases that the judge should be involved in such discussions and that, whenever possible, such discussions should be conducted in the presence of both sides and in open court. It is never proper for a judge to indicate that in the event of a guilty plea he will impose a lighter sentence for this is necessarily coercive and deprives the defendant of his unfettered choice to plead guilty or not guilty. But it may be permissible for the judge to indicate that in any event he will not impose a custodial sentence.

Bargains, whether as to plea or sentence, raise serious issues. On one view there is something in it for all parties. The prosecution gets a conviction without the delay and expense of a trial, the police can close their files on the case, and the defendant gets off more lightly than he might otherwise have done. But there are dangers. An accused, even though innocent, might be tempted to plead guilty to a charge, or to a lesser charge, because he fears the consequences of being found guilty and thus exposing himself to a more severe sentence. And it is obviously important that judges should not be seen to be involved in what are essentially compromises. The function of the judge is to act as an impartial referee motivated only by the dictates of the law; it is not proper that he should be influenced by notions of expediency.

There is no doubt, however, that plea bargaining is extensively practised and that it is seen as having advantages both to the prosecution and the defence. To an extent it must be recognised as a useful device to ensure the smooth running of the criminal justice system. But it has certain dangers and thus far the courts have been unable to articulate guidelines which give rise to complete confidence in the propriety and fairness of its practice.

(10) Course of Trial

A person charged with a criminal offence may be tried on information summarily before a magistrates' court, or on indictment at the Crown Court. The essential difference between the two is that trial on indictment involves trial by jury. In a summary trial the magistrates determine the facts as well as the law; in a trial on indictment it is for the jury to determine the facts while questions of law are the province of the judge.

Otherwise the law and procedure are substantially similar whether the trial is summary or on indictment. The same general rule applies that it is for the prosecution to establish the guilt of the accused and not for the accused to prove his innocence (see above, p. 4). This used to be expressed in the time-honoured phrase of proof beyond reasonable doubt but this particular expression has fallen out of favour and the standard is now expressed by saying that the judges of fact (the jury or the magistrates as the case may be) must be completely satisfied, or feel sure, of the accused's guilt. There are, however, numbers of exceptions (mainly created by statute) to this principle where the burden of proving particular facts falls upon the accused. When this occurs the accused is not required to prove the matter to the same strict standard as applies to the prosecution; it is enough to establish the matter on the balance of probabilities (see above, p. 4).

Normally the prosecution opens the proceedings by outlining the case against the accused and by adducing evidence (which may include real evidence such as finger-prints or the murder weapon, as well as testimonial evidence) to prove that case. The witnesses called and examined by the prosecution may be cross-examined by the defence and may, in turn, be re-examined by the prosecution.

When the prosecution has completed its case it is open to the defence to submit that there is no case to answer. In effect the accused is asserting that, on the basis of the evidence given so far, no reasonable jury (or Bench of magistrates) could find the charge against him proved. If the submission is upheld the judge will direct the jury to return (or the magistrates will return) a verdict of not guilty.

If no submission is made or if the court rules against it, the defence then adduces its evidence; its witnesses will in turn be examined and may be cross-examined and re-examined. The accused, however, is in a special position. While he is free to give evidence, he cannot be compelled to do so, although as we have seen (see above, p. 000), adverse inferences may be drawn if the accused declines to give evidence. If he chooses to do so he is subject to examination in the normal way except that he cannot usually be compelled to answer questions tending to show that he has committed offences other than the one with which he is charged. An accused who chose not to give evidence was once able to make an unsworn statement from the dock. The value of such statements, since they were not subject to cross-examination, was probably small and, by the Criminal Justice Act 1982, s.72, the right was substantially abolished. This is, however, without prejudice to an *un*represented accused making an address to the court or jury which, were he represented, his counsel or solicitor could have made on his behalf. Further-more, the accused upon conviction may make an unsworn statement in mitigation before sentence is passed.

At the conclusion of the defence case and following closing speeches by the prosecution and the defence, the judge, in a trial on indictment, sums up the case to the jury. In his summing-up the judge will review the evidence and direct the jury's attention to the salient points of the case but he must not trespass upon the jury's function of finding the facts. He will always instruct the jury on the burden of proof and may direct them on any matters of law affecting the case.

Magistrates in a summary trial do not direct themselves in this fashion. They may reach a conclusion on guilt or innocence without leaving the bench or they may retire to give the case more detailed consideration.

(11) Form of Trial

Whether a person is to be tried summarily or on indictment depends upon a number of factors. Some crimes (numerically by far the largest class) are of such a minor nature that they may be tried only summarily. Nearly all motoring offences are summary only as are most offences involving a failure to possess a necessary licence (for a television receiver for example) and a host of other offences. At the other extreme there are offences which because of their seriousness are indictable only. These include such offences as treason, murder, manslaughter, infanticide and rape. In between are offences where the seriousness depends not upon the nature of the offence but the particular circumstances of it. An obvious example is theft which may involve property to the value of a few pence or property to the value of millions of pounds. Such offences are made triable either way.

In recent years there has been a tendency to downgrade offences so that offences which were formerly only indictable (e.g. bigamy, unlawful sexual intercourse with a girl under 16) have become triable either way, and offences which were formerly triable either way (e.g. driving with an excessive blood/alcohol concentration, assaults on constables) have become summary only. While this recategorisation is said to be done on principled grounds it has also very conveniently taken pressure off the hard-pressed Crown Court.

Where an offence is summary only or where it is indictable only, the accused has no choice as to the form of trial. Where the offence is triable either way it is in the first place for the magistrates to decide (having regard to such things as the nature of the case, the punishment which they can inflict if the accused is found guilty) whether the case is suitable for summary trial. If they decide that it is not so suitable, the accused cannot gainsay their decision and they proceed to consider whether there is sufficient evidence to commit him for trial on indictment. If they decide that the case is suitable for summary trial, they so inform the accused and tell him that he may consent to summary trial or that he may insist on trial by jury. They must further inform him that if he consents to summary trial and is convicted he may be committed to the Crown Court for sentence if it appears on hearing information about his character and antecedents (for the magistrates will learn of these only *after* conviction) that a greater punishment should be imposed than the magistrates have power to impose.

The above classification and procedure was introduced by the Criminal Law Act 1977 and represents a considerable simplification of the previous position. It may be that it is not entirely logical in that, for example, an accused cannot insist on jury trial for such offences as assaulting a police officer in the execution of his duty nor for driving with a blood-alcohol concentration above the prescribed limit. Both might be thought to be relatively serious offences but both are classified as summary only. On the other hand, if an accused is charged with theft, and even if the value of the property involved is only a few pence, it will be open to him to insist on trial on indictment though summary trial is more appropriate. The Government attempted to meet this difficulty in the Criminal Law Act by proposing that where an offence of theft involved property worth less than £20, it would be triable only summarily. This proposal was overwhelmingly defeated in Parliament (the proposal still has its protagonists and maybe we have not heard the last of it) though Parliament did accept that for offences of criminal damage, where the damage does not exceed a specified sum (presently £5,000), the offence should be summary only. Parliament's reasoning appeared to be that where the offence reflected upon a man's honesty (as theft does while criminal damage does not) he should be entitled to be tried by his peers. In practice minor cases of theft are usually dealt with summarily because the accused consents to being so tried but it is by no means uncommon for cases involving trifling amounts to be tried by judge and jury.

If the accused is charged with an offence which is indictable only or if he is charged with an offence triable either way and the magistrates decide that the case should be tried on indictment, it is the function of the magistrates to decide whether the accused should be committed for trial.

In such proceedings the magistrates sit as *examining magistrates* and conduct a preliminary inquiry into the case against the accused. At one time the prosecution conducted these proceedings much as at the trial on indictment itself, outlining the case and calling witnesses who after examination might be cross-examined and re-examined. This had certain advantages for the accused; he would know the case he had to meet at the trial and might even secure a ruling that he had no case to answer. The latter was, however, unlikely in the extreme because no prosecutor was likely to advise in favour of proceedings unless there was, at the least, a prima facie case and thus the elaborate oral procedure was really a waste of time and money. There was also a possible disadvantage to an accused, especially when the case was one to attract great public interest, that extensive press coverage of the prosecution's case at the committal stage might predispose potential jurors to think him guilty.

Accordingly a new style of committal was introduced by the Criminal Justice Act 1967. It is now possible for magistrates to commit a person for trial "without consideration of the evidence" if all the prosecution's evidence consists of written statements. In practice, the accused's solicitor will have been shown these statements and have satisfied himself that there is a prima facie case. If he is not so satisfied he may submit that there is not a sufficient case for committal and in this event the magistrates will consider the evidence to determine whether a prima facie case is made out. So far as the press are concerned they may publish only specified information such as the name of the accused (unless the charge is rape where the accused's anonymity may be preserved if this is necessary to prevent identification of the complainant), the charge and the decision to commit.

It is, however, still possible for an accused to insist upon the old style of committal proceedings but this is only rarely done in some 7 per cent of cases. It might be done, for example, where the defence believes that cross-examination of the prosecution's witnesses will quickly discredit the prosecution's case. As with the new-style committals, the press is similarly restricted in reporting the proceedings, but it is open to the accused to insist that reporting restrictions be lifted so that the proceedings can be fully reported. This is sometimes done where the defence believes that the publicity given to the case will bring forward witnesses who might help the defence case. Until recently an accused could insist on the lifting of reporting restrictions even though he was charged with co-accused who were opposed to this course; but the

Criminal Justice (Amendment) Act 1981 provides that where one of the co-accused objects to the lifting of restrictions, the court shall make an order for lifting restrictions only if satisfied that it is in the interests of justice to do so.

While committal proceedings, in effect, serve notice of the prosecution's case against the accused, the accused is not obliged to reveal to the prosecution his line, or lines, of defence. One important modification of this principle is that the accused will be told by the magistrates that he will not at his trial be able to adduce evidence tending to establish an alibi (that is that he was somewhere else at the time of the crime) unless he gives particulars of the alibi to the prosecutor within seven days of the order for committal. This is to enable the prosecutor (through the police) to check the alibi and to prevent an accused from springing upon the jury an alibi of doubtful provenance at the eleventh hour which the prosecution has no opportunity to counter.

The Criminal Justice & Public Order Act 1994, however, contains provisions (section 44 and Sched. 4) to abolish committal proceedings and replace them with a procedure to be known as transfer for trial. These provisions, at the time of writing, are not in force but almost certainly will be before the book is published and accordingly need to be noted. When they are brought into force the foregoing account of committal proceedings will be of historical interest only.

Pressure for change came from the Royal Commission on Criminal Procedure (1981) and the Royal Commission on Criminal Justice (1993). The former thought that committal proceedings led to delay and duplication and that if its proposals for the advance disclosure of the prosecution's case and for an independent prosecution service were given effect, as both subsequently were, there was little reason why the prosecution should not determine whether D should be tried on indictment subject only to the defence having the opportunity to challenge the sufficiency of the evidence prior to trial. The latter, following the success of the introduction of transfer for trial provision in limited classes of proceedings, endorsed the former's views and recommended that committal proceedings should be abolished in all cases.

What is envisaged is as follows. In the case of (a) an indictable offence or (b) an offence triable either way where the magistrates' court has decided that the case is more suitable for trial on indictment or where the accused elects trial on indictment, the prosecution will serve on the court and the accused(s) a notice of the prosecution's case. The notice will specify the charge(s), include documents containing the evidence (including oral evidence) and such other information as may be prescribed.

The accused may then apply for the court to dismiss the charge. Normally this application will be considered by the court on the written submissions of the prosecution and the defence without an oral hearing. An oral hearing will be permitted only where the accused is unrepresented or the case is one of unusual complexity. When an oral hearing is permitted only the prosecution and defence may make submissions; the court has no power to call, much less to examine, witnesses.

After considering the written submissions or, where permitted, the oral submissions, the court must dismiss the charge if it is of the opinion that "there is not sufficient evidence against the accused to put him on trial for the offence charged". The court may, for example, dismiss the case if it is satisfied that there is no evidence to support an essential element in the offence or that the evidence is so manifestly unreliable that no jury would convict upon it.

Nearly all trials on indictment follow from committal by magistrates or will in future follow from transfer by trial, but it is possible to circumvent this procedure by what is known as a voluntary bill of indictment. The prosecution may apply to a High Court judge for leave to prefer an indictment and, in substance, the judge performs the functions normally performed by examining magistrates in determining whether there is a prima facie case. This procedure is only exceptionally used. It may be used, for example, where the magistrates have refused to commit but the prosecutor believes that the case is strong enough to justify trial. Or it may be used where the prosecution have evidence implicating A, B and C in a robbery and have secured the committal of A and B while C still remains at large; if C is subsequently apprehended the prosecutor may apply for a voluntary bill so that he can be tried with A and B. In such a case the judge has to balance the disadvantage to C in being brought speedily to trial against the hardship to A and B involved in delay.

(12) Trial by Jury

Trial by jury is the only form of trial for offences tried on indictment. The system has many defenders and some critics but before any appraisal is attempted it is necessary to know the mechanics of the system which are now for the most part contained in the Juries Act 1974.

Every person between the ages of 18 and 65 (the Criminal Justice Act raises the age limit to 70 while allowing persons over 65 to excuse themselves from service if they so wish) is qualified for jury service provided: (i) that person is registered as a parliamentary or local government elector; (ii) has been ordinarily resident within the United Kingdom for any period of at least five years since reaching the age of 13; and (iii) is not ineligible or disqualified for jury service.

Disqualification extends to any person who within the United Kingdom has (a) been sentenced to imprisonment for life (or to be detained during pleasure) or to a term of five years or more; (b) served any part of a sentence of imprisonment of three months or more during the last 10 years, or youth custody; or (c) (an amendment introduced to the Juries Act by the Criminal Justice & Public Order Act 1994, section 40) a person who is on bail in criminal proceedings.

Of those rendered ineligible by the Act the largest class comprises those who are connected with the administration of the law. For obvious reasons, judges, magistrates and police officers are ineligible but so too are many people (clerks and secretaries for example) who are employed (for instance by the Lord Chancellor's Office, the Director of Public Prosecutions, the police) in the day-to-day administration of justice. The other categories of ineligible persons extend to persons in holy orders and the mentally ill.

There is a further category of persons who, though eligible, may claim to be excused as of right. This category recognises that certain people (for example, Members of Parliament, doctors, nurses, and to which the Criminal Justice & Public Order Act adds practising members of a religious society or order the tenets or beliefs of which are incompatible with jury service) may have more important duties than jury service and they may, if they wish, excuse themselves from it. Disabled persons are not, as such, excluded from jury service. If a disabled person is summoned for jury service that person may serve as a juror unless the judge is of the opinion that, on account of the disability, he or she will not be capable of acting effectively as a juror.

The next step is to get together a panel from which juries may be chosen for particular cases. This is done by a person designated as an appropriate officer, who works under instructions issued by the Lord Chancellor. The panel is selected at random under a system devised by the Lord Chancellor's office after consultation with the Royal Statistical Society. Any party to proceedings in which jurors may be called is entitled to inspect the panel from which the jurors are to be drawn. This affords no more information than the names and addresses of the persons comprising the panel but it is in theory open to a party to conduct his own inquiries into the background of these persons to determine whether they are likely to be sympathetic or unsympathetic to his case. In practice this is *rarely* done, partly because of the considerable expense involved in investigating what may be 100–150 persons forming the panel and partly because the parties will normally be confident that the random system of selection will ensure a reasonably impartial jury. This is not to say that it is never done and in a limited class of case ("political" offences involving terrorism and breaches of the Official Secrets Act, and serious offences committed by a gang of "professional" criminals) the Attorney-General may, on the application of the Director of Public Prosecutions, authorise the police to check the names on the panel with certain specified sources to ascertain whether a potential juror is a known associate of the accused or is known to be sympathetic or antagonistic to the accused's cause.

That this practice, known as jury vetting, is legal is clear; whether it is desirable is hotly debated. The Juries Act contains no disqualification of persons who might be subject to improper pressure, nor of persons of extreme political views, and it is argued by some that this form of vetting constitutes a deliberate interference with the principle of randomness which governs jury selection, and that in the nature of things it is a facility available to the prosecution but not to the defence. On occasion, however, the defence has been granted legal aid to make its inquiries into the panel. In one case where prison officers were charged with various offences following a prison riot this was permitted to determine whether there might not be persons on the panel who, though not formally disqualified, from some previous prison experience might be expected to be very hostile to the defendants.

Jury vetting must not be confused with jury challenges though the two are connected in the sense that the information gleaned from vetting might lead to the prosecution standing by, or the defence challenging for cause, a potential juror.

Once the accused is arraigned the charge (or charges) is read to him and he is asked in relation to each charge whether he pleads guilty or not guilty. A plea of guilty to be acceptable must be unequivocal and if it is not, or if the accused refuses to plead, a plea of not guilty is entered. If the accused pleads not guilty, or if such a plea is entered, he is told that the jury will now be called and that if he objects to any of them he must do so as they are called to be sworn.

The accused may challenge all or any of the jurors for cause. The defence is not limited in the number of challenges it may make for cause. The defendant may challenge the whole of the panel (sometimes called a challenge to the array) on the grounds that it has not been selected randomly and impartially. Such a challenge would succeed if, for example, it could be shown that the appropriate officer had selected a panel from people likely to be prejudiced against the defendant or his cause. Such challenges are now almost unheard of. Challenges have been made on the grounds that the panel did not fairly reflect the proportions of whites to blacks known to exist in the area from which the panel had been drawn but the challenge was disallowed; so long as the panel is selected at random it is not a valid ground of challenge that it produces a disproportionate number of whites—or blacks come to that.

Challenges of individual jurors for cause are less rare. "Cause" has never been comprehensively defined but it includes, apart from the grounds which constitute dis-qualification or ineligibility under the Juries Act, any cause which is likely to unfit a juror for the performance of his duties. Most obviously this would extend to any cause which is likely to affect his impartiality (for instance, that he is related to the defendant or belongs to an extreme political organisation opposed to the defendant's cause) but also extends to other matters obviously affecting his fitness (such as that he is hard of hearing or that he has an insufficient command of English to follow the proceedings). The defence cannot examine a juror with a view to determining his suitability, as by questioning him about his attitudes to the offence in issue, or on his racial attitudes and so on. This practice has become established in the United States where the selection of a jury may occupy days of the court's time but it has not been allowed to take root here. In highly exceptional circumstances (see *R. v. Kray* (1969) 53 Cr.App.R. 412), however, such as where jurors may have been influenced by highly discreditable reports in the press concerning the defendant's conduct and antecedents, the examination of jurors may be permitted to ascertain whether they will be impartial.

Until the right was abolished by the Criminal Justice Act 1988, each defendant was able to challenge three jurors without assigning cause. This right, of peremptory challenge, if it was exercised at all, and it was said that only in trials in London was any significant use made of it, was exercised on the "hunch" theory. So, again as it was said, a person called for jury service who wished to avoid it could count on a challenge by being smartly dressed and by carrying a copy of the *Daily Telegraph*. With only three peremptory challenges which the law then allowed there was little chance of affecting the composition of the jury. But if there were several defendants, each with three challenges, the defendants, if on the "hunch" theory they thought it advantageous, might seek to get a young jury, or an all-male jury, or, at the very least, a jury shorn of *Daily Telegraph* readers. Peremptory challenge has its defenders both within and without the profession but their arguments (or hunches) failed to secure the survival of the peremptory challenge.

The prosecution cannot challenge jurors but it can ask jurors to stand by. This is virtually indistinguishable from challenge in its effect except that the prosecution is not required to assign cause until the number left in the panel falls below the number required to compose a jury. It is then a virtually unlimited power of challenge but the Attorney-General has announced that it will be used only (a) to remove a manifestly unsuitable juror; or (b) to remove a juror in a security trial where vetting has been authorised.

The prosecution thus has apparent advantages over the defence in that it may (a) have better access to jury vetting; and (b) need assign no cause to stand by a juror. But it is inconceivable that the prosecutor would use the former without informing the defence and unthinkable that he would use the latter with a view to "packing" the jury.

During the course of a trial the judge may discharge the jury or any individual juror. The former may occur when it is accidentally disclosed to the jury that the accused has previous convictions since this would prejudice the accused's case (see above, p. 146); in such circumstances the trial is recommenced with a different jury. The latter is most likely to occur where a juror falls ill but it may also occur where some impropriety by a juror (in one case the fact that a juror was giving the accused a lift in his car to the court each morning was found to be such an impropriety) has occurred; but discharges must not reduce the number of jurymen below nine.

On completion of the case the jury will retire to consider their verdict. They will be instructed to reach, and ordinarily do, a unanimous verdict and thereafter they must communicate with no one other than the judge in open court.

This is still the general rule but in 1967 the law was altered (it is now contained in the Juries Act 1974) to permit the judge to accept a majority verdict in certain cases. If the jury cannot agree after a reasonable period of deliberation having regard to the complexity of the case (the period must not be less than two hours but the judge may allow much, much longer in a difficult and protracted case) the judge may direct them on a majority verdict. The judge may then accept a verdict: (a) in a case where there are not less than 11 jurors, 10 agree, or (b) in a case where there are 10 jurors, nine agree.

The theory behind the majority verdict is the danger that is said to exist in some cases of a juror being bribed or threatened to hold out against his fellow jurors, or of a juror holding out simply because of his extreme and intractable views. Formerly a single such juror could provoke a disagreement leading to the expense of possible retrial; this risk is now very much reduced. In the nature of things it is difficult to produce affirmative proof of the arguments which led to the adoption of the majority verdict but there are certain types of case in which threats are made to jurymen, or are likely to be made, and from time to time judges order special police protection for the jury.

It is not an easy matter to make an informed judgment about jury trial. As an institution it is hallowed by its very antiquity and must be the sole institution which unites in its approval judges, Members of Parliament and the National Council for Civil Liberties. It is popular with the public but the police are less unflagging in their support. Critics point out that trial by jury has been virtually eliminated in civil cases without any harmful (and arguably only beneficial) effects, and that the vast majority of criminal cases are tried summarily without a jury.

The problem is that the vital information is lacking. We do not know how the jury works. No one is allowed to sit in on their deliberations so that no systematic study can be made. Indeed, by section 8 of the Contempt of Court Act 1981, it is now a contempt of court to obtain or disclose any particulars of a jury's deliberations in any legal proceedings.

This legislation will ensure that disquieting instances which have come to light in the past where it is evident that jurors have not understood the issues in the case or have reached their decision more on prejudice than reason, will no longer surface to embarrass the faith of those who support the institution.

The arguments for and against are accordingly replete with slogans and shibboleths rather than with facts and statistics.

Lord Denning has said that where a man's honour is at stake trial by jury has no equal; yet the same judge believes that juries are entirely unsuitable for civil negligence actions. It is sometimes said that the jury is a bulwark of liberty by which is presumably meant that oppressive prosecutions by the state are divined and checked by juries. While there have been famous historical instances of this, serious research finds little to support the thesis that the jury acts as an effective check on the arbitrary use of power.

One difference, perhaps the critical one, between trial by judge alone and trial by jury is that the judge makes a detailed and explicit finding of fact while the jury returns an "inscrutable" verdict which simply finds in favour of one party or the other. The former is much more open to review by appellate courts because the findings and the inferences of the trial judge can be tested. But when the appellate court is faced, as it is in the case of jury trial, simply with a conclusion it must support that conclusion if the trial has been fairly conducted, if the defence has been given every opportunity to present its case, and if the jury has been properly and fairly directed by the judge in his summing-up.

There have of late been a number of spectacular miscarriages of justice. Since the Court of Appeal is accorded the power to overturn the verdict of the jury where that verdict is unsafe or unsatisfactory the blame for these miscarriages has been laid, not at the door of the jury, though it is the jury which is the supreme arbiter of fact, but at the door of the Court of Appeal for failing to remedy the occasional deficiency of the jury though the Court of Appeal has no access to the jury's deliberations nor its reasoning. Is it entirely unfair to say that the jury is the sacred cow while the Court of Appeal is the whipping horse?

Chapter 5

The Legal System and the European Dimension

This chapter examines the effect on the English legal system of the United Kingdom's membership of the European Community and ratification of the European Convention on Human Rights.

1. The European Communities

Some see the European Union as an embryonic United States of Europe. However, it is important to realise that Europe is a very long way from becoming anything like the United States. When the original 13 American states resolved to form what is now the United States of America, they were intent on forming a political as well as an economic entity. They were prepared to yield as much of their own sovereignty as would be essential to allow the newly formed national government to operate as a single international political force. A balance was therefore struck in the constitution to allow the individual states as much self-government as possible while ensuring that, for example in military matters, the central government spoke for all. It is true that today one still hears the odd dispute over state sovereignty and attempts to return some power to the individual states, but no one would challenge the fact that, on matters external to the United States, the Federal Government in Washington represents the sole policy-making body.

In Europe it is quite clear that many people would like to see a political union of the countries since this would produce a formidable international military and economic force. However, it is equally clear that while there might be some unified political action flowing from the European Communities (such as was seen over Europe's response to the British involvement in the Falkland Islands dispute and the Community's response to the Iraqi invasion of Kuwait), the Communities were intended primarily as economic entities in the first place. Membership almost certainly involves some loss of national sovereignty, but the United Kingdom could probably leave the Community by a simple majority vote in the Westminster Parliament, something which no state in the United States could lawfully do. Certainly the German Federal Constitutional Court held in an important decision in 1993 that, whilst the ratification by the Federal Republic of the Maastricht Treaty was not unconstitutional, Germany could still leave the Communities at a later date. We are still a very long way from a single Parliament for Western Europe with powers to make political decisions for all.

(1) The Composition of the European Communities

In 1951 six founding countries (France, West Germany, Belgium, Luxembourg, Italy and The Netherlands) signed the Treaty of Paris which created the first of the three European Communities—the *European Coal and Steel Community*. Later in 1957 the same six countries signed two further treaties (the Treaties of Rome) to create the *European Economic Community* and the *European Atomic Energy Community*. Over the next eight years the principal governing institutions of these three bodies were gradually unified so that they covered all three communities. There thus emerged the Council, the Commission, the European Parliament and the Court of Justice of the European Communities. The functions of each body are described and governed by the relevant treaty. Of the three, the European Economic Community (E.C.) is by far the most significant and is the subject of this chapter.

In 1973 the United Kingdom, by virtue of the European Communities Act 1972, became a signatory to the three Treaties. Ireland and Denmark joined at the same time. Greece joined in 1981, while Spain and Portugal joined in 1986.

Membership of the E.C. involves participation in all the major institutions of the Community and we must now briefly examine their functions. From the outset it should be emphasised that while comparisons can be made with domestic institutions (*e.g.* it is tempting to compare the Commission with the civil service and the European Parliament with the United Kingdom Parliament) these comparisons are misleading.

(a) *The Council*

Although the four major institutions are supposed to be of equal importance the Council of Ministers is the supreme legislative body, though its power is curtailed by the fact that on most issues it can only proceed on a proposal emanating from the Commission. Its function is to "ensure co-ordination of the general economic policies of the Member States." The Treaty lays down policies in broad, imprecise terms; the Council formulates these into more concrete rules. The Council is composed of Ministers from the national governments of Member States and its presidency rotates amongst them every six months. These Ministers may be the Foreign Ministers of each country or the Ministers responsible for the subject-matter under discussion. Thus the agriculture Ministers will spend much time debating the Common Agriculture or Fisheries policies. The Council's Regulations, Directives and Decisions form part of the law of the E.C., though this is often referred to as secondary legislation to distinguish it from the contents of the Treaties. The Treaty determines which matters may be dealt with by simple majority or by what is called a qualified majority vote. In this latter case each country has a certain number of votes, (France, Germany, Italy and the United Kingdom 10; Spain 8; Belgium, Greece, Portugal and The Netherlands 5; Sweden and Austria 4; Denmark, Finland and Ireland 3; Luxembourg 2) and a decision can only be taken on the basis of 62 votes which means that the big four cannot outvote all the other countries. Under what are known as the Luxembourg Accords a practice has grown up under which, on any important issues concerning the national interests of a Member State, decisions shall be taken only by a unanimous vote. This practice is of doubtful authority and was allegedly broken by a vote in 1989 against the United Kingdom on the adoption of the Community Social Charter.

The Council may be questioned by the European Parliament, but the chief control is exercised by national governments over their Ministers who attend the Council.

It is now normal practice for the heads of government of the Member States to meet to discuss crucial issues and the name given to such meetings is European Councils. Such meetings are now provided for by the Maastricht Treaty on European Union.

(b) *The Commission*

It is tempting to see the Council and the Commission as the legislative and executive branches of the Community, but while there is some truth in this analogy, it is misleading because the Commission has legislative powers and the actual implementation of E.C. policy is carried out, not by the Commission, but by the institutions of the Member States. On the other hand the Commission does in some respects act as the civil service of the Community. Whereas the Council is composed of Ministers who are likely to take nationalistic standpoints, the Commission is the voice of the Community. The Treaty provides that members "shall be chosen on the grounds of their general competence" and that their independence must be "beyond doubt." It is composed of 17 members who are each appointed for four years by general agreement with the Member States. From this number a President and six Vice Presidents are appointed to serve for a period of two years.

> "The Commission is the guardian of the Treaties; it is the executive arm of the Communities; it is the initiator of Community policy and exponent of Community interest in the Council." (Noel, *The European Community: How it Works.*)

That basically summarises the functions of the Commission within the Community.

As stated earlier, generally before any Community law can be made the Council must receive a proposal from the Commission. How the Council then reacts procedurally is determined by the subject-matter of the law. In some cases, where the so-called consultation and veto procedure introduced by the Maastricht Treaty applies, Parliament is entitled to reject definitively a Council proposal. In certain other cases, if Parliament rejects a Council proposal, the Council may still adopt it if it acts unanimously. The latter procedure is called the co-operation procedure. In other cases the E.C. Treaty simply requires Parliament to be consulted. Such consultation may take place even if there is no Treaty requirement for it. Parliament may require the Council to reconsult it where the Council or Commission has substantially altered the proposal on which Parliament was originally consulted or where there has been a significant change in circumstances since Parliament gave its opinion.

In all cases the Council may amend or reject a Commission proposal only by a unanimous vote. Where the Council is not unanimous it may still seek to persuade the Commission, which is represented at all Council meetings, to change its proposal. Thus the Commission is involved at all stages of the procedure and may be delegated its own law-making powers by the Council.

It is the Commission which will see that the obligations laid down in the Treaties are observed. Thus under Article 169 a procedure is laid down to deal with breaches of Treaty obligations by Member States. Where the Commission decides that the Treaty has been infringed (the investigation may have been prompted by a Member State, a government or by an individual) it first gives the State the opportunity to submit observations, and then delivers a reasoned opinion. The State is then given a chance to comply with the opinion after which time the Commission may take the matter before the Court.

The Commission is given certain legislative powers and a large amount of executive powers by the Treaties and the Commission may also be invested with powers to ensure the enforcement of decisions made by the Council. The Commission also represents the Community in its dealings with non-Member States and with international organisations, and is responsible for the administration of Community funds. In order to protect the independence of the Commission it is made answerable to the European Parliament and the European Court of Justice alone.

(c) *The European Parliament*

It often comes as a surprise to discover that the European Parliament is not the supreme law-making body of the Community, though it is hoped that since the introduction of the co-operation procedure under the Single European Act 1986 and the consultation and veto procedure under the Maastricht Treaty it will assume more importance. Originally members of the Parliament were nominated directly to it by the national governments of the Community Members and many were in fact national M.P.s. In 1979 each Member country conducted elections to elect a new Parliament and on this occasion the citizens of the Member States were able to choose the new European M.P.s. The new Parliament met on July 17, 1989 and direct elections are held every five years. The number of members increased as the result of the elections of June 1994. The total number is now 626. Germany now has 99 members; France, Italy and the United Kingdom

87; Spain 64; The Netherlands 31; Belgium, Greece and Portugal 25; Sweden 22; Austria 21; Denmark and Finland 16; Ireland 15 and Luxembourg 6.

Under the Treaty, the European Parliament exercises only "advisory and supervisory" powers. It considers proposals from the Commission before they are discussed in the Council. In addition, the Council is required to undergo a consultation procedure with the Parliament on many important matters before enacting any legislation. Failure to do this would leave the Council's actions open to challenge. However, opinions given have no binding force and when the legislation is introduced, no mention need be made of the Parliament's disapproval.

Despite the co-operation procedure and further powers to put parliamentary questions to the Council and Commission, participation in the legislative process is still rather limited. There is one area in which Parliament is given considerable power: it concerns the Community budget. The Council places the draft proposals for the budget before the Parliament which has power, acting by majority vote, to reject it.

(d) *The Court of Justice of the European Communities*

The Court of Justice is responsible, *inter alia*, for ruling on the validity and interpretation of Community law. It operates as a constitutional supreme court in the sense that it has the power to interpret Community law or to declare invalid any law which has been passed illegally by the Council or Commission. Its decisions, though not binding on itself, can be changed only by its own subsequent decision or by an amendment of the Treaty which would require the unanimous approval of Member States through their own Parliaments. It is thus unlike any court within the English Legal System and in this respect more closely resembles the Supreme Court of the United States.

Under the Treaty there are 15 judges each appointed for a period of six years renewable. Every three years there is a partial replacement of the Bench in that either seven or eight judges shall be replaced or reappointed. The judges may sit in plenary session or in chambers consisting of 3, 5 or 7 judges. They will sit in plenary session whenever the case is brought by a Member State or by an institution of the Community, and the Member State or Community institution so requests, or whenever the chambers do not possess the requisite jurisdiction under the Rules of Procedure. The judges will elect one of their members as President of the Court of Justice for a period of three years; he may be re-elected at the end of that period.

The Court of Justice is assisted by six Advocates General whose duty it shall be, acting with complete impartiality and independence, to make, in open court, reasoned submissions on the cases brought before the Court of Justice in order to assist the Court to ensure that in the interpretation and application of the Treaty the law is observed. It should be stressed that they represent neither the institutions of the Community nor the public, but function only as spokesmen of the law in the context of the Treaties. As such, they have no parallel in the English legal system.

The judges and Advocates General must be persons whose independence is beyond doubt and who would be eligible to assume the highest judicial office in their own countries.

Since September 1989 the full European Court of Justice has been assisted by a new Court of First Instance to deal with specialist economic law cases. More recently the court has been given jurisdiction to hear all direct actions but not Article 177 cases. Judges are appointed on the same basis as the full court to which appeal lies on a point of law.

(2) The Law of the European Economic Community

The law of the E.C. is to be found in the establishing Treaties and in the Regulations, Directives and Decisions of the Council and Commission, and in the rulings of the Court of Justice. According to Article 189 of the Treaty "a regulation shall apply generally. It shall be binding in its entirety and take direct effect in each member state. A directive shall be binding, as to the result to be achieved, upon each member state to which it is directed, while leaving to national authorities the choice of form and method. A decision shall be binding in its entirety upon those to whom it is directed." In addition these bodies issue recommendations and opinions which are not binding. Where a provision is said to be "directly effective" it means that it may be invoked by individual citizens before national courts as well as being binding upon Member States. Thus, it has an effect on an individual's rights and is enforceable before national courts. This feature of European law distinguishes it from general international law which only binds the States.

One of the major questions that must be asked is whether E.C. law takes precedence over the domestic law of the individual Member States.

It is a fundamental principle of British constitutional law that Parliament is supreme, that is, that it can "make or unmake any law whatever; and further that no person or body is recognised by the law of England as having a right to override or set aside the legislation of Parliament." It has been argued that the United Kingdom to some extent surrendered its parliamentary supremacy on joining the E.C..

Under section 2(1) of the European Communities Act 1972 the United Kingdom agreed that existing and future Community law was to be given legal effect in the United Kingdom without the need for further legislation:

> "All such rights, powers, liabilities, obligations and restrictions from time to time created or arising by or under the Treaties, and all such remedies and procedures from time to time provided for by or under the Treaties, as in accordance with the Treaties are without further enactment to be given legal effect or used in the United Kingdom shall be recognised and available in law, and be enforced, allowed and followed accordingly; and the expression 'enforceable Community right' and similar expressions shall be read as referring to one to which this subsection applies."

This provision clearly establishes that all directly effective provisions have the force of law in the United Kingdom. Thus, a potential conflict arises between two doctrines of legal supremacy—what if the Community law is inconsistent with existing United Kingdom legislation? Could the United Kingdom subsequently enact conflicting legislation? The European Court has clearly stated that in the event of a conflict, European law must prevail. An example is provided by *R. v. Secretary of State for Transport, ex p. Factortame* (1991) in which it was held that provisions in a United Kingdom statute (the Merchant Shipping Act 1988) discriminated against community nationals and were thus unenforceable. As a general principle, English judges have recognised this; however, recognition has not always been unqualified. Lord Denning in *Macarthys v. Smith* (1981) drew a distinction between mere inconsistencies and deliberate derogations. Where the incompatibility is inadvertent, he suggested that English courts should apply E.C. law, on the presumption that Parliament intended to fulfil its Treaty obligations. On the other hand, where the incompatibility was deliberate, he was of the opinion that English law should prevail:

"if the time should come that our Parliament deliberately passes an Act with the intention of repudiating the Treaty or any provision in it or intentionally of acting inconsistently with it and says so in express terms then I should have thought that it would be the duty of our courts to follow the statute of our Parliament."

It is clear, moreover, that an English court must now increasingly take account of any possible conflict between domestic and European law. A good example is provided by *R. v. Chief Constable of Sussex, ex p. International Trader's Ferry Ltd* (1995). In the face of intensive protest against the export of livestock the police limited the access of lorries to an English port. The Chief Constable had formed the view that, given limited resources, any other course would interfere with his ability to police effectively other areas of the community. The Divisional Court held that, although his decision could not be challenged as unreasonable under domestic law, it contravened Article 34 of the E.C. Treaty as amounting to a quantitative restriction on exports.

A further problem which arises in the assimilation of E.C. law with United Kingdom law is that of interpretation of the former. Community law is based more on continental legal traditions than British ones. As a result, English judges have faced considerable difficulties because the E.C. Treaty is framed in terms of general principles, concentrating on aims and purposes. It lacks precision, using words without defining them. While the European Court has been recognised as the ultimate arbiter on the interpretation of Community law, some English judges have themselves sought to play a creative role in unravelling the meaning of some provisions. Once again, Lord Denning has been at the forefront of this issue. In his view, judges ought to "divine the spirit of the Treaty and gain inspiration from it. If they find a gap they must fill it as best they can. They must do what the framers of the instrument would have done if they had thought about it." However, if this innovative approach were to be generally adopted it could lead to inconsistency in the interpretation of provisions and undermine the uniformity of approach which is crucial to the success of the European Community.

One view of the influence of United Kingdom membership of the EEC on our municipal law was given by Lord Denning in *Bulmer v. Bollinger* (1974) when he said: "The Treaty is like an incoming tide. It flows into the estuaries and up the rivers.

It cannot be held back." Commenting on this Lord Scarman added:

> "For the moment, to adopt Lord Denning's imagery, the incoming tide has not yet mingled with the home waters of the common law: but it is inconceivable that, like the Rhone and the Arve where those two streams meet at Geneva, they should move on, side by side, one grey with the melted snows and ice of the distant mountains of our legal history, the other blue and clear, reflecting modern opinion. If we stay in the Common Market, I would expect to see its principles of legislation and statutory interpretation and its conception of an activist court whose role is to strengthen and fulfil the purpose of statute law replace the traditional attitudes of English judges and lawyers to statute law and the current complex style of statutory drafting."

The Court has both judicial and advisory functions. In its judicial capacity the Court may hear complaints that a Member State has failed to fulfil its Treaty obligations; such proceedings are normally instituted by the Commission after having given the Member State an opportunity to submit its observations. The Commission has instituted proceedings against the United Kingdom over such things as the unlawful restrictions on the importation of potatoes and UHT milk, discriminatory taxation on wine, and its failure to implement a sex discrimination directive. One notable case which attracted considerable publicity was the *Tachograph* case (1979). A Council Regulation had made the installation and use of tachographs compulsory in lorries. These machines recorded driving periods, speeds and distance covered. The United Kingdom, fearing union opposition, only offered to introduce a voluntary scheme. The Commission did not consider this to be adequate compliance and issued a reasoned opinion requiring speedy compliance with the Regulation. As this failed to produce results, proceedings were initiated before the Court. The Court held that in failing to adopt measures to implement the Regulation, the United Kingdom had failed to fulfil its Treaty obligations. A statutory instrument was subsequently made to give effect to this decision. The Court has power to review the legality of acts of the Council and Commission other than recommendations or opinions. These actions may be brought by Member States, the Council or the Commission on the grounds of lack of competence, infringement of an essential procedural requirement, infringement of the Treaty or of any rule of law relating to its application, or misuse of powers. Such proceedings may also be instituted by a natural or legal person. If the action is well founded the Court shall declare the act concerned to be void.

It is perhaps its jurisdiction under Article 177 that is of supreme interest to students of the English legal system. Under this Article the Court of Justice is given power to give preliminary rulings concerning: (i) the interpretation of the Treaty; (ii) the validity and interpretation of acts of the institutions of the Community; and (iii) the interpretation of statutes of bodies established by an act of the Council where those statutes so provide. Where such a question is raised before a court or tribunal of a Member State, that court or tribunal may, if it considers that a decision on the question is necessary to enable it to give judgment, request the Court of Justice to give a ruling thereon.

It should be emphasised that, in theory at least, the role of the Court of Justice under this procedure is solely to interpret Community law; the application of it is for the national court. Once a ruling has been given, the case is referred back to the national court for decision. This procedure is expensive and time-consuming, often delaying a decision on the case by several months. Hence lower courts have been discouraged from using it and attempts have been made to set down guidelines by which a court could determine when a decision would or would not be necessary. In *Bulmer v. Bollinger* (1974) the Court of Appeal was asked to review a judge's exercise of discretion to refer a question under Article 177. In a nutshell, when was a decision "necessary"? At the outset it was noted that the European Court could not interfere with the exercise of a judge's discretion to refer. Lord Denning took the opportunity of laying down guidelines on the factors which ought to be taken into account in considering whether a decision was necessary. No reference should be made:

(a)   where it would not be conclusive of the case;
(b)   where there had been a previous ruling on the same point;
(c)   where the court considers the point to be reasonably clear and free from doubt;
(d)   where the facts of the case had not been decided.

These guidelines are narrower than those issued by the European Court of Justice and, although they are not stictly binding on English judges, have arguably caused fewer references to be made under Article 177 than in many other

Member States. The first case referred under it was *Van Duyn v. Home Office* (1975).

Miss Van Duyn wanted to take up employment in the United Kingdom with the Church of Scientology. She was refused permission to enter on the basis of the fact that the United Kingdom considered the activities of this sect to be socially harmful, and therefore that her admittance would be contrary to public policy. The English court was uncertain of the meaning of public policy under Community law and thus referred the issue to the European Court. The Court laid down its interpretation of the phrase and the national court then applied it to the facts in question.

Another illustration of this principle in operation is the recent case of *Marshall v. Southampton Health Authority* (1986). In that case the applicant claimed that the Authority was sexually discriminating against women by adopting a policy that employees should retire at state pension age, hence requiring women to retire before men. This policy appeared to be legal under the relevant domestic legislation but was argued to be contrary to a Council directive on the same issue. The national court asked for directions on the meaning of the directive and whether there was a conflict. In its interpretation of the directive, the Court of Justice found that there was a conflict with United Kingdom law. While a ruling is only binding on the case at issue its effects may be more widespread because Member States are obliged to take note of, and act upon, rulings of the European Court of Justice. In this case, the United Kingdom has introduced domestic legislation to bring British law into line with Community law.

Thus where a national court of a Member State is confronted by a point of E.C. law which is said to be of "direct effect" it may seek clarification from the Court of Justice. In this way it is hoped that a uniform approach to interpretation of E.C. law can be achieved throughout the Community. Any court or tribunal may refer a point of law to the Court of Justice for a preliminary ruling which will then enable the national court to reach a decision on the case. It is only where there is no appeal from the national court or tribunal that the reference to the Court of Justice is obligatory and even here there is no compulsion to refer if the national court feels that there is no uncertainty in the interpretation of the point of E.C. law.

The Court of Justice also has jurisdiction in several other matters including disputes between the Community and its servants which are known as staff cases; these are dealt with in the Court of First Instance.

The Court of Justice in its advisory capacity may give its opinion as to whether proposed agreements between the Community and non-Member States or international organisations are likely to violate the Treaties.

2. The European Convention on Human Rights

On December 10, 1948 the General Assembly of the United Nations adopted the Universal Declaration on Human Rights. The Declaration expresses what were thought to be the fundamental rights of mankind and, though the idea of "human rights" has a long history, a precipitating factor was unquestionably the barbaric treatment accorded many millions of people in the Second World War.

Quite what is, or what ought to be, a "human right" is open to argument. In an underdeveloped society pre-eminence is likely to be placed on a right to enough food to sustain life with access to medical care sufficient to preserve it. In a developed society where such things are taken for granted, the emphasis shifts to access to education or, if that too is guaranteed, to sophisticated notions of a fair trial or to rights to privacy. And the most developed societies can experience hard economic times. Should there, then, be a right to a job?

The Universal Declaration makes interesting reading. It does in fact state that everyone has the right to a standard of living adequate for the health and well-being of himself and his family and that everyone has a right to work, as well as to a right to a fair trial and a right to own property. The Declaration, however, binds no one and equally confers rights on no one; it is an expression of ideals.

On November 4, 1950 the Council of Europe adopted the European Convention on Human Rights and the United Kingdom was the first State to ratify this treaty. The Convention is modelled on, just as it was inspired by, the Universal Declaration but there are significant differences. The rights contained in the Convention are basic "civil and political rights," including the right to life, the right not to be subjected to torture or other inhuman or degrading punishment, the right not to be held in slavery or servitude, the right to liberty and security of person, the right to a fair trial, the right to respect for private and family life, the right to freedom of thought, religion and conscience, the right to join a trade union and the right to marry.

A series of separate short treaties, or Protocols, have been drafted to safeguard additional rights by means of the machinery established by the Convention. Britain has ratified the First Protocol, which provides limited protection for the rights to enjoy the ownership of property, to education and to free elections, but has not ratified other Protocols which protect various other rights.

The Convention protects an impressive list of rights but there *might* be thought to be significant omissions. There is no mention of a right to an adequate standard of living though this might be said to be superfluous in modern Western European conditions. There is no reference to a right to work though some might argue that this is more fundamental to the dignity of man than the niceties of a fair trial. These and other "economic rights" are protected by a second treaty, the European Social Charter, adopted by the Council of Europe in 1961. The United Kingdom was the first State to ratify the European Social Charter, but it receives little attention from the media and from lawyers. It imposes less strict obligations upon States which ratify it than the Convention. The Social Charter has not been incorporated into English domestic law. The European Convention is nevertheless an important document which affects the actions of Parliament and the British Government as well as private rights.

It should be noted that these rights are not expressed in absolute terms and they are qualified by limitations. Thus the right not to be held in servitude does not prevent a State from imposing a period of conscription in its armed forces, nor does the right to marry invalidate laws against bigamy or incest.

The Convention further established machinery to protect these fundamental rights—a *Commission of Human Rights* and a *Court of Human Rights*. Where any State which is a party to the Convention feels that another Member State is in breach of the Convention it may report that state to the Commission which then tries to reach a friendly "out-of-court" solution. If this fails the matter may be referred to the Court. If the Member State fails to comply with the report of the Court the ultimate sanction is suspension from the Council of Europe. Private citizens of Member States may also cause a case to come before the Court. The private citizen will first report the alleged breach through the Council of Europe to the Commission, which will investigate the complaint and may refer it to the Court. When Protocol 11 comes into force, *i.e.*

when the 38 members of the Council of Europe have all signed and ratified the protocol, the Commission will be abolished and matters will go directly to the Court. The Court will be able to form chambers to expedite matters. It is thought the protocol will come into effect in 1997. The United Kingdom has already signed and ratified it.

The United Kingdom has on numerous occasions been forced to review its domestic law as a result of actions brought by individuals. In the *Campbell and Cosans* case (1982) parents alleged that the practice of corporal punishment in Scottish state schools which their children attended was a breach of fundamental rights. The Court found in their favour on the basis of Article 2 of the First Protocol. This provides that in the exercise of its functions in education, the State should respect the right of parents to have their child taught in conformity with their own religious and philosophical convictions. As a result of this decision the United Kingdom has introduced legislation forbidding the use of *corporal* punishment in schools. Changes in the law were also introduced as a result of the *Dudgeon* case (1981). A homosexual resident in Northern Ireland claimed that the existence of a law making buggery and gross indecency between consenting males a criminal offence amounted to a breach of his right to privacy, as found in Article 8 of the Convention. The Court upheld this claim. The moral justifications for the retention of the law unchanged were outweighed by the interference with the applicant's private life. Northern Irish law has since been changed in response to this judgment. Other examples have included complaints against dismissals from employment through a failure to join a trade union and complaints concerning the rights of imprisoned persons to have access to legal advice.

While the United Kingdom has ratified the Convention and has thereby agreed to abide by the principles stated therein, no steps have been taken (as they have by some other signatories) to incorporate the provisions of the Convention in English domestic law. It should be emphasised that the European Convention on Human Rights is separate from the system of Community law. Therefore, the Convention, unlike Community law, does not normally have direct effect within the United Kingdom. However, in recent years there have been signs that the two systems are coming closer together. Under Article 169 of the Treaty of Rome the European Court of Justice must ensure the observance of the general principles of law in the interpretation and application of the Treaty. In a number of cases the Court has stated that respect for human rights forms part of the common legal traditions shared by the Members of the E.C. and that the Convention can be looked at as evidence of these; and hence English courts may occasionally be required to apply human rights contained in the Convention *as part of* Community law. However, as regards the attitude of English judges to the Convention, the view of Lord Denning in *R. v. Chief Immigration Officer, ex p. Bibi* (1976) seems to prevail:

> "The position, as I understand it, is that if there is any ambiguity in our statutes or uncertainty in our law, then these courts can look to the Convention as an aid to clear up the ambiguity and uncertainty, seeking always to bring them into harmony with it. Furthermore, when Parliament is enacting a statute or the Secretary of State is framing rules, the court will assume that they had regard to the provisions of the Convention and intended to make the enactments accord with the Convention, and will interpret them accordingly. But I would dispute altogether that the Convention is part of our law. Treaties and declarations do not become part of our law until they are made law by Parliament."

Lord Denning's view was approved by the House of Lords in *Brind v. Secretary of State for the Home Department* (1991). The House refused to accept that Article 10 of the Convention, which gives the right to freedom of expression, forms part of English law. Parliament had chosen not to incorporate the Convention into English law by Act of Parliament. Therefore the judges should not usurp the role of Parliament by incorporating the Convention by means of case law. Nor would the House adopt as part of English administrative law the principle of "proportionality" which had been accepted by the European Court of Human Rights in its judgments. Accordingly the House unanimously refused to hold that the Home Secretary's ban on the live broadcasting of statements spoken by representatives of proscribed terrorist organisations was an unlawful exercise of his powers. The argument that the ban was a disproportional restriction on freedom of expression was rejected.

A good example of the operation of the Convention is provided by *Malone v. Commissioner of Police of the Metropolis (No. 2)* (1979). In criminal proceedings against the plaintiff it was disclosed that the police, acting under a warrant issued by the Home Secretary, had tapped his telephone and in a subsequent civil action the plaintiff alleged that the tap was unlawful both under English domestic law and by virtue of Article 8 of the Convention which conferred on him "the right to respect for his private and family life, his home and his correspondence." Megarry J. held that the telephone tap was not unlawful under domestic law; he did take the view that there had been a breach of Article 8 but since the Convention was "plainly not of itself law in this country" the plaintiff's remedy had to be pursued with the European Commission.

This case did in fact go before the Commission and the Court. The Court found the law on telephone tapping procedures used by the police to be obscure and open to different interpretations. It was not laid down in accessible rules indicating the scope and manner of the exercise of discretion. It was unanimously held that there had been a breach of Article 8. As a result of this decision, the Interception of Communications Act 1985 was enacted to bring United Kingdom law into line with the Convention six years after Malone brought his action against the police.

An example of the controversy which can be caused by the Convention is the recent case of *McCann* (1995). The Court found the United Kingdom to be in breach of art. 2, which guarantees the right to life, over the shooting of alleged terrorists in Gibraltar by the SAS. This decision attracted intense criticism by government spokesmen, yet it is not without interest that it led to an announcement that some compensation would be made to the families of the victims.

The delay and expense involved in taking test cases on human rights to the European Court of Human Rights has led to demands that Parliament should legislate to incorporate the Convention as part of English law. However, the House of Commons has on several occasions refused to pass Bills introduced to achieve this aim. It is possible that the coming into force of Protocol 11 may reduce delays to some extent.

Part Two

Criminal Law

Introduction

The student of criminal law is often puzzled by the fact that the greatest part of his time is taken up with an investigation of so called general principles of criminal liability rather than with a study of specific crimes. The reason for this is quite simple. Although there are obviously hundreds of different criminal offences, there are features common to all prosecutions. Such questions as who can be a party to a criminal offence, how many people can be involved in one single crime, does the prosecution have to prove that the accused intended to bring about the prohibited result, what defences are open to him, are questions which can be asked about nearly every crime and in many cases the answers will be the same whether the crime involved is murder, stealing or assault. Thus in the first chapters we shall examine these general principles. The final chapters will examine certain specific offences.

Students of criminal law should be aware of the recent work of the Law Commission which has resulted in the publication of two important papers; " A Criminal Code for England and Wales" (Law Commission No.177, 1989) and "Legislating the Code—Offences Against the Person and General Principles" (Law Commission Consultation Paper No. 122, 1992). These documents represent the fruits of work begun for the Law Commission by a group of academics under the Chairmanship of Professor Sir John Smith and completed by the Law Commission. It is an attempt to reduce the criminal law of England and Wales to statutory form. It was quite clear the neither political party would find the time needed to enact the Code as a whole and so in the second paper the Law Commission proposed that the Code should be introduced in parts beginning with the proposals relating to Offences Against the Person and allied general principles. These documents provide a wealth of material for classroom discussion and should be regarded as essential reading.

Chapter 6

The Ingredients of a Crime: Actus Reus and Mens Rea

Let us start by considering a particular offence, namely that of rape. Suppose that X has been charged with raping Y. What does his criminal prosecution entail? It is a basic principle of English law that the prosecution must establish the guilt of the accused and that the accused is not expected to establish that he is innocent. Thus the prosecution must prove to the court's satisfaction that the accused, X, raped Y. But what exactly does that mean? In every crime there is what amounts to a set of ingredients which must be established before a verdict of guilty can be returned. The ingredients of rape are to be derived from section 1 of the Sexual Offences Act 1956 and section 1 of the Sexual Offences (Amendment) Act 1976. They are (1) that the accused had unlawful intercourse (2) with a woman or another man (3) without his/her consent. In addition the prosecution must establish that (4) at the time of the act of intercourse he either knew that s/he was not consenting or that he was reckless as to whether s/he was consenting. Factors (1)–(3) are sometimes called the external features of the crime or *actus reus* (literally "guilty act"). Number (4) represents what is called the internal features of the crime or *mens rea* ("guilty mind").

Whatever the crime (whether it be murder at one extreme or dropping litter at the other) there can be no exception to the requirement that the prosecution must establish the *actus reus* (see, *e.g. Dyson* (1908) *Casebook*, p. 101). So in the case of rape the prosecution must establish sexual intercourse, which in the case of rape means that there must have been at least slight penetration of the vagina or anus by the penis. If this cannot be established then the charge of rape must fail, however revolting the circumstances. Equally if the person was actually consenting even though the man thought that she or he was not, then there can be no conviction for rape (though there may be a conviction for attempted rape; see below, p. 329).

183

The reason for this strict requirement is that the law has set its face against imposing criminal liability simply on the basis of the accused's intentions; the law requires, in addition, strict proof of all the elements which the law says constitutes the crime.

The reason for the second requirement—of a certain state of mind—is even more obvious. A broad distinction needs to be drawn between persons who deliberately cause harm and those who cause harm unavoidably and accidentally; the former, it may be supposed are rightly brought within the purview of the criminal law, while the latter are not. In relation to "serious" crimes (sometimes referred to as crimes *mala in se*) this is normally the position; but in relation to "minor" crimes (crimes *mala prohibita*) criminal liability is frequently imposed even though the accused has not deliberately brought about the harm (the *actus reus*). Where liability is imposed though the accused is not at fault, the crime is known as an offence of strict (or absolute) liability. These crimes, and the policies which are claimed to justify their existence, are dealt with later in Chapter 7, though some incidental mention will be made of them in this chapter.

Even if the prosecution establish these two requirements (namely the forbidden act deliberately brought about by the accused) it does not necessarily follow that a crime has been committed. Take a case where the accused is charged with murdering another and pleads that he was acting in self defence. The prosecution may have no difficulty in establishing that the accused has caused the forbidden act and that he did so deliberately; but the accused claims that he killed the victim because, had he not done so, the victim would have killed him. Killing, even deliberate killing, is not always a crime. This is true of other crimes also; the law admits of certain circumstances in which even the deliberate causing of a forbidden act is held to be justified.

Obviously not every case raises an issue of justification but where the issue is raised it is not for the accused to prove the justification, but for the prosecution to negative it. The prosecution will have to prove beyond reasonable doubt that the accused acted without grounds which in law would justify his act (see below, p. 282). This is because lack of justification is regarded as one of the ingredients of the crime—the definition of many offences contains the phrase "without lawful authority or excuse"; for murder the killing must be "unlawful."

As to whether circumstances of justification form part of the *actus reus* or *mens rea* no general agreement exists. What is

clear, however, is that unless the prosecution can *prove* that
there was no justification it will not obtain a conviction. It is
also safe to say that where the accused raises the issue of
justification the prosecution must prove that at the time he is
alleged to have committed the offence the accused was
unaware of the existence of the circumstances of justification.
(*Dadson* (1850)).

In *Miller* (1983) Lord Diplock said that it would be
conducive to clarity in analysing the ingredients of a crime
that was created by statute, as the great majority of criminal
offences now were, if one were to avoid bad Latin and
instead think of and speak about the conduct of the accused
and his state of mind at the time of that conduct, instead of
speaking of *actus reus* and *mens rea*. Clearly to translate *actus
reus* and *mens rea* as "guilty act and guilty mind" would be
misleading. However most lawyers regard the terms as useful
symbols for the various elements of a criminal offence, and
their disappearance from common usage seems rather
unlikely.

1. Actus Reus

Actus literally means "act" but while most crimes require
that the accused commits a certain act this is not always the
case. Criminal liability may also arise through failure to act
and so *actus* can cover an omission as well as an act. Perhaps
it would be better to speak of conduct since conduct can be
taken to include commission and omission. Even this enlarged
meaning of *actus* may not cover all cases since on occasion, as
we shall see (below, p. 191) criminal liability may be imposed
for a state of affairs without any requirement for conduct on
the part of the accused.

A crime, however, requires more than conduct: the *actus*
must be *reus*. If X fires a rifle he is engaged in conduct but to
fire a rifle, without more, is not a crime. Suppose then that X
aims his rifle at Y and deliberately kills him. X has now
brought about a consequence which consequence is normally
proscribed by the law of murder—*normally* but not always.
Whether or not X will be guilty of murder depends upon the
circumstances surrounding the killing. X will not be guilty of
murder if Y is an enemy in time of war or if X is acting in
circumstances of self-defence. Thus we can say of any crime

that it usually involves (a) some conduct (b) a prohibited consequence and (c) certain surrounding circumstances. At first sight it may appear puzzling why one should want to analyse an *actus reus* in this way, but the reason will shortly appear.

(1) Voluntary Nature of the Act

Ordinarily the prosecution must prove that the accused voluntarily brought about the *actus reus* of the crime. To put it another way the act or omission must have occurred because of a conscious exercise of will on the part of the accused. Thus there would be no voluntary act where the act alleged to constitute the crime was performed by the accused while suffering from concussion caused by a blow on the head. In this type of case it is usually said that the accused is acting in a state of automatism (or more accurately non-insane automatism; see below, p. 287). But these are not the only situations in which the act of the accused may be said to be involuntary. For example if X were to hold Y's hand and force him to stick a knife in Z, Y's act could not be said to have been a voluntary one on his part. It is necessary to distinguish the requirement for a voluntary act from the requirement in many, but not all crimes, that the accused intentionally caused the *actus reus*. Whereas the prosecution will always fail if it cannot prove that the accused acted voluntarily, in certain crimes (crimes of strict liability) it will be excused from the need to show that the accused acted intentionally. Suppose that A is charged with failing to stop at a red traffic light. It will be no defence for him to say that he had not seen any traffic lights let alone that they were showing red; this is an offence of strict liability which does not require that the police prove that he knew the lights were red (see below, p. 236). However a plea that he suffered a blackout just before his car reached the lights would, if accepted, mean that there was no voluntary act of driving and this would be fatal to the prosecution's case. It is pointless to worry about whether voluntariness is rightly described as part of the *actus reus* or part of the *mens rea* of a given crime; the point to remember is that it is an essential part of every crime.

Consider the following hypothetical situations:

    (i)   A pushes B so that B loses his balance and falls against C.

    (ii) While driving his car D is attacked by a swarm of bees; in instinctively brushing them away from his face he loses control of his car which mounts the pavement and injures E.

(iii) While sleepwalking F hits G over the head with a video recorder and causes a serious cut;

(iv) H is under the influence of alcohol to such an extent that he is no longer aware of what he is doing. In this state he strikes his friend, J, with a beer glass.

In each of these situations a criminal charge may be laid and in all of them the accused might raise the same defence, namely that there was no voluntary conduct of his which caused the *actus reus*. But it does not necessarily follow that the same result would be reached in all five examples.

In example (i) A may well be liable for assaulting both B and C, but B has not assaulted C since there is absolutely no voluntary conduct at all on B's part. This would clearly result in an absolute acquittal.

Example (ii) differs in that D is the only human agent involved, but his action is purely reflexive and the view would no doubt be taken (*Cf. Hill v. Baxter* (1958)) that it was not a voluntary act—or a sufficiently voluntary act—for D to incur criminal liability either for injuring E or for driving the car without due care and attention.

In example (iii) F is prima facie not guilty for the same reasons; there is no truly conscious control of movements by F during the sleepwalking and thus he cannot be said to have voluntarily attacked G.

In these first three examples the defendant may be said to have raised the defence of *automatism*, or more accurately, *non-insane automatism* (see below, p. 287). The defendant, in each case, is saying that the conduct which is alleged to constitute the criminal offence was not brought about by an exercise of his free will; it was involuntary conduct. Unless the prosecution can prove that the conduct was voluntary, the defendant will be entitled to be found "not guilty." On the face of it, this seems a potent defence. It is surely very easy for a defendant to swear that he blacked out, and extremely difficult, if not impossible, for the prosecution to prove that he did not.

However, in practice, certain factors make the defence of automatism an extremely limited one, In *Bratty* (1963) Lord Denning was able to say that it was confined to "acts done while unconscious and to spasms, convulsions and reflex actions". Two recent cases show just how limited the defence has become. In *Broome v. Perkins* (1987) the defendant had driven his car for a distance of about six miles but was unable to recall the journey at all. Evidence showed that during the drive he had hit small vehicles, but appeared to be able to miss large ones. He suffered from diabetes and evidence was produced that this behaviour was consistent with low blood sugar. The Divisional Court, however, said that this did not amount to automatism because to a certain extent he had exercised conscious control over his vehicle when he reacted to large objects; his driving was not, therefore, totally automatic. This very harsh approach has been approved by the Court of Appeal in *Att.-Gen. Reference (No. 2 of 1992)* (1993) (*Casebook* 103). Here a lorry driver shunted a recovery vehicle parked on the hard shoulder into the rear of another vehicle which had broken down. The drivers of the two marked vehicles were crushed to death between the two vehicles. The lorry driver was charged with causing death by reckless driving (This offence has now been abolished and replaced with causing death by dangerous driving: Road Traffic Act 1988, s.1). The defendant claimed to have been driving in a condition known as "driving without awareness". In such a state the driver's capacity to avoid a collision ceases to exist but he remains capable of driving his vehicle within the road line markings. The driver would be largely unaware of what was happening ahead and largely unaware of steering. However, the unawareness was not total. For this reason the Court of Appeal held that there was no evidence of automatism to be left to the jury.

These two cases illustrate a second factor which limits the defence of automatism. Although the prosecution has to prove beyond reasonable doubt that the conduct of the accused was voluntary, this burden does not arise unless the accused first discharges an evidential burden. This means that he has to introduce evidence which would be capable of creating a reasonable doubt as to whether the accused was acting voluntarily. It will not normally suffice that the defendant has taken the oath and has testified that he blacked out. If that were the case the defendant in most cases would only have to say that he blacked out to leave the prosecution with the almost impossible task of proving that the accused had acted voluntarily. The accused will need to produce something in the nature of medical evidence to support his claim that he acted as an automaton. (See further on evidential burden, below, p. 282).

In both *Broome v. Perkins* and *A.G.'s Reference*, the accused had called medical evidence. However, in neither case did the accused discharge the evidential burden, because the evidence they produced, even if believed, was evidence of only partially automatic conduct. To have the issue left to the jury, the defendant must produce evidence which suggests that his behaviour was totally automatic and this will be very rare. These two cases cast doubts on earlier decisions such as *Charlson* (1955) where a father suffering from a brain tumour struck his small son with a mallet and threw him out of the window. He was acquitted on the basis of automatism, but it is extremely unlikely that Charlson exercised absolutely no control over his movements. (The case would also be decided differently today for a further reason, see below, p. 288).

In *A G.'s Reference*, the Court of Appeal held that in all such cases, the first step was for the defence to lay a proper foundation for the defence of automatism. This will now prove an extremely difficult hurdle to cross. However in our example (iii) (above, p. 187) sleepwalking would be one situation where conduct would be truly automatic. It may seem rather far-fetched that someone who was sleepwalking could hit another over the head with a video recorder, but this was accepted as a possibility in the case of *Burgess* (1991) and the trial judge accepted that a sufficient foundation had been laid. A perhaps more readily accepted situation would be where the accused acts under concussion sustained by a blow on the head.

A third factor is that once we have reached the stage where the defendant has laid a foundation for the defence of automatism, the court will want an explanation as to the underlying cause for the automatic conduct. The reason for this is that if the judge determines that the evidence suggests that the cause of the automatic conduct was a "disease of the mind" then he will direct the jury that the defendant has raised the defence of insanity. If the defence of insanity is accepted, then the defendant will still be acquitted, but on the basis of insanity, and this will enable the court to order his detention for treatment. We shall examine the defence of insanity later (see below, p. 285). For now we can say that if the cause of the automatic conduct is discovered to be external to the accused, such as a blow on the head, an attack by a swarm of bees or the taking of a properly prescribed drug the court is likely to hold that the proper defence is non-insane automatism and that it is for the prosecution to disprove the defence beyond reasonable doubt. Automatic conduct which has been caused by illnesses such as arteriosclerosis, diabetes and epilepsy has been held to amount to a disease of the mind and thus insane automatism or insanity; sleepwalking has also been held to arise from a disease of the mind. The court holds that these are internal factors which affect the mind. It remains to be seen how the court would react to a defence plea that the accused suffered a heart attack or a ruptured appendix and that this caused him to drive through red traffic lights. Surely this would amount to a reflex action as described by Lord Denning in *Bratty*, and hence non-insane automatism. On the other hand it satisfies many of the tests for a disease of the mind (see below, p. 287). If a person acts unconsciously following a blow on the head, this will be treated as an external cause. But what if a week later he blacks out again as a result of the original blow on the head? Is this still an external factor?

There is an important practical consequence to the court's decision as to whether the defence has laid a foundation for non-insane automatism or insane automatism. If the court holds that the basis had been laid for a defence of non-insane automatism, the prosecution will now have to prove beyond reasonable doubt that the accused's conduct at the time of the offence was not automatic. If, however, the judge rules that the accused has laid a foundation for insanity, the accused will bear the burden of proving on a balance of probabilities (a lower standard than required of the Crown) that he is insane. In practice once the judge has ruled that the facts amount to insanity, the accused will often change his plea to one of guilty to escape the possible verdict of not guilty by reason of insanity, which might lead to a lengthy detention in a mental institution.

One final point should be made. Even if the court is prepared to hold that for example, an attack of angina pectoris which causes a motorist to mount a pavement and injure a pedestrian is an example of non-insane automatism, the court will want to know some details of the defendant's history. If this were the first such attack, then he would be entitled to an acquittal. On the other hand, if it turns out that he suffers from frequent attacks, it could most probably be argued that any driving by him is dangerous and that he ought not to drive at all. So in *Kay v. Butterworth* (1945) the accused was found guilty of careless driving even though he had fallen asleep at the time when the accident occurred; his culpability consisted of continuing to drive when he knew he was feeling drowsy. A more refined example is provided by *Jarmain* (1946) where in the course of a robbery J pointed a loaded pistol at a cashier knowing that it had no safety catch and required only a light touch on the trigger to fire. The cashier, a brave woman, told him to go away and this so disconcerted J that, according to his version of the facts, while he was trying to work out what he should do he involuntarily pressed the trigger and the cashier was killed. The court declined to regard J's last action separately from the rest of the transaction. The death was caused by pointing a loaded pistol at the cashier at point blank range, and there was no doubt that this had been done voluntarily. See also *Ryan* (1967)).

Example (iv) is given to draw attention to the fact that automatism arising from the non-medical and voluntary consumption of alcohol or drugs is not generally a defence. There are said to be special policy reasons for treating such cases in an exceptional way (see below, p. 293).

In the result automatism is a defence of limited application. To repeat Lord Denning's analysis it is confined to "acts done while unconscious and to spasms, convulsions and reflex actions" (*Bratty v. Att.-Gen. for Northern Ireland* (1963)).

(2) Criminal Liability in the "State of Affairs" Cases

While there is notionally no criminal liability unless the *actus reus* is brought about by some voluntary act or omission on the part of the accused, there is no rule which says that criminal liability cannot be imposed without some such voluntary act by the accused. Parliament could, for example, make it a criminal offence to be over six feet tall. In such an unlikely event it would be no defence for the accused to claim that he had no control over the mechanisms in his body which had caused him to be over six feet in height. While it is inconceivable that Parliament would create such an offence it has to be acknowledged that it is theoretically open to Parliament to do so and there are, as it happens, some crimes which might be taken to impose criminal liability without proof of any voluntary act on the part of the accused.

Under section 1 of the Road Traffic Act 1974, and for the purposes of ensuring that certain fixed penalties such as parking fines, are paid, "it shall be conclusively presumed ... that [the owner] was the driver at that time ... that acts or omissions of the driver of the vehicle at that time were his acts or omissions." Thus if the accused's son has parked the accused's car illegally, the accused will be liable even though he is sleeping in a bed in New York at the time. It is, however, a defence for the accused to show that the car was in the possession of the other person without the consent of the accused; thus liability is incurred only if the accused consented to the possession of the car. Nevertheless, given an actual consent to possession, the accused is liable for certain crimes committed thereafter without any proof of any voluntary act on his part. It is easy to appreciate what led Parliament to take this unusual step. Many parking tickets were left unpaid and when the police served a summons on the owner they would be met by the impossibility of proving whether it was the owner, his wife or some other member of the family who had been responsible for the illegal parking.

A much more extreme case is provided by *Larsonneur* (1933). A French woman, L, went from England to Ireland where she was arrested by the Irish police and sent back to England where she was taken into police custody. She was charged with being an alien who was "found" in the United Kingdom without permission. Strictly speaking, of course, she was "found" in this country the moment she set foot off the boat from Ireland. However she did not want to come back to England but she was forced back by the Irish police. Once the boat docked here she had no alternative but to get off on to British soil—straight into the arms of the English police—at which stage she was "found" here without permission. There was no voluntary action on her part and nothing she could do to prevent herself stepping on to British soil. Nevertheless she was convicted of the offence. Her conviction was upheld because she literally came within the prohibition. She was "an alien" to whom permission to land was refused and she was "found" here. As a matter of fact her conduct was not involuntary (conduct is not involuntary merely because it is done under duress) but the implication in the judgment is that she would have been convicted even if she had been physically carried into England by the police.

The decision in *Larsonneur* has been justly and universally condemned. Nonetheless a similar decision was reached in *Winzar v. Chief Constable of Kent* (1983) (*Casebook*, p. 109) where the police had been called to remove the accused from a hospital corridor. They found that he was drunk and removed him to a police car which was parked in the highway. He was later charged with being found drunk in the highway, though in reality he was "found" by the police in the hospital corridor. Cases such as these can be defended by a very literal approach to statutory interpretation. Statutory offences rarely specify that such issues as insanity and duress should be a defence but these are implied as a matter of course; it would be no more difficult to read in the fundamental requirement that the *actus reus* must be caused by some voluntary act of the accused. Of course, if, as is the case with section 1 of the Road Traffic Act 1974 (referred to above), Parliament has patently dispensed with the need to prove that the *actus reus* was caused by some conduct of the accused, then that has to be accepted. Obviously Miss Larsonneur would now be liable to be convicted of the offence under section 1 of the Road Traffic Act 1974 if, while on holiday or even imprisoned in Liverpool, her brother, using her car with her permission, had parked it illegally in London. But *Larsonneur* and *Winzar* were not cases where they were made liable (justifiably in view of the difficulties of otherwise enforcing the law) for the acts of others. They were made liable for *their own conduct* in circumstances where that conduct was controlled by others. Are we to say that if, having legally parked her car in a two hour zone and being about to remove it before the time on the meter expires, she is unable to do so because she is kidnapped by terrorists or arrested for theft she is liable for a parking offence? Should it make a difference whether she has been unlawfully abducted or lawfully arrested?

(3) Liability for Failing to Act

In most criminal prosecutions the prosecutor will be seeking to prove that a prohibited situation or result has been brought about by the acts of the accused. However in certain situations it will be the fact that the accused failed to act that led to the prohibited event occurring. For example, if A pushes B under the water in a swimming pool and holds him there until B is dead then it is clear that A's actions have caused B's death. On the other hand if A sees B drowning in the swimming pool in a situation where it would be easy to rescue B, but A does nothing, the result will be the same—B will die. However this time B would have died whether or not A had been there. Should the law therefore hold A responsible for B's death? It would be easy to say yes, for most of us would find the picture of A simply watching B drown morally abhorrent. Yet if we hold, in principle, that A should be liable for failing to act, we would probably cause more problems than the law could handle. It would be easy to hold that A should be liable for the death of B where B is a small child drowning in about two or three feet of water, but such straightforward cases are unlikely to occur. The water may be much deeper, and there may be strong currents, or A may be only a modest swimmer. How much of a risk can the law expect A to take with his own life in order to save another from death or lesser injury? The answer that he should take such risks as the court deems reasonable in all the circumstances would merely involve the courts in a minute examination of all the surrounding factors and possibly A's appreciation of them.

For these sorts of reasons most jurisdictions, including our own, have not adopted a general principle of liability for failing to act. Instead the legislature has from time to time created offences of omission: for example under section 170 of the Road Traffic Act 1988 it is an offence for a motorist in certain circumstances to fail to provide information. Similarly under section 7(6) of the same Act it is an offence for a motorist to fail to provide a police constable with a sample of breath for analysis. In both these situations Parliament has clearly constituted offences which are committed by the motorist failing to act. Other offences which may, at first sight, appear to be offences of omission are not true examples. For example, failure to tax one's car is an offence, but the real offence is driving the car without the necessary tax and this is an act not an omission. Sometimes the courts will have to decide whether Parliament intended that a particular verb within a statutory definition should be interpreted to cover both act and omissions. For example in *Firth* (1990) the Court of Appeal had to decide whether the verb "deceive" in section 2(1) of the Theft Act 1978 (see below) covered a situation in which there had been a failure by the defendant to give relevant information. In holding that the verb was capable of covering such a situation the court was, in effect, saying that the doctor was under a duty to give the correct information.

Thus where the prosecution are seeking to rely on a failure to act as the basis for liability, the court will have to be satisfied that, in addition to the normal requirements of the *actus reus*, (i) the crime is one which, in law, liability may be incurred by an omission; and (ii) that the defendant was under a duty imposed by law to act. As regards (i) a failure to act will probably satisfy most crimes; murder can be committed by a failure to act as can most forms of manslaughter—though not constructive manslaughter (see below, p. 360). Whether or not a person is under a duty to act will depend upon whether he is covered expressly by the terms of the legislation or whether he falls within the general categories of persons whom the courts have held liable because of their status. Sea captains are under a duty to take reasonable steps to protect the lives of their passengers and crew. Parents are under an obligation to look after the welfare of their children and guardians their wards, though the guardian's duty probably arises as much out of the specific undertaking by the guardian. (See *Sheppard* (1980)).

It is possible to bring oneself under a duty to act through contractual obligations. The leading case in this area is

Pittwood (1902) where the accused who was under a contractual obligation to look after a railway level crossing negligently left his post with the gates in such a position as to suggest to road users that no trains were coming. As a result a man was killed when his cart, which was crossing the railway lines, was struck by a train. Clearly the action of the accused could be regarded as grossly negligent and clearly his negligent conduct had lead to the death. He argued that he owed no duty to the users of the level crossing; his contractual obligations lay solely with the railway company. The court, however, held that this contractual undertaking was sufficient to place him under a duty to the road users and thus the prosecution were able to establish the remaining part of the *actus reus* and the accused was convicted of manslaughter.

The courts have also found a duty to exist where the accused has voluntarily assumed responsibility for another's care and then simply failed to fulfil that undertaking. One example of this is the case of *Instan* (1893) where the accused undertook to look after her aged and helpless aunt, but then caused her death by failing to provide for her or summon help when she was ill. Although there may be a contractual situation in relation to the food, the court held that there was also a duty arising out of the voluntary undertaking to look after the aunt.

A doctor is under a duty to look after patients for whom he is responsible, but this duty may be terminated by a patient who refuses to accept treatment. If a patient who has suffered a series of heart attacks makes it perfectly clear that should he have another heart attack, he does not want any medical treatment, not only would the doctor be under no duty to save him following the next heart attack, he may well be guilty of an assault if he disregards the patient's wishes. On the other hand, a doctor who deliberately injected a sick patient with a lethal drug would be guilty of murder, even though it was done at the request of the patient. A patient who took an overdose of drugs would commit no offence, since neither suicide nor attempted suicide are criminal offences; it is, however, an offence to aid, abet, counsel; or procure suicide (see below p. 368) and so a doctor who helped the patient to take the drugs would be guilty of this offence. In other words, so long as the doctor is under no duty to provide medical treatment, he will not be liable for a death he allows to happen, but he will be liable for one he causes by his positive acts.

Where, however, the patient has not given clear instructions the position may be more difficut. In *Airedale National Health Service Trust v. Bland* (1993), Mr Bland (B) was one of the victims of the Hillsborough Stadium disaster in which many football supporters had been crushed to death. B had not died but had never recovered consciousness since the tragedy having suffered irreversible brain damage. He was in a persistent vegative state (PVS), being kept alive by a life support system and fed through a nasogastric drip since he was unable to swallow. The Trust sought a declaration from the High Court that it might discontinue the life sustaining treatment including the feeding, and also all medical treatment except for that which would allow him to die with the greatest dignity and least distress. The declaration was granted at first instance and by the Court of Appeal. The Official Solicitor appealed on the ground that it would constitute murder to discontinue the feeding of the patient.

The House took the view that the cessation of the drip and the medication was an omission rather than an act; hence it would not constitute a criminal offence unless the hospital staff were under a duty to continue the treatment. It is clear that the duty of the doctors is to act in the best interests of the patient and that when B had been admitted it was in his interests that treatment should be started since it was not clear whether or not he could recover. Once it became clear that there was no chance of recovery it could no longer be said that it was in his best interests that the treatment should continue. Lord Goff said that "the question is not whether it is in the best interests of the patient that he should die. The question is whether it is in the best interests of the patient that his life should be prolonged by the continuance of this form of medical treatment or care".

The decision is one arising from a civil action and is not, therefore, strictly binding in criminal cases. However, it would be unlikely that a criminal court would not regard itself bound. The Trust is, in effect, given permission to allow the patient to starve to death. While it is easy to sympathise with the actual decision to allow B to die, the case raises many problems. It is hard to see how the switching off of all the life support systems can be regarded as an omission. This might be the case where the equipment automatically switches itself off after a period of time unless the hospital staff take steps to keep it going. If an intruder were to do exactly that which the hospital staff did to discontinue treatment, would that be regarded as an omission? If not, why should it be so regarded in respect of the medical staff?

The need to phrase everything in terms of an omission will seem strange to the layman. Once a court has ruled that it is permissible to allow B to die, would it not be far more humane to bring about his death by a quick and painless injection rather than to allow him to starve to death over a period of weeks. Is there any meaningful difference between starving someone to death and killing them with poison? The answer is that from a legal point of view there is every difference. The lethal injection is the deliberate killing of a human being and this is murder. Allowing someone to starve is no offence unless you are under a duty to act to prevent that person from starving. It is like allowing a child to drown in a shallow pond; there is no liability unless a duty exists to look after the child. (See also Commentary on *Dr Arthur's Case; Gunn and Smith* [1985] Crim. L.R. 705.)

In some jurisdictions the courts have held that where a person has created a dangerous situation, he is under a duty to take reasonable steps to avert danger. Thus, whereas A, who comes upon a burning house, is under no obligation to take any action to extinguish the fire, if it was he who caused the fire, he would be under an obligation to do his best to get the fire extinguished. A similar situation arose here in *Miller* (1983) where the accused had fallen asleep while smoking a cigarette. He awoke to find that his mattress was on fire, but instead of taking steps to put the fire out, he simply moved to another room leaving the mattress to burn. The House of Lords decided that common sense dictated that he should bear responsibility for the result of his failure to avert the danger and it was necessary to formulate an approach to such cases which Crown Court judges could explain clearly to lay jurors. Thus it was held that where an accused had unwittingly created a risk that the property of another would be damaged or destroyed, he should bear the responsibility for the resulting damage if he subsequently became aware of the risk and failed to take steps to avert it. The prosecution would, of course, have to show that the failure to take action was accompanied by the necessary *mens rea* (see below, p. 218).

Once the prosecution have proved that the accused failed to act in a situation where the law imposes a duty to act then the general principles of criminal liability operate as in any other case. The prosecution will have to establish any remaining elements of the *actus reus* together with any requirements relating to the state of mind of the accused. It is very tempting in situations where the accused has failed to look after someone properly as a result of which the person has died, to say that this will at most amount to manslaughter. However if the prosecution can establish that the accused deliberately withheld food so that the victim would suffer serious bodily harm or death, then this is a proper case for a conviction for murder (see *Gibbons and Proctor* (1918) *Casebook*, p. 112).

This is not intended to be an exhaustive list of duty situations; the courts may well add further categories. The law in this area is, possibly of necessity, imprecise. There is little authority on just how much of a risk people under a duty to act must take in order to perform their duty, but the majority of cases are concerned with situations where no risk at all is involved and the accused has simply abandoned his responsibility. In some American states where there has been codification it has been common to include in the provisions dealing with liability for omissions some such phrase as "or the omission to perform a duty which the law imposes upon him and which he is physically capable of performing," and this is probably implicit in the English decisions.

(4) Causation

Not every crime requires that the prosecution prove that the accused brought about a particular prohibited result. Take, for example, careless driving. A person may be convicted of this offence though no harm is caused to person or property; it is only his conduct in driving the car that matters. Murder on the other hand requires a result; namely that the accused has killed someone and in crimes such as these the prosecution must prove that it was the unlawful act of the accused which resulted in the victim's death. This all seems very simple and indeed in most cases it is, but we shall see that complex situations can arise.

For any given result, there will normally be several contributing causes [often described as factual causes], and our task is to determine what can, in law, be held to be the cause of the prohibited result. For example, I might invite X to my house for dinner and on the way to my house he is run over by Y and killed. You could say that but for my invitation X would not have been killed. Equally you could say that it was the careless way X stepped off the path in front of Y, or the fact that Y was not concentrating or that the road surface was slippery, or that X could have been saved by a more competent surgeon. If we decide to prosecute Y on a charge of causing death by dangerous driving we shall have to prove that his reckless driving was, at least, a factual cause of X's death; in other words the jury must find that but for the dangerous quality of Y's reckless driving X would not have been killed. If the jury reaches the conclusion that even the most careful of drivers would have been unable to avoid hitting X, then the prosecution will fail (*Dalloway* (1847)). If we are prosecuting the surgeon for manslaughter in that he caused X's death by gross negligence, then we must show, at least, that a reasonably competent surgeon would have saved him.

It is, of course, a question for the jury to decide whether the accused caused the death of the victim. But the judge must rule on which of the various factual causes is capable, in law, of amounting to a cause of the victim's death. In the general run of case this presents no problems. It is important to note that in early homicide cases lawyers did not have the benefit of advanced medical testimony as to what medically speaking caused the victim's death. They therefore developed a rough and ready causal test under which the prosecution would have to prove that the death of the victim occurred within a year and a day of the last injury inflicted by the accused. This requirement still exists today and so even if you could establish that X deliberately infected Y with Aids from which Y died two years later, X could not be charged with Y's murder (though he could be charged with an offence under section 18 of the Offences Against the Person Act 1861 which carries life imprisonment). In reaching his decision on what, in law, can amount to a cause of the prohibited result, the judge will exclude factors which can be described as insignificant. In *Armstrong* (1989), for example, the victim, who had already consumed a lethal amount of alcohol, was supplied with heroin by the accused. There was no evidence that the heroin had in any significant way accelerated the victim's death; it could not therefore be held, in law, to be a cause of his death.

Just as there can be several factual causes of a result, so can the judge instruct the jury that they are entitled to find that, in law, more than one factor is responsible. Thus if X and Y attack Z who dies as a result of the combined wounds inflicted by both X and Y, both X and Y can be held responsible as principal offenders in the homicide. One can think of many possible variations, but in the end the test is largely one of common sense. Should the law really hold X's action to be a cause of Z's death? Thus if X poisons Z, but before the poison has any chance to take effect Y shoots and kills Z, only Y will be held liable for the homicide, though X may be found guilty of attempted murder. Most of these problems occur when there is an event which intervenes between the act of the accused and the prohibited result. The question is then whether this intervening event breaks the chain of causation which would otherwise link the accused's acts with the prohibited result. Although the possible factual situations are infinite, certain general principles are discernible.

In the first place the accused may well escape liability if the intervening act is unforseeable. For instance, if X renders Z unconscious and leaves him on a beach where the tide is coming in, Z's subsequent death by drowning is easily foreseeable, but the position would be different if Z were blown up by an undiscovered land mine on the beach.

One application of this type of principle occurs where the accused has acted in such a way as to lead another to take avoiding action, thereby injuring or killing himself. In *Pitt* (1842) it was held that an accused could be held responsible for the death of a victim who had thrown himself into a river to escape harm he reasonably apprehended to be forthcoming from the accused. (Should the same result follow if the victim's response is unreasonable? See *Blaue* below). In *Pagett* (1983) (*Casebook*, p. 129) the accused held a girl in front of himself as a shield and then fired shots at armed police officers. The officers instinctively returned the fire and the girl was killed. The Court of Appeal held that in these circumstances it was perfectly proper to say that the accused's actions caused the death of the girl. The court would almost certainly reach the same conclusion if the police, in returning the shots, had hit and killed an innocent passer-by. In all such cases the accused's eventual liability will depend upon his state of mind at the time that the action occurred.

It is also clear that to a certain extent the accused must take his victim as he finds him. Thus if X injures Z and Z dies partly as a result of those injuries, and partly as a result of failing to take proper care of himself, then X will be held liable for the resulting death. This principle has been recently extended to a case where the victim, a Jehovah's Witness, died as a result of stab wounds inflicted by the accused, because she refused, on religious grounds, to have a blood transfusion *Blaue* (1975) (*Casebook*, p. 127).

Cases involving medical treatment have proved particularly troublesome for the courts. In *Jordan* (1956) the defendant had stabbed the victim, seriously injuring him. The victim responded successfully to treatment and his wounds were almost healed when a series of appalling blunders led to his death from pneumonia. The defendant was tried for and convicted of murder, but on appeal the Court of Criminal

Appeal heard evidence from medical experts who said that death had been caused, not by the stab wound but by the abnormal medical treatment. Jordan's conviction was quashed, but the decision caused anxiety in medical circles. There was worry that if the treatment received in hospital was in any way below the standard which should be expected, the chain of causation between the initial assailant and the eventual death would be broken. However, in *Smith* (1959) the Court re-examined the issue. In that case the victim had been stabbed by Smith during a barrack room brawl and his lung had been punctured. He was then carried to the medical officer's tent where, due to pressure of work, the doctor failed to diagnose the extent of the wounds. As a result the officer prescribed totally inadequate treatment and the victim died two hours after the initial wounding. The Court of Criminal Appeal held that the stab wound was still an operating cause of death despite the poor medical treatment which was received. Lord Parker C.J. said "Only if it can be said that the original wounding is merely the setting in which another cause operates can it be said that the death does not result from the wound. Putting it in another way, only if the second cause is so overwhelming as to make the original wound merely part of the history can it be said that the death does not flow from the wound." In such a case the initial wound more closely resembles the invitation to dinner which causes the victim to be in the place where the real cause of death happens. The Court appears to have gone even further in *Cheshire* (1991) where at the time of the death of the victim the original gunshot wounds were no longer life-threatening. Death, according to one medical witness was due to the negligent (but not grossly negligent) treatment in the hospital. The case thus more closely resembled *Jordan* than *Smith*. However, the Court of Appeal held that the gunshot wound had directly led to the rare medical complication which had not been spotted by the hospital staff and hence the wounding was at least one cause of the victim's death if not the only cause, and this was enough. Beldam L.J. said "Even though negligence in the treatment of the victim was the immediate cause of his death, the jury should not regard it as excluding the responsibility of the accused unless the negligent treatment was so independent of his acts, and in itself so potent in causing death, that they regard the contribution made by his acts as insignificant." This passage is hardly a model of clarity, but it would appear to mean that where a defendant necessitates medical treatment for his victim, he will take the risk of the victim dying from negligent treatment even where the injury itself has ceased to be life-threatening, unless the treatment is very bad.

So where does this leave us? It seems clear that where the initial wounds are still a significant operating cause, the accused will remain liable even if the hospital is guilty of grossly negligent or even reckless conduct which prevents the chance of a good recovery. If, for example, in *Cheshire* the casualty doctor had deliberately failed to attend to the gunshot wounds because he was in a hurry to go for his coffee and the victim had died as a result of the gunshot wounds during the coffee break, there is no doubt that *Cheshire* would be held liable for the death, even though prompt action would almost certainly have led to a full recovery. Of course, the doctor may also be held responsible for the death.

Where, however, the initial wound has ceased to be life-threatening, negligent mistakes by the hospital staff are still unlikely to break the chain of causation since it can still be justifiably said that it is the defendant's fault that the victim has been exposed to the treatment which has led to his death. Only when the treatment is so bad that it can be regarded as independent of the acts of the accused and so potent in itself in causing death will the chain of causation be broken. But when is this point reached? Unless *Jordan* is to be regarded as wrong, a distinction has to be drawn between that case and *Cheshire* and the line drawn accordingly. Possibly the answer is that where the wound is no longer an operating cause, grossly negligent treatment by the hospital will free the initial assailant from liability for the death which follows.

The problem may well arise today where the victim of an assault has suffered irreparable brain damage, but is being kept "alive" on a respirator. If the doctors decide that the victim cannot recover and switch off the respirator, the defendant will nonetheless remain responsible for the victim's death. It may be possible to argue that the doctors are also partially responsible for the victim's death; but it is absurd to imagine that they would be charged with murder. (*Malcherek* (1981)).

2. Mens Rea

Not only must the prosecution show that the accused brought about the *actus reus* of the crime, but they must also, in most cases, prove that he caused the *actus reus* with *mens rea*. Literally translated *mens rea* means "guilty mind," but the expression "guilty mind" is both misleading and too imprecise as a yardstick of liability. This is well demonstrated by the case of *Cunningham* (1957) (*Casebook*, p. 132). In that case a building which had previously been one house had been converted into two; the cellar had been divided by a wall of loose stone rubble. Cunningham's prospective mother-in-law lived in one of these two houses and the other was unoccupied, being the house Cunningham would live in after his marriage. On the occasion in question he entered the empty house, wrenched the gas meter off the wall in the cellar in order to steal the money in it and in so doing he fractured the gas pipe causing gas to seep through the rubble and into the adjoining house. As a result Mrs. Wade, his prospective mother-in-law was partially asphyxiated. He was charged with "unlawfully and maliciously" administering a noxious thing to Mrs. Wade contrary to section 23 of the Offences Against the Person Act 1861. The judge directed the jury that "malicious" meant "wicked—something which he (Cunningham) has no business to do and perfectly well knows it." In this sense Cunningham undoubtedly had a guilty mind. He knew that he was up to no good and there was no doubt that he had committed the crime of theft and possibly burglary into the bargain. Nonetheless this was held, on appeal, to be a misdirection. "Malicious," said the Court of Criminal Appeal, required either that (i) Cunningham intended to administer the noxious thing or (ii) without intending to administer it, he foresaw that by fracturing the pipe he might cause gas to seep through the house to the injury of Mrs. Wade. In *Sheppard* (1980) Lord Diplock held that the word "wilfully" imported the same notions.

Cunningham shows that *mens rea* must not be confused with having a bad motive. Conversely the fact that the accused has the best of motives does not mean that he cannot have *mens rea*. In a tragic case (*The Times*, October 7, 1965), Mr. Gray killed his 11-year old son by administering an overdose of drugs and then gassing him while he was asleep. Mr. Gray was a devoted father and had done this because his son was dying from an incurable cancer and was in such pain that he could not even bear the weight of his bed sheets. On Mr. Gray's conviction for manslaughter (the charge was murder but this was reduced to manslaughter on account of diminished responsibility; see below, p. 289). The judge said to Mr. Gray, "I am perfectly certain that there is not a single person inside this court who will feel that you are in any sense a criminal." One can see what the judge meant but, as the conviction for manslaughter proved, Mr. Gray had committed a crime; he had caused the *actus reus* of an unlawful homicide and in intending to kill his son he had the necessary *mens rea* for murder or manslaughter.

What then does *mens rea* mean? We have already seen that it does not simply mean that the defendant has a guilty mind. You will recall that the *actus reus* of all offences consists of a list of "ingredients." The law relating to *mens rea* requires that in addition to establishing this list of ingredients, the prosecution must prove, what for the moment we can call, culpability on each item in the list. Consider for the moment that X has killed Y. Without further information you are not in a position to say whether or not X is deserving of punishment. In relation to this killing X could be in one of a number of states of mind. For example:

(i) X may have deliberately set out to kill Y. This is known as intention, and is the most culpable state of mind.

(ii) X may have deliberately taken the risk of killing Y without actually desiring Y's death. This is a state of mind often referred to as recklessness and will normally suffice as the basis of liability on all aspects of the *actus reus*.

(iii) X may have failed to realise that what he was doing would kill Y, though a reasonable person would have done. This can be called negligence. Although it is not really a state of mind of the accused, it suffices as the *mens rea* of some crimes.

(iv) X may have been totally blameless, but even here he may still be liable in some crimes.

There are other states of mind which we will meet in the next few pages. For now we can say that *mens rea* is this additional element, be it intention, recklessness or negligence which is normally required on each element of the *actus reus*.

We can now look at the various states of mind in more detail.

(1) Intention

Most crimes can be proved if the accused has acted *maliciously* as defined in *Cunningham* (above, p. 203). In such cases there is no need to pursue a refined distinction between intention and the second state of mind outlined in that case which for the moment we will refer to as *Cunningham recklessness*. There are crimes, however, where proof of intention is required on at least one aspect of the *actus reus*. In these crimes it will be necessary to distinguish between intention and recklessness. Examples of these crimes include any charge of attempting to commit a substantive offence (see below, p. 320), wounding with intent to cause grievous bodily harm contrary to section 18 of the Offences Against the Person Act 1861 (see below, p. 379) and murder (see below, p. 345).

The word *intention* has caused much difficulty in recent years and this is largely due to a reluctance by the courts judicially to define what is, after all, a word in everyday use by ordinary citizens. The problem has been particularly acute in relation to the crime of murder. Until the decision of the House of Lords in *Moloney* (1985) (below, p. 347, *Casebook* p. 301), it was generally assumed that the prosecution would succeed on a charge of murder if it could prove one of four states of mind:

   (i)   intention to kill
  (ii)   foresight that what you were doing was likely (or according to some judges highly likely) to kill
 (iii)   intention to cause grievous bodily harm
 (iv)   foresight that what you were doing was (highly) likely to cause grievous bodily harm.

There was some confusion as to whether categories (ii) and (iv) were a form of intention or whether it was the case that *Cunningham recklessness* sufficed for murder. In practical terms, however, it meant that the *mens rea* of murder was widely drawn. Thus suppose that the accused was charged with planting a bomb on board a transatlantic airliner intending that it should explode when the aircraft was over the sea. The motive behind this was to send some worthless cargo to the bottom of the sea so that the accused could claim on a bogus insurance policy. The aircraft duly exploded and all the passengers and crew were killed. The accused tells the court that he did not want anyone injured. He had hoped that the aircraft would make a forced landing in the sea and that everyone would get into the life rafts before the plane sank. Did he intend to kill the passengers and crew? Under the law of murder defined above, this does not really matter. The jury would have little difficulty in holding that he foresaw that what he was doing was likely, at least, to cause serious bodily harm to those on board and this is sufficient. However in *Moloney* (1985) the House of Lords held that the case which was thought to lay down the four categories of *mens rea* for murder, *Hyam*, had been misinterpreted. The law of murder requires that the prosecution proves that the accused either intended to kill or to cause serious bodily harm and that for this purpose foresight that what you are doing is likely (or even highly likely) to cause death or serious bodily harm is not the same as intending those ends. Thus the House of Lords has, in effect, removed categories (ii) and (iv) from the list. This means we now have to ask whether our bomber intended to kill or seriously injure the crew and passengers; it is not enough that we can say he foresaw that he was likely to kill or seriously injure them. So, if you believe what the bomber has said, do you find that he intended to kill or seriously injure the passengers? If your answer was "yes" then would it differ if the bomb had been placed, not in an aircraft, but on a ship; or if it was a terrorist bomb planted in a pub, a short warning having been given to the drinkers to get out? What would the average person in the street answer if you asked "what is meant by saying that a person intends to kill another?" The answer would probably be that you intend to kill someone when you deliberately set about to produce that result. The strongest situation is where the accused desires to produce a given result. Thus if the accused wants to kill his uncle because his uncle has ill-treated him and to this end holds a gun against his uncle's head and pulls the trigger, we would have little difficulty in finding that the accused intended to kill his uncle.

There is also no difficulty where the accused wishes to bring about a given result but uses a method which he knows has only a limited chance of success. For example if he lies in wait for a victim, intending to shoot him at close range only to find that the victim will pass by on another road which is a lot further away. He fires the gun, knowing the chances of hitting the victim are remote, but he is lucky and the victim is killed. Clearly he intended to kill the victim.

Difficulties begin to arise when the consequence is not wanted for its own sake. In *Steane* (1947) the accused, who had given broadcasts for Germany during the Second World War because of threats to the safety of his family if he did not do so, was charged under regulation 2A of the Defence (General) Regulations with "doing an act likely to assist the enemy with intent to assist the enemy." Delivering the judgment of the court Lord Goddard C.J. referred to British prisoners-of-war who had been forced by their brutal Japanese captors to work on the Burma Road, and considered what the position would have been had they been charged under the same regulation. In such a case, said Lord Goddard, "it would be unnecessary surely ... to consider any of the niceties of the law relating to duress, because no jury would find that merely by doing this work they were intending to assist the enemy." He concluded, allowing Steane's appeal, that the jury should have been instructed that they could find that Steane lacked the necessary intent if they found that he did what he did in subjection to the power of an enemy.

It is easy to sympathise with Lord Goddard's conclusion. No one would want to see those British prisoners-of-war subject to the risk of even a charge, much less a conviction. However, it is an old adage that hard cases make bad law. It is tempting, but wrong, to say that a man who acts under duress does not act intentionally. The prisoners did not choose to build the road but they did build it and they knew that their acts would undoubtedly assist the Japanese. It would certainly be odd to say that they acted unintentionally. What Lord Goddard did was to confuse intention and motive; he talked of an "innocent" and "criminal" intent, but whether conduct is intentional is not determined by the motive with which it is done. The exculpation of such prisoners, and Steane, should be sought in the defence of duress, not in lack of intention.

The same is true where A desires to take an inheritance under the will of his grandfather. He knows the money will be coming to him sooner or later but is desperate to get his hands on it immediately. He is very fond of his grandfather and if there was a way of getting the money without killing the old man he would take it, but there is not and so he poisons him. On a subsequent charge of murder it would be of no avail for him to say that he did not intend to kill his grandfather, because he did not desire the old man's death. He deliberately killed his grandfather and the killing was an intentional one.

Further problems exist where the accused intends to bring about consequence A but realises that in doing so he may well bring about consequence B, which he does not desire. He nevertheless takes the risks and consequence B occurs. Can we say that he intended, to bring about consequence B? Clearly he is reckless within the meaning given above, (p. 203), but if the crime requires proof that the accused intended consequence B this will not be enough. If we return to our example of the bomb on the aircraft, we might be tempted to say that the accused intended to kill the people on board because he knew that it was virtually inevitable that all must die. But the same could not necessarily be said if the bomb were on board a ship or if it had been planted in a pub and a warning, albeit short, had been given.

These problems can arise in any crime where intention is required on at least one aspect of the *actus reus*. They present a special problem in murder because of the House of Lords insistence that murder is a crime which requires an intention to kill or cause grievous bodily harm while at the same time trying to ensure that the word is not given a meaning which would result in the exclusion of many heinous killings from the category of murder.

In *Moloney* Lord Bridge said that in the vast majority of cases where the prosecution had to establish that the accused intended a given consequence it would be sufficient for the trial judge to invite the jury to consider whether the prosecutor had satisfied them that the accused did so intend. The word "intend" is a word in normal everyday use and should need no lengthy explanation. However there would be cases, though these would be rare, where some further guidance would be necessary. These are presumably cases where the jury might need some guidance on the distinction between motive and intention. He said that this can usually be explained by reference to the facts of the case or to some homely example. "A man who, at London Airport, boards a plane which he knows to be bound for Manchester, clearly intends to travel to Manchester, even though Manchester is the last place he wants to be and his motive for boarding the plane is simply to escape pursuit. The possibility that the plane may have engine trouble and be diverted to Luton does not affect the matter. By boarding the plane the man conclusively demonstrates his intention to go there, because it is a moral certainty that that is where he will arrive." In other words a man can intend certain consequences even though he does not desire them. In order to assist a jury in such deliberations Lord Bridge suggested that they be invited to consider two questions.

"First, was death or really serious injury in a murder case ... a *natural* consequence of the defendant's voluntary act? Secondly, did the defendant foresee that consequence as being a *natural* consequence of his act? The jury

should then be told that if they answer yes to both
questions it is a proper inference for them to draw that he
intended that consequence."

As is often the case, one of those "rare" cases in which this
further guidance will be necessary arose almost immediately.
Indeed, it is clear that such cases will not be all that rare. In
Hancock and Shankland (1986) (*Casebook*, p. 307) two Welsh
miners were charged with the murder of a taxi driver. They
had dropped heavy concrete blocks into the path of his
oncoming car from a bridge over the road. They maintained
that they had only meant to prevent the driver from taking a
strike-breaker to his mine. The trial judge rightly identified
this as one of those exceptional cases which would cause the
jury difficulties and so he gave them a direction in the terms
suggested by Lord Bridge in *Moloney*. The accused may
indeed have intended to kill or seriously injure someone in
the car, but as in most cases there was no direct proof of their
actual state of mind. The jury may well have found it easy to
infer that the accused had deliberately taken the risk of
causing serious bodily harm and that this was more than a
slight risk, but *Moloney* has made it clear that this is not the
same as intending to cause that serious bodily injury. The trial
judge, not unreasonably tackled this problem by directing the
jury in the terms suggested by Lord Bridge (outlined above).
The jury convicted the two men of murder. Their convictions
were quashed by the Court of Appeal and the prosecution's
subsequent appeal was dismissed by the House of Lords. So
what had gone wrong? (Convictions for manslaughter were
substituted.)

The House of Lords agreed that a conviction for murder
could be based only upon a finding that the accused intended
to kill or seriously injure another; that foresight by the
accused that what they were doing was likely to cause death
or serious bodily harm was not the same thing. However,
Lord Scarman said that Lord Bridge's guidelines in *Moloney*
were defective in that they referred only to natural consequences and did not advert to the probability of a
consequence occurring. A juror might be misled into thinking
that it was sufficient that a consequence flowed naturally from
the act of the accused. It was clear that Lord Bridge intended
the issue of probability to be considered since elsewhere in his
speech he said that the probability of the consequence must
be little short of overwhelming before it will suffice to
establish the necessary intent. His mistake was in thinking

that such reasoning was conveyed by the word "natural." Lord Scarman thought, however, that jurors needed specific guidance on the probability issue. He said that they needed to be told that the greater the probability of a consequence, the more likely it is that the consequence was foreseen and that if that consequence was foreseen the greater the probability is that that consequence was intended. Unfortunately even here there is a problem. In *Moloney* Lord Bridge said that the awareness had to be of a probability that was little short of overwhelming—or a moral certainty, whereas the Court of Appeal in *Hancock and Shankland* spoke of the high likelihood of the consequence occurring. There would seem to be a substantial difference of degree between the two approaches, and it is unfortunate that the House of Lords in *Hancock and Shankland* did not resolve the matter.

In *Nedrick* (1987) the Lord Chief Justice, Lord Lane, said that whenever the simple direction is not enough, the jury should be directed that they are not entitled to infer the necessary intention unless they feel sure that the defendant's actions made death or serious harm a virtual certainty. However, in *Walker and Hayles* (1990), a case on attempted murder where only an intention to kill would suffice (see below, p. 325) the Court of Appeal held that a direction that the jury were entitled to find D intended to kill if he knew that there was a high degree of probability that his actions would cause death was acceptable though not desirable. The degree of difference between a virtual certainty and a high degree of probability did not amount to a misdirection.

Unfortunately, since *Nedrick*, trial judges have found difficulty in deciding when the simple direction will suffice and when they need to give a more complex direction along the lines suggested by the Court of Appeal in *Nedrick* (see *e.g. Fallon* (1995); *Scalley* (1995)). A *Nedrick* direction will only be necessary in situations where D is alleged to have intentionally brought about result A, but he claims to have had result B in mind. If this is the case then the court should ask whether the defendant knew that it was virtually certain that the attainment of result B would bring about result A and if the answer is that he did, then it is proper to infer that he intended to bring about result A. Trial judges should, however, remember that in the vast majority of cases no such direction will be called for.

The reader will have realised that what the courts have done is not to give a definition of intention; the juror is assumed to understand the meaning of that word. All that is provided is a clear indication that intention is not the same as foresight even where there is foresight of a virtual certainty. However, where the jury believe that the accused saw as a virtual certainty that the outcome of his actions would be death, they would be led almost invariably to conclude that the accused intended to kill. Would it not be simpler if the courts were to say that for the purpose of criminal liability, intention included a state of mind in which the defendant recognised that it was virtually certain that his action would lead to the prohibited result? (A good example of the difficulties faced by trial judges is provided by *Donnelly* (1989)).

(2) Negligence and Recklessness

If you were to construct a descending scale of culpability, then it is clear that intention would be at the top, recklessness would follow and negligence would come after that. It is still clear that recklessness is seen as a more blameworthy state of mind than negligence. However in view of recent developments which have obscured the legal definition of recklessness, it is probably easier to begin with negligence which is relatively straightforward.

(i) *Negligence*

In the civil law the classic definition of negligence is that given by Alderson B. in *Blyth v. Birmingham Waterworks Co.* (1856). "Negligence is the omission to do something which a reasonable man, guided upon these considerations which ordinarily regulate the conduct of human affairs, would do, or doing something which a prudent and reasonable man would not do."

It is thus not a defence in a civil action for the defendant to show that he did not foresee the harm if a reasonable man would have done so; nor even to show that his failure to foresee was due to physical or mental limitations not shared by the reasonable man. Nevertheless it seems probable that the defendant's physical and mental defects may be taken into account in determining whether he is negligent to the extent that they make it impossible for him to take the necessary precautions. Thus it would not avail a man with defective eyesight to attribute a car accident to his inability to judge distances, but if the same man were to fall over and injure the plaintiff's prize poodle when walking along the pavement, the appropriate test would be whether, for a man with defective eyesight, he had taken reasonable care.

So far as the criminal law is concerned there is, of course, no general crime of negligently causing harm. There are, however, particular crimes of negligence. At common law the only instance of a crime of negligence appears to be manslaughter, though in this type of manslaughter the negligence has to be gross (see below, p. 362). Parliament, has, however, thought it appropriate to create certain crimes of negligence. Possibly the best known of such crimes is careless driving contrary to section 3 of the Road Traffic Act 1988. The new offences of dangerous driving under sections 1 and 2 of the Road Traffic Act 1988 are based on a concept of negligence.

Where the crime is one of negligence the test to be applied is probably the same as that in civil cases though in a criminal case (a) the standard of proof required is more stringent (see *ante*, p. 4); and (b) generally there is no need to prove actual harm to person or property. Thus on a charge of careless driving where the accused is a learner driver his driving will be considered careless if he fails to measure up to the standard of the reasonably experienced driver and no allowance is made for the fact that he is a learner; *McCrone v. Riding* (1938). In that case Lord Hewart C.J. said "That standard is an objective standard, impersonal and universal, fixed in relation to the safety of other users of the highway. It is in no way related to the degree of proficiency or degree of experience attained by the individual driver."

Crimes of negligence are exceptional in our law. Sometimes, however, Parliament will create a crime and then make the absence of negligence a defence. Under section 7 of the Sexual Offences Act 1956 it is an offence for a man to have intercourse with a mental defective but by section 7(2) it is provided that the accused does not commit the offence if he does not know and has no reason to suspect the girl to be a defective; the Court of Criminal Appeal made it clear that the accused bore the burden of proof on this defence. Construing this provision in *Hudson* (1966) the Court of Criminal Appeal said that the trial judge was wrong to direct the jury that the test was wholly objective (*i.e.* would a reasonable man have believed that the girl was mentally defective?); the jury should have been instructed to consider whether it was reasonable for Hudson not to have realised that the girl was a defective. This is different from the wholly objective test approved for careless driving in *McCrone v. Riding*. The test in *Hudson* is still objective in the sense that it would not avail an accused to show that he was in fact unaware that the girl was a defective, but it will avail him to prove that persons sharing his limitations, whether physical or mental, would not have realised that the girl was a defective. Under section 7, therefore, a conviction is possible only if the jury concludes that the relevant standard could have been attained by the accused; with careless driving the accused may be convicted even though the relevant standard was unattainable by him.

It must not be thought that whenever a statutory offence is defined with a defence of no negligence, it inevitably follows that the court will adopt the subjective-objective form adopted in *Hudson*. The precise wording of the provision is all important. Under section 7 it is a defence if *"he* does not know and has no reason to believe" (italics supplied) that the girl was a defective. Had the provision been worded, for example, "it shall be a defence to prove that a reasonable person would not in the circumstances have realised that the girl was a defective" the trial judge's direction would almost certainly have been upheld.

Although, manslaughter apart, there are no crimes of negligence at common law, negligence has, at least in the past, had relevance in connection with the defence of mistake of fact. Sometimes courts have held that a mistake of fact is a defence only if it is honestly made *and* that there were reasonable grounds for making it. The result of this can be, in effect, to make negligence a ground of liability even in connection with serious crimes. The matter of mistake is a highly complicated one and is dealt with below (below, p. 227).

(ii) *Recklessness*

You will recall that in *Cunningham* (see above, p. 203) the Court of Appeal held that the jury, in order to convict the defendant of unlawfully and maliciously administering a noxious substance, should be satisfied that either (i) he intended to do the particular kind of harm that was in fact done or that (ii) he had foreseen that the particular kind of harm might be done, and yet had gone on to take the risk of it. The state of mind described in (ii) became known as recklessness. Later statutes began to use the word reckless to indicate the *mens rea* required for new offences and the Court of Appeal appeared to have accepted that it had the meaning ascribed to it in *Cunningham*. Perhaps a simpler way of putting it is to say that it covers a situation where the defendant has taken a conscious risk of bringing about a prohibited result. Thus if the defendant is shooting at a beer can which he has placed on a wall in the street outside his house and he knows that there is a risk he might hit someone passing by in the street, if he does, in fact, hit such a person we can say that he has recklessly hit the person in the street. It should be added that the risk taken must be an unjustified risk. In the example given, there would almost certainly be no justification for risking the safety of passers by. Whether a person is justified in taking a particular risk is a question for the jury and will, to a certain extent, be dependent upon the social utility of the venture. A surgeon, performing a delicate heart operation, may risk killing the patient in an attempt to give him a better future. The risk may be justified here even if the risk of death is high. On the other hand there is no social utility in shooting at beer cans in the street even if the risk of injuring a passer-by is extremely slight.

Thus until 1982 it seemed that the courts would interpret recklessness as indicating a conscious taking of an unjustified risk. However in *Caldwell* (1982) Lord Diplock held that although he was not disposed to challenge the decision in *Cunningham* as a definition of the word "maliciously" he felt that the word "recklessly" when used in modern statutes required a wider, less artificial meaning. Speaking in the context of the Criminal Damage Act 1971, Lord Diplock said that it means that (i) the accused does an act which, in fact, creates an obvious risk that property will be destroyed or damaged and that (ii) he *either* has not given any thought to the possibility of there being any such risk *or* he has recognised that there was some such risk and yet has carried on with his actions.

If we examine this definition we can see that it embraces two distinct tests. The prosecution will succeed if it can establish that D created an obvious risk of damage or destruction and, having recognised the existence of such a risk nonetheless went on with his activity. This, of course, looks very similar to the definition of recklessness given by Byrne J., in *Cunningham* and was probably intended to be so by Lord Diplock; but as we shall see later, even this is not entirely straightforward. Under the second test the prosecution will succeed if it can establish that the accused created an obvious risk of damage or destruction and continued with his activity not having given any thought to the possibility of there being any such risk. The main point to understand in this test of recklessness is that we are no longer concerned to establish that the accused has appreciated the risks of his conduct. It is sufficient that they are obvious risks. In *Lawrence* (1982) which was decided on the same day as *Caldwell*, the phrase "obvious risk" became "obvious and serious risk." It is clear that the words "obvious and serious" qualify the "risk" and not the "destruction or damage", the risk of which has been caused by the defendant. The word "serious" is meant to indicate that the risk must be one which has more than an outside chance of occurring, while the word "obvious" means that the risk is one which should be obvious to a reasonable person.

This direction for juries, handed down by Lord Diplock in the middle of a speech, has been treated subsequently by trial court judges as if it were a carefully drafted piece of legislation. Unfortunately the direction has caused great disquiet among the judges, many of whom have tried to give the jurors long explanations of what the direction means—often with disastrous results. Others have simply left the passage to the jury with no real conviction that the members of the jury would understand what they were being required to find.

One of the reasons given by Lord Diplock for the change was, that he did not think jurors would be able to distinguish *Cunningham* recklessness in its narrow sense from the meaning he was now attributing to it. However, it appears that jurors have been doing just that for well over a century in the context of the Offences Against the Person Act 1861 where *Cunningham* recklessness is required. Furthermore jurors appear to have had no difficulty in convicting defendants on the basis of conscious risk taking despite suggestions by Lord Keith in the recent case of *Reid* (1992) that they would never be sure enough that the defendant actually foresaw the risk.

Reid provided the House of Lords with an opportunity to reconsider the whole question of recklessness as a basis for criminal liability. Reid was charged with the offence of causing death by reckless driving. This offence has now been replaced by the offence of causing death by dangerous driving contrary to s.1 of the Road Traffic Act 1988, but the case is still of relevance for the general observations of their Lordships on the issue of recklessness. The trial judge had directed the jury in line with the direction provided by Lord Diplock for reckless driving in *Lawrence*, which to all intents and purposes is the same as the direction for criminal damage except the obvious and serious risk has to be of causing physical injury to some other person who might happen to be using the road, or of doing substantial damage to property.

The House was clearly not prepared to sweep away all traces of Lord Diplock's definition of recklessness. However, there are indications in the speeches that they were primarily concerned with recklessness in reckless driving and that faced with a case involving criminal damage to property they might reach a different conclusion. For the present, however, Lord Diplock's formulation of the test for recklessness in criminal damage must be taken, at least in substance, to represent the law.

The dangers of relying heavily upon a passage from a judgment in a case can be seen very clearly from the following hypothetical illustration. Imagine that there is a hairpin bend outside a town. So dangerous is the bend, but yet so apparently innocuous to those unfamiliar with it, that the townsfolk have erected large signs "Dangerous Bend: Maximum Speed 15 m.p.h." The signs have been removed by local vandals at a time when D drives round the bend at 40 m.p.h. and collides head on with an oncoming vehicle. Has he recklessly damaged property belonging to the other driver? If he is a stranger to the vicinity then he will presumably have given no thought to the possibility of damaging property belonging to another road user simply by driving at 40 m.p.h. Under Lord Diplock's direction, therefore, everything turns upon whether he has created a serious and obvious risk of damaging or destroying property belonging to another. The answer to this must be that the risk was not an obvious risk because this was why the locals erected such large signs. Would it be different if he knew the area and deliberately took the risk? The answer, you must say, is of course it makes a difference; D is now taking a conscious risk—he is subjectively reckless. However, if you look carefully at Lord Diplock's formulation of the direction to the jury, it would appear that it is in two parts. Part (1) describes the obvious and serious risk which must be created by the defendant's action and this applies to both states of mind outlined in part (2). In other words whether the defendant gives no thought to the risk or deliberately takes the risk, the risk has to be one that is obvious to reasonable people, and we have already said the risk in this case was not an obvious one.

Lord Goff said that Lord Diplock cannot have intended Part (1) to apply to the advertent recklessness part of part (2) and the application of part (1) to both parts of part (2) was almost certainly due to a desire to keep the direction as brief as possible. In reality it was almost certainly a slip of the tongue by Lord Diplock. Lord Goff suggested a reformulation of the direction for future trial judges, and although this does not have the express support of a majority of their lordships in *Reid*, it is suggested that it is a distinct improvement.

Reformulated in terms of criminal damage it can be expressed as follows: (i) he was in fact acting in such a manner as to create a serious risk of damaging or destroying property; and (ii) either (a) he has recognised that there was some risk of that kind (*i.e.* risk of damaging or destroying property) involved, but nevertheless went on to take it; or (b) that, despite the fact he was acting in such a manner, he did not even address his mind to the possibility of there being any such risk, and the risk was in fact obvious.

It is not altogether clear from *Caldwell* to whom the risks must be obvious. On the one hand it could mean that the risks would have been obvious to the accused had he only stopped to think; on the other hand it could mean that the risks must have been obvious to reasonable people. Could this ever be a meaningful distinction? Admittedly there will be few cases in which the risks which would be obvious to reasonable people would not also be obvious to the accused given a moment's thought. In *Elliott v. C.* (1983), however, a young 14-year old girl had spent the evening with a friend and, being unable to stay the night with the friend, had stayed out of doors. During the night she entered a shed and found a bottle of white spirit and some matches. She poured the spirit on the floor of the shed and set fire to it. According to her story she thought it might ignite, but had no idea that it would get out of control and destroy the whole shed. The magistrates took the view that in all the circumstances including the fact that she was somewhat backward, the risk of destruction of the shed was not one which was obvious to her and therefore she did not fall within the meaning of recklessness given by Lord Diplock. On appeal against her acquittal the Divisional Court took the view that the risk had only to be obvious to a reasonably prudent person. It did not have to be a risk which would have been obvious to the defendant had she given any thought to it. However harsh this may seem to be it must be taken as representing the current position.

A further attempt to mitigate the severity of the rule was made by the defence in *Stephen Malcolm R.* (1984) (*Casebook*, p. 142). It was conceded that it was now well established that the jury should not be invited to consider whether the risk was obvious to the particular defendant. However, defence counsel suggested that it would be correct to ask whether the risk would be obvious to a person of the defendant's age with such characteristics of the defendant as affect his ability to appreciate the risk. The Court of Appeal, again reluctantly, held that this was not the approach envisaged by Lord

Diplock. It is clear, therefore, that the prosecution merely have to show that the risk would have been obvious to the reasonable man. In *Reid* Lord Goff discusses the case of a person who might have driven dangerously (*i.e.* in a way which created a serious and obvious risk of physical injury to other road users or substantial damage to property) yet not be guilty of reckless driving because while he was driving he was affected by illness or shock which impaired his capacity to address his mind to the possibility of the risk. How can this be distinguished from the harsh approach adopted by the Divisional Court in both *Elliot v. C.* and *Malcolm R.*

In *Miller* (1983) (above and *Casebook*, p. 139) Lord Diplock said that where recklessness was being used as the basis for liability in a case in which the accused was being charged for his failure to avert a danger he had unwittingly created, he thought that the jury should be directed that the accused was liable "if, when he does become aware that the events in question have happened as a result of his own act, he does not try to prevent or reduce the risk of damage by his own efforts or if necessary by sending for help . . . and the reason why he does not is either because he has not given any thought to the possibility of there being any such risk or because, having recognised that there was some risk involved, he has decided not to try to prevent or reduce it." This is a complex direction. It seems to be saying that the prosecution must prove, at least, that the accused had become aware of the event which had occurred because of his own, albeit unwitting, action. It is not necessary that he realises that he must take action to prevent further harm, merely that there was a risk of damage or further damage happening if nothing was done and that he either gave no thought to this or deliberately decided to do nothing about it. Thus on the facts in *Miller* once he perceived that his cigarette had set fire to this bedding the prosecution simply had to prove that his conduct had created an obvious risk of damage to property which needed attention and that his failure to (for example) call the fire brigade was due either to the fact that he realised that without attention the fire would get worse and deliberately decided to do nothing about it, or that he gave no thought to whether the fire needed attention.

Cunningham or Caldwell Recklessness

Until the decision of the House of Lords in *Caldwell* it was fairly safe to say that the requirement of *mens rea* for most crimes was satisfied if the prosecution could establish intention (or knowledge) or *Cunningham* recklessness in relation to each aspect of the *actus reus*. We must now consider what impact the decision of the House of Lords in *Caldwell* has had upon this proposition. Since *Caldwell* extends rather than restricts liability, it follows that the above proposition remains true. What has happened is that in some cases the prosecution will succeed by establishing something less than *Cunningham* recklessness.

In *Seymour* (1983) Lord Roskill said that the *Caldwell* test should be used wherever recklessness suffices as a basis for liability. How far have the courts accepted this?

1. *Criminal Damage*. Since *Caldwell* is a decision on criminal damage and has recently received the backing of the House of Lords in *Reid*, it is fairly safe to say that recklessness in the Criminal Damage Act 1971 should be given the wider *Caldwell* meaning.

2. *Reckless driving*. This crime no longer exists.

3. *Obtaining Property by Deception* contrary to s.15 Theft Act 1968. In s.15(4) deception is defined as any deception whether deliberate or reckless. Although this would appear, on the face of it, to be the use of the word 'reckless' in a modern statute and therefore likely to be subject to the *Caldwell* definition, this is not the case. The offence can only be committed if the defendant is proved to be dishonest and this must require that the maker of the statement at least took a conscious risk that what he was saying was not true. He can hardly be dishonest if it never occurs to him that the statement may be untrue.

4. *Rape*. Possibly the most contentious area has been in relation to the offence of rape. In s.1(1) of the Sexual Offences (Amendment) Act 1976 the *mens rea* of rape is stated to be that at the time when the accused had intercourse with the woman against her will he either knew that she did not consent or was reckless as to whether she consented to it. This section was passed with the express purpose of giving statutory effect to the decision of the House of Lords in *Morgan* (see below, p. 230) where it was held that a man was not guilty of rape if he honestly but unreasonably believed that the woman was consenting. However, in *Pigg* (1983) the Court of Appeal held *obiter*, that the extended definition of recklessness should apply to the offence of rape. In other words the prosecution would succeed if it could establish that the defendant had given no thought to the obvious and serious risk that the woman was not consenting. Later cases, in particular *Satnam and Kewal* (1984) held that a direction in such terms was more likely to confuse a jury. A man should

not be convicted of reckless rape unless his attitude towards the woman was one of "couldn't care less whether or not she is consenting". Since you cannot "care less" about something you have not thought about, this ruling means that the extended form of *recklessness* does not operate in rape. The jury must be satisfied that the accused deliberately took the risk that the woman was not consenting. This approach, it is submitted, is far more in keeping with the spirit of *Morgan* and the Sexual Offences (Amendment) Act 1976 which is based upon that case.

5. *Offences against the Person Act 1861*. The word reckless does not appear in the offences in this Act; the word used is malice which, as we have seen, has been interpreted to mean either intention or conscious risk-taking. The major offences involved are those under s.18 (unlawfully and maliciously wounding or causing grievous bodily harm with intent) and s.20 (unlawfully and maliciously wounding or inflicting grievous bodily harm). It is clear that the definition of maliciously in *Cunningham* has not been affected by the decision in *Caldwell* and that *Caldwell* has no role to play in the interpretation of the 1861 Act. This was, in fact, made clear by Lord Diplock in *Caldwell* itself and has subsequently been reaffirmed by the House of Lords in *Savage and Parmenter* (1991). However, as we shall see later, a rather strange gloss was put upon its interpretation in relation to s.20 by Diplock L.J. in *Mowatt* (1968) (see below, p. 377).

6. *Assault and Assault Occasioning Bodily Harm*. Although the word assault appears in the 1861 Act it receives no statutory definition there. It has been defined at Common Law to require *Cunningham* recklessness and this was approved by the Court of Appeal in *Venna* (1976). However, following *Caldwell* the Divisional Court in *D.P.P. v. K.* (1990) held that *Caldwell* reckless sufficed. The House of Lords in *Savage and Parmenter* re-affirmed the requirement of *Cunningham* recklessness in these offences and so the position seems fairly settled.

7. *Manslaughter*. Two clear forms of manslaughter evolved at common law—constructive and gross negligence manlaughter. In *Seymour* (1983) and *Kong Cheuk Kwan* (1985) the House of Lords and Privy Council respectively held that judges should no longer use gross negligence as the *mens rea* for manslaughter, but should instead use Caldwell recklessness. Suffice it to say that in *Adomako* (1995) the House of Lords has reinstated gross negligence. *Caldwell*, therefore, has no part to play in manslaughter (see below, p. 362).

8. *Other offences*. There may be other offences where the *mens rea* is satisfied by proof of *Caldwell* recklessness, but it is

now clear that its influence is declining and is today largely restricted to criminal damage.

Conclusion

It is a pretty daft state of affairs when the courts get themselves into a position where juries may have to be told that the same word must to be given two different meanings. If, for example, D pushes a beer glass into C's face, thereby breaking C's glasses and cutting his face, D may be charged with both criminal damage and unlawful wounding. The first is satisfied by *Caldwell* recklessness and the second only by *Cunningham* recklessness. A juror could be forgiven for thinking that the law was an ass. Eventually this mess will have to be sorted out by legislation, but this will not be easy.

Following the work of a Committee under the Chairmanship of Professor Sir John Smith, the Law Commission has recently published a Draft Criminal Code for England and Wales [Law Comm. No. 177; April 1989]. Under such a Code, the mental states would be defined, and future legislation would be construed in accordance with these definitions. It is quite certain that conscious and unconscious risk taking will have to be included in such a code. A major problem, however, will be finding names for these states of mind which will not cause problems for lay juries. It is possible that Parliament may decide that "reckless" should cover a state of mind in which the accused deliberately takes an unjustified risk (as in *Cunningham*), but doubts must remain as to whether this would be wise. The word "reckless" to most laymen probably connotes a high degree of carelessness; it probably does not signify that the person so described had thought about the possible consequences of his actions. If this is correct then the use of the word "reckless" to mean conscious risk taking would be unsafe in jury trials because the jury, in the sanctuary of the jury room, would probably soon forget that they had been instructed that in criminal liability the word had a different meaning from that in every day usage. Having said that, it is not easy to think of a word which does signify conscious risk taking.

Whatever the eventual outcome of the present debate, recklessness will, in the foreseeable future, continue to be risk-taking (either conscious or unconscious), and we should finally note that the risk must be a risk you are not justified in taking. Whether or not the risk is one you are justified in taking will depend upon how the court measures the social utility of your actions. Many doctors operate knowing that the patient might die as a result of the operation. They are therefore taking a conscious risk of killing the patient. But in nearly every case the risk is a justifiable risk, and thus if the patient dies the doctor will not face a charge of manslaughter. On the other hand, if X drives his car down the High Street at 90 m.p.h. in order to evade police capture he risks killing pedestrians and this risk is not one he is justified in taking, even if the risk is very slight, since there is no social utility in his action. Nor would it be a justifiable risk for the driver of an ambulance to risk killing pedestrians in order to get his patient to hospital quickly.

(iii) *The relationship between recklessness and negligence*

We have seen that under the wider definition of recklessness in *Caldwell*, the accused can be held to be reckless not only if he deliberately takes an unjustifiable risk (that is, *Cunningham* recklessness), but also if he fails to give any thought to an obvious risk which he has created. Negligence is often described as failing to foresee that which a reasonable man would foresee. Is there any real difference between the concept of negligence and the second limb of the *Caldwell* test for recklessness; it would, after all, be strange if we were using two names for the same concept?

At one time it looked as if *Caldwell* recklessness would become the general test for recklessness, but as we have just seen it now seems to be confined almost to criminal damage. In those circumstances we have probably already devoted too much attention to it. It is probably safe to say that it is barely distinguishable from gross negligence which is the basis for one form of manslaughter (see below, p. 362). However, there may be a slight difference. It would appear that D will be liable if he consciously takes the risk of causing damage or if he gives no thought to the serious and obvious risk of damage which his activity has created. Where, however, he gives thought to the risk but decides that there is not a risk, he cannot be said to have given no thought to it, nor can he be said consciously to have taken the risk. If this conclusion that there is no risk is made in a grossly negligent fashion, he could be convicted of a crime for which gross negligence is the *mens rea*. In *Reid* (above, p. 215) Lord Goff recognised what has become known as the *Caldwell* loophole, but said that it would not be very often that a jury would believe someone who tried to say that he had given thought to the risk but had concluded that there was none.

Blameless Inadvertence

On principle, it might be thought, a man who causes harm inadvertently and without a scintilla of fault on his part ought not to be convicted of a crime. Thus A should not be guilty of homicide when in driving his car with every care he causes the death of a pedestrian who suddenly steps into the path of his car. Nor should B be guilty of receiving goods which are, in fact, stolen, which he buys in good faith from a reputable dealer. Nor should C be guilty of abducting a girl under 16 if he reasonably believes that she is 18; nor D guilty of selling unsound meat if he has employed a qualified analyst who certifies the meat to be sound. In all these situations the accused would lack *mens rea*, at least as we have defined it, in that he does not intentionally, recklessly nor negligently bring about the elements which constitute the crime.

In reality the position is not quite so straightforward. In the illustrations given A would not be guilty of unlawful homicide; B would not be guilty of receiving stolen goods; but C can be convicted of abduction and D of selling unsound meat. On the face of it this is very unfair to C and D and so some explanation is called for.

What has happened is that as to the quality of the meat and the age of the girl the law has dispensed with the need for *mens rea* and liability on these elements of the crime is said to be strict (or sometimes absolute). These crimes are therefore known as crimes of strict (or absolute) liability. The accused is blamelessly inadvertent as to the quality of the meat or the age of the girl, but he is nonetheless convicted. We shall return to these crimes in the next chapter.

3. Actus Reus and Mens Rea: How do They Relate to Each Other?

Where *mens rea* is required the prosecution must establish that the *actus reus* and the *mens rea* were concurrent. Suppose that the accused intended to shoot X on Friday afternoon, but, for some unforeseen reason, failed to do so, and then on Saturday morning ran over and killed X completely accidentally without realising whom he had hit. Should we allow the prosecution to say that he had the necessary *mens rea* on Friday and performed the *actus reus* on Saturday morning and thus he should be convicted of murder? Clearly not. The prosecution must show that the accused perpetrated the *actus reus* and at that time possessed the necessary mental state. The courts have allowed a certain degree of flexibility, though not sufficient to cover the above case. In *Fagan* (1969) the accused accidentally drove his car onto a policeman's foot and when asked to remove his car from the foot refused to do so immediately. The objection to any charge involving an assault on the policeman is that in this case the *actus reus* would consist of the infliction of unlawful personal violence by Fagan upon the policeman, and the *mens rea* would be that the accused intentionally or recklessly applied force to the person of another (see below, p. 370). Now it is clear that unlawful personal violence was inflicted by Fagan upon the policeman, but at the time when he drove onto the foot he neither intended to do so nor did he realise that there was any risk of so doing. When he realised what he had done and decided to get some fun out of it, it could be argued that the act of inflicting violence was already over. However the court took a common sense view of the situation and resolved that an assault was a continuing offence, in this case beginning when he drove onto the policeman's foot and continuing up to the time when he drove off, and that if *mens rea* was proved to exist at any time while the unlawful force was being applied, the prosecution had made out its case. (Could the courts apply the *Miller* (above, p. 197) approach to this situation. See also *Kaitamaki v. R.* (1985) and *Att.-Gen. for Northern Ireland v. Gallagher*, below, p. 301).

A more extreme example is provided by those cases where the accused has attacked another with the appropriate *mens rea* for murder but has failed to kill the victim and has then disposed of the "body," the act of disposal in the end killing the victim. In *Thabo Meli v. R.* (1954) the accuseds had attempted to kill the deceased by beating him over the head. They had then rolled his "body" over a cliff in an attempt to make it look as if he had died from accidentally falling over a cliff. Medical evidence, however, revealed that he had in fact died from exposure and not from the beating. The problem facing the court was the fact that at the time when the accused possessed the necessary malice aforethought for murder they failed to achieve their objective and when they rolled the body down the cliff they believed that the victim was already dead. However the court held that it was impossible to divide up what was really one series of acts in this way. The court seemed to base its decision upon the idea that there was an antecedent plan and that the victim died as a result of that plan, albeit in a way not anticipated by the accused.

In *Church* (1966) the Court of Appeal extended the reasoning to a case of manslaughter where there was no antecedent plan, and this approach has recently been approved by the Court of Appeal in *Le Brun* (1991). In that case the defendant and his wife had had a serious argument late one night as they were walking to their home. He hit her, thereby rendering her unconscious. In an attempt to drag her out of sight, he dropped her and she suffered a fractured skull from which she later died. It was clear that there was no antecedent plan, nor was there any intention to dispose of a corpse. The Court of Appeal dealt with the case on the basis of the need to link the *mens rea* which existed at the time of the initial assault with the later attempt to conceal the crime or to drag her back into their house against her will. The Court held that where the subsequent acts which caused the death arise out of the accused trying to conceal his initial offence, there is no need for the act which causes death and the requisite *mens rea* to coincide in point of time. Under this approach it would seem that the second injury could be the sole cause of death so long as it occurs during the transaction which commences with the first unlawful blow and continues so long as he is trying to conceal his crime or, in this case force his wife back into their house against her will. The position might therefore be different if the skull fracture had occurred while he was trying to carry her somewhere for proper medical treatment.

Lord Lane C.J. said that the proposition could also be framed in terms of causation. It could not be said that the actions of the accused in dragging the victim away with the intention of evading liability broke the chain of causation which linked the initial blow with the death. Under this view, however, the initial blow must be at least a cause of the death and the skull fracture is a second cause of the death—it is, of course possible for a result to have more than one legal cause. On this approach, since the first assault was perpetrated with *mens rea*, the accused would be liable to be convicted of constructive manslaughter (see below, p. 359) unless it could be held that the skull fracture happened in such a way as to break the chain of causation. The Court of Appeal clearly holds that nothing Le Brun did in the actual case could be said to have broken the chain. It is difficult to see why, on this approach, the dropping of the victim, whether by a stranger or by Le Brun himself, even in an attempt to get the wife to hospital, should be seen as so unforeseeable as to break the chain of causation.

Lord Lane said that he meant to state the law only as it applied to manslaughter, but there seems to be no logical reason why it should not also apply to murder.

It was clear in *Thabo Meli* and *Le Brun* that the victim had been killed as a result of the second of the two acts. In *Attorney-General's Reference (No. 4 of 1980)* (1981) the Court of Appeal was faced with a variant on the problem. There the accused had slapped his girlfriend on the face and this had caused her to fall down the stairs, banging her head. He then put a rope around her neck and dragged her up the stairs, placed her in the bath and then drained off all her blood. Finally he sawed up her body into disposable pieces. The victim died either from the fall, or due to being strangled, or due to having her throat cut; it was not, however, proved exactly how she died as very little of her body was found. The Court of Appeal held that the jury would have been entitled to convict the defendant of manslaughter if they were satisfied that at the time he did each of the acts which could have been responsible for the woman's death, he had the necessary *mens rea* for manslaughter. This is not an application of the *Thabo Meli* principle; that would only be necessary if, for example, the jury were satisfied that he had the necessary *mens rea* for manslaughter only when he pushed her down the stairs. (See also *Att.-Gen. for Northern Ireland v. Gallagher* (1963), below, p. 301).

You should not lose sight of the fact that in the vast majority of the cases the prosecution will establish that the accused caused the *actus reus* with the necessary *mens rea*. The approach suggested in *Le Brun* may be of use when the *actus reus* and *mens rea* are separated in time, but where the series of events can be seen as one transaction.

4. Transferred Malice

Let us imagine a situation in which X intends to kill Y and to this end shoots at him. The bullet misses Y but hits and kills Z. What view should the law take of this? On the one hand you might argue that he only attempted to kill Y and that unless you could find the necessary *mens rea* for a charge in relation to Z (for example that he was reckless or grossly negligent as to the fact that his shot might kill others) there should be no conviction. On the other hand in deliberately trying to kill one man he has unlawfully caused the death of another and should therefore be treated as if he had killed Y. In fact the law adopts the second approach. It is said that the malice X bears towards Y is transferred to Z. X can therefore be convicted of murdering Z even though he only intended to kill Y and was possibly even unaware of Z's presence (see *Latimer* (1886) *Casebook*, p. 64). But suppose that the bullet had missed Y and had struck, not Z, but Z's pet labrador, killing it. Clearly the killing of a dog does not constitute any offence against the person, though it might constitute an offence of criminal damage to Z's property. Can we still join X's *mens rea* against Y to the *actus reus* of destroying Z's property? In *Pembliton* (1874) in the course of a fight outside a public house the accused picked up a stone and threw it at someone, but succeeded only in breaking a window behind his intended victim. He was charged with (the then equivalent of) the offence of criminal damage to property, but his conviction was quashed on the ground that you cannot join the *mens rea* of an offence against the person with the *actus reus* of an offence against property. Does this mean that Pembliton and X in our hypothetical example must go free? In our hypothetical example it is quite probable that you would be able to bring a successful charge against X for attempting to murder Y. Alternatively you might be able to charge X with criminal damage to Z's dog, but on the basis that he recklessly caused damage to the dog and not on the basis that he intended to kill a human being. (A recent example of an extreme form of transferred malice can be found in Att.-Gen.'s reference (No. 3 of 1994) ((1996) see below p. 342). The case also would support the view that if X fires a shot at B and it passes through B and into C killing both B and C, X is liable for two murders.)

5. Mistake: Its Effects on Mens Rea

In some respects the question of mistake ought to be left to the general chapter on defences to criminal charges. On the other hand the defence of mistake is so closely bound up with the *mens rea* of the crime in question, that discussion of it will be included in this chapter. A lot of confusion is caused in relation to the defence of mistake by rather ill-defined use of terminology. The basic rule is, it is suggested, fairly simple. If the accused makes a mistake, the effect of which is to deprive him of the necessary *mens rea* required for that crime, then the mistake is capable of affording him a defence. From this it follows that if the accused makes a mistake as to an issue for which no *mens rea* is required then the mistake will not afford him a defence. Thus, for example, we have seen that the offence of abducting unmarried girls under the age of 16 (Sexual Offences Act 1956, s.20) does not require that the prosecution prove that the accused knew, or was indifferent as to the fact, that the girl was under 16. Thus a mistaken belief, however reasonably held, that the girl was 17 would afford no defence. On the other hand a mistake by a man charged with murder to the effect that he thought he was shooting at an escaped bear would mean that the prosecution would not be able to prove that he intended to kill a human being. We shall see later that complications are caused by the fact that the courts do not seem to be able to make up their minds as to whether the mistake must be an honest mistake or an honest and reasonable mistake (see below, p. 229). Another type of mistake often made is the fact that the accused did not know that what he was doing was a criminal offence. For example, in one case the accused told the court that buggery was not an offence in his country and that as a result he was unaware that it was in this (*Esop* (1836); but see now Sexual Offences Act 1967, s.1). Clearly the accused made a mistake, but it was not a mistake that would affect the necessary *mens rea* of the offence. The prosecution merely have to establish that the accused had sexual connection with the other man and that was what he intended to do. It is not part of the prosecution's case to establish that the accused knew that buggery was an offence. It is often put in the form that the prosecution must prove that the accused was aware of the facts which made the action criminal, but not that he knew that it was criminal. For example in the crime of handling stolen property the prosecution would have to prove that the accused dishonestly received the goods knowing or believing that they were stolen. The prosecution do not have to prove that the accused knew that the handling of stolen goods is a criminal offence. However, if the dependant for some reason, was unaware that receiving stolen property was a crime, the jury might conclude he had not acted dishonestly and therefore the prosecution would fail to establish the necessary *mens rea*. Thus ignorance of the law can occasionally negative *mens rea* (see below).

If, then, it is appreciated that the mistake is one which affects the *mens rea* of the accused, then it will be possible to appreciate that the mistake may take several forms. In the first place it may be one that clearly relates only to factual issues. For example in *Rose* (1884) the accused was charged with the murder of his father. He said he had thought that his father was about to kill his mother and that was why he had killed him. The court found that although his father was not intending to kill the accused's mother, the accused's belief was an honest one (and indeed a reasonable one). If the facts had been as the accused believed them to be he would have had a good defence to the killing (see now Criminal Law Act 1967, s.3, below, p. 304). This was purely a mistake of fact; there was no mistake as to any legal issue whatsoever. On the other hand the accused's mistake might refer to some legal concept which relates to the *actus reus* of the crime. For example where the accused is charged with bigamy (Offences Against the Person Act 1861, s.57) the prosecution must prove that, being married, he married another. It would be a defence for the accused to show that he believed that his first wife was dead, and this would be a mistake of fact. On the other hand he might say that he had been through certain procedures at a solicitor's office and that he believed that as a result his marriage had been dissolved or annulled. Such a belief may be a defence. The mistake, in one sense, is a mistake of fact, namely that he believed that he was a single person. On the other hand it is a mistake as to the effect of certain legal processes and to that extent is a mistake of law. Whichever view is taken the mistake means that the accused did not intend, being a married person, to marry another; his intention was, as a single person, to marry. To reiterate a point made earlier, a mistake that bigamy was not a criminal offence would be no defence whatsoever. Both these mistakes are in a sense mistakes of law; the difference being that one affects the *mens rea* that has to be proved by the prosecution, the other does not. It is for this reason that it is suggested the second type of mistake, that is "I did not realise bigamy was a crime," be called ignorance of the law.

Once it is appreciated that the effect of mistake is to negative *mens rea*, the answer to the question "does it have to be a reasonable mistake, or does it suffice that it was honestly believed?" should be straight forward. We shall see later (below, p. 346) that in murder the prosecution must prove that the accused intended to kill or seriously harm a human being. If the accused *honestly* believed that he was shooting at a bear, then the prosecution will be unable to establish the necessary *mens rea*. The same would be true if *Cunningham recklessness* is required. An assault requires that the prosecutor prove the accused intended to place the victim in fear of immediate harm or foresaw that his conduct would have this effect. An *honestly* held belief that the other person will not be put in fear is therefore totally inconsistent with the necessary *mens rea*. It follows that an honest but totally unreasonable mistake should suffice. On the other hand if we take the crime of driving without due care and attention where the prosecution need show only that the accused's driving did not reach the standard of a reasonable driver, then it will not avail him to say that he honestly thought that the road was clear. If the prosecution can show that reasonable motorists would not have made the mistake, then they have made out their case. Thus where the crime is one of negligence, it follows that a reasonable mistake is required. Unfortunately the courts have not, until recently, followed this simple approach. Problems of proof have become entangled with questions of substantive liability. If we return to the man who said he thought that he was shooting at a bear; how does the prosecution prove that he intended to shoot a human being? On what basis can a jury accept that he honestly thought that he was shooting at a bear? In practice, in the jury room, the jurors will inevitably ask themselves whether they, as reasonable persons, could have made such a mistake. If the answer is no, then they will probably come to the conclusion that the accused did not, in fact, make such a mistake. There is nothing wrong in this type of reasoning. Unfortunately, however, judges in directing juries seem to have strayed into telling them that the mistake must be one which the accused honestly and reasonably held. So what was a perfectly acceptable method of assessing whether or not a mistake was honestly held, becomes an essential part of the defence. Over the years a very uneven pattern emerged; in some cases the judge would tell the jury that the mistake must be one which a reasonable person could have made; in others he would tell them that it sufficed that the accused honestly made such a mistake. Attempts were made by writers to try to find some logical analysis of the decisions, but with little success.

In *D.P.P. v. Morgan* (1976) (*Casebook*, p. 157) the House of Lords appears to have laid the basis for a more realistic approach. In that case Morgan returned home with several friends after an evening's drinking. He invited them to have sexual intercourse with his wife, saying that they should not be put off by any protests she might make as these would only be her way of increasing her sexual pleasure. The facts show that the wife put up tremendous resistance, but was eventually overcome by the men who then had intercourse with her. They were charged with raping her, but pleaded that they believed that she was consenting. The trial judge directed the jury that the accused men would have a defence if they honestly believed that she was consenting to intercourse and furthermore that there were reasonable grounds for such a belief. Not surprisingly the jury convicted the accused and their appeals eventually reached the House of Lords. Their Lordships held that the trial judge should have directed the jury that if the men honestly but unreasonably believed that the wife was consenting to intercourse, then they were not guilty of rape. However, the appeal was dismissed by application of the proviso; in other words their Lordships took the view that on the evidence before the court the jury would have reached the same conclusion even if they had been properly directed. At that time rape was an offence covered only by section 1 of the Sexual Offences Act 1956 which merely provided that "it shall be an offence for a man to rape a woman." The House said that this was clearly an offence requiring *mens rea*. Lord Hailsham said "the prohibited act in rape is non-consensual sexual intercourse, and ... the guilty state of mind is an intention to commit it." It is thus totally contradictory to tell the jury that the prosecution must prove that the accused intended to have intercourse with a woman who he knows or believes is not consenting, while at the same time directing them that if he honestly believed that she was consenting it would still not be a defence unless a reasonable man would have so believed.

The House considered the line of authority relating to bigamy. Statute provides that it is an offence for a person "being married to marry." It is a defence for the accused to show that at the time of the second marriage he believed that, in fact, he was a single person. However the courts have traditionally held that this must be a belief held on reasonable grounds. Were these cases, therefore in conflict with the decision the House had reached in rape cases? Their Lordships held that the bigamy cases were distinguishable. Lord Cross said "If the words defining an offence provide either expressly or impliedly that a man is not to be guilty of it if he believes something to be true, then he cannot be found guilty if the jury think that he may have believed it to be true, however inadequate were his reasons for doing so. But, if the definition of the offence is on the face of it "absolute" (this means the offence requires no *mens rea*—see above, p. 223) and the defendant is seeking to escape his prima facie liability by a defence of mistaken belief, I can see no hardship to him in requiring the mistake—if it is to afford him a defence—to be based on reasonable grounds." Rape, held Lord Cross, comes into the first category and bigamy into the second. In other words he is saying that in law bigamy is a crime requiring only that the prosecution proves that the accused deliberately contracted the second marriage and that a reasonable person would have realised that an earlier marriage was still subsisting. Negligence suffices on this aspect of the *actus reus* and negligence can only be displaced by a reasonable mistake.

The actual decision in *Morgan* led to a great public outcry; the House of Lords, it was said, had published a rapist's charter. A committee under Mrs. Justice Heilbron was established and on the basis of its report the Sexual Offences (Amendment) Act 1976 was passed, which, in effect, gave statutory effect to *Morgan*. By section 1 it provided:

> 1.—(1) For the purposes of section 1 of the Sexual Offences Act 1956 (which relates to rape) a man commits rape if—
> (a)   he has unlawful sexual intercourse with a woman who at the time of the intercourse does not consent to it; and
> (b)   at that time he knows that she does not consent to the intercourse or he is reckless as to whether she consents to it;
> and references to rape in other enactments (including the following provisions of this Act) shall be construed accordingly.

The use of the word "reckless" is perhaps unfortunate in the light of recent developments, but it seems that it will now receive its older *Cunningham* meaning and the section will be interpreted in a way to preserve the decision in *Morgan*.

One area that has caused some confusion since the decision in *Morgan* relates to the issue of self-defence. In crimes against the person the *actus reus* will require that the accused's act was unlawful; where, for example, the jury considers that the accused was merely using reasonable force to defend himself against attack, the prosecution will not be able to make out this element of unlawfulness. Assault, for example, can be said to be the unlawful touching of another (see further, p. 370 below). In the context of assault the prosecutor must prove that there was no consent by the victim of the touching, and that it was not done for the purpose of preventing crime or in self-defence. In *Albert v. Lavin* (1982) the Divisional Court held that whereas it would suffice that the accused honestly, but unreasonably, believed that the victim had consented to the touching, a belief that the accused had a right to use reasonable force in the circumstances in self-defence had to be both honest and reasonable. Eventually in *Gladstone Williams* (1984) the Court of Appeal held that this distinction was untenable. W had witnessed what he considered to be a man, M, beating up a coloured youth. In fact M was trying to arrest the black youth for the mugging of an old lady. M told W, falsely, that he was a police officer effecting an arrest. He could not produce his warrant card and W thereupon tried to protect the black youth. In the course of the struggle M received several injuries. W was charged with an assault and pleaded that he believed that he was acting properly to protect a youth from a beating. The Recorder at the trial directed the jury that the appellant would have a defence only if he honestly and reasonably believed that his intervention and action was needed to save the youth from an unlawful beating. The Court of Appeal held that the mental element necessary to establish guilt was an intention to apply unlawful force to the victim. Force may be applied lawfully where the victim consents, where the defendant is acting in self-defence and where the defendant is using reasonable force either to prevent the commission of a crime or to assist in a lawful arrest. It is for the prosecution to prove that the accused intended to apply the force unlawfully. If the defendant mistakenly believes that the victim is consenting or that it is necessary to defend himself or that a crime is being committed which he intends to prevent, the prosecution have not made out the charge. It is neither here nor there whether the mistaken belief was formed on reasonable grounds except insofar as it helps the jury to decide whether or not the belief was actually formed. The Court of Appeal also stressed that in these cases trial judges must be very careful that they direct the jury properly on the burden of proof. It is very easy to leave the jury with the impression that it is up to the accused to prove that he honestly believed that, *e.g.* the victim was consenting or that he needed to defend himself. The judge must make it quite clear that it is for the prosecution to prove that the defendant did not hold such a belief.

This approach has been recently confirmed by the Privy Council in *Beckford v. R.* (1987); (*Casebook*, p. 162). There, in a murder case, Lord Griffiths gave approval to a model direction of self-defence prepared by the Judicial Studies

Board and which is presently widely used by trial judges. The direction contains the following guidance.

> "Whether the plea is self defence or defence of another, if the defendant may have been labouring under a mistake as to the facts, he must be judged according to his mistaken view of the facts: that is so whether the mistake was, on an objective view, a reasonable mistake or not."

Lord Griffiths commented that some people were concerned that the abandonment of the objective approach (*i.e.* reasonable belief) would result in the success of too many spurious self-defence claims. This simply had not happened. If a jury feels that the belief is unreasonable, they may well conclude that the defendant did not in fact hold that belief. (See *Cogan and Leak* (1976) and *Scarlett* (1993) (below, p. 309); but see also *O'Grady* (1987) below, p. 297, where the mistake was induced by voluntary intoxication.)

6. Proof of Mens Rea

One of the problems facing the prosecution is how to prove that the accused had the *mens rea* required for the offence. The answer is that in most cases this has to be supplied by circumstantial evidence; in other words the prosecution will introduce evidence of what has been observed and the jury will be invited to infer the necessary *mens rea* from this. Suppose X is charged with the murder of Y and the prosecution can produce a witness who saw X stick the knife into Y's back. They can also produce evidence which shows that X had a very good reason for wanting Y dead. From this evidence the jury may well be able to draw the conclusion that X at least intended to cause Y serious harm, and this would suffice as the *mens rea* for murder (see below, p. 309). The sort of reasoning which is often used to reach such a conclusion goes like this. If you stick a knife in someone's back, the natural and probable consequence is that that person will suffer serious injury. It is therefore reasonable to conclude, in the absence of evidence to the contrary, that you intended to cause serious harm. There is nothing wrong in this type of reasoning, but unfortunately it became the practice of judges to direct the jury that if result A was the natural and probable consequence of X's act, the jury were bound to infer that he intended result A. Section 8 of the Criminal Justice Act 1967 was passed to correct this type of direction. It provided

"A court or jury in determining whether a person has committed an offence,

(a) shall not be bound in law to infer that he intended or foresaw a result of his actions by reason only of it being a natural and probable consequence of those actions; but

(b) shall decide whether he did intend or foresee that result by reference to all the evidence drawing such inferences from the evidence as appear proper in the circumstances."

The result of section 8 is that when the definition of a crime requires that the jury have to decide whether or not the defendant intended or foresaw a particular result they may look at all the evidence to see whether the prosecution have established this intention or foresight. They may draw the inference that natural and probable consequences were probably foreseen or intended, but they may not be directed to make this inference (see also discussion of intention above, p. 204; but see also p. 293, below).

Chapter 7

Strict Liability

In the last chapter we noted (see above, p. 206) that on occasion the law imposes liability even though the accused lacks *mens rea* in the strict sense, and that these crimes are called crimes of strict liability. We said that the accused is convicted even though, as to one element at least of the *actus reus*, he is blamelessly inadvertent.

It is worth considering whether it is necessarily unfair to impose criminal liability even though the accused lacks *mens rea* in the strict sense. Let us consider a rather fanciful illustration. In murder the prosecution must establish that the victim died within a year and a day after the last injury inflicted by the accused. Suppose that H poisons W, his wife, using a poison that a brilliant chemist had assured him would take 18 months to take effect. In fact, owing to W's curious metabolism, W dies just inside the year and a day period. Is it to be said that H ought to be acquitted of murder or manslaughter because he did not intend that death or serious bodily harm would occur within a year and a day? On a strict application of the *mens rea* doctrine he must be acquitted of murder. But should we go this far? After all, H does intend to kill—he intends the prohibited act—and is merely inadvertent to a circumstance. Moreover that circumstance has no moral content; it does not alter the fact that H deliberately killed W and there is much to be said for the view that H should take his chances on the death occurring inside or outside the stated period.

Although the above problem might be thought to be far fetched, it was essentially the problem that arose in *Prince* (1875) (*Casebook*, p. 147). William Prince eloped with Annie Phillips, who was aged 13, and was subsequently charged with an offence under section 55 of the Offences Against the Person Act 1861 which provided "Whosoever shall unlawfully take or cause to be taken any unmarried girl, being under the age of sixteen years, out of the possession and against the will of her father or mother or of any person having the lawful care or charge of her, shall be guilty ... " (see now Sexual Offences Act 1956, s.20). The jury concluded that Prince honestly and reasonably believed that Annie was 18-years old but a conviction was directed by the trial judge and that conviction was affirmed by the Court for Crown Cases Reserved. One view that was taken, expressed by Bramwell B., was that Prince did intend to do the prohibited act. He intended to take a girl, not a woman, whom he knew to be in the possession of her parents and further he was aware that he had no lawful authority for the taking. The only factor he was unaware of was the circumstance that she was under 16. Bramwell B. accordingly felt able to hold that Prince had *mens rea*. It is worth noting that when Prince eventually came up for sentencing he was given six months' imprisonment with hard labour; evidently the trial judge was of the opinion that, despite his mistake as to Annie's age, Prince had acted wrongly.

Did Prince get justice? Does not the fact that Prince believed Annie was over 16 take the carpet out from underneath Bramwell B.'s argument? Had Annie been, as Prince supposed she was, 18, Prince would have needed no one's consent—other than Annie's which had been readily given—to take her away. On the other hand Prince knew that her parents would disapprove—why else did he elope with her without telling them? Whether you approve or disapprove of Prince's conviction indicates what you think *mens rea ought* to mean.

It is, however, important to remember that even in crimes of strict liability some mental element will be required. Had Prince believed that Annie was a prostitute and thus not in the care of her parents, he would have been acquitted since in *Hibbert* (1869) the Court for Crown Cases Reserved held that *mens rea* was required on the aspect of the girl being in the control of her parent or guardian. So *Prince* does not decide that no *mens rea* at all is required, only that, in the case of *Prince*, once the prosecution established that he intended to take a girl out of the possession of her parents, then a conviction was possible even though he reasonably believed that she was 18. You may well wonder why such a distinction was drawn between the various elements of the *actus reus* in *Prince*. The answer is probably that these two elements came for discussion at different times and a different mood existed amongst the judges. There can be no logical defence of the distinction.

1. How Can You Identify Crimes of Strict Liability?

It is relatively simple to show how strict liability operates, the difficulty is in being able to identify which crimes will attract strict liability.

With very few exceptions (public nuisance, criminal libel, and contempt of court) crimes of strict liability are statutory offences. It is highly unlikely that we shall see the creation of any new common law crimes of strict liability. In practice we can say that strict liability operates only in respect of statutory crimes. Thus the principles of statutory interpretation operate and the courts are supposed to try to discover the intention of Parliament from the wording of the statute. One principle of statutory interpretation is that in statutes creating criminal offences there is a presumption that *mens rea* will be required even where it is not specifically mentioned. An example of a crime which expressly provides for *mens rea* is section 1 of the Sexual Offences (Amendment) Act 1976 where in the crime of rape it is expressly provided that the accused must either know that the woman was not consenting to sexual intercourse or be at least reckless as to this fact. On the other hand many offences contain no reference at all to the requirement of *mens rea* and here the courts should start from the principle that *mens rea* is required. Thus common assault under section 39 of the Offences Against the Person Act 1861 contains no reference to *mens rea*, but the courts have held that the prosecution must prove that the accused either, intended to cause the victim to apprehend immediate and unlawful violence or that he was reckless as to whether his actions would have this effect.

However this presumption in favour of *mens rea* is rebuttable and we must now examine the factors which are likely to cause its rebuttal.

(1) The Wording of the Act

As with any other statute the court's first duty is to try to ascertain the intention of Parliament, not from any extraneous sources, but from the wording of the Act itself. At present there is no guarantee that any given form of wording will create an offence of strict liability. On the other hand there are one or two discernible patterns. Thus certain words have received fairly consistent interpretations as requiring or dispensing with the need for *mens rea*. We will now have a look at some of these "key" words.

(a) *"Permitting or allowing"*

Where it is an offence to permit or allow another to do a certain act, the prosecution will normally be expected to prove that the accused was aware of the circumstances which made the act unlawful or deliberately avoided finding out. Thus under a statute creating an offence of permitting or allowing another to drive a motor vehicle with defective brakes, the prosecution would have to prove that the accused knew that his vehicle's brakes were defective before he permitted or allowed the other to drive it (see for example, *James & Son Ltd v. Smee* (1955)). You must remember, however, that he does not have to know that it is illegal to permit or allow another to drive a vehicle with defective brakes (see above, p. 228). On the other hand where the statute makes it an offence to drive or use a vehicle with defective brakes the courts have tended to say that the prosecution need not prove that the driver or user knew that the brakes were defective (see for example, *Green v. Burnett* (1955)).

(b) *Cause*

Where statutes create an offence of causing something to happen the courts should, according to the House of Lords in *Alphacell v. Woodward* (1972) adopt a common-sense approach; if reasonable people would say that the accused has caused something to happen then a conviction is appropriate without the need for *mens rea*. Thus in *Wrothwell Ltd v. Yorkshire Water Authority* (1984) it was held that where the accused had poured a toxic chemical down a drain believing, wrongly, that it would find its way into the main sewer when, in fact, it entered a local stream, it was right to say that he had caused a poisonous matter to enter a stream.

In *Southern Water Authority v. Pegrum and Pegrum* (1989) it was held that a defendant could rely on an act of God or an act of a third party as a defence to a strict liability offence. However, the test for the court in such a case would be whether the alleged act of God was so powerful that the conduct of the accused was not a cause at all, but merely part of the surrounding circumstances.

(c) *Possession*

The word possession has caused many problems for the courts over the years. It is the basis of many offences that the accused be *in possession* of a prohibited substance. Since many of the offences involved the possession of prohibited drugs and since these offences were often interpreted as imposing strict liability, the courts from time to time attempted to mitigate the severity that would be caused by strict liability by holding that the word "possession" had a mental as well as physical aspect. For example, would we wish to convict an innocent shopper of being in possession of cannabis when the cannabis had been placed in her shopping bag by a drug supplier who believed that he was just about to be arrested? Is she in possession of the drug? Suppose that just before she left home, and without her knowledge, her husband slipped the keys to the house into her raincoat pocket; is she in possession of these keys while she is walking round the shops? If a pickpocket took the keys out of her pocket, would he not have stolen them from her? Yet is she any more in possession of the keys than the cannabis?

In the realms of possession of drugs the House of Lords in *Warner v. Metropolitan Police Commissioner* (1969), a case under previous legislation but still applicable to the definition of possession, accepted that A would not be in possession of a drug which had been slipped into his pocket or shopping basket without his knowledge. In these types of case we are saying that the prosecution have failed to establish possession. What then of the situation where the accused knows he is in possession of a substance, but is genuinely unaware of the nature of the substance? Suppose A has been given some tablets and told they are aspirin when they are, in fact, heroin. He is clearly in possession of the tablets and this is as far as the mental element in possession goes. Unless the controlling legislation provides that it is an offence knowingly to possess heroin or unless the statute provides a defence of mistake of fact (see, *e.g.* the Misuse of Drugs Act 1971, s.28 below) he is guilty of possessing the prohibited substance. In other words the word "possession" does not involve knowledge of the nature of the thing one possesses.

Does this mean therefore that if you know you possess a substance, but you do not know what it is because it is in a locked container, you are in possession of that substance. Suppose that you believe that it is some photographic equipment, but in fact it is heroin tablets. Can you be said to be in possession of heroin for purposes of section 5 of the Misuse of Drugs Act 1971? The House of Lords took a more lenient view of such container cases. They said that if you were completely mistaken as to the nature but not the quality of the contents, have had no opportunity to examine the contents and do not suspect that there is anything wrong with the contents, then you are not, for the purpose of offences as in section 5, in possession of the contents. The reference to a distinction between nature and quality means that if you believed the contents to be photographic equipment and it was heroin, then this would be a mistake as to the nature of the contents. On the other hand if you thought the package contained aspirin and it turned out to be heroin, then this is a mistake as to quality; you thought it was a drug—and it was, you were merely mistaken as to what sort of drug. Although cases such as *Warner* must now be read subject to the provisions of the Misuse of Drugs Act 1971, *Warner* remains as general authority on the meaning of the word "possesses" in situations where the proscribed goods are in a container. Where, however, there is no container, stricter provisions apply. In *Marriott* (1971) the accused possessed a penknife to the blade of which adhered 0.03 grains of cannabis. On appeal against conviction the court held that the proper direction to a jury in such a case would be that the accused was guilty of possessing cannabis if he knew that there was a substance on the penknife even if he did not know what that substance was. It was not, however, sufficient to prove that he knew he was in possession of the penknife (see also *Searle v. Randolph* (1972)).

These cases dealt with the meaning of the word 'possess." Section 28 of the Misuse of Drugs Act 1971 provided certain defences for those charged with the possession of controlled drugs. For example, section 28(3)(*b*)(i) provides that the defendant shall be acquitted if he proves that he neither believed nor suspected nor had reason to suspect that the substance or product in question was a controlled drug. The Court of Appeal in *McNamara* (1988) appears to have used this provision to find a simpler approach to the container situations which avoids the need to distinguish between differences in kind and quality. The court held that it was for the prosecution to prove that the defendant (i) had control of the container, (ii) knew that he had control of the container and (iii) that the box contained something which was in fact the drug alleged. It was then up to the defendant to bring himself within the provisions of section 28(3)(*b*)(i) by proving that he neither believed nor suspected nor had reason to suspect that the substance or product in question was (any sort of) controlled drug. *Lewis* (1988), however, shows that the word "possession" will continue to cause problems.

(d) *Knowingly*

One would think that the word knowingly could cause few problems and that it would indicate an express requirement for *mens rea*. This is true to the extent that it clearly requires *mens rea* as to the clause it qualifies, but it is not always easy to identify the clause it does qualify. For example in *Hallam* (1957) the accused was charged with knowingly possessing explosives. Does this mean that the accused knows that he is in possession of a substance which is later identified as an explosive even though he thought it was soap powder, or does it mean that he must be both aware that he possesses a substance and that he further knows the substance to be an explosive? In the case cited the court held that the prosecution must prove that the accused knew that the substance was an explosive. Indeed to have held otherwise would have been to render the word "knowingly" superfluous since as we have seen the word "possess" is usually held to require at least the knowledge that the accused has something in his possession. It would have been better had Parliament defined the offence as possession of goods knowing them to be explosives.

In older statutes the words "wilfully" and "maliciously" have been interpreted to require intention or recklessness (see *Cunningham*, above, p. 203).

The word "knowingly" has been used by the courts indirectly to indicate strict liability. In certain offences the word "knowingly" appears in one section but not in the next, or in some but not all subsections of a given section. Where this happens it is tempting to say that this is a clear indication that Parliament must have intended those sections which do not contain the word "knowingly" to impose strict liability. Thus in *Neville v. Mavroghenis* (1984) the accused was the landlord of rented premises and was charged with an offence under section 13(4) of the Housing Act 1961—failure to maintain premises in a proper state of repair. The stipendiary magistrate who tried the case held that since he was unaware of the defects he could not be liable. The prosecutor appealed. The Divisional Court held that section 13(4) could be divided into two limbs. The first limb contained the phrase "knowingly contravenes" and thus clearly required that the prosecution proved that he had knowledge of the defects. The second limb was in the form "without reasonable excuse fails to comply with any regulations." The word "knowingly" did not appear, and thus it was irrelevant that he was unaware of the defects. (See also *Cundy v. Le Coq* (1884) which is to the same effect.) It should, however, be noticed that in *Neville* v. *Mavroghenis* that the words "without reasonable excuse" in the second limb did at least provide the accused with a "no negligence" defence which is a decided improvement on strict liability with no such defence; see below, p. 246). However, you must remember that although the presence of the word "knowingly" in one section and its absence in the next is a pointer in the direction of strict liability it must not be taken to be conclusive. In *Sherras v. De Rutzen* (1895) the accused was charged with selling alcohol to a police constable on duty. The defence submitted that the constable had removed his duty armband and so it was impossible for the accused to know that he was on duty. Against this it was argued that whereas other surrounding provisions of the statute used the word knowingly, section 16(2) of the Licensing Act 1872 did not. The Divisional Court quashed the conviction largely on the basis that without the requirement of knowledge the accused would be defenceless since he would be convicted even if he had asked the constable whether he was on duty and the constable had told him falsely that he was not.

It is important to stress that these sort of "key" words are useful guidelines, but you must not expect complete consistency from the courts.

(2) Crimes and Quasi Crimes

In *Warner v. M.P.C.* (1969) the issue of strict liability received attention for the first time from the House of Lords in a case relating to possession of drugs. The House of Lords gave its approval to the notion of strict liability. In *Sweet v. Parsley* (1970) (*Casebook*, p. 167) four of the same Law Lords appeared to be suggesting a much stronger adherence to the presumption of *mens rea*. The *Sweet* case was not, however, in any sense a denial of strict liability. What their Lordships said was that there were two types of criminal offence: the first were those which could truly be said to be criminal such as murder, rape, theft and assault. These were to be distinguished from those which are not criminal in any real sense, but are acts which in the public interest are prohibited under a penalty. Crimes of this second type have been called regulatory offences, quasi crimes or crimes *mala prohibita*. In other words when Parliament makes regulations to govern the better running of society—such as regulations to ensure that food and drink are sold and served under hygienic conditions or regulations to prevent industry from polluting the environment—then it is common to sanction breaches of such regulations with a penalty, though no one really thinks of the offenders as criminals. The significance of the distinction is that in the former category (true crimes) the presumption in favour of *mens rea* should rarely, if at all, be rebutted, whereas in the second category it is easier to infer that Parliament intended the presumption to be rebutted. Thus whereas in *Sweet v. Parsley* the offence of "being concerned in the management of premises which are used for the purpose of smoking cannabis" was treated as a true crime (*mala in se*) and thus requiring *mens rea*, in *Alphacell Ltd v. Woodward* the House of Lords treated the offence of "causing polluted matter to enter a river" as a regulatory offence and dispensed with the requirement for *mens rea*. The result was that the defendants in *Alphacell*, who had taken great care to ensure that they did not pollute the river, were convicted.

Recently in a case before the Privy Council concerning building regulations in Hong Kong, Lord Scarman found that the law could be summarised thus: "(1) there is a presumption of law that *mens rea* is required before a person can be held guilty of a criminal offence; (2) the presumption is particularly strong where the offence is 'truly criminal' in character; (3) the presumption applies to statutory offences, and can be displaced only if this is clearly or by necessary implication the effect of the statute; (4) the only situation in which the presumption can be displaced is where the statute is concerned with an issue of social concern; public safety is such an issue; (5) even where statute is concerned with such an issue, the presumption of *mens rea* stands unless it can also be shown that the creation of strict liability will be effective to promote the objects of the statute by encouraging greater vigilance to prevent the commission of the prohibited act." (*Gammon (Hong Kong) Ltd v. A.G.*, (1984) (*Casebook*, p. 173).

It is thus important that we are able to identify these crimes which are classified as "quasi crimes" or "offences of social concern." Clearly no definitive list could be provided, but the following areas should serve to provide some indication.

(a) *Sale of food and drink*

Here there are many complicated regulations designed to ensure that hygiene prevails and also to ensure that customers are not given short measure. This area extends to the rules concerning the licensing of public houses. These crimes are prime examples of "regulatory offences" (see *Meah v. Roberts* (1977)).

(b) *Laws governing the environment*

Like clothing, strict liability has its fashions. At times of economic crises we see strict liability being applied in regulations designed to help the economic situation. In the sixties the concern seemed to be with drugs, while in the seventies pollution of the environment became one of the main topics of concern. The argument here seems to be that there is a form of activity which is causing grave public concern and that breaches of the regulations designed to help the community should be subject to sanctions irrespective of whether the transgressor did it innocently or culpably. Such severe action, it is said, will serve to keep people on their toes.

(c) *Drugs*

As mentioned in the previous paragraph, increasing concern over drugs led to strict liability being imposed in the field of possession, etc., of dangerous drugs, but the recognition by the House of Lords that some of these offences fall into the category of true crimes has led to a softer approach being adopted by the courts and by the legislature in the Misuse of Drugs Act 1971.

(d) *Road traffic*

Many road traffic offences are created by regulations and provide sanctions for breaches of rules designed to ensure that the vehicles are in a roadworthy condition; it is a good bet that most of these offences will be interpreted as imposing strict liability. Another group of offences deals with the way in which the vehicles are actually driven on the road. The offences of dangerous and careless driving (ss. 2, 3 Road Traffic Act 1988) require proof of at least negligence. Offences of driving under the influence of alcohol, however, attract strict liability (ss. 4 and 5 Road Traffic Act 1988).

(3) Smallness of the Penalty

Another pointer to the way in which a court will interpret a given offence is the size of the penalty available. As a general rule the larger the penalty the less likely the court is to treat it as a crime involving strict liability. The reasoning behind this is that a heavy maximum penalty is an indication of Parliament's intention that the accused should be shown to be blameworthy. Whereas you can impose fines on blameless individuals, imprisonment should be reserved for those who are at least negligent. In *Gammon (Hong Kong) Ltd v. A.G.* (1984), however, Lord Scarman held that where the regulations were concerned with a matter of public safety it was quite proper that severe penalties could be imposed even for strict liability offences. He thus took the view that strict liability was needed in order to promote greater vigilance among builders and continued, "It must be crucially important that those who participate in or bear responsibility for the carrying out of works in a manner which complies with the requirements of the ordinance should know that severe penalties await them in the event of any contravention or non compliance with the ordinance by themselves. ... "

At the end of the day there is no sure test to discover whether a statute has imposed strict liability. The above principles have been taken from cases. They are not applied consistently but provide some indication of how the courts will react when confronted with a new criminal offence.

2. Defences to Offences of Strict Liability

If we say that the offence is one of strict liability does this mean that the accused can have no defence to it? No, for that would be going too far. We have already said that where an offence is held to be one of strict liability, this usually means that the court has dispensed with the need to prove intention, recklessness or negligence as to one element of the *actus reus*. The practical effect is that on that one element the accused cannot raise the defence of mistake of fact, *even if his mistake was reasonable*. It possibly also means that the defence of impossibility will not apply to that element; thus where the accused is charged with failing, as the owner of a vehicle, to display the excise licence, it will be of no defence to show that it happened without any default of his own while he was away from the vehicle. However, mistake of fact may well apply to other elements of the *actus reus* and the remaining general defences such as infancy, duress, necessity and automatism are possible defences to a charge. Let us consider a hypothetical example. The offence of driving with the level of alcohol in the blood being over the prescribed limit requires that the prosecution prove that the accused was driving on a road or other public place. The notion of driving involves a mental element or at least the concept of voluntary conduct. Thus if the accused were to show that he had received a blow on the head immediately before he started to drive and this had produced a state of automatism, then he would be able to say that he was not "driving" the car. On the other hand a defence that he was unaware that he had consumed any alcohol since a friend had laced his drinks would fail; liability on this element is strict and mistake of fact is no defence.

In Australia the courts have made attempts to lessen the rigours of strict liability by allowing the accused to plead by way of defence that he had taken all reasonable care. If we consider the example of a butcher who sells bad meat (an offence contrary to the Food and Drugs Act 1955, s.8), if such an approach were to be adopted, the prosecution would at first prove that the butcher had sold meat and that this meat had turned out to be bad. If nothing further is said then the butcher will be convicted. However, if he can prove, on a balance of probabilities, that he had taken all reasonable precautions to ensure that the meat sold in his shop was sound, then he would be acquitted. Of course, this would be another exception to the rule in *Woolmington's* case which says that it is for the prosecution to prove guilt and not for the accused to prove his innocence. However, if the alternative is strict liability with no such defence, then it is clearly an improvement from the point of view of the butcher. It would be an even greater improvement if the butcher merely had to introduce evidence that he had taken all reasonable care, leaving the prosecution to prove that he had not taken all reasonable care.

We have not adopted such a general midway position in offences in strict liability. Occasionally the courts have held that a statute, which might have been expected to impose strict liability, did not, in fact impose strict liability, because there was nothing the accused could have done to protect himself. Thus in *Sherras v. De Rutzen* the court held that a statute making it an offence for a licensee to sell alcohol to a policeman on duty did not impose strict liability since this would have left him defenceless had the constable deliberately lied about being off duty. Similarly in *Lim Chin Aik v. R.* (1963) the Privy Council took the view that the imposition of strict liability is pointless unless there is something that the accused can do to prevent himself breaching the regulation.

It is becoming more common today for statutes which impose strict liability to contain express defences. Thus one type of defence consists of allowing the accused to escape conviction if he can prove that the contravention of the regulation was due to the fault of a third party and that he, the accused, took all reasonable precautions against breaking the regulations (see, *e.g.* the Food and Drugs Act 1955, s.113). More generally statutory defences take the form of casting the burden on the accused to prove that he was not negligent; thus we do specifically for some crimes what the Australian approach would suggest we should do for all crimes of strict liability. (See for example Trade Descriptions Act 1968, s.24 and also *Neville v. Mavroghenis* above, p. 242.)

3. Conclusion

There seems no really convincing reason for the perpetuation of these offences. The same result could be achieved by means of imposing liability for negligence; in other words a failure by the accused to take reasonable care. In any event Parliament should make it totally clear in the drafting of legislation, exactly what sort of liability is being imposed. It is hoped that implementation of the Law Commission's Criminal Code would have this effect (see above, p. 181).

Chapter 8

Parties to Criminal Offences

1. Principal and Secondary Offenders

When a criminal offence is committed attention is primarily focused on the perpetrator. In a case of murder the police will look for the killer, in a case of burglary the person who entered the building as a trespasser, in a case of criminal damage the person who caused the damage and so on. However, a moment's reflection tells us that if the criminal law were concerned only with the perpetrator it would be seriously defective. Someone who helps the perpetrator (for example by providing the gun for a killing, or a key for a burglary) ought also to incur liability for the crime. In some cases the helper may indeed have played a much more significant part than the perpetrator for he may have been the one who conceived and planned the offence. On the other hand a point is reached at which the assistance given is so remote that it would be unfair or unrealistic to make the helper a party to the crime. In a well-known civil case (*Lloyd v. Johnson* (1798)) it was held that a laundress could recover from a prostitute the cost of washing expensive dresses and some gentlemen's nightcaps though the laundress knew well that the dresses were used for the purpose of enticing men in public places. In such circumstances the laundress could hardly be regarded as a party to the prostitute's offence of soliciting. Once again the task of the law is to draw the line at the appropriate place.

Our starting point should be section 8 of the Accessories and Abettors Act 1861 (as amended by the Criminal Law Act 1977). This provides "Whosoever shall aid, abet, counsel or procure the commission of any indictable offence whether the same be an offence at common law or by virtue of any Act passed or to be passed, shall be liable to be tried, indicted and punished as a principal offender." There are similar provisions in relation to summary offences. Until 1967 offences were either felonies or misdemeanours and in the case of felonies various degrees of participation were identified. The actual perpetrator of the offence was known as the principal in the first degree, anyone who was present at the scene of the crime and gave assistance was known as the principal in the second degree, while anyone who gave assistance before the commission of the crime but who was not present at the scene was designated an accessory before the fact. A person who gave assistance to the felony after the offence was called an accessory after the fact. With the passing of the Criminal Law Act 1967 the distinction between felonies and misdemeanours was abolished and section 8 of the Accessories and Abettors Act became applicable to all indictable offences, with the resulting disappearance of the above classifications. Today it is more normal to refer to the actual perpetrator of the offence as the principal offender and all the others who assisted in the commission of the offence as the secondary parties, or accessories, and these are the terms we shall use in this chapter. We can say that the general principles of secondary party liability apply to all offences unless they are specifically and clearly excluded by, for example, the statutory provisions creating the offence (*Jefferson* (1994)).

From a procedural point of view it is not necessary to distinguish in the indictment between principal and secondary offenders—all can be indicted as having committed the offence—provided that at the trial the prosecution can prove that the offence was in fact committed by someone and that those on trial are either principal or secondary parties. Once convicted they are all liable to the same penalty. This was brought home in a dramatic way by the case of *Craig and Bentley* (1952) where following a rooftop chase Bentley was arrested by police officers following a robbery. He called out to Craig "Let him have it Chris" and Craig shot and killed a police officer. Both were indicted and convicted of murder. Craig was too young to face the death penalty and he was sentenced to life imprisonment, but Bentley, who was in police custody at the time of the killing, was hanged.

Three points should be noted before we go any further. Firstly, a person does not become a secondary party to a crime until that crime is either committed or attempted by the principal. If B supplies A with a gun in order to kill X, B becomes a party to the murder only when A kills X, though he will be a party to an attempt if A attempts to kill X and fails. Secondly, both section 8 of the Accessories and Abettors Act 1861 and the Criminal Law Act 1967 were designed to improve criminal procedure and not to affect substantive criminal liability. Thus the old cases are authoritative on the question of who is a participant in a given crime. Today, however, we do not need as a general rule to distinguish between the various types of secondary participation. Thirdly, with the abolition by the Criminal Law Act 1967 of felonies, the old offence of being an accessory after the fact to a felony automatically lapsed. However, section 4 of the Act introduces a new offence of assisting arrestable offenders which has similar features to the old offence.

(1) The Principal or Perpetrator

Suppose that A, B and C are charged with murder of X. The evidence establishes that they had agreed to kill X, that all were present at the time of the killing, and that X was killed by a single stab wound. All deny striking the fatal blow and the evidence does not establish who was the perpetrator though it was clearly one of them. It would be the height of absurdity if the law provided in such a case that all three should be acquitted and of course it does not. All three may be convicted of murder and on conviction all three must be sentenced to imprisonment for life.

In this illustration there is no need to isolate the principal but sometimes it is necessary to draw a sharp distinction between the principal offender and secondary party. One such occasion is where the offence is one of strict liability (see above, p. 236). We have seen that a person may be made liable for certain offences even though he lacks *mens rea*. But strict liability is imposed only on the principal offender and is not imposed on secondary parties. In *Callow v. Tillstone* (1900) (*Casebook*, p. 176) the principal offender was a butcher who was charged with exposing bad meat for sale. He had got a vet to examine a carcase of a heifer which had eaten yew leaves. The vet passed it fit for sale and, relying on the vet's certificate, the principal offender put it up for sale. The offence was one of strict liability and the principal offender was therefore convicted. The justices also convicted the vet as they found that he had been negligent in issuing the certificate. On appeal the vet's conviction was quashed since he did not know nor was he reckless as to the meat being bad. It may strike the reader as a trifle odd that the principal offender was held liable even though he was entirely blameless while the secondary party (the vet) was not liable though he was at fault in the sense that he was negligent.

However, the courts have taken the view that strict liability applies only to the principal offender. The reason for all this is that liability for secondary participation arises at common law and criminal liability at common law generally requires *mens rea*. You could argue that this is illogical since if there are good policy reasons for imposing strict liability on the principal there are equally good reasons for imposing it on the secondary offenders—but the law is not always logical.

So how is the principal to be marked off from the secondary party? Normally this presents no problems. A shoots and kills X with a gun provided by B. A is the principal and B is a secondary party to it. C enters a building to steal while D keeps a watch outside; C is the principal offender in the burglary and D is the secondary party. However, it is not always as clear as this. Suppose that E holds Y while F stabs him and Y dies as a result. Is E a principal offender or a secondary party? It is, of course, possible to have more than one principal offender. If E had merely decoyed Y to the place where F stabbed him, then E would clearly only be a secondary party. Does he become a principal by holding Y so that Y cannot defend himself against F's murderous attack? This case is clearly right on the borderline. If the crime had been rape and E had held Y down while F had intercourse with her, you could hardly say that E was the perpetrator of the rape—you could not really say that E raped Y. On the other hand if E holds Y while F punches him you could say that E and F are co-perpetrators of an assault since for E to hold Y against his will is in itself an assault. But where E holds Y so that F can stab him it may be unrealistic to say that E killed Y: what he has done is to help F kill Y.

The principal offender is, therefore, any person (or persons) who by his own conduct directly brings about the *actus reus* of the crime. This formulation may not, however, suffice for all cases. Suppose that A puts poison in X's medicine knowing that B, a nurse, will innocently administer the poison to X in the course of her duties. Or suppose that C persuades D, a nine-year-old boy, to steal from Y. Neither B, since she lacks *mens rea*, nor D, since he is under the age of criminal responsibility, can be charged as parties either to the killing of X or the stealing from Y. In both cases it might be said that A and C did not directly bring about the *actus reus* of the respective crimes. Common sense, however, tells us that A killed X and C stole from Y and the formulation at the beginning of this paragraph should be taken to include such cases. In such cases, B and D are often referred to as innocent agents; thus we say that A killed X through the innocent agency of B. It is probably safer and simpler to say—can we drop B out of the picture and say A killed X? Killing is clearly an offence which can be perpetrated through an innocent agent. On the other hand rape, bigamy and driving offences are equally clearly offences which cannot be so committed (but see *Cogan v. Leak* below, p. 272).

(2) Secondary Parties

From the discussion in the preceding section we can say that a secondary party (sometimes called an accessory) is, broadly speaking, someone who helps to bring about the crime without being the actual perpetrator. Such a broad definition, though it will probably suffice for most cases, is not sufficiently refined to deal precisely with all the cases that can arise.

It might be thought that the position of a secondary party was exactly the same as that of a principal. After all section 8 of the Accessories and Abettors Act 1861 provides that he is liable "to be indicted and tried as if he were a principal offender." However, this is not really so and the liability of the secondary party turns out to be rather more complex than that of the principal. Suppose that A and B are charged with a crime and it is alleged that A is the perpetrator and that B is the secondary party. Against A it has to be proved that he by his own conduct directly caused the *actus reus* with the appropriate *mens rea*. Against B it has to be proved that:

(i) he knew that A would cause the *actus reus* with the appropriate *mens rea*; and
(ii) that he helped A to commit that crime knowing that his conduct would be of assistance to A.

You may say that proposition (ii) includes proposition (i), but this way of setting out the requirements in relation to B serves to emphasise that the *mens rea* of a secondary party extends not only to knowledge of the principal's *mens rea* but also requires a further intention to help the principal; and, in the case of the secondary party, not only has it to be shown that the *actus reus* of the crime was brought about but also that there was some conduct of the accessory which helped the commission of that crime.

It follows, therefore, that B cannot be convicted as an accessory to A's crime merely because he knows that A will commit the crime. B may learn that A plans to murder X or burgle Y's premises but this knowledge alone is not enough to make B a party to the killing of X or the burgling of Y's premises. It can make no difference that, on learning of A's intention, B is secretly delighted because he will inherit under X's will or because Y is someone he hates. An even more extreme illustration is provided by the case of *Allan* (1965). Allan was present when some of his friends became involved in a fight. He knew that his friends were committing a crime, but not only did he approve of their conduct, he had secretly resolved to help them should they require his aid. His conviction, however, as a party to the crimes committed by his friends was quashed because knowledge of the principal's crime coupled with an intention to aid is not enough unless there is also some conduct of the accessory which helps the principal.

So what exactly has to be proved against the accessory to make him a party to the principal's crime? Simply put it must be shown that with knowledge of the principal's crime the accessory did something to help in its commission with the intention of assisting, though in detail the position may be more complicated.

(a) *Knowledge of the type of crime*

First, the requirement of knowledge of the principal's crime does not require that B should know of every detail of A's planned crime. Take a case where A plans to steal money from a safe at a particular factory and needs cutting equipment for this purpose. He contacts B and purchases this equipment from him making no mention whatever of his plans. B, however, knows that A has a record for burglary, that he has no legitimate business for which such equipment could be required and guesses (correctly) that it is required to break into a safe on some premises or other. Nevertheless B supplies the equipment. B may be convicted as an accessory to the burglary committed by A though B has no idea when or where the crime is to be committed. The point is that he knows the essentials of the crime. But *Bainbridge* (1960) (*Casebook*, p. 185) on which the last illustration was based shows that it is not enough to make B liable that he knew that A was up to no good—that would be far too vague. It was also accepted in that case that B would not be liable if his only suspicion was that A planned to commit some different type of crime, such as receiving stolen metal and that the cutting equipment was to be used to break it up.

So the accessory will not escape liability saying that it was a case of no-questions-asked if he, in fact, realised what the principal was up to. Moreover, it is enough that the principal commits one of a range of crimes which was in the contemplation of the accessory. In *D.P.P. for Northern Ireland v. Maxwell* (1978) (*Casebook*, p. 186) Maxwell's task had been to lead Northern Ireland terrorists to a public house in a village where they left a bomb. He claimed that he could not be convicted as a party to the bombing since he did not know what the terrorists had planned to do. The House of Lords held that from his knowledge of the organisation he knew that the mission would take one of a number of forms and it was sufficient that the actual deed that night fell within the bounds of one of the offences he, in fact, contemplated.

In most cases the test propounded in *Maxwell* will provide a ready answer. However, one or two questions remain unanswered. For example if B suspects A is about to commit burglary and the equipment he has supplied will be used to force open the windows of the premises will he be liable if A's plan, which he carries out, is to rape a girl who lives there? Your immediate reaction will be to say that this is an entirely different crime from the one B contemplated. However, where A enters the house as a trespasser with intent to rape someone inside this is burglary contrary to section 9(1)(*a*) of the Theft Act 1968 (see below) and burglary is the very crime B contemplated. Perhaps the courts would take a common sense view in these sorts of cases and hold that B should not be convicted as a party to a particular variant of burglary he almost certainly would not have contemplated. Another problem is that once B has supplied the equipment A can go on using it for the type of crime B had in mind indefinitely. Does B become a party to all the future crimes A commits with the equipment? This may seem rather hard on B but there is nothing technically to stop such liability arising.

We have said so far that the secondary party must know that the principal offender will commit a particular offence or one of a known group of offences. Knowledge here includes wilful blindness and so B would be liable if he guesses that A is about to commit a burglary with the equipment he is supplying and deliberately asks no questions so that he can say that he did not know what A was about. The court appears to have gone even further in *Carter v. Richardson* (1974) where A was a learner driver who was discovered to be driving over the prescribed alcohol limit. His supervisor, B, was held liable as a secondary party even though he could not have known that A was, in fact, over the limit; he was, at best, reckless as to A's alcohol level. B had intentionally assisted A to drive and had deliberately taken the risk that he was over the prescribed limit. (See *Blakely and Sutton* (1991) below, p. 267.)

(b) *Liability for unforeseen consequences*

It follows from the foregoing discussion that while B may be liable for such crimes committed by A as were in B's contemplation, he is not liable for crimes committed by A that he does not contemplate at all. We have just seen that where B supplies cutting equipment to A knowing of its use in connection with a burglary that B becomes an accessory to the burglary. Suppose then, that as part of the burglary, A attacked X, a nightwatchman, and rendered him unconscious. B is not a party to the assault on X which was uncontemplated by him; the fact that B contemplated one crime (burglary) and that during the commission of that crime another (assault) was committed is not enough to make B liable as a party to the further crime. In relation to the assault B is totally lacking in *mens rea*.

In this example it is assumed that B supplies the equipment some days before the burglary and is not present at its commission. Does it, therefore, make any difference if B accompanies A on the burglarious expedition? The answer is that it makes no difference whether B is present at or absent from the scene of the crime. B is liable only for such crime or crimes of A that he contemplates A will commit, intending to assist in their commission. Thus if B had accompanied A but had been totally unaware of the presence of the night-watchman and had never contemplated that force would be used on any person, he could not be a party to A's assault. If, however it could be proved that B had gone along with A foreseeing that in the unlikely event that someone intervened A would use violence to avoid capture, then B will be an accessory to the use of such violence by A.

In these cases it could be said that what is needed is proof that the secondary party joined in a venture contemplating that, for example, violence was a real possibility. The principles relating to joint ventures or enterprises arise in relation to all types of crimes, but the majority of cases involve ventures where violence has occurred. Unfortunately the courts have managed to get themselves into difficulties due, in large measure, to a chance remark by Sir Robin Cooke in *Chan Wing-Siu* (1984). Having said that, in a murder case, the prosecution must prove that the secondary party had joined the venture foreseeing it as a real possibility that the principal might intentionally kill or inflict grievous bodily harm, he then added that this could be expressed in terms of authorisation, *i.e.* the secondary party has authorised the principal to kill or cause serious bodily harm. Now there is potentially a great deal of difference between going on a venture foreseeing that the other party might react with violence and authorising the other to use violence; the latter being far more difficult to prove. If the principal believes that the getaway car driver has no knowledge of the gun that he, the principal, is carrying, whereas in fact he is aware and believes that the principal might use it in an emergency to cause death, it is not possible to say the principal is authorised so to act but we can say that the secondary party joins the venture foreseeing that it might lead to murder.

Following *Chan Wing-Siu* there were decisions of the Court of Appeal which held that the prosecution needed to prove that the secondary party authorised (expressly or tacitly) the use of the violence (see Wakely (1990)).

In *Hui Chi-Ming* (1991) P's girlfriend claimed that she had been intimidated by a man. P got together a group of friends to search for the man responsible; he told them they were going to find someone to hit. Hui Chi-Ming (H), the defendant, was one of the group and was aware that P was carrying a length of metal pipe. Subsequently P hit a man with the pipe and later the man died. P was convicted of manslaughter. Two years later H was put on trial for murder, though it was not alleged that he had himself hit the victim. H refused to plead guilty to manslaughter and stood trial for murder. H was convicted of murder (*Howe* (1987) is House of Lords authority for the proposition that the secondary party can be convicted of an offence greater than that of the principal). H appealed against his conviction *inter alia* on the ground that the trial judge had misdirected the jury by telling them that they could convict H of murder if they were satisfied that he thought there was a realistic possibility that P might use the pipe to cause serious injury. The Privy Council held that this was a perfectly acceptable direction; there was no need to look for any authorisation or agreement, express or implied. It was sufficient that the jury were satisfied that the defendant had lent himself to a venture in which he foresaw that there was a realistic possibility that the principal offender might intentionally inflict grievous bodily harm.

What is a realistic possibility? In *Chan Wing-Siu* Sir Robin Cooke said:

> "What has to be brought home to the jury is that occasionally a risk may have occurred to an accused's mind, fleetingly or even causing him some deliberation, but may genuinely have been dismissed by him as altogether negligible. If they think that there is a reasonable possibility that the case is in that class, taking the risk should not make that accused a party to such a crime of intention as murder or wounding with intent to cause grievous bodily harm."

Clearly, if D has considered the risk of his accomplice intentionally causing grievous bodily harm and has dismissed it entirely, he should not be held liable. In reality, however, if he goes on the venture seeing that there is even an outside chance of such an occurrence, it is unlikely that the court will hold that it was a risk he was entitled to take. (See *Roberts* (1993).)

Hui Chi-Ming makes it clear that it is not necessary for the prosecution to prove that both parties contemplated the use of violence when they set out on their joint venture, though this will usually be the case. Suppose, for example, A and B set out on a burglary expedition. A is armed with a gun which he intends to use merely to frighten anyone who gets in the way. B, on the other hand, knows that A has a gun and expects that A will use it deliberately to kill or seriously injure such a person. If A later, at the scene of the crime, intentionally kills the nightwatchman who intervenes, both will be liable for murder; A because he has intentionally killed the nightwatchman and B because he has gone on the venture contemplating that A might do this.

Is it right, you may be wondering, that against the principal offender it has to be proved that he intended to kill or cause grievous bodily harm but against the secondary party there is only a need to prove that he contemplated this as a realistic possibility (not even a probability)? The answer is that it is perfectly logical. Against the secondary party it has to be proved that he knew that the principal offender might bring about the *actus reus* of murder with the necessary *mens rea* and with this knowledge he deliberately sets out to help the principal offender. If it were to be required that the secondary party foresaw that violence would probably be used, the law would be seriously failing in its duty to protect the public. Consider, for example, a bank robbery in which one of the robbers is, to the knowledge of the others, carrying a gun which in extreme circumstances he will use to kill or seriously injure. It is extremely unlikely that the accomplices could be said to have foreseen death or grievous bodily harm as a probable consequence of the venture since it will only be on rare occasions that someone will intervene to stop them. They do, however, see violence as a possibility and are nonetheless prepared to help. They should be guilty if the violence occurs. (See *Slack* (1989).)

In these cases it is important to keep questions of proof separate from questions of substantive law. What is required is that the prosecution can prove that the secondary party went on the venture with the necessary foresight. Where, as in *Hui Chi-Ming* the overall object of the venture is to injure someone, it is probably easier to infer that the secondary party contemplated that the injuries might turn out to be very serious or even fatal than when the object of the venture was burglary. Equally it is easier to infer that serious violence is contemplated by the secondary party when he knows that the principal is carrying a lethal weapon. However, these are matters of proof and not rules of law. (See *Hyde* (1990).)

In some cases it is not possible to work out which of several defendants actually brought about the *actus reus*. In such cases it is possible for the jury to convict any of the participants against whom it can be proved that he either committed the offence himself or else aided and abetted another to commit the offence. In *Fitzgerald* (1992) it was alleged that the accused had set fire to a motorcycle owned by C. However, at the trial, evidence given by the victim made it unclear as to exactly what had happened. The evidence showed that C had been chased by a car belonging to F in which there was a passenger, H. When C abandoned his scooter on the roadside as he went to seek help from a householder, either F, or, more likely, H, got out of the car and removed the petrol cap from the scooter and then either this same person or the other flicked a match into the tank, thereby setting fire to the scooter. The trial judge left the case to the jury on two factual bases. The first was that it was F who set fire to the scooter by flicking matches out of the car and the second that there was clear evidence of a joint venture. The direction in this case was stricter than in many since the judge directed the jury that they should first consider whether it had been proved that F was the principal. If they could not agree on this they must acquit unless they could all agree that F or H had set it on fire as part of a joint venture. In other cases the jury seem to have been told that it is sufficient that they are all sure that one or other basis is made out *i.e.* it would be sufficient that six found F to have been the principal and six that he aided and abetted H. (See also *Smith v. Mellors and Soar* (1987)).

In general terms, therefore, it can be said that B (even if he accompanies A for the purposes of carrying out the crime) is not a party to other crimes committed by A which were unforeseen by B. This does not mean that B escapes liability because A has deviated from the precise terms of that plan. If B counsels A to kill X by poisoning and A shoots X, B will be a party to the murder of X. If B counsels A to steal X's silver plate and A steals X's gold plate, B will be a party to the theft. Moreover B may be liable for a consequence unforseen by him if that consequence is one for which A is liable even though it was equally unforeseen by him. Suppose that B counsels A to kill X; A shoots at X, misses and kills Y. As we have seen, A will be liable for the death of Y (above, p. 226) by virtue of the doctrine of transferred malice. Since A is liable for the death of Y even though that consequence was unforeseen by him, B will be liable as an accessory even though Y's death was also unforeseen by him. If however, B counsels A to kill C, but A deliberately deviates from the plan and kills D, B cannot be liable for that killing; if, however, he had incited A to kill C he can be charged with that offence (*Leahy* (1985)).

Now we can have a look at a rather more complex example. Suppose that A, B and C plan to burgle X's house in the night at a time when the occupants are expected to be asleep. They plan to steal certain valuable antiques. A and B are to enter the house and C is to remain outside in his car with the engine running. B knows that A carries a loaded revolver; C does not know this but knows that A has a reputation for violence. A and B enter the house. During the enterprise B commits various acts of vandalism by slashing furniture and furnishings with a razor. As they are about to leave they are surprised by X. A fires at him, misses and the bullet travels through the door killing Y, X's wife, who was standing behind it. If we consider the various crimes in turn:

(i) **The burglary.** This presents no problems. A and B are joint principals and C is an accessory. Though the point is unimportant A and B are also joint principals in theft. Could C say that he was not a party to the theft if some of the articles taken were not antiques? Probably not. (He could not deny liability for burglary since this arose the moment A and B entered the house with the intent to steal). He could do so if the compact was for the taking of antiques and nothing else but this is unlikely in the extreme. If C contemplated that other articles would be taken (and he would surely contemplate that A and B would appropriate any money they found lying about the house) he will be a secondary party to the theft of articles other than the antiques.

(ii) **Criminal damage.** B is the principal offender here. Whether C will be held to be an accessory depends upon whether he knows of B's proclivities. It is not at all uncommon for burglars to be given to vandalising the premises they burgle; if C knows that B is given to this activity, he is a party to the criminal damage if there is an understanding that B will damage property in the house. (See C v. Hume (1979).) If C has no such knowledge then he cannot be a party to the criminal damage. A's position as an accessory to criminal damage is essentially the same. The main practical difference is that, in the case of A who was present inside the house, it will be easier for the jury to conclude that the criminal damage was within A's contemplation.

(iii) **Murder and manslaughter.** By virtue of the doctrine of transferred malice A is liable for the death of Y and will be liable to be convicted of murder or manslaughter depending upon his *mens rea;* murder if he intended to kill or cause serious bodily harm, manslaughter if he merely intended to frighten X. As for C, it is clearly not enough to make him liable in respect of Y's death that he knew that A was given to violence. But suppose that C contemplated that the house-holders might be awakened by the burglary and contemplated that A would use force against anyone who disturbed him. Here the fact that C is unaware of the gun is crucial. In *Davies v. D.P.P.* (1954) (*Casebook*, p. 193) there was a fight between two rival gangs on Clapham Common. Basically what started as a punch-up ended with a member of one gang, Davies, stabbing to death a member of the rival gang. Since there were, at that time, special evidential rules governing the testimony of an accomplice, the need arose for the House of Lords to determine whether Lawson, a member of Davies' gang, was an accomplice with Davies in the killing. Since Lawson had been unaware that Davies was carrying a knife, it was held that he was not an accomplice to either murder or manslaughter. It is important to treat this decision with caution. It is not so much that Davies had with him a knife that is important as what the possession of the knife tells us about Davies' state of mind when he embarked upon the venture. Lawson knew that the purpose of the exercise was to inflict actual bodily harm on members of the opposing gang and joined in on that basis. If, for example, Lawson had known that Davies might well attempt to inflict grievous bodily harm or death with his fists, it would have made no difference that Davies in fact used a knife or a gun to inflict death or grievous bodily harm. The point would be that Lawson would have lent his support to a venture in which he saw that there was a realistic possibility that a member of the team would deliberately seek to inflict death or really serious bodily injury. In *Davies* the relevance of the knife was that it was evidence that Davies was prepared to inflict grievous bodily harm and Lawson was unaware of this. The question for the jury is: "What level of violence was Lawson prepared to support?"

It follows in our example that C's ignorance of the gun may well insulate him from liability for the death of Y.

B's position is quite different because he knew that A had loaded the gun. If B realised that in the event of their being surprised by anyone, that A would use the gun to kill or cause grievous bodily harm, then B is a party to murder. If B realised that A would use the gun to frighten and A so used it, then B would be a party to manslaughter. In neither case does it make a scrap of difference that Y's death may have been unforeseen.

Suppose that B thought that A had taken the gun to give himself Dutch courage and that A would not use it. Strictly speaking B would not be a party to the death of Y. As a matter of fact, though, any jury is likely to give short shrift to such a claim by B when he knew of the loaded gun and knew that they were burgling occupied premises in the night. More realistically B may claim that he thought that the gun would only be used to frighten and that A would not use it with intent to kill. What then if it is accepted that B realised that the gun would be used to frighten and A then used it with a deliberate intent to kill or cause serious bodily harm? B cannot be guilty of murder because he does not share, and indeed is quite unaware of A's intent to kill. But surely, it might be said, that B is guilty of manslaughter because he had sufficient *mens rea* for that crime and there is an *actus reus*.

This question has produced a series of irreconcilable decisions. Logically the position could be analysed as follows: If P1 sets out to inflict actual bodily harm on V with fists and

P2 drives him to find V knowing that this is what P1 intends, then

(a) if P1 begins to inflict actual bodily harm but then decides to kill V with his fists, P2 should be convicted as an accessory in that part of the attack during which P1 was only attempting to inflict minor bodily harm. P2 should not be liable for any of the consequences which happened after P1 formed the intention to kill (or seriously to injure) V. If V had died as a result of the injuries inflicted while both parties were intending to inflict only minor injuries, both would be liable for unlawful act manslaughter. On the other hand,

(b) if, as soon as they found V, P1 immediately formed the intention to kill or seriously injure V, then only P1 should be liable for the death. P2 is liable for nothing except any liability there may be for the original conspiracy to inflict minor injuries. He clearly cannot be liable for murder since he lacks the *mens rea* and since he had joined the venture on the basis that it was for the purpose of inflicting only minor bodily injuries he should have no responsibility at all for consequences which resulted from P1 deliberately going outside the scope of the joint venture. He should thus not be held liable even for manslaughter.

This was the approach adopted by the Court of Appeal in Anderson and Morris (1966). The Court commented that the decision would be the same even if M was aware that A had a knife and planned to use it, so long as it was contemplated that the knife would be used to inflict only minor injuries. However, although this decision has received subsequent support, several cases have held that a conviction of P2 for manslaughter would be a possibility in this type of situation. (See *e.g. Stewart and Schofield* (1995). It is now essential that the House of Lords should examine the issue and make a clear ruling on it. The Court of Appeal has certified the following point of law:

> "Where participant A in a criminal joint enterprise contemplates that the carrying out of the joint enterprise may involve the victim suffering some bodily injury, but not a serious injury, and B, another participant in that joint enterprise, forms, independently of the others, an intention to kill or do serious bodily harm to the victim and, with that intention, B does an act which causes the death of the victim, are the jury precluded, as a matter of law, from finding as a fact that that act was done in the course of carrying out the joint enterprise and convicting A of manslaughter?"

If the House gives leave to appeal it is to be hoped that we shall get a clear answer to the question. The House needs to lay down a clear rule whether, on the basis of such facts, the secondary party is or is not guilty of manslaughter. (See the commentary to the case by Professor Smith in [1995] Crim. L.R. 442).

(c) Aids, abets, counsels or procures

In addition to providing that the secondary party knew of the crime the principal intended to commit, the prosecution must prove that the secondary party helped the principal with intent to do so. In fact section 8 of the Accessories and Abettors Act uses neither the words "help" nor "assistance" and imposes liability where the accessory "aids, abets, counsels or procures" the crime. Basically these verbs convey the idea of help or assistance but in the end we have to consider the precise interpretation of the words used in the statute itself. This was the important point made by the Court of Appeal in *Attorney General's Reference (No. 1 of 1975)* (1975) (*Casebook*, p. 177) when it was said that these words must be given their ordinary meaning. Obviously the words overlap to some extent. If A and B meet X and B encourages A to assault X we may indifferently say that B aids, abets, counsels or procures A to assault X. On the other hand each word may contain nuances of meaning not conveyed by the others; *Attorney General's Reference (No. 1 of 1975)* illustrates the point. B added alcohol to A's drink without A's knowledge and A's subsequent driving of a car resulted in him being prosecuted under the breathalyser provisions. It was held that B had procured the commission of the offence by A. The court rejected an argument that the secondary participation always requires communication between the accessory and the perpetrator and held that a crime could be procured (*i.e.* brought about by endeavour) though there was no communication between the secondary and principal offenders. The court did not attempt an exhaustive definition of the remaining verbs but it would now be unwise to assume that they are synonymous.

(i) Conduct amounting to aiding, abetting, counselling or procuring. At all events there must be some conduct of the secondary party which can properly be said to amount to an aiding, etc. *Allan* (above, p. 254) shows that a secret intention to assist without any assistance in fact is not enough. On the other hand very little assistance may, in fact be required, and words alone may suffice. It would have been enough had Allan shouted encouragement to the principals or even if he had said "give me a call if you need a hand."

An interesting problem was posed by the speeches of their Lordships in the case of *Gillick v. West Norfolk and Wisbech Area Health Authority and Another* (1986). It is clear that it is an offence for a man to have intercourse with a girl who is under 16 years of age. It is also clear that it would be an offence for another to aid, abet, counsel or procure that man to have intercourse with the girl. A doctor who prescribes contraceptive pills for a 15-year-old girl knows that he is making it more likely that she will have intercourse. It ought to follow, therefore, that the doctor is a secondary party to that intercourse. Their Lordships recognised this possibility and said that a doctor may, in some circumstances, prescribe for a 15-year-old girl without attracting secondary party liability. They did not, however, explain how this could be so. (See further the commentary by Professor Smith in [1986] Crim.L.R. 113.)

Two particular problems must be considered.

Presence as aiding, etc. If a shout or two of encouragement is enough to constitute aiding, why should not mere presence suffice? A may be just as much encouraged by the presence of B as by a word of encouragement. Clearly B's accidental presence cannot suffice but the reason for this is that B would then lack any intention to aid. But what if B then stays to watch? In 1980 terrorists seized the Iranian Embassy in London and their illegal activities were closely watched for some days by hordes of newsmen and, through the medium of television, by many millions of viewers. In a very real sense the terrorists drew encouragement from this for one of their primary aims was to secure publicity for their cause. Common sense tells us that the newsmen were not accessories to the continued imprisonment of the Embassy staff and the case of *Clarkson* (1971) (*Casebook*, p. 181) strikingly bears this out. In that case B and C did not become secondary parties to rape merely because, to satisfy their prurient interest, they watched fellow soldiers repeatedly rape a girl in their barracks.

Presence, however, if it is not accidental constitutes some evidence of aiding, etc., though it must be considered along with all the other evidence. Thus presence coupled with evidence of a previous conspiracy between the parties to commit the crime will suffice. In *Coney* (1882), however, it was held to be a misdirection to direct a jury that (non-accidental) presence at a fight was conclusive evidence of aiding. No doubt this decision was right, but presence at an illegal activity which requires spectators if it is to prosper at all may more readily give rise to an inference of aiding and abetting than presence at other illegal activities. In *Wilcox v. Jeffrey* (1951) B was convicted of aiding and abetting A (the celebrated jazz saxophonist Coleman Hawkins) to play in public contrary to the conditions on which he was allowed to enter England. The Divisional Court thought it right in such a case to invite the jury to infer aiding from presence throughout the illegal performance together with the fact that B had met A at the airport and had written an account of the performance in the newspaper for which he worked. Suppose then that in *Allan* the trial judge had directed the jury that Allan's continued presence at the fight could be regarded as evidence of aiding, and that the jury had convicted him. Would the Court of Appeal have quashed his conviction?

Aiding, etc., by omission. The last question raises another problem. Is B liable for A's crime because he fails to intervene to prevent it or to put a stop to it? The general answer must be No, because there is no general duty to prevent the commission of crime by others. Exceptionally there may be circumstances where B is under a duty to take positive steps to prevent the commission of a crime by A. In an Australian case *Russell* (1933) it was held that a father was a secondary party to the homicide of his children where he stood by and watched the mother drown them. In *Du Cros v. Lambourne* (1907) (*Casebook*, p. 184) it was held that B could be convicted of aiding A to drive dangerously where A was driving B's car with his permission and was, to B's knowledge, driving it dangerously.

A problem may be experienced where a group of people are sharing a flat and A discovers that B has possession of a controlled drug. Is A expected to leave the flat? If he stays will he be in danger of being held to have given passive encouragement to B? In *Bland* (1988) the Court of Appeal held that you could not get evidence of passive assistance merely from the fact that people live together. You would need evidence that A either encouraged B or that A had the right to control B's activities.

(ii) The mental element in aiding, etc. It has been pointed out that a secondary party's *mens rea* in a sense, requires two elements: (i) knowledge of the principal's *mens rea* and (ii) an intent to aid the principal in the commission of his crime. The former of these requirements has been examined in some detail above; it is now necessary to say something more about the latter. Clearly B does not become a party to A's crime if, knowing of it, he accidentally helps in its commission as where B, knowing that A intends to steal from C's safe, absentmindedly fails to lock the safe. The words "aids, abets, counsels or procures" suggest purposive conduct on B's part.

It is usually said that the accomplice must be proved to have intended to aid, abet, counsel or procure the offence committed by the principal. Is it sufficient that he is reckless as to whether his action will aid, abet, counsel or procure? We saw in *Carter v. Richardson* (above p. 255) that the driving supervisor was convicted on the basis that he intentionally assisted the learner driver to drive the car being aware that he was likely to be over the prescribed alcohol limit. There is no way that he could actually "know" that the driver was over the limit and it seems (*Cunningham*) recklessness in relation to a circumstance provides an adequate basis for liability. In *Blakely and Sutton v. D.P.P.* (1991) the position was, in effect, reversed. Blakely (B) had been having an affair with a married man, T, who occasionally spent the night with her. On the evening in question B and her friend S were having a drink with T at a pub when he announced that he intended to drive home to spend the night with his wife. B and S added vodka to his drink, planning to tell him he would have to spend the night with B since he was now unfit to drive. Unfortunately the plan back-fired. T went off to the toilet and left to drive home before B and S could tell him what they had done. He was breathalysed and found to be over the limit. There is no question of T's criminal liability; he had committed a strict liability offence and his lack of knowledge of the lacing of his drink was no defence (though it might save him from mandatory disqualification). The question for the court was whether B and S were parties to the offence. Their convictions for procuring T's driving over the prescribed limit were quashed on the ground that the magistrates may have convicted on the basis of *Caldwell* recklessness. Whereas in *Carter v. Richardson* the accomplice *intended to aid and abet* the learner driver to drive the car, being reckless as to whether the level of alcohol in his blood was too high, (*i.e.* reckless as to a circumstance of the offence), Blakely and Sutton deliberately set about to ensure that T was over the prescribed limit, but the last thing they wanted was for him to drive; they were at most reckless that he might do so. The decision in the case is blurred by a lengthy discussion of whether *Caldwell* recklessness sufficed, the Divisional Court holding that if recklessness were appropriate it would need to be

Cunningham recklessness. The convictions were quashed because the magistrates may have convicted on the basis of *Caldwell* recklessness. There is, however, a suggestion in the case that they would have been convicted had it been proved that they were aware that he might drive (*i.e. Cunningham* recklessness). But should *Cunningham* recklessness suffice as the basis for secondary party liability? There is support in the Draft Criminal Code for the proposition that recklessness as to circumstances (as in *Carter v. Richardson*) should suffice, but the Code proposes that the prosecution must prove that the accessory intended to "aid, abet, counsel or procure". There are statements in other cases that where, at least, procurement is concerned, the prosecution will need to prove that the accomplice intended to procure the commission of the offence by the principal and it is suggested that this should be the position in relation to the other methods of participation. (See *Millard*, below, p. 273).

Suppose, however, that A plans to burgle X's house and he asks B to drive him to a specified destination. B does so and A burgles the house. B's liability may be considered on various hypotheses:

(1) If B believes that A's enterprise is an innocent one then B cannot incur criminal liability.

(2) If B knows what A plans and is willing to drive him to and from the scene of the crime he is evidently a party to A's crime.

(3) B is a taxi driver whom A has engaged at the normal commercial rates. B knows that A plans to burgle C's home but considers that this is none of his business. B reasons that if he refuses his services then another taxi driver (who does not have B's knowledge of A's intentions) will be readily found by A. Why, B asks himself, should he lose a fare when the crime will be committed anyway? A problem similar to this arose in *National Coal Board v. Gamble* (1959) (*Casebook*, p. 189) where the defendants, the National Coal Board, had supplied X with coal. The procedure was that X's drivers filled up their lorries at the Coal Board's depot and then drove the loaded lorries on to a weighbridge. If the weight shown was correct the weighbridge operator issued the driver with a ticket at which time the court held that ownership of the goods passed to X. Under the Motor Vehicle (Construction and Use) Regulations it is an offence to drive a lorry on a public road when the load exceeds a certain weight. On the occasion in question the weighbridge operator saw that the lorry was overloaded and commented on this fact to the driver. The driver replied that he would take the risk and a

ticket was issued. The driver committed the offence immediately he drove on to the road, but the difficult question was whether or not the Coal Board was liable as a secondary party (through the action of their employee). It seems clear that although the weighbridge operator did not want to help the driver commit an offence, he could not have cared less whether the driver was picked up for contravening the regulations or not. On the other hand he did know all the facts which constituted the offence and his action in issuing a ticket enabled the driver to commit the offence. The Divisional Court held that this was enough to make the weighbridge operator (and therefore the Board) a secondary party. Thus it is sufficient that X performs an act which he knows will assist Y in the commission of a crime.

(4) Now suppose that B hopes that A will be unable to commit the burglary; let's say that he hopes that on arrival at X's house they will discover that it is occupied and that A will thereupon call off the enterprise. It seems that this will not save B. In *D.P.P. for Northern Ireland v. Lynch* (1975) (*Casebook*, p. 247) Lynch drove some terrorists to a place where they shot and killed a man. Lynch said that he was hoping that the crime—or any crime—would not be committed but it was said that this would be no defence. Would it make any difference that B spent the journey to X's house trying to persuade A not to burgle the house? *Fretwell* (1864) suggests that it might, for there B was held not guilty for the self-murder by A where he gave her the wherewithal to procure an abortion whilst earnestly entreating her not to use it. This decision is, however, questionable. In *N.C.B. v. Gamble*, Devlin J. thought, surely correctly, that if B sold a gun to A knowing that A intended to murder his wife, B would be an accessory to the murder even though his interest was only in the profit he would make on the sale and was utterly indifferent to the fate of A's wife. It is unlikely that Devlin J. would take a different view of B's participation if B had sold the gun to A with a plea for matrimonial reconciliation. This brings us full circle to the case we were discussing at the outset of the laundress who washed and returned clothes to a prostitute knowing that she would use them to ply her trade in public. It seems unlikely that we should convict the laundress as a party to the prostitution and therefore a line has to be drawn. Of course in these cases B can always refuse to sell the gun and wash the clothes, but what if A is asking for the return of the gun he lent to B? If B refuses can he be sued for wrongful retention of A's property? It is unlikely that a civil court would uphold such an action and in any case *Garrett v. Arthur*

Churchill (Glass) Ltd (1970) would imply that such a plea would be no defence to B if he returns the gun. How then do we distinguish between the sale of the gun and the washing of the clothes. The only really practical solution is to say that liability in this type of situation will depend upon the severity of the contemplated crime. Thus if B returns the gun to A knowing that he plans to shoot his wife he will be liable, but not if he knows that A plans a bit of illegal poaching. This hardly seems satisfactory but it is submitted it is the only practicable solution.

Thus far an attempt has been made to describe participation in crime and to show why we need to distinguish between the principal offender and secondary offenders and how the distinction is to be made. This does not exhaust all the problems which arise in connection with participation in crime and some mention must be made of these.

(3) The Need for an Actus Reus

It may happen that the police have been unable to catch the principal offender but they have arrested the man they think aided the principal. Is it now permissible for them to bring the secondary party to trial in the absence of any principal offender? This raises several related problems which we can now examine.

(a) *No principal offender*

Provided that the prosecution is able to prove that the *actus reus* of the crime in question was caused by someone then the jury are entitled to convict B as a secondary party even though the prosecution have not been able to produce the principal offender.

(b) *Previous acquittal of the principal offender*

If the principal offender has already been tried and acquitted it is still possible for the prosecution to bring to trial the secondary offender provided that the evidence against him is not identical to the evidence upon which the previous jury acquitted the principal offender.

(c) *Joint trial of principal and secondary parties*

It is usual for the principal and secondary parties to the offence to be tried together. So the question then arises as to whether the jury could acquit the principal offender and convict the secondary party. This, to an outsider, would look rather odd and indeed there are suggestions that this course is not open. However, such action is probably not as absurd as it may first appear. If the evidence against the parties is the same then it would be improper for the jury to acquit the principal and convict the secondary party. On the other hand, some evidence may only be admissible against the secondary party. For example, the secondary party may have made a voluntary confession to the police which he now denies. This, under the rules of evidence, would be admissible evidence against the secondary party who made it, but not against the others since in relation to them it would be inadmissible hearsay. In these circumstances there would be no illogicality in the jury convicting the secondary party even though they felt that they were not satisfied with the case against the principal offender.

One point needs to be remembered. In any of these cases if the acquittal of the principal is tantamount to a finding that the jury are not satisfied that the *actus reus* of the crime was committed by anyone, then obviously they cannot convict someone of being a secondary party. Thus in *Thornton v. Mitchell* (1940) the driver of a bus had been trying to reverse his vehicle with the help of signals on the bell from his conductor. On the given signal he reversed the bus and collided with two pedestrians. He was charged with driving without due care and attention and the conductor was charged with aiding and abetting. Now it is quite clear that the responsibility for what happened lay with the conductor, but he could not be charged with careless driving (even through the innocent agency of the driver) since he had not, in fact, been driving the bus. Thus he was charged as a secondary party to the driver's careless driving. However, the charge against the driver was dismissed, and this could only be on the basis that there was no careless driving, since the offence does not require any subjective *mens rea* on his part. The finding, therefore, was that no crime of careless driving had been committed. It was consequently impossible to convict the conductor as a secondary party to a non-existent crime. Was there any offence with which the conductor could have been charged? If he had intended or seen as likely the injury to the pedestrians then he could have been prosecuted for some form of assault (see below, p. 370). Had the pedestrians died he could probably have been prosecuted for manslaughter as the principal offender (see below, p. 362) but since there is, at present, no offence of negligently causing injury it seems that he committed no offence. If, however, the principal offence has been committed but, the principal offender is, for some reason, exempt from prosecution, then it is still possible to prosecute a secondary offender. This was the position in *Austin* (1981) where the Court of Appeal held that the effect of a statutory provision was that the perpetrator could not be prosecuted; it did not mean that he had not committed the offence.

In the case of *Bourne* (1952) where a husband forced his wife to have sexual connection with a dog, the wife would be the principal offender in the crime of buggery, but because of the duress factor she was not charged and would have been acquitted had she been charged. There was, however, the *actus reus* of buggery and it was held that the husband could be charged with and convicted of this offence.

In *Cogan and Leak* (1976) where the facts were similar to those in Morgan (see above, p. 230) the accused had invited a friend to have intercourse with his wife telling him that his wife was a willing partner. During the intercourse the wife lay passively with her face covered. The jury found that the friend had honestly but unreasonably believed that the woman was consenting and so, following the decision in *Morgan* his conviction for rape was quashed. At the time of this case a husband could not be indicted as a principal offender in the rape of his own wife and so he had been prosecuted as a secondary offender. (The marital exemption rule for husbands no longer exists. In *R. v. R.* (1991) the House of Lords declared that it had been based upon a concept of marriage which no longer existed; see further [1991] All England Law Reports Annual Review pp. 107 ff). The question in *Cogan and Leak* for the Court of Appeal was whether the husband could be convicted as a secondary party to the rape of his wife when the only principal offender had been acquitted on the grounds of lack of *mens rea*. The Court of Appeal held that he could, but unfortunately based this decision largely upon the doctrine of innocent agency. In other words the Court was saying that the husband raped his wife through an innocent agent, namely his friend. This is an unfortunate approach; innocent agency should only be used where the innocent agent is being used as a sort of weapon by the real perpetrator of the crime. Thus X hands Y a poisoned apple to give to Z. Y hands it over to Z without any awareness of the poisonous contents and Z is killed. In that case it makes complete sense to say that X killed Z. It does not make any sense in *Cogan* to say that the husband raped his wife. He did not; his friend raped the wife assisted by the husband. Like the word "drive" in *Thornton v. Mitchell* (above) "intercourse" is another word which does not lend itself to the concept of innocent agency. Furthermore the decision is open to the objection that the use of the innocent agent approach would render the husband liable as the principal offender and at that time he could not be indicted as a principal offender in his wife's rape. It is submitted that Lawton L.J. was on safer grounds when he said: "If we are right in our opinion that the wife had been raped (and no one outside a court of law would say that she had not been), then the particulars of the offence accurately stated what Leak had done, namely that he had procured Cogan to commit the offence." The use of the word "procured" does describe precisely what the defendants in both *Bourne* and *Cogan* had done and this approach received the approval of the Court of Appeal in *Millward* (1994). In *Millward* an employer (P2) instructed his employee (P1) to drive a tractor and trailer belonging to P2. Because the hitch was defective, the trailer broke free and caused the death of another road user. P1 was acquitted of causing death by reckless driving, but P2 was convicted on the basis that he had procured the offence by instructing P1 to drive the tractor. The Court of Appeal upheld the conviction. An accessory can be liable provided that there is the *actus reus* of the principal offence even if the principal offender is entitled to be acquitted because of some defence personal to him or because he lacks *mens rea*. P2 had procured the *actus reus* of the offence. It is to be observed that, if procure means to achieve by endeavour, it can hardly be said that P2 procured the death in the way that Cogan procured the rape, but this point appears to have been overlooked. It is also not clear whether this principle is confined to procuring or whether it extends to other forms of secondary participation. It is, however, a significant development in the principles of liability (see commentary in [1994] Crim. L.R. 528.).

Can the secondary party be convicted of an offence greater than that of the principal?

Suppose that A and B return to A's house one night and discover A's wife in bed with X. Let us suppose that B sees that A is boiling over with rage and so he hands him a poker and urges A to smash in X's skull. If A were to do this, then he would be charged with murder and B would be charged as a secondary party. A, however, is likely to raise, probably successfully, the defence of provocation which will mean that he will be convicted only of manslaughter. B, however, cannot rely on such a defence. Can he therefore be convicted of murder while A, the principal is convicted of manslaughter. Theoretically this would seem quite logical, but until recently it appeared that the Court of Appeal favoured a general rule that it was not open for a jury to convict the secondary party of an offence greater than that of the principal offender (*Richards* (1974)). However in *Howe* (1987) the House of Lords expressed its disapproval of *Richards* and, although the statements concerning *Richards* were *obiter dicta*, it seems fairly safe to assume that in our example of the adulterous spouse a jury could properly find A not guilty of murder but guilty of manslaughter on the ground of provocation, while convicting B, who cannot raise the defence of provocation, of murder. In this example both defendants have the same *mens rea*; the difference lies in a mitigating defence available only to A. The same result should follow in a case where A, the secondary party, has the *mens rea* of murder, while B, the principal offender has the *mens rea* only of manslaughter. For example, if A and B were escaping from the scene of the crime in a car driven by B, when a police officer stepped out into the road and signalled to B to stop. Suppose that A had urged B to run over the officer, but B had made an unsuccessful attempt to avoid hitting him and the officer was killed. It may well be, if B's driving were sufficiently bad, that B could be convicted of manslaughter (see below, p. 362); he cannot be convicted of murder since he lacks the necessary *mens rea*. A, however, is a party to the *actus reus* of unlawful homicide (the *actus reus* for murder and manslaughter is the same, see p. 341) and since A possesses the *mens rea* of murder he should be convicted of that offence. (See also, *Hui Chi-Min* above, p. 257).

(4) Victims as Parties to an Offence

When A is charged with raping B we can say that in a very real sense B is the victim of the crime and no one would suggest that B is a party to rape. On the other hand, if A is charged with having unlawful sexual intercourse with his 15-year-old girl friend, B is again the victim, but this time a very willing one and so why should she not be charged as an accessory to A's crime? The reason why B cannot be so charged is the rule in *Tyrell's* case (1894) which provides that where a statute is designed to protect a certain class of individual, then such an individual cannot be held to be a party to the crime however willing she was for the crime to be committed against her. The scope of the rule is uncertain but it has been applied mainly in the sexual area. It only protects, however, the victim of the particular crime. If B, a 15-year-old girl helps A to have intercourse with C, another 15-year-old girl, then B can be charged as a party to that intercourse, but C cannot.

(5) Repentance by a Secondary Party before the Crime is Committed

As we have said, the secondary party becomes liable only when the principal commits the offence in question or attempts to commit it. There may be, therefore, a fair amount of time between the act of assistance rendered by the secondary party and the commission of the offence by the principal. Is it therefore possible for the secondary party to escape subsequent liability by washing his hands of the crime?

It obviously makes sense to allow a person to avoid criminal liability by withdrawing from a criminal venture before it takes place. On the other hand, where an accused has given help to others who then commit a crime, it should not suffice that the accused has simply resolved to have nothing more to do with the venture. What therefore constitutes an effective withdrawal? This will depend upon the nature of the assistance given, the type of crime involved and the timing of the withdrawal (*Becerra* (1975) (*Casebook*, p. 203). Where the accused's part in the crime has consisted solely in giving advice and encouragement, then he can effectively withdraw simply by telling the other parties that he is withdrawing his encouragement. (*Whitefield* (1984)). Where the accused decides to withdraw long before the commission of the offence, it may suffice that he makes it very clear to the others that any further activity will go ahead without any further assistance from the accused. Where the offence is about to be committed it may well be that the accused must try, by force if necessary, to prevent the commission of the offence. If his assistance has been in the form of supplying a gun for the murder, then the court would certainly require something more than mere communication by the accused to the would-be killer that the accused wants nothing more to do with the offence. In such a case, or where communication with the other parties is impossible, it may be that the only effective action the accused can take to withdraw is to inform the police so that the crime can be stopped.

The mere fact that the police have already arrested the secondary party does not mean that he can no longer give assistance to the principal (see *Craig and Bentley*, above, p. 250).

2. Vicarious and Corporate Liability

We shall conclude this chapter with a look at the way in which a master can be prosecuted for the crimes of his servants and a limited company can be prosecuted as if it were a human defendant.

(1) Vicarious Liability

In civil actions a master (usually covered today by the word "employer") is liable for the wrongs of his servants (employees) which were committed by the servants during the course of their employment. This usually enables the victim of the torts to sue a defendant who is more likely to be able to pay should liability be proved. There is no general application of vicarious liability in criminal law where we are normally trying to attach liability to the people directly responsible for the commission of a criminal offence and where compensation of the victim is not the primary concern. However, it does occur in the following situations:

(a) *Express statutory vicarious liability*

Occasionally Parliament provides expressly for the imposition of vicarious liability. For example, section 163(1) of the Licensing Act 1964 provides: "A person shall not, in pursuance of a sale by him of intoxicating liquor, deliver that liquor, either himself or *by his servant or agent*, from any van, barrow, basket or other vehicle or receptacle. . . . "

(b) *Implied vicarious liability*

In some cases the courts treat the acts of the perpetrator as the acts of his employer. This they will do when the word used in the statute is one which, without too much of a strain on its meaning, can be interpreted to cover persons other than the actual perpetrator. Such words as "sell," "supply" and "use" have frequently received this extended meaning. Thus when a lorry driver takes a lorry out for his employer, it is not unreasonable to say that both the driver and the employer "use" the lorry. So both could be said to have used a lorry with defective brakes. This form of vicarious liability is found only in cases where the statute imposes strict liability.

It cannot be used, in offences requiring *mens rea*, to transfer the *mens rea* of the actual perpetrator to his employer.

In *James & Sons Ltd v. Smee* (1955) the offence in question was using, or causing or permitting to be used, a vehicle in contravention of the Motor Vehicle (Construction and Use) Regulations 1951. The Divisional Court held that there were in effect three different crimes of which permitting to be used clearly required *mens rea* and using clearly did not. Thus if A, an employee, sets out in one of his employer's lorries which has defective tyres, the employer, B, can only be convicted of permitting the use of the vehicle if he knows that the tyres are defective whereas A can be charged with using the vehicle even if he is unaware of the defect. Furthermore, if the police rely on the "using" offence they can hold B vicariously liable—they can, in effect, say that B was using the lorry. They may charge both A and B in which case they will be co-principals. If, however, the regulation had provided that it was an offence to drive a vehicle with defective tyres, then the police could charge only A as a principal offender. B could not be held vicariously liable since the word "drive" is not really capable of an extended meaning—you could not really say that B had driven the lorry. In this case it would only be possible to charge B as a secondary party and then only if he had knowledge of the defect. (See also *Coppen v. Moore (No. 2)* (1898)).

(c) *The delegation cases*

Most people are aware that before a public house can sell alcohol to the public there will have to be a licence obtained from the local magistrates permitting such a sale. This licence has to be issued to a person and not to a company so it will be issued either to the tenant of the pub or, in most cases today, the manager who draws his salary from one of the breweries. The sale of alcohol is governed in the main by the Licensing Act 1964 under which there are many offences which can only be committed by the holder of the justices' licence. This means that he will have to be named as the principal offender and if he does not commit the offence then the offence is not committed which means that there is no chance of charging the actual perpetrator (*e.g.* a barman) as a secondary party. There are not many pubs or establishments operating under these licences where the licensee is the sole person working. Most places employ staff and so there is a good chance that it will be these staff that perpetrate the acts which if done by the licensee would be an offence. Thus without vicarious liability many offences would be virtually unenforceable.

Some of the offences under the Licensing Act are offences of strict liability and where this is the case it may be possible to hold the licensee vicariously liable under the principles discussed in section (b) above; e.g., selling alcohol to a person under the age of 18 years. The courts, however, do not seem to have taken this course in licensee cases. On the other hand some of the offences are offences requiring *mens rea*. We saw in Chapter 7 (above, p. 236) that the offence of selling alcohol to a policeman on duty requires that the offender knows that the policeman is, in fact, on duty. The offences of permitting drunkenness and permitting prostitutes to congregate also require *mens rea*. The courts have not allowed the type of vicarious liability we saw in the previous section to be used where the offence requires *mens rea*. Thus the courts have developed a second type of vicarious liability which is now used almost entirely to impute the guilty mind of the licensee's employees to the licensee himself. This operates only when the licensee has delegated general responsibility to his staff for at least part of the pub and is himself not present in that part when the offence is committed. The principle is not restricted to the Licensing Act, but this is where it has been largely developed.

We can see how this delegation principle works in relation to an offence requiring *mens rea*. Let us suppose that members of the local rugby club are in the lounge celebrating a victory that day. They are now all well and truly drunk. It is an offence for the licensee to permit drunkenness on the licensed premises (the Licensing Act 1964, s.172(1)). B, who is the senior barman on duty in the lounge, has been instructed by A that under no circumstances must he permit such behaviour. B, however, knows most of the players and consequently does nothing. Has an offence been committed? This will depend upon whether we can impute B's knowledge to A under the delegation principle. This raises two questions. Has A delegated authority for the general running of the lounge to B and is A absent? Of course, if he has gone out for the night he will have delegated authority to someone and he will not be present. But is it enough that he is simply in another room? Most of the cases on this topic suggest that it is sufficient that the licensee is not in the room in question at the time the offence is committed and that in his absence another is in charge (see *Howker v. Robinson* (1973)). However, in *Vane v. Yiannopoullos* (1965) the House of Lords held that there had not been delegation when the licensee of a restaurant was not in the room in question, but had gone up on to another floor. Since there was no delegation the House of Lords did not give a final ruling on the delegation principle, but their comments suggested that they were not altogether happy about the idea of imputing *mens rea* to a licensee in this way. As Lord Donovan said "If a decision that 'knowingly' means that 'knowingly' will make the provision difficult to enforce, the remedy lies with the legislature." But the lower courts have continued to apply the delegation principle.

If the drunken men were in the bar where A was clearly in charge then the delegation principle does not operate. So, in our example, if the drunken men were in the bar and only D is aware of their state, D's knowledge cannot be imputed to A. In such a case the prosecution will have to prove that it was A who personally permitted the drunken men to remain and that he knew that they were drunk.

One final point can be made here. Suppose that various customers continue to drink after closing time with the knowledge of the bar staff. The point to remember is that the offence is drinking after hours and not permitting customers to drink after hours. Thus it is the customer who is the principal offender. Any of the staff who knowingly permit this to continue will be liable as secondary parties, but if A is absent the knowledge of his staff cannot be imputed to him under the delegation principle; you cannot be vicariously liable as a secondary party (*Ferguson v. Weaving* (1951)).

(2) Corporate Liability

Limited companies possess what is known as legal personality. This means that the company can hold property as if it were an ordinary human being and that it can sue and be sued in the civil courts in its own name. The question for us to consider now is whether the company can be a party to criminal proceedings. Of course when a criminal offence is committed, the actual act must have been perpetrated by an ordinary human being and he will be liable as an individual for the criminal act, but the courts have held that in certain circumstances the limited company can also be held liable in the criminal law for the acts of one of the member individuals.

There are two ways in which a limited company can be held liable for criminal acts:

(i) The company can be held to be vicariously liable for the crimes of its employees in just the same way that a human employer can be held responsible for the crimes of his employee. Thus, as we saw earlier this will only apply in statutory crimes of strict liability where the court has been able to give an extended meaning to words such as "sell" or "use."

(ii) The company can be held liable by what is known as the doctrine of identification. What this means is that in each company the court recognises certain senior individuals as being the company itself and the acts of these individuals when acting in the company's business are treated as the acts of the company. It has been said that certain members of the company can be regarded as its brain and the others as its hands. This tells us that we are looking for people who have the power to control the company's actions. Thus in most companies we can say that the managing director and the other directors will be regarded as being in a position of control and this might even extend to the company secretary and non-director managers if they have sufficient executive power. But the line is not easy to draw with any degree of certainty and this was illustrated by the case of *Tesco Supermarkets Ltd v. Nattrass* (1972). In that case an old age pensioner was trying to buy a packet of soap powder at the reduced price being offered by one of Tesco's shops. He could not find any packets priced at the lower price and the shop refused to sell him a packet at anything other than the full price. He complained to the inspector of weights and measures who brought a prosecution against Tesco Supermarkets Ltd under the Trade Descriptions Act 1968, s.11(2). Tesco sought to put the blame on the branch manager who had failed to ensure that packets at the reduced price were on display, despite the control exercised by the firm and its detailed instructions to managers as to how to deal with such matters. One of the issues confronting the House of Lords was whether or not the store manager could be identified as the company. If this was the case then Tesco would be liable for the offence. The House of Lords held that because of the strict controls exercised by the company over its branch managers they were left with so little power that they could not be regarded as part of the "brains" of the company. This meant that Tesco Ltd was able to show that the offence was, in fact, committed by a third party—namely their manager—and thus it could rely on section 24 of the Act which provided that it would be a defence to a person charged under the Act to show that the commission of the offence was due to the act or default of another person and that he himself took all reasonable precautions to prevent the commission of such an offence by himself or any person under his control. (See defences to strict liability above, p. 246.) This is not a true example of the third-party defence since there is no need for the third party to be joined in the proceedings. It is sufficient that the defendant can give sufficient information to the prosecution to enable the true culprit to be prosecuted.

Liability of individual

If the firm is held to be liable because of the acts of one of its members, can the member be joined as a party to the proceedings? The answer to this is clearly yes. In both types of corporate liability he may be joined as a co-principal.

Are there any crimes a company cannot commit?

A company can be convicted of any offence provided that the sentence can be in the nature of a fine. You clearly cannot send a company to jail, let alone hang it. Thus the penalty must take the form of a fine which will fall upon the shareholders. The only crimes where this will not be possible are treason, murder and some forms of piracy where imprisonment is mandatory.

Theoretically this means a company can be convicted of all offences against the person except for murder. In *P & O European Ferries (Dover) Ltd* (1991) Turner J. held that an indictment for manslaughter could lie against a company. In November 1994 the first conviction of a company for manslaughter was reported. It involved the drowning of four young persons while taking part in an adventure holiday. The directors were held to have been grossly negligent in allowing the young persons to have sailed in dangerous seas. Both the company and the managing director were convicted. It is, however, difficult to imagine that a company director acting in furtherance of his company duties could ever render the company liable for rape. However, if Z, the managing director of X Co. Ltd, a film company, supervises the filming of intercourse between M, an 18-year-old male with N, a 15-year-old girl, there is no reason why Z and hence the film company should not be convicted as secondary parties to the unlawful sexual intercourse.

Chapter 9

General Defences

Although specific crimes may be provided with special defences of their own, there are several defences which are of general application to criminal offences and these will be examined in this chapter. Most defences are, in fact, allegations by the accused that the prosecution has failed to establish one or more elements of the *actus reus* or *mens rea*. In some cases the defence relates to a part of the *actus reus* or *mens rea* that is so central that the accused does not even have an evidential burden to discharge before the judge is bound to leave it for consideration by the jury. Thus if X is charged with the murder of Y and he says either that it was another man who shot Y or that the gun went off accidentally, he is doing nothing more than saying that the prosecution cannot prove that he caused Y's death or that he had the *mens rea* needed for murder. Both of these issues are issues upon which the prosecution have the duty to introduce evidence and also the duty to prove their case to the court's satisfaction. It would obviously be advisable for the accused to introduce any evidence he possesses in support of such defences, especially where the prosecution appears to have a good case. On the other hand if the prosecution's case is weak he may be advised to say nothing, since the judge is bound to direct the jury that the prosecution must prove that the accused was the man who pulled the trigger and that he did so with the necessary *mens rea*. A second group of defences although relating to the *actus reus* or *mens rea* of the crime are not so central to the prosecution's case and here the accused may well bear an evidential burden, which means that unless, by the end of the case there is evidence which could create a reasonable doubt, the judge will not give the jury any direction on that issue. This is the case with the defences of self-defence, provocation, duress, necessity, automatism and intoxication. Finally there are those defences in which the accused bears not only an evidential but also a legal burden; here the accused will not only have to introduce evidence of this defence, but he will also have to prove to the jury that it was more likely than not that factors amounting to such a defence existed. Under this category come the defences of insanity, and diminished responsibility (there are others but these are by far the best known).

If we discount for the moment those defences in the third category, it is probably not inaccurate to say that in order for the prosecution to secure a conviction, it must prove *actus reus*, *mens rea* and absence of a defence. Thus if X is charged with the murder of Y, the prosecution will have to prove the *actus reus* of the crime and this will include proof that the killing was unlawful. If X gives no evidence and the prosecution establish that X shot Y and that Y died as a result, the jury would conclude that the prosecution had also proved that the killing was unlawful. On the other hand if X believes that he acted in self-defence the judge will only direct the jury to consider whether the prosecution have failed to rebut self-defence beyond reasonable doubt if, by the end of the case for the defence, there is some evidence to support such a finding. It does not matter whether this has been raised specifically by the defence or whether it has emerged from various sources during the course of the trial so long as there is evidence adduced upon which a jury could entertain a reasonable doubt.

1. The Mentally Abnormal Offender

(1) Insanity and Unfitness to Plead

The defence of insanity is raised by a defendant who is claiming that at the time he was alleged to have committed the offence he was suffering from a mental condition which would excuse him from criminal responsibility. Where a court reaches such a conclusion it returns a verdict of not guilty by reason of insanity. If it is obvious that the defendant is totally unfit to stand trial, there are powers to commit him directly to a mental hospital (sections 47 and 48 Mental Health Act 1983). Where it is less obvious and he is sent for trial, the court may determine that he is unfit to plead. A person is unfit to plead when he is unable to recognise the charges that have been brought against him and is unable to appreciate the difference between pleas of guilty and not guilty. If he is able to understand these issues he is fit to stand trial even if he is unable to recall any of the events to which the charges relate (Podola (1960)). Where the issue is raised by the defendant he has the burden of proving on a balance of probabilities that he is unfit to plead; where it is raised by the judge or prosecution, the prosecution bears the burden of proving beyond reasonable doubt that the accused is unfit. Until very recently once a trial court held that the defendant was insane or unfit to plead, it had no discretion but to make an order admitting him to a mental institution coupled with a restriction direction forbidding his release without the Home Secretary's approval. As a result very few defendants were inclined to use these pleas. For this reason the Criminal Procedure (Insanity and Unfitness to Plead) Act 1991 makes important changes by way of amendment to the Criminal Procedure (Insanity) Act 1964.

The 1991 Act provides that no jury may make a finding that the accused is insane or unfit to plead unless it has received evidence from at least two qualified medical practitioners, at least one of whom must be approved by the Home Secretary as having special experience in the diagnosis or treatment of mental disorder. In the case of unfitness to plead, the issue should normally be dealt with at the beginning of the trial by a jury different from that which will hear the case should the trial proceed. However, the trial judge may delay considera-tion of the issue of unfitness to plead right up until the start of the defence case. If before the defence opens, the jury has already acquitted the defendant (*i.e.* on a submission of no case to answer), the issue of unfitness to plead may not be tried. If the issue of unfitness is dealt with after the start of the trial of the offences, the judge will decide whether it will be heard by a separate jury or the jury which is trying the case. Once a jury has returned a finding that the defendant is under a disability and hence unfit to plead, the jury will then determine, on the evidence already received or now adduced, whether they are satisfied that the defendant did in fact do the act or make the omission charged against him. The jury will either make such a finding or return an acquittal.

Where the court reaches a verdict of not guilty by reason of insanity or unfitness to plead coupled with a finding that he did the act or made the omission with which he was charged, it is no longer restricted to making an order confining the defendant indefinitely to a mental hospital. It may make (i) an order admitting him to a hospital (with or without a restriction order); (ii) a guardianship order under the Mental Health Act 1983; (iii) a supervision and treatment order under schedule 2 of the Criminal Procedure (Insanity and Unfitness to Plead) Act 1991 or (iv) an absolute discharge. In murder, however, it must make an admission order coupled with an indefinite restriction direction.

Where under its powers under sections 6 and 14 of the Criminal Appeal Act 1968 the Court of Appeal, on an appeal against conviction or acquittal on the grounds of insanity, substitutes a verdict of not guilty by reason of insanity or unfitness to plead together with a finding that the accused did the act, it may make any of the orders available to the court of trial.

It is hoped that these new provisions will make the defence of insanity more acceptable to defendants who could benefit from the wide treatment which is now available.

(2) The Defences of Insanity and Diminished Responsibility

Now we can look at the scope of the defence of insanity, under which the accused claims that because of his mental state at the time he allegedly committed the offence, he was not truly responsible for his actions. The defence of insanity is of common law origin and its requirements are to be found in what are known as the M'Naghten Rules 1843 (from M'Naghten's Case (1843) Casebook, p. 216). We shall see that insanity is a relatively narrow defence and does not provide for many mentally abnormal offenders. This led Parliament in the Homicide Act 1957 to provide a special defence, applicable only to murder, known as diminished responsibility which, when successfully pleaded, means that the accused will be convicted, not of murder, but manslaughter.

(a) Insanity

The word "insanity" is not a medically recognised term which describes a particular mental state; it is a legal term for a legally defined state of mind which will lead in any criminal offence to a verdict of not guilty by reason of insanity.

The starting point is the presumption that the accused is presumed sane until the contrary is proved. The burden of proving insanity lies on whoever wishes such a finding to be made by the jury. Thus if the accused raises the defence he must prove that it is more likely than not that he is insane. If the accused pleads diminished responsibility the prosecution will be entitled to argue that the accused was insane. If the jury decide that the accused was insane they will return a verdict of not guilty by reason of insanity. Since this is technically an acquittal it is provided by section 12 of the Criminal Procedure (Insanity) Act 1964 that the accused may appeal against the verdict.

The fact that before the Criminal Procedure (Insanity and Unfitness to Plead) Act 1991 a verdict of not guilty by reason of insanity meant hospitalisation, very few defendants chose to raise it directly, except as a defence to very serious charges. In murder cases it was virtually superseded by the defence of diminished responsibility. However it may arise indirectly. Firstly, as we have already seen, it may be raised by the prosecution in answer to the defendant's plea of diminished responsibility. Secondly the accused, in seeking to raise some other defence such as automatism or even lack of *mens rea*, may provide an explanation for his conduct which may be seen by the trial judge as evidence of insanity. In such a case the trial judge will be bound to leave the defence of insanity to the jury. Where the defence realises that this will happen, he may change his plea to guilty to avoid any possibility of a verdict of not guilty by reason of insanity and the risk of incarceration in a mental hospital.

The side bearing the burden of proof must prove that the accused was, at the time he committed the act, "labouring under such a defect of reason, from disease of the mind, as not to know the nature and quality of the act he was doing, or if he did know it, that he did not know he was doing what was wrong." Thus there are various elements which must be established.

(i) **Defect of reason.** The defendant (or prosecutor if it is the prosecutor who is seeking to establish the defendant is insane) must show that the defendant was suffering from such a defect of reason that he did not know the nature and quality of the act he had committed or, if he did know, that he did not know that what he was doing was wrong.

Clearly anyone who is acting in a state of automatism will not know the nature and quality of his act. More generally the reference to nature and quality of the act is another way of saying that the accused lacked the necessary *mens rea* for the crime. Traditional examples given include the man who cut a woman's throat thinking it was a loaf of bread, and the nurse who put the baby on the fire thinking it was a log of wood.

If the accused is relying on the second limb—that he did not know he was doing what was wrong—then he must prove that he did not know that it was legally wrong (*Windle* (1952)). Thus, even though the accused believed that what he was doing was morally abhorrent and that people in general would not approve, he is entitled to a verdict of not guilty by reason of insanity if he can show that he thought that it was legally permissible. It is useful to remember at this point that in the case of a sane adult, it is no defence to prove that he was unaware that his actions constituted a criminal offence (see above, p. 228). Thus if X's disease of the mind caused him to think that three of his friends, A, B and C were members of an assassination squad who had to be killed before they could kill him, then he would succeed on a defence of insanity, because his delusion caused him to think that he was legally entitled to kill A, B and C. If, on the other hand, his disease of the mind caused him to think that he was Jack the Ripper and so led him to go round killing prostitutes, he would not succeed with a plea of insanity because, as Jack the Ripper, he would know that he was not entitled to kill random prostitutes. He might now, however, be able to plead diminished responsibility.

(ii) **Disease of the mind.** Not every defect of reason will lead to a defence of insanity. The defect of reason must have been caused by a disease of the mind. Where, for example, the defect of reason has been brought about by the defendant consuming 15 pints of beer, he may be able to plead intoxication (see below, p. 293) but the defence of insanity will not be available. Where, therefore, the accused has relied on a blackout at the time of the alleged crime, the court will want information as to the cause of the blackout. If this explanation reveals that the cause was a disease of the mind, then the defendant will be taken to have raised the defence of insanity. What, therefore, constitutes a disease of the mind? In *Sullivan* (1983), in the House of Lords, Lord Diplock said:

" 'mind' in the M'Naghten Rules is used in the ordinary sense of the mental faculties of reason, memory and understanding. If the effect of a disease is to impair these faculties so severely as to have either of the consequences referred to in the latter part of the rules, it matters not whether the aetiology of the impairment is organic, as in epilepsy, or functional, or whether the impairment itself is permanent or is transient and intermittent, provided that it subsisted at the time of the commission of the act."

Thus any condition which produces these effects on the mind can and will be classified as a disease of the mind; remember it is a disease of the mind and not a disease of the brain which is required. In the later cases of *Quick* (1973) and

Hennessey (1989) the Court of Appeal made it clear that the basic question for the courts is whether the condition was caused by internal or external factors. For example, it is clear that where the condition is caused by illness such as epilepsy or diabetes it will be classified as a disease of the mind. (The case of *Charlson* (1955) in which a state of automatism produced by a brain tumour was held to be non-insane automatism must now be considered to be wrong.) The distinction between external and internal factors is not, however, entirely straightforward. In diabetes certain conditions such as hypoglycaemia (low blood-sugar level) can be caused by failure to eat sufficient food or the administration of incorrect levels of insulin. Where this has happened the condition will be ascribed to external factors and will not therefore be classified as insanity; (see, *e.g. Bingham* (1991)). In *Hennessey* (1989) *(Casebook* p. 213) the defendant was suffering from hyperglycaemia (high blood sugar level) at the relevant time. This, the Court of Appeal held, was brought about not by any external factor, but by the illness (diabetes) itself. It was therefore a disease of the mind. In cases where the condition has been triggered by external factors such as alcohol, failure to eat properly or administration of too much insulin, the jury should consider whether this is the first time it happened. If it has happened in the past, the accused might be said to have been reckless in his behaviour.

The courts have indicated that those causes which are prone to recur are more likely to be treated as internal causes. In other words external factors which cause automatism are likely to be unexpected occurrences such as a blow on the head, which are not likely to recur and hence which are not susceptible to treatment. Thus in *R. v. T.* (1990) the Court of Appeal held that the recent rape of the defendant which had caused Post Traumatic Stress Disorder and a dream-like state of mind at the time of the offence now alleged was a prime example of an external factor. In *Rabey* (1978) on the other hand, where the defendant had sought to rely on rejection by his girlfriend as a cause of his automatism, the court held that this was the sort of stress that everyone had to be able to come to terms with. It was not so much the rejection (clearly an external factor) but his failure to cope with it which had caused the automatism and this was part of his psychological make-up and hence an internal factor.

It is clear what the courts are trying to achieve. They are trying to distinguish between cases where the defendant can be safely acquitted and allowed to resume his everyday life and cases where the defendant should not be convicted of the offence but should nevertheless be obliged to undergo treatment to ensure the public's safety in the future. Thus where the defendant has acted as an automaton because of a blow on the head, or because he has been attacked by a swarm of bees, or because he has failed to eat in conjunction with his insulin, he can be expected to behave normally in the future, and can therefore be acquitted. Where, however, the automatism has been caused by an internal factor which is likely to recur, it is felt that the court should have the power to ensure that he receives treatment for the condition. His acquittal is therefore a qualified acquittal. Consider, however, a case in which the defendant is charged with assaulting a football referee thereby occasioning him actual bodily harm. His defence is that he had just been kicked on the head and he had acted in a state of automatism. If he can produce evidence to support this claim, the court will treat the matter as one of non-insane automatism. However, suppose that in the next two football matches he blacks out again and strikes the referee. What would the court's reaction be to a defence that this also was non-insane automatism brought about by the kick on the head in the first match?

Until recently sleepwalking had been cited as a clear example of non-insane automatism. However unless it stems from external factors it will be treated as arising from internal causes and hence insane automatism. If the defendant has killed another while sleepwalking the public clearly need protection (*Burgess* (1991)) (*Casebook* p. 218).

Insanity is a legal and not a medical term. Its use in many of these cases is highly offensive. Clearly the courts need to have the power to protect the public from possible danger, but is it essential to label as insane a diabetic whose illness has caused him to take goods from a shop while in a state of automatism?

The question of whether a given condition amounts to a disease of the mind is a question of law for the judge.

(b) *Diminished responsibility*

Such was the narrowness of the legal test for insanity that Parliament introduced a special defence which would apply to charges of murder only. This was known as diminished responsibility and a successful plea leads to the accused being convicted of manslaughter rather than murder. As with insanity, the burden of proof lies on the accused to prove that it was more likely than not that he was suffering from diminished responsibility at the time he committed the offence. In *Campbell* (1987) the Court of Appeal held that a trial judge who thought that the evidence raised the issue of diminished responsibility should inform the counsel for the defence of his opinion in the absence of the jury. In effect, it is rather like provocation in that it enables the jury to return a verdict of guilty of manslaughter but not a complete acquittal. (Recent cases have shown that the defences of provocation and diminished responsibility may often arise on the same facts; see *e.g. Cox* (1995).) Once the jury has returned a verdict of guilty of manslaughter, the judge then has a wide discretion over what should happen to the accused. He can commit him to prison for up to life, he can have him detained in a mental institution, he can put him on probation or even give him an absolute discharge. The net result is that diminished responsibility has almost entirely replaced insanity as a defence. In reality, insanity was only raised as a defence to a charge of murder and we shall see that any state of mind that can constitute insanity would also amount to diminished responsibility. Until the 1991 Act (above) a verdict of insanity meant indefinite hospitalisation whereas, following a success-ful plea of diminished responsibility, there is every chance that the judge will pass a determinate prison sentence.

What, then, must the accused prove in order to establish the defence? Section 2(1) of the Homicide Act 1957 provides:

"Where a person kills or is a party to the killing of another, he shall not be convicted of murder if he was suffering from such abnormality of mind (whether arising from a condition of arrested or retarded development of mind or any inherent causes or induced by disease or injury) as substantially impaired his mental responsibility for his acts and omissions in doing or being a party to the killing."

This looks all very technical. What is the judge supposed to do? Is he to try to define the terms of the section for the jury? The Court of Criminal Appeal eventually resolved that it was wrong for a trial judge simply to read the section to the jury and leave them to make what they could of it. He should give them whatever guidance they require to understand it (*Byrne* (1960)). Basically, three factors have to be established:

(i) **The accused must have been suffering from an abnormality of mind.** In effect, the judge should ask them whether the accused's mind seems normal—would they say that he appeared to them to be normal. If he appears "mad" or "insane" (as a layman would use these words) then he can be said to be suffering from an abnormality of mind. Thus it was apt to cover the accused in *Byrne* (1960) (*Casebook*, p. 223) who had strangled a young girl and had then horribly mutilated her body. His defence was that from early years, he had suffered from overwhelming perverted desires which he found very difficult—if not impossible to resist. He submitted that he had killed the girl under the influence of such an urge. It is interesting to pause here for a moment. Could Byrne have successfully pleaded insanity? The answer is that he could not. Whether or not he could have established that he was suffering from a disease of the mind, the evidence suggested that not only did he appreciate what he was doing, but that he also realised that it was wrong. His trouble was that he found it very difficult to stop himself.

In *Seers* (1985) where the defendant had pleaded diminished responsibility on the basis of reactive depression the Court of Appeal said that *Byrne* (above) should not be taken as laying down an immutable rule that juries should, in every case where diminished responsibility is raised, be asked whether or not the defendant could be described in popular language as partially insane or on the borderline of insanity. Even if "insane" were given a broad meaning, it was inappropriate to describe every condition which might properly be described as an "abnormality of mind." The trial judge should always relate his direction to the jury to the particular evidence in the case.

(ii) **Cause of the abnormality of mind.** The abnormality of mind must have arisen from a condition of arrested or retarded development of mind or any inherent causes or must have been induced by disease or injury. This is clearly a very wide provision. Is it wide enough to cover an abnormality of mind caused by excessive drink or drugs? It would seem for this to be possible, the accused would have to argue that the alcohol had injured his mind; possibly, therefore, a condition such as alcoholism caused by long-term drinking might be covered, but not an accused who was simply drunk at the time he committed the offence. In *Gittens* (1984) the court was faced with a situation in which the abnormality of mind had been caused in part by inherent causes and in part by drink and drugs. In such a case it would seem that the jury should be asked whether they were satisfied, on a balance of probabilities, that if the accused had not taken drink (i) he would have killed as he in fact did? and (ii) he would have been under diminished responsibility when he did so. In other words the jury have to try to discount the effect of the voluntary consumption of alcohol. In *Tandy* (1987); (*Casebook*, p. 226) where the defendant tried to prove that the diminished responsibility was caused by alcoholism, the Court of Appeal said that the issue for the jury was whether her abnormality of mind was induced by disease, namely the disease of alcoholism. She would have to prove that the drink taken on the day in question had been taken involuntarily as a result of her condition. If the jury found that she took the first drink of the day voluntarily, they should conclude that the defence of diminished responsibility was not open to her.

(iii) Effect of the abnormality of mind. The accused must prove that the abnormality of mind substantially impaired his mental responsibility for his acts and omissions in doing or being a party to the killing. In *Byrne*, the accused had relied on perverted sexual urges which he alleged caused him to kill the girl. Clearly, if the evidence had shown that he found these urges to be irresistible, the defence would have been established. But this would amount to a total impairment of his responsibility and the Act says that he need only prove a substantial impairment. What, therefore, does the Act mean by "substantial?" In *Egan* (1993), the Court of Appeal approved directions given in *Lloyd* (1966) to the effect that (i) the jury should approach the word in a broad common-sense way or (ii) the word meant more than some trivial degree of improvement which does not make an appreciable difference to a person's ability to control himself, but it means less than total impairment (see *Mitchell* (1995)).

Procedural note

Under section 6 of the Criminal Procedure (Insanity) Act 1964, it is clearly provided that if the accused raises the defence of insanity or diminished responsibility the prosecution shall be entitled to prove the alternative defence. But here the standard of proof required of the prosecution is the criminal standard—proof beyond reasonable doubt.

(3) Hospital Orders

After a successful plea of diminished responsibility has resulted in a manslaughter conviction, the court, as one of its sentencing options, may make a hospital order under the Mental Health Act 1983. Where the court, in such a case, feels that the accused is particularly dangerous, it can make a restriction order which has the effect of necessitating the consent of the Home Secretary before he can be moved or released.

2. The Intoxicated Offender

You will recall that under section 8 of the Criminal Justice Act 1967, where the definition of the offence requires that the prosecution prove that the accused intended or foresaw that a given result would be a consequence of his action (*i.e.* that sticking a knife into Y would cause Y's death) then the jury should be entitled to take into account any evidence which may help them reach such a conclusion. The same sort of proposition should be true in relation to knowledge or foresight of circumstances. One such factor immediately springs to mind, namely that the accused has drunk so much alcohol or has taken such a large quantity of heroin that he really could not have been fully aware of what he was doing. Is this therefore a factor the jury are entitled to take into account? Why should it be any different from any other factor which might affect the accused's ability to form the necessary *mens rea* required? One reason is that many members of society would find it abhorrent that a person who has caused the *actus reus* of a criminal act should escape liability because he has got himself into such a state that he did not know what he was doing. Should the law, therefore, allow such a defence only if the court is satisfied that the accused was not at fault in becoming intoxicated or drugged; if, for example, his drinks had been laced? We shall examine first of all those situations in which the accused has knowingly consumed alcohol or drugs and seeks to adduce this as evidence that he should not be held responsible for the act he committed. After that we shall look at the situation where the intoxication was involuntary. (In this section we shall use the word intoxication to cover both drink and drug induced states.)

A. Voluntary Intoxication

If the basic common law principle of requiring the *actus reus* to be accompanied by the necessary *mens rea* before there could be a conviction were to apply in relation to defendants who had consumed quantities of alcohol, then it would follow that if the accused has consumed so much alcohol that he did not form the requisite *mens rea* for the offence he should be acquitted. But as we have already said, such a rule would be unacceptable to many. Objection could be taken on the ground that such a defence would be easy to raise and hard to rebut, or simply that people who get drunk should learn to accept the consequences, and possibly this last notion is at the base of the uneasy compromise that has been drawn by the courts in this area.

If there were no special rules relating to voluntary (or self-induced) intoxication, it would not necessarily follow that such intoxication would afford a defence of a criminal charge. It would only afford a defence if it negatived the requisite *mens rea* for the offence. Thus it would not have availed *Prince* (1875) (above, p. 236) to have said that he made his mistake about the girl's age because he was drunk. Liability in relation to her age was, and is, strict. It follows that a mistake about her age, however caused, is irrelevant. Where liability is based upon negligence, as in the offence of careless driving (contrary to s.3 of the Road Traffic Act 1988) it would be of no use for the defendant to say that had he been sober he would have seen the other car coming; the drunkenness affords all the evidence needed of negligence on the part of the driver. Also where liability can be established by the wider meaning of recklessness in *Caldwell* (above, p. 214) drunkenness will be irrelevant since the prosecution will merely have to prove that the defendant gave no thought to an obvious and serious risk; it matters not why he gave no thought. In fact in all these cases it will not matter whether the defendant was suffering from voluntary or involuntary intoxication.

Where, however, the prosecution has to establish intention or *Cunningham* recklessness (or the narrower meaning of recklessness within the *Caldwell* definition see above, p. 214), intoxication could clearly negative the *mens rea* required. Thus if X is accused of intentionally killing Y, the fact that he was intoxicated could explain why he thought Y was a wax works model. Also, if there is a *Caldwell* loophole (see above, p. 222) then D would be able to say that he gave some thought to the possibility of there being a risk, but, because of his drunken state, he concluded that there was no risk. The question, therefore, is whether the courts are prepared to allow the defendant to plead that he did not form the necessary *mens rea* in these cases because he was drunk. Section 8 of the Criminal Justice Act 1967 (see above, p. 235) would seem to suggest that the jury should be entitled to consider any facts which might help them decide whether or not the accused possessed the necessary *mens rea*, and intoxication would appear to be a very relevant consideration. On the other hand many citizens would be gravely offended at the proposition that a person could escape criminal liability on the basis that he had got himself so drunk that he did not know what he was doing. Current public opinion is probably moving even more towards the condemnation of intoxication, and it is this which explains the law's approach to voluntary intoxication as a defence. We shall see later that the courts will probably be prepared to take a far more tolerant approach to cases where the accused is not responsible for his intoxication (see below, p. 301).

The general position can be stated thus. Where the prosecution has to establish intention or *Cunningham* reckless-ness (and probably to a case where the *Caldwell* loophole applies) the answer depends upon whether the crime is classified as one requiring *basic* or *specific* intent. In *Majewski* (1977) the House of Lords held that voluntary intoxication could be a defence only to crimes requiring *specific* intent; in relation to a crime of *basic* intent it was irrelevant. The question, therefore, is what do we mean by a crime of *specific* intent? As a general rule, these are crimes where, on at least one element of the *actus reus*, the prosecution will succeed only if it can establish intention. Crimes of basic intent are those crimes where the prosecution will succeed if it can establish either intention or recklessness on every aspect of the *actus reus*. However, it would be unsafe to suggest that this is a watertight definition or that the courts have adopted a consistent approach in this area. Before *Moloney* (above, p. 206) the above definition would have suggested that murder was a crime of basic intent, but the courts have always classified murder as a crime of specific intent. The crime of rape requires an intention to have intercourse, yet this is treated as a crime of basic intent. The safest answer is that crimes of specific intent are those crimes where the courts have permitted the defence of voluntary intoxication and crimes of basic intent are those in which the courts have refused to accept the defence of voluntary intoxication. We can safely say that the following have been held to be crimes of specific intent; murder, wounding or causing grievous bodily harm with intent, robbery, burglary with intent, theft and an attempt to commit any offence (but in relation to attempt see *Khan* (1990) below, p. 326). There are others but these will suffice for our purposes. The following have been held to be crimes of basic intent: manslaughter, rape, maliciously wounding or inflicting grievous bodily harm, assault occasioning actual bodily harm, indecent assault, criminal damage (Criminal Damage Act 1971, s.1(1)). The recent case of *Hutchins* (1988) has added kidnapping and false imprisonment to this list. The effect of these rules is that where the defendant is charged with a crime of basic intent the court will not allow him to assert that he lacked the necessary *mens rea* for the offence when he is basing this claim upon the fact that he was suffering from self-induced intoxication. This is a rule of substantive law which, in effect, says that where there is evidence that the accused had become voluntarily intoxicated, the prosecution is relieved of the need to prove the *mens rea* of the offence; the result is that section 8 of the Criminal Justice Act 1967 is irrelevant.

Despite the outrage that these rules perpetrate upon the general principles of *mens rea*, it is possible to see some sort of logic, at least in relation to offences against the person. Where the defendant is charged with murder or an offence under section 18 of the Offences Against the Person Act 1861 (*e.g.* wounding with intent) he will be able to plead intoxication as a defence. This may mean that he escapes conviction for the offence charged, but the jury will in these cases be able to convict him of alternative offences which are crimes of basic intent where intoxication is irrelevant. Thus where a husband pleads intoxication on a charge of murdering his wife, the jury may hold that he did not intend to kill her, but nevertheless convict him of manslaughter, a crime of basic intent where intoxication cannot be raised. The Courts in these cases take note of the public outrage that would be likely to follow if the defendants were totally exonerated. However, if this was the reasoning of the courts it would have made more sense had rape been classified as a crime of specific intent with indecent assault as its basic intent counterpart.

So far we have said that where the crime is one of specific intent, the accused may rely on self-induced intoxication to negative the *mens rea*, and where the crime is one of basic intent, he may not. Now we have seen in an earlier chapter (above, p. 204), that in most crimes there are several parts to the *actus reus* and the prosecution, must establish *mens rea* in relation to each. Thus in murder the prosecution must establish the unlawful killing of a human being within the Queen's Peace. Murder is a crime of specific intent because in relation to the killing of a human being the prosecution must establish an intention to kill or cause serious harm—nothing short of intention will do. In relation to the other elements it is fairly certain that *Cunningham* recklessness will suffice. Can the defendant rely on intoxication to negative the *mens rea* on these other elements?

Recent decisions of the Court of Appeal would suggest that the defence of intoxication may well be a defence only if it negatives the specific intent of the crime; in murder this is the intention to kill or seriously injure a human being. This can be seen in the case of *O'Grady* (1987). You will remember that in crimes such as murder the prosecutor must establish that the killing was unlawful and that this means that the prosecutors must establish the absence of any circumstances of justification such as self-defence. In relation to this aspect of the *actus reus* the courts have held that a sober man is entitled to be judged on the facts as he believed them to be (*Williams* (1983) and *Beckford* (1987); see above, p. 233). In *O'Grady* two friends who had been drinking heavily fought each other. O'Grady said that he could remember being attacked by his friend and that he had taken what steps he had considered necessary to save his own life. He had later fallen asleep and when he awoke he found his friend to be dead. On appeal against his conviction for manslaughter Lord Lane C.J. said that the issue of mistake should be kept apart from the issue of intent. Where the jury are satisfied that the defendant was mistaken in his belief that any force or the force which he in fact used was necessary to defend himself, and are further satisfied that the mistake was caused by voluntarily induced intoxication, the defence must fail. The question of basic or specific intent was irrelevant to this issue. Although the case involved a manslaughter conviction, Lord Lane indicated (*obiter*) that the same would be true of murder. If this is so then it means that a man who, because of voluntary intoxication, mistakenly believes he is shooting at a gorilla will have a defence to murder if he kills a human being, whereas a defendant will have no defence if he mistakenly believes, because of voluntary intoxication, that he is about to be violently attacked by a man whom he consequently shoots. It is hard to justify such a distinction or to see how you can keep the issues of mistake and intent apart since they are merely different ways of looking at the same issue. It would surely make greater sense to say that intoxication can be raised in relation to any element of the *mens rea* in a crime of specific intent and not at all in a crime of basic intent.

Despite general criticism of the statements in relation to murder, the Court of Appeal felt bound to follow them in

O'Connor (1991). The statements again were strictly *obiter dicta* since the actual decision in the case was that the trial judge had misdirected the jury by telling them that the effect of the intoxication must be to deprive the accused of the ability to form the necessary specific intent. It was enough that because of the drink he had not, in fact, formed the necessary intent.

Insofar as crimes of basic intent are concerned it would appear that involuntary intoxication can prove no defence whatsoever (see *e.g. Fortheringham* (1988)). No defence, that is, unless the wording of a particular statutory defence to a crime of basic intent leads the court to believe that Parliament must have intended otherwise. In *Jaggard v. Dickinson* (1981) the defendant had damaged property belonging to another because in her drunken state she thought that she was trying to enter the house of X who had told her to treat the place as her own, whereas she was, in fact, damaging the property of Y. She was charged under section 1(1) of the Criminal Damage Act 1971 which makes it an offence intentionally or recklessly to damage or destroy another's property. It was quite clear that *Caldwell* recklessness governs this provision and that it would have been of no use to say that in her drunken state she did not realise she was damaging property. However under section 5 of the Act it is provided that the defendent would have a lawful excuse if she thought that the person entitled to consent to the damage would have done so had he known the circumstances. The Divisional Court held that the provision was so worded that it provided her with a defence even though her mistaken belief was due to intoxication. With respect to the Court this does create very anomalous results and it is very hard to follow the actual statutory interpretation adopted by the Court. The case means that a person who because he is drunk does not intend to damage property, or mistakenly believes it to be his own, will be guilty; but a person who mistakenly believes that the owner would have consented will not.

We have said earlier that where there is evidence of drunkenness in a crime of basic intent the prosecution is relieved of the need to prove *mens rea*. This, however, raises further questions. What do we mean by drunkenness? At what point on the scale of intoxication does the judge say the prosecution is relieved of the need to prove *mens rea*? Can the prosecutor seek to lead evidence that the accused was drunk as an alternative to proving *mens rea*? It would seem that the effect of *Majewski* is to make drunkenness the basis for liability in crimes of basic intent where it is raised, and so it would seem to follow that the prosecution should be entitled to lead evidence which would establish such liability. However, we should remember that *Majewski* was the case of a defendant raising drunkenness by way of defence and furthermore it was the case of a defendant saying that he was so inebriated that he did not have the necessary *mens rea*. Most adults are aware that it takes a lot of alcohol to reach the stage where you simply do not know what you are doing. It is submitted that only where there is evidence that the accused had reached this extreme state should the prosecution be relieved of the need to prove *mens rea*. Equally, if the prosecution is to be allowed to adduce evidence of intoxication instead of *mens rea*, it should only be where there is evidence that the defendant had drunk so much he did not form the necessary *mens rea*. We should remember that the defence is the defence of drunkenness or intoxication and although there is no definition of these terms, they are not appropriate to cover the case of the defendant who has had the odd drink. It would be adsurd if a defendant, charged with assault, could be convicted without the evidence of *mens rea* simply because he admitted to having had a half pint of beer. However it can be said that where D is charged with a crime of basic intent, he would be well advised to keep quiet about the fact he had been drinking; such evidence can only harm his case.

Self-induced automatism. A similar problem may arise in relation to self-induced automatism. In *Bailey* (1983) (*Casebook*, p. 236) the accused suffered from diabetes for which he was receiving insulin treatment. On the day in question he complained of feeling unwell and drank a mixture of water and sugar, though he did not eat any food. Shortly afterwards he struck the victim a blow on the head. He claimed that he had been acting in a state of non-insane automatism caused by hypoglycaemia brought on by his failure to eat food. It was accepted that since the attack was caused more by the failure to eat rather than the diabetes itself, that this was not a disease of the mind. However the trial judge held that self-induced automatism was no defence either to wounding with intent nor to the alternative charge of unlawful wounding. The Court of Appeal took the view that since wounding with intent was an offence of specific intent to which voluntary intoxication would be a defence, by analogy the same must be true for self-induced automatism. His conviction for wounding with intent was, therefore, quashed. Unlawful wounding, however, is a crime of basic intent to which voluntary intoxication is no defence. Did it therefore follow that the accused's self-induced automatism should be equally inadmissible? The Court of Appeal thought there was a distinction between the two situations. Where the accused lacked the necessary *mens rea* in a basic intent crime because of voluntary intoxication, the court relieved the prosecution of the need to prove *mens rea*. It has been said that people should realise that they will react in violent and dangerous ways when they are drunk and so the necessary *mens rea* is supplied by their voluntary action in getting into the drunken state. But the same cannot necessarily be said of the man who fails to eat after taking insulin. If the accused realises that such a failure may lead to aggressive, unpredictable and uncontrollable conduct and nevertheless deliberately runs the risk or ignores it, this will amount to recklessness. However, there is no evidence to suggest that such consequences are common knowledge even among diabetics. It followed that his self-induced automatism should have been left to the jury on this basis, even on the basic intent charge of unlawful wounding.

In *Hardie*, the accused had taken valium tablets after being told by the woman with whom he had been living that they were old stock and harmless. He set fire to a bedroom while the woman and her child were in the sitting room. He was charged with causing damage to property being reckless as to whether life would thereby be endangered contrary to s.1(2) Criminal Damage Act 1971 (see Casebook p. 401). Insofar as the prosecution rely on recklessness, this is an offence of basic intent. The trial judge dealt with the case on the basis of voluntary intoxication being raised to a crime of basic intent. The Court of Appeal, however, held that where the drug was non-dangerous in that it was not likely to cause unpredictability or aggression, the defendant should be entitled to rely on it to explain the absence in this case of *Caldwell* recklessness. It is rather extraordinary that in determining whether the defendant gave no thought to an obvious and serious risk the jury may take into account the fact that the defendant had consumed non-dangerous drugs, but not that the defendant would have been unable to give any thought to such a risk because she was mentally backward (see *Elliott v. C.* above, p. 217). The consumption of non-dangerous drugs is, in effect, treated as involuntary intoxication. However, if the accused is reckless in the taking of the non-dangerous drug, it will provide no defence for him except insofar as it negatives specific intent. It is not entirely clear what is meant by recklessness in the taking of the drug. Presumably it means that if the defendant is charged with an offence such as an assault it means that he was aware that the taking of the drug might make him aggressive. If he is charged with dangerous driving, it means that he is aware that it might make him unpredictable or sleepy.

Dutch courage. Should the accused, having formed the intention to kill another person, drink in order to give himself courage to perform the deed and thereby pass into a state in which, although he is no longer capable of forming the intent to kill, he kills that person, then he will not be able to rely on his mental state as a defence (*Att.-Gen. for Northern Ireland v. Gallagher* (1963)). Thus if X determines to kill his wife, drinks half a bottle of whisky to steady his nerves and thereby brings to the surface his quiescent insanity, he may not rely on the insanity as a defence.

B. Involuntary Intoxication

Finally we must consider the case of the person who brings about the *actus reus* of a criminal offence while under the influence of alcohol or drugs, but where he was not responsible for being in that condition. He may have got into that state because someone has laced his drinks or in some other way induced him to take alcohol or a drug wthout his knowledge. Equally the accused may have been forcibly injected with a drug or forced to consume alcohol. A person who has voluntarily consumed alcohol cannot claim that his drunkenness was involuntary simply because he had not appreciated the strength of the alcohol he was drinking (*Allen* (1988)). Involuntary intoxication would also cover a person on a medically prescribed course of drugs who was unaware of the effect the drugs might have upon him, particularly if combined with alcohol (see *e.g. Bailey* above, p. 299).

How should the law deal with a person who has brought about the *actus reus* of a crime when suffering from involuntary intoxication? Since the policy reasons for severely restricting the defence in relation to voluntary intoxication do not exist here, the most obvious answer would be that involuntary intoxication should be a defence if it negatives the *mens rea* required for the offence. Should the defence go further? Should it provide a defence for an accused who formed the *mens rea* required by the offence, but did so only because he was drugged or for an accused whose inhibitions were removed by involuntarily intoxication? The matter has received surprisingly little information until the recent case of *Kingston* [1994] 3 All E.R. 353. In that case P had lured a 15-year-old boy to his flat and had rendered him unconscious by a drugged drink. He then invited K to abuse the boy while the boy was unconscious. P, for the purpose of blackmailing K, photographed and tape-recorded K as he indecently assaulted the boy. P and K were charged with indecently assaulting the boy and K pleaded that he had also been drugged by P, otherwise he would never have acted in the way he did. The trial judge directed the jury that K was entitled to an acquittal if, because of involuntary intoxication, he had not formed the intention indecently to assault the boy. He was not, however, entitled to an acquittal if they were of the opinion that he did have the necessary intent, because a drugged intent was still an intent. The Court of Appeal quashed the conviction on the ground that where a defendant commits a crime with the necessary *mens rea*, and where his inhibitions are overcome by a drug unlawfully administered to him by a third party, he shall have a complete defence to that crime.

The Crown appealed to the House of Lords where the decision of the Court of Appeal was reversed and K's conviction restored.

In examining the reason given by the Court of Appeal, Lord Mustill said it was necessary to see involuntary intoxication in the light of intoxication generally. It was accepted that voluntary intoxication was no defence to a crime of basic intent. There were two ways of rationalising this approach. The first was that in a crime of basic intent the absence of the necessary intent is cured by treating the intentional taking of drink without regards to its possible effects as a substitute for the mental element ordinarily required by the offence. The second is to hold that the defendant cannot rely on the absence of the mental element when it is absent because of his own voluntary acts. Where, however, the intoxication is involuntary, these two reasons for restricting the defence disappear. The first disappears because there is no voluntary consumption of alcohol to substitute for the necessary mental element, the second because there is no reason to deny the opportunity to the defendant to rely on a mental condition he was not responsible for. The defendant is therefore able to rely on his intoxication to show why he *did not* (not "*could not*") form the *mens rea* for the offence. But that is as far as the defence goes. It does not provide a defence for a defendant who has the *mens rea* of the offence but was disinhibited by a drug.

The House examined other approaches which could have led the Court of Appeal to its decision and rejected them. That left the final question of whether the House of Lords should create a new defence to cover this type of situation.

Lord Mustill had no hesitation in saying that it would be entirely inappropriate. On the whole, law reform should be the responsibility of Parliament where all the possible implications of a new defence can be carefully analysed. The questions involved in *Kingston* were highly complex and completely unsuitable for resolution in a Court of Law.

3. Self-Defence, Necessity and Duress

These defences all have a common feature; they are all based on the concept of necessity. In other words the defendant is alleged to have committed a criminal offence but he pleads that he was forced to commit the offence. The three defences reflect the different ways in which this "force" arises. For example, suppose that D (the defendant) is a member of a mountain climbing team. As they ascend the mountain they are roped together. Ahead of D are A, B and C and behind D is E. D is alleged to have cut the rope between himself and E, sending E hurtling down the mountain side and seriously injuring him. D has been charged with causing grievous bodily harm with intent (contrary to section 18 of the Offences Against the Person Act 1861 (see below, p. 379)): If his defence was self-defence, D might, for example, plead that E had a gun and was about to shoot D, and so D cut the rope to protect himself. If the defence was duress, D might plead that both he and his family had been threatened with violence if he did not seriously injure E. If the defence was necessity, he might plead that E had slipped and was gradually pulling the others with him and so D cut the rope to protect the others. We shall see that although the concept of necessity is the basis of the well recognised defences of self-defence and duress, until recently the courts have been reluctant to admit the existence of a general defence of necessity.

A. The Use of Force in Public and Private Defence.

We have seen (see above, p. 184) that a common element in offences against the person is a requirement that the use of force was unlawful. The law recognises that the use of force is sometimes justified and when this occurs, the act will not be unlawful. The best-known justification for the use of force is the common law defence of self-defence. Allied to this is the defence of property, also a creation of the common law. Under s.3 of the Criminal Law Act 1967 there is provision for the use of force in the prevention of crime and in the effecting of lawful arrests. Today it is common to refer to the common law defences as private defence and the defences under s.3 as public defence. Thus we talk of the use of force in public and private defence. It is for the prosecution to prove that there was no justification; the defendant bears an evidential burden to introduce evidence of justification. In the next few pages we must examine these provisions to determine whether the same principles apply to all or whether there are differences between the various defences.

(1) Prevention of Crime

This was originally covered by common law rules, but is now covered by section 3 of the Criminal Law Act 1967 which provides:

> "(1) A person may use such force as is reasonable in the circumstances in the prevention of crime, or in effecting or assisting in the lawful arrest of offenders or suspected offenders or of persons unlawfully at large."

The crux of the provision is determining what is reasonable in the circumstances of the particular case being tried, and this is a question of fact to be determined by the jury. Thus where the accused is charged with assaulting another and seeks to rely on section 3, the question for the jury is whether they are "satisfied that no reasonable man (a) with knowledge of such facts as were known to the accused or [honestly] believed by him to exist (b) in the circumstances and time available to him for reflection (c) could be of the opinion that the prevention of the risk of harm to which others might be exposed if the suspect were allowed to escape, justified exposing the suspect to the risk of harm to him that might result from the kind of force that the accused contemplated using." (*Reference under s.48A of the Criminal Appeal (Northern Ireland) Act 1968 (No. 1 of 1975) (Casebook,* p. 263); *per* Lord Diplock interpreting a provision identical in terms with s.3; in para. (a) the word [honestly] has been substituted for the word "reasonably" which appeared in the original quotation. This, it is suggested, is necessary in the light of the decision of the Court of Appeal in *Williams* (1984) and *Beckford,* above p. 233). Thus in *Cousins* (1982) the Court of Appeal held that, in appropriate circumstances, it could be reasonable to threaten to kill another when, for example, it is believed that this would forestall a planned attack on oneself. Whether or not such a threat is reasonable is always a question of fact for the jury. Clearly a threat to kill may be reasonable in circumstances where the implementation of such a threat would not be.

What, then, if the accused was mistaken in thinking that the man he assaulted was about to commit a crime? Suppose that X was drinking in a bar when he saw Y pick up a broken glass and wave it menacingly in front of Z. It would not be unreasonable for X to suppose that Y meant to harm Z and for him to take action to prevent such injury to Z. However, it turns out that Y was just telling Z of an incident which had happened in the bar on the previous evening. Lord Diplock's statement would indicate that the jury must consider the facts as they were known to X or as he honestly believed them to be. Thus, in our example, if the jury considers that X honestly thought that Y was about to attack Z, they should proceed to consider whether it was reasonable for him to have acted in the way he did (see below for problems relating to the case of excessive force).

(2) Self-defence and Defence of Others

Although in many cases where the accused pleads self-defence the situation could be covered by section 3 in that if the accused's story is correct he is merely trying to prevent the other man from committing a crime—namely attacking the accused—this is not necessarily so. If D is attacked by a child he knows to be below the age of criminal responsibility then he cannot say that the force he used on the child to stop the attack was force used in the prevention of crime. He would, however, be able to rely on the common law defence of self-defence. It is clear that the common law defence of self-defence survives section 3, but since the area of overlap is, to all intents and purposes, total, it would be absurd if the common law defence were to be governed by principles different from those controlling section 3. It is therefore submitted that where the accused, who is charged with an offence against the person, relies on the common law defence of self-defence, the court will approach the question in the same way as a defence brought under section 3. (See also O'Grady (1987) above, p. 297.)

Under the common law rules relating to self-defence the accused was expected to retreat before resorting to force; he was also expected to show that the expected violence was imminent and not a mere threat of what might happen at some time in the future. It is now clear that these are now merely facts which the jury should take into account in assessing whether the accused's use of force was reasonable in the circumstances (see *Bird* (1985) *Casebook*, p. 276).

Normally self-defence describes a situation in which X has been attacked by Y and takes action to defend himself. There may, however, be situations in which it will be justified to take pre-emptive action. Thus in *Finch and Jardine* (1983) two police officers approached a car in which they believed was an armed man who was extremely dangerous. It was held that in such situations it may be unreasonable for the police officers to wait for the suspect to shoot first.

(3) Defence of Property

Again this is probably covered sufficiently by section 3 and the same principles will apply; was the force used by D to protect his property reasonable in the circumstances? Can it ever be reasonable to kill in order to defend your property? (See *Hussey* (1924).)

(4) Excessive Force

Now that we have looked at the various forms of self-defence, we can turn to a problem that has been hinted at in the preceding sections. We have seen that if the accused mistakenly believes that there is a need for force, he will be able to rely on the defence provided that he used only so much force was reasonable in the circumstances he believed to exist. Thus, if the accused rightly believes X is about to attack him, but wrongly, though honestly, believes that X plans to use a knife, the amount of force which would be reasonable will be assessed on the facts the accused believed to exist. But the more difficult problem is the one in which the amount of force used was unreasonable even in the circumstances he believed to exist. Two types of problem may arise here:

(i) X believes that he is about to be attacked by Y and reasonably decides to shoot Y in the leg as he approaches. Unfortunately, his aim is bad and Y is killed. If X is charged with murder, the first thing to remember is that the prosecution must prove that X had the necessary *mens rea*. That aside, the jury should be asked to consider the reasonableness of what the accused contemplated doing. In our case, they should ask whether it was reasonable for X to try to shoot Y in the legs to prevent the attack (see the passage of Lord Diplock, above).

(ii) X believes that poachers are taking trout from his lake during the night. He therefore lies in wait with a twelve-bore shotgun and when he sees Y taking trout from the lake he shoots at him and kills him. In other words, we have a situation in which the jury would have probably sanctioned the use of some force, but not the killing of Y. Where does X stand now? Does this finding mean that he has no defence at all? The problem is only likely to be acute in the cases where the charge is murder, since in all other cases, if it is held that excessive use of force means that the defence fails, the judge can take the facts into account when passing sentence. However, where the accused is charged with murder, if the defence fails the accused will be convicted of murder (if the prosecution establishes the necessary *mens rea*), in which case he receives life imprisonment.

The position in England has recently been reviewed by the House of Lords in *Clegg* (1995). Clegg (C) was a soldier on patrol in Northern Ireland. The soldiers' mission was, although it may not have been explained to C, to look out for joyriders. A car ignored an order to stop and was driven towards C and his colleague, Pte Aindow (A), with its headlights full on. C fired four shots at the car. Forensic evidence showed that three were fired as the car approached and the fourth some time after the car had passed C. The fourth bullet lodged in the back of a rear seat passenger and was a substantial cause of her death. The trial judge (sitting without a jury), accepted that the first three shots were fired by C in defence of himself and A. There could be no such justification of the fourth shot and indeed C admitted that he had no cause to fire at the car once it had passed him. The trial judge concluded that C was guilty of murder. The Court of Appeal held that there was a possibility that C had fired in order to arrest those inside following injuries sustained by A. Even if this were true, the amount of force used was grossly disproportionate and meant that no miscarriage of justice had occurred. In the House of Lords, Lord Lloyd reviewed the position of excessive force in self defence, even though this question was not raised by the facts since C admitted that the fourth shot had not been fired in self-defence or defence of A. However, Lloyd held it was the starting point for the whole issue of the use of excessive force. He held that the law was correctly stated by the Privy Council in *Palmer v. R.* (1971) and the Court of Appeal in *McInnes* (1971). The issue of whether or not the force used was reasonable in the circumstances, which existed or which the accused believed to exist, was a question of fact for the jury. If a jury concluded that the accused had used unreasonable force in the circumstances, then the defence failed. This may seem at first to be somewhat harsh, but in many cases the charge against the accused will be of a non-fatal offence and in such cases the trial judge can take account of the fact that the defendant overreacted in a tight spot in passing sentence. In murder, of course, no such course is available; if the defence fails and the accused is convicted of murder the trial judge must pass a mandatory life sentence. In *Shannon* (1980) the trial judge had left the jury with the simple question "Are you satisfied that the appellant used more force than was necessary in the circumstances?" However the Court of Appeal said that they should have been reminded of Lord Morris' qualification to this test which he propounded in *Palmer v. R.* namely, that, if they concluded that the appellant honestly thought without having to weigh things to a nicety, that what he did was necessary to defend himself, they should regard that as "most potent evidence" that it was actually reasonably necessary.

> "In other words, if the jury concluded that the stabbing was the act of a desperate man in extreme difficulties, with his assailant dragging him down by his hair, they should consider very carefully before concluding that the stabbing was an offensive and not defensive act, albeit it went beyond what an onlooker would regard as reasonably necessary."

It should also be remembered that on a murder charge, the prosecution must be able to prove the necessary *mens rea* and it is also possible that there is some evidence that the accused was provoked (see below, p. 350). Lord Lloyd said that the principles which were applicable to the use of excessive force in self-defence were also applicable to the use of force in the prevention of crime and effecting of arrests under s.3.

The English Courts have refused to follow an approach at one time favoured in Australia (*Howe*) (1958) and *McKay* (1957)) that where the jury concluded that the accused was entitled to use some force, but that he had used excessive force, then he should be convicted of manslaughter. Such a conviction would enable the judge to take account of the circumstances in passing sentence. In *Zecewic* (1987) this halfway house approach was abandoned by the Australian courts because the jurors appeared to have difficulty in applying the principles. They have subsequently reaffirmed the principles stated in *Palmer v. R.*. Lord Lloyd in *Clegg* considered whether the halfway house approach should be adopted by the English Courts and decided that although such a step would have much support, it was a change that should only be made by the legislature. It should also be noted that in *Scarlett* (1993) the Court of Appeal appeared to say that where a publican had killed a man by throwing him out of his pub, the jury should ask themselves whether *he* thought the force he was using was reasonable in the circumstances he believed to exist. Such a decision is completely at variance with the law stated in *Palmer v. R.* and it is strange that it was not discussed in *Clegg*. However it cannot stand with *Clegg* and must be considered to have been overruled. It was cited by the Court of Appeal in *Owino* (1995) where it was said to have been misunderstood—a polite way of saying that it should be consigned to the waste bin. This is an area which requires parliamentary attention. However, it should not be thought that by simply removing the mandatory life sentence from murder the problem will be solved; there still remains the stigma of a murder conviction. Many believe that murder is the wrong label for a person who is adjudged to have been entitled to use some force but who has overestimated the amount of force required.

B. Necessity

The basic question here is whether A, confronted by a choice between committing a criminal offence or allowing what he considers to be far worse to occur, would have any defence if he chooses to commit the criminal offence. In some situations it would seem just that he should have a defence. For example, if the accused is charged with failing to stop at traffic lights we might be very tempted to say that he should have a defence if the reason for this failure was that he could see someone in need of immediate help in a burning building beyond the lights. We might wish to be satisfied that he exercised all reasonable care in the circumstances, but otherwise this seems to be an excellent case for a defence of necessity. Suppose, however, that A and B were out mountain climbing. Suddenly B, who is roped to A, loses his footing and falls. A realises that he will soon be pulled off the mountain unless he cuts the rope holding B, but equally that this will result in B's certain death. The case for a defence of necessity may now seem less clear cut. The number of such hypothetical examples is limitless. But what does English law say of this?

We cannot say that the law never recognises a defence of necessity because the well known defences of duress and self-defence are, in reality, species of necessity, though they are cases where the necessity is imposed by a deliberate human agency. Where the necessity is not of this kind English law appeared reluctant to recognise such a defence.

The leading case is *Dudley and Stephens* (1884) (*Casebook*, p. 244) where the two accused together with another crew member and a cabin boy were forced to take to the lifeboat. After 20 days adrift, the last eight of which were without food, Dudley and Stephens killed the cabin boy and the three survivors fed on his flesh and blood. The cabin boy was by this time by far the weakest and most likely to die if help did not arrive soon. Four days after the killing they were rescued. They were later tried for and convicted of murder, though their death sentences were commuted to six months imprisonment without hard labour.

While the case is not noted for the clarity of its judgments, it is almost certainly authority for the proposition that necessity is no defence to anyone charged either as a principal or accessory to murder. It is often cited as authority for the more general proposition that necessity is no defence to any criminal charged. Harsh as this may seem the Law Commission recommended that no general defence of necessity should be introduced into English Law (Report No. 83; 1977). While it is perfectly understandable that, in the interests of consistency with the similar defence of duress (see below, p. 281) the defence of necessity should not be available to a person charged with murder, it may seem harsh that a motorist who disobeys a red traffic light in order to save a person's life would not be able to plead necessity. However, we shall see in the next section that recently the courts have been prepared to allow a limited version of the defence of necessity in what is called duress of circumstances. In classifying this as a variant of duress the court have been able to allow what, in reality, is a defence of necessity, but a defence subject to all the stringent requirements of the defence of duress (see below, p. 315).

C. Duress

English law has long recognised the defence of duress—but its scope has recently received attention from the House of Lords. The general basis of the defence is that the accused, who is alleged to have committed a criminal offence, claims that he did so because of threats made against him by another. Thus two questions need to be answered; (i) is duress a defence to all charges of crime, and (ii) what constitutes duress?

(i) Scope of the defence

Over the last few years it has been generally accepted that duress is a general defence to any crime, subject to the qualification that it was not available to a person charged as a principal offender in murder and to a person charged with treason (see *D.P.P. for Northern Ireland v. Lynch* (1975) and *Abbott v. R.* (1976)). Thus a man charged with murder could plead duress, but the jury would be instructed that if they found him to be a principal offender in the crime they must ignore the plea. The reasoning behind this distinction between the principal and secondary offender to murder was that the law could excuse a person who had taken a subsidiary role in the killing of another human being, but that it could not excuse the actual killer. In other words no threat could be serious enough to cause you to take another person's life. The dividing line between a principal and a secondary offender may be exceedingly hard to draw, but on it could rest the difference between a conviction for murder or a complete acquittal. This was clearly an unsatisfactory state of affairs and the House of Lords took the opportunity to review the position in *Howe* (1987) (*Casebook*, p. 246). In effect, the House saw the decision lying between an extension of the defence to all murderers or a complete withdrawal of the defence in murder cases. In the result the House decided that it should not be available to anyone charged with murder whether as a principal or secondary offender. The decision clearly simplifies the law, but it will lead to some harsh decisions. For example if the defendant is threatened with the instant death of his wife and children if he does not drive the terrorists to a spot where they will ambush and kill a political leader he must now choose between the death of his family and his own conviction for murder. It is easy to see the public policy decision behind this case; where the defence of duress is available it will be easier to coerce innocent people into providing aid. Possibly when the law is codified, there will be a chance to consider a half-way house solution, namely a conviction for manslaughter in cases where the defendant has either killed or aided a killer under duress. It is, of course conceivable, that a jury faced with a hard case might simply refuse to convict the accused of murder, and return a verdict of manslaughter instead.

In *Gotts* (1991; Casebook p. 255) the accused was charged with attempted murder and with wounding with intent to do grievous bodily harm (section 18 Offences Against the Person Act 1861). The jury convicted G of attempted murder and on appeal the House of Lords held that duress was no defence to attempted murder. There was no evidence that the common law had drawn a line under murder and treason as the only offences to which duress could not be raised as a defence; there was no reason to distinguish attempted murder, in which the defendant must be proved to have had the intention to kill, from murder. The Court of Appeal, however, thought that different reasoning might be applied to incitement or conspiracy to murder since they were a stage further away from the completed killing than attempted murder.

The major problem, it is suggested, is whether duress should be allowed on a charge under section 18 where the prosecution is alleging that the accused intended to do grievous bodily harm. This problem did not face the court in *Gotts* since the jury convicted the defendant of attempted murder and thereby must have found he had an intention to kill. It is, however, slightly illogical that D could be charged with an offence of wounding with intent to do grievous bodily harm to which he might successfully raise the defence of duress and on the day after his acquittal the victim could die rendering D liable to a murder charge to which duress would be no defence. Lord Jauncey commented that in the current climate of violence and terrorism, Parliament would do well to review the availability of the defence in the case of all very serious crimes.

It would appear that duress remains unavailable to a person charged with some forms of treason.

(ii) *What constitutes duress?*

Where the accused seeks to rely on the defence of duress he bears the burden of introducing evidence on it and it is then up to the prosecution to prove beyond reasonable doubt that the accused was not acting under duress. Many of the statements on what constitute duress speak of the need for the will of the accused to have been overborne by threats of death or serious personal injury so the commission of the alleged offence was no longer the voluntary act of the accused. Whatever the earlier courts may have meant by the use of the word "voluntary" it is now clear that it is not to be used in the sense we saw it used in relation to automatism namely an act he was not really in control of. What we are concerned with is a situation in which the accused was faced with a choice of two evils and under that pressure he chose what to him seemed the lesser of the two and deliberately committed a crime. The question is whether the court should take account of the pressures and if so what sort of pressure should be needed.

In *Graham* (1982) (*Casebook*, p. 254) the Court of Appeal recommended the following approach. First was the defendant, or may he have been, impelled to act as he did because, as a result of what he reasonably believed the threatener to have said or done, he had good cause to fear that he might be killed or seriously injured? Secondly, if so, have the prosecution made sure that a person of reasonable firmness sharing the same characteristics as the accused (*Cf. Camplin*, below, p. 355) would not have responded in the way that the defendant did? The test set out in *Graham* was approved by the House of Lords in *Howe* (1987) where it was said accurately to record the objective element.

In *Bowen* the Court of Appeal held that in applying the *Graham* test it may in some cases be appropriate for the trial judge to indicate to the jury that they should take into consideration characteristics of the particular defendant which made him less courageous and less able to withstand threats and pressure. Age and sex were obviously examples; a young person may well not be so robust as a mature one and a woman may be less robust than a man. Serious physical disabilities and psychiatric disorders may also constitute such characteristics. On the other hand the jury should not take into account the fact that the accused was simply more vulnerable or timid than the average person nor that his timidity was caused by self-imposed abuse such as drugs or alcohol. Where characteristics are raised which the jury might be tempted to think relevant, the trial judge should modify the Graham direction to make it clear whether they are relevant or not. In *Bowen* the Court of Appeal did not see how Low I.Q. short of mental impairment could be said to be a characteristic which lowered the resistance of those who had it. The approach of the Court of Appeal here is similar to that taken in relation to "control characteristics" in provocation (see below p. 356).

In *Graham* the court was considering duress as a defence to a charge of murder, a situation which is no longer possible. Where, however, a lesser crime is committed under duress, are threats of consequences less than death or serious bodily harm sufficient? It could be argued that a sliding scale of threats would be fair, though it would inevitably introduce an air of uncertainty. However, in *Valderrama-Vega* (1985) where the accused had been charged with being knowingly concerned in the fraudulent evasion of the prohibition on the importation of a controlled drug, it appeared that his will may have been overcome by a combination of factors including (1) threats of death or serious injury against him and his family, (2) threats to expose his homosexual tendencies and (3) fear of financial ruin. It was held that the defence of duress was available so long as it was reasonably possible to say that the threat of death or serious bodily injury was a *sine qua non* of his decision to offend, although it need not have been the only factor. This would suggest that threats of anything less than death or serious bodily injury will not suffice whatever the offence. (See also *D.P.P. v. Bell* (1992)).

It is generally accepted that the threats do not have to be against the safety of the defendant himself. Threats to kill or seriously injure the defendants family, and possibly anyone with whom he has a special relationship, will suffice.

It is not entirely clear how specific the person imposing the threat has to be about the crime to be committed. Take a fairly common type of situation. D has become heavily indebted to a drugs dealer and is told that he must pay the arrears within a week or his throat will be slit. D replies he does not know how to get the money. If the reply is that he should steal some clothes from a particular shop, this will undoubtedly be sufficiently specific. It is, however, more likely that he will be told to try shoplifting with no particular shop nominated. Is this sufficient? The case of *Ali* (1995) would seem to suggest that it is. Should it therefore suffice that the dealer had said "I don't care how you get it as long as you have it within a week" and D could think of no method to obtain the money other than by shoplifting?

A further restriction is that the defence of duress should not be open to the accused if it was open to him to avoid the threatened consequences of not committing the criminal act. Thus, if there is an opportunity for him to place himself under police protection, even if he does not believe that the police will be able to protect him, then failure to avail himself of the opportunity will mean that the defence of duress will fail. A rather benevolent application of this rule was seen in the case of *Hudson* (1971) where two girls were charged with committing perjury. They claimed that they had been threatened with injury if they made certain statements at the trial in question, and that during the course of the trial they had seen one of the men who had made the threats in the public gallery. Of course, they would have been able to have asked, then and there, for police help, but the Court of

Appeal held that the defence of duress should have been left to the jury. The decision seems to have been based upon the notion that police protection could not guarantee to be effective and that the threats were no less immediate because they could not be carried out until the girls had left the courtroom. However, it could be said that police protection will rarely, if ever, be able to guarantee permanent protection. The Law Commission recommend that the defence should not be available where the accused has had an opportunity to seek official protection for himself or another and it is irrelevant that he believes such protectin would be ineffective. This would clearly reverse *Hudson* but does such a rule mean that if a man's daughter is being held hostage and threatened with death if he does not join the kidnappers on a robbery that because there will be a chance to call in the police, he cannot rely on the defence of duress? It would seem at present that a defence of duress would be available in these circumstances; would this also be altered? It may seem a harsh recommendation, but it must be seen against the policy argument that to widen the scope of the defence is to provide villains with even more incentive to use threats to gain their ends. If a person subjected to threats knows that he will have no defence to a criminal prosecution, then he is less likely to yield to those threats.

In *Sharp* (David) (1987) the Court of Appeal held that where the accused had committed a crime after voluntarily joining an organisation with full knowledge that it was the sort of organisation which was likely to put pressure on its members to commit the type of crime with which the accused was now charged, the defence of duress should not be available. However, if he was not aware of the risks when he joined, or he was compelled to join he is entitled to use the defence. In any event if there is evidence that the accused acted under duress, the jury should decide on the exact facts (*Shepherd* (1987); *Ali* (1995).)

(iii) *Duress of circumstances*

In *Jones* (1963) the court was not prepared to allow a defence of duress in a situation where the defendant claimed to have driven dangerously because he thought he was being chased by men who wanted to attack him; his pursuers were, in fact, police officers. The court ruled that the defence was only open to someone who had been ordered to commit a crime, and no-one had ordered Jones to drive dangerously (see also *R. v. Cole* [1994], which examines the difference between duress by threats and duress of circumstances). However, more recent decisions have tended to support the possibility of a defence of duress in these circumstances. In *Conway* (1988) C was charged with and convicted of reckless driving. He claimed that he honestly believed that the two men, who were, in fact, plain clothes police officers who approached his car planned to kill his passenger T. T had been involved in a shooting incident several weeks earlier, and C believed that T had been the real target for the attack at that time. After a high speed chase through a built up area C was eventually forced to stop. On his appeal against conviction C argued that the jury should have been directed on the defence of necessity. The Court of Appeal was of the opinion that it was not entirely clear whether or not there was a general defence of necessity and if so when it was available. The court held that it was only available in cases of reckless driving where it amounted to duress of circumstances. What this means is that the court is saying that it would accept a defence of duress (provided that all the requirements of that defence were satisfied, see above, p. 313) but that this defence was unlike the ordinary defence of duress where the defendant is told to do something "or else." In duress of circumstances the duress is applied by the surrounding circumstances. Woolf L.J. agreed with a comment of Lord Hailsham L.L. in *Howe* where he remarked that it could make no difference whether the accused does something because he is told to "or else" or whether he does it because he perceives that in view of the circumstances he has no choice.

The position after *Conway* was somewhat obscured by the discussion in that case of two earlier decisions in which the court did not seem to appreciate the true nature of the defence that was emerging. However following the decision of the Court of Appeal in *Martin* (1989) (*Casebook*, p. 260), it seems fairly safe to assert that we now have a general defence of necessity, the scope and requirements of which are those of the defence of duress. In *Martin* the defendant was charged with driving while disqualified. The trial judge refused to allow the defence of necessity and so the defendant pleaded guilty and introduced, by way of mitigation, the facts he would have used to support his defence of necessity. He said that on the morning in question his wife asked him to drive her son (his stepson) to work as he was late and in danger of being fired. His wife had previously tried to commit suicide and she now threatened to do so again if he refused. He thus felt obliged to drive, although he had been disqualified. Allowing his appeal against conviction, the Court of Appeal said that Martin had discharged his evidential burden in relation to the defence of duress of circumstances and the trial judge should therefore have left it to the jury. The jury should have been asked two questions. (1) Was the accused, or may he have been, impelled to act as he did, because as a result of what he reasonably believed to be the situation he had good cause to fear that otherwise death or serious bodily injury would result. (2) If so, would a sober person of reasonable firmness, sharing the characteristics of the accused, have responded to that situation by acting as the accused did? Was *Martin* really a case of duress of circumstances? In *Cole* (1994) the Court of Appeal said that the defence required a degree of immediacy and directness between the suggested peril and the offence charged. In *Willer, Conway* and *Martin* the offence committed was virtually a spontaneous reaction to the physical risk arising.

In conclusion we can say that the defence of duress of circumstances is a limited form of a defence of necessity. Limited in that by classifying it as duress it means that it is not available on a charge of murder or attempted murder and the requirements of the defence are the partially objective requirements of the defence of duress. It seems fairly clear that the fear of death or serious bodily injury does not have to be for oneself (see *Conway* above) and it is suggested that it could cover a situation in which there is no relationship between the defendant and the person for whose safety he fears (for example the motorist who goes through a red light to save a child from a fire; above, p. 310). Later cases may need to explore the relationship between this new defence and existing defences such as self-defence and prevention of crime. (See further Smith, *Justification and Excuse in the Criminal Law*, p. 84; also *D.P.P. v. Bell* (1992)).

4. Infancy

Brief mention should be made of the defence of infancy. In *C. v. D.P.P.* (1995) the House of Lords has confirmed that the position is as follows.
(a) *Children under 10 years of age.* There is an irrebuttable presumption that children under the age of 10 cannot commit criminal offences.
(b) *Children 10 years of age but under 14 years of age.* There is a rebuttable presumption that they cannot commit criminal

offences. This presumption is sometimes referred to as *doli incapax* (incapable of committing crime). However, a person over 10 but under 14 can be convicted if the prosecution can rebut this presumption. This requires that the prosecution proves beyond reasonable doubt that the defendant committed the offence with the necessary *mens rea* and additionally that the defendant knew what he was doing was seriously wrong and not just that it was naughty. This additional element has to be proved by discrete evidence. In other words it cannot be inferred simply by proving the elements of the offence; there has to be additional proof. The House of Lords expressed a hope in *C. v. D.P.P.* that Parliament would re-examine this presumption as a matter of urgency.

Chapter 10

The Inchoate Offences

In Chapter 8 we saw that a secondary party to a criminal offence could be held liable for acts of assistance he had performed sometime before the commission of the offence; but his liability does not arise until the offence is actually committed or attempted. The law would be seriously deficient if liability only arose when the offence was actually committed. It would mean that if the police were aware that X intended to assault Y they would have to choose between preventing the offence and prosecuting X. Obviously we would not wish to prosecute a man simply for dreaming up criminal plans in his head, but as soon as he begins to commit overt acts which evidence his intention to put the plan into operation it is arguable that the law should be able to intervene. This, basically, is the role of the inchoate offences of incitement, conspiracy and attempt. Consider, for a moment, the following set of events; (i) X conceives in his mind a plan to burgle Barclays Bank; (ii) he approaches Y and tells him of his plans; (iii) he encourages Y to help him and to find a getaway driver; (iv) Y agrees to help and they formulate a plan in collaboration with Z who will be the getaway driver; (v) on the night in question they render the alarm on the outside of the bank inoperative; and (vi) they enter the bank.

Clearly at stage (vi) they commit the completed offence of burglary the moment they enter the bank with intent to steal from it. No offence is committed at stage (i) for our law does not punish a man for his thoughts; nor at (ii) in disclosing his thoughts to Y does X commit a crime because this is still too remote from the commission of the contemplated crime. But at stage (iii) X oversteps the mark; in seeking to persuade Y to join him he commits the crime of incitement. At stage (iv) the agreement reached by X, Y and Z is a crime; they have conspired to commit burglary. At stage (v) they may be guilty of attempted burglary. When the prosecution gain a conviction of inciting, conspiring or attempting to commit a criminal offence the convicted person is generally speaking liable to receive the same penalty he would have incurred had he been convicted of the completed offence.

319

It is important to remember that these offences do not exist in the abstract; the indictment must always contain reference to the completed offence. Thus it would be wrong to say in the indictment "X is charged with conspiracy" it should be "X is charged with conspiracy to murder, steal, etc."

1. Attempts

Liability for attempting to commit criminal offences in general is covered by section 1(1) of the Criminal Attempts Act 1981 which provides:

> "If, with intent to commit an offence to which this section applies, a person does an act which is more than merely preparatory to the commission of the offence, he is guilty of attempting to commit the offence."

The effect of this provision is that a person can be charged with attempting to commit any offence which is triable on indictment; see section 1(4). It follows that a person cannot, under this provision, be charged with attempting to commit an offence which is triable only summarily. If it is thought necessary to provide such liability, it will have to be created specifically. Thus under section 5 of the Road Traffic Act 1988, it is specifically made an offence to drive *or attempt to* drive over the prescribed alcohol limit (the breathalyser offence).

There are further restrictions on the scope of attempted criminal liability under the Act. These can be summarised as follows:

1. It is possible to attempt to incite another to commit a substantive offence, but it is not possible to attempt to conspire (s.1(4)(a)).
2. It is possible to be a secondary party to an attempt, but it is not possible to attempt to become a secondary party (s.1(4)(b)). Occasionally the principal offender will be someone who aids, abets, counsels or procures (*e.g.* aiding and abetting suicide contrary to the Suicide Act 1961). Where this is the case, it is possible to attempt to aid and abet under section 1(1) Criminal Attempts Act 1981.
3. It is not possible to attempt the commission of the offences under sections 4(1) and 5(1) of the Criminal Law Act 1967 (helping arrestable offenders after the

commission of the offence); (s.1(4)(c) Criminal Attempts Act 1981).
4.   There are some crimes which, because of their very
     nature, it is impossible to attempt to commit. It is
     generally accepted that it is impossible to attempt
     to commit involuntary manslaughter (see below,
     p. 319). This is because it would require proof that
     the defendant intended to kill and this would render
     him guilty of attempted murder.

What therefore constitutes an attempt to commit a
substantive offence? As in any other offence we must consider
both the *actus reus* and *mens rea*. After that we must consider
whether it is possible to be convicted of attempting something
which it is impossible to achieve.

(1) Actus Reus

Suppose that X wishes to kill Y. He buys a gun, loads it,
goes to Y's house, rings the door bell, points the gun at Y and
pulls the trigger. If the bullet strikes and kills Y then X will be
convicted of murder. Suppose however, that either Y does not
die from the wounds, or that X is stopped before he can pull
the trigger. At what stage can we say that he has attempted
to kill Y? The 1981 Act says that he must do an act which is
more than merely preparatory to the commission of the
offence. This may seem unduly vague and not particularly
helpful, but the view is held that it is for the jury and not for
the judge to decide whether the accused can be said to have
attempted to kill. It would be wrong for a judge to say to the
jury "if you find the following acts proved, then you will find
that the acts of the accused go beyond mere acts of
preparation." This would be usurping the jury's function
(*D.P.P. v. Stonehouse* (1978)). On the other hand the judge
may tell the jury that certain acts are mere acts of preparation
and not sufficiently proximate to the completed offence to
constitute an offence. Thus in *O'Brien v. Anderton* (1984) Kerr
L.J. said:

> "The words 'more than merely preparatory' have re-
> placed the various ways of seeking to define the concept
> of an attempt which one finds in many earlier authorities.
> In my view, whether an act is more than merely
> preparatory to the commission of an offence must be a
> question of degree in the nature of a jury question.
> Obviously, acts which are merely preparatory, such as a

reconnaissance of the scene of the intended crime, cannot amount to attempts. They must be more than merely preparatory. If they go close to the actual commission of the offence, they may still form part of the acts necessary to carry out the complete offence, and may, in that sense, still be preparatory. But if they are properly to be regarded as more than merely preparatory, then they constitute an attempt."

In other words the jury should ask themselves "is he getting ready to commit an offence or is he in the process of attempting to commit it?" There will be many cases in which a jury, properly directed, could reasonably convict or acquit. In these cases the appellate court will not interfere.

Before the passing of the Criminal Attempts Act the courts had evolved several tests designed to help a jury to decide whether the stage of a criminal attempt had been reached. In *Jones* (1990) the Court of Appeal said that the courts should not rely on the old tests, they should read the words of the Statute. In most cases if the judge were simply to ask the jury whether they thought that the defendant was merely getting himself ready to commit the crime or whether he was attempting to commit the crime, they would be able to reach a sensible conclusion. Where, however, the trial judge feels that there is no evidence upon which a jury could find that the defendant had got beyond acts of preparation he can direct the jury to find that the prosecution have failed to make out an attempt.

Three recent decisions will help to show where the dividing line comes between acts of preparation and attempts. In *Gullefer* (1987) the accused had placed money on a dog race. When he realised that his dog would not win, he ran onto the race track in order to distract the dogs. His intention was to cause the race stewards to declare the race null and void and so entitle those who had bet on the race to claim back their stakes. In fact the stewards did not declare the race void, but Gullefer was charged with attempted theft. (The charge of attempted *theft* is puzzling since it is not at all clear that at that time had he obtained the money he would have been guilty of theft; he would, however, have been guilty of obtaining money by deception. See below, p. 425.) The Court of Appeal held that there was no evidence on which a jury could find that he was attempting to steal; there was much more he needed to do. He was simply making preparations.

In *Jones* (1990) Jones' mistress had left him in favour of another man, F. Jones purchased several guns and shortened the barrel of one. He went to where he knew he would find F and got into F's car with him. He then pulled out the gun with the sawn off barrel and pointed it at F at close range. F managed to get the gun away from Jones and threw it out of the car. On a charge of attempted murder Jones argued that the stage of attempt had not been reached; he had still to remove the safety catch, put his finger on the trigger and pull it. The trial judge rejected his submission and the Court of Appeal agreed that there was sufficient evidence on which a jury could find that Jones was attempting to kill F.

A more difficult decision is that in *Campbell* (1991) where the police had received a tip off that a post office was to be robbed. They kept the post office under surveillance and saw C behaving suspiciously. He eventually walked towards the entrance and put his hand in his pocket where the police thought he had a heavy object. They arrested him outside the post office and he was charged with attempted robbery. When he was searched he was found to be carrying an imitation pistol. The Court of Appeal held that he was still in the act of preparing to commit the crime of robbery; he was not, as yet, on the job since he had not even entered the building. However logical this decision might be it will be worrying for the police and those like the counter assistants in the post office who are at risk of being the victims of armed robbery. By acting too early the police had lost the chance to gain a conviction for attempted robbery. This presumably means that the suspect must be allowed to proceed further before he is apprehended with all the risks to the safety of the assistants that this will entail. Fortunately, in this case, the court was able to convict him of unlawfully possessing an imitation firearm. Should the prosecution have charged him with attempted burglary (see below, p. 442)?

A further example is provided by *Att.-Gen.'s Reference No. 1 of 1992 under s.36 of the Criminal Justice Act 1972* (1993). In that case the defendant was charged with attempted rape. The facts alleged by the prosecution were that the complainant and the defendant were walking home late at night and that both had been drinking. The defendant had dragged her off the path and behind a hedge where he forced her to the ground and lay on top of her, threatening to kill her if she did not stop screaming. A nearby householder raised the alarm when he saw a man dragging a woman away from the road. When the police arrived, the complainant was on her back, her skirt pulled up and her breasts exposed. Her knickers were found nearby. The accused was kneeling on the ground a little way off. When (he stood up it was seen his trousers were round his ankles, but his penis was not erect. Medical examination revealed that the complainant had bruising around her private parts and the defendant had corresponding bruising to his penis, though this had not necessarily been caused by the accused trying to penetrate the complainant. He said that he accepted that the complainant had been in no fit state to consent and that he had not asked her. He had been unable, due to drink, to have intercourse. On these facts the trial judge ruled initially that there was evidence which could be left to a jury to decide whether he had in fact gone beyond acts which were merely preparatory to the commission of rape. However he later changed his mind and told the jury that for attempted rape there had to be some evidence of an attempt by the accused to insert his penis into the complainant's vagina. On this basis he directed the jury to acquit. The Court of Appeal was asked "whether on a charge of attempted rape, it is incumbent upon the prosecution, as a matter of law, to prove that the defendant physically attempted to penetrate the woman's vagina with his penis". The Court said it was not necessary. It was sufficient that there was evidence that the defendant had the necessary intent and that the prosecution had established facts from which a jury could conclude that the accused had gone beyond mere acts of preparation; the evidence in this case satisfied those requirements. In his commentary in the Criminal Law Review, Professor Smith asks whether, since rape is the physical penetration of the woman's vagina by the man's penis, is it not a contradiction in terms to say he did not attempt to penetrate her, but he did attempt to rape her? The answer he suggests is that in the law of attempt we must give the word "attempt" a wider meaning than we have so far allowed.

> "If D is pulling his gun from its holster with intent to kill P when he is arrested we do not need the Criminal Attempts Act to tell us that D is attempting to kill P, although D still has to aim the gun and pull the trigger. It is the same if D takes out his penis with intent to insert it into P. He is attempting to penetrate her even though he may still have more than one physical movement to make before he does so"

Is this case reconcilable with *Campbell*?
One of the previous tests, which was used to determine whether the stage of an attempt had been reached, was known as the "last act" theory. Under this the question for

the jury was whether the accused had done the last act required of him to bring about the crime; if so he was guilty of an attempt to commit that crime. This test has been rightly criticised as being too restrictive since there will be occasions where the defendant is guilty of an attempt before he does the last act. For example a poisoner who is slowly administering arsenic to his wife will be guilty of attempted murder when he administers the first of many doses. However, in the case of the principal offender, it is probably safe to say that where the accused has, in fact, done the last act required of him, there will be evidence upon which a jury can find he has gone beyond mere acts of preparation. This will not necessarily be true of secondary parties. Consider, for example, a wife who has hired a killer to murder her husband. She has done the last act required of her, but she cannot be liable for attempted murder until the principal offender attempts to kill her husband.

(2) Mens rea

In many respects it might be thought desirable in the interests of simplicity to require that the *mens rea* for the attempted offence should be the same as that for the completed offence. On the other hand that might lead to odd results. If a terrorist who is torturing a prisoner shoots him in the kneecaps, he clearly intends to cause him serious bodily harm and if the victim dies there is nothing wrong in holding that the terrorist should be guilty of murder. However, if the victim does not die, it might sound odd to hold the terrorist liable for attempting to murder him because this would imply that the terrorist was trying to kill the victim, which he was not. In other words if you say that someone is attempting to bring about a result you are saying that he intends to achieve that result.

Section 1(1) of the Act says that the prosecution must prove that the accused did the act with the intention to commit an offence to which the section applies. This will clearly be interpreted to mean that, for example, in the crime of attempted murder, the prosecution must prove that the accused intended to kill the victim; proof that he intended to cause the victim serious bodily harm will not suffice (*Whybrow* (1951)). It is also clear that in the basic offence of criminal damage, contrary to section 1(1) of the Criminal Damage Act 1971, which provides that it is an offence intentionally or recklessly to damage property belonging to another, the attempted offence will require proof that the defendant intended to destroy property belonging to another (*Millard and Vernon* (1987)).

The crime of attempted offences thus inevitably confronts the trial judge with the meaning of intention. In straightforward cases it will probably be simplest to ask the jury if the prosecution has satisfied them that the accused was trying to bring about the prohibited result. In more complex cases where the attempted crime was merely the means of achieving some ulterior purpose the trial judge should give the jury the type of direction outlined in *Nedrick* (1986) (see above, p. 210). For example, if the defendant is charged with attempted murder for trying to blow up a passenger airliner in mid-flight in order to recover insurance money on the cargo, the judge should tell them that if they find that the defendant saw it as virtually certain all the passengers on the aircraft would be killed, they were entitled to draw the conclusion that he intended to kill them.

Unfortunately this is not the end of the matter. You will recall that we said that the *actus reus* of most crimes comprises several elements and that *mens rea* might be required on each of the elements. You will also recall that the degree of culpability required might vary from element to element. Take, for example, the crime of rape. The *actus reus* consists of unlawful intercourse with a woman who is not consenting. As far as the *mens rea* for the completed offence is concerned, the prosecution must prove that the accused intended to have intercourse with the woman, and that he knew or that he was at least reckless as to whether or not she was consenting. Suppose that he is charged with attempted rape. It is clear that the prosecution must prove he intended to have intercourse with the woman, but will recklessness as to her lack of consent suffice? Section 1(1) of the Act requires that the accused intend to commit the offence and in the context of rape that would seem to mean he intended to have intercourse with a non-consenting woman. In *Khan* (1990) the Court of Appeal held that in the crime of attempted rape the prosecution had to prove that the accused intentionally had intercourse with a woman, but that as far as her lack of consent was concerned it was sufficient to prove that he was reckless. What the Court appears to be saying is that in every crime there is a central prohibited act and where the charge is attempting to commit a particular crime, the prosecution must prove that the defendant intended to bring about that prohibited act. Thus in criminal damage the defendant must intend to damage or destroy property belonging to another, it would not be sufficient that he was reckless as to the ownership of the property. In rape the prohibited act is the intercourse with a woman. As far as the elements outside the prohibited act are concerned it would appear that whatever *mens rea* suffices for the completed offence will suffice for the attempted offence.

With the greatest respect to the Court of Appeal this decision is likely to cause great confusion. Is the decision to be confined to the crime of attempted rape? That seems unlikely. How, then, are we to decide exactly what constitutes the prohibited act—the core of the crime? Did not the House of Lords in *Morgan* (see above, p. 230) say that the prohibited act in rape was having intercourse with a non-consenting woman. Suppose that I find a book and I do not know whether it belongs to me or to you. I decide that I am going to burn it irrespective of the ownership. If I am stopped just as I am about to throw it on the fire, am I guilty of attempting to destroy your book? It would appear not since in *Millard and Vernon* (above) it was clearly held that the prosecution must prove that I intended to destroy your property, which means that they must establish that I knew the book was yours. It seems absurd that I can be convicted of attempted rape if the prosecution can establish that I could not care less whether the woman was consenting, but not of criminal damage if the prosecution can prove I could not care less whether the book belonged to you or to me.

The Court of Appeal had another chance to review this area of the law in *Att.-Gen.'s Reference No. 3 of 1992* (1993) and appeared to find yet another way to identify the *mens rea* in attempted crime. In that case the owners of property, which had been the subject of attacks, had arranged for a night time watch to be kept from a patrol car. The defendants had arrived upon the scene in a van containing petrol bombs, matches, a petrol can and some rags. The defendants threw a petrol bomb towards the night patrol car, its four occupants and two people talking to them on the pavement. Fortunately the bomb missed the car and hit a garden wall behind. No-one was injured. The defendants were charged, *inter alia*, with the offence of attempted aggravated arson contrary to section 1, subsections (2) and (3) of the Criminal Damage Act 1971 (see Casebook p. 401). To gain a conviction for the completed offence the prosecution must prove that the defendant intentionally or recklessly (*Caldwell*) damaged or destroyed property (this property may belong either to another or to the defendant) with intent to endanger life or being reckless (*Caldwell*) as to whether life is thereby endangered. Subsection

(3) provides that if the damage is caused by fire, the charge is arson. The trial judge had directed the jury that for the prosecution to succeed on the attempted offence they must prove not only that the defendant intended to damage or destroy property (*Millard and Vernon* above, p. 326), but also that the defendant intended to endanger life. In other words, recklessness was insufficient on any limb of the attempted offence. Following the acquittal of the defendants on this charge, the Attorney-General sought the opinion of the Court of Appeal as to whether the trial judge's direction had been correct, and whether she had been right to say that this case was distinguishable from *Khan* (above, p. 326). The Court held that there was no reason to distinguish *Khan*. The *mens rea* of an attempt was an intention to bring about that which was missing from the completed offence. In attempted rape it is the intercourse which is missing; the prosecution therefore have to prove an intention to have intercourse. In attempted aggravated damage (or arson) it is the damage or destruction which is missing; it has therefore to be proved that the defendant intended to damage or destroy property. As far as the *mens rea* of the other elements of the *actus reus* was concerned, it sufficed that the prosecution could establish the *mens rea* required of the completed offence. Thus as far as the absence of consent in attempted rape was concerned, it sufficed that the prosecution could prove the accused knew or was reckless (*Cunningham*) as to the lack of consent. In aggravated damage, it was sufficient that the prosecution could prove that the defendants intended or were reckless as to endangering life, and apparently here *Caldwell* recklessness suffices. It would seem to be the position, therefore, that if D does an act intending to endanger life, but not intending in the process to damage property he cannot be convicted of attempted aggravated damage endangering life, but that if he intends to damage property he can be convicted even though he was unaware that anyone was inside the property he was trying to damage as long as a reasonable person would have realised that what he was doing created an obvious and serious risk of endangering life.

If the prosecution must prove that the accused intended to bring about that which is missing from the completed offence, consider the following situation. D intends to have sexual intercourse with V, not caring whether or not she is consenting. In fact she is consenting. D cannot be convicted of rape since V is, in fact, consenting to the intercourse. He can, however, be charged with attempted rape (see below

p. 329) but what mens rea will be required? What is the missing element? This whole area is in need of attention.

(3) Are all attempted offences crimes of specific intent?

You will recall that earlier we said that attempted offences were crimes of specific intent and that therefore the defence of intoxication was a relevant defence if it negatived the specific intent. This was true even where the completed offence was a crime of basic intent since in the attempted offence the prosecution has to prove that the accused intended to bring about the completed offence. Thus in the offence of battery the prosecution must prove that the accused either intentionally or recklessly applied unlawful force, but in the attempted offence only an intention to apply unlawful force will suffice. The picture is no longer so clear. The statement would still seem to be true in relation to criminal damage since the completed offence can be committed either intentionally or recklessly, but the attempted offence is satisfied only by an intention to damage or destroy property. The same cannot, however, be said in relation to attempted rape. The completed offence requires an intention to have intercourse with a woman, knowing or being reckless as to whether or not she is consenting. According to *Khan* (above) this is also the *mens rea* for the attempted offence. Since the completed offence is a crime of basic intent, it is hard to see how the attempted offence could be said to be different. It therefore seems that the crime of attempted rape is an offence of basic intent. Would it make any difference that the charge of attempt arose, not out of the accused's failure to have intercourse, but his failure to appreciate that the woman was consenting?

(4) Attempting the Impossible

Sometimes an accused fails to commit the full offence because he is either stopped before he can do so or because his plan goes astray. These are perfectly proper areas to charge the accused with attempting to commit the offence in question, provided he has gone beyond acts of mere preparation. On the other hand he may fail to commit an offence because what he is trying to do is impossible. In this section we shall look at four different situations in which the accused may be said to have tried to do something which is impossible. In each case the question to be asked is whether the Criminal Attempts Act 1981 renders his activity criminal.

(a) A is caught trying to open the night safe at a bank with a can opener. It is quite clear that the bank's money is safe from him. On the other hand, if he were to succeed he would commit the offence of theft. This is not so much a case of attempting the impossible, as incompetently attempting the possible. Provided that the jury think that he is beyond merely preparing to commit the offence he can be convicted.

(b) B is a pickpocket operating around King's Cross railway station. He sneaks up behind V and inserts his hand into V's pocket, but it is empty, having been emptied by C another pickpocket. Once again, if B were to achieve his purpose he would commit the offence of theft, but since there is nothing in the pocket this is impossible. This type of case is sometimes referred to as attempting the factually impossible. It is fairly certain that the general public would view this conduct as attempted theft and would be highly surprised if the law provided otherwise. In *Anderton v. Ryan* (1985) the House of Lords held, *obiter*, that such conduct amounted to attempted theft. Had the accused been able to achieve his purpose he would have committed theft, he only fails because there is nothing in the pocket. Section 1(2) of the Act provides "A person may be guilty of attempting to commit an offence to which this section applies even though the facts are such that the commission of the offence is impossible." This section was clearly intended to cover such cases as trying to steal from empty pockets and it is suggested that it is quite adequate to do so. The pickpocket has clearly got beyond the stage of preparation and it makes perfect sense to say that he is attempting to steal from the pocket.

(c) D has intercourse with his girlfriend. Although she is, in fact, 16 she has always told him she is 15 in order to dampen his approaches. On the evening in question, however, he has broken down her resistance and they have had intercourse, but she has not informed him that she is 16 and that he will not be committing any offence. Now if the girl had been 15 he would have committed a criminal offence. Unlike the situation in (b) D has done everything he set out to do; it is unlikely that he will feel disappointed when he realises that she is 16. This type of case is sometimes said to be attempting the legally impossible and occurs most frequently where the accused receives non-stolen goods in the belief that they are stolen. Again it is clear that the drafters of the Act thought that such conduct should constitute a criminal attempt and that the Act, as drafted, would criminalise such conduct. However, in *Anderton v. Ryan* (1985), the House of Lords reached a contrary conclusion. In that case Mrs Ryan had received a Video Cassette Recorder believing it to be stolen property, whereas it was not, in fact, stolen. She could not be charged with the offence of handling stolen property contrary to section 22 of the Theft Act 1968 (see below, p. 451) since that requires proof that she handled property which was, *in fact*, stolen, knowing or believing it to be stolen. She was therefore charged with attempted handling. She was convicted, but when her appeal reached the House of Lords her conviction was quashed. Their Lordships held that handling non-stolen property was no offence and that a belief that the property was stolen could not render the person liable for a criminal offence unless such liability was created by the Criminal Attempts Act. They could find nothing in the Act which was sufficiently clear to do this. In *Shivpuri* (1986) (*Casebook*, p. 283) the House of Lords had another chance to examine this area of law. Here the accused was convicted of an attempt to be knowingly concerned in dealing with and harbouring a prohibited drug. Shivpuri admitted that he thought that the substance in his possession was such a drug, but on investigation it turned out to be a harmless substance rather like snuff. The House of Lords said that they considered that they had reached the wrong conclusion in *Anderton v. Ryan*, and although Lord Hailsham said that he could distinguish the two cases on the facts, their Lordships preferred to invoke their power to overrule previous decisions of the House of Lords. Lord Bridge said that the correct way to approach such problems was first of all to ask whether the defendant intended to commit the offence which he was alleged to have attempted; in *Shivpuri* he clearly intended to be knowingly concerned in dealing with and harbouring prohibited drugs with intent to evade the prohibition on their importation. The second question is whether he, in relation to these offences, did an act which was more than merely preparatory to the commission of the offences? Lord Bridge held that the acts relied on were more than merely preparatory to the commission of the *intended* offence and this was sufficient. Where the facts were such that the commission of the offence was impossible, it would never be possible to prove that the accused had done an act which was more than merely preparatory to the commission of the *actual* offence and this would render section 1(2) otiose.

There has been much heated debate over this issue; suffice it to say that *Shivpuri* seems to have settled this issue for the moment in favour of the prosecution. However, in *Galvin* (1987) the Court of Appeal quashed the defendant's conviction for unlawfully receiving a document contrary to section 2(2) of the Official Secrets Act 1911 because there was evidence that the Government's own wide distribution of the document may have impliedly authorised anyone who came into possession of it to use the document as he saw fit. Thus, to put it simply, Galvin believed he was receiving the document unlawfully, when, in fact, he was not. It is strange that with *Shivpuri* still ringing in our ears, it did not occur to the Court of Appeal that this was a case of attempting to receive the document unlawfully. (See also *D.P.P. v. Huskinson* (1988) and the comments of Professor Smith in [1988] Crim.L.R. 620.)

Since nearly all the examples of this type of attempting the impossible occur in the areas of handling or drugs, it would be more satisfactory to amend the substantive offences so that the accused commits a full offence. Thus if handling were amended so that it was an offence to receive property knowing or believing it to be stolen, Mrs Ryan would have committed the offence of handling—there would be no need to rely on attempts at all.

(d) E has intercourse with his 17-year-old girl-friend believing it to be a crime to have intercourse with girls under the age of 18. This is not an offence, either full or attempted; there is no such crime which he could attempt to commit.

2. Conspiracy

While a decision by one person to commit a crime, even if there is clear evidence of his intention, is not an offence, it has long been the law that an *agreement* by two or more to commit a crime is an offence. Perhaps the reason is that where two or more persons have agreed on a course of action it is much more likely that the planned course of action will be carried out. Certainly courts have taken the view that confederacies are especially dangerous. So dangerous, in fact, that criminal conspiracies were not restricted to agreements to commit crimes. In *Kamara v. D.P.P.* (1974) for example, it was held by the House of Lords that an agreement to commit the tort of trespass to land, if accompanied by an intention to inflict more than merely nominal damage, was indictable as a criminal conspiracy.

That it should be a crime in certain circumstances even to agree to commit a civil wrong was thought by many to be objectionable. The Law Commission considered the matter and at first the Commission essentially expressed the idea that only agreements to commit crimes should be indictable as conspiracies. This proposal was in turn criticised as being too narrow. In particular it would have restricted the operation of conspiracy to defraud because, on the common law view of this crime, there could be a conspiracy to defraud even though there was no conspiracy to commit a crime. Take *Scott v. Metropolitan Police Commissioner* (1975) for example. Here A, B and others made copies of films without the consent of the copyright holders with a view to making a profit for themselves by showing the films without paying the copyright holders. In such a case as this it may have been difficult to prove that A and B had committed some crime under the Theft Acts. They did not steal anything from the copyright holders nor was there any deception of the holders. But it was held that their conduct fell within the wide net of conspiracy to defraud—"an agreement by two or more by dishonesty to deprive a person of something that is his or to which he is or would be or might be entitled and an agreement by two or more by dishonesty to injure some proprietory right of his."

The Law Commission therefore proposed that criminal conspiracy should extend to: (i) agreements to commit crime, and (ii) that the common law conspiracy to defraud should be retained, at least for the time being. Had this proposal been accepted all common law conspiracies other than conspiracy to defraud would have ceased to be criminal. But the government of the day thought it best to postpone a final decision on conspiracies to corrupt public morals and conspiracies to outrage public decency pending the outcome of another review. The result, not altogether a happy one, is embodied in the Criminal Law Act 1977. The Law Commission's proposals have been implemented to create statutory offences of conspiracy but the common law conspiracy to defraud was retained and agreements to corrupt public morals and outrage public decency were excepted from the statutory scheme as well. We thus have statutory conspiracies and common law conspiracies.

One problem that has troubled the courts since the introduction of statutory conspiracies in 1977 is the overlap between the new statutory conspiracies and those common law conspiracies which were not abolished. For instance, if A and B, two buffet stewards on British Rail, were to agree to sell their own homemade sandwiches and to keep the money they obtain from the travellers by the deception that the sandwiches are British Rail Sandwiches, they would have agreed to commit an offence under section 15 of the Theft Act, 1968 (see below, p. 425). It should therefore follow that they should be charged with a statutory conspiracy. However, they have also committed the common law conspiracy to defraud and the question for the courts is whether such a charge would, in the circumstances, be wrong. After several unsuccessful attempts by the courts to answer this question clearly, the matter has now been resolved by section 12 of the Criminal Justice Act 1987. Section 12 provides that it is perfectly permissible to charge a defendant with conspiracy to defraud even though the facts reveal a statutory conspiracy. Although this was not the intention of the drafters of the original statute it does seem the simplest solution to a potentially difficult problem.

The whole area of conspiracy is complex and what follows is simply an outline of the general principles involved.

(1) Mens Rea

It was established by the House of Lords in *Churchill v. Walton* (1967) that conspiracy at common law involves *mens rea* in the full sense—strict liability does not apply. Thus if in *Prince* ((1875) above, p. 236) Prince and another agreed to take the girl out of the possession of her parents, both believing she was over 16, neither could be convicted of conspiracy to abduct.

Section 1 of the Criminal Law Act was intended to embody the identical principle for statutory conspiracies and provides:

"1.—(1) Subject to the following provisions of this Part of this Act, if a person agrees with any other person or persons that a course of conduct shall be pursued which will necessarily amount to or involve the commission of any offence or offences by one or more of the parties to the agreement if the agreement is carried out in accordance with their intentions, he is guilty of conspiracy to commit the offence or offences in question.

(2) Where liability for any offence may be incurred without knowledge on the part of the person committing it of any particular fact or circumstance necessary for the commission of the offence, a person shall nevertheless not be guilty of conspiracy to commit that offence by virtue of subsection (1) above unless he and at least one other party to the agreement intend or know that that

fact or circumstance shall or will exist at the time when the conduct constituting the offence is to take place."

These are complex provisions but they should be interpreted to reflect the common law position. Thus in the example just given Prince and his friend are not guilty of a statutory conspiracy. Section 1(2) makes it clear that even if the completed offence can be committed without knowledge of a "particular fact or circumstance" (in this case that the girl is under 16) there can be no conviction for conspiracy unless that fact or circumstance is known to those charged with conspiracy.

Section 1(1) is intended to make it clear that on a charge of conspiracy, *e.g.* to murder or to cause criminal damage, it must be shown that the alleged conspirators had agreed on a course of conduct which will necessarily result in murder or criminal damage if the agreement is carried out in accordance with their intentions. There is no difficulty whatever if A and B agree to kill X by poisoning or to break Y's windows. But suppose that A and B agreed to "knee-cap" X. A and B would here be guilty of a conspiracy to cause grievous bodily harm and if X dies they would be guilty of murder since an intention to cause grievous bodily harm forms part of the *mens rea* of murder (see below, p. 345). Are A and B thus guilty of conspiracy to murder? The answer is No. The course of conduct they have agreed on will not necessarily result in death; indeed it is rare for death to occur as a result of "knee-capping." Another example could be where, in a street fight, A and B agree to attack X and Y by throwing stones at them, both realising that they might miss X and Y and break windows in the street. A and B are guilty of a conspiracy to assault X and Y but they are not guilty of a conspiracy to commit criminal damage. In other words conspiracy is an intentional crime in the same sense as attempt (see above, p. 325).

(2) Actus Reus

The *actus reus* of conspiracy consists in an agreement by two or more persons: (i) to commit a crime; (ii) to defraud; (iii) to corrupt public morals; or (iv) to outrage public decency. The Criminal Law Act governs conspiracies falling within (i), but (ii), (iii) and (iv) are common law conspiracies.

It is common ground to both statutory and common law conspiracy that there must be an agreement by two or more persons.

As to the latter of the requirements it is a truism to say that a man cannot conspire with himself. It was accordingly held in *McDonnell* (1966) that A, the managing and sole director of A Ltd, could not be convicted of conspiring with A Ltd even though A Ltd could have been convicted of the substantive crime committed by A (see above, p. 254). On the other hand it is perfectly possible to convict A, A Ltd *and* B on a charge of conspiracy; or to convict A Ltd of conspiring with B Ltd.

For reasons of policy one spouse cannot be convicted of conspiring with the other spouse if these are the *only* parties to the agreement. So husband and wife do not commit a crime in agreeing to murder X, but if their son, A, becomes a party to the agreement then all three are guilty of conspiracy. This was the rule for common law conspiracies (*Mawji v. R.* (1957)) and by section 2(2)(*a*) of the Criminal Law Act 1977 the same rule is applied to statutory conspiracies. In *Chrastny No. 1,* (1992) it was held that it was sufficient that the wife was aware that others were conspiring with her husband and that she had also conspired with her husband. It is not necessary to prove that she entered into an agreement with a person other than her husband. It is also provided in section 2(2) of the Act that a person cannot be convicted of conspiracy if the *only* other party is (*b*) a person under the age of criminal responsibility; or (*c*) an intended victim of the offence. There is no common law authority on agreements falling with (*b*) or (*c*); the Law Commission was of the view that at common law a conviction for conspiracy was at least theoretically possible in both cases. The Law Commission further proposed that a person should not be liable for conspiracy if the only other party was himself or herself exempt from liability for conspiracy to commit the offence in question. Had this proposal been implemented it would have reversed the decision in *Duguid* (1906) where it was held that A could be convicted of conspiring with B to abduct a child from his guardian even though B, as the mother of the child, was exempt from liability. Since it was not implemented it continues to be the law that a non-exempt party can conspire with an exempt party even though the exempt party cannot be convicted.

As to the former requirement, the agreement, what is required is a compact. Negotiations, however far advanced, will not suffice without a compact to effect a criminal purpose. Nor is it enough that A gives help to B knowing of his criminal purpose. In *Bainbridge* ((1960) above, p. 254) B in knowingly supplying oxygen cutting equipment to A became a secondary party to the burglary committed by A, but, on those facts alone, it could hardly be said that B had agreed with A to commit burglary.

In relation to statutory conspiracy, section 1 requires that A and B should have agreed on a course of conduct which if it is carried out as planned will necessarily amount to a crime. Suppose that A and B agree to go on a shoplifting expedition tomorrow. Between now and tomorrow many things may go wrong and thwart the plan. They may fall ill, or the shops may be closed by a strike or by a power failure. Have they, then, agreed on a course of conduct which if carried out in accordance with that intention will *necessarily* result in the commission of a crime? Of course they have and the fact that their intentions are thwarted for some reason cannot affect the matter. Nor are they any the less guilty of conspiracy to steal because they have not decided upon the particular shop or shops from which they will pilfer, nor because they have not yet specified the goods they will steal.

When A and B are the only parties to the alleged conspiracy it is necessary to show a meeting of their minds. But if there are three or more parties it is unnecessary to show that each conspirator was in contact with every other conspirator. A agreed with B to rob X leaving it to B to get someone to provide transport and B engaged C in the enterprise. A and C have now conspired to rob X though neither may have met or even known of the other's identity, provided C knew he was joining such an enterprise and that there were other members of the gang even if he did not know their names. On the other hand, there must be a nexus between A and C in relation to the conspiracy charged. If A and B plan to kill X as well as rob him but only the intention to rob X is disclosed to C, A has conspired with C to rob X but there is no agreement between them to murder X.

Criminal conspiracies are now confined to agreements: (i) to commit crime; (ii) to defraud; (iii) to corrupt public morals; and (iv) to outrage public decency. For the sake of completeness it should be added that an agreement (v) to commit murder abroad is indictable here though not agreements to commit other crimes abroad.

Little needs to be said of (i). We have seen (above, p. 333) that (ii) is wider than (i) in embracing certain dishonest activity which would not be a crime if perpetrated by one person. As to (iii) and (iv) these seem to go much further than (i) in embracing all sorts of vague conduct which would not necessarily be a crime if committed by one person. But this may not be so. There is almost certainly a substantive offence of outraging public decency (*Knuller v. D.P.P.* (1973)) and if this is so (iv) adds nothing to (i). It is not clear whether there is a substantive offence of corrupting public morals (see *D.P.P. v. Withers* (1975)) but if there is then (iii) adds nothing to (i). These are matters which still await judicial decision or, for preference, clear statutory restatement.

As with attempts, so with conspiracy, issues of impossibility arise (see above, p. 329); it is possible for persons to agree to steal from a safe which is, in fact empty, or to receive goods which are no longer stolen. By section 5 of the Criminal Attempts Act 1981 the law of conspiracy on this point is brought into line with the new law on attempts; there can be a conviction for conspiracy in both of these cases.

3. Incitement

We saw at the beginning of this chapter that if X were to conceive in his mind a plan to burgle Barclays Bank and even if he were to outline his plan to Y he would commit no offence. However if the prosecution can prove that he tried to persuade Y to join him in the venture this would amount to the common law offence of inciting Y to commit, in this case, burglary. The basis, therefore, of incitement is an attempt to persuade another to commit an act which, if committed by that other, would amount to a criminal offence. As with the other inchoate offences incitement is divisible into *actus reus* and *mens rea*.

(1) Actus Reus

The prosecution must establish that the accused by word or deed encouraged another to commit a criminal offence. One who incites another to commit a criminal offence will become a party to the offence when it is committed by that other, but the reverse is not necessarily true. If X supplies Y with a gun to kill Z, X will be a party to the killing, but he is not necessarily guilty of incitement since this requires that he urged Y to kill Z. Thus if Y approached X for the gun telling him that he was thinking about killing Z, but he had not yet made up his mind, and if X then tries to remove the lingering doubts in Y's mind X will be guilty of both incitement immediately and murder when the crime is committed.

The persuasion can be by both words and deeds and it can take the forms of encouragement or threats. It can be to a particular person or to people in general. Thus even though the government has approved the use of citizen's band radios it would constitute incitement for a seller to advertise his radios by saying that the problems of police radar speed traps were almost eliminated by careful use of the equipment. In such an advertisement there would be implied encouragement for motorists to break the speed regulations.

(2) Mens Rea

As with conspiracy and attempts, incitement requires that the accused has *mens rea*. Thus the prosecution will have to show that the accused intended that as a result of his persuasion another person would commit an act which would be a criminal offence, though, of course, there is no need to prove that the accused knew that the act in question was a crime (above, p. 228).

In the following examples it is accepted that X has tried to persuade Y to receive some watches and to sell them.

(i) If we assume first that the watches are, in fact, stolen at the time of the incitement then if X is unaware of this fact he cannot be guilty of inciting Y to handle stolen property since X is unaware of the fact which would make Y's receiving of the watches a crime. Similarly if X does not tell Y that the watches are stolen and has no reason to suppose that Y knows this, then this will not be incitement by X since Y will not be guilty of any criminal offence—in other words the act incited is not a crime.

(ii) If we assume that the goods are not, in fact, stolen, and if X, believing them to be stolen, tells Y that the watches are stolen and encourages Y to receive them he will be inciting Y to do an act which will not, in fact, be a crime since the watches are not stolen property. Here again the problem of impossibility arises. But unlike impossibility in attempts (see above, p. 429) and statutory conspiracies (see above, p. 338), the matter is governed by the common law. On common law principles X cannot be convicted of *inciting* Y to handle stolen goods since the goods are not stolen (this is a case of so-called legal impossibility, see above, p. 330); but, odd though it may seem, Y can be convicted of *attempting* to handle stolen goods. Factual impossibility is also a defence to incitement in some circumstances; X is not guilty of incitement, for example where he incites Y to steal from a safe that is empty. But here the critical time is the time of the incitement; if the safe contains money at the time of the incitement X may be guilty of incitement even though the safe is subsequently emptied and contains nothing when Y tries to steal from it (*Fitzmaurice* (1982)).

Chapter 11

Unlawful Homicide

Homicide simply means the killing of a human being by a human being and there is no crime called homicide. It is homicide where one person kills another in lawful self-defence but this is not a crime. So what the law does is single out certain homicides which are considered to be unlawful or unjustifiable or inexcusable and makes crimes of these. These homicides are called variously murder, manslaughter, infanticide and causing death by dangerous driving. In this section we shall look at the crimes of murder and manslaughter.

In this country we have seen fit to attempt to reflect the varying degrees of heinousness of unlawful homicides by dividing them into two categories; murder and manslaughter. By our definition of these two offences we try to classify as murder those killings which we consider to be the most heinous, and as manslaughter those killings which are less serious but still deserving of punishment. Until 1965 we subdivided murders into those which attracted the death penalty and those which were punished by life imprisonment. Today, following the abolition of the death penalty all convicted murderers are sentenced to life imprisonment. This means that they will stay in prison until the Home Secretary orders that they may be released on licence. The trial judge may, in very serious cases, impose a recommendation that the Home Secretary should not review the case for a minimum number of years. Those convicted of manslaughter may receive any sentence up to life imprisonment.

1. The Actus Reus of Murder and Manslaughter

In all cases of murder and manslaughter the prosecution will have to prove that the accused unlawfully caused the death of a human being who was within the Queen's peace and that the victim had died within a year and a day of the last act causing death performed by the accused. Murder and manslaughter are exceptional crimes in that any citizen of the United Kingdom and Colonies who is alleged to have committed murder or manslaughter may be tried in this country wherever the killing was alleged to have occurred. Our courts also have jurisdiction over any such crimes alleged to have been committed by non-British subjects in the United Kingdom or on a British ship or aircraft.

(1) Human Being

In the normal run of events it will be obvious whether the accused has killed another human being. Difficulties may, however, arise at each end of life's spectrum. At what precise moment does a child come under the protection of the law of homicide? It is established that the child must be expelled entirely from the mother's body and that it must have an existence of its own. It is difficult to be any more precise, for although there are authorities to suggest that the after-birth need not have been expelled or severed, there are authorities which say that the child must have breathed and others which say that independent breathing is not required since this may start several minutes after the child has been expelled from its mother. There are, of course, separate offences to deal with the killing of a child not yet independent of its mother.

If the foetus is intentionally injured within the womb and is then born alive, but later dies from the injuries received in the womb, may the assailant be convicted of murder or manslaughter? This question was squarely put to the Court of Appeal in *Att.-Gen.'s Reference No. 3 of 1994* ([1996] 2 All E.R. 10). In that case D stabbed his girlfriend who was 26 weeks pregnant. Hospital examination revealed that the wall of the uterus had been cut in the attack, but the doctors decided, wrongly, that the foetus had not been injured; it had, in fact been cut by the knife. They attended to the cut in the uterus wall and the girl made a good recovery. However she later gave birth prematurely. The infant received exemplary surgical care, but died after 120 days. D admitted a charge of wounding the mother with intent to cause her grievous bodily harm and was sentenced, before the baby died, to four year's imprisonment. Following the death of the baby he was charged with murder. The trial judge found that the knife wound to the child had been repaired and made no direct contribution to the death of the child; death was a result of being born prematurely. It was, therefore, necessary to prove that he intended to cause death or grievous bodily harm to a person in being. The trial judge directed that these facts could not amount to murder or manslaughter and the matter was referred to the Court of Appeal under the reference procedure.

It seems clear that the defendant was aware that his girlfriend was pregnant, and therefore it is possible that he intended to injure the foetus. If he had intentionally killed the foetus in the womb this would be abortion or child destruction, but not murder since he did not intend to kill a person in being nor had he done so. If D attacked the woman with the view that the child should be born alive but should die after birth as a result of the prenatal injuries, this would be murder. It would, however, be a very rare factual situation.

Lord Taylor C.J. approached the problem on the basis of transferred malice. Whether D intended death or really serious bodily harm to the woman or to the foetus, he could be taken to have intended really serious bodily harm to the woman since at this stage the foetus is as much a part of her body as her arms or legs. If the mother dies he can be convicted of murder without the need for the doctrine of transferred malice on the basis that he intended to cause her really serious bodily harm. If, however, the child is born alive but then dies as a result of the prenatal injuries, the malice against the mother (or the foetus or the foetus and mother since they are all in effect the mother) can be transferred to the living child. Lord Taylor says that their Lordships saw no reason to hold that malice could be transferred only where the person to whom it was transferred was alive at the time of the act causing death. Nor was he prepared to hold that transferred malice could only apply where the eventual result was reasonably foreseeable. In these circumstances the defendant can be convicted of murdering both the mother (if she dies) and the child who dies after being born alive.

It also follows that it would not have mattered that D was unaware of his girlfriend's pregnancy, but it goes further. The evidence showed that the knife wound to the child did not directly contribute to the child's death. This, however, makes no difference. As long as it can be shown that the initial stabbing was a substantial cause of the child's death that is sufficient. Suppose that D, intending to cause serious bodily harm to his girlfriend, stabs her. Unbeknown to him she is pregnant. The stab wound does not extend to the foetus, but it does cause the girlfriend to give birth prematurely to a child who lives for a week and then dies. It would appear that the defendant could be charged with the murder of the child. There must obviously be some connection between the initial stabbing and the ultimate death; in our example the premature birth caused by the stabbing would suffice. It is not essential to show that the foetus was injured in the womb.

How far can we go? Suppose that D punches his girlfriend in the stomach. She is not pregnant but becomes pregnant ten days later. As a result of the punch she gives birth prematurely and the child is too weak to survive for more than 10 days? Is he to be convicted of murder?

Lord Taylor C.J. held that although the Court had been primarily concerned with a charge of murder, there was no reason why the same principles should not be applied to a charge of manslaughter, though of course the *mens rea* requirement would be less. Had the child in the present case survived, it is suggested a charge of attempted murder would not be appropriate since such an offence would require proof that D intended to kill a person in being which he did not. He could, however, be charged with wounding the mother with intent to cause really serious bodily harm.

At the other end of life's span it is not difficult to think of problems which might occur as to the precise moment at which a human being died and thus ceased to be capable of being killed. With the advancement of medical science it is now quite possible to maintain heart beats and breathing by artificial means even though the patient has no chance of making a recovery or of even regaining consciousness. The issue has been further complicated by the fact that organs for the use in transplants need realistically to be taken from a body in which the heart is still beating. The question could therefore arise where the accused has seriously wounded the victim who is then artificially maintained on a respirator. If another person then turns off the respirator, who has killed the victim? The initial assailant or the person (possibly a doctor) who has turned off the respirator? Although there is no definitive statement on the law relating to this issue, it seems likely that in future the courts will accept the test as being that of "brain death" rather than cessation of heart beat. Brain death occurs where medical evidence shows that the brain has been irreparably damaged and that none of its major centres is functioning (see *Malcherek* (1981) *Casebook*, p. 123).

(2) Queen's Peace

If the accused has killed an enemy during the heat of war and in the exercise thereof the killing will not be an unlawful homicide.

(3) Death Within a Year and a Day

The old definitions of murder and manslaughter provide that the prosecution must prove that the victim died within a year and a day of the wounds inflicted by the accused and if this was a series of wounds within a year and a day of the last. This rule still persists today (see *Dyson*, (1908) (*Casebook*, p. 101) and above, pp. 9 and 183).

(4) Unlawful

The inclusion of the word "unlawful" indicates that the courts recognise that there are certain situations in which the killing can be said to be justified. Thus where the accused kills X because X was about to kill the accused, the accused's killing of X may be said to be "not unlawful," and hence he may be acquitted. (See above, p. 303.)

2. Murder

The distinguishing feature between murder and manslaughter is the requisite *mens rea*. It is in this way that the law seeks to identify the most heinous killings and classify them as murder. Many of the older authorities refer to the *mens rea* of murder as the malice aforethought of murder. You will recall that in Chapter 7 we said that unless the law has dispensed with the need for *mens rea* on a particular element of the *actus reus* (*e.g. Prince* above, p. 236) the accused must be shown to have possessed *mens rea* on each element of the *actus reus*. This can probably be best illustrated by assuming, for the moment, that in murder the prosecution must establish intention on each element of the *actus reus*. This would mean that the prosecution could not obtain a conviction for murder unless it could show that the accused intended to kill a human being, that he knew that there was no justification for the killing (the word "know" is used here as the equivalent of "intend" since it is not usual to say that a person intended a circumstance), that he knew the victim was under the Queen's Peace and that he intended the victim to die within a year and a day. We shall see that the prosecution will not be required to prove intention on every element of the *actus reus*, but hopefully the illustration serves to demonstrate the way *mens rea* operates. We can now examine exactly what *mens rea* is required on each limb of the *actus reus*.

(1) The Killing of a Human Being

This is the very core of the offence and it might be thought that the law would require proof that the accused intended to kill another human being. Unfortunately this area of the law has been the subject of a great deal of judicial debate and the present position is far from satisfactory. Until 1957 and the Homicide Act of that year the prosecution would succeed if they could establish that the victim had died as a result of a felony perpetrated by the accused and that the accused had the *mens rea* of that felony. Thus if the accused were raping a woman and suffocated her by trying to stop her screaming, he could be convicted of murder if it could be proved that he had the *mens rea* of rape. This was known as the felony murder rule. It was abolished by section 1 of the Homicide Act 1957 (though it is still found in several jurisdictions of the United States). This Act was thought to leave two other heads of liability, namely express and implied malice. Express malice indicated that the accused intended to kill the victim and implied malice indicated that the accused intended to cause the victim grievous bodily harm. If we pause here for a moment, you may well be asking how implied malice differs from the felony murder category which has been abolished. After all, the intentional infliction of grievous bodily harm is a crime in its own right and the *mens rea* of that crime is the intention to inflict the harm. Indeed in the House of Lords decision in *Hyam* (1975) Lord Diplock strenuously argued that to convict a man of murder on the basis that he intended to cause the victim grievous bodily harm was to use the felony murder rule and that had been abolished. However in *Cunningham* (1981) the House of Lords held that this was not the case and that an intention to cause grievous bodily harm sufficed as the *mens rea* for murder. Thus it seemed safe to say that a man was guilty of murder where he either intended to kill or intended to cause grievous bodily harm. It only remains to add in relation to grievous bodily harm, that this

expression means nothing more than really serious bodily
harm. What constitutes really serious bodily harm is a
question of fact for the jury.

In *Hyam v. D.P.P.* the House of Lords appeared to say that
it would also suffice if the prosecution could foresee that what
he was doing was likely to cause death or serious bodily harm
(see above, p. 205). It was not entirely clear whether this
meant that *Cunningham* recklessness sufficed as the basis for
murder or whether the House of Lords was saying that
intention included this state of mind. All in all it meant that
where an accused had deliberately taken the risk of killing or
seriously injuring a human being in an attempt to achieve
some objective he could be convicted of murder if he foresaw
that the risk of doing this could be described as sufficiently
great. It mattered not whether you said that he intended to
produce the result or was reckless as to producing it; he
satisfied the test of *mens rea*. In *Moloney* (1985) (*Casebook*,
p. 301) the House of Lords said that the speeches in *Hyam*
had been misunderstood. In *Moloney* a young soldier home on
leave had blown off his step-father's head with a shotgun. It
appeared that following a party, when all the other guests
had gone to bed, M's stepfather had challenged M to a race to
see who could load and fire a shotgun the faster. M had won
and had pointed the gun in the direction to the stepfather to
indicate he had finished. He was then apparently taunted by
his stepfather who had said that he knew M hadn't got the
guts to pull the trigger. At that M pulled the trigger and the
stepfather was killed instantly. It was clear that M had been
drinking quite heavily at the party and at his trial he said that
he had not aimed the gun at his stepfather and that he had
certainly not intended to cause him any harm. The trial judge
told the jury that they could only convict Moloney of murder
if they were satisfied that he intended either to kill or to
seriously injure his stepfather. However, for this purpose
intention included foresight that death or serious bodily harm
would probably result whether this was desired or not. His
direction was clearly based on the decision of the House of
Lords in *Hyam*. Moloney was convicted of murder, but this
conviction was replaced by one for manslaughter by the
House of Lords. The appeal was allowed by their Lordships
because of a failure by the trial judge adequately to place the
accused's defence before the jury. However, as we have
already seen (above, p. 206) the House took the opportunity
to reconsider the whole question of the *mens rea* of murder.
Their Lordships held that the prosecution could only succeed
by proving that the accused either intended to kill or seriously

harm another human being and that for this purpose intending a result was not the same as foreseeing that result. (For fuller treatment of this aspect of the *mens rea* of murder see above, p. 205).

Thus we can safely say that on this aspect of the *mens rea* the prosecution must establish that the accused intended either to kill another human being or seriously to harm that human being.

(2) The Other External Elements

The major difference between the mental state required on the other external elements and the element just discussed is that whereas the prosecution will always have to lead evidence that the accused intended to kill or seriously harm a human being, once this is established it will be assumed that the necessary mental element on the other external factors exists unless the accused actually introduces some evidence to the contrary. However once the accused has introduced evidence that he did not possess the necessary mental state on one of the other elements it will be up to the prosecution to prove beyond reasonable doubt that he did. We can take the other three elements in turn.

(a) *That the victim should die within a year and a day*

Although there is no authority on this point it seems likely that no mental element is required here at all. It is unlikely that a court would be sympathetic to a defendant who said that he was not guilty of murder since he did not intend his victim to die within a year and a day; the poison he had introduced was meant to take 18 months to kill him. Since we have already said that an accused can be convicted of murder when he intends to cause serious harm it would be highly illogical to introduce a requirement that the accused must intend or even foresee that death would occur within a year and a day. This external element is one upon which the accused simply takes his chance. The death must actually occur within a year and day, but no mental element is required on this eventuality.

(b) *That the victim should be with the Queen's Peace*

It is suggested that the prosecution would succeed if they can prove either that the accused knew that the victim was within the Queen's Peace or that he realised there was a risk that the victim was within the Queen's Peace. In other words intention or *Cunningham* recklessness suffices on this element.

(c) *That the killing should be unlawful*

Clearly where the accused raises a defence of justification it will suffice if the prosecution can prove that the accused did not know of the existence of any circumstances which would, in law, justify the killing. Equally if the accused thought it probable that no circumstances of justification existed the prosecution would also succeed on this issue. Something less than intention suffices on this element; (see *Beckford* (1987) above, p. 233).

Thus it is suggested that only on the central element of the offence is liability restricted to intentional conduct. On the other elements something less suffices, namely *Cunningham* recklessness. On one element no *mens rea* at all is likely to be required.

3. Manslaughter

Although there is only one offence known as manslaughter, a conviction for this offence can be reached in several ways. Where the accused is convicted of manslaughter he can receive a maximum sentence of life imprisonment, but, unlike a convicted murderer, he can receive as little as an absolute discharge. This explains the first category of manslaughter, often referred to as voluntary manslaughter (though the American term "mitigated murder" probably better describes the type of killing). In these cases the accused is charged with murder and he may well possess the necessary *mens rea*. There exists, however, a mitigating factor such as provocation or diminished responsibility which entitles the jury to return a verdict of manslaughter rather than murder. Such a verdict enables the judge to avoid the mandatory life sentence which he must pass in cases of murder; he may thus give some account to the mitigating factor when passing sentence.

The second category of manslaughter covers those unlawful killings where the prosecution feels unable to establish the *mens rea* necessary for murder. In this situation the accused will be indicted for manslaughter. This category is normally referred to as involuntary manslaughter.

It is worth noting that where an accused is indicted for murder it is always open to the jury to return a verdict of not guilty of murder, but guilty of manslaughter. This means that where, on a charge of murder, the accused is acquitted altogether, he cannot subsequently be charged with manslaughter on the same facts since he has already been in jeopardy of such conviction; he would, if charged with manslaughter be entitled to plead "autrefois acquit." We shall see that there are at least several types of involuntary manslaughter, but there is no need for the indictment to specify which type is alleged. It is sufficient that the indictment simply accuses the defendant of manslaughter and reveals sufficient information to show the defendant whom he is alleged to have killed unlawfully.

A. Voluntary Manslaughter

In this section we shall consider the defence of provocation. Of the other well-known mitigating factors, diminished responsibility was discussed in Chapter 9 (above, p. 289); suicide pacts are covered by section 4 of the Homicide Act 1957 and deal with a situation in which the defendant who is charged with murder pleads that the killing was part of an agreement between himself and the victim in which both resolved to die. All three defences allow the jury to return a verdict of manslaughter instead of murder and hence the trial judge is enabled to take account of the mitigating factor when passing sentence. (See also Infanticide, below, p. 368.)

Provocation

The basis of provocation is that the accused has killed another during a loss of self control. However, the courts have been unwilling to allow a purely subjective approach to the defence and hence the classic definition of provocation given by Devlin J. in *Duffy* reveals a dual test. "Provocation is some act, or series of acts ... which would cause in any reasonable person, and actually causes in the accused, a sudden, and temporary loss of self-control, rendering the accused so subject to passion as to make him or her for the moment not master of his mind." Although this definition has been subsequently modified, the idea of a sudden and temporary loss of self-control is still at the heart of the defence today.

Under the common law defence of provocation, the trial judge would withdraw the issue from the jury if he concluded that while the accused may have lost his self-control a reasonable person would not have acted in the way the accused did. It was held that a reasonable person would not be provoked by words alone. He would still react proportionately to the degree of provocation; he would not in other words repay the provocation with interest. He would not have any abnormal characteristics such as impotence, so that if as in *Bedder* (1954) the accused had lost his self-control because of taunts about his impotence, the trial judge would ask himself whether a reasonable man, who was not impotent, would react in the same way as the accused. The law was modified by section 3 of the Homicide Act 1957 which provided

"Where on a charge of murder there is evidence on which a jury can find that the person charged was provoked (whether by things done or by things said or both together) to lose his self-control, the question whether the provocation was enough to make a reasonable man do as he did shall be left to be determined by the jury; and in determining that question the jury shall take into account everything both done and said according to the effect which, in their opimon, it would have on a reasonable man."

As a result the defence of provocation is partially controlled by statute and partially by common law. It is important to remember that provocation is a defence only to a charge of murder; it is not a defence even to a charge of attempted murder. The reason for this is that on a conviction for murder, the trial judge must pass a mandatory life sentence allowing no scope to take account of the provocation as mitigation. On a conviction for manslaughter, or indeed for any non-fatal offence against the person, the judge may impose any sentence up to a given maximum and can thus take account of provocation in mitigation of the sentence. Many have argued for the abolition of the mandatory life sentence for murder and this would certainly allow the judge to take provocation into account by way of mitigation. However, there is the important question of stigma. Should a person who has killed under provocation be classed as a murderer?

It is important from the outset to understand the framework in which the issue of provocation will be considered. (i) The trial judge must decide whether there is any evidence that the accused was provoked and if there is he is bound to leave the issue to the jury. (ii) The jury must be asked to consider (a) whether the accused was in fact provoked so as to lose his self-control and (b) whether the provocation was sufficient to make a reasonable man do as the accused did. We can examine each of these steps in turn.

(1) *Is there evidence that the accused was provoked*

The judge must decide on all the evidence in the case whether there is evidence that the accused was provoked. The accused bears an evidential burden to introduce evidence of provocation and this means that if at the end of the case there is no evidence of provocation the trial judge will not leave the issue to the jury. In many cases the evidence of provocation will not be raised directly by the accused since he will be relying upon another defence, such as self-defence which would lead to a complete acquittal. However, the evidence which is produced to support a defence of self-defence may very well also raise the issue of provocation. In such a case the trial judge will have to leave the issue to the jury even though the accused has not specifically relied upon the defence.

The Court of Appeal in *Baillee* (1995) has recently endorsed the approach of Russell L.J. in *Rossiter* (1992) where he said

> "The emphasis in (s.3 of the Homicide Act 1957) is very much on the function of the jury as opposed to the judge. We take the law to be that wherever there is material which is capable of amounting to provocation, however tenuous it may be, the jury must be given the privilege of ruling on it".

This makes it clear that the trial judge has no right to withdraw the issue because *he* believes that the accused was not acting under provocation or that no reasonable man would have acted in the way the accused has done. Getting the issue past the judge and into the province of the jury is to not be seen as a very great hurdle.

In *Stewart* (1995) Stuart Smith L.J. found that there was evidence in the circumstances of the killing which pointed to a frenzied attack rather than a cool premeditated one. He said it would have been rather a messy way to carry out a premeditated killing (c.f. *Wellington* (1993). In *Doughty* (1986) the Court of Appeal held that there was evidence that the accused had been provoked by the crying of his 17-day-old baby; this was capable of constituting "things done". It is unlikly that s.3 would cover provocation caused entirely by non-human forces such as a bolt of lightning which damages the accused's property. In *Cocker* (1989), on the other hand, the accused eventually gave in to his terminally ill wife's requests that he should kill her. The Court of Appeal held that there was no evidence that he had been provoked, he simply did what his wife wished. A difficult case is that of *Dryden* (1995) where the accused had been ordered by the planning authority to pull down his dream house. Over a lengthy period of time he formed the conclusion that the planning inspector and the local authority solicitor had behaved improperly and he let it be known that should they try to achieve their object by force he might not be able to resist using violence. On the morning when the excavators moved in, he went into his house, returned with a rifle and killed the planning inspector and went after the solicitor. The Court of Appeal held that there was no evidence of provocation; he had planned this attack for some time. While there was certainly an element of preparation, it is hard to conclude that he did not lose his self-control.

The question which has troubled the courts for several years is that of self-induced provocation. The situation envisaged is where the accused, by his acts, causes the victim to act in a provocative way towards the accused who thereupon loses his self-control and kills the victim. It had been felt by some that it would be wrong to allow the accused to rely on the provocation when he had caused it. Such a rule would be clearly against the wording of the Act which says that once there is evidence that the accused has been provoked to lose his self-control the issue of provocation must be left to the jury. The Act does not say that this is restricted to provocation for which the accused was not responsible. Thus in *Johnson* (1989) *Casebook*, p. 331 the Court of Appeal accepted that the accused was not debarred from relying on the defence of provocation even though he had caused the victim to act in a provocative manner. It would, however, be a factor that the jury would take into consideration in deciding whether the provocation was such as to make a reasonable man act in the way that the accused had acted. It would also be taken into account by the trial judge in determining sentence should the defence succeed.

Once the judge has decided that there was evidence of provocation, he must leave the two questions to the jury and he will need to analyse the evidence of provocation and indicate which evidence they may take into account.

(2) *The first jury question*

The first question for the jury is whether the accused lost his self-control. This should be approached from a purely subjective point of view. We shall see later that the accused will not be able to shelter behind a very volatile nature or behind the fact that he has voluntarily got himself intoxicated. These matters, however, should be left for consideration of the second question. The first question is simply: "did the accused lose his self-control ?" In *Thornton* (1992) the accused killed husband after she claimed she had suffered years of physical and mental abuse at his hands. There was evidence that shortly before the stabbing she had armed herself with a knife from the kitchen and had sharpened it. Such evidence is inconsistent with a requirement of a sudden and temporary loss of self-control. Equally evidence of a cooling-off period between the last provocative act and the killing may make it difficult to find that the killing took place under provocation. Thornton argued that it was inappropriate today to require a finding that the accused had suffered a sudden and temporary loss of self control. particularly in cases where there was a long history of abuse. However, the Court of Appeal held that this had been a requirement of the defence of provocation for many years and any changes should be made by the legislature. When Thornton appealed again to the Court of Appeal in 1995 (*Thornton No. 2* (1995)), this argument was not pursued.

It is important to remember that it is the loss of self-control which must be sudden and temporary; not the provocation. A history of violence or teasing or bullying may explain why a particular provocative act, not in itself particularly strong, may have been the last straw. Provocation can clearly be cumulative. A jury might more readily find that there was a loss of self-control triggered by even a minor incident, if the defendant has endured abuse over a long period (*Thornton No. 2* (1996)).

(3) *The second jury question*

The jury must then consider whether the provocation, which they have found caused the accused to lose his self-control, was sufficient to make a reasonable man do as the accused did. At this point we can return to the case of *Bedder* mentioned above (p. 351). How would such a case be decided today? There would be clear evidence that the accused was provoked and so the matter would become a jury question. The jury would have little difficulty in finding that he killed during a loss of self-control. Then comes the second question: would a reasonable man have reacted in the way that Bedder reacted? How can a juror answer this question? Is the juror to assume that the reasonable man in this case is reasonable but impotent? It has been said that a juror cannot put himself in the shoes of an impotent man, but does it make any sense to ask how would a non-impotent reasonable man react to taunts about his impotence?

The position was examined by the House of Lords in the case of *D.P.P. v. Camplin* (1978). In *Camplin*, the accused who had been drinking went to the house of a middle-aged Pakistani, K, whom he had been blackmailing over a homosexual relationship K was having with a friend of the accused. While he was there the accused was buggered by K, according to the accused, by force. After the act of buggery the accused claimed that he was overcome with remorse and shame, especially when he heard K laughing over his sexual triumph and he hit K over the head twice with a heavy chapati pan, thereby killing him. The accused was charged with murder and at his trial rested his defence solely on the issue of provocation, thus seeking to reduce the offence to manslaughter. From the point of view of the case the major factor in dispute was whether the jury should have been advised not to pay any regard to the fact that at the time of the killing the accused was only 15 years old. In the event the jury were directed to apply the criterion of whether a reasonable man of full age would in like circumstances have acted as the respondent had done. The accused was convicted of murder but this was reduced on appeal to a conviction for manslaughter. The Court of Appeal certified that there was a point of law of general public importance involved in the case namely

> "whether on the prosecution for murder of a boy of 15, where the issue of provocation arises, the jury should be directed to consider the question, under s.3 of the Homicide Act 1957, whether the provocation was enough to make a reasonable man do as he did by reference to a 'reasonable adult' or by reference to a 'reasonable boy' ".

In the eventual appeal the House of Lords confirmed the decision of the Court of Appeal. Their Lordships took the view that if the accused possesses one characteristic which is relevant to the provocation the jury must be able to take it into consideration. Lord Diplock suggested that the proper test for a jury would be as follows:

"The judge should state what the question is, using the very terms of the section. He should then explain to them that the reasonable man referred to in the question is a person having the power of self-control to be expected of the person of the sex and age of the accused, but in other respects sharing such of the accused's characteristics as they think would affect the gravity of the provocation to him, and that the question is not merely whether such a person in like circumstances would be provoked to lose his self-control, but also would react to the provocation as the accused did."

The judge should only draw the age of the accused to the attention of the jury where the age might be relevant to the way in which the accused responded to the provocation. In *Camplin* it was the fact that a 15-year old would clearly find it harder to cope with the provocation than would an older man which made it essential for the jury to consider the accused's age. In *Ali* (1989), however, the Court of Appeal held that there was no reason for the trial judge to draw attention to the fact that the defendant was 20 years of age since the provocation in the case would have affected a 20-year old no differently from a man of any other age.

Camplin provided an excellent starting point for a systematic development of the defence, but unfortunately the opportunity was not taken. The issue is what characteristics can be accredited to the reasonable man in order to understand the gravity of the provocation to him. It should have been clearly recognised that there are two entirely distinct groups of characteristics. The first are those such as age and sex which may explain why the accused reacted in a particular way. In *Camplin* the House of Lords accepted that you cannot expect the same restraint from a 15-year old that you can expect from a fully grown adult male; you cannot expect an old head on young shoulders. Such characteristics have nothing to do with the provocation in that it is not targeted at that characteristic; Camplin was not being taunted for being 15. These characteristics could be labelled as "control characteristics" in that they explain the degree of control that can be expected of a person with the characteristic. As we shall see later the courts are clear that the defendant cannot rely on voluntary intoxication or his very short temper as control characteristics.

The second group of characteristics are those which explain the gravity of provocation because the provocation is directed at that characteristic. In *Bedder*, for example, the provocation was aimed at his impotence. Lord Diplock would therefore allow the jury in answering the second question to consider whether the provocation was sufficient to make a man who was impotent but in all other respects "reasonable" do as the accused did. These characteristics could be labelled as "response characteristics."

In *Newell* (1980) the Court of Appeal held that in order to be a relevant characteristic the feature must have a degree of permanence and the provocation must be targeted at the feature. Since in that case the characteristic relied upon was chronic alcoholism and the provocation was directed at his relationship with a woman, the court held that the alcoholism was not a relevant characteristic. Unfortunately the Court of Appeal failed to realise that the defendant was relying upon his alcoholism as a control characteristic, and not as a response characteristic, in the same way that Camplin had been allowed to rely upon his age to explain his reaction. It would undoubtedly have been possible for the Court of Appeal to hold that as a matter of policy alcoholism could not be a control characteristic, but this point was not taken.

In *Morhall* (1995) the defendant was a glue-sniffing addict and had killed another who had been taunting him about his habit. This clearly raised the question of addiction as a response characteristic since the provocation was aimed at it. The Court of Appeal held, however, that there was a limit to the characteristics which could be ascribed to the reasonable man. One limiting factor was that you cannot ascribe to the reasonable man a characteristic which is repugnant to the concept of a reasonable man. It is one thing to say that a reasonable man is impotent; this in no way offends the concept of a reasonable person. It is quite another matter to say that the reasonable person in this case is an addicted glue-sniffer.

On appeal to the House of Lords (1995) Lord Goff held that most of the problems stemmed from a misunderstanding of the use of the word "reasonable" in s.3. It is there to introduce, as a matter of policy, a standard of self-control which has to be complied with if provocation is to be established in law. It would be better to use, as Lord Diplock had done in *Camplin*, the word "ordinary". What the jury should be asking is whether the provocation would have made a person having the self-control of an ordinary person do as the accused did. There is nothing in the speeches in *Camplin* to suggest that response characteristics are limited to those which are not repugnant to the concept of an ordinary or reasonable person. In fact as far as response characteristics are concerned there would appear to be no restrictions. Lord Goff converted that even where the defendant is taunted about having been intoxicated on a previous occasion "[in] such a case, however discreditable such a condition may be, it may where relevant be taken into account as going the gravity of the provocation. Even transient conditions such as exzema can clearly be the response characteristics if the provocation is directed at the accused's spotty face.

As far as control characteristics are concerned we can say that where relevant the jury should be told to ascribe the accused's age or sex to the reasonable person. It is equally clear that for public policy reasons the accused is not entitled to rely on the fact that he was voluntarily intoxicated or high on drugs as a control characteristic. Lord Goff recognised that this could lead to difficulties. Suppose that the accused, a glue-sniffing addict, was high on solvent abuse at the time the victim taunted him about his addiction. The jury should be told that they should consider the effect such taunts would have on an ordinary man addicted to glue-sniffing but who at the time of the killing was not under the influence. It is also clear that the accused may not rely upon his volatile nature as a control characteristic; this is the whole purpose of the reasonable man test in section 3. What should be the position if the accused is suffering from a complaint such as exzema which, from time to time, causes the accused to be volatile? Can this be relied upon as a control characteristic; we have seen it can be a response characteristic? Professor Smith ([1995] Crim. L.R. 892) argues that the answer should be no. Eczema merely explains why the defendant is more short-tempered than the ordinary person and shortness of temper is generally considered to be irrelevant.

> "It is suggested that increased provocativeness is relevant, increased provacability is not. All exceptional irascibility must be due to some cause—perhaps a nagging wife, a prodigal son, an overbearing employer, unemployment ... and if that cause, whatever it be, is to be attributed to the reasonable man of section 3, then we have indeed eliminated the objective test".

Such a view is hard to reconcile with decisions already taken. The relevance of age and sex mentioned in *Camplin* must be that they explain why a person with those characteristics is more likely to lose his self-control than for example, someone who is older. In *Dryden* (1995) the Court of Appeal held that his obsessiveness and eccentricity were relevant characteristics; in *Humphrys* (1995) immaturity and attention-seeking were relevant characteristics but not her explosive character since this was simply another way of saying that she lacked the normal powers of self-control. In *Thornton No. 2* (1996) the Court of Appeal held that the trial court should take account of a personality disorder (battered woman syndrome; but see *Luc* 1996 P.C.) and the effect of abuse over a long period of time. All of these characteristics have been accepted as control characteristics. They are all matters which explain why the defendant lost his self-control, and are surely indistinguishable from exzema.

B. Involuntary Manslaughter

Involuntary manslaughter is the name given to those unlawful killings in which the prosecution is unable to prove the necessary *mens rea* for murder, but where it is felt that the defendant's culpability warrants classifying the killing as manslaughter. This area of criminal law has never been noted for its clarity, and the present position can only be described as chaotic. The current difficulty stems from the fact that following decisions of the House of Lords and Privy Council in 1983 and 1985 it appeared that the category of manslaughter known as gross negligence manslaughter had been replaced by a new category based on *Caldwell* recklessness. Unfortunately, since that time the Court of Appeal has either not heard of this development or has chosen to ignore it. The result is that all we can say with certainty is that there are at least two categories of involuntary manslaughter, and possibly three. In this section we shall look at the three categories in turn.

(1) Constructive or Unlawful Act Manslaughter

We have already mentioned that there existed a doctrine known as felony murder. Under this doctrine killings in the course of committing (violent) crimes were automatically murder, the only mental state the prosecution had to prove being that of the felony. Alongside this doctrine grew up a similar one for killings that occurred during the commission of lesser wrongs; this has been named constructive manslaughter, unlawful act manslaughter or misdemeanour manslaughter. In this country during the last century the accused could be convicted of manslaughter by this doctrine if he caused the death of another whilst committing any unlawful act including wrongs which were tortious but not criminal. Eventually the doctrine was modified so that it can now be confidently asserted that the unlawful act has to amount to a crime; and during this century it has been further qualified by decisions that the act must be an act likely to cause some harm. The doctrine receives its clearest statement in the judgment of Edmund Davies L.J. in *Church* (1966), where he said "the unlawful act must be such as all sober and reasonable people would inevitably recognise must subject the other person to, at least, the risk of some harm resulting therefrom, albeit not serious harm."

What therefore must the prosecution prove to make out a charge of manslaughter under this doctrine?

(i) They must prove that the accused committed an unlawful act (it would appear that failure to act will not suffice as the basis for constructive manslaughter, *Lowe*, (1973); see p. 193 for liability generally for failing to act). This act must be an act which is unlawful in itself and not one that would have been lawful but for the negligent way in which it was performed. For example, driving a car is a lawful act, but if the car is driven negligently then it becomes a criminal offence. This is not the sort of unlawful act which would suffice for the doctrine of constructive manslaughter. If the driver kills someone while driving badly the prosecution will have to charge him either with causing death by dangerous driving (see Road Traffic Act 1991) or with reckless or gross negligence manslaughter described below (*Andrews v. D.P.P.* (1937)). On the other hand an assault is an unlawful act in itself and indeed most cases of constructive manslaughter will be based on some form of assault.

(ii) The next step is to prove to the court's satisfaction that sober and reasonable people would inevitably recognise that the act would subject the other person to, at least, the risk of some harm, albeit not serious harm. It must be noted that it is not necessary to establish that the accused himself foresaw the possibility of any harm to the victim. Since the decision in *Church* there have been instances where it was thought that the Court of Appeal was saying that the accused himself must foresee that his actions would harm the victim, but the House of Lords in *D.P.P. v. Newbury* (1976) (*Casebook*, p. 336), where youths had thrown paving slabs from a bridge on to a passing express train thereby killing the guard, re-affirmed the law as expressed by Edmund Davies L.J.

One problem that has arisen in several cases is whether the reasonable man is taken to know any special facts that might make it more likely that the defendant will, by his act, cause some physical harm. For instance in *Dawson* (1985) where three men held up a petrol station attendant who died from a heart attack shortly afterwards, the trial judge told the jury that they could convict the accused of manslaughter if they thought that the attack was likely to cause the attendant to suffer emotional disturbance. The Court of Appeal said that this was a misdirection; the jury had to be satisfied that the attack was likely to cause physical harm. Since the accused had no reason to know that the attendant had a heart complaint, this factor should not be taken into account by the jury in deciding whether the attack was likely to cause physical harm. In *Watson* (1991), however, the court held that, since by the end of a burglary the defendant had realised that the victim who was in the house was a frail and elderly man, the jury should ask themselves whether the burglary and subsequent visit of the police was likely to cause some harm to such a frail person. A similar decision was reached in *Ball* (1989) where the defendant loaded a shotgun with cartridges he had grabbed from the pocket of his overalls and then fired the gun to frighten G off his land. G was killed by pellets from the shotgun, but the defendant said that he thought he had only put blank cartridges into the shotgun since he had only meant to frighten G. The defendant knew, however, that the pocket contained both live and blank cartridges and the jury were thus entitled to take that fact into account in deciding whether D's unlawful act was likely to cause some harm. It would have been different if D had only kept blanks in the pocket and his wife had inadvertently slipped some live ones in without telling her husband.

(iii) Finally the prosecution must prove that it was the unlawful act of the defendant which caused the death of the victim. In *Williams* (1992) where a hitchhiker leapt to his death from a moving car in which he had accepted a lift, the prosecution needed to show that it was an unlawful threat to rob the victim which led him to jump. In these "fright and flight" type cases (see above, p. 200) the jury will have to consider whether the victim's reaction was foreseeable in the light of what was being done to him or whether it was a daft thing to do. In reaching this conclusion the jury should bear in mind any relevant characteristic of the victim and the fact that in the agony of the moment he may do the wrong thing. With the greatest of respect to the Court of Appeal all of this is covered by the direction in *Church*. Unfortunately the Court saw fit to hold that in this type of case the judge should first direct the jury on the issue of causation and then on the law relating to manslaughter.

(2) Gross Negligence Manslaughter

As we have just seen that constructive or unlawful act manslaughter is based upon a perception that killings caused by the deliberate performance of an unlawful and dangerous crime should be treated as manslaughter. Gross negligence manslaughter is based upon the notion that whereas those who negligently injure others do not incur criminal liability, even where the negligence is very bad, if *death* results from very negligent conduct there ought to be criminal liability.

While the *actus reus* of this offence is that of murder, it has been the definition of the *mens rea* which has caused the courts much difficulty. Traditionally the *mens rea* was said to be gross negligence and in *Bateman* (1925) Casebook p. 337. Lord Hewart C.J. explained this by saying

"... in order to establish criminal liability the facts must be such that, in the opinion of the jury, the negligence of the jury went beyond a mere matter of compensation between subjects and showed such disregard for the life and safety of others as to amount to a crime against the state and conduct deserving punishment ..."

This can be illustrated by a simple example. Suppose that D has killed a child while driving through a village. If it is considered to be safe to drive at 30 m.p.h. along that stretch of road, then the more D exceeds that speed limit, the more negligent his driving becomes. At 40 m.p.h. we could say that there was an increase in the likelihood that he would injure someone; at 60 m.p.h. this risk has increased significantly. At 80 m.p.h. the public would probably say that it would be a miracle if D did not kill or at least seriously injure another. At some point on this scale the law says that it is no longer sufficient that the defendant's conduct should be the subject for damages in the civil courts; the criminal law should be able to punish D for the death he has caused. Of course you will be aware that there is an offence of causing death by dangerous driving (s.1 Road Traffic Act 1991 which replaced the offence of causing death by reckless driving). In the majority of cases where D has caused death by bad driving, he will be charged with the offence of causing death by dangerous driving or causing death by careless driving when under the influence of drink or drugs (s.3A Road Traffic Act 1988). But there will come a point where the driving is so bad that a jury will be prepared to convict of the much more serious offence of manslaughter and herein lies the alleged deficiency in this form of manslaughter. Whereas murder and unlawful act manslaughter provide the judge with a set of ingredients to leave to the jury with the direction that if they find those elements proved they will convict the defendant, in gross negligence manslaughter the trial judge will have to tell the jury that offence is made out when they consider that the defendant's conduct deserves to be treated as criminal. In other words it is circuitous; D will have committed an offence if his conduct can be described as grossly negligent and that stage will be reached when the jury considers that he should be treated as having committed a crime.

It is for this reason that the House of Lords in *Seymour* (1983) and the Privy Council in *Kong Cheuk Kwan* (1985) attempted to replace gross negligence manslaughter with reckless manslaughter, based upon *Caldwell* recklessness. In *Seymour* the House of Lords, dealing with a defendant who had killed his wife in a driving incident, held that the offence of "motor manslaughter" required a direction to the jury in virtually the same terms as a direction for causing death by reckless driving and this involved a direction in terms of *Caldwell* recklessness. In *Kong Cheuk Kwan* the Privy Council appeared to extend it to manslaughter in general and said that judges should no longer direct juries in terms of gross negligence since that was unhelpful. The direction should be in terms of *Caldwell* recklessness (that the accused had failed to give any thought to the serious and obvious risk that his conduct might cause personal injury to others).

There is little need to explore the confusion which followed since the Court of Appeal in *Adomako* (1994) started out on the road back to a test of gross negligence. In *Adomako*, the appellant was acting as the anaesthetist during an operation. He failed to notice that the supply of oxygen had become disconnected. As a result the patient died. It was conceded at the trial that Adomako had been negligent; the question was whether his conduct had been criminal. (There was no suggestion that he had performed an unlawful act and so this was not a case of constructive manslaughter; in any event constructive manslaughter cannot be based upon a failure to act; see above, p. 360). Lord Taylor C.J. in the Court of

Appeal, bound by the decision of the House of Lords in *Seymour*, held that in the future, whereas cases of motor manslaughter should continue to receive the *Seymour* direction, in all other cases of what he described as breach of duty manslaughter cases the jury should he directed in terms of gross negligence.

In the appeal to the House of Lords (1995). Lord Mackay L.C. held that since the legislation upon which the cases of motor manslaughter had been based had been repealed (reckless driving and causing death by reckless driving were abolished by the Road Traffic Act 1991) the distinction drawn by Lord Taylor C.J. was unnecessary. There was no longer any reason why cases of motor manslaughter should receive different treatment from other forms of manslaughter. It is a great shame that Lord Mackay felt the need to invoke the change in legislation as his reason for this decision. It is a pity that he could not simply have said that there is not nor never had been a special category of manslaughter reserved for those who kill using a motor vehicle.

Lord Mackay signalled a return to gross negligence manslaughter. He saw it as the duty of the House to lay down a test which would be user friendly for both judges in the Crown Courts and their juries. Judges should direct their juries in accordance with the following principles. Firstly they should use the ordinary principles of negligence to determine whether or not the defendant was in breach of a duty of care towards the victim who has died. In the civil law of negligence citizens are said to owe a duty of care towards persons whom it is reasonably foreseeable might be affected by their activities. For example road users owe a duty of care to other road users, food manufacturers to the customers who buy their products, etc. If such a breach is established the second question was whether that breach of duty had caused the death of the victim. If this was the case the final question was whether the breach of duty could be categorised as gross negligence and therefore as a crime. The answer to the final question would depend upon the seriousness of the breach committed by the defendant in all the circumstances in which the defendant was placed when the breach occurred.

Lord Mackay recognised that his approach would contain an element of circularity, but this has always been the case in gross negligence manslaughter: He concluded "The essence of the matter which is supremely a jury question is whether, having regard to the risk of death involved, the conduct of the defendant was so bad in all the circumstances as to amount in their judgment to a criminal act or omission."

The quotation reveals that there is another element to be proved by the prosecution, namely that the accused's act or omission gave rise to a risk of death. Of course, the fact that the victim has died might lead jurors to conclude that there must have been a risk of death. However it is clear that Lord Mackay was indicating that the jury must be satisfied that the act or omission of the defendant had caused a serious risk of death. It is also important to keep separate the seriousness of the risk from the culpability of the defendant for that risk. For example it was accepted in one case that an injection of a certain drug into a patient's spine created a very real risk of death to that patient and this was evident from the doctor's reaction when he realised what had happened. However, he should only be liable to be convicted of manslaughter if his treatment of the patient could be said to have been grossly negligent—a perfectly blameless act could have led to a serious risk of death. This requirement that the act or omission of the accused gave rise to a serious risk of death may have reduced the scope of this type of manslaughter from what it was perceived to be under cases such as *Bateman* (see above, p. 362). At that time it was generally agreed that, a risk of serious bodily harm would also suffice.

Lord Mackay said that trial judges might use the word "reckless" to explain this type of manslaughter to jurors, but he stressed that they should not use the complex formulas associated with the *Caldwell* type of recklessness. In reality a trial judge would be well advised to steer well clear of the word "reckless" when directing a jury; it has caused nothing but trouble.

In summary we can say that in order to get a conviction for gross negligence manslaughter the prosecution must prove that the defendant caused the death of the victim by an act or omission which created a serious risk of death and where the act or omission of the defendant could be said to have been so negligent it should incur criminal liability.

We can conclude by asking whether such a general category of manslaughter is needed. From a purely logical point of view it could be argued that grossly negligent conduct resulting in serious injury does not constitute a criminal offence, so why should grossly negligent conduct resulting in death warrant liability. The answer is that the public sees the causing of death in a totally different light from the causing of serious injury even though the culpability of the accused may be the same. Recently the managing director of an activity centre was gaoled for three years following the drowning of four teenagers while under supervision at the centre. His company was also convicted and became the first company to be convicted of manslaughter (see above, p. 281). Had the young people suffered serious injury but made full recoveries the desire for criminal prosecution would have been much less and compensation through the civil law might well have been considered the more approriate approach. It is suspected that the public would expect to see those who kill through the mis-operation of ferry services, fairgrounds or adventure holidays subject to some form of criminal liability and this would extend to doctors who kill their patients though negligence. Gross negligence manslaughter provides this opportunity and despite the claims of its circuitous nature, juries do not seem to encounter any inseparable problems in its application. . . .

(3) Do we need any other categories of involuntary manslaughter?

After the decision in *Moloney* (see above, p. 347) foresight of death or grievous bodily harm no longer suffices as the *mens rea* for murder. It is clear that a person who kills another foreseeing that he might kill or seriously injure the victim must be guilty of manslaughter and it is possible that they would always come within constructive or gross negligence manslaughter.

However, just in case a case should arise in which this was not the case, it has been suggested that there should be a separate category to cover these two states of mind.

(4) Future Reforms

It is possible that the law of manslaughter will be overhauled in the not too distant future. The Law Commission has just published a package of reforms as part of its mission to produce a Criminal Code (Legislating the Criminal Code: Involuntary Manslaughter; Law. Com. No. 237, 1996). In outline it proposes that the present form of unlawful act manslaughter should be abolished. There should be two separate offences of unintentional killing—(*Cunningham*) reckless killing and killing by gross carelessness. Killing by gross carelessness would have two forms, one of which would be similar to the present gross negligence manslaughter and the other a restricted form of unlawful act manslaughter. The separate offences to deal with killings by motorists would be retained. There would be an offence of corporate killing broadly corresponding to the proposed individual offence of killing by gross carelessness.

An illustration

It will probably help if we conclude this section with an illustration of how these rules work in practice. The case of *Lamb* (1967) (Casebook p. 334) provides a useful vehicle for discussion. In that case two teenagers were playing with a revolver. Lamb, who was holding the revolver, knew that there was one live round in the chamber, but mistakenly believed that the chamber revolved after the gun had been fired. He saw that the live round was not opposite the firing pin and so, aiming the gun at his friend, he pulled the trigger. In fact the chamber revolves as the trigger is being pulled and this meant that a live round was opposite the firing pin at the crucial moment. A shot was fired and his friend was killed. In the actual case Lamb's conviction for manslaughter was quashed by the Court of Appeal. If the same facts were to occur today, what would be the outcome? It is fairly clear that he cannot be convicted for murder since he did not intend to kill or seriously injure his friend. On a charge of constructive manslaughter the prosecution would have to prove that the accused intended to do an unlawful act which was likely to expose his friend to the risk of some harm. The only possible unlawful act on these facts is an assault, and since neither thought that the gun would fire, it would be impossible to prove that Lamb foresaw that his friend would fear for his personal safety (see below, p. 370). There would thus be no assault and therefore no unlawful act. If he were to be charged with gross negligence manslaughter it is likely that the court would take the same view that it actually took in the case, namely that the mistake Lamb had made was understandable for someone not experienced in the workings of guns. It is unlikely that the court would have taken such a lenient view had Lamb been older.

4. Other Offences Involving Killing

Space permits only an examination of murder and manslaughter. There are, however, other offences which involve killing or allied concepts. These include:

(1) Causing death by dangerous driving and causing death by careless driving when under the influence of drink or drugs (Road Traffic Act 1988 as amended).

(2) Abortion (Offences Against the Person Act 1861, s.58, subject to the Abortion Act 1967) and child destruction (Infant Life Preservation Act 1929, s.1) are offences to deal with the killing of a child in the womb right from the time of conception up till and including the time at which it is being delivered, after which it is capable of being the subject of murder and manslaughter.

(3) Suicide. Suicide itself is no longer a crime, but it is a crime to aid, abet, counsel or procure the suicide of another (Suicide Act 1961, s.2). If a defendant charged with murder can prove that he killed the deceased as a party to a suicide pact in which he also, at the time of the killing, intended to die, the jury should return a verdict of manslaughter (Homicide Act 1957, s.4).

(4) Infanticide. Where a mother has killed her child within 12 months of its birth and while the balance of her mind was still affected from the effects of giving birth, she may either be prosecuted for infanticide or, if prosecuted for murder, may raise the defence of infanticide (Infanticide Act 1938).

Chapter 12

Non Fatal Offences Against the Person

Any criminal justice system requires a set of offences to deal with acts of violence perpetrated by one person against another. These offences should cover situations ranging from fairly trivial incidents to those falling just short of murder and manslaughter. In England and Wales these are known as the non-fatal offences against the person and are contained for the most part in the Offences Against the Person Act 1861. However, the current provision is far from perfect and the Act has been described as "piecemeal legislation," which is a "ragbag of offences brought together from a wide variety of sources with no attempt, as the draftsman frankly acknowledges, to introduce consistency as to substance or form". The Law Commission's proposals contained in its Consultation Paper on Offences Against the Person (No. 122), if implemented, would provide us with a properly graded set of offences. In the meantime we are left with the offences under the 1861 Act set out below in what is agreed to be their ascending order of gravity.

1. Common assault and battery (now covered by s.39 Criminal Justice Act 1988; summary only offences; maximum sentence—6 months imprisonment and/or a fine of £5,000).

2. Assault occasioning actual bodily harm (s.47 Offences Against the Person Act 1861; either way offence; maximum sentence 5 years).

3. Unlawful and malicious wounding or infliction of grievous bodily harm (s.20 Offences Against the Person Act, 1861; either way offence; maximum sentence 5 years).

4. Unlawful and malicious wounding or causing of grievous bodily harm with intent to do grievous bodily harm (or resist arrest) (s.18 Offences Against the Person Act 1861; indictable only offence; maximum sentence—life).

1. Assault and Battery

At common law there were two basic offences of assault and battery. Technically assault is the offence of causing another to apprehend immediate and unlawful personal violence. Thus if X puts up his fists to strike Y, if Y apprehends that he is going to be hit, then we can say that X has assaulted Y. When Y is, in fact, hit on the nose, this constitutes a battery. However over the years criminal lawyers have come to use the word "assault" to cover both assaults and batteries. In *Att.-Gen.'s Reference (No. 6 of 1980)* (1981) the Court of Appeal approved with a slight addition the definition of assault given by James J. in *Fagan v. M.P.C.* (1969): "the actual intended use of any unlawful force to another person without his consent (or any other lawful excuse)".

Both assault and battery are crimes of basic intent to which the defence of self-induced intoxication does not apply. We shall look separately at the *actus reus* of assault and battery and then at the *mens rea*.

(1) The Actus Reus of Assault

The prosecution must establish that the victim was put in fear of immediate and unlawful personal violence. Thus a very clear example of an assault would be where X, during the course of an argument, raises his clenched fist as if to punch Y in the face. Y would be in fear of immediate personal violence for which there would be no lawful excuse. The requirement that the fear be of immediate personal violence has, over the years, been given a fairly generous interpretation. In *Smith v. Chief Superintendent, Woking Police Station* (1983) it was held that magistrates were entitled to find that a woman who saw the defendant looking through the window of her bedsitting room late at night apprehended immediate violence. The same was true in *Lewis* (1970) where the husband was threatening violence to his wife who was on the other side of a locked door, though in this case the court may have been over anxious to find an assault in order to uphold a conviction under s.20 of the Offences Against the Person Act 1861 (see below, p. 376). It is clear, however, that immediate fear of future violence does not suffice.

There is some authority for the view that words alone cannot constitute an assault, but it is suggested that in appropriate circumstances there is no reason why they should not. For example, if X, a prostitute, was walking home in the dark one evening when a man said to her "I am continuing Jack the Ripper's crusade against prostitutes", it would be absurd if this were not to be treated as being capable of constituting an assault. However, in this case it could be argued that there is something which could be classified as an act as opposed to words alone. Would there be an assault if X telephones Y and tells Y that he has planted a bomb in the telephone Y is holding and that it will go off in two seconds?

For the purposes of common assault the personal violence is not unlawful if the accused was acting in self-defence (or if one of the allied defences applied; see above, p. 303) or if the defence of consent was available. We shall see later (below, p. 380) that in some cases a person may consent to another doing what would otherwise be an assault or battery. Suffice it here to say, however, that consent is more likely to be in issue in relation to battery. It did, however, arise in *Lamb* (above, p. 367) where the victim clearly consented to Lamb pointing the gun at him; though in that case the absence of an assault is equally explicable on the ground that Lamb lacked *mens rea* since he did not intend to put the other in fear of immediate harm and neither did he foresee that his friend would apprehend such harm.

(2) The Actus Reus of Battery

Here the prosecution must prove that the accused inflicted unlawful personal violence on the victim. There is no need to show that the amount of force was great or that injury was caused; in fact, any touching of another without that other's consent amounts to a battery (for the defence of consent see below, p. 387), but consent is generally implied in the sort of bodily contact that happens in ordinary everyday life. Thus we generally assume that people walking about in the street accept that others will inevitably bump into them; that others may tap them on the shoulder to attract their attention; and that in the course of conversation there are people who need to touch the other to emphasise what they are saying.

The most simple example of batteries are those cases in which the accused hits his victim either with a fist or with an object he is holding. But it is also a battery to dig a hole for someone to fall into or to cause people to fall down stairs by turning out the lights (*Martin* (1881) see below, p. 376). There is no need for the victim to be aware that he is about to be struck; thus it would amount to a battery where X removes the chair Y is about to sit on, or hits him on the head from behind.

As with assault, the application of force is not unlawful if it is by consent or in circumstances of justification.

(3) Mens Rea of Assault and Battery

Although the elements of assault and battery are not elaborated in the Offences Against the Person Act 1861, it is generally accepted that both assault and battery are basic intent crimes requiring proof of intention or *Cunningham* recklessness. In *Venna* (1976) the Court of Appeal confirmed that this was correct. However, in *Kong Cheuk Kwan* ((1985) above, p. 363) Lord Roskill said that the word "recklessness" should receive the same definition whether it appeared in a statute or elsewhere and that the definition should be the one given by Lord Diplock in *Caldwell*. In *D.P.P. v. K. (a minor)* (1990) Parker L.J. said, *obiter*, that the *mens rea* of assault and battery would be satisfied by proof of *Caldwell* recklessness. Subsequently the Court of Appeal in *Spratt* (1991) held *D.P.P. v. K.* to be wrong and that the position was as stated in *Venna*. In *Savage and Parmenter* (1991) the House of Lords overruled Spratt on other grounds, but held that recklessness in assault was to be given the subjective *Cunningham* meaning. As a result we can safely assert that the prosecution must prove that the accused **either** intended to apply unlawful force (battery) or to put the victim in fear of the immediate application of unlawful force (assault): **or** consciously took an unjustified risk that what he was doing might result in the unlawful application of force (battery) or might cause the victim to fear the immediate application of unlawful force (assault).

In assault it is the effect the accused intentionally or recklessly creates on the victim that is central to the offence; it does not matter that the accused had neither the intention nor the ability to carry out the threat. Thus where X holds up Y, a bank cashier, with a water pistol, if X intends that Y should fear for his personal safety and Y is so affected then X has committed an assault. It is no defence for X to say that there was no assualt because Y was never in any danger. In *Lamb* ((1967), above, p. 367) the defendant was not guilty of an assault in pointing the gun at his friend since neither believed that the gun would fire; Lamb had no intention to cause his friend to apprehend force, nor was he reckless, and the friend apprehended no force.

Where in assault or battery the defendant relies upon the defence of consent (see below, p. 380) or self-defence (or one of its allied defences, see above, p. 303), it is sufficient that he honestly believed that the victim was a consenting or that he was about to be attacked. If the jury believes that he honestly held such a belief it is irrelevant that there are no reasonable grounds for such a belief (*Williams* (1987)).

2. Assault Occasioning Actual Bodily Harm

Under section 47 of the Offences Against the Person Act 1861, it is an offence for a person to assault another thereby causing that person actual bodily harm.

(4) Actus reus

The actus reus of the offences requires (i) proof of a common assault or battery (see above) and (ii) that the assault or battery was the cause of the actual bodily harm. What, therefore, do we mean by "actual bodily harm"? In *D.P.P. v. Smith* (1961) the House of Lords was considering the phrase "grievous bodily harm" and said that the words "bodily harm" needed no explanation and that "grievous" meant really serious. It was thus taken to follow that "actual bodily harm" was something less than "really serious harm". In *Chan-Fook* (1993) the Court of Appeal said that "harm" was a synonym for "injury" and that "actual" indicated that indicated that, although there was no need for the injury to be permanent, it should not be so trivial as to be wholly insignificant.

The issue for the Court in *Chan-Fook* was whether "bodily harm" could embrace psychiatric injury. Care should be taken so as not to distract from the central issue namely that the offence requires proof of an "injury". In some cases it might be necessary to instruct the jury as to what was covered by the phrase "*bodily*" injury. The Court of Appeal held that the inclusion of the word "bodily" did not limit the harm to harm to the skin, flesh and bones of the victim. The body of the victim included all parts of his body, including his organs, his nervous system and his brain. Bodily injury might therefore include injury responsible for his mental and other faculties. Thus actual bodily harm was capable of including psychiatric illness, but it did not include mere emotions such as fear, distress or panic. Nor would it include an assault which had caused an hysterical and nervous condition. Judges should avoid using phrases such as "state of mind of the victim" in considering whether a psychiatric injury had been caused since this might lead a jury to think that something which was no more than a strong emotion such as fear would constitute actual bodily harm; it did not.

(5) Mens Rea

The prosecution must establish the *mens rea* of an assault and that is all; it is not necessary to show that the accused intended to cause or took a conscious and unjustified risk of causing actual bodily harm. This had been the accepted position following the decision in *Roberts* (1972) and indeed was the view taken in the Court of Appeal by Glidewell L.J. in *Savage* in 1991. In *Savage* the prosecution alleged that the defendant had not only deliberately thrown the contents of a glass of beer over the victim, but had also let go of the glass itself. The glass struck a table and the victim's wrist was cut by flying glass. Glidewell L.J. observed that the verdict of the jury in the Crown Court showed that they clearly believed that she had let go of the glass, but due to the direction they received from the trial judge it was not clear whether they thought the release of the glass was deliberate or accidental. It was thus impossible to say whether the jury thought the accused intended or foresaw any bodily harm as a result of her actions, since the drenching with beer could not in itself amount to actual bodily harm. The Court of Appeal, however, held that the defendant had committed an intentional battery (the soaking with beer) and this was the only *mens rea* required. It was not necessary to prove that she either intended to cause bodily harm or that she consciously took an unjustified risk in doing so.

It is amazing that with this offence on the statute book for 130 years that within hours of this decision another section of the Court of Appeal was reaching the opposite result, namely that the offence under section 47 required proof that the accused either intended to cause or consciouly took an unjustified risk of causing some bodily harm. This was the decision in *Spratt* (1991) which was shortly thereafter endorsed by the Court of Appeal in *Parmenter* (1991). In the combined appeals to the House of Lords in *Savage and Parmenter* (1991) the House of Lords held that the position had been correctly stated in *Roberts* and *Savage*. Thus the only *mens rea* required for the offence under section 47 is that of common assault.

The result of this is that the only difference between section 47 and common assault is the causing of some bodily harm required for section 47. This harm may be very slight and completely accidental, but it provides the court with four and a half more years in terms of sentencing power.

3. Offences Against the Person Act 1861, s.20

> "Whosoever shall unlawfully and maliciously wound or inflict any grievous bodily harm upon another person, either with or without any weapon or instrument, shall be guilty of an offence triable either way and being convicted thereof shall be liable to imprisonment for five years."

The first thing that should strike you about this offence is that although it sounds far more serious than that under section 47 (assault occasioning actual bodily harm) it carries precisely the same maximum penalty. This is a result of the Offences Against the Person Act being a haphazard consolidation of offences, but it does make the law look a trifle illogical.

(1) Actus Reus

The prosecution must establish that the accused unlawfully inflicted grievous bodily harm or that he unlawfully wounded the victim. The word unlawfully means that the offence is not committed if the accused was acting in self-defence or possibly if the victim had consented (see below, p. 380). Wounding will rarely cause problems: here the prosecution must prove that as a result of the accused's actions the inner and outer skin of the victim were severed. Would it suffice therefore that the accused has caused internal bleeding in his victim? If, for example, the accused has caused bleeding inside the accused's mouth this will be· classified as a wounding, but probably not if he has caused a rupture of the victim's stomach lining or a bruise. The difference is that the inside skin of the lips and cheeks are readily accessible from the outside; you can trace the continuity of the skin with your finger. In no way is this true of the stomach lining. The matter is not likely to cause many problems since an attack which caused internal bleeding is likely to be said to have inflicted grievous bodily harm—or at least actual bodily harm in the case of a bruise.

We have already seen that grievous bodily harm means that the victim suffers bodily harm which can be described as really serious. Here there need be no breaking of the skin, and it is a question of fact for the jury whether the harm is or is not really serious. However it will be seen that in section 20 the accused must be shown to have "inflicted" grievous bodily harm, whereas under section 18 he must be shown to have "caused" grievous bodily harm. Is any significance to be drawn from the use of these different verbs? The answer is that no such distinction may have occurred to the original drafters of the provisions, but in interpreting them the courts have more often than not held that the word "inflicts" means that the act of the accused which results in the grievous bodily harm must itself be an assault. In the majority of cases this causes no problems since the accused usually produces the grievous bodily harm by striking the victim with his fists or a weapon. In *Clarence* (1888), however, the accused who was suffering from a communicable form of venereal disease had intercourse with a woman without revealing his condition to her. It was held that he could not be convicted of "inflicting grievous bodily harm" on her since she had consented to the intercourse and hence there was no assault (see below, p. 387 for meaning of consent). Recently in *Wilson* (1984) (*Casebook*, p. 366) the House of Lords has held that the word "inflicts" did not necessarily include an allegation of assault. This still leaves open the question of whether the word "inflicts" has a meaning different from "causes" and it is possible that "inflicts" might be held to require the application of some force, whether by an assault or not, and may not therefore cover a situation in which grievous bodily harm has been caused by the secret administration of poison.

Whatever the eventual decision in cases of poisoning and cases such as *Clarence*, the decision in *Wilson* removes doubts from other earlier cases in which convictions under section 20 had been upheld despite the absence of any obvious assault. Thus in *Martin* (1881) the accused had caused panic in a theatre as the audience was leaving after a performance, by extinguishing all the lights on the stairs and placing a bar across the doors at the bottom. In the ensuing chaos several persons were injured when crushed against the doors which would not open. The court seems to have assumed that there was an assault, though it is difficult to see how they were placed in fear of immediate and unlawful violence. Possibly there was a battery of the type involved where a pit is dug for somebody to fall into. If, however, the word "inflicts" does not require proof of an assault there will be no difficulty in holding that the accused has inflicted grievous bodily harm on the victims. Similarly many of the problems of holding that there has been an assault in cases, in which the victim has caused grievous bodily harm upon himself in trying to escape from the accused, will disappear. In *Halliday* (1889) the accused advanced in a threatening manner towards his wife who tried to jump out of an upstairs window. Her daughter prevented her fall by trying to hold on to her, but the accused ordered her to let go whereupon her mother fell to the ground below. It was held that the father had inflicted grievous bodily harm. In that case it would be possible to say that there was an assault since both the mother and daughter were put in fear of immediate harm; but this is more difficult in the case of *Lewis* (1970) where the husband who was threatening the wife was on the other side of a locked door. Again the court held that there was an assault although the wife was not in fear of such immediate harm because of the locked door. The decision in *Wilson* means that a conviction in such cases as these can be upheld without the need to give an unduly wide meaning to the requirement in assault that the accused should place the victim in fear of "immediate" harm.

(2) Mens Rea

The prosecution must prove that the accused acted maliciously. We have already seen that maliciously does not mean that the accused acted from evil motives; it generally indicates that *mens rea* will be required (*Cunningham*, above, p. 203). If this is the case then one would have supposed that the prosecution would have to prove that the accused intended or foresaw that his actions would wound or inflict grievous bodily harm. However in *Mowatt* (1968) (*Casebook*, p. 362) the Court of Appeal held that it was sufficient if the accused foresaw that some physical injury would be caused to some person albeit of a minor nature. The accused did not have to foresee that it would be a wound or grievous bodily harm. The accused did not have to foresee that the harm would be to wound or grievous bodily harm. Diplock L.J. purporting to follow Byrne J. in *Cunningham*, said that when Byrne J. referred to the particular kind of harm, he was not referring to the degree of injury, but rather to the fact that the prosecution must prove that the accused foresaw his acts would cause bodily injury rather than damage to property. This decision has been heavily criticised; the prosecution merely has to prove that the accused intended or foresaw the harm which suffices as the *actus reus* of a lesser offence, namely that under section 47. Although both offences carry the same maximum sentence, it is quite clear that the section 20 offence is regarded as a much more serious charge and it would be preferable if the *mens rea* related to the degree of harm described in the *actus reus*, namely a wound or grievous bodily harm. This is not the end of the problems caused by the decision in *Mowatt*. In explaining that the accused does not have to intend or foresee a wound or grievous bodily harm, Diplock L.J. added "it is enough that he should have foreseen some physical harm." Since *Mowatt* several cases have appeared on appeal in the Court of Appeal in which the trial judge has directed the jury that they have to be satisfied that the accused *should have* foreseen some harm. Such a direction could clearly lead a jury to believe that they are not being asked to decide if the accused actually intended or foresaw some harm but whether he ought, as a reasonable person, to have foreseen some harm. Despite confusion in his judgment it seems fairly clear that Diplock intended that the offence required at least *Cunningham* recklessness.

In the combined appeals of *Savage and Parmenter* the House of Lords said that two matters needed to be resolved. Firstly was it enough that the accused should have foreseen the requisite degree of harm and secondly what is that requisite degree of harm? As to the first the House held that the prosecution must prove that the accused intended or foresaw (*i.e.* consciously took an unjustified risk of causing) the requisite degree of harm; in other words maliciously meant what Byrne J. had said it meant in *Cunningham* and this had not been affected by the decision in *Caldwell*. However, as to the degree of harm, the House said that *Mowatt* had been correctly decided. The prosecution had to show that the accused intended to cause some harm (albeit slight) or consciously took an unjustified risk of causing some harm. Suffice to say that none of the reasons advanced for this part of the decision are convincing. Section 20 is a serious offence and a person should not be convicted of such an offence unless he at least foresees that what he is doing may cause the degree of harm outlined in the *actus reus* of the offence.

In *Sullivan* (1980) the Court of Appeal confirmed the correctness of the decision in *Mowatt*, and went on to hold that an intention to frighten the victim, without more, would not suffice as the *mens rea* for section 20. Where, for example, A drives his car perilously close to B intending to scare him, A may well realise that he might cause some injury to B. Unless, however, he does realise that there is a risk of injury there is no offence under section 20, though there may be an offence under section 47.

4. Offences Against the Person Act 1861, s.18

"Whosoever shall unlawfully and maliciously by any means whatsoever wound or cause any grievous bodily harm to any person with intent to do some grievous bodily harm to any person, or with intent to resist or prevent the lawful apprehension or detaining of any person, shall be guilty of an offence, and being convicted thereof shall be liable to imprisonment for life."

The maximum possible sentence of life imprisonment clearly shows that this offence is reserved for the most culpable of offenders against the person.

(1) Actus Reus

The *actus reus* of this offence is to a large extent identical to that of the offence under section 20. It should be noted however that this section speaks of the accused "causing" rather than "inflicting" grievous bodily harm, and thus there is no question of the need to show an assault here.

(2) Mens Rea

The prosecution must prove (i) that the accused intended to do grievous bodily harm or intended to resist arrest, and (ii) that he acted maliciously.

(i) The prosecution must prove that the accused caused the *actus reus* with the intention either of doing grievous bodily harm to some person or with the intention of resisting or preventing the lawful apprehension or detaining of any person. *Belfon* (1976) makes it clear that nothing short of intention will suffice on this part of the *mens rea*; thus the prosecution must establish that the accused intended to achieve one of these ends though they may be able to infer intention if they find he foresaw the result as virtually certain (see above, p. 210). In relation to intention to resist, etc., we can safely say that if the accused believes that the arrest is unlawful and it is, in fact, unlawful, he will have a defence.

The position is less clear if he believes the arrest is unlawful, but it is in fact lawful. On principle he should have a defence as long as his belief is genuine. This would seem to follow from *Morgan* (above, p. 230) but there is old authority to the contrary (*Bentley* (1850)).

(ii) In addition to the intent described in (i) above the prosecution must establish that the accused was acting "maliciously." In *Mowatt* (1968) the Court of Appeal said, *obiter*, that this word is superfluous in section 18, presumably thinking of a case in which the accused is charged with maliciously causing grievous bodily harm with intent to do grievous bodily harm. And similarly it would not add much to wounding where this was charged coupled with an intent to do grievous bodily harm. Where, however, the accused is charged with wounding or causing grievous bodily harm with intent to resist arrest it has a full part to play. Consider a situation in which X, in trying to resist lawful arrest pushes the arresting officer who falls and is seriously injured. If the word malicious is given no role to play it means that the only *mens rea* required of X would be his intent to resist arrest and this would be satisfied even if he intended to use only the slightest force to break away. This would surely be wrong. Thus the word maliciously should be employed so as to require that in addition to the ulterior intent the prosecution should also have to prove that the accused at least foresaw that what he was doing would cause at least some physical harm. This would give maliciously the same meaning as in section 20. Despite the criticism of this meaning of maliciously, it is unlikely the courts would be happy to give a different meaning to the word, especially since it has been subject to recent examination in the House of Lords. Equally, however, it would be just as illogical to say it had no meaning whatsoever in section 18. Thus in our illustration X would only be liable on an indictment charging him with causing grievous bodily harm with intent to resist arrest if he did intend to resist arrest and if he also foresaw that his act would cause some physical harm.

5. Consent as a Defence to Offences Against the Person

The questions we must ask in this section are whether consent can ever be relied upon as a defence to offences against the person and, if so, what does the criminal law mean by the term "consent"?

(1) Is consent any defence to a charge involving an offence against the person?

We have already seen (above, p. 230) that consent has a major role to play in the offence of rape. It is perfectly lawful for a man to have sexual intercourse with a woman who is consenting. If she does not consent and he is at least indifferent as to whether or not she is consenting, then he commits the offence of rape and, although this is likely to be academic, the offence of battery. On the other hand there are activities which are unlawful whether or not the parties are willing participants. For example, if the woman turns out to be under the age of 16, then the man commits the offence of unlawful sexual intercourse and although the woman's consent may prevent a charge of rape it will be no defence to the charge of unlawful sexual intercourse.

In the field of non-sexual offences against the person, the position is less well-defined. While it is generally accepted that consent may be a defence to a charge of common assault or battery and is not a defence to charges of murder or manslaughter, there is no clearly defined theoretical framework to cover the offences in between. It is likely that most citizens would think that the law would not sanction the consensual infliction of serious bodily harm, but such a rule, without some exempting provision, would outlaw boxing and perhaps surgical operations. Until the recent decision by the House of Lords in *Brown* (1993) the position was controlled by the decision of the Court of Appeal in *Att.-Gen's Reference (No. 6 of 1980)* (1981). In that case two youths had resolved to settle an argument by a fight, during the course of which the defendant caused the other to suffer a bleeding nose and bruised face. It would appear that the accused was charged with common assault. (This is not entirely clear from the report and in *Brown*, Lords Jauncey and Lowry stated that the charge was assault occasioning actual bodily harm, while Lord Mustill was of the opinion that it was common assault.) The Court of Appeal held that while consent would normally be a defence to common assault, there might be cases where the public interest demanded otherwise. Such a case was where people try to cause or cause each other bodily harm *for no good reason*. While the Court might have rested its decision on the potential of such fights to cause a breach of the peace, it did not do so saying that the same rule applied whether the fight had occurred in public or in private. The italicised words *"for no good reason"* are a reference to the exceptions to the rule such as boxing matches where there is deemed to be a public interest in allowing such activity (see below, p. 385).

The whole issue of consent was brought dramatically before the House of Lords in the case of *Brown* (1993). In that case a group of homosexual males had been discovered to be participating in sado-masochistic practices. The practices usually involved the recipient being manacled so as to be powerless while another member of the group carried out such activities as the nailing of the recipient's scrotum to a board or the burning of his penis with a candle. It is clear that the recipients were fully willing participants and that the group had created code words which would be used by the recipients when they wished the activities to stop. It also appeared that younger people had been introduced to these practices by the group and that video recordings had been made, not for sale, but for viewing by members of the group who had missed the particular events. The defendants were charged with numerous offences, but the House of Lords was concerned only with the charges of assault occasioning actual bodily harm (section 47) and unlawful wounding (section 20). It is worth noting that four of the men had pleaded guilty to keeping a disorderly house and had received custodial sentences for that offence. One had also been sentenced for two counts of publishing an obscene article (the video recordings). It is further worth noting that it was clear that the men had indulged in what the House described as even more revolting sexual practices, but that no charges had been brought in respect of these since they could not be brought within the scope of any recognised offence. At best these other activities constituted battery, but since no injury was caused, consent would be a defence under *Att.-Gen.'s Reference* (see above, p. 381). The charges brought under section 47 and 20 concerned activities where bodily harm or wounding had occurred.

The defendants argued that consent should be a defence to all the charges since the injuries fell short of serious bodily harm. By a majority of three to two the House of Lords held that consent was no defence. The approach of the majority was that, on the face of it, the activities fell within the definition of the offences and that since harm was both intended and caused, consent was irrelevant unless the court could find that there was good reason to allow such activity. In other words the majority considered that they were being asked to extend the defence of consent to cover the intentional infliction of bodily harm in the course of sado-masochistic practices. The majority held that there were several good reasons why they should not do so. In the first place it was only luck that these men had not suffered any really serious injuries or infections. Secondly there was the risk of spreading such diseases as AIDS. Thirdly there was the danger that young people could be drawn into these unnatural practices. There was therefore no public interest in permitting such activities. It had been suggested that the court should allow consent as a defence to actual bodily harm, but not serious bodily harm. This was rejected since wounding under section 20 might amount either to actual bodily harm or to grievous bodily harm and it was felt undesirable to draw a line through the middle of section 20. It made more sense to draw the line between no bodily harm and some bodily harm. Therefore, the position would appear to be that whether you are charged with common assault (including battery), assault occasioning actual bodily harm or unlawful wounding or infliction of grievous bodily harm, consent will be no defence, if bodily harm is intended or caused, unless there is held to be "some good reason for it". The pursuit of sado-masochistic pleasures does not constitute a good reason.

The minority approached the case from an entirely different angle. Lord Mustill observed that the involvement of the Act of 1861 was purely adventitious.

> "This impression is reinforced when one considers the title of the statute under which the appellants are charged, 'Offences *Against* the Person'. Conduct infringing sections 18, 20 and 47 of the Act of 1861 comes before the Crown Courts every day. Typically it involves brutality, aggression and violence, of a kind far removed from the appellant's behaviour which, however worthy of censure, involved no animosity, no aggression, no personal rancour on the part of the person inflicting the hurt towards the recipient and no protest by the recipient. In fact, quite the reverse."

"Of course", he continued, "we must give effect to the statute if it's interpretation covers what these men have done". His review of the earlier cases led him to the conclusion that there was nothing to prevent the House from looking afresh at whether the public interest required s.47 to be interpreted so as to include the conduct of these men. In other words, he was of the opinion that the consensual infliction of actual bodily harm was not caught by s.47 unless there was good public reason to stop this type of conduct. Lord Slynn was of the opinion that consent could even extend to charges of wounding under s.20, so long as the wound did not represent a serious injury. Neither felt that there was any clear public interest argument which necessitated the extension of liability under the 1861 Act to cover these practices, though both were at pains to point out that they were not condoning the activities. If Parliament considered, having carefully researched the position, that the conduct ought to be made criminal, then it would be for Parliament to pass the necessary legislation.

It would seem therefore, under the view of the majority, that consent is only relevant as a defence to common assault and battery and only when no injury is intended or caused (cf *Wilson* 1996). It is not entirely clear whether lack of consent is seen as an essential element of assault or whether it is raised by way of defence. It is probably correct to say that the majority perceived it as a defence which means that the defendant would have an evidential burden to introduce evidence of consent before the prosecution is required to prove that there was no consent.

In cases of common assault the relevance of consent turns upon whether or not injury was intended or caused. If it is the prosecution's case that consent is irrelevant because bodily harm was, in fact, caused, is it necessary to show that the defendant was at least reckless as to the causing of it? In *Boyea* (1992) the defendant inserted his hand into the complainant's vagina and twisted it thereby causing her injury. On a charge of indecent assault the judge directed the jury that consent was irrelevant if the conduct was likely or intended to cause harm. (An indecent assault requires proof of a common assault or battery). On appeal the defendant argued the judge should have asked the jury to consider whether he knew or was aware that he might cause harm. The appeal was dismissed. The Court of Appeal reasoned, by analogy with *Savage and Parmenter* (above, p. 374), that since in the offence of assault occasioning actual boldily harm no *mens rea* was required as to the occasioning of bodily harm, none was required in the present case. The analogy is at least questionable. In *Savage* there was clearly an intentional battery; the question for the court was whether the battery had caused actual bodily harm. In *Boyea* the question is whether there was a battery at all and a battery is the intentional or reckless (*Cunningham*) infliction of non-consensual force. It would, of course be no defence for Boyea to say that he did not know the law did not permit the defence of consent when injury was caused, but surely it must at least be proved that he was aware of the facts which rendered consent irrelevant. In other words unless he consciously took the risk of harming the girl, he foresaw only a consented-to, non-injurious application of force and that is not a battery.

So far we have been considering what may be described as the general starting point, namely that a person may not consent to any activity which is intended to or which actually causes harm for no good reason. We must now look at those situations in which the law has decided that there is good reason. (The special categories are dealt with fully in the speech of Lord Mustill in *Brown*.)

Sporting activities

Without some relaxation of the general rule stated above, any contact sports would be illegal. It is in the public interest that people engage in sporting activity both as a means of gaining exercise and also in the cause of providing entertainment for the public at large. The law has to strike a balance between what are and what are not acceptable risks. Brutality cannot be licensed under the name of sport. In many sports there is simply an acknowledgment that the participants may be accidentally hurt, though the expectation is that this will be rare. This is true, for example, of athletics and sports such as tennis. At the other end of the spectrum is boxing in which each opponent is aware that the other intends to cause him serious bodily harm. In the middle lie contact sports such as soccer and rugby in which the players are aware that deliberate contact (tackles) may have unintended effects, conceivably of sufficient severity to amount to grievous bodily harm.

Let us consider first boxing.

"For money, not recreation or personal improvement, each boxer tries to hurt the opponent more than he is hurt himself, and aims to end the contest prematurely by inflicting a brain injury serious enough to make the opponent unconscious, or temporarily by impairing his central nervous system through a blow to the midriff, or cutting his skin to a degree which would ordinarily be well within the scope of section 20. The boxers display skill, strength and courage, but nobody pretends that they do good to themselves or others. The onlookers derive entertainment, but none of the physical and moral

benefits which have been seen as the fruits of engagement in manly sports" (*per* Lord Mustill).

Boxing's predecessor was prize fighting (fighting with bare
fists) this was made unlawful in the early nineteenth century
when it was felt no longer in the public interest to tolerate it.
Boxing today is perhaps best regarded as an activity which for
the time being stands outside the ordinary law of violence,
because society chooses to tolerate it.

Contact sports such as rugby and soccer often involve quite
violent bodily contact. Obviously those who take part in such
sports consent to fair tackles even though these may
sometimes lead to quite serious, but unintentional, injuries. It
would seem also to be the case that the participants accept the
risk that they may be tackled and thereby injured in a way
that constitutes a foul against the laws of the game. Do the
participants, however, consent to the intentional infliction of
any degree of bodily harm? It is clear that they do not consent
to the deliberate infliction of serious bodily injury and
probably the courts would hold that consent is not given to
the deliberate infliction of any degree of bodily harm in such
sports. However, the problem is more likely to arise in
relation to recklessly inflicted injuries. Consider the position
of the soccer player who tackles an opponent from behind in
such a way as to break the opponent's leg; or jumps in a
group of players for a high ball with his elbows protruding
and thereby blinds another player. In either case the
deliberate causing of such injuries would constitute offences
under ss.18 and 20 and no court would allow a defence of
consent. It is suggested that the answer should be the same if
the offender consciously took the risk of causing this type of
harm.

In the case of milder sports the participants are taken to
have consented to the possibility that they might be injured
by the other players.

Medical Treatment

With the express, or implied consent of the patient a
surgeon may do things to the patient which, if performed by
anyone else, would constitute very serious bodily harm. We
allow such activity because its aim is the well being of the
patient. While we do not allow euthanasia, we do permit
patients to consent to medical treatment where there is a risk
of death or serious injury. For example, a patient may consent
to a heart transplant operation even though this might be

unsuccessful. The risk of death is considered to be a justified risk in that the treatment is the only way in which the patient can be given a chance of leading a normal life. What would be the position of a surgeon who amputated a patient's leg at the request of a patient who said he wanted to take part in the disabled persons' Olympic Games? The courts would take the view that there was no public interest in allowing the defence of consent to such an operation and the doctor would commit an offence under section 18 of the Offences Against the Person Act 1861. What attitude do the courts take to cosmetic surgery, for example an operation to reduce the size of the patient's nose? At first it was said that such operations served no therapeutic purpose, but the psychological benefit of such operations is now recognised and so the patient can give a valid consent. Sex change operations and sterilisations which were once regarded as being against the public interest are now generally recognised as valuable operations.

Rough Horseplay

The courts apparently believe it is necessary to allow scope for the sort of rough horseplay that occurs in school playgrounds and in military barracks, usually among men. In *Jones* (1987) two young boys were thrown into the air by two other youths in a school playground and were seriously injured when they hit the ground. It was held to be a defence that the defendant believed however unreasonably, that the victims were consenting. This must be seen as an area in which the courts feel that the public interest demands a relaxation of the normal principles enunciated in *Att.-Gen.'s Reference* (see above, p. 381).

(2) What is Consent?

We have seen that consent is a defence to some offences. but not to others. Where it is capable of being a defence, what exactly do we mean when we say that D consented to a particular course of conduct? It will be convenient to begin the discussion with an examination of cases relating to the defence of consent to a charge of rape. We shall see later (below p. 389) that the scope of the offence has been widened, but for the moment we can say that the actus reus of rape is unlawful sexual intercourse with a women who does not consent. Where force is used by the defendant to secure intercourse, the jury may have little difficulty in reaching the conclusion that the woman did not consent. However, neither force nor threat of force is essential. In

Olugboja (1981) the victim submitted to intercourse through fear of what might happen to her if she did not, although the court accepted that no specific threats were made. The Court of Appeal held that she had not consented to the intercourse.

There are situations where a woman would not have consented to the intercourse but for fraud practised on her by the defendant. He might, for example, have told her that he was wealthy or that he would marry her if she had intercourse with him. He might falsely tell her that he was cured of a sexually transmitted disease. In *Linekar* (1995) the accused had persuaded a prostitute to have intercourse with him on a promise to pay for the services. In each of these situations the victim is under no misapprehension as to the nature of the act which is requested, nor as to the person with whom it will be committed, though she may have accredited him with attributes he does not possess. In each of these cases the court will hold that she has consented to the intercourse and it does not constitute rape, even though she would not have consented to have intercourse, and the defendant may well realise she would not have consented, had she known the truth.

Where, however, the victim is mistaken as to the nature of the act or as to the identity of the person with whom the act will be performed, her consent to intercourse is not effective or real. Suppose that the defendant persuades the victim to have intercourse with him by telling her that it will improve her singing ability. Should the victim be too young to understand the nature of the act, she will be held not to have consented to intercourse. If on the other hand, she is well aware of the nature of the sexual act, but is led to believe that it can help improve her singing voice, she will be held to have consented to intercourse. (See *Williams* 1916.)

For many years it has been accepted that if the defendant persuades the woman to have intercourse by impersonating her husband, this will be rape. In this situation she is mistaken as to the identity of the other party. In *Elbekkay* (1995) the Court of Appeal has said that such mistakes are not confined to a belief that she is having intercourse with her husband. In an act such as intercourse, the identity of the other party is crucial and so it would also negative consent if the victim mistakenly thought she was having intercourse with her boyfriend. Although this is a logical extension there are serious difficulties to it. Section 142(3) of the Criminal Justice and Public Order Act 1994 provides that "A man also commits rape if he induces a married woman to have intercourse with him by impersonating her husband". Such a provision would suggest that impersonating persons other than the husband will not suffice and it may be that further attention will be paid to this by the courts.

The case of Linekar (see above, p. 388) makes it clear that it is not the fraud which is the crucial element in these cases. What is important is the nature of the mistake. Only mistakes as to the nature of the act and to the identity of the other party will be effective to negative consent.

By section 134 Criminal Justice and Public Order Act 1994 rape is extended to cover non-consensual intercourse per vaginam or per anum with a man or woman; the requirement that the intercourse is unlawful is removed. It is suggested that the principles in relation to consent remain the same. It must, however, be noted that only a man can be the principal offender in a charge of rape; a woman who persuades a man to have intercourse by impersonating his wife does not commit rape.

Where a man has sexual intercourse with a willing girl of 15, her consent to the act will be a defence to rape. It will not however, provide a defence to most other sexual offences such as indecent assault or the offence of unlawful sexual intercourse (often referred to in other jurisdictions as statutory rape); for this offence her consent is, by law, considered to be ineffective.

Consent generally

A similar approach to consent has been adopted by the courts in offences against the person generally. In the Canadian case *Bolduc and Bird* (1967) a woman patient submitted to a vaginal examination having agreed that a medical student could observe. In fact the medical student was simply a friend of the doctor who wished to see a vaginal examination. Not surprisingly when the patient discovered what had happened she was very upset and the doctor together with his friend were prosecuted for indecent assault. A prosecution for indecent assault requires that an assault or battery can be established (see above). The Court held that the woman was fully aware of the nature of the act, a vaginal examination conducted by a doctor, and had consented to it. The fact that she would not have consented had she known that the observer was not a medical student was irrelevant. Had the examination been carried out by a person passing himself off to be a doctor, there would be no consent since there would have been a mistake as to the nature of the act—the act would not have been a medical examination. Would there be consent if the patient had been expecting an examination from Doctor X, but had actually been examined by Dr Y passing himself off as Dr X? As we have seen a mistake as to the identity of the person with whom you are having intercourse negatives consent. Could it be argued that mistake as to identity is less relevant outside the sexual arena; it is at least arguable, despite *Elbekkay* (above, p. 388) that only a mistake that you are having intercourse with your husband will suffice? It is suggested that *Elbekkay* is right in principle and should extend to other, non-sexual, offences.

Reform

In its recent Paper, "Consent in the Criminal Law", the Law Commission has sought views on a wide variety of proposals for reform in relation to the defence of consent (Law Commission Consultation paper 139, 1995).

Chapter 13

Offences Under The Theft Acts 1968 and 1978

The Theft Acts of 1968 and 1978 provide us with a fairly comprehensive list of offences which broadly speaking involve the dishonest dealing with other people's property. Taken together with the Criminal Damage Act 1971 and the Forgery and Counterfeiting Act 1981, it may be said that there is now a code dealing with all the principal offences against property.

The Theft Act 1968 implemented an overhaul of the then existing assortment of offences which had become rather complex and unwieldy. The 1978 Act created three new offences to replace a subsection of the 1968 Act which had been found to be unworkable. Between them the Acts have produced a simplification of the law in this area and we can say from the outset that the great majority of cases brought under them present very few difficult legal problems. However it is probably impossible to construct a totally simple code for property offences. Take theft for example; this consists in the interference with the property rights of another. These property rights are controlled at the outset by the civil law and so in theft cases it is sometimes necessary to take account of difficult civil law rules before criminal liability can be sorted out. Occasionally judges have said that complex rules relating to property rights have no place in the criminal law, but it would be impossible to divorce the law of theft from the property rights it is seeking to protect.

In this chapter we shall concentrate mainly upon the offences of theft and deception and the chapter will conclude with a summary of the other well-known offences.

I. THEFT

The offence is defined by section 1 of the Theft Act 1968.

"(1) A person is guilty of theft if he dishonestly appropriates property belonging to another with the intention of permanently depriving the other of it; and 'thief' and 'steal' shall be construed accordingly."

Sections 1 to 6 of the Act amplify the meaning of words and phrases used in this definition and section 7 provides that the offence of theft shall be punishable with a maximum of 7 years' imprisonment. It should be borne in mind that the offence of theft covers all cases of stealing whether it be of a great or a small sum; we have no division into petty theft and grand theft; though theft is an offence which is triable either way (see above, p. 152). There is no separate offence of shoplifting; this is a colloquialism used to describe a particular form of theft, which has the unfortunate tendency of suggesting that there is a separate, less serious offence.

From the definition in section 1 we can see that the *actus reus* comprises (a) an appropriation (b) of property (c) which property belongs to another. The *mens rea* requires (a) dishonesty and (b) an intention permanently to deprive the other of property.

1. The Actus Reus of Theft

(1) Appropriates

This requirement is defined in section 3(1) of the Act as follows: "any assumption by a person of the rights of an owner amounts to an appropriation." Attempts to explain what is meant by "appropriates" have probably caused more problems for the courts than the rest of the Act put together. The Eighth Report of the Criminal Law Revision Committee, upon which the Theft Act was based, makes clear that the meaning intended to be conveyed was that of an unauthorised dealing with another's property. This being so, there was no need for the draftsman to incorporate words such as "without the consent of the owner," which appeared in the old Larceny Act, because an unauthorised dealing clearly would be without the consent or authority of the owner. The courts, nevertheless, appear in this instance to have ignored the Committee's report. This is somewhat strange in view of the House of Lords new-found willingness, revealed in *Pepper v. Hart* to consider parliamentary debates as an aid to discovering the intention of the legislature. The result has been, as we shall see, a very wide interpretation of the notion of "appropriation". It is not essential that the defendant must have assumed *all* of the owner's rights. The decision of the House of Lords in *Gomez* (1992) (see below, p. 396) now makes clear that it is enough to assume *any* of those rights and that the consent or authorisation of the owner may be irrelevant.

To begin with we can consider the most commonly occurring form of appropriation, the case of appropriation by taking. A enters B's bookshop and takes a book belonging to B; C enters D's room and takes D's watch; E puts his hand in F's pocket and removes F's wallet. In these cases it is as clear as can be that A has appropriated the book, C the watch and E the wallet. A, C and E are treating themselves as owners of property which belongs to B, D and F.

But two things need to be noticed. The first is that although taking is so far the most common mode of appropriation that laymen still think of theft as a taking, it is not the *only* mode of appropriation. The definition says that "*any*" assumption of the rights of an owner amounts to an appropriation. Strictly, therefore, it amounts to an appropriation to destroy another's property. Thus if A pushes B's car over a cliff and thereby destroys it, it can properly be said that he has appropriated the car. Most laymen would not recognise this as a case of theft (and no doubt A would be charged under the Criminal Damage Act 1971), but a charge of theft could be supported on such facts. This is clearly an appropriation (what could be a clearer assumption of B's rights than destroying his car?) and section 1(1) makes it clear that the prosecution does not have to establish on a charge of theft that A intended to make any gain from his action. The wide meaning given to "appropriates" is probably at odds with many people's instinctive, though erroneous, feeling that theft involves some form of unauthorised taking. This may have led the Court of Appeal into error in *Gallasso* (1992). There a nurse opened a new bank account for a patient and paid into it a cheque belonging to the patient who could not look after himself. The prosecution's case was that she had done this to facilitate later unauthorised withdrawals by her. The Court of Appeal held that this was not an appropriation. Probably they thought it seemed more like an act of preparation which had not yet reached the stage of an attempt. But payment in of the cheque was the exercise of a right of the owner. It may have been an act authorised by the patient but authorisation is, according to *Gomez*, irrelevant for the purposes of appropriation. The Court of Appeal was clearly wrong to hold that a taking was required; the defendant in the light of *Gomez* had indeed appropriated the cheque.

The second point to note is that while the layman might think that, in the examples first given, A, C and E appropriate the property when they take it *away*, *i.e.* when they remove the goods from the control of B, D and F and into their own control, in law the appropriation has occurred at an earlier stage. When, for example, E put his hand on the wallet inside F's pocket, and *before* he removes it, he may be said to have appropriated because, at that instance, he is assuming the rights of the owner, F. One of F's rights is to enjoy the undisturbed possession of his wallet; in asserting a right to possess it himself, E is assuming F's right. This point may be further illustrated by reference to *Corcoran v. Anderton* (1980). A and B attacked a woman intending to take her bag. A got his hands on her bag and there was a struggle for its possession during which the bag fell to the ground. A and B then ran off empty handed. This to the layman might look like a case of *attempted* robbery because the youths failed to get what they were after but they were convicted of the full offence. Robbery is theft accomplished with force and the theft was complete when the handbag was appropriated, *i.e.* when A grabbed it and tried to take it from her—that conduct was an assumption by A of the owner's rights.

The decision in *Gomez* affirms the correctness of this approach but, it also has the effect of reversing some earlier decisions on appropriation. The point is made by *Skipp* (1975), where the accused, posing as a genuine haulage contractor, was instructed to pick up three loads of oranges from different places in London and to deliver them to Leicester. All the time he was collecting the oranges he intended to abscond with them, thereby depriving the owner permanently of his property. The Court of Appeal, however, held that he did not appropriate the property until he did an act inconsistent with the owner's instructions even though the owner would not have let him take the oranges had he known of his intentions. It now seems that Skipp did appropriate the goods on each of the three occasions that he took delivery of the oranges. He had assumed a right of the owner in taking delivery; the fact that the act was to outward appearances only what he was authorised to do is irrelevant. Coupled with the required mental element it was theft. Similarly in *Fritschy* (1985) the defendant was authorised to collect Krugerrands in England and to take them to Switzerland, which he did. The prosecution alleged he had collected the coins with the dishonest intention of keeping them. Nevertheless the reasoning in *Skipp* led to the conclusion that no unauthorised act had occurred in this country. Theft, if it had been committed at all, had been committed in Switzerland. The House of Lords, in overruling this case, made clear in *Gomez* that there was a theft of the gold in England. Authorisation or consent is irrelevant to whether or not there has been an appropriation.

In line with *Skipp* was *Eddy v. Niman* (1981). A and B went into a supermarket with the intention of stealing goods and in pursuance of this plan they took goods from the shelves which they placed in the receptacle provided by the store. B then had a change of heart and left the store. It was held that he could not be convicted of theft because there was nothing that could be described as an appropriation; in doing what he was authorised to do, albeit with a dishonest intention, he had not yet assumed the rights of the owner. This is, of course, a situation similar in principle to *Fritschy*. A court would now say that B had already committed the full offence of theft before he left the store. There had been an appropriation coupled with the requisite intent. For practical reasons (such as to negative a possible defence of forgetfulness or mistake or accident) store detectives do not usually challenge the customer until he has left the store but the appropriation occurs not when he leaves the store but when he assumes a right of the owner.

A case that was hard to reconcile with *Skipp*, but would now be seen as correct in its result, was *Monaghan* (1979). There a checkout cashier was seen to place money given her by a customer for the purchase of goods in the till but without ringing up the purchase. When questioned she admitted that she was acting dishonestly and that it was her intention to take from the till an equivalent sum of money at a *later* stage. It was held that she had appropriated the money when she failed to ring it up and she was convicted of theft. It seems that there was an appropriation at the time she took delivery of the cash.

What reference to these cases show is that prior to the decision in *Gomez* there were essentially two conflicting approaches to the meaning of appropriation, both of which could claim the authority of the House of Lords. One view, reflected in the label switching case of *Morris* (1984) was that appropriation connoted doing something inconsistent with the owner's rights or without his authority. This was the approach in *Skipp* (see above, p. 394). The other view was that it meant no more than possession of an article and that such possession need not necessarily be antagonistic to the rights of an owner. Support for this approach was found in *Lawrence* (1972). There the accused, a taxi driver, picked up an Italian student, Occhi, who had just arrived at Victoria station and whose grasp of English was very poor. Occhi indicated he wished to be taken to Ladbroke Grove and produced a £1 note. Lawrence said it would cost a lot more and took a further £6 from the wallet which Occhi held open. The correct fare would have been 50p. Like many difficult cases on theft it arose because the prosecution failed to bring the obvious charge, obtaining the fare by deception contrary to s.15 of the Theft Act. Nevertheless the House of Lords upheld the charge of theft. Lawrence had appropriated property which, at the time he took it from the wallet, belonged to Occhi. He was clearly dishonest and intended to deprive the student of the money. Even if Occhi had consented to the removal of the money from his wallet there would still, it was said, have been an appropriation. It was noted that, as mentioned earlier, the Theft Act, 1968 contains no requirement that an act be "without the consent of the owner".

These two lines of authority were, on the face of it, irreconcilable and went to a matter at the very heart of the operation of the Theft Act. *Gomez* resolves the matter in favour, as has been seen, of the approach supported by *Lawrence*. What happened was that D1, the assistant manager of a shop, was approached by D2 and asked to sell goods whose value exceeded £17,000 and to accept two stolen building society cheques as payment. D1 was told by his manager to check with the bank and D1 falsely reported that the bank had said the "cheque was as good as cash". As a result the transaction was approved and D2 took delivery of the goods. The same happened in relation to a second cheque. The cheques were eventually returned as stolen and the defendants were then charged with theft. Despite a vigorous and scholarly dissent by Lord Lowry the House decided that *Lawrence* was correctly decided and that the contradictory statements in *Morris* were *obiter dicta* and incorrect. The statements were *obiter* because the act of switching labels was an adverse interference with or usurpation of the owner's rights. There was thus no need to express the opinion that mere removal from the shelf of an article would not amount to an appropriation. A person may therefore appropriate property belonging to another even by an act which is expressly authorised, as happened in *Gomez*, by the person to whom the property belongs or their agent. It is enough to assume just one of the owner's rights to consistute an appropriation.

The result of this case is that the net of appropiation is cast very wide. Take the case of the person who switches labels on goods in a supermarket with the intention of obtaining goods at the lower and false price indicated on the substituted label. It would appear that he is now guilty of theft when he first gets hold of the item whose label he intends to remove and even before he makes any effort to change the label. This is so even though he is merely doing what all shoppers are by implication authorised to do, namely to pick goods off the shelf. It might be objected that it is difficult to see how by picking up the item he intends by that act to deprive the owner of property, since it is his plan to present the item at the counter. However, the courts will now presumably hold that by picking up the goods with a dishonest intent he has appropriated the property of the store owner and it is sufficient that it is his ultimate aim to deprive the owner permanently of the property. Of course, there may be practical problems of proof at this stage and the fact that labels have indeed been switched would provide some evidence of dishonesty. The logic of the decision in *Gomez* is that a shopper appropriates property belonging to another every time he handles items in a shop, although he will not be guilty of theft unless he additionally has a dishonest intent.

As noted at the beginning of this chapter, some of the intricacies of the Theft Act stem from the involvement of civil law concepts concerning right of ownership over property. For example, fraud does not always render a contract of sale a complete nullity which means that even a fraudulent buyer who obtains a voidable title to goods may obtain ownership of the goods (see below, p. 550). Generally speaking one cannot steal one's own property (although see below, p. 402) so the precise point when an appropriation occurs might before *Gomez* have been crucial (and see below, p. 427). In other words if the appropriation took place after the contract of sale it was hard to see how one could be appropriating anybody else's property and therefore be guilty of theft.

An interesting case which raises this point is *Dip Kaur* (1981). In that case the defendant was looking at a display of shoes in a shop. She noticed that one pair had been incorrectly labelled. One heel had a price label for £6.99 while on the other was a label for £4.99. She apparently realised that the higher price was correct. She took the shoes to the counter with the cheaper label uppermost and was sold the shoes for £4.99. A store detective stopped her afterwards because he thought she had been switching labels. She admitted dishonesty and was ultimately prosecuted for theft. The Divisional Court held that the mistake on the part of the cashier rendered the contract only voidable, not void, and so Kaur became owner of the goods before she did any act which could amount to an appropriation. Following *Gomez* it would now seem that she committed theft when, having formed the dishonest intent, she took the shoes to the cashier. The real issue in such a case is probably whether the defendant's conduct was dishonest. Nevertheless, it seems that the appropriation on those facts now clearly precedes any point at which ownership of the goods might have passed.

Thus far it has been suggested that an appropriation requires some *conduct* on the accused's part. Certainly it is difficult to see how a pure omission could amount to an assumption of the user's rights. If, for example, A has mislaid his umbrella, B could hardly be said to have appropriated it because he knows where it is and fails to tell A—even if B hopes that A will fail to find it so that he, B, can make off with it later on. On the other hand section 3(1) goes on to say that there is an appropriation where a person has come by the property (innocently or not) but without stealing it and has assumed a right to it " ... by keeping it or dealing with it as owner." This is meant to deal with the sort of case where A "comes by" (A may have borrowed it, or found it or had it delivered to him by mistake, etc.) B's property and decides to keep it. A's mental resolution to keep it is probably not enough; the section says that A must keep it "as owner." Suppose then that A borrows B's lawn mower or bicycle or book for a week. At the end of the week A fails to return the goods and his intention is never to do so. Probably this will not make A a thief; but A will become a thief if, with the necessary intent, he removes the lawn mower to his new premises, or he continues to drive the bicycle, or he writes his name in the book. On the other hand, the fact that the draftsman specifies that there may be an appropriation in these circumstances when A has come by the property without stealing it rather implies that there is no fresh appropriation when a person has already stolen the property and subsequently deals with it. This was the approach taken by the Court of Appeal in *Atakpu* (1994). There the defendants hired cars in Germany and Belgium and then returned the cars to England, still within the period of hire, with the intention of selling them in England. Their conviction of conspiring to steal the cars in England was quashed because, following *Gomez*, the cars were appropriated and stolen as soon as the defendants hired them with an intent to steal.

The theft had therefore occurred outside the jurisdiction of the English courts, and a thief cannot re-steal goods which he has already stolen.

Where, however, A receives the property in good faith from B for consideration, if it later turns out that B had no right to sell the property, no assumption of the rights of an owner by A over that property can amount to an appropriation for the purposes of a charge of theft (see s.3(2)). Thus if A buys a car from B in circumstances where A believes that B is the lawful owner of the car, then if he is later told that C is the rightful owner of the car and that B had stolen it, A's refusal to restore the car to C would not amount to theft (see *e.g. Adams* (1993)). However, if A later sells the car to D, he may be guilty of obtaining property by deception contrary to section 15 (see below, p. 425) since he will have impliedly represented that he had title to sell, when he clearly did not.

(2) Property

The definition of what can amount to property for the purposes of being stolen is to be found in section 4. The general position is covered by section 4(1) which provides that "property" includes money and all other property, real or personal, including things in action and other intangible property. The reference to real property means that land is included in the definition of property, but subsection 2 specifically provides that with one or two exceptions land cannot be stolen (it can, however, be obtained by deception; see p. 426). Before we look at the special problem with land we ought to mention one or two points in relation to the general definition. The effect of subsection 1 is that virtually all tangible property with the exception of land is capable of being stolen. One or two difficulties may, however, arise:

(a) *Gas, water and electricity*

Gas and water are clearly within the definition of property in section 4(1) and are thus capable of being stolen. Electricity, on the other hand, does not constitute property and cannot therefore be stolen. There is a separate offence to deal with the unlawful abstraction of electricity in section 13.

(b) *Intangible property*

Section 4(1) makes it clear that choses in action and other intangible property are capable of being stolen. Choses in action are rights which can only be enforced by taking legal action. Thus if X owes Y £50, X can sue Y for the £50 and this right to sue is known as a chose in action. Other examples of choses in action are copyrights and trademarks; patents are not choses in action but they are clearly a form of intangible property. It is perhaps not immediately apparent how such things can be stolen, but if X purports to sell a copyright which belongs to Y, he will have stolen that copyright.

(c) *Intellectual property*

In *Oxford v. Moss* (1979) a student borrowed an examination paper and photographed the questions. He could not be charged with stealing the question paper since he intended to return it and the court held that he could not be charged with theft of the confidential information since this did not amount to property under section 4(1). It would seem to follow that trade secrets are not property which is capable of being stolen.

(d) *Land, wild plants and wild creatures*

While property is widely defined in section 4(1), certain modifications to the generality of the definition are made by section 4(2)–(4) which provides—

"(2) A person cannot steal land, or things forming part of land and severed from it by him or by his directions, except in the following cases, that is to say—
(a) when he is a trustee or personal representative, or is authorised by power of attorney, or as liquidator of a company, or otherwise, to sell or dispose of land belonging to another, and he appropriates the land or anything forming part of it by dealing with it in breach of the confidence reposed in him; or
(b) when he is not in possession of the land and appropriates anything forming part of the land by severing it or causing it to be severed, or after it has been severed; or
(c) when, being in possession of the land under a tenancy, he appropriates the whole or part of any fixture or structure let to be used with the land.
For the purposes of this subsection "land" does not include incorporeal hereditaments; "tenancy" means a tenancy for years or any less period and includes an agreement for such a tenancy, but a person who after the

end of a tenancy remains in possession as statutory tenant or otherwise is to be treated as having possession under the tenancy, and "let" shall be construed accordingly.

(3) A person who picks mushrooms growing wild on any land, or who picks flowers, fruit or foliage from a plant growing wild on any land does not (although not in possession of the land) steal what he picks, unless he does it for reward or for sale or other commercial purpose.

For purposes of this subsection "mushroom" includes any fungus, and "plant" includes any shrub or tree.

(4) Wild creatures, tamed or untamed, shall be regarded as property; but a person cannot steal a wild creature not tamed or ordinarily kept in captivity, or the carcase of any such creature, unless either it has been reduced into possession by or on behalf of another person and possession of it has not since been lost or abandoned, or another person is in course of reducing it into possession."

The general effect of this provision is that land, as such, can be stolen only in exceptional circumstances. Apparently it is not unknown for purchasers of building plots to move the boundary markers in order to enlarge their plots at the expense of neighbouring plots; this practice, though dishonest, does not constitute theft. Nor do people who pick mushrooms or wild growth become thieves unless they do it for gain; strictly they appropriate property of another but it was considered too harsh to make such conduct theft. The last exception, in effect, favours poaching; poachers cannot steal the wild animals that they take though they may commit other offences.

(3) Belonging to Another

The prosecution must establish that at the time of the appropriation the property belonged to another. This seems an obvious requirement as theft is generally understood to be the taking of someone else's property. What then do we mean by the phrase "belonging to another"? Clearly it must include the case where the property is owned by the victim at the time when the accused takes it. But that alone would be too restricting. Suppose that X dishonestly appropriates a television set which A rents from B. Does X steal the set from A or from B? If we said that belonging to another meant only "owned by another" then the indictment would have to charge X with stealing the television from B. This might present few problems in our illustration, but there will be cases where the true owner would be hard to identify. In any case a law of theft which in our example would allow X to defeat a charge of stealing from A on the ground that A was not the real owner would be open to ridicule. Suppose that it was B, the owner of the television set, who secretly took it back from A, intending both to resell the set and claim the cost of a new set from A. Should we not in such a case be able to charge B with stealing the set from A? It is for reasons such as these that the phrase "belonging to another" receives a much wider definition in section 5 of the Act.

Section 5(1) provides "Property shall be regarded as belonging to any person having possession or control of it, or having in it any proprietary right or interest (not being an equitable interest arising only from an agreement to transfer or grant an interest)."

Thus property can be stolen from a person who owns, possesses or has control over it. In the example of the television set it can therefore be stolen from either A, who has possession of it under a rental agreement or from B who owns it. If A takes the set to C for repairs it could also be stolen from C while it was in his premises awaiting repairs. But then the question arises, can one of the persons with a recognised interest in the property steal it from one of the others? If A, the person renting the set, sold it and told B that it had been stolen, could A be charged with stealing it from B? If B, the owner, took it from A and claimed that A had lost it and was therefore under a contractual obligation to pay for it could B be charged with stealing it from A even though B is the owner? The answer to both of these questions is clearly yes. In *Turner* (1971) the accused had left his car for repair with a garage. Later he returned after it had been repaired and took it from outside the garage intending not to pay the bill. Despite the fact that the car belonged to Turner it was held that the garage had sufficient control of it to come within the phrase "belonging to another," and so Turner's conviction for theft was upheld (*cf. Meredith* (1973)). Another example is provided by *Philippou* (1989). In that case the sole directors and shareholders of a company were convicted of theft from that company. Although this case was once thought to present difficulties on the issue of appropriation, its correctness was confirmed by *Gomez* and it illustrates the principle that a limited company is a separate "person" from whom property can be stolen even by those who control it.

Does the victim need to be aware of the property? It is obvious that most people have property in their homes they have long forgotten that they possess.

In *Woodman* (1974) the X company were running down one of their factories and sold off a quantity of scrap metal to Y company. This gave Y company the right to enter the factory and remove the metal. Y company did, in fact, remove most of the scrap metal but left some there as not being worth the cost of salvaging it. X company remained owners of the site and put up a barbed wire fence and notices to discourage trespassers. It became clear that X company was not aware that any scrap remained at the site. Some two years after X company's business had ceased at the factory, Woodman entered the site and took some of the scrap metal. He was charged with stealing the metal from X company. The trial judge took the view that there was no case to go to the jury on the basis that X company owned or possessed the property, but there was a case of theft which could be left to the jury on the basis that X company controlled the property. The accused was convicted and appealed on the basis that X company could not be said to control the scrap metal since they were under the impression that it had all been removed by Y company. The Court of Appeal held that in the ordinary case if "it is once established that a particular person is in control of a site such as this, then prima facie he is in control of items on the site even though they were unaware of the existence of specific items." It might be that if the scrap metal had been placed there by a third party after the barbed wire had been erected then a different result could follow, but that was not the case here. In one sense the property was abandoned, but at least in relation to Woodman the X company could be said to be in control of it (see *Small* (1987) below, p. 411).

Sections 5(3) and 5(4). Subsections 3 and 4 of section 5 provide for two further situations in which the phrase "belonging to another" is given an extended meaning in order to widen the scope of the offence in section 1. It should be remembered that in both cases the provisions of section 5 enable the accused to be prosecuted for the offence of theft under section 1; they do not create separate offences of theft; the tendency to speak of charging the accused under section 5(4) is therefore inaccurate.

Section 5(3) provides "Where a person receives property from or on account of another, and is under an obligation to the other to retain and deal with that property or its proceeds in a particular way, the property or proceeds shall be regarded (as against him) as belonging to the other."

The subsection and the problem it is supposed to solve are probably best explained by looking at the facts of one of the leading cases: *Hall* (1973). The accused ran a travel agency and in the course of business had taken various sums of money from customers in return for which he promised to book them on flights to America. Later he was forced to tell these customers that his business was in trouble, that he had not booked the flights and that there was no money with which he could refund their deposits. He was charged with stealing money from the customers. Now it was not alleged that he had all along intended to default on his obligation towards these customers, otherwise he could have been charged with obtaining their money by deception (contrary to Theft Act 1968, s.15: see below). The appropriation relied on the misuse of the money and it is here that the difficulty arises. The appropriation must be of money *belonging to another*. Thus at this point we must consider the civil law. When a customer hands over his money to a travel agent it is quite clear that the agent becomes the owner of the property and can pass a good title to it on to a third person. Thus since Hall became owner of the money, when he later misused it he was appropriating money which belonged to himself. Section 5(3) provides that even where the accused has become the owner of the property before it is appropriated he can none the less be regarded as appropriating someone else's property if, but only if, he is expected to deal with that property in a particular way. At first it may appear that this will cover the travel agent, but, unfortunately, it is not as simple as that. When a customer hands over his deposit to the agent he cannot expect that the agent will put the money in a marked envelope and use it solely to book that customer's flight. If the customer thought for a moment, he would realise that all the receipts from all customers go into the business account and money is drawn from that account as needed to make bookings. The customer's only right is that he can expect that a booking will be made or an equivalent amount of money will be returned. Thus the Court of Appeal held that Hall was not covered by the provisions of section 5(3). A more recent application of the same principle is found in *D.P.P. v. Huskinson* (1988). There a tenant spent his housing benefit on himself rather than in payment of rent. He was acquitted of theft because the relevant legislation imposed no legal duty to use the money only for payment of rent and section 5(3) was therefore again of no assistance to the prosecution. So what sort of situation would be covered by section 5(3)? It applies only where ownership in the property has been transferred to the accused and where he must use that very property in a particular way. The property will nearly always be money, so we are looking for a situation in which the accused was expected to use *that* money for a particular purpose. Thus if the accused is painting A's house and asks A for £5 to buy more paint, it is likely that the court will hold that he was expected to use that £5 note to buy the paint. Similarly the treasurer of a social club might be held to receive money which he is to put in a special fund for the club purposes only. If this is the case, any appropriation of that money will be theft.

It is sufficient that he is obliged to keep in existence a fund equivalent to that which he has received. Thus in *Davidge v. Bunnett* (1984) the Divisional Court held that it was sufficient the defendant was under an obligation to keep a fund of money which would cover the gas bill. A similar principle was applied by the Court of Appeal in *Wain* (1993) to the case of someone who collected money for a charity. The collector was under an obligation to retain at least the proceeds of the actual notes and coins collected. When he took money credited to a separate account into which he had paid those receipts and moved it to his own personal bank account he had appropriated what was still the proceeds of the money collected and accordingly s.5(3) applied.

Whether or not an obligation arises is a matter of law for the judge since the obligation referred to is a *legal* obligation. While it is for the jury to find the facts, it is for the judge to rule on which facts give rise to an obligation (*Mainwaring* (1981)).

Section 5(4). This is possibly one of the most complex provisions of the entire Act yet arguably one of the least needed. It is supposed to cover the situation in which due to a mistake by the victim "ownership in the property passes to the rogue before any act of appropriation" so that when the appropriation occurs he is appropriating his own property. The subsection provides:

"Where a person gets property by another's mistake, and is under an obligation to make restoration (in whole or in part) of the property or its proceeds or of the value

> thereof, then to the extent of that obligation the property
> or proceeds shall be regarded (as against him) as
> belonging to the person entitled to restoration, and an
> intention not to make restoration shall be regarded
> accordingly as an intention to deprive that person of the
> property or proceeds."

It might be easiest to understand the workings of the
subsection if we first consider the case of *Moynes v. Coopper*
(1956) which it was designed to overrule. In that case the
accused was given an advance on his wages during the course
of the week. At the end of the week the wages clerk paid him
a full salary, totally unaware that he ought to have made a
deduction for the amount already advanced. When Moynes
later discovered the error he decided to keep all the money.

At this point it is necessary to consider the *civil* law. No one
can doubt but that Moynes was acting in a thoroughly
dishonest way but, as we have just seen, dishonesty is not
enough. So far as the civil law is concerned the fact that the
person delivering property makes a mistake does not
necessarily prevent ownership from passing and, of course, if
ownership passes the recipient cannot steal the property
because it is his own property. Generally, a mistake will
prevent ownership from passing only where the deliveror is
mistaken as to the identity of the recipient or the identity of
the property. The clerk in *Moynes v. Coopper* was mistaken in
neither of these senses: he intended to pay the Moynes the
exact amount he in fact paid.

Prima facie, therefore, Moynes was merely a dishonest
debtor—he owed his employers the amount of money (some
seven pounds) which had been overpaid—but the law stops
short of making thieves out of dishonest debtors. Moynes,
however, was not quite like other dishonest debtors. He did
not merely owe seven pounds to his employers: he was under
a quasi-contractual obligation to restore either the actual seven
pounds or its *proceeds or its value*. Section 5(4) is there to deal
with this sort of case or where, say, a bank account is
erroneously credited with a payment which the customer then
dishonestly spends. It is not there to deal with the case where
A is under an obligation to pay money to B (because that
would make thieves of all dishonest debtors) but only where
A is under an obligation to restore B the *very* property which
he received from B or the proceeds or value of *that* property.
Whether A is under such an obligation can be a very
complicated question but the complications arise in the civil
law not the criminal law. For our purposes it is enough to

note that section 5(4) will be necessary in very few situations, primarily because in most cases the mistake will have been caused by the defendant's fraud and hence the more appropriate charge will be obtaining property by deception (see further *Att.-Gen.'s Reference, No. 1 of 1983* (1984)).

2. Mens Rea

The Act provides that the prosecution must prove that the appropriation of property belonging to another was dishonest and that at the time of the appropriation the accused had the intention of permanently depriving the other of the property. There is no requirement that the accused did it for personal gain; it could be theft if the accused simply smashed the victim's valuable Ming vase (s.1(2)).

(1) Dishonesty

Dishonesty is peculiarly difficult to define. Dishonest conduct is conduct which is regarded by people generally as dishonest. In most cases, of course, there is general agreement as to what is viewed as honest or dishonest. No one doubts but that it is dishonest to take goods from a store without paying for them, or surreptitiously to remove books from a library, or to get goods from a machine by using a washer instead of coinage, and so on. But cases can arise, and arise not infrequently, where views may differ as to whether particular conduct is dishonest.

The Theft Act does not attempt a comprehensive definition of dishonesty. Section 2 provides only a partial definition and details three cases where a person's conduct is not to be regarded as dishonest. Before these are examined, it will be noted that in addition it is provided by section 2(2) that a person's appropriation of property *may* be dishonest notwithstanding an intention to pay for it, and by section 1(1) that it is immaterial that the appropriation is not made with a view to gain. Suppose A wants to purchase a painting from B which B refuses to sell; A may be convicted of theft if he takes the picture though he leaves in its place money which more than represents its value. Alternatively A may wish merely to deprive B of the painting without intending to enjoy it himself or to sell it for his own profit; A may be convicted of theft because he intends the painting to be lost to B though he has no view to a gain for himself.

Section 2(1) states that an appropriation is not to be regarded as dishonest in three cases: (i) where he believes that he has in law the right to deprive the other of it on behalf of himself or another; (ii) where he appropriates the property in the belief that he would have the owner's consent; and (iii) where he appropriates the property in the belief that the owner cannot be traced by taking reasonable steps.

Where the accused relies on one of the three claims in section 2(1) the trial judge should specifically direct the jury in relation to the plea; it will not suffice for him merely to direct the jury on the issue of dishonesty generally. In other words he must direct them that the prosecution must, in this case, prove that the defendant does not believe, *e.g.* that the owner would have consented to the appropriation (s.2(1)(*b*)).

(a) *Belief in legal right*

The only belief that is relevant here is a belief in *legal* right. That A feels that he has a moral claim to the property, or that he is in some vague way justified in taking it, is not relevant under this head though it may be otherwise relevant to the issue of dishonesty. If A believes he has a *legal* right, his conduct cannot be accounted dishonest though his claim is entirely unreasonable or even though the claim is one which the law does not recognise. An honest belief in legal right, however arrived at, is inconsistent with dishonesty (see *Robinson* (1977), p. 440).

(b) *Belief in consent*

If A honestly believes that B, the owner, would have consented to his appropriation, his conduct cannot be regarded as dishonest. That A's belief is unreasonably arrived at is irrelevant except to the extent that it may cast doubt on the honesty of his belief (see *Holden* (1991)).

(c) *Belief that owner cannot be traced*

This provision essentially deals with property which is found by A; he is not to be treated as a thief if he appropriates that property in the belief that the owner cannot be traced by taking reasonable steps. If, for example, A finds a £5 note in the street it could only be exceptionally that he would believe that the owner can be traced so that in appropriating it he would not be guilty of theft. If, however,

A finds in the same street Goya's portrait of the Duke of Wellington, he is unlikely to believe that the owner cannot be traced by taking reasonable steps. Nevertheless, if A is a Philistine who regards the painting as worthless so that it does not occur to him to take steps to trace the owner, he cannot be convicted of theft. If it does occur to A that the owner might be traced, he may be convicted of theft if he fails to take *reasonable* steps. He is not required to take every conceivable step; no doubt the most usual reasonable step would be to hand the property to the police on the assumption that the owner, if he cares about his loss, will have reported it to them.

(d) *Dishonesty in other cases*

The partial definition does not of course provide for all cases and the question arises as to how dishonesty is to be defined in circumstances not falling within the partial definition. The courts have considered the matter in a number of cases: *Feely* (1973); *Boggeln v. Williams* (1978); *Landy* (1981); *McIvor* (1982) and in *Ghosh* (1982) (*Casebook*, chap. 8) the Court of Appeal, recognising that the law was in a complicated state, attempted a restatement.

The Court of Appeal held that whether conduct is to be regarded as dishonest is a matter for the jury to determine. The judge should, however, direct the jury that A acts dishonestly if (a) his conduct would be regarded as dishonest by the ordinary standards of reasonable people; and (b) A realises that his conduct is so regarded. If (a) and (b) are satisfied then (c) A's conduct is dishonest however he might regard his conduct; A cannot set up a personal standard which he knows to be at variance with the general standard.

As to (a) the issue is one for the jury who have only their own knowledge and experience to guide them. No doubt on any given set of facts most juries would reach the same decision, but on certain facts juries may reach different conclusions. Take cases where A "borrows" money from B without permission. A may take 75p from B's, his employer's, till to pay a taxi driver because he has no small change; C may take £5 from B's till to lay a wager on a horse (*Feely* (1973)); D may take £200 from B's safe to pay a deposit on his holiday (*McIvor* (1982)). All intend to pay the money at a later stage but, of course, the money which they take is not "borrowed" but is appropriated since B is deprived permanently of the notes and coins taken (*Velumyl* (1989)).

Would any or all of these takings be regarded as dishonest by the generality of reasonable people? No doubt the jury would wish to consider such factors as whether B had expressly forbidden "borrowing," the extent to which A, C and D had an ability to repay, whether the borrowing was done openly or secretly and so on. It seems difficult to lay down a general principle for such cases (but see Elliott [1982] Crim.L.R. 395) so it may be that different juries would reach different conclusions.

As to (b) the jury is concerned to find whether the defendant is aware that his conduct is generally regarded as dishonest. It is generally regarded as dishonest to travel on buses with intent to avoid paying the fare but, as the court pointed out in *Ghosh*, a person who came from a country where public transport was free, would not act dishonestly if he boarded a bus here believing that public transport here was similarly free.

If, then, a modern Robin Hood thought it was right for him to rob the rich in order to feed the poor, he would be acting dishonestly if he realised, as is the fact, that people generally regard such a taking as dishonest. But if he is out of touch with community standards and genuinely thinks that people generally do not regard such conduct as dishonest, then his conduct cannot, it seems, be accounted dishonest. Cases where the defendant is mistaken about the prevailing standards of dishonesty will be exceptional but they may occasionally happen.

(2) With Intention Permanently to Deprive

During the period of debate before the Theft Act 1968 was enacted, it was suggested that the prosecution should no longer have to prove the accused intended permanently to deprive the other of his property. This would have had the effect of making dishonest borrowing theft. It was finally decided that the requirement should be retained and that cases of unlawful borrowing were better dealt with by the civil law. (But sections 11 and 12 penalise some instances of unlawful borrowing, for example motor vehicles.)

Thus the prosecution must prove that at the time of the appropriation the accused intended permanently to deprive the owner of the property. This ordinarily presents no problems because when A takes money from B's pocket or when C takes a book from D's shop the prosecution is usually not hard pressed to prove that A and C intended to deprive permanently. Equally where the accused believed that the property has been abandoned, he cannot be said to have intended permanently to deprive another of it (*Small*, 1987). But *evidential* difficulties can occur. Where C takes the book from the university library, his claim that he intended to return the book at the end of term may be plausible and the prosecution may in such a case have difficulty in proving the intent. It has been known even for law students to take books from the law library without signing for them and then to leave them at the end of term outside the library door. This is a deplorable practice but it is not theft for it is obvious that the miscreant does not intend the university to lose the books permanently. What, then, if the miscreant left the books in the students' union or on the London underground? Given that the books were stamped as the property of the university of X, the probability is that they would be returned to the university in the first case, though this is much less likely in the second. But in either case the test of C's liability is the same: did he *intend* to permanently deprive the university of its books? If C believes that by leaving the books where he does they will be returned to the university he cannot be said to intend permanent deprivation even if he leaves them in a place which makes it highly unlikely that they will ever be returned.

In the normal run of case, then, the intent permanently to deprive raises only evidential problems. But in exceptional cases it can raise legal problems. Such cases tend to be those where A takes property of B's which, in a sense, he returns to B but only after A has treated himself as owner of that property. It is for these exceptional cases that section 6 is there to provide:

> "A person appropriating property belonging to another without meaning the other permanently to lose the thing itself is nevertheless to be regarded as having the intention of permanently depriving the other of it if his intention to treat the thing as his own to dispose of regardless of the other's rights; and a borrowing or lending of it may amount to so treating it if, but only if, the borrowing or lending is for a period and in circumstances making it equivalent to an outright taking or disposal."

Consider the following examples:

(1) A is a shopkeeper who stores empty bottles, on which he has paid the refund, in his yard. B enters the yard, takes some bottles and then enters A's shop where he gets a refund

on the bottles. Such a case as this is perhaps best treated as obtaining by deception, but B may alternatively be convicted of stealing the bottles. In a sense he intends that A should get his bottles back but only after A has paid for them. B is clearly treating the bottles as his own to dispose of regardless of A's rights; A can get his own bottles back only by paying for them.

(2) D, a first-year medical student, takes a copy of Gray's *Anatomy* from the library intending to return it on completion of his course in five years' time. Can it be said that D has treated the book as his own to dispose of regardless of the other's rights? According to the second part of section 6(1) a borrowing can only be so treated if it is equivalent to an outright taking. Five years is a long time, so can it be said that D's "borrowing . . . was for a period and in circumstances which made it equivalent to an outright taking or disposal"? The difficulty with this view is that it could leave the courts with an impossible task in determining what period of borrowing would be so equivalent. The section says it must be *equivalent* to an outright taking. Borrowing for a fixed term falls short of being so equivalent. Thus the courts have held it to be a misdirection for a judge to direct a jury that X may be convicted of stealing Y's goods where X intends to borrow those goods indefinitely (*Warner* (1970)). A taking or borrowing is equivalent to an outright taking only where all the value of the property is consumed. So if X takes Y's season ticket to a football ground, intending to use it for *all* the games for which it is valued and then return the ticket to Y, X has stolen the ticket, for the borrowing is now equivalent to an outright taking. In *Lloyd* (1985) a cinema projectionist handed over to an associate, films which were currently being shown at the cinema. The associate produced a master video tape of the films which were then returned to the cinema in time for their next showing. It was clear that there was no intention permanently to deprive the owner of the films, and so there was no theft, since they were returned none the worse for wear; they had lost none, let alone all, of their virtue.

In *Coffey* (1987) the prosecution alleged that the defendant had obtained a machine from the victim by deception (a worthless cheque). Although this was a charge under section 15 of the Act, namely obtaining property by deception, it also required that the prosecution prove that the defendant intended permanently to deprive the other of the machine. It appeared that the defendant was in dispute with the owner of the machine and had obtained the machine so as to give himself a bargaining counter in the negotiations. It was not altogether clear what would have happened to the machine if the negotiations were not settled to the defendant's satisfaction. It was held that this was a situation in which the trial judge should give the jury a full direction on section 6(1). The prosecution would have to satisfy the jury that the defendant intended not to return the machine until he got what he wanted, or at least, that he intended to keep it so long as to be regarded as an outright taking of it; in other words, till all the virtue had gone out of the thing.

(3) H hires a car from J for a week. K takes the car, uses it for a week and then returns it to J. No doubt K would be charged under section 12 (taking a conveyance) but he may also be guilty of theft. He has not stolen the car from J but so far as H is concerned he has deprived H of the whole of his interest.

(4) A takes B's silver goblets and pawns them. He keeps the money he receives from the pawnshop intending to redeem it later. This is covered by section 6(2) which gives a further extended meaning to the phrase "with the intention permanently to deprive."

> "If any person in possession of another's property (whether lawfully or not) parts with that property under a condition he may not be able to perform he may be regarded as treating the property to dispose of regardless of the other's rights."

A recent case which might be thought of as rather overextending the meaning of "dispose of" in section 6 is *Lavender* (1994). The defendant took two doors from a council property undergoing repair and used them to replace two damaged doors in another council property. He was convicted of theft on the basis of disposing of the doors regardless of the owner's right not to have them removed. But is this really a "disposal" of the property in the natural sense of the word? If I swap the door on my office for the door on another office of the same company's building, which could be regarded as essentially the same as this case, I may have re-arranged the property but it seems somewhat harsh to say that I have stolen it.

(3) Conditional Intention

A problem which has caused much controversy in recent years has been that of so-called conditional intent. In a sense all intention may be said to be conditional. A may set out with the firm intention of stealing B's painting but his intention will be subject to certain conditions such as that he will be able to effect an entry to the place where the painting is kept or that B will not be guarding the painting. But it would be quite unrealistic to say that if A leaves empty handed because he cannot effect an entry or because B was on guard that he therefore did not intend to steal the painting.

But what if the painting is not in the building at all because B has moved it to another place? Until recently this sort of case caused a problem because of a House of Lords ruling (in *Haughton v. Smith* (1975)) that a person could not be convicted of attempting to commit a crime which was physically impossible of achievement. This ruling has been reversed by the Criminal Attempts Act 1981 (above, p. 320) and now a person may be convicted of an attempt even though, in the circumstances, he could not have effected the complete crime. So if A is found in the room where the painting used to hang he may be convicted of attempting to steal it; moreover in entering the building with intent to steal it he commits the crime of burglary.

A somewhat similar problem arose where A has not yet made up his mind whether and what to steal. Take the case of the rogue, A, whose practice it is to search other people's cars to see whether there is anything that takes his fancy. In B's car he finds nothing at all; in C's car he notices that there is a copy of the Bible but he is not interested in that; in D's car he finds a handbag but having ascertained that the contents (lipstick, handkerchief, nail file) are of no value to him he returns the handbag to its place. In none of these cases can A be convicted of theft since he has stolen nothing. Now that the rule in *Haughton v. Smith* has been changed by statute, A may be convicted even though it was impossible for him to commit the completed crime (theft) owing to the fact that there was nothing he was remotely interested in stealing. But there is another matter to consider. A cannot be charged with stealing nothing, nor with attempting to steal nothing. He must be charged with attempting to steal some property belonging to another. Nor can he be properly charged with attempting to steal property which he just does not intend to steal. A cannot be charged with attempting to steal C's Bible or the lipstick from D's handbag because his conduct proves that he had no intent to steal these.

But when A saw the handbag in D's car he no doubt hoped that it would contain money and, had it done so, it is certain that he would have taken it. If so, A can be charged with and convicted of attempting to steal money from D. In the other two cases it may be that A had no expectation of finding money, nor did he find anything else that took his fancy. But if A had found something that had taken his fancy he would certainly have taken it, and in such a case it is proper to charge him with attempting to steal "property belonging to" B or C without specifying any particular property (*Bayley v. Eastbrook* (1980)).

It really boils down to this. If, in the indictment, you charge A with stealing or attempting to steal a specific item of property, you must prove that he actually intended to steal that item. In a case where you are alleging that A has committed the completed offence of theft, you will obviously need to specify the property, alleged to have been stolen, in the indictment. In cases of attempted theft, however, where you are faced with the sort of problem illustrated above in which A has been looking through the boots of cars, the court will allow an indictment which simply alleges that A has attempted to steal property from B. A similar problem occurs in burglary where the accused is charged under section 9(1)(*a*) of the Theft Act 1968 (see below, p. 442). In this type of burglary the prosecution may have to prove that at the time the accused entered the building he intended to steal property from within. Again it has been held that there is no need to specify particular items of property in the building, nor would it be fatal to the prosecution that the building turned out to be empty. (See *Attorney-General's References Nos. 1 and 2 of 1979* (1980); and *Smith and Smith* (1986)).

II. OFFENCES INVOLVING DECEPTION

So far we have been considering the offence of theft which is concerned largely with those situations in which the accused has taken property belonging to another. In this section we shall be concerned with those situations where the accused has, by fraud, induced the victim to act in a way he would not, but for the fraud, have acted. Under the Theft Act 1968 there are two basic offences of deception. Under section 15 it is an offence to obtain property by deception and under section 16 it is an offence to obtain a pecuniary advantage by deception. Common to both offences is the need to establish that the property or the pecuniary advantage was obtained as a result of the deception practised by the accused. The need for two sections arises from the fact that Parliament saw it necessary to distinguish between those situations in which the accused obtained property and those in which he obtained a financial advantage but nothing tangible. For example, if you go into a car rental agency and by showing a false driving licence and insurance you induce him to rent you a car for the day, you will have obtained possession of the car by deception and this is clearly the obtaining of property. If, however, when it comes to paying for the car which the garage has already let you take away you trick the owner into giving you time to pay then you have not obtained any property by deception, you have gained a financial advantage—namely more time to pay. Under the Theft Act 1968 "pecuniary advantage" was defined to mean three things under section 16(2)(a), (b) and (c). Unfortunately section 16(2)(a) gave rise to so many difficulties that it was thought better to repeal it and replace it with three new offences to be found in the Theft Act 1978. Under the new Theft Act it is an offence to obtain services by deception, to evade liability by deception and to make off without paying. The resulting position is that there are now four offences of deception and these are the dishonest obtaining by deception of:

  (i)   property (Theft Act 1968, s.15);
  (ii) pecuniary advantage (the unrepealed parts of section 16 of the Theft Act 1968—*viz*. s.16(2)(b) and (c) which deal with defined cases and which have as yet given rise to few problems);
  (iii) services (the Theft Act 1978, s.1);
  (iv) evasion of liability (the Theft Act 1978, s.2).

Finally there is the offence of dishonestly making off without paying (Theft Act 1978, s.3—but this offence does not require any deception). In this section we shall first consider the elements common to the deception offences and then examine the four things which have to be obtained. We shall then consider the offence of making off.

1. Elements Common to Deception Offences

There are three basic elements which the prosecution must prove in all four crimes, namely (i) deception; (ii) that the deception was instrumental in the obtaining of, *e.g.* the property; and (iii) dishonesty.

(1) What Constitutes Deception for the Purposes of the Theft Acts?

In the majority of cases it will be quite clear that the accused has deceived the victim into handing over some property or into performing some task and there will be no problem over the definition of the word "deception": the accused will have made a statement of fact which he well knows to be false. Thus if A, a well-known art dealer, tells B, a customer, that the picture he is interested in is a genuine Constable, when he knows full well that it is a reprint, then this will be a deception within the meaning of the Acts. If this is so, then what about the television commercial which says that X soap powder washes whiter than any other brand? Are we saying that if A buys this brand because of the advert and discovers that it washes no whiter than any other brand, that the advertiser obtained his money by deception? If not, what is the difference between this case and the art dealer? There are two points to be made here. In the first place, we should note that section 15(4) says that "deception" means any deception (whether deliberate or reckless) by word or conduct as to fact or law. ... " This means that in relation to commercials the deception must involve a false statement as to an issue of fact. It could be argued that television commercials are statements of opinion and not of fact. If A therefore falsely tells B that he believes one car to be better than another this is a statement of opinion and not of fact and is not within the definition of deception. However, many statements of opinion are simply statements of fact expressed as opinion. For example, in the case where A tells B that he thinks that one car is a better buy than another he may have no factual basis for saying this. On the other hand, he may be aware of facts which make one car better than the other; for example, he may be aware that the second car's engine will need replacing in about a thousand miles. If, knowing this, he deliberately tells B that he thinks that the car with the faulty engine is a better car and B buys on the strength of that opinion, then he should be held to have deceived B. To the purchaser of a car from a salesman, the statement "This car is a better buy than the other one" implies to the buyer that the seller is saying that he is not aware of any facts which would prove otherwise.

The second point to note concerning commercials is that in today's world there is the general assumption that most television watchers are immune to sales pressures through adverts and there is the general view that no one actually believes the inflated claims of the advertisers. However, this does not mean to say that in appropriate circumstances commercials could not be the basis of a deception charge. Much greater care can rightly be expected where the adverts are directed at children. Equally, if it can be shown that the advert makes a false statement of fact, such as "X Co. ball point pens last longer than Y Co. ball point pens," then if it can be shown that viewers were induced to buy the product for this reason, there is no reason why a deception charge should not be made. (See *Bryan* (1857)).

(a) *Misrepresentation of law*

It is quite clear from the definition of deception in section 15(4) that a deliberate or reckless misrepresentation of law can amount to a deception for the purposes of these offences. Thus if a solicitor deliberately misrepresented the effect a certain clause in a will would have, so that he became a beneficiary under the will, he would, on receipt of the legacy, have obtained property by deception.

(b) *Statement of intention*

X offers to paint Y's house for £100 cash in advance. He intends all along to abscond with the money without painting the house. This is a statement of intention of what he will do in the future if Y gives him £100, and not a statement of fact. Under the pre-1968 law this could not amount to a deception, but section 15(4) concludes that deception includes a "deception as to the present intentions of the person using the deception or any other person." Thus in our example X's present intentions are to take the money and leave and thus the statement is capable of amounting to a deception within the Act.

In *Silverman* (1987) the defendant gave an excessively high quotation for work to be done on property owned by two elderly sisters. The defendants had worked for the family in the past and it was clear that the negotiations had taken place in an atmosphere of mutual trust. The question for the court was whether his excessively high quotation could amount to deception for purposes of section 15. Obviously the court was mindful of the implication of holding that high quotations could constitute deception. However, it held that, in the special circumstances of this case where there was a relationship of trust, a representation of a fair charge which the defendant, but not the sisters, knew to be dishonestly excessive could amount to a deception. In one respect the statement was a statement of opinion, but it amounted to a representation of the present state of his mind. In these circumstances his silence was as eloquent as if he had said that he was going to make no more than a modest profit.

(c) Does there need to be words; will conduct suffice?

We have already seen above in the definition of deception under section 15(4) that conduct can amount to a deception. This will be conduct which the accused knows or believes will cause another to draw certain conclusions. Thus in *D.P.P. v. Ray* (1974) the House of Lords held in a case where Ray left a restaurant without paying for a meal he had just eaten, that there was evidence which could support a finding that by staying in his seat after forming the intention not to pay, Ray had caused the waitress to leave the room, enabling Ray to walk out. Similarly, if you were to drive into a self-service station intending not to pay when you had filled up your tank, then you would be inducing in the attendants, by your conduct, a belief that you would be paying when you had got your petrol. When you sit down in the hairdresser's chair you are impliedly telling him that you will be paying for the haircut.

What of the accused who tenders a cheque or cheque card in payment? Let us consider the straightforward unaccompanied cheque first. Following the decision in *M.P.C. v. Charles* (1977) it would appear that, in the absence of any statement to the contrary, a person who tenders a cheque is impliedly stating that to the best of his knowledge, the cheque will be met when it is presented to the bank. This is not without its difficulties, since you are really saying that your bank manager will authorise payment of the cheque when he sees it. As we have already said, the deception must be as to a question of fact or present intentions and this is a statement concerning how you believe someone else will act in the future. Nevertheless, it does represent a statement of the presenter's present beliefs. He is saying that at that precise moment he has no reason to think that the cheque will not be met. Thus, for example, if he knows that he no longer has an account at that bank or that the manager has specifically told him that all future cheques presented will be dishonoured, it is suggested that this will amount to a deception within the meaning of the Act.

We shall see that cheque cards and credit cards present special difficulties owing to the way in which they operate (see below, p. 423). It is suggested, however, that the presenter of such a card is stating that he has the authority to use it.

A slightly different situation was presented in *Hamilton* (1990) where the balance of the defendant's bank account consisted of the proceeds of forged cheques. When he signed withdrawal slips to obtain the money the Court of Appeal held that he had made a false representation that he was owed that amount by the bank, which clearly he was not.

(d) *Can there be a case of deception by silence?*

In many cases of sales the seller is aware that the buyer labours under a misapprehension as to the qualities of the goods he is about to purchase. Is the seller therefore guilty of obtaining property by deception if he fails to correct the buyer's misapprehension? There exists at civil law the motto *caveat emptor*, which translated means, "let the buyer beware"; in other words, he must take the risks. It would be odd if the criminal law were to punish the seller for simply following a civil law maxim. However, the seller must do nothing actively to promote the mistake. If the customer were to say "I am going to use this for outside work" and the shopkeeper knew it was extremely unsuitable for that purpose, his silence could be taken as an implied statement that the product was suitable for outside work. It is suggested that this should amount to a deception within the Act. Similarly, if X warrants that the car he is selling Y is roadworthy but discovers before Y pays him the money that there is a serious defect in the car which makes it extremely unsafe, X would be guilty of obtaining the money by deception if he failed to draw this to the attention of Y before he received the money.

(e) *Can you deceive a machine?*

The simple answer to this question is: not for the purposes of these four offences. The deception must cause a human being to act in a way he would not have done but for the deception. Thus, if you insert a valueless metal disc into a cigarette machine for the purpose of getting cigarettes out for nothing, then you have stolen the cigarettes just as much as if you had forced the machine open with a crowbar; but you have not obtained them by deception. However, if the machine is used to deceive a human being, there may be a deception. For example, if X takes the afternoon off work and alters the machine which prints his time of leaving so that his record card shows that he left at the proper time, when he gets paid his full amount at the end of the week it will be because he had used the machine to deceive his employers. Thus he will be guilty of obtaining property from his employers by deception.

(2) The Causal Link

It is not sufficient for the prosecution to prove that the accused practised a deception on the victim and that he then obtained an item of property from the victim. They must prove that the deception was the reason why the accused obtained the property. In other words there must be a causal link between the deception and the obtaining of the property. A few illustrations will help to make this clearer.

(a) A offers to sell B his copy of *Smith and Hogan's Criminal Law*. He tells B that it is the current edition when he knows full well that there has just been a new edition and that B will need the new edition for his classes. The jury should only convict A of obtaining the property (*i.e.* the sale price) by deception if they are satisfied beyond reasonable doubt that B would not have bought the book but for the deception. If, on the other hand, they find that B knew that the book was out of date but that he had some reason for still wanting to buy it, then despite A's belief that he has duped B, his attempt to deceive B did not cause B to buy the book and so the purchase price was not obtained by A's lies. In *Laverty* (1970) the accused sold B a stolen car on which he had changed the number plates. The prosecution alleged that P was induced to buy the car because of the accused's representation by his conduct that this was the original car with those number plates. However, the Court of Appeal held that P bought the car because he thought that the accused was authorised to sell it and that there was no evidence to prove that B would have been in any way influenced by the knowledge of the change of number plates.

(b) C drives into a petrol station. He intends to fill up with petrol and then drive off without paying. If the jury are satisfied that his representations caused the petrol station attendants to believe that C intended to pay and thus allowed him to fill his car then clearly C has obtained the petrol by deception.

(c) D writes a begging letter to E saying that she is the impoverished widow of a sailor who was drowned at sea. E knows whom the letter is from and that it is an attempt to trick him. Nevertheless E sends D the money in an attempt to trap D. Care is needed here. D has told E lies and E has sent D some money, *but* it was not D's deception which caused the money to be sent because E was aware it was a trick (*Hensler* (1870)). That was a relatively easy case in which to see the absence of a causal link between the deception and the obtaining, but it is not always so simple. Let us consider a case in which A and B who are travelling on a train from London to Leeds, go to the buffet car for a snack. In the buffet car a bystander tells them that he suspects that the attendant is selling his own sandwiches and keeping the money. A says that he will only buy a sandwich if it is a British Rail sandwich, for which the money will have to go in the till. B, on the other hand, says that he could not care less who made the sandwich as long as it is fresh. They ask the attendant whose sandwiches are on sale and he falsely tells them that they are British Rail sandwiches. Both are deceived by the attendant, but the deception is material only to A since B would have bought the sandwiches even if the attendant had told them that he had made the sandwiches himself. The attendant obtains property only from A by deception.

An interesting illustration of this point was provided by the case of *King and Stockwell* (1987). In that case the defendants were charged with attempting to obtain property by deception from a 68-year-old woman to whom they had falsely represented themselves as employees of a reputable firm of tree surgeons. They told her that certain trees on her property needed felling as they could cause damage to the foundation of her house and to her gas supply. They argued that they had committed no offence since any money paid over would have been in return for the felling of trees; the lies they had told merely gave them the opportunity to do the work and had, in effect, ceased to be operative. The Court of Appeal held that this reasoning was fallacious. The question in every case is: was the deception an operative cause of the obtaining of the property? There was plenty of evidence in the present case that had the attempt succeeded, the money would have been paid over by the victim as a result of the lies told to her by the defendants. In the present case it would seem that the work recommended was unnecessary and so it is easy to say that the deception was an operative cause of the obtaining of the payment. However, it would be less clear cut if the work was essential and if the defendants had performed it well and at a reasonable price. The deception need not be the only reason for the handing over of property, but the jury must be satisfied that but for the deception the property would not have been obtained by the defendant.

A similar situation may arise where credit or cheque cards are used. You will know that one common feature of these cards is that a shopkeeper who sells goods to a person using one of these cards is guaranteed payment provided that he has fulfilled the regulations relating to them. In the case of credit cards these regulations require that the shopkeeper checks the signatures, checks that the card number is not on a stop-list, and telephones the company if the money involved is over a certain amount. In the case of cheque guarantee cards the seller must ensure that the signatures are in order. In both cases he should not actually be aware that the customer is no longer authorised to use the card. Where a person uses such a card he is impliedly representing that he is authorised to use the card. Thus if the shopkeeper is induced by a false representation that the card holder is authorised to use the card to sell the goods, the holder has obtained the goods by deception. Before the introduction of such cards many shopkeepers were reluctant to accept cheques or grant credit. One purpose of the cards is to remove his fears that he will not be paid for the goods. As long as he is not actually aware that the authority to use the card has been withdrawn by the bank or credit card company, he will be paid. It is no longer necessary for him to ask embarrassing questions to ensure the customer's bona fides. He is, in theory, allowed to be like B on the train; he need not care whether the customer is authorised to use the card, so long as he does not actually know that the authority has been withdrawn. So when he accepts a cheque from X backed by a cheque guarantee card does he do so because of X's implied assertion that he is authorised to use the card, or because he knows that he will be paid whether or not X is in fact authorised to use the card? If the prosecution cannot prove that he was influenced by the implied assertion of authority to use the card there is no causal link between X's deception and the obtaining of the property.

There have been two recent cases on this issue. In *Charles* (1977) the House of Lords was concerned with cheque cards and in *Lambie* (1982) with a credit card. In both cases the accused had pretended to be authorised users of the cards, when they both knew that this was not the case. In both cases the evidence that there was any causal link between the deception and the obtaining was extremely weak. In *Charles* the House upheld a conviction of obtaining (a pecuniary advantage) by deception, but in *Lambie* the Court of Appeal found a distinction between cheque cards and credit cards (based on the differences in the way they each secure payment for the shopkeeper) and held that this enabled them to distinguish *Charles* and hold *Lambie* not guilty because there was no evidence that the shopkeeper had been influenced by the implied representation that the accused was authorised to use the card. Suffice it to say that the House of Lords, in *Lambie*, held that there was no relevant distinction to be drawn between cheque and credit cards. The question then remained of whether Lambie had obtained a pecuniary advantage by holding herself out as an authorised credit card user. The House took the view that had the shop assistant been asked whether, if she had known that Lambie was acting dishonestly and had no authority to use the card, she would have completed the transaction, she would obviously have answered "No." The House found this answer irresistible. But it is not at all clear from the reports that this answer was irresistible. The effect of this decision appears to be that the courts will fictitiously imply that all those who permit their customers to use credit and cheque cards do so motivated by the belief that their customers are authorised to use the cards.

(d) X buys a book from Y and hands Y a cheque in payment. The following day X discovers that the cheque will not be met by the bank, but he does not inform Y. There is no obtaining of a book by deception since no deception was practised before the book was obtained. If, however, X did not take possession of the book until after he has discovered that the cheque will not be met then his silence would amount to a deception in that he would be impliedly representing that there is no reason to think that Y will not get his money and this would cause Y to hand over the book.

(e) X sells Y a car and makes several representations about its qualities. All the representations are true except for the one in which X tells Y that the car has never been involved in a serious accident. Could X defend himself against a charge of obtaining property by deception on the basis that Y bought the car acting on representations most of which were true? This is a question of fact for the jury. If they are satisfied that Y would not have bought the car had he known about the serious accident then the charge is made out.

(f) X drives into a petrol station intending to pay. When he has filled the tank he discovers that he has left all his money at home. He therefore simply drives off without paying. Even if you could find any form of deception here it would be at a time when the ownership in the petrol had already passed to X (it passes to him when he puts it in the tank) and so it would be impossible to say that he obtained the property by deception. Nor is it theft because the property in the petrol has already passed to him before he dishonestly appropriates it. This is now dealt with by the Theft Act 1978, s.3 (below, p. 436).

(3) Dishonesty

All deception offences require dishonesty. The partial definition of dishonesty which is provided in section 2(1) for the purposes of theft is not made applicable to the deception offences. Obviously this partial definition is for the most part inapt for deception offences but otherwise the concept of dishonesty is the same for the deception offences as it is for theft. So a person would not commit a deception offence if he used a deception with a view to obtaining something to which he believed he was legally entitled. But just as a person's conduct may be accounted dishonest for the purposes of theft notwithstanding any intention to pay for the property, so too a person may dishonestly obtain though he gives full value for what he obtains. If, for example, A sells Christmas cards by pretending that the profits will go to charity, he may be convicted of obtaining by deception though his cards are fair value for the price charged (see *Potger* (1970)).

The foregoing constitute the common elements in deception offences. Their differences lie in the nature of what is obtained. In order to constitute a deception offence it must be proved that as a result of the deception the accused obtained:

(1) property (Theft Act 1968, s.15); or
(2) a pecuniary advantage (Theft Act 1968, s.16); or
(3) services from another (Theft Act 1978, s.1); or
(4) the evasion of liability (Theft Act 1978, s.2).

2. Obtaining Property by Deception

The most common of the deception offences is that under section 15 of deception by dishonestly obtaining property belonging to another with the intention of permanently depriving the other of it.

(1) Property

Property for the purpose of section 15 is as defined by section 4(1), that is *without* the exceptions which apply in the case of theft by virtue of sections 4(2)–(4). This means, for example, that while wild mushrooms cannot usually be stolen, they may be obtained by deception. For practical purposes, however, the important point to note is that land, which in general cannot be stolen, may be obtained by deception.

Property is obtained for this purpose when A obtains ownership, possession or control of B's property with the relevant intent. Thus if A by deception causes B to lend him property (for example, he procures the hire of a television receiver) A is guilty of this offence *if* he intends to deprive B permanently of it. Merely to obtain a loan by deception is not an offence under this section (though it will usually be an offence under section 1 of the 1978 Act) if A intends to return the goods at the end of the period of loan or otherwise has no intention of permanently depriving the owner of it.

(2) Mens Rea

Apart from (i) dishonesty which has been discussed above, it must also be proved that (ii) the deception was deliberate or reckless; and (iii) that there was an intention permanently to deprive.

A classic case to illustrate how the issue of dishonesty may cause difficulties in this context is *O'Connell* (1991). The defendant had been part of a mortgage fraud by which building society cheques were obtained by false representations. His defence was effectively that he always intended to repay the loans so that there would no loss to the building society. Although the proviso was applied to sustain the conviction, this appears to be just the sort of case where a jury should consider the issue of dishonesty in the light of *Ghosh*.

As to (ii) there must be a representation which is in fact untrue which the maker knows to be untrue or which he makes not caring whether it be true or false. This requirement is really an essential adjunct of the requirement for dishonesty. It follows that D does not commit the offence where he is merely negligent for no amount of negligence can make an honest man a dishonest man. It would appear clearly to follow that the objective test of recklessness endorsed in *Caldwell* (above, p. 214) can have no place in this context.

(3) Is There an Overlap between the Offences of Theft and Obtaining Property by Deception?

It should be noted at the outset that there is no reason why there should not be an overlap between these offences. After all the Criminal Law Revision Committee did at one stage consider whether to define theft in such a way as to include cases of obtaining by deception. In the end they decided against this course but at least some members of the Committee thought it possible to subsume the deception offence within a more broadly drawn definition of theft. But having decided on two separate offences, the Committee never had it in mind so to define them that there could be no conceivable possibility of overlap. The fact that in particular circumstances the defendant might be convicted of either theft or deception is of no great consequence.

Suppose, then, that A obtains a television set from B on a hire-purchase term, that A has no intention of paying the instalments and makes off with the set. This looks like, and is, a case of obtaining by deception contrary to section 15. It is also a case of theft. Under a hire-purchase transaction the purchaser gets possession but does not get ownership of the goods hired. The ownership here remains in B so when A makes off with (*i.e.* appropriates) the set he is then appropriating property belonging to B. So there are at least some cases in which the defendant may be convicted of theft or deception. What we need to explore is the extent of this overlap.

The first question that arises is whether *all* cases of theft can be charged as deception. The answer must be an obvious "No." If A puts his hand in B's pocket and abstracts B's wallet this is theft, but by no stretch of the imagination can it be said to be an obtaining of the wallet by deception. Thus by far the most common form of theft (*i.e.* theft by taking) cannot fall within deception—because there is no deception.

The second question is whether *all* cases of deception can be charged as theft. It would certainly be surprising if this turned out to be the case, if only because the Criminal Law Revision Committee, though it anticipated some overlap, can hardly have thought that the offence of deception was entirely superfluous. Sometimes, though, statutory provisions do not always have the effect they were intended by their framers to have and the logic of the House of Lords decision in *Gomez* would now suggest that nearly all cases of obtaining by deception are also theft. This follows from the very wide meaning given in that case to "appropriation" and the fact that the consent or authorisation of the owner of the property to the transaction is apparently irrelevant (see above, p. 396). Indeed *Gomez* was just the sort of case where it might once have been thought that it was essential to preserve the distinction between theft and obtaining property by deception (which includes obtaining ownership of the property) because the defendant had obtained a title to the goods under the principles of the civil law. It might have been a voidable title, since it had been induced by fraud, but it was nevertheless a title valid until set aside, and a person cannot normally be said to steal property of which they are the owner. Nevertheless, as we have seen, the House of Lords came to the conclusion that there was an appropriation and a theft.

In at least one respect there is no overlap. The range of property which is capable of being obtained by deception is wider than the range of property which can be stolen. Land, for example, can be obtained by deception but it cannot be stolen (see above, p. 426). If, then, A obtains Blackacre from B by deception he may commit the offence under section 15 but not the offence of theft under section 1. The court's decision, therefore, can only be applied to cases where the property involved can be both obtained by deception and stolen. Even so, this seems strange. It is a reflection of the fact that the House of Lords chose, for reasons that are not obvious, not to have regard to the Eighth Report of the Criminal Law Revision Committee when construing the Act. The controversy and uncertainty which previously existed over the conflicting House of Lords decisions in *Morris* and *Lawrence* have been resolved in favour of the latter with the result that cases such as *Skipp* have been expressly overruled.

Even if there is an almost complete overlap between theft and obtaining property by deception there may still be reason to prefer a charge of section 15 where there has indeed been deception. In the first place, criminal charges should surely reflect as nearly as possible the essence of the criminal conduct and crimes of deception are different in kind to theft and so should be charged as such. It is also possible that prosecutors may wish to take advantage of the fact that the maximum penalty for a section 15 offence is 10 years imprisonment whereas for theft it is only seven years. From a procedural point of view prosecutors may also prefer to bring a charge under section 15 where the facts warrant it. If for some reason the deception element cannot be proved beyond reasonable doubt there is still the possibility of a conviction on the alternative verdict of theft. This would follow from the fact that obtaining property by deception would appear to be after *Gomez* an aggravated form of theft.

3. Obtaining a Pecuniary Advantage

If X goes into a hairdresser's and allows the hairdresser to cut his hair intending not to pay when the haircut is over, you could say that he has obtained the haircut by deception. But is a haircut property? Clearly not within the definition of section 4 of the Theft Act 1968. Of course, if shampoos or conditioner have been used you could say that he obtained those items by deception. It would, however, be absurd to say that liability should depend upon whether the haircut involves the use of shampoos. Similarly if A gives false information on an application form for a job and as a result of that false information he obtains the employment, what has he obtained by deception? So far he has obtained the right to work for the firm. At the end of the month when he is paid, this will be for the work he has done during the month and not because of the deception, so does he commit no offence?

These examples should show that whereas theft can be limited to items of property (albeit a widened definition to cover such property as things in action) the definition of property is just not suitable to cover the examples given above. If was therefore felt necessary to include a separate offence to cover situations where the accused by his deception obtains some form of financial advantage. Thus section 16 provided a criminal offence of obtaining a pecuniary advantage by deception. The phrase pecuniary advantage was defined in three ways by section 16(2)(a)–(c). Paragraphs (b) and (c) provided for a fairly restricted range of situations and these will be discussed below. Paragraph (a) was a wide-ranging definition of pecuniary advantage which was intended to cover, for example, the cases like the hairdresser described above. Unfortunately this section caused the courts so many problems, being described at one stage as a "judicial nightmare," that Parliament repealed this one small part of the Theft Act and replaced it with three new offences under the Theft Act 1978. The end result is that the offence of dishonestly obtaining a pecuniary advantage survives in section 16, but the definition of pecuniary advantage is now limited to paragraphs 16(2)(b) and 16(2)(c). There is, of course, only one offence under section 16.

What Therefore is a Pecuniary Advantage for the Purposes of Section 16?

(a) *Section 16(2)(b):*

> "He is allowed to borrow by way of overdraft, or to take out any policy of insurance or annuity contract, or obtains an improvement of the terms on which he is allowed to do so";

Thus if X falsely tells his bank manager that he is expecting a cheque from his father in five weeks' time and as a result is allowed to create an overdraft, then even before he has begun to take advantage of the overdraft facilities he has committed the offence under section 16 of obtaining a pecuniary advantage by deception. It is the obtaining of the facility that is the crux of the offence.

If Y gives false information about his state of health and thereby obtains a life insurance policy, he has committed an offence at the time he is granted the policy.

(b) *Section 16(2)(c):*

> "He is given the opportunity to earn remuneration or greater remuneration in an office or employment, or to win money by betting."

Our earlier example of the applicant for a job who gives false information on the application form which induces the employer to give him the job will be caught by this definition of pecuniary advantage. Similarly a university lecturer who gains promotion by supplying the university with a false list of publications would also commit the offence under section 16.

4. Obtaining Services by Deception

Section 1 of the Theft Act 1978 provides:

(1)   A person who by any deception dishonestly obtains services from another shall be guilty of an offence.

(2)   It is an obtaining of services where the other is induced to confer a benefit by doing some act, or causing or permitting some act to be done, on the

understanding that the benefit has been or will be paid for.

This offence is based on the notion that a man's services have a value and that it is wrong by deception dishonestly to cause him to confer the benefit of his services on another where there is no intention that he shall be recompensed. "Services" are widely defined and extend to any act, or causing or permitting some act to be done. The operation of this section may be explained by reference to a number of examples.

(i) X deliberately allows a hairdresser to cut his hair, fully intending to leave without paying. Clearly the barber is "induced to do some act" by the deception and there is obviously an understanding that the service will be paid for when it is completed and before the customer leaves the shop. If he decides to leave without paying only after the haircut is completed then he will commit an offence under section 3, (see below, p. 436).

(ii) The following example is based on a newspaper report. E was a student at school Y where he was studying for his A level examinations. He was dissatisfied with the instruction he was receiving in history and so, putting on the school tie of Z school, he attended the history lessons at that school. The history master at Z school did not realise that there was an interloper in the class and gave the lesson. Did E commit an offence under section 1?

(a) Is he dishonest? This is a question for the jury (see above, p. 407). His wearing of Z school tie tends to suggest that he knows he has no right to be there. But is that enough?

(b) Is there a deception? Clearly he wears the tie to deceive the authorities at Z school into allowing him on to the premises.

(c) Does he obtain a service by the deception? Presumably F was going to deliver his class that day for his own pupils, in which case it would be rather straining the section to say that E's deception deceived F into conferring a benefit upon E. If F had spotted E before the class he would no doubt have expelled E, but that does not seem to be the same as saying that E caused F to perform the act. There is a further difficulty. The Act says that the act must be done on the understanding that it has been or will be paid for. Now F will be paid by the Local Authority (if it is a state school) for his work as a teacher. He therefore gives each class on the understanding that he will be paid. It is submitted, however, that this is not what the Act means. It surely means that an understanding exists between the deceiver and the deceived that there will be payment though not necessarily payment made by the deceiver. If X were to go to a car repairers and falsely tell them that he worked for a firm which had an account with that garage, when the mechanics repaired the car it would be because the deception had created in their minds the understanding that they would be paid, not by the rogue, but by his firm. In our school example no such understanding exists and it is submitted that no offence under section 1 is committed.

(iii) H sneaks into a cinema without being observed by the ticket seller. It is probable that this does not amount to an offence under this section. The section requires that somebody provides a service because they have been deceived, but since no one has seen him enter, how can it be said that anyone has been deceived?

(iv) J by deception persuades his neighbour to drive him to the station. This would only be an offence under this section if there was an understanding between them that J would pay for the service and this is unlikely. If J gets into a taxi intending not to pay at the other end he will obtain the service by deception, but if, by deception at the beginning of the ride, he persuades the taxi driver to carry him free then no offence under section 1 will be committed.

(v) K and his secretary book into a local hotel as husband and wife. They know that the hotel is run by people with strict moral principles who would never allow them to stay there if they knew what was afoot. After their night of passion they pay the bill and leave. If the prosecution can establish that K and his secretary were dishonest and that the services were provided because the hoteliers thought that K and his secretary were man and wife, it would appear an offence under section 1 has been committed. Normally, of course, the deception will concern payment for the services, but the statute does not limit it to this. It suffices that the deception causes the service to be performed and that it is a service which is performed on the understanding that it will be paid for.

(vi) A visits B, a prostitute, for the purpose of having sexual intercourse and intends to walk off without paying. It is submitted that an offence under section 1 is committed; the section makes no reference to the payment needing to be one which is legally enforceable. (If he so decides after the act of intercourse he would not commit an offence under section 3 of the Theft Act 1978; see below, p. 439.)

In conclusion we should note that there is a good deal of potential overlap between this section and section 15 of the

Theft Act 1968. Thus if D books into a hotel for bed and breakfast intending never to pay, he obtains both goods and services by deception. Again there is no harm in such an overlap provided that common sense is used. In all cases where the accused has obtained property by deception he could be said to have obtained a service, but this is clearly not what is intended. In most cases, however, the correct charge should be obvious.

5. Evasion of Liability by Deception

Section 2 provides an offence to cover the situation where the accused dishonestly and by deception evades a financial obligation. Although the section contains only one offence it may be committed in one of three ways and the prosecution would be expected to make clear in the indictment in which of the three ways it was alleged the accused committed the offence.

Section 2(1)(a)

Section 2(1)(a) covers the situation where D, by any deception, "dishonestly secures the remission of the whole or any part of any existing liability to make payment, whether his own liability or another's."

D's girl-friend, E, is £45 in arrears in the rental payments on her flat. D goes to her landlord and falsely tells him that E's mother is slowly dying and that E is having to spend nearly all her money in travelling to care for her mother and this is the reason for her rental arrears. Out of kindness the landlord tells D that he will accept £20 in full settlement of the arrears.

D has committed an offence within the meaning of section 2(1)(a). The subsection makes it clear that it does not matter whether the liability evaded is his own or another's. The £45 rental arrears is an existing liability which D has dishonestly tricked the landlord into reducing. Most commentators seem to suggest that the use of the word "remit" in section 2(1)(a) indicates that there must be an agreement by the person deceived either to wipe the slate clean as far as the existing liability is concerned or to make a reduction in the amount of money that will have to be paid. It would not be sufficient that the landlord is tricked into believing that he has already been paid. (This might amount to inducing the landlord to forgo payment under s.2(1)(*b*)). He must be aware that there is an existing liability and decide to extinguish or reduce that liability. If the landlord also says that he will accept half rent until the situation alters, this would be an offence under section 2(1)(*c*).

Section 2(1)(b)

Section 2(1)(*b*) covers the situation where by any deception the accused "with intent to make permanent default in whole or in part on any existing liability to make payment, or with intent to let another do so, dishonestly induces the creditor or any person claiming payment on behalf of the creditor to wait for payment (whether or not the due date for payment is deferred) or to forgo payment."

(i) A has rented a television set from B Ltd for the last four years, paying monthly instalments. He is now five months in arrears of payments and the shop manager has called round to tell him that if he does not give the money owed they will take immediate possession of the set. A is about to emigrate to Australia in three days' time, but is very eager to see the Cup Final on his set the day before he leaves the country. He therefore hands the manager a cheque for the full amount, knowing full well that he has closed that account and that the cheque will be dishonoured. He believes, however, that by the time the cheque is returned to the television company, he will have seen the Cup Final and have left the country for good.

Has he dishonestly and by deception induced the manager to wait for payment on an existing liability? Has he not, in fact, paid the manager by the cheque? Section 2(3) expressly provides for a case in which the creditor is given a cheque in payment; he is to be treated not as one who has been paid but one who has been induced to wait for payment. The answer to the initial question is, therefore, yes. There is, however, one more requirement: the accused must have the intention to make permanent default in whole or in part on any existing liability. In our example, this condition is clearly met. He is simply buying himself time so that he can get out of the country and avoid payment altogether. If, on the other hand, A was short of money and not about to emigrate and so sent his son to the door to tell the manager that his father was away for a few days, intending to pay the bill when he received his monthly salary, then this would not amount to an offence since he had no intention to make permanent default. This is a difficult area. The father who sends his son to the door to tell the rent collector that "dad is out" is clearly dishonest, but should he be treated as a criminal? Parliament decided that he should not be so treated unless the deception was practised with the intention that the debt would never be paid.

(ii) Let us imagine another type of debt situation but one in which the liability A evades is to a prostitute C, for services rendered. Unfortunately for C, A commits no offence under section 2 because liability is defined in section 2(2) as "legally enforceable liability" and under the law (see below, p. 582), the prostitute could not sue A for the recovery of the money owed for her sexual services. And this applies to all three types of evasion of liability under section 2.

(iii) X, while driving his car, runs into the back of Y's car, causing about £5 worth of damage. X denies that he was to blame, but he tells Y that to save any bother he will give him a cheque for £30, knowing that the cheque will not be met. Section 2(2) provides that throughout section 2, liability does not include a liability which is not accepted or established to pay compensation for a wrongful act or omission. Since X has not accepted that he was to blame for the accident, there is no offence committed under section 2.

(iv) A, who owes B's bookshop £20, dishonestly and falsely tells them that he has paid them already. The manager accepts that his sales staff have made a mistake and enters "paid" in the accounts. This would be an example of dishonesty and by deception inducing another to forgo payment.

Section 2(1)(c)

Section 2(1)(c) covers the situation where the accused by any deception "dishonestly obtains any exemption from or abatement of liability to make a payment."

Unlike the other two types of evasion in paragraphs (b) and (c) this provision makes no reference to an existing liability. It is therefore suitable to cover a situation in which the deception is practised before any liability is incurred with the result that either the liability which is eventually incurred is less than it should have been or that no liability at all is incurred.

(i) A and his friend B are desperate to catch a train. The local station is next to the hospital and so B pretends to be taken ill while A flags down a passing taxi driver. The driver agrees to take them to the hospital free of charge. This would clearly amount to an offence under this provision. But for the deception A and B would have incurred a financial liability for the ride.

(ii) A local authority passes a by-law under which senior citizens who satisfy certain financial requirements can obtain a pass which will enable them to travel free on local buses. C, a senior citizen, misrepresents the true state of his finances and as a result he is issued with a pass. He commits an offence under this section. He would be liable to pay his fares on any bus journey but for the deception which he has practised on the local authority.

(iii) D gets on board a local bus by flashing a fake season ticket at the driver as he enters. Arguably this case differs from the two previous cases in that here the driver would regard the "season ticket" as evidence that this passenger was under no liability to pay since he would assume that payment had already been made. There is thus no conscious decision on the part of the driver to grant any exemption from or abatement of D's liability to make a payment since he believes that there is no such liability. It would seem more appropriate to charge D with an offence under section 2(1)(b) (by deception inducing the driver to forgo payment) or with making off without payment (section 3, Theft Act 1978 below) when he leaves the bus at the end of the journey. However, the Court of Appeal has held that this would amount to an offence under section 2(1)(c) (see *Sibartie* (1983)).

III. MAKING OFF WITHOUT PAYMENT

Before the Theft Act 1978 came into effect there was a common, and quickly growing, fraud for which the 1968 Act made inadequate provision. The fraud was simplicity itself and consisted merely in making off without paying for goods or services provided. Typical examples are provided by the motorist who, having filled up his tank with petrol, drives away without paying; or by the customer who, having consumed a meal in a restaurant, runs off without settling his bill. If the goods or services are obtained by deception there will usually be an offence under section 15 of the 1968 Act or under section 1 of the 1978 Act but if no deception is made before the goods are obtained or the service provided then these provisions are inapplicable.

On the other hand the law does not in general make it an offence for a debtor dishonestly to resolve not to pay his debts. It is not an offence dishonestly to resolve not to pay the quarterly gas or electricity bill. But since the gas and electricity bodies know with whom they are dealing, they can be left to pursue their *civil* remedies and there is no need to make a crime of such conduct. Moreover, if such conduct was made criminal there is a real danger that people who cannot pay, as opposed to those who will not pay, would find themselves in the criminal courts.

Section 3 is accordingly not aimed at dishonest debtors in general but at the kind of debtor who, if he cannot be brought to book on the spot, may never be traced and made to pay. Hence the offence of making off is made an arrestable one because without a power of arrest it would, as a practical matter, be impossible to give effect to the section.

Section 3(1) provides "a person who, knowing that payment on the spot for any goods supplied or service done is required or expected from him, dishonestly makes off without having paid as required or expected and with intent to avoid payment of the amount shall be guilty of an offence."

Again we can examine the working of the offence in relation to some hypothetical examples.

(i) A eats a meal in a restaurant fully intending to pay. At the end of the meal he discovers that he has come out without any means of paying and so he simply runs out intending to avoid payment. Before the Theft Act 1978 the prosecution would have had to discover some deception on A's part which enabled him to make his escape. Under section 3 no such mental gymnastics are required. The prosecution must prove that the accused knew that payment on the spot was required. It is clear that people eating in a restaurant will expect to pay before they leave. Even if they expect to arrange for credit or to use a credit card, this will clearly be covered by the section as long as the customer knows that he must make some deal with the restaurant owner before he leaves. Secondly, the prosecutor must prove that the accused made off from that spot. (For where payment is expected or required (see *McDavitt* (1981); *Brooks and Brooks* (1983)). What will constitute making off will depend upon the facts of the individual case; but there will be no difficulty in holding that a person who runs out of a restaurant without paying has "made off." Thirdly, the prosecutor must establish that the accused was dishonest and fourthly that in making off he did so *with intent to avoid payment*. This last phrase is somewhat ambiguous. It could be interpreted to mean that it was sufficient that the accused intended not to pay when expected or it could mean that the prosecutor must establish that the accused intended never to pay. In *Allen* (1985) the House of Lords held that this ambiguity should be resolved in favour of the defendant; no offence shall be committed unless the prosecutor proves that the accused intended never to pay.

From a practical point of view it may be easier to use this offence even where you suspect that the accused intended to avoid payment even before he ate the meal. Technically, he should be charged with obtaining property by deception which carries a much higher penalty. On the other hand where it is obvious that no use will be made of this greater sentencing power, it may well prove attractive to the prosecution to avoid the need to prove that the deception occurred from the outset. Similarly where the accused drives off from a petrol station without having paid, he may well have committed offences of theft, deception and making off, but the prosecution may well settle for the making-off charge.

(ii) G pays for a repair to his car with a cheque which he knows will be dishonoured when presented. The garage owner, however, is quite happy and hands G the keys to the car and G leaves intending never to pay. The issue raised by this example is whether the concept of "making off" is satisfied when the accused leaves with the consent of a person who has been tricked into thinking that he has been paid or does "making off" cover only those cases where the accused leaves without the consent of the victim? This point has not yet been settled by the courts.

(iii) X travels each evening between Leeds and Menston on a local pay train (on such trains the guard issues tickets in the same way that tickets are issued on buses, there being no station staff to collect such tickets at the local stops such as Menston). One evening the train is particularly full and the guard has not reached X by the time the train reaches Menston. X gets out of the train and walks off without paying.

This may seem an obvious example of an offence under section 3, but is it? He clearly makes off without paying (would hiding in the toilet constitute a making off?); a service has been provided for him and payment on the spot was expected. However, the section requires that the accused should have acted dishonestly and with intent to avoid payment. You will recall that the word "dishonestly" is a question of fact for the jury (above, p. 407); they will have to consider whether people in general would regard such conduct as dishonest and, if so, whether the defendant knew that this conduct would be so regarded by people in general. It is therefore quite on the cards that a jury would not find the accused to have acted dishonestly. Further it is rather hard to say that he made off with the intention of avoiding payment. Experience may have taught him that it is not advisable to stay on the train to look for the guard since the train will probably move on as soon as other passengers have dismounted. Clearly if he gets off at an earlier station because he sees that the guard will reach him before the train gets to Menston then it will be possible to say that he has dishonestly made off with intent to avoid payment. This may also be the position if, when he alights from the train at Menston he sees the guard standing on the platform ready to receive fares from those who have not yet paid and then deliberately avoids taking the opportunity to pay. This problem clearly raises issues as to the duties owed by persons travelling on buses or such pay trains; is there a duty to seek out the fare-collector? Considerations such as these will affect how the jury tackles the requirements of dishonesty.

(iv) X has just had intercourse with a prostitute who now requires payment. X simply walks off saying "Take me to court and try and get your money." There is no difference in principle between this example and that in number (i). However, section 3(3) provides that if the supply of goods or the doing of the service is contrary to law, or if the service done is such that payment is not legally enforceable, then the offence is not committed. Here the prostitute would not be able to sue X to recover damages for breach of contract and so X commits no offence when he walks off. However, if from the outset he intended not to pay, X would probably commit the offence of obtaining services by deception contrary to section 1 of the Act, since no such qualification is expressed in section 1 (above, p. 430). Thus in *Troughton* (1987) where the defendant had allegedly made off without paying a taxi fare, it was fatal to the prosecutor's case that the taxi-driver had broken his contract by not taking the accused to his desired destination. In those circumstances he was in no position to demand payment on the spot.

IV. ROBBERY

Section 8 of the Theft Act provides:

"(1) A person is guilty of robbery if he steals, and immediately before or at the time of doing so, and in

order to do so, he uses force on any person or puts
or seeks to put any person in fear of being then and
there subjected to force.

(2)   A person guilty of robbery, or of an assault with
intent to rob, shall on conviction on indictment be
liable to imprisonment for life."

In order to succeed on a charge of robbery the prosecution
must establish (a) that the property was stolen; and (b) that
the theft of it was accomplished by force. Thus all the
defences open to one charged with theft are open on a charge
of robbery. If the jury believe that the accused honestly
thought that he had the right to take the property they must
acquit him of theft, and therefore of robbery. In *Robinson*
(1977) the accused was owed £7 by I's wife. The prosecution
alleged that R and two others approached I in the street and
that R was brandishing a knife. In the course of a fight which
followed, I dropped a £5 note. R picked it up and asked for
the remaining £2 he was owed. The judge directed the jury
that for a defence under section 2(1) of the Theft Act the
accused should honestly believe he had the right to take the
money in the way he did. His appeal against conviction for
robbery was allowed by the Court of Appeal. The prosecution
had to establish the basic offence of theft and it would be a
defence to that charge that the accused honestly believed he
had a right in law to deprive I of the money, even if he knew
he was not entitled to use a knife to get it. If the prosecution
failed to prove theft, then an indictment for robbery must also
fail.

What then turns an act of theft into one of robbery? In the
first place the prosecution must prove that in order to steal
the accused used force on any person or sought to put any
person in fear of such force being then and there used on
him. It is important to note that the section does not say that
the force or threat has to be used to the person from whom
the property is stolen. It can be used on any person provided
that it is used "in order to steal." Thus if the accused sees Mr.
and Mrs. A walking along the street, it would be robbery if he
knocked Mr. A unconscious and snatched Mrs. A's handbag.
It is not sufficient that the defendant has simply taken
advantage of a victim by stealing, when the victim has been
rendered powerless by others without any complicity on the
part of the defendant (*Harris* (1988)). The prosecution must,
however, establish that the force was used against a person
though very slight force will suffice. It is enough to constitute
robbery that there is a struggle for possession of the goods

and that A pulls them from B's hands (*Corcoran v. Anderton* (1980)). It is a question for the jury whether in these circumstances the defendant has used force *on the person* in order to steal (*Clouden* (1987)). Before the Theft Act 1968 the law required that the force be used to overpower the victim and prevent his resisting, and not merely to gain possession of the goods stolen. The drafters of the Act intended that this distinction should remain, but the present decision does much to undermine the distinction. Where the defendant has grabbed a bag which has a strap around the victim's shoulder and neck, it is possible to say that the force needed to break the strap will also constitute force applied to the victim's body, but it is surely more akin to pickpocketing than robbery.

The Act, however, says that the force or threat of force must be used immediately before or at the time of stealing, and this raises difficult problems of fact and degree. What does the Act mean by immediately before? If a gang intend to break into a factory and one of the gang knocks out the night-watchman before the main part of the gang break in to steal, this would be robbery. If, on the other hand, they were to threaten the night-watchman with a beating up if he did not draw them a plan of the factory so that they could steal from it a week later, this would not be robbery since force or threat of force was not used immediately before the stealing.

At the other end of the time span, the Act says that the force must be used (immediately before or) at the time of the stealing. Here it is important to remember the other qualification that the force or threat must be used in order to steal. A strict interpretation would mean that once the theft is complete, in the sense that the accused could be charged with the substantive offence of theft, the use of force will not turn the crime into an offence of robbery. For example, if X is a pickpocket and has got his hands round Y's wallet and is in the process of removing it from Y, we have said that since he has now assumed rights of an owner over (*i.e.* appropriated) the wallet the offence of theft is complete even though he has not yet removed it totally from Y. If Y now realises what is being done, resists and is hit in the stomach by X, does this mean that it is not robbery because the force is used after X has stolen the wallet? Could X argue that since the theft was complete the force was not used "in order to steal?" Clearly, the words must be given a wider meaning than "up to the time where there is a completed act of appropriation." Similar problems arise in handling (see below, p. 455), where the phrase "otherwise than in the course of stealing" appears) and presumably a uniform answer should be given. It must be robbery when the accused uses force on the victim to enable him to get the wallet out of his control, or to get the goods off the premises in a bank raid (see *Hale* (1978)). Even though there is already a completed act of theft when the accused assumed the rights of the owner, it would still be robbery if X hit Y to stop him immediately recovering the wallet and the House of Lords decision in *Gomez* on appropriation does not affect the principle that appropriation is a continuing act (see *Lockley* (1995)). Even if there is a complete theft at the instant of appropriation the theft continues at least for the duration of what one might call the transaction in question. On the other hand, if X has got hold of Y's wallet and is running down the street when he is stopped by P.C. Z, force now used on P.C. Z would be after the commission of the theft and would not turn the offence into robbery. "At the time of" committing the theft must be viewed in a common-sense way; the test is whether X can sensibly be said to be stealing the goods when the force is used on Y.

V. BURGLARY AND AGGRAVATED BURGLARY

1. Burglary

Burglary is traditionally thought of as breaking and entering a dwelling-house in the night with intent to steal. It was once so defined and separate provision was made for less serious entries where the building was entered by day or where buildings other than dwellings were entered. All these distinctions have been swept away.

Burglary can now be committed in buildings generally, and nothing turns upon whether the entry (for there is no longer any requirement for a breaking) was during the day or night (except the more alarm the burglars cause the heavier the eventual sentence they may receive). Section 9(1) of the Theft Act 1968 provides for two distinct ways in which burglary may be committed, namely by a person who

> "(a) enters a building or part of a building as a
> trespasser and with intent to commit any such
> offence as is mentioned in subsection (2) below.

(These are stealing from the building or part of the building, inflicting grievous bodily harm on any person therein, raping any woman therein, or unlawfully damaging the building or anything therein), or

(b) having entered any building or part of a building as a trespasser he steals or attempts to steal anything in the building or that part of it or inflicts or attempts to inflict on any person therein any grievous bodily harm."

Burglary is, in effect, a form of aggravated trespass. In both types of burglary the prosecution have to prove that the accused has entered a building (or part of the building) either knowing, or being reckless as to the fact that, he is a trespasser. If the charge is brought under section 9(1)(a) the prosecution must, in addition, prove that at the time he entered the building the accused intended (and here recklessness will not suffice) to commit one of the offences specified in section 9(2) which are listed above. If the charge is brought under section 9(1)(b) the accused must be shown to have actually committed one of the offences specified in paragraph (b) and at the time of committing the offence he either knew that he entered as a trespasser or was reckless as to that fact.

We shall now consider the elements which are common to both forms of burglary, namely (1) entry; (2) trespassing; (3) a building; (4) part of a building.

(1) Enters

In both forms of burglary the prosecution must prove that the accused entered the building as a trespasser. Under section 9(1)(a) they must prove that the accused intended to enter and that at the time he either knew that he was a trespasser or was reckless as to that fact. Under section 9(1)(b) the prosecution must prove that at the time of committing the specified offence he knew that he had entered as a trespasser or was at least reckless as to that fact.

The prosecution must prove that the accused actually entered the building in question. As with many elements of criminal offences this will pose no great problems in the general run of cases since the accused will be apprehended in the building or some days later when he has actually removed property from the building. However, on occasion it may be difficult to say whether or not there has actually been an entry into the building within the meaning of section 9.

There are various possible views as to what constitutes an entry. One view is that entry requires that the accused, A, should be entirely within the building. On this view, if he still had so much as a foot on the window ledge outside the building he would not be guilty of the complete offence though he would be guilty of an attempt. Another view is that A has entered if any part of his body is within the building; on this view A would be guilty should his hand, or even his fingertips, penetrate beyond the door or window. The one case on this point (*Collins* (1973) *Casebook*, Chap. 8) holds that there must be "an effective and substantial" entry which seems to suggest a half-way house between these two views. As a practical test it seems to be less satisfactory than either of the two first suggested tests because it is not clear cut. Whether A's body is entirely within the building or whether any part of his body has penetrated the building, admit of definite answers; but whether enough of his body is within the building so as to constitute an effective and substantial entry must be something on which views may differ. The subsequent decision of the Court of Appeal in *Brown* (1985), in which it was said that "substantial" did not materially assist in the matter, but that a jury should be directed that in order to convict they must be satisfied that the entry was "effective," would appear to add little in the way of clarification to the matter (and see *Ryan* (1996)).

A further complication is introduced where A employs an innocent agent. A might, for example, employ a child below the age of criminal responsibility to enter the building and bring out property to him. In such a case it must be tempting to use the innocent agency principle (above, p. 252) and conclude that this is to be treated as an entry by A himself. Suppose, then, that A, while remaining outside the building, uses some instrument to withdraw property from the building. Is it to be said that, by parity of reasoning, the implement is to be regarded like the boy so that its insertion into the building is to be regarded as an entry by A himself? Since burglary may now be committed when there is an entry with intent to do serious bodily harm, is A guilty of burglary when the bullet from his gun, fired from the highway, enters the victim's house?

If regard is paid to the wording of section 9, it would appear that these last two illustrations cannot constitute burglary. A person is guilty of burglary if "he enters" with certain intents, or "having entered ... he" commits certain offences. To hold that "he" enters or has entered when an instrument is inserted by him would seem to be at odds with what the section expressly requires.

It is further suggested that the natural meaning of the words employed in the section requires a complete entry by A. "Enters" or "having entered" means just that; it can hardly be supposed to mean "being in the process of entering" or "having half-entered." If A is in the process of entering he may always be convicted of an attempt.

Where an innocent agent (the child under the age of criminal responsibility) is employed the same argument should hold good. The "he" referred to in section 9 is the person who is charged with burglary and "he" has not entered the building.

(2) As a Trespasser

"Trespass" is a civil law concept. Essentially it requires entry on to property which is in the possession of another without the consent of that other. At civil law it would not be a defence to show that you had entered by mistake. So does this mean that for purposes of burglary the prosecution need show only that the accused was, by civil law definitions a trespasser? Fortunately the Theft Act seems to be one area in which the courts have adopted a subjective approach and in prosecutions under section 9 the prosecution will have to prove that the accused was at least reckless as to the fact of being a trespasser; in other words he was aware of facts which might mean he was trespassing. If the prosecution is brought under section 9(1)(a) of the Theft Act the prosecution must prove that he was reckless as to being a trespasser at the time he entered the building (see e.g. Laing (1995)). In the case of a prosecution under section 9(1)(b) the prosecution would have to prove that at the time he committed the offence inside the building he then realised that he had entered the building as a trespasser. If the accused mistakenly thinks that he has the consent of the owner to entering, even if his mistake is unreasonable, he should not be convicted; equally if he believes that he is entering his own house, since then he would not even consider the issue of consent. More problematical is the situation where the accused is invited into the house by a person who has no right to give that consent. Again the answer should be that if the accused honestly believes that he has entered with the consent of someone who he believes is entitled to give that consent he should not be convicted. So in Collins (1973) (Casebook, chap. 8) it was held that Collins was not a trespasser where he accepted an invitation from the householder's daughter to enter the house. The case might have been differently decided on this point had Collins known that the householder would not have permitted him to enter. It is instructive to contrast *Jones and Smith* (1976) where the accused and an accomplice were charged with and convicted of burglary, the offence consisting of stealing TV sets from the house of Smith's father. At the trial it was accepted that Smith's father had given his son a sort of blanket permission to enter his house. So how could you say he entered as a trespasser? James L.J. said that the jury were entitled to hold that the son and his friend were trespassing if they found they had entered the premises of another knowing that they were entering in excess of the permission that had been given to them, or being reckless whether they were so entering. Here it is clear that his father's permission to enter did not extend to entry for the purpose of stealing and the son well knew this.

Usually a trespasser enters by stealth but it is by no means unknown for a person to gain entry by tricking the owner into giving his assent to entry. X may, for example, gain entry to Y's house by pretending to be the gas meter reader. In a way he enters not by stealth but with the consent of the owner, but on the other hand he is fully aware that the owner would not have let him in had he known the truth. It is suggested that there should be no difficulty in saying that X entered knowing that he was a trespasser. Does this mean that if X enters a supermarket intending to steal from within, he commits burglary as he enters? X knows that if the shopkeeper knew of his intentions he would not allow him into the shop and his case is thus not really different from the example of the gas meter reader. The major difficulty here is that the jury will have to be sure that he had that intention when he entered the store; this will be difficult to prove unless X is specially equipped for stealing as where, as once happened, an enterprising rogue inserted false arms in the sleeves of his overcoat so that store detectives would not notice what his real arms were doing.

(3) A Building

Under the law before 1969 burglary could only be committed from a dwelling-house. The new Act is not so restricted, and burglary can be committed in a building or part of a building.

Little would be gained here in trying to give an exhaustive definition of what constitutes a building. It is a word generally used to convey some idea of permanence, and probably there is a requirement of a roof, but beyond this no firm guidelines can be given. Clearly burglary can now be committed from such places as offices, barns, garages. A tent, on the other hand, although it may constitute a dwelling is probably not sufficiently permanent to be regarded as a building (see *B. and S. v. Leathley* (1979)).

The Act specifically extends the definition of buildings to cover inhabited vessels or vehicles, including the times when the person who inhabits them is not there. The word "inhabited" does, however, seem to require that the vehicle at the time of the entry is used as a dwelling, and it would not therefore cover an ordinary car or a motorcaravan which is being used as a form of transport at the time. But if a family use their motorcaravan as an ordinary form of transport for 50 weeks in the year but as a holiday home for the other two, it would be an inhabited vehicle for those two weeks. In *Norfolk Constabulary v. Seekings and Gould* (1986) the definition of "building" did not extend to two articulated lorry trailers which for a year were used by a supermarket as temporary storerooms. Although they remained static, with steps attached and with an electricity supply, the court held they were still vehicles and as such they only constituted "buildings" if they were inhabited.

(4) Or Part of a Building

The Act provides that the accused must have entered a building or part of a building as a trespasser. This second part is designed to cover situations where the accused is lawfully entitled to be in one part of the building but not in another. For example if X is a student in a hall of residence he will be entitled to enter his own room and those parts of the hall designed for common use and connecting corridors, but he would not be entitled to enter a fellow student's room without permission. Thus if he goes into student Y's room to steal money from his desk, he would enter Y's room as a trespasser. He has therefore entered a part of the building as a trespasser and thus he would commit burglary as well as theft. One problem arising out of the use of the concept of parts of a building, is that where the prosecution are alleging that the accused has entered part of a building as a trespasser with intent to steal, they must prove that he intended to steal from that part. Suppose that X enters a department store intending only to purchase some gardening equipment. While in the store, where he is legally entitled to be, he conceives a plan to steal money from the manager's office. To reach this office he must first pass through the staff common room which like the manager's office is out of bounds. If X is apprehended in the staff room and confesses that he was on his way to the manager's office can we say that he has entered a part of the building intending to steal in that part, or is the manager's office another part? Possibly the most sensible answer in cases such as these is to treat the building as having two parts—one part where customers are entitled to be, and the other part which is for staff only. If this interpretation is adopted, then as soon as X enters the staff room he has entered a part of the building he is not entitled to enter, and this part includes the manager's office. In *Walkington* (1979) the accused was charged with burglary from a till in a department store. The till was standing on a three-sided counter and the questions for the jury were (1) did the management regard the floor area within the three sides of the counter as being restricted to staff; (2) if the answer to (1) was yes, then did the accused realise that this area was so restricted and (3) if he did, did he enter it with the intent to steal from it?

(5) Mens Rea

Apart from a trespassory entry which has already been considered the offence of burglary requires an intention to commit one of the specified offences. Burglary is no longer confined to cases where the intention is to commit theft and it will be noted that this range of specified offences is wider under section 9(1)(*a*) than under section 9(1)(*b*) (see above, p. 443).

2. Aggravated Burglary

Section 10 of the Theft Act 1968 provides for the offence of aggravated burglary which carries a possible maximum sentence of life imprisonment. A person is guilty of aggravated burglary if he commits any burglary and at the time has with him any firearm, any weapon of offence, or any explosive. Whereas burglary under section 9 is in some senses a form of aggravated trespass, section 10 is designed both to deter would-be burglars from taking offensive weapons with them when they burgle a house and to enable the court to reflect in the sentence the fact that burglary where offensive weapons are carried is a far more serious offence than when they are not.

VI. MAKING UNWARRANTED DEMANDS WITH MENACES: BLACKMAIL

Section 21 of the Theft Act provides:

"(1) A person is guilty of blackmail if, with a view to gain for himself or another or with intent to cause loss to another, he makes any unwarranted demand with menaces; and for this purpose a demand with menaces is unwarranted unless the person making it does so in the belief—

(a)   that he has reasonable grounds for making the demand; and

(b)   that the use of menaces is a proper means of reinforcing the demand."

The word "blackmail" is a word commonly used in everyday language to describe a situation in which X is threatening Y with unpleasant consequences unless Y does what X wants. This is, in fact, the gist of blackmail under section 21, but as we shall see the scope of the offence is somewhat more restricted than the everyday use of the term.

(1) There Must Be a Demand

This will generally present no problems and the word will be given its ordinary meaning. What is required is that the accused acts in such a way as to demonstrate that he wants the victim to do something. It does not matter whether the request is made in the form of an order or a humble plea. The offence is demanding with menaces and so it does not matter whether the request is complied with or even that it was heard, provided that it was made. It is immaterial whether it was made orally or in writing. Where it is made in writing and sent through the post the demand is made as soon as the letter is posted and it continues to be made until it is received. Thus if A posts, in England, a demand to B in America, the demand is made and therefore the offence is committed in England; if the facts are reversed the offence is committed in England at the latest when the letter reaches England (see *Treacy* (1971)).

(2) The Demand Must Be Accompanied by Menaces

This does not mean that there must be a threat of violence; it is sufficient that something detrimental or unpleasant is threatened (*Torne v. Motor Traders Association* (1937)). The use of the word "menaces," however, rather than "threats" suggests that there might be certain threats which would be too trivial to be classed as menaces. In *Garwood* (1987) the Court of Appeal considered threats made by the defendant to a youth the jury considered to be unduly timid. The court held that in the majority of cases the judge would not need to spend time in defining "menaces." However, there were two cases where guidance would be needed. The first was where the threats, although likely to affect the mind of a normal person, did not affect the defendant's; this would clearly amount to "menaces." The second is where the threats are unlikely to have affected the mind of a person of normal stability, but have affected the particular victim because he was unduly susceptible. In this type of case it all depends upon the knowledge of the defendant. If he knows the likely effect of his actions on the victim, then what he has done constitutes menaces. Thus a threat to expose A's sexual perversions would probably influence most stable citizens, but a threat to poison A's pet budgie may be an example of a threat which would only be a menace if the accused knew that A, an old lady, was very timid and devoted to the budgie.

(3) The Demand Must Be Made with a View to Gain for the Maker or Another, or with Intent to Cause Loss to Another

The words gain and loss are defined by section 34(2) of the Act as being restricted to gains and losses in money or other property; the gain or loss may be temporary or permanent. Gain includes a gain by keeping what one has, as well as a gain by getting what one has not; and loss includes a loss by not getting what one might get as well as a loss by parting with what one has. Thus if A threatens to expose B's cheating in an examination if she does not have sexual intercourse with him, this will not be a gain under section 21, but if his demand is for the £50 which she owes him then it will be a demand under section 21 even though the money is legally owed to him. If A threatens to expose B to his wife as an adulterer if she does not get promoted, this would be an offence since she expects to make a monetary gain from the promotion. However, it may be that the monetary gain can become too remote, as where A threatens Professor B that he will expose him as a homosexual if he does not give him a place as a student in the University Law School. Presumably A will be hoping to earn good money with the law degree he will obtain in a few years' time—but it is possible that the court might hold that this monetary gain is too remote.

(4) The Demand Must Be Unwarranted

If the accused raises the issue that the demand was not unwarranted then the prosecution must prove either that the accused did not believe that he had reasonable grounds for making the claim or, if he did, that he did not believe that it was proper to use menaces as a means of reinforcing the demand. In the majority of cases it is likely that the accused will believe that he had reasonable grounds for making the claim. Even a prostitute or bookmaker who knows that the court would not enforce the demand may genuinely believe that they have the right to demand payment for a "debt of honour." It is far more likely that the accused will know that he should not have used menaces as a means of reinforcing the demand. In *Harvey and Others* (1981) the Court of Appeal held that no act which the accused believed to be a crime could be considered by him to be a proper means of enforcing the demand. However, even here, it is for the jury to decide what the accused actually believed. Thus, in practice, the more serious the threat, the less likely the jury are to believe that the accused considered his conduct to be "proper."

VII. HANDLING

When thieves have got away with their stolen property, the next step is to dispose of it. Clearly, if the stolen property is money there will be no difficulty, but where the property is readily identifiable there is every danger that the thief will get caught trying to sell it or use it. It is for this reason that specialist criminals exist whose function is to dispose of the goods for the original thieves. These are the persons regularly known as "fences." In some respects these people are a greater social menace than the original thieves since without them the thieves would have to dispose of the stolen property personally and might find the whole enterprise less attractive and rewarding. Most fences probably commit theft in relation to the property they deal with, but this is not always the case and this fact coupled with the generally accepted need to be able to punish big-time fences more severely than the thieves for whom they act has led to the creation of a separate offence. Until 1968 this was known as "receiving" but under the Theft Act 1968 its scope has been increased and it is now termed "handling." The basic offence is defined by section 22 of the Act which provides:

> "(1) A person handles stolen goods if (otherwise than in the course of the stealing) knowing or believing them to be stolen he dishonestly receives the goods, or dishonestly undertakes or assists in their retention, removal, disposal or realisation by or for the benefit of another person, or if he arranges to do so."

It should be noted that while there are about 18 methods of handling stolen goods outlined in this section, there is only one offence.

1. The Actus Reus of Handling

(1) Stolen Goods

"Goods" for the purposes of section 22 are defined to include "money and every other description of property except land, and includes things severed from the land by stealing" (s.34(2)(b)). Subject to minor exceptions "goods" which may be handled extend to the same property which may be the subject of theft.

Such goods must be "stolen" and for this purpose goods are not only stolen when obtained in circumstances amounting to theft but also when they are obtained by blackmail or by deception contrary to section 15(1) (s.24(4)). Provision is also made for goods stolen abroad which are brought to this country.

Not only must the prosecution establish that the goods were at some time "stolen" as defined in section 24, they must prove that they were "stolen" at the time of the handling. Section 24 provides that goods which may have been "stolen" within the meaning of section 24(4) may cease to be stolen in one of three ways, namely where:

(i)   they have been restored to the person from whom they were stolen; or
(ii) they have been restored to other lawful possession or custody; or

(iii)   the person from whom they were stolen (or anyone claiming through him) ceases to have any right to restitution of the goods.

Other lawful possession or custody in (ii) covers the situation in which the police recover the stolen property. Here and in (i) the major difficulty is to decide when the property has actually been restored either to its owner or to other lawful possession. The problem was considered in *Att.-Gen's Reference (No. 1 of 1974)*. A police officer suspecting, correctly as it turned out, that the goods in the back of a car were stolen, immobilised the car and kept watch for the driver. When the driver arrived the officer questioned him and, because the driver's replies were unsatisfactory, he arrested him. It was held that in such a case the jury should be invited to consider whether the officer had taken custody of the goods before the driver returned or whether he had postponed a decision to take custody until he had the chance of confirming or disaffirming his suspicions by questioning the suspect. Merely to prevent the suspect from having access to the goods until questions are asked is not necessarily to take possession of the goods.

Sometimes the owner, or the police, become aware that A has stolen goods but, with a view to catching the handler as well, follow the goods to their destination. Such conduct by the owner or the police does not constitute a resumption of possession and the receiver may be convicted of handling.

An illustration of property ceasing to be stolen under (iii) would be where X has obtained property from Y under a contract which is voidable because of X's deception. If, when he realises what has happened, Y ratified the contract, he would cease to have any rights in the property and at that stage the property would cease to be stolen.

Section 24(3) contains some rather complex rules concerning the proceeds of stolen goods. Two examples will serve to illustrate the general idea of the section. If X steals a car and then sells that car, the money he receives in exchange will be stolen goods and so will the car. Equally, if the handler of stolen property exchanges it for other property, the newly acquired property will be classified as stolen goods. Where, however, stolen property comes into the hands of someone who is not a thief or handler (for example because he is totally unaware that the property is stolen) then although the property is still stolen property, anything he acquires in exchange for it does not become stolen property.

(2) A Handling

The prosecution must prove that the accused handled the stolen property. While goods may be handled in a wide variety of ways, these ways fall into two groups:

(a) **Received or arranged to receive.** This is the clearest example of handling. If the prosecution allege that the accused received the goods they will have to show that he took them into his possession whether personally or by his agents. It is a question of fact and degree for the jury to decide whether the alleged receiver had possession or control of the goods. If the accused has not actually received the goods and has not yet done enough to be charged with an attempt he may nevertheless have arranged to receive. Thus a typical case of arranging to receive would be where the thief has got in touch with a fence and has arranged to deliver the property to the fence who will then dispose of it.

(b) **Undertakes or assists in their retention, removal, disposal or realisation by or for the benefit of another person, or arranges to do so.** This form of handling casts the net very wide. Assist would seem to suggest a situation in which the accused joins forces with the thief or other handlers and works with them; undertakes, on the other hand, would seem more suitable to cover the situation where the accused has acted on his own. A few illustrations will serve to show how this part of the section works.

X negotiates with Y that Y will buy stolen property from the thief Z. X has undertaken the disposal of stolen goods on behalf of Z.

X helps Y, the thief, store stolen property in a barn where it will stay until the police search dies down. X will have assisted Y in the retention of the stolen goods.

X lends Y, the thief, a van to take the stolen goods abroad. X has assisted Y in the removal of the stolen goods.

The section, however, goes further; if X arranges to do any of the above acts he will also be guilty of handling. Thus, in the first example, if X agreed with Z that he would try to find him a buyer, X has arranged to undertake the disposal of the goods for Z.

Where the prosecutor is relying on forms of handling other than receiving or arranging to receive, he must prove that the acts were done by or for the benefit of another person. In each of the examples discussed above the acts were done by or for the benefit of another. On the other hand the person who steals the goods does not become a handler by disposing of the goods for his own benefit even if some benefit incidentally occurs to another. If A steals a car and sells it to B there will, no doubt, be profit in the transaction both to A and B. But the thief is not a handler because some benefit accrues to B, even if he realises that some benefit accrues to B. The words "for the benefit of another" were inserted to make it clear that a disposal of the goods for the thief's own benefit would not constitute him a handler (*Bloxham* (1982)).

(c) **Otherwise than in the course of the stealing.** All forms of handling are subject to the requirement that the act which constitutes the handling must not be in the course of stealing. If these words were not present, it would mean that if X and Y were to burgle Barclays Bank and X handed Y the money from the safe, Y would be guilty of handling. This phrase is similar to that used in the definition of robbery and it is suggested that it should be given the same interpretation (see above, p. 441). Thus, in our example of X and Y burgling Barclays Bank, the stealing would presumably be deemed to continue until at least they have left the premises and possibly whilst they are making their getaway.

2. Mens Rea of Handling

A person is guilty of handling if he dishonestly receives, etc., the *stolen* goods knowing or believing them to be stolen. Notice that the goods must be proved to be stolen goods at the time of the handling. It is not enough to prove this element of the offence that D believed the goods to be stolen unless there is also evidence, such as the circumstances in which the goods were acquired, which points to the fact that they must have been stolen (*Barnes* (1991)). A person may also believe goods to be stolen even where they are not; such a person cannot be convicted of the completed offence of handling though by virtue of the Criminal Attempts Act 1981 (above, p. 329) he may be convicted of an attempt.

(1) Knowing or Believing that the Goods were Stolen

The expression *knowing or believing* has caused many problems for the courts and the Court of Appeal has shown a great reluctance to give clear guidance to trial judges on the correct way to direct juries on this issue. However in *Hall* (1987) the court said that a person might be said to *know* that goods were stolen when he was told by someone with first-hand knowledge. Belief is something short of this, but not much short. It might be the state of mind of a man who said to himself, "I cannot say I know for certain that those goods are stolen, but there can be no other reasonable conclusion in the light of all the circumstances of all that I have heard and seen." It would even be enough that the defendant had said to himself, "despite all that I have seen and heard, I refuse to believe what my brain tells me is obvious." What will certainly not suffice is a finding that the accused *suspected* that the goods were stolen. Possibly the trial judge will not go far wrong if he follows the statement of Glanville Williams "The preferable view is that [the section] extends the notion of knowledge to the case where the defendant, while lacking explicit information, is virtually certain in his own mind that the fact exists" (*Textbook of Criminal Law* (2nd ed., 1983), p. 875). In *Toor* (1987) the Court of Appeal said that it will often be unnecessary for the trial judge to give a full direction along the lines of *Hall*. However, where in the trial much reference has been made to suspicion, the trial judge should ensure that the jury fully appreciate the meaning of the word "believing" (see *e.g. Brook* (1993)).

(2) Dishonesty

This is a question of fact for the jury though it will normally add nothing to the requirement that the prosecution must prove that the accused knew or believed that the goods were stolen. However, if X received goods knowing that they are stolen, but intending to return them to their true owner, the jury would no doubt find that X was not dishonest.

(3) Proof of Mens Rea

Proving *mens rea* in cases of handling may be difficult. Accordingly, the so-called doctrine of recent possession states that, where the defendant is found to be in possession of recently stolen goods, a jury may infer from that fact that he acquired them knowing or believing that they were stolen. This is really no more than an invitation to the jury to make a common-sense inference from circumstantial evidence. Additionally, section 27(3) of the Theft Act 1968 exceptionally makes evidence of the defendant's past conduct as a handler or a thief admissible to prove *mens rea*. This is unusual because a person's previous criminal record is normally inadmissible at his trial.

Part Three

Contract

Chapter 14

Introduction

When a man gives his word he is expected to keep it, and usually he does. Nor should we be so parochial as to think that it is only the Englishman's word that is his bond because the notion that a pledge is to be honoured is understood and accepted by all people and has been so understood and accepted for many thousands of years.

Up to a point promises are self enforcing; even without the enforcement machinery of a legal system most people would honour their promises most of the time. Apart from the feeling that it is dishonourable not to keep one's word, there is the practical consideration that a person is placed at a serious disadvantage in their dealings with others if they acquire a reputation for being untrustworthy.

But in an ordered and developed society rules need to be created and fashioned to regulate the enforcement of promises. Even if everyone was prepared always to honour their word, and of course there are always numbers who do not, it would still be necessary to establish a legal framework. To say that a man's word is his bond is too simplistic. Both parties may subscribe unreservedly to this maxim but they may legitimately dispute exactly what was promised. A says that he understood one thing by his promise, B claims that he understood something else. A may say that he made his promise not to B, but to C, B may claim that C was acting as his agent so that he, B, may enforce the contract. A may say that he was mistaken about the subject-matter of the contract, B may claim that he was misled by A. So it can be seen from these few examples that even parties acting in complete good faith will have genuine differences of opinion about the interpretation of their contract; the law of contract is fashioned to resolve these differences.

It needs to be noted at this introductory stage that our law does not enforce all promises even if they are seriously made and intended to be binding. English law became imbued, it is not entirely clear why, with the notion that promises were enforceable only so far as they formed part of a bargain. The

461

law is a law of contract not a law of promise. To be enforceable a promise must be "bought." So a promise to sell goods is bought by a promise to pay the price but it must not be thought that promises can only be bought for money. A person may offer one sort of goods in exchange for another, or he may offer services in return for goods or money. These are *bargains* which the law will enforce. But the law will not generally enforce gratuitous promises, that is a promise given for nothing in return. This may seem strange because many (perhaps most) of us would think that a promise seriously given and intended to be binding should be enforceable even though given without any compensating promise from the other party. Keeping my word means keeping my word without thought to some compensating advantage to me. But in English law bargain is fundamental to enforceability and a gratuitous promise is usually enforceable only if it is made in a special solemn form, by deed (see below, p. 484).

In the development of contract law, form has always played an important part. Form may range from a simple handshake to an elaborate ritual accompanying the signing of a treaty of peace. Formalities may be used to give added solemnity to the promise, to make it clear that the promise is not casually given and that a breach of it will be considered a very grave matter. Thus a promise may be reduced to writing and sealed by the party making the promise. As we have just noticed, even a gratuitous promise is enforceable if made by deed; the solemn form may be said to make up for the lack of the bargain usually required. But there is another reason for reducing a contract to writing which is that the parties have a record of its terms and thus avoid the problems which arise from the uncertain recollection of an oral bargain. This is not to say that written contracts do not give rise to difficulties of interpretation but they may have obvious advantages over an oral agreement. If a contract is for the sale of a newspaper or a packet of bacon a written contract would be entirely inapropos and would only hamper daily business; if it is for the sale of an aircraft or for chartering a ship it would be highly unusual for the parties, given the likely complexity of the contract, to rely on an oral agreement.

There is no general requirement under the law that a contract should be in a prescribed form, but to this rule there are exceptions. For example, a lease for three or more years must be made by deed (see below, p. 484.) An important exception is the long-standing requirement, now embodied in section 2 of the Law of Property (Miscellaneous Provisions) Act 1989, that a contract for the sale of land must be in writing, otherwise the agreement is unenforceable. Ironically it is this rule, which was originally intended to discourage fraudulent claims to land, which facilitates the practice of "gazumping." In practice, however, a contract is likely to be reduced to writing whenever the transaction is one of some complexity while routine everyday contracts are concluded by word of mouth, or even by conduct without a word said on either side.

Suppose, then, we take the case of a contract for the sale of goods when the transaction is concluded by the seller wrapping and delivering the goods in exchange for the price. Though not a word is exchanged a valid contract has been concluded. But what are its precise terms? What if the dress is thought by the buyer's wife to be an unsuitable colour, or the shoes pinch when worn, or the pie is mouldy, or the pork when eaten causes trichinosis?

At one time our law took the view that it was for the parties to specify the terms and if the buyer did not bargain for terms warranting the quality of goods then so much the worse for him: *caveat emptor*—let the buyer beware. This view may be acceptable where the parties have equal bargaining strength and deal at arm's length. It is a less attractive view where one party enjoys a bargaining advantage not shared by the other. Another example is provided by contracts of service. In the famous case of *Somersett v. Stewart* (1772) it was held that a slave who was confined to a ship on the Thames about to sail for Jamaica must be set free. In a ringing judgment Lord Mansfield said that slavery was so odious that nothing could be suffered to support it "and therefore the black must be discharged." Yet throughout the Industrial Revolution the courts and the legislature tolerated appalling working conditions for men, women and children at grossly inadequate rates of remuneration. Such practices could be tolerated in the name of freedom of contract and economic policies of laissez-faire, but with the economic power in the hands of the few it would be idle to pretend that the labourer enjoyed any real freedom of contract.

In the context of sale of goods it is significant that the maxim *caveat emptor* called upon the *buyer* to beware with the inference that the seller would be capable of looking after himself. Recognising this imbalance the courts in the nineteenth century began to imply terms, especially in contracts for the sale of goods, to ensure that the buyer got a fair deal. As Lord Ellenborough (*Gardiner v. Gray* (1815)) once put it, it can hardly be supposed that a buyer purchases goods in order to lay them on a dunghill. Consequently terms relating to the fitness and suitability of goods (now to be found in the Sale of Goods Act 1979, below, p. 631) were implied by the courts.

But these implied terms could be expressly excluded. The general rule remained that it was for the parties to make the contract. People (most especially corporate enterprises which by the twentieth century had come to dominate the market for the provision of goods, services and utilities) realised that they could draw up a written contract entirely favourable to them which the consumer had little option but to accept, and no option whatever if the provider enjoyed a monopoly.

Faced with this development, the courts could, and did, construe such contracts strictly, against the party dictating the terms, and showed not a little ingenuity in finding ways of obviating the grosser forms of exemption clause (see below, pp. 511 and 646). But only Parliament could launch the frontal assault necessary to ensure a fair deal for the consumer. This it did in such legislation as the Supply of Goods (Implied Terms) Act 1973, the Consumer Credit Act 1974, the Unfair Contract Terms Act 1977 and the Supply of Goods and Services Act 1982. More recently European law has led to the passing of the Unfair Terms in Consumer Contracts Regulations 1994 which strengthen still further the rights of the consumer across a broad range of everyday transactions. This legislation is examined in more detail below but the broad effect is to ensure that in contracts for the sale and supply of goods, hire-purchase and credit-sale transactions, and in contracts for the supply of services, the consumer's interests are protected. In the field of employment, the restoration of the employee's bargaining position owes more to trade unions than it does to either the courts or Parliament, but legislation now closely regulates conditions of employment, prohibits discrimination, provides for compensation on redundancy and affords remedies for unfair dismissal. The law of landlord and tenant has been similarly revised by Parliament to afford the tenant more security of tenure and a mechanism for ensuring a fair rent.

Thus "freedom" of contract has been progressively constrained by legislative intervention. The broad aim of such legislation, which is to secure reasonable terms for a party who by reason of social and economic circumstances cannot secure them for himself, is clearly an acceptable one though there is always room for argument about the precise details of such legislation. It is against a background of increasing legislative intervention, which shows little sign of diminishing, that the modern law of contract must be viewed.

Chapter 15

Offer and Acceptance

The English law of contact is dominated by the indivisible trinity of offer, acceptance and consideration. That it should have developed in this way was not inevitable, as the rather different approach of Scots law shows. Sometimes the resolution of a factual situation into these classical terms of legal analysis leads to a degree of artificiality which is somewhat out of touch with modern conditions, but then it might be said that any rule of general application will have to cover marginal areas which will not fit readily into a conceptual framework. The problem which the application of these rules does help to solve, however, is essentially one of identity. When and under what circumstances does a legally enforceable contract arise as opposed, for example, to some preliminary discussion or identity of mutual interest which may only later ripen into a fully fledged legal agreement? If I place a "For Sale" notice on the windscreen of my car, at what point am I irrevocably bound to hand it over to a purchaser? What of an auction or tender to carry out work on my house? It is in identifying the point when the contractual bond is finally tied that the basic rules of offer and acceptance come into play.

1. Offer

(1) Offer and Invitation to Treat

Not every "offer" in the sense in which that word is often used will constitute an "offer" for the purposes of contract. In particular, an "offer" needs to be distinguished from an "invitation to treat" (or as it is described in some of the older cases an "offer to chaffer"). In other words the "offer" must show that the offeror intends to be bound by the precise terms of his offer, and is not merely taking a tentative preliminary step towards a later agreement. An illustration of

465

such a mere "invitation to treat" is revealed in *Partridge v. Crittenden* (1968). Mr. Partridge placed an advertisement in a periodical which read, "Bramblefinch cocks, bramblefinch hens, 25s. each." As this bird was a member of a protected species, he was charged with unlawfully offering for sale a wild bird contrary to the Protection of Birds Act 1954. The Divisional Court quashed his conviction on the grounds that this was not indeed an "offer for sale" but a mere "invitation to treat." The business reality that may to some extent lie behind this view is that unless catalogues and advertisements were considered in this way, a supplier would find himself in the embarrassing position of being sued if demand for an article ever exceeded supply.

The same principle is illustrated in a different context in *Pharmaceutical Society of Great Britain v. Boots Cash Chemists (Southern) Ltd* (1953) (*Casebook*, chap. 1). Two customers in a "self-service" shop placed in their wire baskets articles selected from the open shelves. These articles were medicines which it was an offence for Boots to sell except by or under the supervision of a registered pharmacist, who was therefore under instructions to supervise the transaction at the cash desk and if necessary to prevent a customer from removing such an article from the shop. The prosecution case was that the display constituted an "offer" which the customers "accepted" when they put the article in the basket. They alleged a contract was completed at that point, although payment was postponed until the customer reached the cash desk. The Court of Appeal did not agree. They decided that the shelf display was, like an advertisement, merely an invitation to treat. It was the customer who made the "offer" when the article was presented to the cashier. The shop accepted the customer's offer only at the cash desk where a pharmacist was available, and accordingly no offence was committed. The result illustrates the fact that, contrary to what one might have thought, it is the customer who makes an offer which the shopkeeper then chooses either to reject or accept. No-one can demand to buy the contents of a shop.

(2) Offers to the Public at Large

Most offers will be made to particular people on a particular occasion, for example A offers to sell B his car. This will typically be a so-called "executory" agreement, that is, a promise to sell is matched by a promise to buy. Sometimes a promise is exchanged for an act (on which see later), and is known as a "unilateral" contract. There will nevertheless be other occasions, where a unilateral as opposed to executory agreement is involved, when the offeror may not wish to limit his offer to a particular person or persons. In these cases placing an advertisement is likely to be the only way such an offer can in practice be made, and hence such an action will be regarded as an offer and not a mere invitation to treat. The most famous example of this type of offer is in *Carlill v. Carbolic Smoke Ball Co.* (1893) (*Casebook,* chap. 1). The defendants were the sellers of a medical preparation called "The Carbolic Smoke Ball." They placed an advertisement in the *Pall Mall Gazette* stating that they would pay £100 to anyone who used the ball according to their directions, but still contracted influenza. They mentioned that they had also deposited £1,000 with their bankers to show their sincerity in the matter. The plaintiff used the ball as prescribed and contracted flu. She thereupon sued the defendants for her £100. She succeeded. One of the points taken by the defendants was that the advertisement was a "mere puff." The Court of Appeal rejected such an argument and held that this was a true offer. It was an offer made to all the world, which ripened into a contract only with those people who accepted and acted upon the terms of the offer.

It is instructive to note that there was a contract in this case based on the advertisement and the use of the smoke ball even though she had not bought it directly from the defendants.

2. Acceptance

If A offers his car to B for £2000, and B says to A, "I accept," this would clearly have the makings of an enforceable contract. Unfortunately, many cases are not as clear cut as this. Often, for example, there will be protracted negotiations in which it is difficult to ascertain when, if at all, a contract was concluded. Accordingly, the legal rules elucidate how an acceptance can be recognised. There must in fact be an acceptance, although the communication of that acceptance may take various forms.

(1) The Fact of Acceptance

For an acceptance to be valid, it must precisely fit the terms of the offer. If it does not, then it may well be a further step in negotiations, but cannot lead to a firm contract. Sometimes the negotiations are so ambiguous that the existence of a contract can only be inferred from the conduct of the parties, as in *Brogden v. Metropolitan Rail Co.* (1877). After Brogden had supplied the defendant company with coal for a number of years without any formal agreement, the parties decided to regularise the situation and draw up a formal contract. The company sent Brogden a draft agreement, and after inserting what amounted to a new term in the agreement, he returned it marked "approved." The company's agent put the draft in his desk drawer, where it remained for the next two years. It might have stayed there but for the fact that eventually a dispute arose between the parties. The difficult question at issue was to discover when, if at all, there had been mutual consent to the terms of the agreement. Clearly Brogden had not accepted unconditionally the terms of the offer as he had inserted a fresh term. But how could the subsequent delivery of coal be explained except with reference to a contract? The House of Lords therefore decided that an acceptance by conduct could be inferred from the parties' behaviour, and a valid contract came into existence either when the company first ordered a load of coal after the receipt of the draft from Brogden or, at the latest, when he supplied the first load.

Other clear examples of acceptance by conduct are provided by so-called unilateral contracts where, instead of A exchanging a promise with B, B simply does something on the strength of A's promise. *Carlill* (above) is such a case, as are offers of a reward for the return of some article that has been lost. They are further discussed below under problems related to the communication of acceptance.

When a party makes what one might call a qualified acceptance, as did the plaintiff in Brogden, the party is in reality making a counter-offer, the effect of which is to destroy the original offer. So if A offers to sell his car to B for £2,000, and B offers £1,950 for it, then although A and B might be thought close to agreement, as a matter of law there is as yet no contract. The point is illustrated in *Hyde v. Wrench* (1840) (*Casebook*, Chap. 1). Wrench offered to sell an estate to Hyde for £1,000. Hyde made an offer of £950 which the defendant refused. Accordingly Hyde wrote saying that he was prepared to pay the original asking price of £1,000, and sued Wrench in an attempt to enforce the sale at that price. The court rejected the plaintiff's claim. Hyde's counter-offer of £950 had destroyed the original offer; there was therefore no longer any offer in existence which he could subsequently "accept."

Why, therefore, was there a contract in *Brogden v. Metropolitan Rail Co.*, but not in this case? If in *Brogden* the defendants had noticed that the plaintiff had inserted a new term, they could have refused his counter-offer. But they *behaved* as though they had accepted it; Brogden was entitled to assume from their subsequent conduct in taking deliveries that they had accepted his new term. This illustrates the way in which parties can be held bound to a contract by an "objective" view of their actions, that is to say, how their actions would have appeared to a disinterested outsider. This objective approach of the courts is a theme which needs constantly to be born in mind.

A less obvious but similar type of problem has recently been presented by the "battle of forms" cases. Many commercial concerns seek to save time and money by contracting on standard terms which are printed on their own forms. If the parties' terms are identical there is clearly complete agreement, but what if they conflict? This situation arose in *Butler Machine Tool Co. Ltd v. Ex-Cell-O Corp. (England) Ltd* (1979) (*Casebook*, Chap. 1). The seller offered to sell one of their machines to the plaintiff on their standard terms, printed on the quotation, which were stated to prevail "over any terms and conditions in the Buyer's order." The buyer replied by placing an order which was stated to be on their own terms and conditions, which *inter alia* contained a crucial clause as to price in conflict with the seller's terms. The sellers acknowledged receipt of the order on the buyer's form, and a contract was undoubtedly thereupon concluded. The difficulty arose, on whose terms had the contract been concluded? Was it on those of the buyer or the seller's?

The Court of Appeal applied the principle in *Hyde v. Wrench* and held that the buyer's reply on their own form constituted a counter-offer which the plaintiff had accepted by agreeing to supply the goods. Hence, although it will not always be the case, it will often be true that in the "battle of forms" the party who fires the last shot wins.

A difficult problem of construction may sometimes arise to decide whether a reply is a counter-offer or merely a request for information. If it is the latter, then the original offer remains open. The point arose in *Stevenson v. McLean* (1880) (*Casebook*, Chap. 1). The defendant offered to sell iron to the plaintiffs, the offer to be open until Monday. The plaintiffs replied by asking if they might buy the goods on credit. No reply was received, so on Monday afternoon they telegraphed the defendant accepting the offer. By this time the defendant had sold the goods to a third party, and the plaintiffs sued for breach of contract. Although it could be regarded as a marginal case, the court held that this was "a mere inquiry, which should have been answered and not treated as a rejection of the offer." The defendant's offer, therefore, remained open until it had been effectively revoked which, by the time of acceptance, it had not been.

A simple and convenient test for distinguishing between a counter-offer and a mere inquiry has been proposed by Professor Smith, namely: could the "enquiry" be accepted? If not, it can hardly be interpreted as an offer. On the facts of *Stevenson v. McLean*, it is difficult to see how the plaintiffs message could possibly have been accepted, bearing in mind the rather uncertain and general nature of their request.

(2) The Communication of Acceptance

It is not enough that a party has made a mental decision to accept a certain offer. There must be something more, an external indication that the party intends to be bound by the terms of the offer. This is sometimes explained by the statement that English law takes an objective rather than subjective view of the transaction. In other words, the court looks at the matter from the point of view of a disinterested bystander, and draws inferences on the basis of how events would appear to such a person. The way in which such acceptance can be communicated will nevertheless vary greatly according to the circumstances.

(a) *Silence*. It follows from what has been said that silence alone cannot constitute consent, and the authority usually cited to support this proposition is *Felthouse v. Bindley* (1862) (*Casebook*, Chap. 1), the facts of which were earlier outlined (above, p. 6). One way of explaining the case would be to say that there had been no acceptance of the plaintiff's offer, and the action therefore failed. Even though the nephew appeared to have made a mental reservation to sell the horse to his uncle, the failure to communicate this acceptance in some way meant that the contract was never concluded. Contracts generally require agreement and there can hardly be agreement without communication.

(b) *Waiver*. The facts of *Carlill* (above) show that there may nevertheless be circumstances in which the offeror waives the communication of acceptance. In that case the waiver was by implication, since it would clearly be a practical absurdity if everyone on seeing such an advertisement was obliged dutifully to write a letter communicating their acceptance. In other cases, it may be expressed directly by the parties.

Paradoxically, if the nephew today sued the uncle in *Felthouse v. Bindley* (above) it seems likely he would succeed. The uncle had clearly waived the need for communication of acceptance. The result in the case itself could also, and perhaps better, be explained by the fact that there was in 1861, although not now, a requirement that the sale of goods above a certain value required the agreement to be evidenced in writing. On the facts there was just insufficient evidence of such a written memorandum between the uncle and the nephew.

(c) *Ignorance of the offer.* What if someone does an act which in fact complies with the terms of an offer, although he is unaware of such an offer? For example, if an insurance company offers £100 for information leading to the conviction of a criminal, and a member of the public supplies it in ignorance that any reward was made, can he claim the money? In principle the answer would appear to be No. The underlying rationale of the rules of offer and acceptance is that there should be an agreement, and agreement hardly seems possible when the respective parties are mutually ignorant of each other's intention. There is no clear English authority on the matter. It was a slightly different issue that arose in *Williams v. Carwardine* (1833). The defendant had offered a reward for information leading to the discovery of a certain murderer, and handbills were posted in the area where the plaintiff lived declaring the fact. The plaintiff apparently knew of the offer, but gave the information for a different reason. She believed she had only a short time to live and wished to ease her conscience. It was held that she was entitled to the reward. She had complied with the terms of the offer, of which she was aware, and her motive was not material. Had she completely forgotten the reward at the time she gave the information then the result might well have been more difficult to justify, as the Australian decision in *R. v. Clarke* (1927) indicates. In that case the defendant's only object in giving the information was to clear himself of a murder charge, and at the time he had no intention of claiming the reward. The Australian court accordingly dismissed his claim. The borderline between these two cases is obviously a thin one.

(d) *Prescribed communication.* Whilst an offeror may waive communication of acceptance altogether, he may also on the other hand prescribe the way in which it is to be made. If the offeror made it clear that one and only one method of acceptance was possible, for example telephoning at a precise time and date, then it seems that any other purported mode of acceptance would be invalid. What of the case, however, where A prescribes that B should reply immediately by letter, but B replies a day earlier by fax instead? It would seem absurd to say that there was no contract in this situation. The general principle would seem to be that if the offeree accepts in the prescribed mode or a manner equally efficacious or better, then the offeror should be bound.

(e) *No prescribed mode of communication.* Where no particular means of communication has been prescribed, then the form of acceptance will depend entirely on the circumstances in which the offer is made. If, to adopt the examples given by Lord Denning in *Entores Ltd v. Miles Far East Corporation* (1955) (*Casebook*, chap. 1), A shouts an offer to B across a river, and does not hear B's reply because of the noise from a passing aircraft, then no contract is concluded. B will have to repeat his reply so that A can hear it. Equally if B's reply is inaudible because of interference on a telephone line, there is no contract until B has made an effective reply.

(f) *Acceptance by post.* Very commonly the medium of communication will be the post, and the courts have inevitably developed a set of rules which regulate the moment at which acceptance takes place. The almost insoluble dilemma which has to be solved is to balance on the one hand the offeror's need to know whether he is bound by the offeree's acceptance, and the latter's need to know that he had done enough to comply with the offer and can therefore rely on it. The courts' response has been to lay down a rule on the basis of convenience rather than principle. The general rule is that an acceptance by post takes effect as soon as it is posted, and was established in *Adams v. Lindsell* (1818). On September 2, 1817 the defendants wrote to the plaintiffs offering to sell a quantity of wool and requiring an answer "in course of post." Unfortunately the defendants misaddressed the letter which consequently did not arrive until the evening of September 5. The plaintiffs posted a reply the same evening which reached the defendants on September 9. It appeared from the evidence that a properly addressed letter would have elicited a reply "in course of post" by September 7. The defendants, having heard nothing at that time, sold the wool to a third party on September 8. The crucial question in the case was whether a contract had been concluded before the sale to the third parties on September 8. The court held that a contract was concluded as soon as the acceptance was posted. Various views have been advanced as to the theoretical basis of the court's decision. The court may have been influenced by the consideration that it was the defendant's fault that the letter had been misaddressed, and that they should therefore bear the burden of any loss. It remains true, however, that any solution to the problem would have tended to operate harshly against one of the parties, and as a practical matter, it is easier to prove the posting of a letter than its receipt, or that it has in fact been brought to the attention of the offeror. What if the letter of acceptance to the offeror has been misaddressed? Although, curiously enough, there is no direct authority on the point, it would seem reasonable to assume that under those circumstances the normal postal presumption would not apply. Acceptance might then be effective, if at all, only when the wrongly directed letter is actually received.

The logical development of this rule can work very harshly against the offeror as was shown in *Household Fire, etc. v. Grant* (1879). In this case the letter was lost in the post and never delivered. Nevertheless, it was still held to be an effective and binding acceptance. "Posting" means placing the letter in a postbox or into the hands of a Post Office employee authorised to receive letters. It is not "posting" if the letter is merely placed in the hands of a postman authorised to deliver letters as happened in *Re London and Northern Bank, ex p. Jones* (1900).

Telegrams were treated similarly to letters. Communication by telex (and now, no doubt, fax) being almost, if not quite completely, instantaneous has been treated by the courts as more akin to a conversation, either direct or by telephone. Consequently, in *Brinkibon Ltd v. Stahag Stahl* (1982) the House of Lords approved the earlier Court of Appeal decision in *Entores Ltd v. Miles Far East Corporation* (1955) and decided that acceptance, as a general rule, takes place when the acceptance was received and not when it was sent. The underlying rationale would seem to be that once a telegram had been dictated or handed to the Post Office, nothing further could be done to ensure its delivery. In the case of telephone or telex it should be immediately obvious to the sender of a message if something has gone wrong in its despatch, and so it is only sensible that it is the sender's duty to ensure that any ambiguity or failure in the message is immediately corrected.

In order to prevent the offeror being unfairly prejudiced the operation of the postal rules is subject to the consideration that the post must be a means of communication which in all the circumstances is reasonable. Clearly, if an offer comes by post, it is reasonable to employ the post to reply. If the offer was made orally by a next-door neighbour the post would hardly seem appropriate. An intermediate situation was posed in *Henthorn v. Fraser* (1891–94). The plaintiff lived in Birkenhead, and the defendant was based in Liverpool. The defendant handed him an offer in Liverpool, which the plaintiff accepted by posting a letter from Birkenhead. It was held in this case that, even though the offer was not made by post, because the parties lived in different towns the use of the post to reply must have been within their contemplation. The contract came into being as soon as the plaintiff posted the acceptance.

If a party did not wish to be bound by the postal rules, it would always be possible to spell this out expressly. There may undoubtedly be other circumstances when, even if it is not so stated directly, it is quite apparent that the parties did not intend the postal rules to apply. In that case whatever the parties themselves envisaged will have to be complied with.

A difficult point is raised if B accepts A's offer by post, but then changes his mind and telephones A seeking to withdraw. Can B escape from the contract? Surprisingly, there is no authoritative English decision on the point. In principle it would seem that the contract is concluded, and that it is therefore too late to decline the offer. On the other hand, does permitting withdrawal in this situation lead to either party being put at a disadvantage, since A will not yet know of the "acceptance?"

3. Termination of Offer

Quite apart from the obvious case of an outright refusal, and the more difficult problem of a counter-offer which has been discussed above, there are a number of ways in which an offer may lapse.

(1) Revocation

It has long been the law that an offer may be revoked at any time before acceptance, but that the revocation must be effectively communicated to the offeree. It is not enough that A has simply changed his mind about contracting with B. In *Byrne v. Van Tienhoven* (1880) (*Casebook*, Chap. 1) the defendants in Cardiff posted a letter to New York offering to sell the plaintiffs 1,000 boxes of tinplates. On October 8 they posted a letter revoking the offer. On October 11 the plaintiffs received the first letter and immediately telegraphed their acceptance. The second letter eventually arrived on October 20. It was held that the revocation came too late. The postal rules apply only to acceptance, not to an offer, and by the time the second letter reached the plaintiffs a contract had already been concluded.

Although the revocation must actually be communicated to the offeree, it seems that the information does not have to come from the offeror himself. In *Dickinson v. Dodds* (1876) the defendant made an offer to sell a house for £800, "to be left over until Friday, June 12, 9 a.m." On Thursday, June 11, the defendant sold the house to a third party, Alan. The plaintiff came to know of the sale through a fourth man. Before 9 a.m. on June 12 the plaintiff handed the defendant a letter purporting to accept the original offer. The Court of Appeal held that the offer had already been revoked, and there was no contract. Dickinson, it was said, "knew that Dodds was no longer minded to sell the property to him as plainly and clearly as if Dodds had told him in so many words." The case could give rise to difficulties. What if the offeree had merely heard a rumour that the property was no longer for sale? It seems that the question of whether the information was inconsistent with the continued existence of an offer would have to be considered as a question of fact in each case as it arose.

(2) Revocation in Unilateral Contracts

A special difficulty arises in the case of unilateral contracts. If before anyone had had a chance to purchase a smoke ball in *Carlill* an advertisement had appeared stating that the whole offer was a meaningless publicity stunt then no great harm is done. But suppose A offers B £10,000 to walk from John O'Groats to Lands End, the money to be paid over when the walk is completed. Just as B is limping through Truro, A says that he is revoking his offer. Since it is generally assumed that in cases such as these there is no acceptance until the act is completed, and a revocation can be made at any time prior to acceptance, it might seem that A is within his rights in so acting. There does not seem to be a completely satisfactory solution to the problem, but in *Errington v. Errington* (1952) an attempt was made to mitigate the injustice of such a rule. A father let his son and daughter-in-law live in a house which he had purchased with the aid of a building society mortgage. He told them that if they paid off the mortgage instalments the house would then be conveyed to them. They paid the instalments as they became due even though they did not bind themselves to do so. The father later died and his personal representatives sought to withdraw the offer. The Court of Appeal held it was too late. Lord Denning explained this by saying, "The father's promise was a unilateral contract—a promise of the house in return for their act of paying instalments. It could not be revoked by him once the couple entered on performance of the act, but it would cease to bind him if they left it incomplete and unperformed, which they have not done." This suggests that partial performance can amount to acceptance of the contract, although complete performance is the necessary consideration (consideration is considered later in Chapter 16). If this view is correct, then A's purported revocation in Truro would also come too late if B were minded to go on to Lands End. Such an approach also gains support from the *obiter dicta* of the Court of Appeal in *Daulia Ltd v. Four Millbank Nominees Ltd* (1978).

(3) Lapse of Time

If an offer is stated to be open for a specific period, then clearly it will lapse after that time. When no period has been laid down then the offer will lapse after a reasonable time. Quite what a reasonable time will be depends entirely on the circumstances of the case. An offer to sell fruit which will deteriorate is likely to lapse more quickly than that relating to a piece of antique furniture (see, *e.g. Ramsgate Victoria Hotel v. Montefiore* (1866)). There may be difficult questions of fact in between these extremes. The problem is closely related to the earlier discussion of the mode of acceptance which the parties contemplated. If the offeror uses the telephone or telex as a means of communication, a reply by letter might well be thought to be defeated by the fact that the offer has lapsed.

(4) Failure of a Precondition

An offer, just like an acceptance, may be conditional. Consequently if the condition fails, then there is no offer capable of acceptance. The point arose in *Financings Ltd v. Stimson* (1962). The defendant, in effect, made an offer to a Finance Company that they should purchase a car. Before the company accepted the car was stolen and badly damaged. In ignorance of this, the Finance Company signed the agreement. It was held that no contract had been concluded. As Donovan L.J. said: "There must ... be implied a term that until acceptance the goods would remain in substantially the same state as at the date of the offer; and I think that is both good sense and good law."

(5) Death

The effect of death is more ambivalent in law than in life. It is not the case that an offer automatically ceases with the offeror's death. It seems that the precise effect varies with the subject matter of the contract. If the offer is to provide a service such as performing at a concert, which only the particular person can provide, then the offer must lapse on death. But in the case of something that is not "personal" to the offeror, for example an offer to sell a chair, then if the offeree is unaware of the offeror's death there seems no reason why a contract is not concluded which can be satisfied from the deceased's estate. A contract of guarantee was held not to be invalidated by the death of the offeror in *Bradbury v. Morgan* (1862). There appears to be no English authority on the corresponding effect of the offeree's death, but the prevailing view appears to be that the offer would then lapse.

4. Certainty

A contract assumes that there has been agreement on the central issues of the bargain, and clearly if the "agreement" is in such ambiguous terms as to be without real meaning, or if issues vital to a complex commercial arrangement have been left unspecified, then there has been no true consensus. In effect the parties are still negotiating. One could analyse such a failure in terms of offer and acceptance; in other words an unambiguous offer has not been met by a clear and unqualified acceptance. Since, however, the failure of certainty might equally effect "offer" or "acceptance" it is convenient to consider it as a separate issue.

At one extreme a provision that a sum of money should be paid if a horse proved "lucky" was held to be too vague to be enforceable in *Guthing v. Lynn* (1831). A less obvious case was *Scammell v. Ouston* (1941) where Ouston wished to acquire a van from Messrs. Scammell "on hire-purchase terms." The House of Lords decided that notwithstanding the courts desire to uphold a bargain if in truth there was one, these terms were too vague to signify an agreement. There were many different permutations on "hire-purchase terms" and it was impossible to say what precisely, if anything, had been agreed. In other words, the parties were still negotiating. Similarly an agreement to negotiate cannot constitute a legally binding contract. It simply lacks the necessary degree of certainty and, as a practical matter, it would be impossible for the courts to force people to negotiate through to an agreement with each other (see *Walford v. Miles* (1992)). On the other hand an agreement *not* to negotiate with third parties for a fixed period of time is sufficiently unambiguous to be enforceable, as happened in *Pitt v. P.H.H. Asset Management Ltd* (1993). A buyer might, for example, wish to be certain that something requiring an expensive survey will not be sold before he has had a chance to consider the results of the survey.

In *Hillas v. Arcos* (1932), however, the House of Lords upheld an agreement where Hillas had contracted to buy timber from Arcos for the season 1930, stated to be "of fair specification," with a further option to purchase the following year. The further option contained no specific references to the kind or size of timber, but the House of Lords decided that having regard to the parties' previous course of dealings and "the legal implication in contracts of what is reasonable" that the terms used were sufficiently certain. Wherever possible, as Lord Tomlin observed, the courts are anxious not to "incur the reproach of being the destroyer of bargains." This approach is shown in the later case of *Nicolene Ltd v. Simmonds* (1953) where an agreement to purchase steel was couched in perfectly clear terms except for a reference to the fact that the transaction was subject to "the usual conditions of acceptance." It was found that this phrase was quite meaningless as there were no such conditions. That being so the reference could be ignored. Otherwise, any insertion of meaningless words would effectively allow defaulters to escape from their contractual obligations.

5. Auctions, Tenders and the Sale of Land

The general rules applying to auctions, tenders and the sale of land are no different from those that apply to any contract. Their precise application in these circumstances, however, requires some elucidation.

(1) Auctions

Normally the two parties to an auction sale are the bidder and the owner of the goods who is simply making use of the auctioneer's services.

An advertisement that an auction is to take place at a certain time is not an offer which those who attend at the specified time thereby accept. This was decided in *Harris v. Nickerson* (1873), where the plaintiff failed to recover damages for travelling to an auction which was subsequently cancelled. The effect of the advertisement was merely a declaration of intention, not a contractual promise. At an auction it is the bidder who is the offeror, each bid effectively revoking the previous one, and it is the auctioneer who accepts the offer by the fall of the hammer or in any other customary way (Sale of Goods Act 1979, s.57(2)). The result is that up until the moment of acceptance the bidder is free to retract his bid, as is the auctioneer to withdraw the item from sale. It is different where the sale is advertised "without reserve," that is a sale where an item does not have a minimum reserve price below which it will not be sold. In *Warlow v. Harrison* (1859) it was said that the auctioneer makes an offer that the lot will go to the highest bidder, and the bidder making his bid relying on this, accepts. There is thus a contract quite separate to the main agreement, for breach of which an action will lie against the auctioneer. If this is the case, it is strange that if no sale at all took place he could not be sued, the basis of *Harris v. Nickerson* (above), but this approach was implicitly approved by the decision of the House of Lords in *Harvela Investment Ltd. v. Royal Trust Co. of Canada Ltd* (1985). Here the sellers of shares in a company sent telexes to two prospective purchasers stating. "We confirm that if the offer made by you is the highest offer received by us we bind ourselves to accept ... " Both prospective purchasers then made bids to buy the shares. Although this was not an auction it can be seen that it presented a somewhat analogous situation. The House of Lords' analysis of the telexes sent by the sellers was that this constituted an offer under a unilateral contract which would become binding upon them by the buyer's act of submitting the highest bid. This would then be followed by a bilateral contract between the seller and the highest bidder for the transfer of the shares.

A further issue raised by the case is relevant to the discussion of Tenders (below). One of the two bids made for the purchase of the shares was a "referential bid" or a bid formed by reference to other bids. In this case one of the purchasers tendered "$101,000 in excess of any other offer." The court rejected this ingenious stratagem as an invalid offer which was inconsistent with the purpose of a sale by fixed bidding, which is to provoke the best price from purchasers regardless of what others might be prepared to pay. Any other decision would also have had an unacceptable practical result. If everyone had made referential bids it would have been impossible to ascertain any offer; if only one party had made such a bid then, in reality, no other party would have had a valid opportunity to have his bid accepted.

(2) Tenders

If A asks B, C and D to tender, for example, to supply coal to a hospital for the next 12 months, then clearly A is not making an offer. He is merely inviting B, C and D to make offers to him. If A accepts B's offer, then the precise legal effect will depend upon what sort of tender is involved. If it is to supply 100 tons on July 1, then clearly A and B are bound to pay and deliver respectively at the due date as soon as A accepts B's offer. If the tender was to supply up to a maximum of 100 tons "if and when" required, then the result is quite different. B has made what is called a standing offer. A may order no coal at all, or spread delivery over several instalments. Each time A places an order, he accepts B's offer, and a separate contract is concluded on each occasion. An example of such a transaction is contained in *Great Northern Rail Co. v. Witham* (1873). The result is that B is bound to supply within the terms of the offer as required, but revocation is always possible prior to acceptance by A.

Someone who invites tenders is not generally under any obligation to accept any of them. An offeree might consider properly, or even quite capriciously, that none of the tenderers would be a suitable or competent contractor. This statement must, however, be qualified by what has already been said in (1), above. It also requires examination in the light of the decision in *Blackpool and Fylde Aero Club Ltd v. Blackpool Borough Council* (1990). In that case the council sought tenders for a concession to operate flights from their airport. The invitations were directed to a few selected parties who were to reply in the envelopes provided. These envelopes, not bearing any identifying mark, were to be returned to the Town Hall by a certain deadline under an ordered and familiar procedure. The plaintiff returned his bid before the deadline but the council mistakenly thought it had arrived late, refused to consider it and awarded the contract to one of the other parties. The Court of Appeal upheld the plaintiff's claim against the council for breach of contract. True, the council was not obliged to accept any tender at all. On the other hand, the terms of their invitation amounted to an offer or contractual promise, which was accepted by anyone who submitted a tender on time and in accordance with the council's terms, that the council would at least *consider* all properly communicated tenders on an equal footing. This amounted to a unilateral contract which the council had clearly breached.

(3) Land

Although land is bought and sold in principle like any other commodity, the application of the rules of contract to its transference are dealt with by the courts in a rather strict manner. Most importantly section 2 of the Law of Property (Miscellaneous Provisions) Act 1989 requires that a contract for the sale of an interest in land must be made in writing. Any oral understanding will not therefore constitute a legally enforceable agreement. This is the reason why "gazumping" is not necessarily unlawful.

In negotiations for the sale of land it is common to find the phrase "subject to contract." This is a well understood form of words to denote the fact that neither party is bound, even where for example their arrangement has been recorded in writing, unless and until a definitive formal contract is executed. Hence the phrase "Sold subject to contract" or "I accept subject to contract" has no binding effect whatsoever. Although the phrase is most commonly found in the context of land, it can be used in any other form of contract, but if an alternative formula is used, there may be a difficulty of construction over its legal effect.

6. Two Problem Cases

(1) Cross Offers

What if A offers to sell his car to B for £900 and B offers to buy it for £900, and the letters cross in the post? Do these cross offers constitute a contract? The point has never been decided but there are *obiter dicta* in *Tinn v. Hoffman* (1873) which suggest there is no contract. Although the parties are, unknown to each other, in a sense *ad idem*, they are making offers without reference to each other. This seems to offend against the orthodox view that there must be an offer by one party followed by an acceptance from another. Lord Denning has recently said in *Gibson v. Manchester City Council* (1979) that (on the facts of that case) there was, "no need to look for a strict offer and a strict acceptance. You should look at the correspondence as a whole and at the conduct of the parties, and see therefrom whether the parties have come to an agreement on everything that was material." In the case of cross offers there does appear to be a mutual intention to contract on identical terms in respect of the same subject matter. If the courts were to take Lord Denning's broad approach, would not cross offers lead to a contract?

(2) The "Satanita"—The Fringes of Offer and Acceptance

A classic example of another area at the fringes of the concept of offer and acceptance is provided by the case of *Clarke v. Dunraven* (1897). Two yacht owners entered a race and undertook in a letter to the club secretary to obey the rules. These club rules contained an obligation to pay "all damages," caused by fouling. The "Satanita," whilst manoeuvring, fouled and sank the "Valkyrie." The owner of the Valkyrie sued the defendant who claimed that he was only liable to pay the lesser damages laid down for such an eventuality by a statute. The plaintiff claimed that, by entering the competition in accordance with the rules, a contract had been created between the competitors which obliged him to pay "all damages." Was there a contract between the two owners? The House of Lords answered in the affirmative. A contract was created when they entered for the race, or at least when they sailed. Each competitor had accepted the rules as binding on each other.

It is far from easy to analyse the case in terms of the conventional doctrine of offer and acceptance, although the courts upheld the contract. It is perhaps an illustration of the way in which the courts are prepared in problem cases to descend to some degree of artificiality to produce a result that satisfies the requirement to find a binding agreement. Both in regard to what has been said already, and in the ensuing discussion of consideration, it is important to have in mind Lord Wilberforce's statement in *New Zealand Shipping Co. Ltd v. A.M. Satterthwaite & Co. Ltd* (1975, P.C.) that: " . . . English Law, having committed itself to a rather technical and schematic doctrine of contract, in application takes a practical approach, often at the cost of forcing the facts to fit uneasily into the marked slots of offer, acceptance and consideration."

Chapter 16

Consideration

In addition to offer and acceptance English law requires the presence of consideration and an intention to create legal relations before it will enforce an agreement as a binding contract. The latter will be considered in Chapter 17, but we now need to consider the former since it bears a specialised legal meaning which our ordinary use of the term "consideration" does not always reveal.

The term consideration was defined in *Currie v. Misa* (1875). It was there stated that: "A valuable consideration in the sense of the law may consist either in some right, interest, profit or benefit accruing to one party, or some forbearance, detriment, loss or responsibility given, suffered or undertaken by the other." The same idea is expressed more concisely if less comprehensively by Patteson, J. in *Thomas v. Thomas* (1842) where he declares: "Consideration means something which is of value in the eye of the law, moving from the plaintiff; it may be some detriment to the plaintiff or some benefit to the defendant." The terms "benefit" and "detriment" themselves bear in this context a less than obvious interpretation. The benefit and detriment can be very slight, and are often merely alternative ways of describing the same thing from different view points. For example, A offers to buy B's car and B accepts saying that he will bring it to A the next day. If B fails to deliver the car, A can sue B even though no payment has yet been made by A. A's promise to pay B for the car is a benefit to B and a detriment to A. The law would thus regard such a promise as valuable consideration. However, as we shall see, if A had merely offered 50p for the car and B had accepted this would still be sufficient to complete the contract.

The existence of the concept of consideration is one which at various times has been criticised by the courts. Doubtless this is due partly to the distaste felt at relieving parties from obligations following promises which might be thought binding in conscience, and partly due to the fact that there is a high degree of artificiality in certain marginal applications.

483

The rationale behind the legal requirement for consideration can be expressed as the need for a *quid pro quo*. In other words, central to the English law of contract is the need for a bargain and the law will rarely enforce a gratuitous promise. There must be something in return for which an offer or promise is made. That "something" is the required element of consideration. The fact that the adequacy of the consideration will not be inquired into reflects the historical reluctance of the courts to inquire into bargains once they have been made by the parties.

A distinction encountered in reading the cases is made between "executory" and "executed" consideration. In a bilateral contract, in other words a contract where there is a promise in exchange for a promise, the consideration is said to be executory. The promise itself is the consideration, and is "executory" in the sense that it has yet to be fulfilled. "Executed" consideration arises in the case of a so-called unilateral contract where there is a promise for an act or a forebearance to do something. Typically this might be the case of a reward. For example, A offers £10 for the return of his lost dog. If B returns it, then his act is the response to A's offer and the complete act of returning the vagrant animal is the executed consideration. The detriment to B in returning the dog, and the benefit to A in receiving it, has actually been carried out. The consideration in this case is executed.

1. Agreement By Deed

There is a separate category of agreement, where there is no obvious consideration, which is nevertheless enforceable. This exception to the general requirement is a so-called agreement "by deed," formerly also known as an agreement "under seal." This is described as a "formal" contract or a contract of "specialty," whereas every other type of contract is described as a "simple" contract. The formalities for executing a deed are laid down by section 1 of the Law of Property (Miscellaneous Provisions) Act 1989 and typically require a formal document to be signed in the presence of another witness who attests the signature.

The reason for such a class of document is typically to give binding legal effect to what might otherwise be a gratuitous gift unenforceable for lack of consideration. If A promises B that he will give B £100 next week, B cannot compel payment if A subsequently refuses. It is otherwise if the declaration is made "by deed." It is perhaps easier to regard such a transaction as not so much an exception to the need for consideration, as an example of a *sui generis* legal device which produces the consequences of a contract without necessarily containing all the ingredients. Declarations of trust are frequently made by deed.

2. Sufficiency and Adequacy of Consideration

In normal speech most people would not draw a distinction between the meaning of "sufficient" and "adequate" but the law of contract does. Whilst the word "adequate" has acquired no precise legal connotation, "sufficient" is used in a technical way to describe consideration which the law considers sufficient to form the basis of a contract. If in the example already mentioned A pays B 50p for the car, no-one in all probability would regard this as an adequate consideration. It would nevertheless be "sufficient" consideration in law. The law merely seeks the presence of *some* consideration; it does not seek to rectify a bad bargain made by the parties. So in *Thomas v. Thomas* (1842) the defendants agreed with the plaintiff that she could live in her deceased husband's house provided she paid £1 a year and kept the house in good repair. This was held to be sufficient consideration to enable the plaintiff to succeed in an action for breach of contract.

In the bizarre case of *Bainbridge v. Firmstone* (1838) (*Casebook*, Chap. 2) the plaintiff, at the defendant's request, allowed him to weigh two boilers. The defendant agreed to return the boilers in perfect condition, which he failed to do. The plaintiff sued and the defendant claimed there was no consideration for the promise to return the boilers in perfect condition. The court, however, held that the plaintiff had suffered detriment in parting with his boilers, but in any event the defendant had obtained a benefit by being enabled to weigh them. The court was not concerned to investigate what this agreed benefit actually was. The omission to do so, though clearly correct in principle, has done nothing to assuage the curiosity of generations of law students who have wondered why anyone should want to weigh someone else's boilers. A further illustration of the disparity between adequate and sufficient consideration is provided by the reasoning in *Chapell & Co. Ltd v. Nestle* (1960). Nestle's offered a record for sale at a price of 1s. 6d. plus three wrappers from their 6d. bars of chocolate. When the wrappers were received by Nestle's they were thrown away. It was still held that they were part of the consideration for the contract between the record buyers and the chocolate manufacturers. It would logically follow that if these wrappers could be part of the consideration they could just as easily in an appropriate case be the entire consideration.

3. Consideration must Move from the Promisee

In the typical case of a breach of contract the plaintiff (the promisee) will be suing the defendant (the promissor) for a failure to honour the defendant's promise in some way. To succeed he must prove that consideration moved from (that is to say, was provided by) him. To have a different rule would, it might be thought, enable someone to obtain the benefit of a "gift" rather than the earned consequence of a "bargain." Hence if A, B and C agree that B will mow A's lawn in return for C giving him £10, then this agreement cannot be enforced by A. He has provided no consideration.

A similar example is provided by the facts of *Tweddle v. Atkinson* (1861) (*Casebook*, Chap. 7). William Guy and John Tweddle agreed with *each other* that they would each provide a sum of money for William Tweddle. Guy died without having paid and so William Tweddle sued his executors. The court held that his action must fail as he was "a stranger to the consideration." In a sense he failed on two grounds, both that he had not provided consideration, and that he was not even the promisee. He was to benefit from the agreement, but he was not the person to whom the promise was actually made.

This case raised a further issue which will be dealt with later, the question of privity (see Chapter 21). It is generally stated that a person who is not a party to an agreement cannot sue on it. Some writers have sought to separate this doctrine from the rule that consideration must move from the promisee. Others, it is thought more realistically, regard the two concepts as different ways of describing the same thing. If the promisee cannot enforce an obligation when there is lack of consideration, then *a fortiori* it cannot be done by someone who is not even a party to the agreement.

4. Past Consideration

It is generally stated that past consideration is not sufficient. It would perhaps be more accurate to say that it is no consideration. It is, however, important not to confuse this with executed consideration discussed earlier. In the case of returning the lost dog, then when B meets A it is true that the consideration is in the past. Nevertheless the law regards this as valid, because it was not "in the past" when A's original offer was made and on which B relied and acted.

A classic illustration of the rule is the old case of *Roscorla v. Thomas* (1842) (*Casebook*, Chap. 2). The defendant had sold the plaintiff a horse without, it seems, any warranty that it was a sound animal. Subsequently, the defendant claimed that it was "sound and free from vice." It seems that this somewhat overstated the horse's virtue, and the plaintiff sued. It was held that the promise was not supported by fresh consideration, and the action therefore failed. If the plaintiff had bought the horse after the statement then the result would have been different. As it was, the only consideration was the "past consideration" of the sale which had already taken place and was over.

A modern illustration of the same principle is *Re McArdle* (1951), where a man left his house in his will to his wife for life, then to his children. While the mother was still alive the son and daughter-in-law lived in the house and spent money improving it. Later the other children signed a document in which they stated: "in consideration of your carrying out certain alterations and improvements to the property, we hereby agree that the executors shall repay to you from the estate, when distributed, the sum of £488 in settlement of the amount spent on such improvements." The Court of Appeal held that the document did not produce a binding contract. When the letter was signed, the work had already been done. It was therefore "past consideration."

A different situation arises if the act was carried out at the request of the promissor, and the situation is such that it can be assumed that payment was all along contemplated for the act. It seems misleading to describe these cases as ones where past consideration is sufficient. Rather the cases seem to be rationalised upon the assumption that the act was always effectively a response to the promissor's original request.

In *Lampleigh v. Braithwait* (1615), Thomas Braithwait had killed a man and asked Anthony Lampleigh to obtain a pardon for him from the King. Lampleigh went to considerable trouble at his own expense "riding and journeying to and from London and Newmarket." Doubtless buoyed up by the euphoria of absolution, Braithwait promised him £100. He failed to pay and Lampleigh sued. The court gave judgment for the plaintiff and explained that whilst "a mere voluntary courtesy" would not have led to liability, the fact that the services were performed at the request of the defendant with, apparently, the tacit assumption that they would be paid for rendered the transaction a valid contract. A modern illustration of the principle is to be found in *Re Casey's Patents, Stewart v. Casey* (1893). A and B owned certain patent rights. They wrote to C saying that, in consideration of his services in relation to the patents, they would give him a one-third share of them. Later they claimed that, as their promise was made in relation to C's past services, it was "past consideration" and therefore invalid. The court, however, took the view that the services were always meant to be paid for, and rejected A and B's argument. Their statement merely made it easier to fix the level of C's remuneration.

5. Forbearance to Sue

A type of valuable consideration of practical importance is forbearance to sue. Suppose B injures A, with the result that A may recover damages for injury against B if he were to bring an action against him. Instead, A agrees not to sue B if he will pay him £1,000. If B subsequently defaults, A may recover the money. The forbearance to sue is consideration, and contributes to the bargain which the parties have made. One way of looking at it is to say that A has conferred a benefit on B by agreeing not to expose him to the hazards of litigation.

Forbearance to sue will only be sufficient consideration when the prospective plaintiff at least has a *bona fide* belief in the possibility of bringing an action. Where a claim is totally invalid as in the case of an illegal contract (see Chapter 22), and the plaintiff knows this, he is clearly not giving up anything of value. In such a case, declining to bring an action would be no consideration.

6. Performance of an Existing Duty

We have seen that the requirement of consideration may at times be rather artificial, but it must be regarded as in some way the price of defendant's promise. That is the result of the underlying concept of bargain. A problem is therefore raised when the purported consideration is in fact the performance of some duty which the plaintiff was obliged to render anyway. At first sight all such cases would appear to fail, since what extra element is the defendant receiving from the bargain? Nevertheless, the courts have sometimes found it possible to discover consideration in such circumstances. The problem is likely to arise under four main headings, of which the fourth has given rise to intense modern development and controversy.

(1) Performance of a Duty Imposed by Law

The general rule would appear to be that where a person, for example a policeman, is merely carrying out his legal duties, then he provides no consideration in so doing, or in agreeing to do so. The point is made in *Collins v. Godefroy* (1831). The plaintiff had, in effect, been put under a legal duty to give evidence at a trial. The defendant allegedly had promised to pay him six guineas for his attendance which he failed to do. The plaintiff's action failed because it was said he had given no consideration. He was bound to attend regardless of any inducement from the defendant. There is a suggestion that the case can also be explained as based upon public policy (on which see Chapter 22).

This case can be contrasted with the decision in *England v. Davidson* (1840), which at first sight seems somewhat surprising. A reward had been offered for information leading to the conviction of a criminal. The plaintiff, a policeman, gave the requisite information but was refused the reward. He sued, and it was argued against him that it was against public policy to make such a reward to a policeman and that he had only done his duty anyway. The court rejected these arguments. The judgment is brief in the extreme, but the court seems to have assumed in this case that the plaintiff did render services which went beyond the call of duty, and could therefore justify the claim.

Exceeding one's public duty is undoubtedly regarded as consideration. In *Glasbrook Brothers v. Glamorgan County Council* (1925) a difficulty arose over adequately protecting a coal mine during a strike. The company requested the police to provide a higher degree of protection than the police considered was reasonably necessary, and they agreed to pay the additional cost of £2,200 thereby incurred. Subsequently the company refused to pay claiming absence of consideration on the part of the police. The House of Lords rejected this defence and gave judgment for the plaintiffs. They said that, in providing more protection than they considered necessary, they had provided consideration in return for the promise of extra payment. Identifying the point at which the police go beyond their general public duty to maintain law and order may of course give rise to difficulty, as is illustrated by the litigation in *Harris v. Sheffield United Football Club Ltd* (1987).

The case of *Ward v. Byham* (1956) (*Casebook*, Chap. 2) illustrates the willingness of the courts to find evidence of some consideration. The defendant, the father of the plaintiff's illegitimate child, wrote to her offering to pay £1 a week in maintenance "providing you can prove that she will be well looked after and happy and also that she is allowed to decide for herself whether or not she wishes to come and live with you." The mother was at that time under a specific statutory duty to maintain the child in any event. The defendant eventually defaulted on payment, and when sued by the plaintiff, pleaded absence of consideration. The majority of the court held that there was a valid contract, and that she had promised to do more than was required by the statute by agreeing to "Look after the child well" and see that it was "happy." Lord Denning even put forward the view that: "a promise to perform an existing duty, or the performance of it should be regarded as good consideration because it is a benefit to the person to whom it is given." This view now seems to be supported by some dicta as well as the tenor of the decision in *Williams v. Roffey Bros.* (1990) (see below). If so, it would appear that performance of a duty imposed by law could now amount to valid consideration. Even so, such a principle might still be qualified by the requirement that the transaction should not be contrary to the public interest. *Collins v. Godefroy*, for example, might then still be decided in the same way.

(2) Performance of a Contractual Duty owed to the Promissor

Obviously, if A is already bound to carry out certain duties as a result of his contract with B, then it is difficult to see how A's performance of those duties can amount to consideration. There is no fresh element of bargain. The point is neatly illustrated by contrasting two nineteenth century shipping cases.

In *Stilk v. Myrick* (1809) two seamen deserted from a ship on a voyage from London to the Baltic and back. The captain, being unable to find substitutes, promised the crew extra wages if they would work the ship back short-handed. They agreed, but were subsequently refused the extra money. It was held that the crew were doing no more than their duty in meeting the normal contingencies of a voyage. Lord Ellenborough expressly stated that he based his decision on lack of consideration. This can be contrasted with the later case of *Hartley v. Ponsonby* (1857). A ship left England with 36 crew, but reached Port Philip with only 19. The captain promised the plaintiff extra money if he would help work the ship to Bombay. He did so, but the defendant subsequently refused to pay. It was held in this case that the plaintiff was entitled to recover the extra money since he had furnished consideration. The shortage of seamen had made the rest of the voyage so dangerous that the plaintiff was performing duties well beyond the normal hazards of a voyage. The danger had relieved them from their old contract, and they were therefore free to enter a new agreement in which their promise to serve was the fresh valid consideration.

Unfortunately this area of the law has been thrown into some disarray by the Court of Appeal's decision in *Williams v. Roffey Bros.* (1990) (*Casebook*, Chap. 2). The plaintiff had contracted to carry out certain carpentry work for the defendants. Before the work was completed it became clear that the plaintiff would not be able to complete the work on time. The defendants accordingly offered the plaintiff payment in addition to the agreed contract price in return for completing the work on schedule. The court held that the plaintiff was entitled to recover the extra payment.

At first sight, and even upon close examination, it is difficult to find any consideration for the defendants' promise. The court apparently took the view that consideration was to be found in the advantage the defendants undoubtedly obtained from having the work completed on time. This, however, was surely no more than they were entitled to demand under the original contract. Although none of the judges thought they were overruling *Stilk v. Myrick* it is difficult to see how the two cases can sensibly be reconciled. The result is therefore that performance of a contractual duty owed to the promissor, at least in the absence of duress, may after all amount to consideration. On the other hand, the difficulty of fitting this decision into the received learning on the topic may tempt the courts to consider this area again.

(3) Performance of Contractual Duty owed to a Third Party

It might seem surprising in view of what has already been said that where A makes a promise to B to do something which A is already bound to do by a contract with C, A is nevertheless regarded by the law as having supplied consideration by such a promise. This principle has been authoritatively confirmed by the Privy Council in *Pao On v. Lau Yiu Long* (1980) and is illustrated by *Scotson v. Pegg* (1861). In *Scotson v. Pegg* the plaintiffs had entered into a contract to supply a cargo of coal to X or to the order of X (meaning anyone whom X nominated). X directed the plaintiff to deliver the coal to the defendant. The defendant promised to unload the coal at a stated rate, which he failed to do. The plaintiffs sued and claimed that the defendant's promise to unload the coal was matched by their promise to deliver it to him. There was therefore executory consideration. The defendant replied by saying that as a result of the contract with X, the plaintiffs had to supply the defendant anyway. In other words, there was no consideration for their promise to unload. The court upheld the plaintiffs' claim. It did so on the basis that either the delivery of the coal was a benefit to the defendant, or that there was a detriment to the plaintiffs. Whatever the theoretical difficulties of such cases, the result is obviously satisfactory from a commercial point of view.

(4) Part Payment of a Debt

This category is essentially a particular example of the duty discussed in (2) above. There are, however, certain specific rules which have developed in this area and which therefore make it easier to consider the topic separately.

Suppose A owed B £10. A is in financial difficulties and asks B if he will accept £5 in full and final satisfaction of the debt. B agrees. On the face of it, there is nothing to stop B changing his mind a week later and suing A for the balance of the money. A has given no consideration for B's promise; there is no element of bargain. A has merely obtained a gratuitous promise which, as we have seen, the law will not normally enforce. On the other hand, as a matter of justice or even "fair play" the situation might be thought to bear rather harshly and unfairly on A. The law has therefore developed in a way that tries to reconcile these opposing considerations and inevitably the development has involved legal controversy.

(a) *The rule in Pinnel's case—the common law approach.* The basic legal proposition has become known as the rule in *Pinnel's* Case (1602). It was there stated that, "Payment of a lesser sum on the day in satisfaction of a greater cannot be any satisfaction for the whole." There is simply no consideration in such a case. The rule was approved by the House of Lords in *Foakes v. Beer* (1884) (*Casebook*, Chap. 2). Mrs. Beer was owed £2,090 on a judgment debt by Dr. Foakes. She agreed that if he would pay the money by instalments, she would not "take any proceedings whatever on the judgment." A judgment debt bears interest until it is fully paid, but the agreement made no reference to the interest. Dr. Foakes did eventually pay off all the money, and Mrs Beer then claimed the interest as well. He refused, pointing to the agreement. She sued, claiming there was no consideration for it. The House of Lords, applying the so-called rule in *Pinnel's* Case, upheld Mrs Beer's claim. Even if Mrs Beer had promised to forgive the interest her promise was unenforceable for want of consideration.

It has been seen that *Williams v. Roffey Bros* may have an impact on (1) above. If category (4) is really only a specialised example of the duty imposed in (2) then it would seem arguable that part-payment of a debt might also sometimes furnish consideration. The consideration in *Williams* seems to have been the undoubted practical benefit which both parties derived from the arrangement. The main contractor got the job done on time without being sued for late completion, a loss he might not have recovered in full from the subcontractor, who in turn perhaps received a reasonable price for the job. In the same way there may be a pragmatic advantage in the certainty of receiving £5 of a £10 debt owed today instead of £10, or perhaps nothing, next week. In his dissenting speech in *Foakes v. Beer* Lord Blackburn makes the point that businessmen all the time enter into such an arrangement. This argument seems nevertheless to have been rejected in *Re Selectmove Ltd* (1995). In this case part of the argument concerned whether a company's promise to pay the Inland Revenue what it owed them under statute could constitute consideration. The Court of Appeal held that *Foakes v. Beer*, a decision of the House of Lords, bound them and that there was no consideration. *Williams* was distinguished on the basis that it concerned goods or services, not payment of a debt.

Whilst this is a distinction one may wonder whether it is in principle a particularly meaningful one. The case does at least suggest that if payment of all the company owed could not be consideration for an alleged promise from the Inland Revenue, it is *a fortiori* the case that there is no sufficient consideration where less than the full amount due is promised or indeed paid.

The situation is nevertheless more complex than the result of these cases might suggest.

(b) *Two exceptions to the rule.* (i) The first exception relates to the fact that if the debtor supplies some new element at the request of the creditor together with or instead of the lesser sum then the rule does not apply. This much was stated in *Pinnel's* Case itself, where the court made clear that, "the gift of a horse, hawk, or robe etc., in satisfaction is good. For it shall be intended that a horse, hawk or robe etc., might be more beneficial to the plaintiff than the money in respect of some circumstance, or otherwise the plaintiff would not have accepted it in satisfaction ... " Accordingly, if the creditor accepts £5 today for a debt not due until next week, or £5 in London under an agreement to pay £10 in say Newcastle, or a book instead of the £10, in each of these cases the law will not permit the creditor to go back on his word. In effect, the parties have struck a fresh bargain which the courts will enforce. They are not concerned to see that it is also a good bargain for the parties. A further development of the principle applies when the creditor's claim is unliquidated (which means that there is a valid claim against the debtor, but the precise amount is uncertain). If the creditor accepts a lesser sum than he might have hoped to obtain if he had sued the debtor to judgment, this will still lead to a binding agreement. Of course he may have obtained more than he would have got in a completed action, but even if this is not the case, it is clear that there is considerable practical benefit to a creditor in sometimes agreeing to such an arrangement and avoiding the vagaries of litigation.

(ii) A second exception relates to composition agreements with creditors. It not infrequently happens that A owes money to B, C and D and it becomes apparent that A is insolvent and cannot pay everybody what he owes them in full. B, C and D will often therefore agree to take a "dividend" (that is a certain amount in the pound which is less than the full debt) in full and final settlement of their claims against him. Such an agreement has long been held binding by the courts although it is difficult, if not impossible, to see where the consideration comes from. Clearly if one creditor went behind the others and sued for the full amount this would act as a fraud upon the others, but this observation rings more like a justification of a practical rule rather than an adequate theoretical basis.

A similar principle, or perhaps one should say lack of principle, applies when part of a debt is paid by a third party in full satisfaction of the original debt. This was the situation in *Hirachand Punamchand v. Temple* (1911). An army officer was indebted to a moneylender. The officer's father sent a draft for a smaller amount "in full settlement" of the debt. The moneylenders accepted the draft, but nevertheless subsequently sued the son for the balance. The Court of Appeal rejected the moneylenders' claim. It is equally difficult in this case to detect any consideration for the agreement, but is similar to the last case in that it would clearly have been a fraud on the father to have allowed recovery of the balance from the son. Perhaps both cases can be most easily regarded as exceptions to the general requirement of consideration.

(c) *The doctrine of promissory estoppel—Equity's solution.* We have seen earlier that equity has always sought to mitigate the rigour of a common law rule where it might work an injustice. The development over recent years of the doctrine of promissory estoppel, as it has become generally known, serves as an illustration of the way in which this process is worked out in the courts. "Promissory estoppel" essentially means an impediment or bar to action brought about by a promise, but its meaning becomes clearer after reading the "*High Trees*" case later. A study of the relevant cases also provides an insight into both the advantages and disadvantages of our system of judge-made law. On the one hand it provides a flexible response to practical problems. On the other hand, there is the difficulty that as the courts develop or revitalise a new set of principles there is inevitably doubt about how far these principles extend. In this area law is still very much in the making. This process is clearly evident in the development and doubts which surround promissory estoppel.

The case which is often regarded as the modern starting point for the doctrine is the decision by the House of Lords in *Hughes v. Metropolitan Railway Co.* (1877). In October 1874 a landlord gave his tenant six months to repair the premises, or else his lease would be forfeited. In November the landlord started negotiations with the tenant for the purchase of what remained of the lease. During this time the tenant did nothing about carrying out the repairs, and the negotiations were ultimately broken off at the end of December. At the end of the six-month notice period the landlord claimed that the lease was forfeited and brought an action to enforce his claim. The House of Lords, however, took the view that the negotiations between the parties amounted to a promise by the landlord that as long as they continued he would not enforce the notice. It was on this basis that the tenant had failed to carry out the repairs, and consequently the six months' notice only ran from the date when negotiations finally failed.

Lord Cairns, holding that the tenant was entitled in equity to relief, made the now famous statement that:

> "It is the first principle upon which all Courts of Equity proceed, that if parties who have entered into definite and distinct terms involving certain legal results—certain penalties or legal forfeiture—afterwards by their own act or with their own consent enter upon a course of negotiation which has the effect of leading one of the parties to suppose that the strict rights arising under the contract will not be enforced, or will be kept in suspense, or held in abeyance, the person who otherwise might have enforced those rights will not be allowed to enforce them where it would be inequitable having regard to the dealings which have thus taken place between the parties."

It is important to note that the tenant was not relieved from his duty to repair, he was merely in effect given extra time to do so.

The principles of the case were applied 70 years later by Denning J. (as he then was) in *Central London Property Trust Ltd. v. High Trees House Ltd.* (1956) (*Casebook*, Chap. 2). In September 1939 the plaintiffs had leased a block of flats to the defendants. Due to the ensuing wartime conditions there were many vacancies in the flats, and the landlords agreed in 1940 to accept half-rent only. By 1945 the flats were full again, and the plaintiffs claimed the full rent for the last two quarters of 1945. The last two quarters only were claimed as a "test case" for all the other monies which the plaintiffs alleged could now be recovered. The court decided in the plaintiff's favour. The 1940 agreement was a temporary expedient to reflect wartime conditions and was no longer applicable. Accordingly, the original rent fixed by the 1939 contract was payable.

The main interest of the case, however, is contained in what Denning J. went on to say *obiter dicta*. He considered that had the plaintiffs tried to recover the rent for the period 1940–45 they would have failed in accordance with the principle in *Hughes* (above) in that the landlord would have been estopped. But a moment's thought shows that this view carries the principle of *Hughes* case one stage further. In the earlier case the landlord's rights were essentially temporarily suspended; in *High Trees* Denning J. asserted that the landlord's claim for the period 1940–45 had been extinguished. If Lord Denning's view is correct, then the landlord had lost his right to claim for arrears of rent, it had not merely been put into temporary abeyance until the tenant found himself in a position to pay. Part, at least, of the reasoning is based on the fact that the traditional concepts of offer, acceptance and consideration, and especially the latter, although appropriate ingredients in the formation of a contract, need not be applied in quite the same way when, as here, the defendants are not seeking to enforce a contract but merely to establish a defence. Such a view might be regarded as part of a wider criticism that contract law tends to be more concerned with the establishment of a strict contract than with the subsequent practicalities of its discharge or variation.

The doubts and difficulties associated with the doctrine enunciated in *High Trees* have only been partially alleviated by many of the subsequent cases, in which Lord Denning himself has frequently been a leading proponent. In *Combe v. Combe* (1951) the court made clear that, in keeping with orthodox doctrine, promissory estoppel can only be used as a defence and not as a means of establishing a new cause of action. Lord Denning explained it thus: "The principle stated in the *High Trees* case ... does not create new causes of action where none existed before. It only prevents a party from insisting upon his strict legal rights, when it would be unjust to allow him to enforce them, having regard to the dealings which have taken place between the parties ... " Hence the principle has been described "as a shield and not as a sword," although such a formulation appears as a simplification in which there is potential for subsequent change or development.

A problem which still remains is whether obligations are merely suspended or extinguished by the doctrine. Lord Denning is of the view that the latter result is produced. He reiterated this view in *D. & C. Builders v. Rees* (1966) (*Casebook*,

Chap. 2) where he stated that: "the principle may be applied, not only so as to suspend strict legal rights but also so as to preclude the enforcement of them." In the later case of *Alan v. El Nasr* (1972) he appears aware of the difficulty, but is still insistent that rights can be extinguished when he commented that the creditor's rights are, "at any rate suspended ... but there are cases where no withdrawal is possible. It may be too late to withdraw; or it cannot be done without injustice to the other party." Nevertheless, it is difficult to reconcile Lord Denning's view with the orthodox interpretation of the doctrine and it hardly seems to fit easily with *Pinnel's* case. In *Hughes* itself the rights were clearly suspended and not extinguished. In *High Trees*, this aspect was not part of the *ratio decidendi* of the decision. The consideration of the issue of promissory estoppel by the House of Lords in *Tool Metal Manufacturing Co. Ltd v. Tungsten Electric* (1955) seems if anything to favour the standard interpretation of *Hughes* that future obligations are only suspended, but this case also suggests that existing claims may be lost for ever. This would be important where there are periodic payments such as rents or royalties; payments due in the past which have been waived may be irrecoverable whereas the right to claim full payment in the future may be revived upon giving reasonable notice. In the Privy Council case of *Emmanuel Ayodei Ajayi v. R.T. Briscoe (Nigeria) Ltd* (1964) the view was expressed that the promise only becomes final and irrevocable if the promisee cannot resume his original position. The result of the cases, and bearing in mind the traditional doctrine of consideration, therefore seems to support the view that rights are suspended rather than extinguished by the doctrine. It would, however, be rash to regard this yet as clearly established law. What if the obligation were suspended until the limitation period had expired? There has yet to be a case on such facts, but if that were to happen, then it seems the Limitation Acts would be an effective bar to further action.

A further unsolved issue is what precisely the promisee must have done to invoke the doctrine. Is it necessary that he should act to his detriment in some way, or is it enough that he has merely acted in reliance upon the promise? If the notions of "bargain" and "consideration" are to mean anything at all, it might be suggested that acting to the promisee's detriment ought to be an essential requirement. It was certainly a factor present in the *Hughes* case in that the tenant had acted to his detriment in relation to the landlord in failing to repair. In *Emmanuel Ayodei Ajayi v. R.T. Briscoe (Nigeria) Ltd* the Privy Council talked of the promisee altering his position, and by many this was understood as meaning *"for the worse."* Lord Denning, on the other hand, has consistently taken the view that acting to one's detriment is not an essential ingredient. In *W.J. Alan & Co. v. El Nasr Export and Import Co.* (above) he commented: "I know it has been suggested in some quarters that there must be detriment. But I can find no support for it in the authorities cited by the judge." More recently in *Brikom Investments Ltd v. Carr* (1979) he stated: "The principle extends to all cases where one party makes a promise or representation, intending that it should be binding, intending that the other should rely on it, and on which the other does in fact rely, by acting on it, by altering his position on the faith of it, by going ahead with a transaction then under discussion, or by any other way of reliance. It is no answer for the maker to say: 'You would have gone on with the transaction anyway.'" However, a note of caution in relation to the "new estoppel," as it has been called, was sounded by Lord Roskill who noted; "it would be wrong to extend the doctrine of promissory estoppel, whatever its precise limits at the present day, to the extent of abolishing in this back-handed way the doctrine of consideration." There seems, therefore, to be an obvious difference of approach between the expansionist assertions of Lord Denning in relation to a creature which might be thought to a large extent to be of his own making, and the rather more cautious view of other members of the judiciary towards promissory estoppel. It remains to be seen which approach will ultimately command final approval.

Although the doctrine has often been stated in wide terms, two cases illustrate the way it can be restricted. In *D. & C. Builders Ltd v. Rees* (1966) the plaintiffs were a small firm of jobbing builders who were owed £482 by the defendant. They pressed for payment over several months, but received nothing. Eventually, knowing that they were in financial difficulties, the defendant offered the plaintiff £300 in final settlement saying that if they refused this offer they would get nothing. The plaintiffs reluctantly agreed. They later sued for the balance of the original debt, and the court awarded judgment in their favour. As Lord Denning graphically put it: "The debtor's wife held the creditor to ransom." Under these circumstances it would hardly have been equitable to allow the defendant to succeed in a claim of promissory estoppel. Equity is concerned to do justice between the parties, not to facilitate a settlement procured by intimidation. A second case, which simply serves as an illustration of the way the courts approach the business of examining representations, is

China Pacific S.A. v. Food Corpn. of India (1980). In a complicated commercial dispute there had been considerable correspondence and dealings between the parties. For the defendants it was alleged that a promissory estoppel existed based on a letter and what was said in a discussion between counsel prior to arbitration. The court, on the facts of the case, rejected the defence of estoppel. Megaw L.J. took the opportunity to emphasise that: "for a promissory estoppel, apart from other conditions, it has to be shown that there is something which is a quite unequivocal statement." It seems that the representation relied on must therefore be in clear and unambiguous terms.

(d) *Promissory estoppel and the future of consideration.* Various aspects of the doctrine of promissory estoppel seem somewhat surprising when measured against some notions of legal orthodoxy. One of the interesting facets is that the doctrine has been established more by way of authoritative *obiter dicta* than the clear *rationes decidendi* of cases. Many of the regularly cited authorities on the matter in fact turn on, or are explicable upon, other points of law. It is, unless one takes a very restricted view of the meaning of "law," clear that it is something of an oversimplification to say that our system always proceeds on the basis of building one *ratio decidendi* upon another.

Some of the controversial areas of the doctrine expose fundamental difficulties in the English notion of contract. The discussion on the issue of the requirement for merely "acting" or "acting to one's detriment" is a reflection of this. Clearly the latter view seems to reflect more closely established views on the requirement for consideration and the need for benefit and detriment. On the other hand, if the doctrine of promissory estoppel is compared to the phenomenon of the unilateral contract (that is, a promise for an act) the rather artificial nature of "detriment," as it is often used, becomes apparent. In a unilateral contract it is essentially the act which forms the basis of the contract, and the notion of any real detriment (or sometimes benefit) seems somewhat unreal. The law often seems to be finding a convenient mechanism for enforcing a gratuitous promise. Perhaps no great disservice to the law would be caused by dropping any requirement of "detriment" from the law of promissory estoppel.

Consideration has often received astringent criticism from the Judges. In the late nineteenth century, Jessel M.R. observed: "According to English Common Law a creditor may accept anything in satisfaction of his debt except a less amount of money. He might take a horse, or a canary or a tom-tit if he chose, and that was accord and satisfaction; but by a most extraordinary peculiarity of the English Common Law, he could not take 19s. 6d. in the pound; that was *nudum pactum*" (*Couldery v. Bartrum* (1881)). The contrary view has been put by Professor Hamson when he said: "So far from being an accidental and unnecessary mystery, an accidental tom-tit in an otherwise rational theory of contract, consideration in its essential nature is an aspect merely of the fundamental notion of bargain, other aspects of which, no less but no more important, are offer and acceptance. Consideration, offer and acceptance are an indivisible trinity, facets of one identical notion which is that of bargain."

The reality is perhaps more subtle than either of these quotations might suggest. Of course consideration is a central ingredient of the notion of bargain that underlies much contract law. However, it is only one strand, albeit a crucial one, in weaving the web of a binding agreement. As we have seen, sometimes the element of bargain looks more fictional than substantial. Moreover, concentrating on the rules relating to the *formation* of a contract may distract attention from considering the very different problems that arise often much later when for some reason contractual performance as originally envisaged becomes mutually inconvenient. In those cases a practical solution to the parties' new situation might be thought to be more in keeping with the tradition of the pragmatic response of English Contract Law to business efficacy than insistence on an often rather technical doctrine of consideration. Quite how the doctrine of promissory estoppel will develop is something only the subsequent case law is likely to show, at least in the absence of some legislative intervention.

Chapter 17

Intention to Create Legal Relations

Although offer, acceptance and consideration are essential prerequisites, there is a further element which must be present in order to constitute a binding contract, namely an intention to create legal relations. The view was expressed in somewhat ponderous language by Lord Stowell in the early nineteenth century that contracts, "must not be the sports of an idle hour, mere matters of pleasantry and badinage, never intended by the parties to have any serious effect whatever." The matter can be put more clearly by an example. If I offer to give you dinner tomorrow if you will come and bring a bottle of wine, prima facie all the elements of a contract would seem to be present. I make an offer, and there is acceptance and consideration when you arrive with the wine. However, it would be contrary to commonsense and most people's expectations to say that there was a binding contract here. Nobody would contemplate legal action if I failed to provide dinner after you had turned up with the wine. Consequently, in a situation such as this, the decided cases make clear that there is no binding agreement since there is no intention to create legal relations. Of course many factual situations are more ambiguous than the fictional example and, in order to ascertain whether or not an intention to contract will be assumed by the courts, it is convenient to distinguish between domestic and social agreements on the one hand and commercial transactions on the other. In the case of the former, the court will generally need to be persuaded that formal legal relations were intended. As regards the latter, the presumption is that the parties did intend to bind themselves by their agreement.

1. Domestic and Social Agreements

Although many social and family arrangements are clearly made without thought for legal consequences, difficult borderline cases may sometimes arise. For example in *Merritt v. Merritt* (1970) a husband left his wife in order to live with another woman. The husband and wife met to settle various financial arrangements, and eventually the husband signed a piece of paper which stated: "in consideration of the fact that you will pay all charges in connection with the house ... until such time as the mortgage repayment has been completed I will agree to transfer the property into your sole ownership." The wife duly paid off the mortgage; the husband failed to convey the house. The Court of Appeal upheld the wife's claim. In this case the couple were not living in amity at the time of the agreement and the court held that the parties had intended to create formal legal relations. This case can be contrasted with the attitude of the court in *Balfour v. Balfour* (1919). The defendant was a civil servant stationed in Ceylon. While on leave in England the wife was taken ill, and it became clear that the husband would have to return on his own. He therefore agreed to pay an allowance of £30 a month as maintenance while he was away. The wife later sued for his failure to pay, but the Court of Appeal refused to uphold the agreement. Lord Atkin commented: " ... one of the most usual forms of agreement which does not constitute a contract appears to me to be the arrangements which are made between husband and wife ... and they are not contracts because the parties did not intend that they should be attended by legal consequences." Although as an illustration of a general principle *Balfour v. Balfour* is still entirely valid, it probably represents a decision on the legal borderline. Given this, and the changes in social assumptions which have taken place since 1919, it is far from certain that on similar facts the actual result of the earlier case would be followed.

Similar types of problems may arise between parent and child as those between husband and wife. In *Jones v. Padavatton* (1969), the mother, Mrs. Jones, wished her daughter to give up her job in Washington and qualify as a barrister in England. She therefore agreed to pay the daughter a monthly allowance while she studied. The daughter accepted the offer and came to England. Mrs. Jones later bought a house in London and the daughter lived there although she persistently failed to complete the Bar examinations. The mother and daughter eventually quarrelled and a dispute arose over possession of the house. There were then two agreements, neither of them in writing. The first was to pay the daughter a monthly sum in return for travelling to England to read for the Bar. The second permitted the daughter to live in the house while she studied. The Court of

Appeal considered that neither agreement was intended to create legal relations, it was merely a family arrangement depending upon the good faith of the promisors. One judge, however, thought that although this was true of the second agreement, the first was a binding contract intended to last for a reasonable time which had now elapsed. Having regard to the serious consequences of the daughter's move there seems much to be said for such a view.

A domestic agreement where the parties were not related existed in *Simpkins v. Pays* (1955). A grandmother, granddaughter and lodger took part each week in a newspaper competition. The entries were actually made in the name of the defendant, and one week she obtained a prize of £750. The plaintiff, the lodger, claimed a third of the sum as his share of the prize. The grandmother refused, claiming there was no intention to create legal relations. The court upheld the claim of the plaintiff, considering that each had contributed to the competition in the expectation of sharing any prize.

2. Commercial Agreements

Because the presumption operates in favour of assuming that the parties do intend to create legal relations, the courts require evidence of a clear contrary intention before holding that no binding agreement exists. Nevertheless, problems may be caused by the extravagant language used in, for example, advertising. It is unlikely that a disappointed customer could sue for breach of every claim that is made in the course of promoting the sale of goods, although naturally everything depends on the facts of an individual case. This was one of the difficulties raised in the case considered earlier (p. 467) of *Carlill v. Carbolic Smoke Ball Co.* (1893). Amongst the defences unsuccessfully raised by the defendants was the assertion that their statement was "a mere puff," in other words, an advertising gambit not to be taken seriously. The court rejected this interpretation, saying that the mention of the deposit of £1,000 with their bankers "to show their sincerity" was strong evidence that they did indeed contemplate legal liability when they placed the advertisement.

If the parties expressly make it a term of their agreement that there is no legal liability then the courts will not interfere. One of the clearest examples of this is the case of *Rose and*

Frank v. Crompton Bros. (1923). In 1913 the parties made an unexceptional agreement for the sale of goods. There was, however, one unusual feature, the "Honourable Pledge Clause." This stated: "This arrangement is not entered into ... as a formal or legal agreement, and shall not be subject to legal jurisdiction in the law courts ... but it is only a definite expression and record of the purpose and intention of the parties concerned, to which they each honourably pledge themselves." In 1919 the defendants terminated the agreement without giving the specified notice and the plaintiffs sued. The House of Lords refused to uphold the claim. Scrutton L.J. commented: " ... I can see no reason why, even in business matters, the parties should not intend to rely on each other's good faith and honour, and to exclude all idea of settling disputes by an outside intervention ... "

So-called "honour clauses" are frequently found on football pools coupons. Although prima facie the submission of such a coupon would obviously be regarded as part of a commercial transaction, it has been held that the presence of the words "binding in honour only" is sufficient to prevent a disappointed punter being able to sue the promoter. Strange though it may seem, a pools company who uses such a clause is therefore under no legal obligation to pay out money to a winner.

Nevertheless, where there is an ambiguity in the words used, the courts will favour the interpretation which gives the agreement binding effect. An example of this is contained in *Edwards v. Skyways Ltd* (1969). As part of a redundancy agreement the plaintiff's employers promised that they would make him an *ex gratia* payment of a specified amount. Later the employers refused to make the *ex gratia* payment saying that the words used showed that there was no intention to create legal relations. The Court of Appeal rejected such an interpretation. This was a commercial agreement and there was therefore a strong presumption in favour of creating legal relations. All the words *ex gratia* signified was that the employers were not admitting any pre-existing liability; it did not mean that they were not bound by the agreement.

3. Collective Bargaining

One type of commercial agreement, which has frequently led to political controversy, is treated by the law in a rather special way. Collective agreements between employers and trade unions are not generally enforceable contracts. The point was raised in *Ford Motor Co. Ltd v. Amalgamated Union of Engineering and Foundry Workers* (1969). A written and carefully worded agreement was drawn up between the Ford Co. and various trade unions. One clause in effect stated that a strike should not be called before certain negotiating procedures had been carried out. The defendants issued strike notices in breach of the agreement and the plaintiffs sought to restrain them. The court declined to do so, relying mainly on "the climate of opinion voiced and evidenced by the extra judicial authorities." In other words, public policy was the determining factor. Of course, if terms and conditions of employment negotiated by a trade union are later incorporated into the individual employment contract between an employer and employee then these terms are legally binding on both parties.

The legal position after the *Ford* case has effectively been affirmed by statute. Under section 18 of the Trade Union and Labour Relations Act 1974 a collective agreement is presumed not to create a legally enforceable contract unless it is in writing and the agreement expressly provides that the agreement is to be legally enforceable. In practice it seems that the presumption is rarely, if ever, displaced.

Chapter 18

Contractual Terms

The terms of a contract provide the map which delineates the area of subject-matter to be covered, and they make clear what duties and obligations will arise at various stages in the performance, or indeed non-performance, of the agreement. At first sight it might seem obvious that in the case of straightforward written contract the parties will simply agree between themselves what is to be included and what is to be left out. Matters are not always, however, quite so easily dealt with. What if the parties have forgotten to include a crucial term? Can a court repair the omission? What if the parties are not really on an equal footing, can one party "impose" a term on the other? What is the relative importance of different terms? At what stage does a statement become a term of the contract, if at all? Can the law itself imply a term into an agreement, regardless or even against the wishes of the parties? Related to these problems is the effect of so-called "exclusion clauses" on the duties and obligations that might otherwise have arisen.

Many of these problems are considered later (in Chapters 26–27) and consequently what follows must be read in the context of and with an awareness of the further material in later chapters. Two matters will be dealt with at this stage: (a) the incorporation of terms into a contract, and (b) the relative importance of contractual terms.

I. INCORPORATION OF TERMS INTO A CONTRACT

The fact that a certain statement is not considered to be a term of the contract does not necessarily rob it of all legal significance. As we shall see in Chapter 19, a misrepresentation made before a contract is concluded may well give rise to a remedy which can give relief to the victim of such a statement. Nevertheless, it is only where a term of the actual contract is broken that the plaintiff can sue for breach of contract and claim the appropriate remedy. It must not be forgotten that, with the possible exception of certain terms implied by law, the underlying purpose of deciding whether or not a statement is a term of the contract is to give effect to the intention of the parties. The intention of the parties, however, as we saw earlier in the context of offer and acceptance, is considered objectively. In other words, the matter is viewed from the position of an interested and reasonable bystander.

The approach of a court to the problems raised in this area will inevitably be affected by whether the contract is written or oral. Where it is completely in writing, then it should be obvious what terms are involved, and it will be for the judge merely to decide as a matter of law what is their effect. Where the contract is oral there is a preliminary issue of fact whether the relevant statement was made at all. Only when this initial hurdle has been surmounted will the court then go on to consider its effect. Sometimes a contract may be partially contained in a written document, and partly set out in various oral undertakings. In this case the court has to combine elements of both approaches in order to ascertain the intention of the parties.

1. Representations and Terms

The law has long drawn a distinction between "mere" or "non-contractual" representations, for example various statements made in the course of negotiations, and statements which are actual terms of the contract. Although the distinction between them, as we shall see in the next chapter, no longer has quite such significance as in the past, it is still a matter of importance. In an ideal case the parties might, after prolonged negotiations, embody their eventual accord in a comprehensive written agreement. Often this does not happen, and so the courts have developed various guide-lines in order to assist in making what may be a difficult assessment of whether a statement is a representation or a term.

(1) Does the Representor have Special Knowledge?

The courts will in general place more weight on the words of an expert than on a similar statement made by an amateur or someone who has no special knowledge. This can be seen by contrasting two cases involving the sale of cars.

In *Oscar Chess v. Williams* (1957) the defendant wished to trade-in his Morris car for a new Hillman Minx. Obviously the price allowed for the Morris depended on its age, and relying on the information in the vehicle's registration book (the forerunner to the present car owner's document) the defendant innocently stated that it was a 1948 model. On this basis the plaintiffs allowed him £290. They later discovered that the registration book had presumably been fraudulently altered by someone in the past, and the car was in fact only a 1939 model worth £175. They thereupon sued the defendant for the difference in price between the two valuations on the grounds of breach of a contractual term that the car was in fact a 1948 model. The Court of Appeal rejected their claim. The seller was a private individual who had simply relied in all innocence on the contents of the registration book. The buyers on the contrary were experts who as professional car dealers were in a position, if anyone could, to discover its true age. Consequently, the defendant's statement was not a contractual term.

A different approach was adopted in *Dick Bentley Productions Ltd. v. Harold Smith (Motors) Ltd* (1965) where the defendant was a car dealer. The plaintiffs said they were looking for a "well-vetted" Bentley car, and the defendant stated that this particular car had only done 20,000 miles since it had been fitted with a replacement engine and gearbox. It later emerged that the car was unsatisfactory and had done almost 100,000 miles since then. In this case the Court of Appeal said the defendant's statement was a term of contract.

(2) Does the Representee Place Special Importance on the Issue?

If the representee lets it be known that he attaches special importance to some particular fact, then it is not difficult to see that the court may well regard that fact as a term of the contract. This point is illustrated in *Bannerman v. White* (1861.) A prospective buyer of hops asked the seller if any sulphur had been used in their treatment. He explained that, if it had, he would not even trouble to ask the price. The seller said no sulphur had been used, and a contract of sale resulted. It later transpired that it had been used. The court held that the seller's statement as to the absence of sulphur was a term of the contract of which he was therefore in breach.

(3) When was the Statement Made?

Although the cases show that it can be no more than an approximate guideline, it may be a matter of some significance when the statement in question was actually made. If it was made in the negotiations some time before any contract it is more likely that the court will regard this as a non-contractual statement. For example, in *Routledge v. McKay* (1954), the parties had been discussing the sale of a motor-cycle. Both were private persons with no special knowledge and the defendant, relying on the registration book, asserted that it was a 1942 model. A week later a written contract was drawn up which did not mention the date. In fact, it was a 1930 model. The buyer unsuccessfully claimed that the date of manufacture was a term of the contract. In this case not only was there a pronounced interval between the negotiations and the ultimate contract, but it was also significant that the date of the model was not part of the later written agreement. If the parties draw up a written contract but fail to include an earlier statement, it may be reasonable to assume that they did not regard it as of great significance.

Nevertheless, if the intention of the parties as gathered from all the evidence shows that they regarded a particular term as of special or indeed of no significance, the courts will not hesitate to regard such general indications of the kind being considered as inconclusive.

(4) How Strong was the Inducement?

A point can be made with more or less force. If the representor makes a statement with some diffidence, this is less likely to be relied upon as a contractual term than is an emphatic direction. In *Ecay v. Godfrey* (1947) the seller of a boat said that it was sound, but suggested to the prospective buyer that he should have it surveyed. The court held that this indicated the statement was not intended to be a term of any contract. This can be contrasted with *Schawel v. Reade* (1913). The plaintiff, who wished to buy a horse, started to examine it. The defendant said to him: "You need not look for anything: the horse is perfectly sound." Accordingly the plaintiff stopped his examination. Eventually, three weeks later, the sale was concluded. In fact, the horse was quite unsuitable. The House of Lords was agreed that under the circumstances the seller's statement was a contractual term. It is note-worthy that in this case the obvious strength and importance of the statement negated any suggestion that the length of time involved between negotiation and sale indicated that this was something other than a contractual term.

2. Incorporating Terms

Even if a statement is made that is clearly intended to be a term, it must of course be apparent to both parties *before* the contract is concluded. One party cannot unilaterally impose terms on another. Where there is no signed contractual document, a term will only be incorporated into a contract if one of two conditions are fulfilled: (a) the affected party knew of the clause or (b) reasonable steps have been taken to bring the term to his notice. If the contract is in writing, we shall see later that different considerations apply. Although problems of notice are often dealt with in the context of "exemption clauses" (see Chapter 27), this may give a misleading impression. What is said about notice applies to any term, regardless of its function.

As one would expect, a considerable body of case law has built up on what are "reasonable steps" in bringing a term to someone's notice. The answer in any case is likely to turn upon two issues: (1) what degree of notice was given, and (2) when was the notice given? If the degree of notice is too little, or the term comes too late, it will not form part of the contract.

(1) The Degree of Notice

A person will not receive notice if he is handed something which is clearly not a contractual document. If, on the other hand, he is handed a document which is clearly meant to contain contractual terms, then he is likely to be bound even if he fails to read them. This problem arose in *Chapelton v. Barry U.D.C.* (1940). The plaintiff wished to hire two of the defendants' deck chairs in order to sit on the beach. A notice requested the public to obtain a ticket from the attendant and retain it for inspection. The plaintiff collected his two tickets which he thrust into his pocket without reading. When he sat down on the chair it collapsed, injuring him. He sued the council who relied on a term printed on the back of the ticket stating that they were not liable in the event of "any accident or damage arising from the hire of the chair." The Court of Appeal held the defendants liable. No reasonable person would have thought he was receiving anything other than a receipt for the hire. If, however, the council had put up a prominent notice warning of this clause, then this could have been regarded as a contractual document giving reasonable notice and so might have exempted the defendants in this case.

Many of the cases on "notice" arose out of nineteenth century decisions on, for example, the contractual effect of railway tickets. Hence they are often referred to as "the ticket cases." One case, however, is generally regarded as being of fundamental importance in eliciting the guiding principle, *Parker v. South Eastern Railway* (1877) (*Casebook*, Chap. 4). The plaintiff left a bag in the defendant's cloakroom, paid the 2d. charge and received a ticket in return. The front of the ticket contained details such as opening hours of the office, but also the words: "See back." On the back was a clause limiting the company's liability in the case of loss of the bag to £10. Later that day, when the plaintiff presented his ticket, it was discovered that the bag was lost. The value of the bag was £24 10s., and this was the amount claimed from the railway company. They claimed that liability was limited to £10. The Court of Appeal said two questions needed to be considered. Did the plaintiff read or was he aware of the term? If the answer was "yes," then the matter was clear. If the answer was "no," then a second question needed to be answered: did the defendant do what was reasonably sufficient to give the plaintiff notice of the term? Accordingly, in each case it will be necessary to consider the facts and see if the test is satisfied. If, for example, the ticket or notice contained terms which were illegible or obscured by an obstruction or obliterating date stamp, then the court is likely to find that the notice was inadequate (see, *e.g. Sugar v. L.M. & S. Railway* (1941)). Further, the more onerous or unusual the term the more explicitly it must be drawn to the other party's attention. In *Interfoto Picture Library Ltd v. Stiletto Visual Programmes* (1989) (*Casebook*, Chap. 4) the court clearly approved Lord Denning's statement that: "Some clauses ... would need to be printed in red ink on the face of the document with a red hand pointing to it before the notice could be held to be sufficient."

One way in which a plaintiff may be considered to have notice of a term is through a previous course of dealing between the parties. In *Hollier v. Rambler Motors (A.M.C.) Ltd* (1972) the plaintiff took his car to a garage where it was destroyed by fire as a result of the defendants' negligence. On the three or four previous occasions in the last five years when the plaintiff had used the garage he had been asked to sign an invoice containing the words: "The company is not responsible for damage caused by fire to customers' cars on the premises." The defendants argued that this term was imported into the contract even though on this occasion nothing had been signed. The Court of Appeal held that there was an insufficient course of previous dealing to justify the inclusion of such a clause. One wonders what the position might have been if, say, the plaintiff had used the garage six times in the last two years?

Although the frequency of previous dealing is one fact from which the courts may deduce that a party is aware of a term, this will also be readily accepted if the parties are dealing in the same trade or business. Even if they have not done business before with each other a knowledge of the usual trade terms can often be assumed. Hence in *British Crane Hire Corporation Ltd v. Ipswich Plant Hire Ltd* (1975) (*Casebook*, Chap. 4) the hirer of a crane was liable for the expense of extracting it from marshy ground even though, at the time when the crane became stuck, the written terms had not reached the hirer. The court held that both parties knew that this was a usual term in the business and their oral agreement was therefore made with this in mind.

(2) The Time when the Notice was Given

A clause can only become part of the contract if notice of it is given either before or at the time of contracting. If it comes later than this then it will be without legal effect. This is simply illustrated in the case of *Olley v. Marlborough Court Ltd* (1949). A husband and wife booked into a hotel for a week and then went up to their allotted room. On the wall was hung a notice effectively excluding the liability of the hotel for loss of guests' property. The wife's property was in fact wrongfully taken, but the hotel relied on the clause contained in the wall notice to exempt them from liability. The Court of Appeal held that the notice came too late. By the time the guests had reached their room the contract was already completed. A new term could not then be unilaterally imposed on the other party.

In *Olley* the gap between contract and term was obvious. A more difficult case, although one that poses similar problems in principle, is *Thornton v. Shoe Lane Parking* (1971) (*Casebook*, Chap. 4). In this case the plaintiff wished to use the defendant's car park, to which admission could be gained by way of an automatic barrier. He drove up to the barrier, the machine automatically produced a ticket, and he was permitted to drive in. The ticket referred to various exempting terms and the defendants pleaded one of these was a defence to a claim by the plaintiff. An immediate problem was to break down this modern feature into the standard analysis of offer and acceptance, and so decide when the contract was complete. The old "ticket cases" were somewhat different in that one person was dealing directly with another; here, the "other" was a machine. Lord Denning analysed it in this way. The offer was made by the proprietor of the machine holding it out as ready to receive custom, in this case by the notice at the entrance to the garage. Acceptance took place when the customer through driving up to the machine activated it enabling him to gain entry. The contract was then complete, and the terms printed on the ticket which was thrust at him by the machine came too late. This is obviously a sensible rationalisation of the situation. It would be unrealistic to expect a motorist to stop and read through a large number of terms at the threshold of the garage while he reflected upon whether or not to contract. By the time he reaches the machine he is likely to be effectively committed.

The decisions in both of these cases might have been different if the plaintiffs had been regular users of the respective services. Then it might be inferred from the previous course of dealing that the parties were both aware of the relevant terms and were therefore bound by them.

3. Written Contracts

(1) The Rule in L'Estrange v. Graucob

A special rule applies to the effect of terms in a contractual document which has been signed. This is known as the rule in *L'Estrange v. Graucob* (1934) (*Casebook*, Chap. 4) after the case in which the rule was strikingly illustrated. Its effect is that a party is bound by the terms in a document which he has signed and it is immaterial that he may never have read the document. He is still bound as though he had and was aware of the contents. In the case itself the plaintiff bought a vending machine from the defendants by signing a "sales agreement." The machine proved to be unsatisfactory but the defendants claimed the protection of a clause, "in regrettably small print but quite legible." The court held that they were protected by the clause. The plaintiff had signed the document and was bound. The result shows how important it is to read a legal document with the utmost care before signing it.

(2) The Parol Evidence Rule

The effect of this "rule" is that extrinsic evidence cannot be introduced to contradict, add to or vary the contents of a written agreement. The obvious basis of such a rule is that if the parties have taken the trouble to put their contract into writing then they presumably intend that it should contain all the terms, or at least all the important ones. Accordingly, if two statements made by the parties conflict then that contained in the written agreement will generally be regarded as conclusive.

Nevertheless, it is a "rule" with so many exceptions as to make clear that it is only a common sense starting point. It is qualified by the fact that if, for example, the written evidence is clearly inconsistent with what the parties really agreed, then the agreement can be rectified to reflect this. If the written agreement was never intended to be the whole contract, then again evidence may be admitted to clarify the rest of the agreement. Another important qualification to the rule is the possibility of effectively side-stepping it by the use of a "collateral contract" (on which see p. 518 later). The result is that exceptions to the rule are likely to be just as important as the rule itself.

4. Implied Terms

The express terms of a contract may not contain every particular of the parties' agreement. Sometimes a term may be omitted through mere inadvertence, at other times the parties may have tacitly assumed its existence and thought it too obvious to be worthy of mention. In such cases the courts can intervene under certain circumstances to repair the omission. A term may also enter a contract through the operation of a particular statute. There are therefore various ways in which terms may be implied into a contract.

(1) Custom

Custom, especially in the past, was a fruitful source of implied terms. Indeed the common law itself developed as the customary law of the land. In particular, it has played an important part in the development of commercial law. Nevertheless, in consumer and everyday transactions, it is somewhat unlikely to be encountered in modern conditions.

We have already considered the effect of a previous course of dealing in incorporating terms into a contract, and this is in a sense merely incorporating into the contract the customary usages as between the parties. Custom, on the other hand, even if it may sometimes be limited to a specific locality, is clearly wider in its effect in that it does not depend upon previous transactions between the particular parties.

(2) Statute

Many terms are implied into agreements by specific statutes. An obvious example is the terms implied by sections 12–15 of the Sale of Goods Act 1979. The other side of the coin is represented by the Unfair Contract Terms Act 1977 which renders certain terms designed to limit liability ineffective. Both these areas are considered later in detail (Chapters 26 & 27) in the context in which they are likely to arise in normal consumer dealing. There are, however, a very large number of statutory interventions of this kind which may be relevant to many different kinds of agreement. To take only one example, many leasehold agreements contain a term that the property will not be assigned (that is transferred to someone else) without the landlord's consent. Section 19(1)(a) of the Landlord and Tenant Act 1927, where it applies, implies a term that "such consent is not to be unreasonably withheld." Such a term is implied even if the understanding of both parties is to the contrary.

(3) Terms Implied by the Courts

These terms readily fall into two main categories; those the courts will imply into specific classes of agreement, and those which may be implied into contracts generally. A brief and helpful summary of the law is to be found in *Shell (U.K.) v. Lostock Garages* (1977) (*Casebook*, Chap. 4).

(a) *Specific types of contract*

It would not be possible to catalogue all the cases where a court, always subject to any contrary expression of the parties, will imply a term. For example, it has long been held to be a standard implied term in a contract for the lease of a furnished house that it is reasonably fit for habitation at the beginning of the term. A graphic example in another context was posed by *Samuels v. Davis* (1943). The plaintiff, a dentist, agreed to make a set of false teeth for the defendant's wife.

The defendant refused to pay for them on the grounds that they were so unsatisfactory that they were unusable. One of the problems that arose, which is dealt with later in Chapter 25, was whether this was a contract for the sale of goods or for services. A contract for the sale of goods would have carried an implied statutory term that the goods were fit for the purpose for which they were supplied. The court held that the distinction was irrelevant. If it was for sale of goods then the statutory term would be implied; if it was for services, then on the analogy of the Act (which was a codification of the earlier common law) a similar term would be implied into such a contract by the court.

(b) *Contracts generally*

Parties who have drawn up a written contract may well have provided in clear terms for the general nature of their obligations but simply have overlooked, or failed adequately to formulate, a term to allow for a contingency which later arises. In these circumstances the courts will willingly imply a term to make the contract work, or in the phrase used by judges, to give the contract "business efficacy." This is an aspect of another theme which underlies the law of contract. Where possible the courts claim to be the upholders of bargains, not the destroyers of them.

A famous case which illustrates the role of the courts is *The Moorcock* (1889) (*Casebook*, Chap. 4). The defendants, who operated a wharf on the Thames, contracted to allow the plaintiff to discharge his vessel at their jetty. Both parties knew that at low tide the vessel would ground. During the unloading the vessel did settle on the bottom and was damaged by a ridge of hard ground beneath the mud. Their contract did not expressly provide that this was a safe anchorage. Nevertheless, the Court of Appeal implied into the contract a term that the defendants undertook that, so far as reasonable care could make it, the river bottom was in such a condition as not to endanger the vessel.

The principle has often been applied by the courts and was explained by Lord Pearson in *Trollope and Colls Ltd v. North West Regional Hospital Board* (1973) when he said: "An unexpressed term can be implied if and only if the court finds that the parties must have intended that term to form part of their contract: it is not enough for the court to find that such a term would have been adopted by the parties as reasonable men if it had been suggested to them: it must have been a term that went without saying, a term necessary to give business efficacy to the contract, a term which although tacit, formed part of the contract which the parties made for themselves." It follows from this that, since it is the presumed intention of the parties which is the underlying rationale, a term cannot be implied if it is inconsistent with some other term agreed by the parties. Equally, if one party is completely ignorant of some fact which is peculiarly within the other's knowledge, a court can hardly imply a term that would result in both parties being bound. Such a term could not be said to be an accurate reflection of their mutual intention (see, *e.g. Spring v. N.A.S.D.S.* (1956)).

5. Collateral Contracts

The doctrine of the "collateral contract" is a device developed by the courts which has become increasingly important as a means of varying or supplementing what appear to be at first sight the clear terms of a contract. It may operate in a number of ways. For example, it may provide the mechanism for the avoidance of an exemption clause (on which see Chapter 27 later) or have the effect of importing into a contract a term quite inconsistent with a later written agreement. It may therefore be relevant to the problem of when a statement has become part of the contractual bond, to the effect of terms in an agreement, and to the more specialised problem of exemption clauses. The difficulty of assessing under what head it should most appropriately be considered only emphasises its importance. The point becomes clearer by examining a recent case.

In *City & Westminster Properties (1934) Ltd v. Mudd* (1959) (*Casebook*, Chap. 4) the defendant had been the plaintiff's tenant for some years. The lease related to a shop, and annexed to it was a small room in which, as the plaintiffs knew, the defendant slept. Later on a new lease was negotiated which contained a clause restricting use to business purposes only. The defendant received an oral undertaking that if he accepted the lease, notwithstanding this clause, he could still sleep on the premises. The defendant thereupon signed the agreement but the plaintiff later sued for breach of the covenant relating to use of the premises. The court held that the defendant had a good defence despite the clear words of the written document; he could plead the collateral contract made before the lease was executed. The landlords could not resile from this earlier agreement.

The term "collateral contract" in this context may be slightly misleading. There was a proper complete contract before the lease was signed which contained all the essential elements of offer, acceptance and consideration. The situation could be analysed in terms of a promise not to enforce the particular term of the lease in exchange for a promise to sign it. The term "collateral" merely draws attention to the fact that in reality the first contract operates to modify or amplify another agreement. It is still, quite clearly, a complete independent contract the consideration for which is an agreement to enter another contract.

A slightly different example of the same principle can be seen in *De Lassalle v. Guildford* (1901). The parties were negotiating over the lease of a house. The plaintiff refused formally to agree the lease unless he was assured that the drainage system was in order. The defendant declared that it was and the plaintiff thereupon agreed to the lease. In fact, the drains were defective. The plaintiff successfully sued the defendant for damages. The basis for this action was not the tenancy agreement, the lease not containing any express conditions as to the state of the drains, but rather a prior collateral contract. That again could be stated as deriving from an exchange of promises. You promise that the drains are in order, I therefore (impliedly) promise to execute the lease. The strength of the doctrine is shown in the way that whereas in the first case it was used as a "shield" so to speak, in the latter it was wielded as a "sword." It is, as can be seen, a device that can be used not only to undermine the effect of the parol evidence rule, but also as an alternative approach to the problems of the distinction between a term and a "mere" or "non-contractual" representation.

II. THE RELATIVE IMPORTANCE OF TERMS—CONDITIONS, WARRANTIES AND INNOMINATE TERMS

In any contract some terms are likely to be more important than others so that breach of a term will not always be regarded with the same degree of seriousness. The law has reflected this by labelling the terms in a contract as being either "conditions" or "warranties" (although as we shall see this is not an exhaustive categorisation) and attaching different consequences according to the type of term which is broken. The discharge of a contract by breach is dealt with in detail later (in Chapter 23) but the essential distinction between the two terms is that whereas for breach of either monetary damages may be recoverable, in the case of breach of a condition the wronged party is entitled to regard the contract as repudiated and so is absolved from future performance. Hence, breach of a condition is regarded as a failure to perform some really important obligation, or at least one which the parties themselves regard as important, whereas breach of a warranty is felt to be a relatively minor failure which can adequately be compensated by an award of damages. It is often said that the contract has been terminated by a breach but it is important to remember that this is only a shorthand way of describing the situation. Parts of the contract (for example a clause setting out a scale of damages payable on breach) may survive; it is only the innocent party's obligation to carry out his part of the contract that is ended, and this only if he elects to treat the contract as repudiated. A party may treat a breach of a condition as equivalent only to a breach of warranty and simply sue for damages.

The terms "condition" and "warranty," used in the sense described above, have crystalised as a result of their incorporation into what is now the Sale of Goods Act 1979. In the case of an uncomplicated contract the employment of these labels to describe the relative importance which the parties attach to their terms is likely to lead to a readily understood and predictable set of legal consequences. There are, however, a number of difficulties which give rise to formidable complications. These stem partly from the fact that "condition" and "warranty" are not always used in the limited way so far described and partly from the fact that the parties themselves do not always make clear how they regard a particular term. Even if they appear to do so, the courts may regard their labelling of the term as inconclusive. Furthermore, there has recently emerged a third category of term, the "innominate" or "intermediate term." It is these difficulties and developments which now need to be examined.

1. Meaning of "Condition"

In the older cases, especially those decided before 1893 when the forerunner of the present Sale of Goods Act was passed, terms such as warranty and condition were often used without reference to the comparatively clear distinction that is now made between them. Although this difficulty is no longer a source of confusion, there is a sense in which "condition" is still used which is distinct from that so far described. It is sometimes employed to denote the existence of some fact or event which is a pre-requisite to contractual liability arising or continuing. Just as we say passing examinations is a condition for entry to a university, so some eventuality may be a prior condition to the existence of a contract. The case of *Carlill* yet again furnishes an example of this. The purchase of the smoke ball by the customer on the terms of the offer made in the advertisement undoubtedly brought about a binding contract. Nevertheless, no action could arise unless and until the user contracted flu despite using the device. This was a condition precedent to the plaintiff's action for breach of contract.

A modern illustration of the same principle would be an agreement to buy land subject to the vendor obtaining the requisite planning permission. In this sort of case, where satisfaction of the condition lies within the power of one of the parties, the courts are very willing to imply a further promise that the appropriate party must use his best endeavours to bring about fulfilment of the condition.

2. What Sort of Term is it?

If the parties have drawn up a formal written agreement, then the fact that the words "condition" or "warranty" are used to denote the status of certain terms will almost always be conclusive. This is no more than an acknowledgment of what, on the face of it, is the parties' common intention. Nevertheless, there may be rare occasions when even this fails to solve the difficulty. In *Schuler A.G. v. Wickman Machine Tool Sales Ltd* (1973) the parties concluded an agency agreement in which the respondents undertook to visit certain manufacturers at least once a week. This was stated to be a condition of the agreement, although it is clearly the sort of term that could be broken with varying degrees of seriousness. The House of Lords decided that condition was a word that had more than one specific meaning, and in this particular contract it was not being used as a term of art to denote that any breach could lead to repudiation. Taken as a whole, the contractual document showed that this was not the discernible intention of the parties.

Even if the parties do not expressly or by implication (for example by their emphasis upon or failure to consider some point) make clear the status of a term, it may sometimes be possible to discover this by reference to a rule of law. For example, the Sale of Goods Act 1979 provides in sections 12–15 that certain terms such as those relating to title to the goods or their fitness for the purpose for which they are sold are not only implied into such an agreement but are regarded as conditions as opposed to warranties. Where a statute fails to give guidance the problem may be solved by reference to judge made law. In *The Mihalis Angelos* (1970) the owners of a vessel let it on charter (in other words on hire) by a charterparty (the name for the contract document in such a case) which contained the clause, "expected ready to load under this charter about July 1, 1965." It transpired that the ship could not have been ready by this time when the agreement was made, and in the event was not ready until July 23. Clearly, the owners were in breach of the term, but what sort of term was it? The House of Lords decided that the distinction between conditions and warranties was a valuable one and that this "expected readiness" clause in charterparties was a condition. An important consideration in reaching their conclusion was undoubtedly that, in commercial agreements where bargains are struck by people who meet on an equal footing, predictability and certainty are ultimately the crucial factors. No businessman wants to await the vagaries of a complicated and uncertain course of litigation.

The final possibility, is that the term is classed as an "innominate," or "intermediate term." The starting point for this doctrine is the decision in *Hong Kong Fir Shipping Co. Ltd v. Kawasaki Kisen Kaisha Ltd* (1962) (*Casebook*, Chap. 4). The plaintiffs chartered a ship to the defendants for two years by an agreement that contained a clause stating that the ship was "in every way fitted for ordinary cargo service." In fact, the engines were dilapidated and the crew was incompetent. The result was that several months of the charter were wasted whilst the ship underwent various repairs. The defendants accordingly claimed that the agreement was at an end and repudiated the charter. The plaintiffs, whose ship it was, sued for damages for wrongful repudiation and the Court of Appeal upheld their claim. At first sight it might appear that the court merely regarded this as a simple case of a breach of warranty as opposed to breach of a condition. However, the importance of the case lies in the fact that the Court of Appeal expressed the view that some terms, and this was one of them, did not lend themselves to the traditional form of legal analysis. Diplock L.J. stated: "the problem in this case is, in my view, neither solved nor soluble by debating whether the shipowner's express or implied undertaking to tender a seaworthy ship is a 'condition' or 'warranty.' " The correct approach was to look at what had happened as a result of the breach and then decide if the charterers had been deprived of "substantially the whole benefit which it was the intention of the parties they should obtain."

The significance of this decision goes further than giving rise to a new type of "innominate" term. In the past, as we have seen, the courts have set out to determine what was the status of a particular term at the time the parties made their contract, and having decided that, to assess the consequences of the breach. In the *Hong Kong Fir* case the court has approached the problem, so to speak, the other way round. The relative importance of the term is derived from the consequences, whatever they turn out to be, which perhaps much later emanate from the breach. This approach was clearly thought to be valuable when one is dealing with a term, like the seaworthiness clause in a charterparty, which can be broken in a wide variety of ways ranging from the trivial to the really serious. However, the obvious difficulty in such a doctrine is its inherent uncertainty. Until the breach has occurred, it may not be clear what kind of term is involved. As between commercial parties of equal standing the benefits of such an approach are less certain.

In subsequent cases the courts seem to have determined not to give the doctrine too wide a scope. In the *Mihalis Angelos* (above) which was decided after the *Hong Kong Fir* case, the court decided the common "expected readiness to load" clause was a condition, not an innominate term. However, in *Cehave N.V. v. Bremer Handelsgesellschaft mbH. (The Hansa Nord)* (1975), a dispute arose over 12,000 tons of citrus pellets which under the contract were to be shipped "in good condition." Some of the cargo was damaged, though it seems that the defects were not particularly serious. It was argued that in a contract for the sale of goods, which is therefore governed by the Sale of Goods Act from which the classic modern distinction between conditions and warranties is derived, there was no place for the "intermediate" or "innominate" term. The Court of Appeal rejected this and held that the clause was indeed an "intermediate" term following the principles of the *Hong Kong Fir* case. On this basis, because the breach was not serious, the buyers were not entitled to repudiate the contract. In other words, this was equivalent only to a breach of warranty since it did not deprive the buyers of substantially the whole benefit intended under the contract.

Clearly the invocation of the notion of an innominate term does serve a valuable purpose in cases where the parties are not of equal bargaining power or where the breach is of a very technical nature and is being used, in effect, as a way of escape from what has simply become a bad bargain. In *Reardon Smith Line v. Hansen Tangen* (1976) the respondents agreed to charter an as yet unbuilt tanker identified as "Osaka No. 354." This description merely related to who had built the ship and the yard number. In fact, due to pressure of work, the ship was satisfactorily completed by another shipyard who acted as sub-contractors so that the vessel became known as "Oskima 004." The appellants, to whom the vessel had been sub-chartered, wished to reject the vessel as the tanker market had collapsed in the meantime. Accordingly, they claimed that the vessel did not accord with its contract description. Although it might be thought there was little merit in the argument, it could be supported to some extent by reference to cases on description in the sale of goods. The House of Lords decided that the breach was of a very technical nature and did not entitle the appellants to reject the ship. Although the case does not squarely raise the issue of innominate terms, the House endorsed the reasoning and approach of *The Hansa Nord* (above) which clearly in a case such as this is calculated to try and ensure that an injustice is not perpetrated by a mechanical application of rigid rules.

Nevertheless, in commercial dealings between parties of equal bargaining power, a different approach may be justified. For example in *A/S Awilko v. Fulvia SpA di Navigazione (The Chikuma)* (1981) (*Casebook*, Chap. 4) a charterparty, in a form commonly used, provided that unless "punctual and regular payment" of the hire charge was made the owners were entitled to withdraw the vessel from the charterers. On one occasion the charterers paid in a way that in effect gave the owners an overdraft facility for the amount of the monthly hire as opposed to an equivalent to an unconditional cash payment. Had the owners wished to draw on the money immediately it would probably have cost them no more than $100 in interest charges in the context of a monthly payment from the charterers of nearly $69,000. The owners, however, claimed that, because of the technical failure to make an unconditional payment, they had not been punctually paid and were entitled to withdraw the ship. The House of Lords agreed. Even though the decision appeared to work harshly in this particular case, the overriding consideration in a commercial agreement such as this was that the legal effect of any term should be quite clear so that the parties know exactly where they stand and a long course of expensive and uncertain litigation could be avoided in other cases.

Chapter 19

Misrepresentation

In the last chapter reference was made to the distinction between "representations" and "terms." Although much of the discussion was concerned with the way in which the law classifies various statements or promises made in the course of negotiations into one or other of these categories, it is important to grasp that breach of a term is not the only way in which a contract can come to an end or a plaintiff recover compensation. If one party has been induced to enter into a contract by some factual statement which turns out to be untrue, (in other words a misrepresentation) the injured party may have a remedy despite the fact that the inaccurate statement never actually became a term of the agreement. It is this situation with which we are now concerned and which has given rise to the cluster of overlapping legal principles brought together under the heading of "Misrepresentation."

The justice of allowing someone who has been misled into entering a contract the opportunity of escaping from it is more obvious than the legal devices which try to achieve this aim. It is unfortunate that the Misrepresentation Act 1967 far from clarifying and codifying the various legal remedies at that date appears to have added another layer of complexity on the uncertain foundation of the previous common law. Nevertheless, there are clearly two issues which require attention, namely: (1) What sort of statement or conduct will amount to a misrepresentation? and (2) What redress does a plaintiff have in these circumstances? The rather complex range of remedies available is a reflection of the fact that a misrepresentation can range from the outrageously fraudulent to the entirely innocent and therefore more than one solution may be appropriate.

1. The Meaning of Misrepresentation

In the simplest type of case nobody could doubt the existence of a misrepresentation. Suppose that A wishes to sell his armchair to B. A untruthfully tells B that it was a personal gift by the Queen to A, and B thereupon buys it. Assuming that this was not a term of the contract of sale (an assumption that is made of any misrepresentation throughout this chapter) and that it was an inducement to B's purchase, then clearly this is a misrepresentation which gives rise to legal consequences. In some areas, however, the legal usage of the term "misrepresentation" is rather narrower than its use in every day speech, in others perhaps a little wider. A misrepresentation to be of legal effect must be of fact, not of opinion, intention or law; but in some cases silence itself will be regarded as a misrepresentation. These areas now require to be examined in more detail.

(1) Fact rather than Law

To come within the legal definition of a misrepresentation the statement must relate to a matter of fact not law. At first sight this appears perfectly straightforward. To say that the Sale of Goods Act 1979 relates to consumer as well as commercial contracts is a clear statement of law; to state that this blanket has a hole in it is a statement of fact. But suppose one makes a statement which combines fact and law, such as "these blankets can be rejected because they are not of satisfactory quality." Is this a statement of fact or law? Probably this can best be regarded as a statement of fact about the condition of the blankets, and of law in relation to the consequence of rejection. In daily life, where such statements are comparatively common, it may frequently be difficult to disentangle the two.

(2) Fact rather than Opinion

The statement of an opinion, that is to say a view expressed on a matter that is either incapable of proof or as to which the speaker does not have conclusive evidence, cannot found an action for misrepresentation. So in *Bisset v. Wilkinson* (1927) (*Casebook*, Chap. 5) Bisset was selling two plots of land in New Zealand to Wilkinson for the purpose of sheep farming. Bisset expressed the view in the course of negotiations that if the land were worked properly it could carry 2,000 sheep. Ordinarily one would regard such a statement as giving rise to a remedy on the grounds of misrepresentation. A farmer's statement as to the quality of his land in some particular area looks every much like a statement of fact. Nevertheless in this case it was regarded merely as a matter of opinion. Both parties knew that the land concerned had never been used before for sheep-farming. Consequently, in the circumstances of this case, the statement could only be regarded as one of opinion not fact.

This case must be distinguished from the facts in *Smith v. Land and House Property Corporation* (1884). The plaintiffs wished to sell an hotel and claimed that it was let to a "Mr. Frederick Fleck (a most desirable tenant)." This, on any view, was an optimistic assessment of Mr Fleck's solvency since it was discovered that he had been seriously in arrears with his rent and had only paid "by driblets under pressure." Here the Court of Appeal allowed the action for rescission (a remedy for misrepresentation where the pre-contractual position of the parties is restored which will be discussed later). Bowen L.J. explained this by saying, "In a case where the facts are equally well known to both parties, what one of them says to the other is frequently nothing but an expression of opinion ... But if the facts are not equally well known to both sides, then a statement of opinion by the one who knows the facts best involves very often a statement of material fact, for he impliedly states that he knows facts which justify his opinion." The material facts known by the vendors about Mr. Fleck clearly did not justify the expression of an opinion of him as a good tenant.

(3) Fact rather than Intention

A promise to do something in the future is not regarded as a representation. If the promise is a contractual term then it may give rise, for example, to an action for breach but it will not lead to rescission on the grounds of misrepresentation. Nevertheless, a statement of intention to do something in the future may sometimes imply a present state of mind which can be regarded as a fact. A famous example was provided in *Edgington v. Fitzmaurice* (1885). The directors of a company sought to raise money on the basis that this would be used to improve and extend their buildings. In truth they intended all along to pay off the company's existing debts. The court regarded this as a dishonest statement of fact. As Bowen L.J. said. "There must be a misstatement of an existing fact: but the state of a man's mind is as much a fact as the state of his digestion."

(4) Silence

It may seem strange that silence could ever be regarded as a representation and normally, as one would expect, it signifies nothing. Hence the general rule is *caveat emptor* (let the buyer beware), although of course that maxim is not a licence to make false replies to a purchaser's questions. Even if one contracting party knows that the other is labouring under a misapprehension there is not necessarily any duty to disabuse him. In *Fletcher v. Krell* (1873), at a time when such things were felt to be important, a woman applied for a post as a governess without revealing the fact that she had previously been married. The court held that silence in that case did not amount to a misrepresentation.

In some instances, however, the law does impose a duty to disclose information and to remain silent can therefore amount to a misrepresentation.

(a) *Contracts uberrimae fidei*

Certain types of contract are said to require the utmost good faith (*uberrima fides*) and so to involve a duty to disclose certain information. For practical purposes the most important example of this type is the insurance contract. The basis for the rule is that the relevant facts are likely to be peculiarly within the knowledge of the insured and it is therefore necessary to ensure that one party does not have an unfair bargaining position over the other. Ironically, the rule has sometimes been abused by those it was meant to protect. Insurance companies have been known to specify that the *accuracy* of the information supplied shall be a condition of the validity of the policy. Consequently a proposer who honestly but inaccurately answers a question, or fails to make a disclosure, may find that the policy is later avoided despite his own good faith and integrity. As always, care is necessary in assessing the precise terms of the contract.

The obligation to disclose "all material facts" in such a contract is interpreted by the courts to mean a factor which would, "influence the judgment of a prudent insurer in fixing the premium, or determining whether he will take the risk" (Marine Insurance Act 1906, s.18(2)). A clear example of the rule, which incidentally makes the point that the loss does not have to be a result of the non-disclosure, is the case of *Seaman v. Fonereau* (1743). The assured here concealed the fact that the ship involved was in a position of danger when last sighted. In fact it escaped from that difficulty but was subsequently captured by the Spaniards. It was held that the failure to disclose was sufficient to render the contract voidable.

(b) *Subsequent falsity*

A statement once made will generally be regarded as having effect up to the time the contract is made. If a statement although true when made subsequently becomes false, then silence under these circumstances can amount to a misrepresentation. In *With v. O'Flannagan* (1936) a doctor wished to sell his medical practice and quite truthfully stated in January that it was worth £2,000 a year. Subsequently the doctor became ill and by the time the contract was signed in May the value had dwindled to almost nothing. It was held that the failure to disclose the subsequent events amounted to a misrepresentation.

(c) *Partial revelation*

A slightly different problem is posed by the statement of one who literally tells the truth, but who thereby conveys a totally misleading impression of the real situation. In *Dimmock v. Hallett* (1886) a vendor of property stated that the farms on his land were let, but failed to reveal that the tenants had given notice of their intention to leave. This failure to disclose so distorted the positive information given that the court held there had been a misrepresentation.

(d) *Other cases*

Sometimes the relationship between the parties, as opposed to the type of contract concerned, gives rise to a duty to disclose. There may be such a "fiduciary relationship" in the case of, for example, a parent and child, solicitor and client or trustee and beneficiary. A similar duty to disclose certain information exists, by virtue of legislation, between the promoters of a company and the public.

2. The Misrepresentation must be Operative

A misrepresentation does not become actionable unless it is at least one of the reasons for which the plaintiff entered the contract. If the other party never heard or read the statement, even though it was made, then there is no cause of action. Similarly if even though there was a misrepresentation the other party did not rely on it then the contract cannot be avoided. This was the case in *Attwood v. Small* (1838). The vendors of a mine made exaggerated claims as to its capacity in order to sell it but the purchasers appointed their own surveyors to check the accuracy of the statements. They reported, quite wrongly, that the claims were correct and relying on this the purchasers bought the property. It was held by the House of Lords that an action for rescission must fail on the basis that no reliance had in fact been placed on the vendor's statement. The purchasers had relied on their own enquiries.

It should not be assumed from this that anyone who has had the opportunity to check the facts does not rely upon the misrepresentor's statements. Both in contract and in criminal deception it is no defence that the victim could have found out the truth had he gone to even a little more trouble (see, *e.g. Redgrave v. Hurd* (1881)).

Although the misrepresentation must be an inducement to enter the contract, it need not be the only one. In *Edgington v. Fitzmaurice* (1885) the plaintiff loaned money to a company induced (1) by a misstatement in the prospectus about how the money would be used and (2) by a mistaken belief of his own that the type of transaction involved gave him a charge on the company's property. Even though he admitted that he would not have lent the money but for (2) it was held that (1) was still an operative misrepresentation.

3. Different Types of Misrepresentation

Depending upon the state of mind of the maker a misrepresentation may be either fraudulent, negligent or wholly innocent. The distinction matters because the remedies for each type of misrepresentation differ.

(1) Fraudulent Misrepresentation

The classic definition of a fraudulent statement was provided by the House of Lords in *Derry v. Peek* (1889) as being a false statement made: (i) knowingly; or (ii) without belief in its truth; or (iii) recklessly whether it be true or false. More simply, this amounts to saying that a fraudulent statement is one that the maker does not honestly believe to be true. It must be more than foolish, inaccurate or unreasonable; an allegation of fraud is a serious matter and there must, to borrow the language of the criminal law, be *mens rea*. Negligence, as the House of Lords made clear, is never sufficient to found an allegation of fraud although, as in criminal law, the fact that a belief was highly unreasonable may be evidence that it was not honestly entertained.

The remedy for fraud is twofold. The plaintiff may (1) claim damages, and (2) rescind the contract. Although damages and rescission are available as we shall see for other types of misrepresentation there are special features of both in their relation to fraud. The damages for fraud are not a contractual remedy as such but are recoverable under the tort of "deceit." The measure of damages is therefore that of tort not contract. In other words, the object of the award is to put the plaintiff in the position he would have been in had the fraud not been practised upon him, not the position he would have been in had the fraudulent statement been a contractual promise (see, *e.g. East v. Maurer* (1991)). More of this will be said later in Chapter 24. Quite apart from suing for damages, the injured party may also elect to avoid the contract and if necessary apply for an order of rescission to ensure that any property handed over is restored to him. There is, however, one special feature relating to fraud. If the fraudulent party sues for rescission the other can use fraud as a defence and decline to hand back what he has obtained under the contract. If for example someone defrauds an insurance company into giving him cover, then the company would be entitled not only to avoid any liability under the policy but also to keep any premium the fraudulent proposer had paid over.

(2) Negligent Misrepresentation

Until recently the remedy provided by the law for a careless misrepresentation was extremely limited but two developments have altered this. One is the development of the tort of negligent misrepresentation, the other, the Misrepresentation Act 1967. The first of these has had enormous ramifications in the law of tort and its consequences are still being explored by the courts. For present purpose only the way it impinges upon the law of contract is examined.

(a) *Negligence at common law*

At the time when *Derry v. Peek* was decided, and for long afterwards, it was assumed that no damages could be recovered at common law for loss due to a careless misstatement. This was part of a wider doctrine in tort that no damages were recoverable for pure economic loss because the consequences might be so far reaching. This orthodoxy was dramatically dispelled by the House of Lords in *Hedley Byrne & Co. v. Heller & Partners Ltd* (1964). The plaintiffs here entered into certain advertising contracts on behalf of Easipower in a way which rendered them liable if Easipower failed to pay. They obviously wished to check the company's credit worthiness and so contacted their bankers for a credit reference which was not unfavourable. Easipower did in fact default and the plaintiffs sued the defendant bankers. Although the plaintiffs lost their action because the reference was given "without responsibility" (although such disclaimers of liability when giving advice may now fall foul of the Unfair Contract Terms Act 1977, see, *e.g. Smith v. Eric S. Bush* (1989) (H.L.)), the House of Lords decided that there could be liability for negligent misrepresentation on the normal tort principles enunciated in *Donoghue v. Stevenson* (1932) as long as there was a "special relationship" between the parties. It is still not completely clear what precisely this means, and the rationale behind such a qualification may be to limit liability within reasonable bounds. The essence of the relationship is perhaps that the person giving the information must be someone who can normally be expected to have knowledge of the kind required, and that it is reasonable for such information to be relied upon. Such a relationship was certainly held to exist in *Esso Petroleum Co. Ltd v. Mardon* (1976) (*Casebook*, Chap. 5). Here Esso's very experienced sales representative assured the defendant that a new garage development would have a throughput of petrol of some 200,000 gallons. The defendant doubted this but ultimately in reliance on the representative's estimate signed the tenancy agreement. In fact the throughput was less than half the estimate and in the course of the resultant litigation the defendant claimed for Esso's negligent misstatement and won. It seems clear from this case that where a contract is brought about by the careless misstatement of an "expert" on whom the other party relies, then the victim has a cause of action in negligence. It does not matter that at the same time there may be liability in contract as well.

(b) *Negligence under the Misrepresentation Act 1967*

Section 2(1) of the Misrepresentation Act 1967, a piece of legal draftmanship not noted for its clarity or elegance, has the effect that a negligent misstatement provides a plaintiff with a remedy of damages and rescission unless the other party can prove that he had, "reasonable ground to believe and did believe up to the time the contract was made" that the facts represented were true. It is now clear that damages are to be assessed on the same basis as the tort of fraudulent misrepresentation (*Royscot Trust Ltd v. Rogerson* (1991)). The great advantage for a plaintiff in proceeding under the 1967 Act is that it is for the party who made the misrepresentation to show that he did act reasonably, not the victim of the misstatement to prove negligence (see, *e.g.* the earlier discussion at p. 4). In fact unless some special circumstance exists such as the contract being void *ab initio* for mistake (on which see next chapter) or there is some advantage in circumventing the restricted meaning of misrepresentation in the context of contract (see above, p. 526), or in the case of fraud benefiting from the more generous limitation period given a plaintiff, it is unlikely that an action for negligent misstatement or deceit at common law will be brought.

Whilst the Act has not led to large numbers of reported cases a good example of the operation and difficulties inherent in the Act and its relationship to common law is *Howard Marine and Dredging Co. Ltd v. A. Ogden & Sons (Excavations) Ltd* (1978) (*Casebook*, Chap. 5). In this case contractors wished to hire some barges for removing large quantities of clay. The carrying capacity of the barges to be used was crucial as this would affect, for example, how quickly the job could be done. The contractors approached a firm which hired out barges and on enquiring as to their capacity received an oral reply which turned out to be too high. The reason for the wrong estimate was that the person making it had relied on the entry in Lloyd's Register (which was usually accurate) instead of looking at the ship's documents in their possession. A majority of the Court of Appeal held that the maker of the inaccurate statement was liable under section 2(1) of the 1967 Act. The case suggests that the statement's maker must discharge a considerable burden. Bridge L.J. stated: "the statute imposes an absolute obligation not to state facts which the representor cannot prove he had reasonable ground to believe." On the further claim for common law negligence the Court was divided. Shaw L.J. thought there was liability in the context of a business transaction whose nature made it clear just how important was the capacity, but Lord Denning thought there was here no special relationship. Unfortunately this interesting point is left undecided by the case as the third member of the Court, Bridge L.J., did not reach a conclusion upon it.

(3) Innocent Misrepresentation

In the event of an innocent misrepresentation the injured party may still rescind the contract, but this right has now been qualified by section 2(2) of the 1967 Act which gives the court a discretion to award damages in lieu of rescission, "if of opinion that it would be equitable to do so." This would cover the case of a misrepresentation of comparatively minor importance where complete rescission would be a remedy out of all proportion to the damage done (see e.g. *William Sindall plc v. Cambridgeshire County Council* (1993)).

There is also an overlap at this point between subsections 2(1) and 2(2). A court could if it wished even in the case of a negligent misrepresentation award damages in lieu of rescission under section 2(2).

4. Rescission

Frequent mention has been made of this term in the preceeding pages since all three types of misrepresentation give rise to a right to rescission and it is now helpful to look more closely at just what rescission is and how the right to it may be lost.

The effect of misrepresentation is generally to make a contract voidable not void, that is, the contract continues unless and until the injured party chooses to have it set aside. This may be done either (1) by the representee making it clear to the representor that he no longer intends to be bound by the contract's provisions, or (2) by doing something which reasonably leads to that inference. Once the representee has done this the contract is terminated once and for all *ab initio* as if it has never existed. Not unnaturally the representor is sometimes hard or impossible to find and an example of the operation of (2) is provided by *Car and Universal Finance Co. Ltd v. Caldwell* (1965). A rogue bought a car from its owner using a cheque which later was dishonoured. By the time the seller discovered this the rogue and his car had disappeared so he immediately requested the police and the A.A. to find the car. It was held that this showed a sufficient intention on the part of the seller to rescind the contract and so re-vest the property in the car in himself (in this particular case resulting in no one else being able to acquire ownership of the goods and a subsequent "sale" by the rogue therefore being invalid; cf. *Lewis v. Avery* (1972) (*Casebook*, Chap. 5)).

It is not strictly necessary, as we have seen, for a victim of a misrepresentation to go to court to rescind the contract. He may do it himself and from that date the contract is a nullity and consequently any property exchanged re-vests in its former owner. If, however, the other party disputes the position or fails to hand back property which has been transferred under the previously existing contract then it is possible to apply to the court for a formal order of rescission. The court will then seek to put the parties back into the position they were in before the contract was made. This is sometimes described as restoring the *status quo ante* (the position before) or *restitutio in integrum* (complete restitution). Sometimes this can best be done by ordering a payment of money, but it is important to realise that this is not damages. The law draws a strict distinction (although its importance is lessened by for example the Misrepresentation Act 1967 which does permit a statutory claim for damages) between damages which can properly be recovered for breach of contract, and a mere indemnity which is designed to restore the position upon rescission.

The point is illustrated by the case of *Whittington v. Seale-Hayne* (1900). The plaintiff bred prize poultry and leased certain property from the defendants in order to carry on this business. Although it was not contained in the lease and therefore not a term of the contract, the plaintiffs had previously represented orally that the premises were in a sanitary condition. In fact the water was poisoned so that the poultry died, the manager of the farm became ill and the local authority required the drains to be repaired. The plaintiffs claimed for the lost stock, loss of profits and removal and medical expenses. In all, it was a claim of some £1,525. The defendants offered £20 to pay for the rent, rates and repairs to the drains which under the terms of the lease the plaintiffs were bound to pay. The court accepted the defendant's view. The other claims did not inevitably arise under the terms of the lease; there would have been no breach of contract if the plaintiffs had failed to carry on business. Unless therefore the expense is an inevitable part of the contract, it will not be compensated.

Although on these facts a different result might be reached today (for example there may have been a negligent misstatement) the authority is still valid on the point that in the case of rescission only an indemnity, not damages, can be awarded. It might, for example, still be of relevance when a representor has discharged the burden of proof under section 2(1) of the 1967 Act and a court does not order damages in lieu of rescission under section 2(2).

5. Bars to Rescission

Rescission is in many ways a more drastic remedy than damages since it involves disentangling completely what may have become a complex web of connections. Not surprisingly therefore the right to rescind may be lost in certain circumstances where it would plainly be unreasonable to return to the *status quo ante*.

(1) Affirmation

If the victim of a misrepresentation decides to affirm the contract with full knowledge of what has happened either by declaring his intention to continue with the agreement or by doing some act from which such an intention may reasonably be inferred then the right to rescind is lost.

(2) Lapse of Time

Lapse of time is not, in itself, a bar to rescission, but it may provide evidence that the representee in fact intended to affirm the contract. In any event, rescission is an equitable remedy and so a court would have a discretion to refuse to grant it if, for example, other people had altered their position on the reasonable understanding that the contract was to remain in existence. One case involving the sale of goods suggests that lapse of time without more can be a crucial factor. In *Leaf v. International Galleries* (1950) the plaintiff bought a painting of Salisbury Cathedral after being told that it was by Constable. Five years later when he wished to sell it he discovered that it was by someone else. There was no suggestion of fraud and the plaintiff applied for rescission of the contract as soon as he discovered the truth. Nevertheless the Court of Appeal refused to grant the remedy and stated that: "it behoves the purchaser either to verify or, as the case may be, to disprove the representation within a reasonable time, or else stand or fall by it." No doubt the position would have been quite different if the misrepresentation had been fraudulent. In that case it seems likely that time would only have started to run once the fraud had been discovered.

(3) Restitutio in Integrum

The object of restitution is compensation so that each party gets back what it has given to the other. If the property has been consumed, destroyed or for example in the case of a mine, exhausted, then *restitutio in integrum* has become impossible and rescission will not be granted. It does not, however, matter that the property is not still in its original pristine state. If substantial restitution is possible then the court may order return of the property with a further order of monetary compensation for any deterioration.

(4) Third Party Involvement

If a third party has acquired a title to the property under a contract made in good faith and for value (*i.e.* consideration) then the right to rescind is again lost. In effect someone else now owns the property and it is no longer there to be restored. The situation might arise in this way. If a contract is void *ab initio* for some reason no property can pass. But if the contract is merely voidable (*i.e.* valid until set aside), as in the case of a misrepresentation, it is perfectly possible that, before the victim of the misrepresentation has had a chance to rescind, the property has been sold on by the buyer to somebody else. Restitution has now become impossible.

6. Misrepresentations and Terms

The difficulties that were thought to exist in the law over the relationship between terms and representations have been swept away by section 1 of the Misrepresentation Act 1967. The result is that if a misrepresentation is made in the negotiations which later becomes a term of the contract then a plaintiff may have a cause of action both for misrepresentation and breach of contract. If facts similar to the case of *Leaf* were to recur, as they did in *Peco Arts Inc. v. Hazlitt Gallery Ltd* (1983), the pleadings might well contain an allegation that a condition or warranty as to the painter's identity had been breached (although see below, p. 633). This would open up a claim for damages even if it was too late for rescission. Sometimes, however, an action for misrepresentation might be more beneficial than a claim for breach of contract. In *Naughton v. O'Callaghan* (1990) the plaintiffs bought a horse whose pedigree had been hopelessly misdescribed and which subsequently turned out to be a poor racer worth much less than the 26,000 guineas paid for it. The problem was that, even if accurately described, it might still have been worth a similar amount at the time of sale. There was therefore an argument that the plaintiffs had suffered no loss of bargain as a result of the breach. This was avoided by bringing the claim under the head of misrepresentation. The plaintiffs had bought and kept the horse because of the misrepresentation concerning its pedigree. Had they known the truth at the time of sale they could have sold the horse immediately with almost no loss. Because they had kept it instead, by which time it had become much less valuable, they had suffered the loss of the difference between its value at the time of sale and at the date of judgment. This was recoverable as damages which flowed directly from the misrepresentation.

7. Exempting Liability

The remedies available to a plaintiff would clearly be of no use if it was possible to insert into a contract a term excluding all liability for misrepresentation. Section 3 of the 1967 Act as amended accordingly states that if a contract contains a term which would exclude or restrict any liability or remedy for misrepresentation, "that term shall be of no effect except in so far as it satisfies the requirement of reasonableness as stated in section 11(1) of the Unfair Contract Terms Act 1977; and it is for those claiming that the term satisfies that requirement to show that it does." More will be said of the Unfair Contract Terms Act 1977 in Chapter 27 but it is noteworthy that the onus rests firmly on the claimant relying upon it to show that it was reasonable and that, unlike the 1977 Act which excludes certain types of contract (*e.g.* insurance) from its ambit, section 3 of the 1967 Act has general application.

An example of the application of section 3 occurred in *Walker v. Boyle* (1982). The vendor of a house made an innocent but incorrect statement that there were no disputes regarding the boundaries of the property. This was an incorrect misrepresentation which on the face of it gave a right to rescission of contract. The contract had, however, been concluded using the National Conditions of Sale which contained a clause 17(1) stating, "no error, mis-statement or omission in any preliminary answer concerning the property . . . shall annul the sale." The vendor therefore relied on this term as excluding his liability. The court granted rescission. One of the grounds for the judgment was that clause 17(1) was an unreasonable exclusion clause. Not only does the case illustrate the operation of section 3 of the 1967 Act but it is also of interest in that the occurrence of the offending term in a common-form clause in a long used standard form contract did not prevent its demise in the circumstances of the case. As Dillon J. commented, "I do not think it can be said that its precarious survival until 1977 entitles it to the automatic accolade of fairness and reasonableness."

Chapter 20

Mistake

At first sight it might seem obvious that if an agreement has been concluded on the basis of a mistake by one or both of the parties then the law will release them from their obligations. Such an approach, however, could never represent the law. Some mistakes are trivial, others fundamentally alter the basis of the contract. It would not be feasible or sensible to dissolve whole contracts merely because one party was labouring under a slight misapprehension as to some peripheral matter. Justice must not only embrace the interests of the immediate parties but also the requirements of certainty. If other parties have relied upon the existence of a contract, which on the face of it is perfectly valid, it may cause inconvenience and hardship to declare it invalid. For all these considerations the operation of the legal doctrine of "mistake" is a much more circumscribed notion than the use of the word in common speech would suggest. The result is that when things go wrong with a contract the doctrine of mistake is not likely to be the first thing a lawyer turns to. In order for it to be relevant, there must in general be something very seriously defective about the agreement or the subject-matter of the contract. Even where there is quite serious error the only remedy may be equitable rather than legal.

"Mistake" covers a wide range of situations and some have doubted whether there really is a single doctrine of mistake at all. Many of the cases could be explained on the basis of a breakdown in the conjunction of offer and acceptance, albeit a breakdown of a serious kind. Some of them, however, would not readily lend themselves to this approach. If, for example, the parties reach perfect agreement on an entity which has ceased to exist then it is difficult to see how a failure of offer and acceptance is to blame for the resulting nullity. Moreover the willingness of courts of equity to intervene in certain circumstances does seem consistent with the growth of an equitable doctrine of mistake. In what follows therefore the subject will be treated in the traditional way as a topic in itself, but it should not be forgotten that many of the cases could with equal validity be analysed in a slightly different way.

One of the matters which makes this area of the law confusing is the quite separate legal rules developed by the courts of common law and equity for the resolution of the same problem. In many cases the distinction between equitable and legal rules is no longer central. Professor Ashburner's statement in 1902 that: "the two streams of jurisdiction ... , though they run in the same channel, run side by side and do not mingle their waters," was criticised by the House of Lords in *United Scientific Holdings Ltd v. Burnley Borough Council* (1978). Lord Diplock commented, "this metaphor has in my view become both mischievous and deceptive. ... If Professor Ashburner's fluvial metaphor is to be retained at all, the waters of the confluent streams of law and equity have surely mingled now." Despite this co-mingling the distinction still matters in the area of mistake. In those rare cases where the common law recognises the operation of mistake, the effect is that the contract is *void*. This has the drastic consequence that the whole transaction is a complete nullity so that not only the parties themselves will have to return to the status quo but others who have derived rights under the void agreement may also find themselves with no title or interest in the relevant property. Where equity intervenes the effect is to render the contract liable to be set aside on the grounds that it is "voidable." This means that the contract may be set aside but that those who have bona fide acquired rights under the temporarily valid agreement are protected. Indeed unless the voidability has crystallised into a declaration of invalidity the contract remains a perfectly valid agreement. Equity also has the further advantage that a contract may be set aside on terms. It is therefore not possible to inquire simply as to the ultimate solution provided by equity; it is still necessary to consider the effect of the mistake, if any, at common law.

There seem to be as many ways of describing types of mistake as there are judges or authors. Broadly speaking two threads can be followed through the web of terminology. One describes the situation where the parties agree between themselves but for some reason the contract is incapable of performance as they envisage it. In a sense the contract is frustrated (on which see Chapter 23) before it has even got off the ground. The second situation that may arise is where there is in fact no real *consensus ad idem* between the parties. These situations will be examined in turn.

1. Mistake as to the Basis of the Contract

The essence of this type of mistake is that although the parties may be in complete accord as to the terms of an agreement, neither party would have entered a contract if they had realised the falsity of some underlying assumption.

(1) Absence of Subject-Matter

Perhaps the clearest example of a fatal common mistake is that the very subject-matter of the contract never or no longer exists. The matter is then described as *res extincta* (the thing is destroyed). An example is provided by *Scott v. Coulson* (1903). Both parties entered into a contract for the sale of a life policy in the belief that the assured, Mr. A. T. Death, was alive. Unfortunately Mr. Death was dead at the time of the contract. The agreement was therefore held to be completely void at common law. Similarly in *Galloway v. Galloway* (1914) a man and woman entered into a separation agreement on the assumption they were married to each other. Rather surprisingly to them, it transpired that they were not. The wife of the husband by an earlier marriage turned out to be still alive. Such a common mistake led to the agreement being void.

In *Couturier v. Hastie* (1852) it was found that the parties had agreed the sale of a specific cargo of corn which they believed to be on board a boat from Salonica to the United Kingdom. In fact the cargo had by then already been sold by the ship's master to a buyer at Tunis. Although the language of mistake is never actually used by the House of Lords, the finding that there was no contract here is often thought to rest on the basis that as the entire content of the contract no longer existed, it must be void.

The common law relating to the sale of goods in such circumstances is now contained in section 6 of the Sale of Goods Act 1979 which declares: "Where there is a contract for the sale of specific goods, and the goods without the knowledge of the seller have perished at the time when the contract is made, the contract is void."

An analogous case which extended the principle of *res extincta* to the slightly different circumstances of *res sua* (the thing is his own) is shown in *Cooper v. Phibbs* (1867). Here one party took a lease of property from another which, unknown at the time to both of them, actually already belonged to the lessee. It was said by the court that the agreement "ought to be set aside" which Lord Atkin at least, in a later case, understood to mean was void at common law. It is simply quite impossible to give someone something he already has.

Two other decisions of the courts at first sight similar raise slightly different issues. In *Amalgamated Investment & Property Co. Ltd v. John Walker & Sons Ltd* (1977) the plaintiffs negotiated the purchase of a warehouse, which they wished to redevelop, for £1,710,000. In fact the day after the signing of the contract the Department of the Environment made the property a listed building (a planning device restricting development of buildings of special interest) so reducing its value to some £210,000. Neither party were aware of this during their negotiations, but the Court of Appeal refused to intervene. The agreement was in fact valid; at the time of the agreement both parties were perfectly correct in their belief that the building was not listed. The mistake, quite apart from being sufficiently serious, at the very least must pre-date the contract. Even if the listing had taken place prior to the contract it seems likely that the agreement would not have been void at law, although it might have led to consideration of the application of equity's doctrine of mistake exemplified in *Solle v. Butcher* (*Casebook*, chap. 6) (which is considered later).

Not every case of non-existence of the subject-matter will lead to the contract being void. If in *Couturier v. Hastie* the agreement had been to purchase not specific goods but the risk that there were such goods then the contract would have been perfectly valid. The parties would have agreed where the risk of non-existence was to fall in that event. In the Australian case of *McRae v. Commonwealth Disposals Commission* (1951) the Commission agreed to sell the plaintiff "an oil tanker lying on Jourmand Reef, which is approximately 100 miles north of Samarai." The plaintiff fitted out an expensive salvage operation and it was then discovered that not only was there no oil tanker in such a place but there was also no place known as Jourmand Reef. The court decided that the Commission had in effect impliedly promised that such a tanker existed and could therefore be sued for breach of contract. The result seems entirely fair and the facts could be distinguished from *Couturier v. Hastie* in that in *McRae* the goods could not be said to "have perished" within the meaning of section 6 of the Sale of Goods Act 1979. They simply never existed. *McRae* nevertheless poses the question of what the famous case of *Couturier v. Hastie* did decide. Does section 6 accurately embody the *ratio* of the case? Is that statutory provision dispositive of the issue or is it only a rule of construction which yields to the contrary intention of the parties? In principle there seems no reason why the existence of the subject matter should not be made a term of the contract, as *McRae* decided. If section 6 does apply so as to render an agreement void, is there any way round this? One approach now open to an English court in dealing with facts such as occurred in *McRae* would be an action for negligent misrepresentation (see above; p. 532).

(2) Mistake as to Quality

It is not difficult to see that if the subject-matter does not exist then the contract can be void for mistake. A more difficult problem arises where, although the thing exists, it lacks or possesses some quality which makes it impossible to achieve the result the parties originally envisaged. We shall see later that a mistake as to quality where there is a failure as to the agreement, as in *Smith v. Hughes* (1871) (*Casebook*, Chap. 6) will not absolve the parties, what of a common mis- take as to quality? The position is not altogether clear. It seems certain that the courts are, at the very least, reluctant to apply the doctrine of mistake in such circumstances. The difficulty arises over whether they are prepared to countenance it at all.

The crucial case upon which discussion turns is *Bell v. Lever Bros. Ltd* (1932) (*Casebook*, chap. 6). Lever Brothers appointed Bell as managing director of a company in which they had a controlling interest at an annual salary of £8,000 for a period of five years. Due to a merger Bell became redundant and Lever Brothers paid him £30,000 as compensation for his loss of employment. They then discovered that during his employment he had committed various acts which would have entitled them to terminate his employment without any compensation at all, although it was found that Bell had not been fraudulent in failing to reveal these actions. Not surprisingly Lever Brothers sued for the recovery of the £30,000, amongst other things on the basis of a common mistake rendering the contract void. The mistake claimed was that this was a service contract which could only be terminated by paying substantial compensation. The trial judge and Court of Appeal held that it was void for mistake; the House of Lords decided by a majority of three to two that it wasn't. The difficulty that arises is how to interpret the various speeches of their Lordships.

One view is that the case decides that there is no doctrine of operative mistake as to quality. There is no doubt that the parties had made a fundamentally wrong assumption about the factual basis of their agreement. If the doctrine of mistake did not operate in these circumstances, then when could it ever be relevant? This view could be supported by, amongst other cases, the Court of Appeal's judgment in *Solle v. Butcher* (1950) (*Casebook*, Chap. 6). Here A agreed to let a flat to B for a rent of £250 a year on the assumption that the flat was not subject to the Rent Acts. On this they were mistaken, and the maximum rent permissible was only £140. Again this could hardly be denied to be a fundamental mistake as to quality since the application of the Rent Acts to property is a crucial consideration. Nevertheless the court purported to follow *Bell v. Lever Brothers* and held that the agreement was not void for mistake *ab initio* (from the beginning). In *Leaf v. International Galleries* (1950) the Court of Appeal also denied that the contract was void for mistake.

On the other hand the issue of mistake was never squarely raised in *Leaf's* case and the comments are therefore *obiter dicta*. Surely it is false apparently to regard a picture merely as a physical conglomeration of paint and canvas and not take account of the fact that it is often identified solely by reference to the painter? In *Nicholson & Venn v. Smith-Marriott* (1947) some table napkins were put up for sale as having been the authentic property of Charles I and consequently fetched £787. In fact they were much later and so only worth £105. Although the case was disposed of on other grounds Hallet J. said that the contract could have been held void for mistake. The buyers presumably wanted not just old napkins but an authentic Carolean relic. Surely this would come within Lord Atkin's statement in *Bell's* case that, " . . . a mistake will not affect assent unless it is the mistake of some quality which makes the thing without the quality essentially different from the thing as it was believed to be." Moreover, quite apart from *dicta* in *Bell's* case that are consistent with the wider view of there being a general doctrine of common law mistake, there is at least one case decided since *Bell v. Lever Brothers* and *Solle v. Butcher* where the court did decide that a contract could be held void for a mistake as to quality. In *Sheikh Bros. Ltd. v. Ochsner* (1957) A agreed to deliver at least 50 tons of sisal a month to B who would then process it and they would both share the profits. In fact the land could not produce at this rate; they had made a mistake as to its quality which was essential to the agreement. The Privy Council purporting to follow the decision in *Bell* decided that it was void. Although this decision is not technically binding on English courts, its persuasive value is surely very high. More recently in *Associated Japanese Bank (International) Ltd v. Credit du Nord SA*

(1988) (*Casebook*, Chap. 6). Steyn J. was unwilling to give what he regarded as an artificially restricted interpretation to the speeches in *Bell*. Accordingly, one of the grounds of his decision rested on the basis that there had been a mistake sufficient to render the contract void at common law, on the basis of common mistake, when certain machinery, whose existence was central to the operation of a lease and guarantee, was shown to have never existed.

Although there is no doubt that any doctrine of mistake at common law is extremely limited, it would therefore seem against the weight of authority to deny its existence altogether.

(3) The Intervention of Equity

The very narrow ambit of the doctrine of operative mistake at common law is to some extent relieved by the intervention of equity. Notwithstanding that an agreement is not *void* it may be set aside on the grounds that it is *voidable* in equity. Substantial justice between the parties is also aided by the fact that a court may set aside the agreement on terms.

A clear illustration is provided by *Solle v. Butcher*. Although as we have seen the agreement was held to be valid at law, the Court of Appeal declared it to be voidable. It did, however, set it aside on terms to ensure that neither party was unfairly prejudiced. Essentially, the tenant was given the choice of either leaving the flat or remaining on the same terms but at the increased rent of £250 a year. A similar approach was adopted in *Grist v. Bailey* (1967) where the mistake in a sale of property was as to the protection of the tenant under the Rent Acts and in *Magee v. Pennine Insurance Co. Ltd* (1969) over mistakes in an insurance proposal.

The underlying rationale in the case was explained in *Huddersfield Banking Co. Ltd v. Henry Lister & Son Ltd* (1895) by Kay L.J., " ... both on principle and authority, when once the court finds that an agreement has been come to between the parties who were under a common mistake of a material fact, the court may set it aside." The obvious difficulty with this very important equitable jurisdiction is to know just when it will be exercised. Certainly a court will not intervene if any of the events which bar rescission for misrepresentation has occurred. Probably the courts would not wish to tie themselves too closely to a set of rigid principles when the whole object of the exercise is to do broad justice as between the parties, but this clearly produces an unfortunate degree of uncertainty. If the facts of *Bell's* or *Leaf's* cases were to recur, would they now be disposed of under this jurisdiction (and see below, p. 633)? In any event, if the outcome of *Bell's* case leaves a lurking sense of injustice, it should be remembered that the plaintiff in such a case may still have a remedy of some other kind. For example, a defendant might be compelled to account for the profits earned through a breach of duty and repay them to an employer. Recovery of the money paid may also be possible if, as happened in *Sybron Corp. v. Rochem Ltd* (1983), it is established that the senior employees involved have acted dishonestly.

2. Mistake as to Agreement Between the Parties

As we saw in Chapter 15, when two parties are agreed on the same subject-matter in the same terms then they are bound. Sometimes, however, despite the appearance of agreement the parties are not really *ad idem*; a firm acceptance has not really connected on the same terms with the offer. For example, if I offer to sell you my "crop," meaning my riding whip, and you accept thinking you are buying the produce of my farm, then there is no real *consensus* despite the apparent verbal conjunction of offer and acceptance. As we shall see, the law would provide a remedy for such a mistake. Nevertheless the operation of a doctrine of mistake in this area is severely limited. It is not sufficient that a party is not getting what he anticipated from the bargain. The test which the law applies to the parties' dealings is objective. As Blackburn J. said in *Smith v. Hughes* (1871) (*Casebook*, Chap. 6): "If whatever a man's real intention may be, he so conducts himself that a reasonable man would believe that he was assenting to the terms proposed by the other party, and that other party upon that belief enters into the contract with him, the man thus conducting himself would be equally bound as if he had intended to agree to the other party's terms." Even if one party knows the other is labouring under a self-induced delusion this will not invalidate the agreement if to all outward purposes it is apparent that agreement has been reached. In the case itself the defendant was shown some oats by the plaintiff. He wanted old oats as the plaintiff apparently knew, but these were new oats. The defendant bought them labouring under the mistake that they were old oats which were the only kind he had any use for. There was no fraud and the plaintiff had done nothing at all to induce the erroneous belief in the defendant. The court held that the mere fact of the buyer's mistake as to the quality of the oats, even though known to the seller, did not invalidate the contract. Any reasonable onlooker would have drawn the reasonable inference that both parties were in agreement on the same terms on the precisely identified subject-matter.

Nevertheless, there are certain circumstances where the mistake is so fundamental and important to the parties that the law will regard the apparent agreement as void.

(1) Mistake as to Identity

A mistake as to identity renders the contract void if the true identity of the party is a crucial factor. If, for example, A visits his broker to take out an insurance policy on his car the actual identity of the insurance company may be a matter of complete indifference to him (see, *e.g. Mackie v. European Assurance Society* (1869) as long as his car is insured. Consequently a mistake as to the identity of the other contracting party would not have legal consequences. There may be other cases where identity is important, and not surprisingly some of the leading cases in the area involve confidence tricksters purporting to be well known and reputable figures.

In *Cundy v. Lindsay* (1878) (*Casebook*, Chap. 6) a respectable firm of merchants called "Blenkiron & Co." carried on business at 123 Wood Street, London. A rogue called Blenkarn hired a room, also in Wood Street, and placed an order for handkerchiefs with Lindsay & Co. The order came on a letter which gave his address in Wood Street and contained a signature which might have been read as "Blenkiron & Co." The plaintiffs forwarded the handkerchiefs to the rogue on credit and needless to say received no payment. Blenkarn had sold the handkerchiefs to Cundy, who acted in good faith, and Lindsay sued Cundy for conversion (*i.e.* wrongful dealing with the handkerchiefs). If the contract between Lindsay and Blenkarn was only voidable for Blenkarn's fraud Cundy would have a defence because at the time of the sale to them Blenkarn had a title to pass on. If, however, the contract was *void* then Cundy was bound by the normal rule that a person cannot effectively sell something to which he has no title. The House of Lords decided that there was no contract. The plaintiffs, as the rogue well knew, intended only to deal with the respectable firm of "Blenkiron & Co." and nobody else. Blenkarn was a completely different entity and the contract was therefore void. This can be contrasted with the decision in *King's Norton Metal Co. v. Edridge, Merrett & Co. Ltd* (1897). A rogue called Wallis adopted the name "Hallam & Co." His notepaper showed a large factory and claimed that "Hallam & Co." had depots and agencies in Belfast, Lille and Ghent. Using this notepaper he ordered goods from the plaintiffs which were delivered but never paid for. Again the issue arose as to the status of the agreement between the rogue and the plaintiffs. The court held that there was a contract. The plaintiffs intended to contract with the writer of the letter. There was nobody else. Their only mistake was not as to *identity* but as to the *attributes* of the rogue, in particular his credit-worthiness. This was not sufficient to render the contract *void*, but of course as was shown in Chapter 19 the agreement would be *voidable* for fraudulent misrepresentation. As was noted earlier, the vital difference is often in the rights that third parties will obtain in the latter but not in the former case.

Both the above cases involved parties dealing by letter. The situation is rather less clear where there is fraud and the parties are dealing *inter praesentes* (face to face). Does one look to the physical party standing in front of you, or to the entity he represents? The three crucial cases are not altogether easy to reconcile.

In *Phillips v. Brooks Ltd* (1919) a rogue called North entered a jeweller's shop and selected some pearls worth £2,550 and a ring at £450. He wrote out a cheque saying, "You see who I am, I am Sir George Bullough." The plaintiff had heard of Sir George as being a rich man and asked if he wished to take the articles with him. With some aplomb North replied that he would give an opportunity for the cheque to be cleared and just asked to take the ring for his wife's birthday. The cheque was subsequently dishonoured and North pawned the ring. In suing the pawnbroker for its return the agreement between the plaintiff and North fell to be considered. Was it a contract? The court said it was because the plaintiff, "had contracted to sell and deliver the ring to the person who came into his shop. ... His intention was to sell to the person present and identified by sight and hearing." The plaintiff had made a contract with the person in front of him, even though it might be voidable for fraud.

In *Ingram v. Little* (1961) three sisters advertised their car as for sale. They were visited by a rogue calling himself "Hutchinson" who made an offer of £717 for the car. As he was about to write a cheque, Elsie Ingram indicated that the deal was off as she was not prepared to take a cheque in payment. He thereupon falsely claimed to be a Mr. P. G. M. Hutchinson and gave an address. Hilda Ingram checked in the telephone directory that there was a person of that name at that address. They then allowed him to take the car. The cheque was later dishonoured and the rogue sold the car to a third party. The Court of Appeal held there was no contract. The plaintiffs intended only to deal with P. G. M. Hutchinson not the person who stood in front of them. It was not a mere mistake as to credit-worthiness, but as to identity.

Lewis v. Averay (1972) (*Casebook*, Chap. 6) involved another rogue who claimed to be Richard Green, an actor who portrayed the part of Robin Hood. The rogue offered to buy the plaintiff's car and signed the cheque "R. A. Green." The plaintiff asked for evidence of his identity and the rogue produced a Pinewood Studios pass with his name and photograph on it. The plaintiff handed over the car, the cheque was dishonoured and the rogue sold the car. Here the Court of Appeal said there was a contract, albeit voidable. The agreement was reached with the very person present.

How can one reconcile these three cases? Lord Denning in *Lewis v. Averay* thought that on their facts they were indistinguishable and the court preferred the approach of *Phillips v. Brooks*, which therefore seems to represent the present law. A further point of interest is that this appears to be an example of the Court of Appeal having to make a choice between two previous conflicting decisions (see above, p. 84.

The result is therefore that at least where parties are face to face there is a presumption that the parties intend to deal with the person who is physically present.

(2) Mistake as to Subject-Matter

If A intends to sell commodity X, and B intends to buy commodity Y, then clearly both parties are labouring under a mistake as to the subject-matter of the contract. This is in effect what happened in *Scriven Bros. & Co. v. Hindley & Co.* (1913). An auction contained two lots of hemp and tow respectively. Tow is inferior in quality to hemp. The cataloguing and wording of the separate lots was not altogether clear and the bidder wrongly thought both lots contained hemp and made an extravagant bid for the inferior quality tow. The plaintiff therefore intended to sell tow, but the defendant bidder intended to buy hemp. Neither party realised the mistake of the other. Clearly there was no genuine *consensus* between the parties, but was there a contract when the situation was looked at objectively? The court decided there was no contract. The circumstances were so ambiguous that it was impossible to be certain what commodity was being contracted for. The parties were not *ad idem*.

A similar situation arose in the leading case of *Raffles v. Wichelhaus* (1864). The buyer agreed to purchase a consignment of cotton to arrive "ex Peerless from Bombay." Unfortunately there were two ships called "Peerless" leaving Bombay at about the same time. The seller intended to deal in the cotton on board the ship leaving in December; the buyer intended to buy from the ship sailing in October. The case turned on the pleadings and the actual reason for the court's decision in favour of the buyer (when sued for refusing to accept the December shipment) is not clear, but it is commonly thought that there was no contract because it would not be open to a reasonable person to determine the sense of any agreement between the parties. The facts could be regarded as entirely ambiguous; the appropriate offer simply did not "connect" with the acceptance.

An agreement mistake merely as to the quality of the subject matter will not be sufficient as *Smith v. Hughes* (1871) shows. On the other hand if, as might be said in the case of *Nicholson & Venn v. Smith-Marriott* (1947), the mistake of quality was so great as to amount to a common mistake as to the identity of the subject matter then this would be an example of the other kind of operative mistake considered previously.

(3) Mistake over the Terms of the Contract

In general there is no relief if a party mistakenly interprets the effect of the agreement or one of its terms. So in *Wood v. Scarth* (1858) the plaintiff accepted the defendant's offer to lease a public house for £63 a year. The defendant thought his clerk had made it clear that a premium of £500 should be payable in addition, but he had in fact failed to do this. The court held that the agreement must stand. Any reasonable observer would have seen a precise and unambiguous offer and acceptance which the defendant's mistake could not be seen to vitiate.

However, the position is different where a party's mistake as to the terms of the deal is known to the other party. In *Hartog v. Colin & Shields* (1939) the defendants intended to sell skins at a certain price "per piece" as was apparently the custom in the trade and the basis of their negotiations. By a mistake they offered them "per pound" which worked out much cheaper. The buyers purported to accept this offer. The court held that there was no contract. The buyers were aware of the seller's mistake; there was no genuine offer to accept.

(4) Intervention of Equity

In principle the intervention of equity in this type of mistake is much more limited. The court has looked at the bargain and determined for itself the sense of the promise. Either there has been no real offer and acceptance so the contract is void, or there has so that it will be valid. One area where equity can, however, intervene is in refusing a decree of specific performance. Since like all equitable remedies it is discretionary the court may always withhold it if it is thought fairer to do so, but this would not prevent a claim for damages at law as indeed happened in *Wood v. Scarth* (1855). Equity even so would not refuse specific performance merely because one party found he had made a worse bargain than he thought as, for example, in *Tamplin v. James* (1880).

3. Rectification and Non Est Factum

In the case of written documents the law provides two further remedies where there has been a mistake.

(1) Rectification

In general a person who signs a document is bound by its terms whether or not he has understood or even read them, and no oral evidence is admitted to contradict such written terms. The former is sometimes described as the rule in *L'Estrange v. Graucob* (1934) (*Casebook*, Chap. 4) which provided a particularly harsh illustration of the principle, and the latter the parol evidence rule. Sometimes however a document will be executed which does not accurately reflect the prior agreement of the parties. In that case an application can be made to have the document rectified. As Cozens-Hardy M.R. stated in *Lovell & Christmas Ltd v. Wall* (1911): "The essence of rectification is to bring the document which was expressed and intended to be in pursuance of a prior agreement into harmony with that prior agreement." It is important to note that the court is not varying the agreement or remaking the bargain. It is merely ensuring that the document is an accurate record of the agreement already reached. In *Joscelyne v. Nissen* (1970), for example, a father and daughter who shared the same house agreed that the daughter should take over the father's car hire business and in return pay certain household expenses including gas, electricity and coal. The subsequent written document did not specifically refer to these expenses. After paying them for a while she refused to continue. The father brought an action for rectification of the agreement to include these specific payments. The Court of Appeal found for the plaintiff. There was a common continuing intention up to the time when the written document was executed. It could therefore be amended to ensure that it accurately reflected what the parties had in fact agreed.

(2) Non Est Factum

The plea of *non est factum* (this is not my deed) provides another exception to the rule that a person is bound by the terms of any document he has signed. The plea originated in the mediaeval common law to protect, for example, people who might have signed a document which they could not read and whose effect had been misrepresented to them. As social conditions have changed the ambit of the plea has been steadily reduced. It now operates only in somewhat extreme cases but it still remains a specific common law plea quite distinct from the law of misrepresentation and mistake. Its effect is that the purported agreement is completely void.

The whole area was thoroughly considered by the House of Lords in *Saunders v. Anglia Building Society* (1971) (*Casebook*, Chap. 6). Mrs. Gallie was a 78-year-old widow who had a nephew called Wally Parkin. She had left the house to Parkin in her will and handed over the deeds to him so that he could raise some money on the security of the house. Parkin and an acquaintance called Lee called at the house and asked her to sign a document. She was told that the deed was an assignment of the lease to her nephew to enable him to raise the money. Because she had broken her glasses she did not read the document, but did not object to her nephew raising money in that way. In fact it was a deed of sale to the dishonest Mr. Lee who failed to pay Mrs. Gallie or Parkin and mortgaged the house to a building society. After Lee defaulted on the mortgage repayments the building society sought possession of the house (the normal result of failure to keep up mortgage payments). Mrs. Gallie claimed that the assignment to Lee was void on the ground of *non est factum*. The House of Lords decided that the assignment was valid. Certainly Mrs. Gallie had been tricked, but she was not mistaken as to the "object of the exercise." She intended to enable Parkin to raise money. If Lee had not been dishonest, the transaction would have achieved this. The burden on a plaintiff to establish the plea is therefore a very heavy one. The Law Lords used various terms to describe the type of mistake required but it seems that the document must be fundamentally different in character from that which the signatory believed it to be. An example of the type of mistake required is provided by the case of *Lewis v. Clay* (1897). Here one Neville showed some documents to Clay which were largely covered by blotting paper except for some small gaps. Clay was told that his signature was required as a witness to a family arrangement; in fact they were documents which on their face made Clay liable for a payment of £11,113 to one Lewis. The court here in effect upheld a plea of *non est factum*.

The House of Lords also laid down a second requirement that a plaintiff would have to satisfy, in effect overruling an earlier case which had cast doubt on the matter. He must prove that he did not act negligently (not in the technical way that word is used in the tort of negligence but simply meaning "carelessly") in signing the document.

Identical principles apply to the person who signs an agreement in blank leaving someone else to fill in the details as in *United Dominions Trust v. Western* (1976). In such a case one would have thought that it will be almost impossible to prove that the person had not been careless in signing such a document. The result will be, as happened in the case, that the signatory will be bound by a contract which does not necessarily represent what he had agreed to.

Chapter 21

Privity

1. The Meaning of Privity

The doctrine of privity of contract states that no one who is not a party to the contract can either enforce it or be made liable upon it. It is something that was mentioned in Chapter 16 in the context of the requirement that consideration must move from the promisee. In other words, it is an aspect of the emphasis in English contract law on the element of "bargain." No one who has not put something into the contract can either take action or be sued upon it. We now need to examine this concept in more detail.

If A and B make a contract which purports to place some obligation upon C it is not difficult to see why the law would not enforce it. No one would think it right that C should have some obligation foisted upon him. But suppose A and B agreed that B should confer some benefit on C. Can C compel B's adherence to the contract? In this situation it is more difficult to see why C should not have a right of action. Nevertheless, the result of the doctrine of privity at common law is that C cannot enforce the agreement. He is a "stranger," as it is said, to the contract. The case of *Tweddle v. Atkinson* (1861) (*Casebook*, Chap. 7) (discussed in Chapter 16 above, p. 486) provides a simple illustration of that situation, and the House of Lords has on a number of occasions reaffirmed the general principle. In *Dunlop v. Selfridge* (1915) (*Casebook*, Chap. 7) the plaintiffs, Dunlop, sold tyres to Dew & Co. under a contract which stated that the buyers would not sell the tyres below a certain price and that a similar term would be part of any agreement between Dew & Co. and subsequent purchasers. Dew & Co. sold tyres to Selfridge who agreed not to sell below the fixed price and to pay Dunlop £5.00 for every tyre sold in breach of this agreement. Selfridge later supplied tyres to customers below the fixed price. Dunlop brought an action against Selfridge for damages and an injunction to restrain further breaches of contract. The

House of Lords gave judgment for Selfridge. There were in fact three distinct contracts; the first between Dunlop and Dew, the second between Dew and Selfridge, and the third between Selfridge and their customer. No doubt Dew could have sued Selfridge for failing to keep the contract made with them but Dunlop could sue neither Dew nor Selfridge. They could not sue Dew because Dew had honoured their contract by obtaining a promise from Selfridge that they would not sell the tyres below the stated price (note that Dew had not as part of their bargain with Dunlop promised that they would additionally seek to restrain Selfridge from selling below the stated price) and they could not directly proceed against Selfridge because they had struck no bargain with them. Their reasoning can easily be grasped by looking at the diagram.

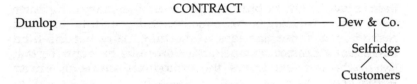

CONTRACT
Dunlop ————————————————————————— Dew & Co.
                                                    |
                                             Selfridge
                                              ╱ ╲
                                           Customers

It was as if Dunlop were trying to take advantage of somebody else's agreement.

Like many legal rules, much of the complication arises from attempts by the courts to relieve parties from the injustice of an over-strict application of the general principle. An example of the difficulties imposed by the doctrine of privity is provided by *Jackson v. Horizon Holidays Ltd* (1975) (*Casebook*, Chap. 7). The plaintiff contracted with the defendants for a holiday in Ceylon for himself, his wife and children. It was a less than euphoric experience. The hotel plumbing did not work properly and there was mould growing up the walls. The defendants were clearly in breach of contract, but the damage extended not only to the maker of the agreement but also to his family who were not parties to the contract. Lord Denning at least thought that the plaintiff could recover damages on behalf of both himself and his family, but this is difficult to square with orthodox privity of contract. As was pointed out by the House of Lords in *Woodar Investment Development Ltd v. Wimpey Construction U.K. Ltd* (1980) the award of damages to Mr Jackson for the loss suffered by his family could be supported on the basis that his family's failure to enjoy their holiday was itself a loss to the original contracting party, Mr. Jackson. His own personal distress could be said to have been increased by witnessing the distress of his family.

Some elucidation of this area has now been achieved by the decision of the House of Lords in *Linden Gardens Trust Ltd v. Lenesta Sludge Disposals Ltd* (1993). There the plaintiff was said to be entitled to damages both because of his own loss and because this type of building contract fell within an exception to the rule that a plaintiff could not recover for loss suffered by a third party. Lord Browne-Wilkinson regarded it as "apparently established that, if a defective meal or holiday is supplied, the contracting party can recover damages not only for his own bad meal or unhappy holiday but also for that of his guests or family".

Whilst therefore approving Lord Denning's innovative approach in *Jackson* this decision leaves for subsequent case law an exploration of just what those exceptional cases are. What it does make clear is that the third party has no independent right to bring an action. If the contracting party does recover damages he may be under a duty to make restitution of those damages to the third party but the third party himself cannot compel an action to be brought. To that extent the decision leaves the orthodox doctrine of privity untouched.

Nevertheless, what follows shows some of the ways the law has sought to mitigate the effects of the doctrine of privity or to recognise legitimate limitations upon it such as the law of agency.

2. Limitations to the Doctrine of Privity

(1) Implying a Trust

Suppose A gives £1,000 to B with instructions that, while A is abroad, the money is to be spent on C's welfare. This creates the legal mechanism of a "trust." B (the trustee) holds the money on trust for C (the beneficiary of the trust). C as the person entitled under the trust can sue B in equity for the performance of his obligation as trustee. One of the contributions of equity to the problems created by the doctrine of privity is to extend the notion of a trust affecting property such as money to that of the benefit of a promise. The promise is the "property" which is the subject-matter of the trust. Accordingly a beneficiary, C, can enforce the trust against say, B, where A has contracted to vest some property or benefit in B for the benefit of C. The principle becomes clearer if we examine a case where the House of Lords approved it.

In *Les Affréteurs Réunis S.A. v. Walford* (1919) Walford, a broker, negotiated a charterparty (a contract for the use of a ship) between the owners of a ship and the charterers (the people who wanted to use it). The agreement made between the owners and the charterers contained a term that the owners would pay Walford a 3 per cent. commission on the estimated gross amount of hire, which was not in fact paid. Walford sued the owners for this commission. He also applied to join the charterers as parties and the action proceeded as if this had been done. The House of Lords gave judgment for Walford, Lord Birkenhead declaring "in such cases charterers can sue as trustees on behalf of the broker." The reasoning, as can be seen from the diagram, was that since the charterers were trustees of the promise to pay Walford commission, Walford as the beneficiary could enforce his claim either by getting the charterers to join him as co-plaintiff or by compelling them to act by joining them as co-defendant. Either way the beneficiary could enforce his interest despite not being a party to the original contract between the owners and charterers.

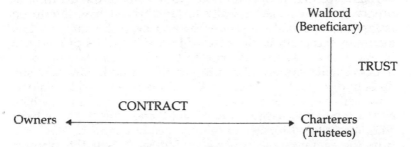

If this idea had been developed then there is no doubt that the doctrine of privity could have been robbed of much of its effect. The behaviour of the courts since *Walford's* case has, however, been to make scant use of the machinery of the constructive trust as it is called. No doubt this is partially owing to the fact that a trust must be irrevocable (in other words, it cannot subsequently be altered) and many of the situations which at first sight might be thought to be amenable to the constructive trust analysis turn out to contain elements which the parties would never wish to make unalterable. For example, in *Re Schebsman, Official Receiver v. Cargo Superintendents (London) Ltd and Schebsman* (1944) Schebsman had been employed by two companies. He entered into an agreement with them whereby he, or in the event of his death his wife and daughter, was to receive a sum of £5,500. Schebsman first went bankrupt then died and one of the arguments advanced in the subsequent litigation was that the deceased held the company's promise as trustee on trust for his wife and daughter. This argument, if it had succeeded, would have enabled them directly to enforce the trust. The Court of Appeal rejected the argument. Lord Greene M.R. said: " ... it is not legitimate to impart into the contract the idea of a trust when the parties have given no indication that such was their intention. To interpret this contract as creating a trust would, in my judgment, be to disregard the dividing line between the case of a trust and the simple case of a contract made between two persons for the benefit of a third."

Such a view seems to indicate that the constructive trust is not likely to pose much of a threat to the orthodox doctrine of privity.

(2) The Restrictive Covenant

Land and interests over land generally have a degree of permanence that people do not. The results of the doctrine of privity if applied mechanically to land would have produced highly inconvenient consequences and even the common law made an exception in the case of leases. If A lets property to B, and B later assigns his lease to C, then C can be bound by the covenants and terms that originally bound B. C would still be bound to the new lessor if A sold his interest to D. Equity, however, has made a later and separate contribution which clearly operates in the case of land and which some have sought to extend further to other types of contract.

In the famous case of *Tulk v. Moxhay* (1848) the plaintiff owned several plots of land in the middle of Leicester Square. He sold the garden in the centre to one Elms who agreed as part of the contract not to build upon the garden. The land was conveyed a number of times until it eventually came into the possession of one Moxhay who knew of the original covenant but nevertheless proposed to build on the land. The plaintiff realised that on orthodox principles he could not succeed at common law so he sought an injunction in equity to restrain the building. The court granted the injunction on the basis that it would be unconscionable to allow the defendant to disregard a contractual obligation which he knew about at the time of purchase. Although the doctrine has been modified and developed somewhat since then, the case provides a basis for the principle that negative covenants (*e.g.* a restriction on building) can be made to run with the land itself so as to bind subsequent purchasers who have notice of the restriction, even though they were not parties to the original agreement.

In two areas in particular, that of price control and the use of a chattel (in this sense any property other than land), an attempt has been made to apply similar principles to those which restrict the use of land.

(a) *Price control*

The difficulty in imposing price control as a result of the doctrine of privity has already been seen in *Dunlop v. Selfridge*. In *Taddy v. Sterious* (1904) a more determined attempt was made. The plaintiffs, tobacco manufacturers, attached a printed sheet to each packet stating, as a term of the contract of sale, that the tobacco was only sold "on the express condition that retail dealers do not sell it below the prices above set forth." If the retail dealer had bought through a wholesaler, then the latter was stated to be regarded as the plaintiff's agent (more will be said of agency later). The agency argument was rejected, but the second argument advanced was that the principle of *Tulk v. Moxhay* should be applied to the price restriction. The court roundly rejected this. Swinfen Eady J. said: "Conditions of this kind do not run with goods and cannot be imposed upon them. Subsequent purchasers, therefore, do not take subject to any conditions which the court can enforce."

This area is now in any event governed by statute. After a rather complicated legislative history the law has been consolidated in the Resale Prices Act 1976. The effect of Parts I and II of the Act is that minimum price clauses are void unless they fall within a class of goods which the Restrictive Practices Court is prepared to exempt. So at common law the rule was that while A could by contract with B enforce a minimum price at which B was to sell the goods, A could not enforce a similar undertaking given by C who bought the goods from B. Now, as the result of statutory provisions directed against resale price maintenance, A cannot oblige B to sell the goods at any particular price.

(b) *Use of a chattel*

An attempt was made to apply the doctrine of *Tulk v. Moxhay* to a ship in *De Mattos v. Gibson* (1858). Knight Bruce

L.J. expressed himself in broad terms that certainly favoured the application, although it should perhaps be borne in mind that at the time of this statement the principle in *Tulk v. Moxhay* was comparatively recent and had not yet reached the degree of development it has later achieved. In particular, requirements have been appended to the notion of the restrictive covenant in respect of land which were not apparent in the years after 1845 and which suggest that it is a doctrine of narrower application than might have been thought soon after the decision. Nevertheless, the Privy Council in *Lord Strathcona Steamship Co. v. Dominion Coal Co.* (1926) approached another shipping case in a way that suggests they were seeking to apply the restrictive covenant doctrine. The case has, however, been heavily criticised. In a subsequent case, *Clore v. Theatrical Properties Ltd* (1936), Lord Wright M.R. commented that the *Strathcona* principle should be restricted "to the very special case of a ship under a charterparty" and in *Port Line Steamers Ltd v. Ben Line Steamers Ltd* (1958) Diplock J. (later Lord Diplock) expressed the view that the *Strathcona* case was wrongly decided. Even so, the doctrine gets some support from the observations of Browne-Wilkinson J. in *Swiss Bank Corp. v. Lloyds Bank Ltd* (1979).

The result of the cases therefore seems to be that whilst the doctrine of the restrictive covenant is not altogether unarguable in the case of charterparties, it would require a substantial dose of artificial respiration to bring it back to full vigour. Outside this area it seems unlikely that the doctrine has any application.

(3) Statutory Interventions

In some cases Parliament has intervened to resolve the problems posed by the doctrine of privity, especially in the area of insurance. For example section 11 of the Married Women's Property Act 1882 states that where a husband or wife insures his or her life for the benefit of their spouse or children this will create a trust in favour of the objects of the policy. This section therefore provides the spouse or children with an enforceable right of action even though they are not parties to the original agreement.

One statutory provision which has caused difficulty in the past is section 56(1) of the Law of Property Act 1925. On the face of it, this provision appears to state that someone who is not named as a party to a "conveyance or other agreement" can take the benefit of the agreement. Lord Denning interpreted the section as making at least a large dent in the orthodox doctrine of privity but the House of Lords did not agree. The point arose for determination in *Beswick v. Beswick* (1968). Peter Beswick sold his business to his nephew John on terms that Peter would receive a weekly payment for the rest of his life and in the event of his death his widow was to receive £5 per week. After Peter's death John made only one payment to his widow. She thereupon sued (i) as administratrix (a person appointed to administer the estate of the deceased) of her husband's estate, and (ii) in her personal capacity. In the House of Lords the second argument was rejected. Section 56(1), their Lordships decided, was limited in effect to covenants relating to land. Although the words could literally have supported Lord Denning's contention it was felt that Parliament could not possibly have intended to make such a major change in the doctrine of privity in contract generally in a statute devoted to reforming the law of real property (see above, p. 73). Nevertheless the House upheld the claim on the first argument and granted a decree of specific performance of the agreement. In effect, Mrs. Beswick was not suing as a third party benefiting under a contract but rather as the representative of the original promisee. The result therefore was satisfactory and within the spirit of the doctrine of privity.

(4) Agency

The law of agency is an extensive legal topic which warrants a book to itself but it does have an important relevance to the present discussion.

The essence of agency is that one person is appointed to be the representative of another. The commercial convenience of such an arrangement has long been recognised and indeed the present law of agency is largely derived from the custom of merchants. To some extent, however, it does appear to conflict with the doctrine of privity and this is why it needs to be considered at this point. Normally, as we have seen, if A contracts with B these are the only two parties who can enforce the agreement. Yet if A is the agent of someone else, P (called in law the principal), then P becomes able to sue or be sued upon a contract which he has not personally made. In most cases this will not be thought of as offending anything but the strict letter of the privity doctrine. After all, B may know perfectly well that A always acts as the agent of P and therefore it accords with the expectations of everyone involved that the real contract is between P and B. A is simply an intermediary who drops out of the picture. In a sense, he is the crucial link in a chain that really binds only the parties P and B together. Such an approach fits many of the situations in which the concept of agency operates, but the law goes somewhat further than this.

Quite apart from the occasions when A has actual authority to enter into a contract on behalf of P the law also recognises so-called "ostensible" or "apparent" authority. Lord Denning explained this concisely in *Hely-Hutchinson v. Brayhead Ltd* (1968) when he said: "Ostensible or apparent authority is the authority of an agent as it appears to others. It often coincides with actual authority. Thus, when the board [of a company] appoint one of their number to be managing director, they invest him not only with implied authority, but also with ostensible authority to do all such things as fall within the usual scope of the office. Other people who see him acting as managing director are entitled to assume that he has the usual authority of a managing director. But sometimes ostensible authority exceeds actual authority. For instance, when the board appoint the managing director they may expressly limit his authority by saying he is not to order goods worth more than £500 without the sanction of the board. In that case his *actual* authority is subject to the £500 limitation, but his *ostensible* authority includes all the usual authority of a managing director. The company is bound by his ostensible authority in his dealings with those who do not know of the limitation." Accordingly if the director orders goods worth £5,000 in breach of his *actual* authority the seller may still sue the company for payment if it appeared to the seller that he had apparent authority. This moves a little further from the doctrine of privity in that P finds himself bound by a contract that he at least had no wish to make as well as not being personally involved with the transaction. But such a claim must be based on some sort of conduct by P: it cannot rest solely on false representation by the agent about his authority (*Armagas v. Mundogas* (1986)).

An even greater deviation from the notion of privity is the doctrine of the undisclosed principal. If A has in fact been authorised to act as P's agent but A makes a contract with B where to all outward appearances A is acting entirely for himself, P can nevertheless sue and be sued as the undisclosed principal. In this case of course not only does B not intend to benefit or burden P, he does not even know he exists. The justification for such a rule appears to rest on the basis that it has been found a convenient practice in business. Diplock L.J. in one of the leading agency cases, *Freeman &*

Lockyer v. Buckhurst Park Properties Ltd (1964), explained it thus: "It may be that this rule relating to 'undisclosed principals,' which is peculiar to English law, can be rationalised as avoiding circuity of action, for the principal could in equity compel the agent to lend his name in an action to enforce the contract against the contractor, and would at common law be liable to indemnify the agent in respect of the performance of the obligations assumed by the agent under the contract." Whatever its explanation it is an undoubtedly valid doctrine which does not readily square with orthodox notions of privity.

(5) Assignment and Negotiability

Both these topics would require extensive space to cover in any detail. They are here examined merely to see how they relate to the doctrine of privity.

(a) *Assignment*

In view of what we have seen about the way the doctrine of privity operates it may seem surprising that it is possible to assign the benefit of a contractual arrangement. This was a development of equity which has since been assisted by statute. For example, suppose A owes B £1,000. A is described as the debtor and B the creditor in this situation. It is possible for B to assign the debt to C who can then enforce it directly against A. B has in effect given away (as one might sell or give away any item of valuable property) his right to enforce the debt and so drops out of the picture. A debt is the most obvious form of such a right but there are others. Such "choses in action" as they are described (that is, intangible property or rights which can only be obtained or enforced by bringing an action in court) also include copyrights, patents, shares in a company, insurance policies or benefits under a trust. Of course it is possible for the parties to include a term in the contract that the rights or benefits arising under it shall not be assignable, and certain rights as a matter of policy cannot be assigned. For example, a wife cannot assign any right to maintenance payments. A further limitation is that although the benefit of a contract can be assigned, the burden cannot be. So in the above example A could not, even with D's consent, assign to D the obligation to pay B.

Equity's development of this area can again be explained by the common law's failure to meet the demands of business convenience. A simple and reliable machinery for assignment is supplied by section 136(1) of the Law of Property Act 1925. This provides that where an assignment of any chose in action is (i) absolute (*e.g.* complete and not, say, conditional upon something else happening), (ii) written, and (iii) notice in writing has been given to the debtor, then this will be effective to pass the whole legal interest in the thing in action to the assignee.

(b) *Negotiability*

Some types of contractual benefit are so readily assignable as to become negotiable, and such written choses in action are called negotiable instruments.

They arose out of business convenience and special rules relating to them are found largely in the Bills of Exchange Act 1882. The distinction and advantage of negotiable instruments over normal assignments is that various technicalities which might inhibit exchange do not apply to them. For example, it is never necessary to inform the debtor that there has been a transfer. In addition, the person to whom the instrument is transferred is said to take "free from equities". This means that the bona fide holder in due course of the instrument, *i.e.* the transferee, is not at risk of having its value reduced by, for example, a set-off between the original parties to the transaction. In other words, it avoids the risk that the real value of the instrument is less than its apparent face value.

Promissory notes, certain types of bonds and share certificates are all examples of negotiable instruments. Cheques also fall into this category but their negotiability has been curbed as a practical matter by the Cheques Act 1992. Section 1 states that a cheque crossed "account payee" shall not be transferable, meaning that the recipient cannot endorse the cheque and transfer it to a third party. In practice high street banks routinely supply cheques with these words printed across their face.

3. Conclusion

Despite Lord Scarman's dictum in *Woodar Investment Development Ltd v. Wimpey Construction U.K. Ltd* (1980) that: "If the opportunity arises, I hope the House will reconsider *Tweddle v. Atkinson* and the other cases which stand guard over this unjust rule". The doctrine of privity has shown considerable resilience. It has not suffered the erosion of subsequent cases which sometimes renders a general principle the insubstantial ghost of its original form. Most of the authoritative decisions of the courts, such as for example *Beswick v. Beswick*, have in the end tended to reaffirm the orthodox doctrine rather than to undermine it. There are, as we have seen, various inroads both common law and statutory into the integrity of the principle but they tend to be well established and relatively clearly demarcated. For an old doctrine, it still shows a youthful vigour.

Chapter 22

Incapacity, Illegality, Duress and Undue Influence

So far we have examined the various ingredients which are required to constitute a contract and some of the things that can go wrong so as to make it defective. Before leaving consideration of how contracts are formed we need to examine briefly a further set of rules which may come into play. Notwithstanding that all the formal requirements of a contract are present and that there has been no question of misrepresentation or mistake a contract may still be invalid, either in part or in whole, as a result of the incapacity of a party to make a contract or the illegality of the transaction itself or the fact that undue pressure has been brought to bear on one of the parties. In all these areas the underlying rationale is that of public policy. Certain classes of person are thought of as requiring protection or special consideration and certain types of transaction break the law because they offend moral or economic values which society considers to be worth protecting.

I. INCAPACITY

Generally speaking anyone is capable and competent to bind himself by any contract which is not in itself illegal or contrary to public policy. Certain persons, however, are said to lack capacity to contract freely. The unlikely assortment which makes up this group includes minors, corporations, the mentally disordered and drunkards. Of these only the first will be looked at in any detail.

1. Minors

The term "infant" used to be applied to anyone under the age of 21 but by virtue of the Family Law Reform Act 1969 the age of majority was reduced to 18. The Act also replaces the rather outworn terminology "infant" with "minor" and although these terms are effectively interchangeable, the latter is the one used in modern statutes. One might have expected the law in such a basic area to be straightforward and long settled. Unfortunately it is somewhat involved even after the reforms introduced by the Minors' Contracts Act 1987. Amongst other changes, this Act repealed the tortuous provisions of the Infants' Relief Act 1874. In its place, a somewhat unusual reform for a modern statute, the pre-existing common law has been restored. The result is that contracts with minors fall into three broad categories. There are those that are perfectly valid; those that can be disaffirmed; and those that cannot be enforced against a minor even without his prior disaffirmation. These will be examined in turn. It is the special rules relating to contracts with minors which explain why so many order and booking forms include a term that the signatory must be over 18. No supplier of goods or services wants to find himself in difficulties recovering the price because he has sought to contract with a minor.

(1) Contracts Which are Valid

These are agreements where the minor's liability to sue or be sued is effectively the same as anyone else of full capacity. They fall into two categories; (a) contracts for so-called "necessaries," and (b) contracts of service.

(a) Contracts for necessaries

It has long been the law that a minor can be sued for the price of "necessaries." These not only include such essentials as food and clothing but also those articles or services which are appropriate to one in his station in life. As regards goods, the Sale of Goods Act 1979, s.3(2) states that: " 'necessaries' means goods suitable to the condition in life of the minor or other person concerned and to his actual requirements at the time of sale and delivery." The common law applies a similar test to services.

The operation of the law is illustrated by the leading case of *Nash v. Inman* (1908). A Savile Row tailor supplied a Cambridge undergraduate with, "eleven fancy waistcoats at two guineas each." When he sued for payment he was met with the plea of infancy. The Court of Appeal gave judgment for the defendant. Although he was, "the son of an architect of good position" so that the clothing might well have been "suitable to the condition in life of the minor," the plaintiff failed to satisfy the second limb of the statutory definition. They were not suitable to his actual requirements at the time. His father had given uncontradicted evidence that he was already adequately supplied with clothes.

Necessary services include such matters as legal and medical advice and education. A further illustration is supplied by *Chapple v. Cooper* (1844). An undertaker sued a widow, who was an infant, for the cost of her husband's funeral. It was held that this was a necessary for which the widow was liable. Obviously this involves a slight, though doubtless sensible, extension to the concept of what is necessary since in a sense there is no direct personal benefit to an infant in the burial of a deceased person.

The range of necessaries clearly cannot be a closed category and will vary with the status of the minor and the subject-matter of the contract.

The precise legal basis for a minor's liability is strangely not entirely clear. Some have suggested it is simply contract; others quasi-contract. In other words, liability rests on the basis that the infant has been supplied with goods and should not be unfairly enriched (see for example Fletcher Moulton L.J. in *Nash v. Inman*). Whatever view is correct there is one other anomaly concerning contracts with minors at least in respect of the sale of goods. Section 3(2) states that a minor need only pay "a reasonable price" for goods delivered. Hence an agreed contract price may turn out to be more than that which the minor can lawfully be compelled to pay.

(b) *Beneficial contracts of service*

The law is designed to protect a minor, not prevent him from earning a living. Hence it has long been the case that a minor can bind himself by a so-called beneficial contract of service. This really means a contract of employment which, taken as a whole, is substantially to his advantage even though it may contain some term or terms which are disadvantageous to him. Two contrasting cases bring out the principle which a court applies.

In *De Francesco v. Barnum* (1890) a 14-year-old girl entered into an indenture (meaning agreement) of apprenticeship with De Francesco to be taught stage dancing. The agreement was, to say the least, somewhat one-sided. She was not to marry during the seven-year period of the agreement; she could not contract professional engagements without written consent; she was entirely at the disposal of her master. He on the other hand made no commitment to employ her and even when he did the rate of pay was very low; he could send her to work abroad; if at any time he considered her unfit he could put an end to the agreement. Fry L.J. concluded: "Those are stipulations of an extraordinary and unusual character, which throw, or appear to throw, an inordinate power into the hands of the master without any correlative obligation on the part of the master." The court held the contract to be invalid as not being for the infant's benefit.

In *Clements v. London and N.W. Rail Co.* (1894) an infant was employed by a railway company as a porter. The company operated an insurance scheme amongst its employees whereby in exchange for giving up his right to sue the employer for personal injuries under the Employers' Liability Act 1880 he received certain benefits. Although the level of compensation was lower than that which might be obtained under the Act, it did not depend upon proving negligence and embraced a wider range of possible accidents. When the infant was injured in an accident the validity of the agreement fell to be considered. It was held to be valid. Taken as a whole, the contract was for the infant's benefit and binding upon him.

The trend in recent cases has been to extend the notion of contract of service to analogous situations. So in *Doyle v. White City Stadium Ltd* (1935) the infant plaintiff entered into an agreement with the British Boxing Board to obtain a fighter's licence. One of the terms of the licence was that in the event of a foul and disqualification the fighter should only receive his travelling expenses and not the "purse." Doyle was disqualified for hitting below the belt. The court held that even though in this case the contract had deprived him of a £3,000 "purse" the agreement as a whole was analogous to a beneficial contract of service and was therefore binding upon him.

(2) Contracts Which are Voidable

These are contracts which although valid at the moment they are made, the minor may repudiate before he is 18 or within a reasonable time afterwards. There is no sanction against his repudiation as would be the case with anyone else. The types of contract which come within this category include contracts concerning land (for example for a lease of property), company shares, partnership and marriage settlements. The common denominator in all these transactions is that they concern relatively durable arrangements in respect of property.

If the minor repudiates the agreement before any obligations have arisen under it then there is no doubt that the whole arrangement is a nullity. It is as if it had never happened. Two problems, however, may arise: (i) what of obligations that have accrued before the minor's repudiation, and (ii) what of money that the minor may have paid over under the avoided contract?

As regards (i), there is a curious lack of conclusive authority and conflicting dicta in cases and textbook writers alike. Pending a conclusive decision the balance of opinion favours the view that a minor is liable on a contract debt that has arisen *before* repudiation. Such a view would seem at least to minimise the disruptive effect of a minor's privilege to repudiate.

The recovery of money paid under the "contract" depends upon whether or not there has been what is called a total failure of consideration. In other words, he must have got nothing at all out of the arrangement. Two contrasting cases make the point. In *Corpe v. Overton* (1833) a minor agreed to enter into a partnership and paid a £100 deposit which would be forfeited if he failed to execute (*i.e.* sign so as to make operative) the deed. Before the deed was executed the minor repudiated the agreement. He was held entitled to the return of his £100. At the time he repudiated, he had received nothing. The situation was different in *Steinberg v. Scala (Leeds) Ltd.* (1923). Here a minor bought shares in Scala which were not fully paid up. When shares are not fully paid up the company can subsequently require a shareholder to make payments up to the nominal value of the shares. This was done by Scala and the minor paid a further £250 on the shares. She now wished to repudiate the contract and reclaim the £250. Her claim failed. Even though she was freed from any future obligation to make payment, there had not been a total failure of consideration and she could not recover past payments. She had applied for the shares and she had got them.

(3) Contracts Which are Unenforceable

The general rule at common law, subject to the two qualifications considered above, is that a contract made by a minor does not bind him. Even so, the transaction is not necessarily without legal consequences. First, the contract may bind the other party. Secondly, if the minor pays money to the other party in performance of the contract he may not be able to recover it, at least unless there has been a total failure of consideration. Thirdly, if a person over 18 ratifies a contract entered into whilst he was still a minor he then becomes liable. Sometimes these contracts are described as "voidable" but this is clearly something of a misnomer. Normally the description "voidable" means that the contract is valid unless and until it is repudiated. This certainly applies to the cases discussed in (2) above, but inappropriately describes a transaction which is only binding on the minor if he chooses to affirm it whilst the other party has no right to avoid the contract.

A loan is an obvious example of a contract which cannot be enforced against a minor and indeed it is an offence under section 50 of the Consumer Credit Act 1974 to send literature to a minor inviting him to borrow money or obtain goods or services on credit. One exception to this general rule exists where the money loaned has been used for the purchase of necessaries. In this case the lender can maintain an action in equity for the money actually laid out in the purchase of the necessaries.

In the light of the above rules it is easy to see why retailers might be reluctant to have dealings with minors. Even a guarantee of the minor's contractual obligation given by an adult was rendered unenforceable and so worthless by the Infants' Relief Act 1874. Section 2 of the 1987 Act therefore enacts a significant reform by providing that such a guarantee will no longer be unenforceable merely because the contract with the minor cannot be enforced. This benefits the minor who might now be expected to have less difficulty obtaining a loan or credit whilst at the same time protecting the other party to the transaction who can now rely upon a valid guarantee.

(4) Contract and Tort

Generally speaking an infant is liable in tort in the same way as an adult. The significance of this is that in some contexts tort and contract overlap, and it has accordingly been held that where a tort is directly connected with a contract, suing the infant in tort cannot be used as a way to get round the unenforceability of the contract. An example is *Fawcett v. Smethurst* (1914). Here the infant defendant hired a car for a specific journey but in the event drove it further than was agreed. The car was damaged on the journey but the plaintiff's claim for damages in tort failed. Success would have meant that the plaintiff could get indirectly what he could not get directly (see also *Leslie Ltd v. Sheill* (1914)).

(5) The Intervention of Equity

A law designed to safeguard minors against exploitation could easily work an injustice against people of full capacity who contract with them. Accordingly even the common law developed the doctrine of quasi-contract to allow recovery of money paid where the effect was to unjustly enrich the recipient, for example money paid over on a mistake of fact. Nevertheless an action in quasi-contract will not be enforceable against a minor if its effect is indirectly to enforce an unenforceable contract. So in *Leslie v. Sheill* an infant fraudulently represented that he was of full age and thereby obtained a loan of £400. Clearly this could not be recovered under contract law, but the plaintiffs also rested their claim on the tort of deceit and quasi-contract. Both these claims failed.

Equity has made an important contribution in the doctrine of restitution. The principle is that those who have been unjustly enriched should be made to disgorge their profits, and this principle can be applied to infants. So if an infant fraudulently obtains goods and remains in possession of them, an order for restitution will be made to restore them to the plaintiff.

In practice this equitable remedy is likely to be superseded by the new power granted by section 3 of the Minors' Contracts Act 1987. This provision enables courts to order restitution of property acquired under an unenforceable or repudiated contract, "if it is just and equitable to do so." The important departure from previous law is that the court's power to make such an order is no longer restricted to the case where the minor has acted fraudulently. If the minor has sold or exchanged the property he may still be compelled to pay the price or hand over the goods received in exchange. If, however, the minor no longer possesses the goods or their proceeds, for example he may have already consumed them, then no order for payment of the purchase price or value of the goods can be made. To do so would have the practical effect of circumventing what is still an unenforceable agreement.

One equitable remedy not available to a minor is specific performance. Since mutuality is a precondition of this remedy, and specific performance cannot be enforced against a minor, so he cannot obtain this remedy against anyone else.

2. Corporations

A corporation is a legal entity which is treated by the law as being separate from the person or persons who constitute it. They may be created by Royal Charter or statute. Universities for example tend to be created by Royal Charter. The most common form of statutory corporation is a registered company under the Companies Act 1985. The law regards a corporation as just as much an individual as a natural person, but places certain restrictions on their capacity. Corporations created by statute may only contract *intra vires* (within the power) which the statute or memorandum of association of the company authorises, otherwise the contract is void. The rationale behind this is that shareholders and creditors should be protected against directors who employ company resources for unauthorised objectives. Nevertheless the practical effect of this doctrine is reduced by the fact that the memorandum of association of a company can be (and usually is) widely drafted. Further, section 35 of the Companies Act 1985, as amended by the Companies Act 1989, states that a transaction is *deemed* to be within the capacity of the company where the other party deals in good faith. A company can no longer therefore escape from a contract on the grounds that it was *ultra vires*, at least where the other party acts bona fide. The wording of the section, "In favour of a person dealing with a company . . . " leaves open the possibility that *ultra vires* could be pleaded as a defence by a party against whom a company seeks to enforce a contract.

3. The Mentally Disordered

If a person was suffering from such a degree of mental disability that he was incapable of understanding the nature of the contract, then the contract is *voidable* at the election of the person of unsound mind provided he can show that the other party knew of his disability (see, *e.g. Hart v. O'Connor* (1985)). The last proviso does not apply where the contract is for necessaries, but by virtue of section 3(2) of the Sale of Goods Act 1979 he is then only obliged to pay a "reasonable price."

4. Drunkenness

The general view appears to be that drunken persons are in a similar position to those suffering from a mental disorder, and section 3(2) of the 1979 Act also applies to them. One obvious difference is that it is never likely to be a problem to show that the other party was aware of the drunkenness. If one party was so intoxicated that he did not know what he was doing then this ought to be quite obvious to the other party.

II. ILLEGALITY

A full, or even adequate, treatment of the way in which certain transactions may offend some legal rule and thereby become defective lies outside the scope of the present work and is to some extent peripheral to the central principles of contract law. But it is still important to note that sometimes agreements which on the face of it might be thought of as binding are not recognised as effective by the courts for reasons other than the incapacity of the parties. The terminology of this complex area is not always used with complete accuracy or consistency but the major distinction which is normally drawn is that between contracts which are "void" and those that are "illegal." An illegal agreement cannot be enforced because it is of a kind that is in effect prohibited. A void contract (in this context) is one that is simply unenforceable or denied its full validity. One result of this distinction is that although an illegal contract taints any other transaction that depends upon it, a void one being only unenforceable does not necessarily do so. It is convenient to consider first void and then illegal contracts both of which can arise either by statute or common law.

1. Void Contracts

(1) Contracts Which are Void by Statute

Numerous transactions are rendered void by statute and reference has to be made to specialised works to discover how statutory provisions affect a transaction. Two obvious examples are wagering and restrictive trading agreements.

(a) *Wagering agreements*

The whole area of wagering and gambling is heavily regulated by statute. An example is section 18 of the Gaming Act 1845 which provides:

> "All contracts or agreements, whether by parole or in writing, by way of gaming or wagering, shall be null and void, and no suit shall be brought or maintained in any Court of Law or Equity for recovering any sum of money or valuable thing alleged to be won upon any wager. ..."

The result of such a provision is that although a wagering transaction is not illegal in the sense that it is proscribed, it simply cannot be enforced if a party to it refuses either to pay the agreed stake or hand over the winnings. For the purposes of this section a wagering contract is one where there are only two parties so that, for example, a football pool is not within the section. Nevertheless, as we saw in Chapter 17, such a transaction is usually unenforceable for the reason that the parties choose to exclude a legally binding relationship (see, *e.g. Jones v. Vernon's Pools Ltd* (1938)). A further result of the section is that if the wagering transaction is paid by cheque which the drawer subsequently "stops" then the payee cannot sue on the cheque even though this would normally be an ordinary recoverable contract debt.

Even an indirect way of enforcing such a transaction has been held to be invalid. In *Hill v. William Hill (Park Lane) Ltd* (1949) a race-horse owner owed some £3,635 in unpaid debts. He was ordered by Tattersalls to pay the debt by instalments or else, in effect, be blacklisted. He failed to pay. Later in exchange for a promise not to enforce the order he promised to pay. Even though there was therefore a separate agreement with fresh consideration the House of Lords held the arrangement to be void. In substance it was an agreement to recover a sum of money won upon a wager and therefore within the terms of the section.

(b) *Restrictive trading agreements*

Restrictive trading agreements are governed by several statutes and may also fall foul of the provisions of Article 85 of the Treaty of Rome if they result in unfair competition within the EEC (see, *e.g. Publishers Association v. EC Commission* (1989)). An example is section 1 of the Restrictive

Trade Practices Act 1976 which requires ceratin agreements to be registered with the Director General of Fair Trading. This Act is intended to control agreements as to such matters as the price charged for goods or services or the persons or areas to be supplied. Once registered the Director General msut submit the agreement to the security of the restrictive Practices Court. Such an agreement is presumed to be contrary to the "public interst" and the parties have the onus of rebutting the presumption. If they fail to do this (and most such agreements are considered by the Court to be contrary to the public interst) then the provision is declared to be void.

A similar type of restriction (although the effect is actually to render the agreement *illegal* not just void) is that imposed by the Resale Prices Act 1976 (discussed in the context of privity above, p. 561) which effectively renders unlawful restrictions intended to ensure that goods can only be sold by reatilers at fixed prices.

(2) Contracts Void at Common Law

The courts have long taken the view that certain classes of contract are void on the grounds of "public policy." as early as 1824 one judge described this notion as "a very unruly horse" and the result has been that there are three important areas where such a potentially nebulous concept has crystallised into a rule.

(a) *Contracts ousting the jurisdiction of the courts*

The courts have looked crictically at any attempt to limit by contract a person's right of access to the courts. Consequently even though an agreement may make some domestic tribunal the ultimate arbiter on questions of fact, if it purports to limit the adjudication of the courts on matters of law it will be, to that extent at least, void. An agreement that in the first instance a dispute will go to arbitration rather than the courts is lawful (see, *e.g. Scott v. Avery* (1856)) although this area is now affected by the provisions of the Arbitration Act 1979.

(b) *Contracts prejudicial to marriage*

This head of policy renders void contract which seek to restrict a person's right to marry, involve charging a fee for procuring a marriage partner or which make provision for a future separation between husband and wife. One might wonder whether in relation to the last two areas public opinion may have moved somewhat ahead of the law.

(c) *Contracts in restraint of trade*

This is an important area which frequently comes before the courts and the overall approach has been to lean against agreements which either place fetters on an individual's deployment of skills or the ability to trade freely.

The two areas where such contracts are most likely to be encountered are in the context of employment contracts or in the sale of a business. If an employee or apprentice has gained valuable commercial information or training there may be an understandable desire on the part of the employer to restrict his ability to set himself up in competition. Equally the purchaser of a business might wish to protect himself against a well-known and successful vendor simply setting up business again close by and so destroying the purchaser's custom.

The result of leading cases such as *Nordenfelt v. Maxim Nordenfelt Guns and Ammunition Co.* (1894) and *Esso Petroleum Co. Ltd v. Harper's Garage (Stourport) Ltd* (1968) is that every covenant in restraint of trade is prima facie void unless it can be shown that the agreement is reasonable as between the parties and that it is not unreasonable as regards the public interest.

Two contrasting cases illustrate the point. In *Mason v. Provident Clothing Co. Ltd* (1913) the House of Lords held that a restriction on an employee against working in a similar capacity within 25 miles of London was void. It was wider that that which could reasonably be required to protect the business of the employer. In *Fitch v. Dewes* (1921) the restriction upon a solicitor's former managing clerk against being similarly employed for the rest of his life within a seven-mile radius of Tamworth Town Hall was held to be valid. In the circumstances of this case it was reasonable. Nevertheless each case will depend upon its facts and covenants which are too widely drafted will be struck out. A prohibition against practising some trade or profession within seven miles of Tamworth Town Hall might be reasonable. A similar restriction measured as a five-mile radius from, say, Leicester Square might be considered quite unreasonable embracing as it does a major portion of the business area of the capital.

2. Consequences of a Contract being Void

(1) By Statute

This will depend upon the particular wording of the statute (for example there are special provisions relating to wagering contracts) but many of the principles applied are analogous to those of common law.

(2) At Common Law

(a) *Severance*

The fact that one part of a contract is void does not necessarily mean that the entire contract fails. If, of course, the entire promise is indeed void then there may be a total failure of consideration which renders the whole agreement void. If only one of several or merely part of a contractual promise is void, then the court may sever the void area and leave the rest of the contractual obligations intact. This will not be done, however, if the real effect of such severance is to alter the whole nature of the agreement (see, *e.g.* the contrasting cases of *Goldsoll v. Goldman* (1915) and *Attwood v. Lamont* (1920)).

(b) *Money paid over*

The prevailing view is that money paid over under a void term or contract can be recovered. There is a certain lack of authority, but the proposition is supported by the decision in *Hermann v. Charlesworth* (1905).

3. Illegal Contracts

(1) Contracts Which are Illegal by Statute

Numerous transactions are rendered illegal by particular statutes which may often be concerned with such matters as economic controls or the licensing of certain activities. An example is that of an agreement for the collective enforcement of price control under Part I of the Resale Prices Act 1976 (see above, p. 561).

Even if a statute does not specifically prohibit a transaction it may be construed as having that effect by implication. This is illustrated by the contrasting cases of *Cope v. Rowlands* (1836) and *Archbolds (Freightage) Ltd v. S. Spanglett Ltd* (1961). In the former a statute made it an offence for a stockbroker to act in the City of London without first obtaining a licence. The broker did some work for the defendant and sued for payment. The action was dismissed for the reason given by Parke B. that "The clause ... must be taken ... to imply a prohibition of all unadmitted persons to act as brokers, and consequently to prohibit by necessary inference all contracts which such persons make. ... " In the latter the Road and Rail Traffic Act 1933 required a carrier of goods to have an "A" licence which permitted him to carry other people's goods. The carriers, who did not have such a licence, agreed to transport a cargo of whisky for the plaintiffs who were unaware of the defendants' failure to obtain a licence. The defendants subsequently argued that the contract was prohibited under the Act. Clearly it was not expressly prohibited, but the Court of Appeal rejected the argument that it was even impliedly illegal. The object of legislation was to regulate those who provided transport. This could be done through criminal penalties against those in breach and did not require every agreement made contrary to the licensing provision to be invalid.

(2) Contracts Illegal in Their Performance

Even though a contract may be perfectly valid at its inception, the mode of performance may subsequently render it illegal. This happened in *Anderson Ltd v. Daniel* (1924) where a statute provided that in sales of artificial fertilisers the seller was required to give the buyer an invoice giving details of certain chemicals contained in it. The sellers delivered the fertiliser without such an invoice and the defendants successfully resisted an action for the price of the goods. Although there is, of course, nothing inherently wrong in selling fertiliser, the way it was actually done in this case rendered the transaction unlawful. This case may be contrasted with *Shaw v. Groom* (1970) where a landlord, in breach of statute, failed to provide a rent book. In an action for rent arrears the defendant alleged that the contract was unlawful but the Court of Appeal rejected this view. The Act might render the landlord liable to a fine for his failure, but the central intention of the legislature was not to prevent a landlord from recourse to the courts to recover payment.

Although the cases just considered involved statutes, similar considerations apply when a contract is illegal at common law.

(3) Contracts Which are Illegal at Common Law

In the same way that the courts have held certain agreements to be void, so more serious infringements of what have been regarded as rules of public policy will render the contract illegal. Broadly speaking, there are three main areas:

(a) *A contract for crime, tort or fraud*

A striking example of this category is the old case of *Everet v. Williams* (1725). An agreement between two highwaymen to rob a coach and share the loot was held to be illegal so that one could not sue the other for the appropriate share. Nevertheless, in the unusual and colourful circumstances that arose in *Howard v. Shirlstar Container Transport Ltd* (1990) a plaintiff was held entitled to recover payment under a contract which involved him committing a criminal offence. The significant feature here was that the plaintiff's primary purpose in pursuing the criminal course of conduct was to escape with his life.

(b) *Contracts prejudicial to the state*

This includes a wide range of activities including agreements with enemy aliens or damaging to foreign relations; agreements prejudicial to the administration of justice, such as those involving maintenance or champerty; and agreements which encourage corruption in public life. An example of the latter was *Parkinson v. College of Ambulance* (1925) where the plaintiff unsuccessfully claimed the return of £3,000 paid to a charity for a knighthood he had "bought" and which was not forthcoming.

(c) *Contracts to promote sexual immorality*

This is an area where the courts may well be less willing to intervene now than in the different moral climate of, say, a hundred years ago. Nevertheless, it seems clear that a prostitute cannot sue for the price of her services nor could a landlord who supplied premises for prostitution sue for his rent (see, *e.g. Pearce v. Brooks* (1866) *Casebook*, chap. 8). It has been held that a promise of money for past sexual immorality made under seal (otherwise the contract would fail on the grounds of "past consideration") is valid. This is perhaps explicable on the grounds that the provision of support for a former partner, for example, is something to be encouraged, not prohibited. On the other hand, stable, unmarried relationships are now regularly held to give rise to legal consequences such as the acquisition of property interests via trusts and it may well be that contracts made in such relationships are perfectly valid—provided, of course, there is an intention to create legal relations.

4. Consequences of a Contract being Illegal

The crucial distinction here is not so much between law and statute as it is between a contract illegal from its inception and one that is only rendered illegal by its performance. Common to both types of illegality is the problem of whether it is possible to sever the illegal part of the contract from the rest. The orthodox view in the past has been that a contract tainted with illegality fails completely. A more recent view is that adopted by Templeman J. in *Ailion v. Spiekermann* (1976) who decided that severance was a possibility in a proper case stating that "the absence of precedent does not worry me so long as there is no lack of principle." The trend therefore seems to be in the direction of allowing severance in appropriate cases.

(1) Contracts Illegal in Themselves

The general result is that the contract is treated as a complete nullity, although there are various exceptions which are particularly necessary to protect an innocent party from the drastic effects of illegality.

(a) *Parties cannot sue*

Because the contract is treated as if it had never been made, neither party can sue or be sued upon the agreement. Consequently one might think that property can never pass under such a contract. In principle this seems correct, although the Court of Appeal (in *Belvoir Finance Co. Ltd v.*

Stapleton (1971)) seem to have cast doubt on this idea by stating that at least in an agreement involving the Sale of Goods Act property may pass under an illegal contract. The better view would seem to be that it cannot in general do so. In many cases where the property has already been delivered the decision would make no difference in any event since property handed over under an illegal contract is irrecoverable. So in the *Parkinson* case (above) Mr. Parkinson could not recover his £3,000. The principle is sometimes expressed in the maxim: *in pari delicto melior conditio defendentis* (where both parties are equally at fault, the defendant is in the better position).

There are exceptions to the above.

(i) *Illegality not vital to the cause.* If a plaintiff can rely on some cause of action not dependent upon the illegal contract, then the property can be recovered. So in *Bowmakers v. Barnet Instruments Ltd* (1945) the parties entered into an illegal hire-purchase agreement. Nevertheless, since the plaintiffs' rights as the hirer of goods did not depend upon the illegal agreement they were able to claim damages for the conversion of the goods. A similar approach was recently adopted by the House of Lords in *Tinsley v. Milligan* (1993).

(ii) *Parties not in pari delicto.* Where the parties are not equally at fault the court may sometimes allow the relatively innocent party to recover. Examples would be where one party has used fraud or oppression against another or where a rule is designed to protect a class of persons. Accordingly, a tenant can recover an illegal premium paid to a landlord. But there is no general rule that an "innocent" party may enforce the contract and it is more satisfactory when the statute itself deals with the civil consequences. Thus under section 132 of the Financial Services Act 1986 an insured person can enforce an insurance contract which the insurer was not authorised to make even though at common law the contract was wholly void (*Phoenix General Insurance v. Hahenon Insurance* (1987).

(iii) *Repentance.* If a party to an executory contract repents before the contract has been substantially performed, he may also recover. (See, *e.g. Taylor v. Bowers* (1876)).

(b) *Related transactions*

Related transactions are tainted by the illegality and are also unenforceable. This problem may arise where one contract is dependent for its performance upon another. So in *Fisher v. Bridges* (1854) an illegal contract for debauchery invalidated the promissory note to pay for it.

(2) Contracts Illegal in Performance

Where both parties are equally guilty then the same considerations outlined in relation to initial illegality will govern this form of illegality. Repentance will not, however, be a problem since if a party repents before he has yet carried out an illegal performance, then of course no illegal performance will ever have happened.

The real distinction between the two types of illegality resides in the fact that in the case of illegal performance one party may be entirely innocent and quite unaware of the other's illegal mode of performance. In this situation the innocent party has all the usual contractual remedies against the other. An example is provided by *Marles v. Trant* (1954). Here X sold some seed as "spring wheat" to the defendants. In fact, in breach of contract, it was winter wheat. The defendants then sold the wheat on to the plaintiff failing to supply an invoice with the goods so rendering the contract illegal. The plaintiff, when he discovered he had been delivered the wrong type of wheat, was nevertheless able to sue the defendant for damages under the contract which was illegal as performed. So also could the defendant sue X for his breach of contract. One may contrast this case with *Anderson v. Daniel* (above, p. 581). In that case the seller lost because he was not innocent; in this case the buyer won because he was.

Sometimes the difficulties may be circumvented by a collateral contract as in *Strongman v. Simcock* (1945). The plaintiff builders agreed with the defendant architect to do certain building work for the latter who would obtain the licences then required. He failed to do so with the result that the main contract was illegally performed. Although the builders could not recover on the main illegal contract, they were entitled to succeed on the collateral contract. There was a promise on the part of the architect to obtain the appropriate licence matched by the promise of the builders to do the work on that basis. The law of misrepresentation must also be borne in mind. In *Saunders v. Edwards* (1987) the plaintiffs set up a flat-purchase transaction in such a manner that it was possibly tainted with illegality but they were still allowed to sue for the vendor's fraud (a claim in tort) in misdescribing the flat. This case may indicate a rather more flexible attitude to illegality, under which the seriousness of the wrongdoing has to be balanced against the consequences of denying relief.

III. DURESS AND UNDUE INFLUENCE

It is not hard to see that if parties have not willingly consented to enter into a contract, or at least to all outward appearances have not done so, then there can hardly be said to exist a valid agreement. Intimidation and threats of violence are the most blatant form of coercion and come within the province of the common law doctrine of duress. The more subtle means of exercising an undue level of persuasion or influence upon another are dealt with by the equitable doctrine of undue influence. In either case, the effect is to render the transaction voidable rather than void.

1. Duress

Traditionally, the common law doctrine of duress has been limited to violence, or threats of violence, against the person. It is rare for such an extreme case to come before the courts, but a striking example is provided from Australia by *Barton v. Armstrong* (1975) (*Casebook*, Chap. 8). Armstrong threatened Barton with death if he did not agree to buy out Armstrong's interest in a business on terms that strongly favoured the latter. Even so, there was some evidence that Barton in fact executed the deed because he thought it was a satisfactory business arrangement. Nevertheless, the Privy Council decided that on these facts the disposition was voidable on the grounds of duress. It was enough that the threats of Armstrong contributed to Barton's decision to sign the deed even if they were not the only reason.

Probably of much greater practical significance is the recognition by the courts in recent years of a doctrine of economic duress. In *Pao On v. Lau Yiu Long* (1980) (*Casebook*, Chap. 8) Lord Scarman stated, "there is nothing contrary to principle in recognising economic duress as a factor which may render a contract voidable, provided always that the basis of such recognition is that it must amount to coercion of will which vitiates consent. It must be shown that the payment made or the contract entered into was not a voluntary act." Subsequently the House of Lords explicitly recognised the doctrine in *Universe Tankships of Monrovia v. International Transport Workers Federation* (1983), although Lord Scarman commented, "in life, including the life of commerce and finance, many acts are done 'under pressure, sometimes overwhelming pressure': but they are not necessarily done under duress. That depends on whether the circumstances are such that the law regards the pressure as legitimate." Identifying what the law regards as "legitimate" will no doubt be the subject of further cases in an area where the law has only just begun to develop. At least in the context of arm's length dealing between two trading companies, where the party making the threats bona fide believes its demands are valid, the Court of Appeal in *CTN Cash and Carry Ltd v. Gallaher Ltd* (1995) has said that it would be difficult to maintain an action for economic duress. A case where the plea did succeed, is *Atlas Express Ltd v. Kafco (Importers and Distributors) Ltd* (1989) (*Casebook*, chap. 8). Here a small company entered into an agreement with a national firm of carriers. The carriers subsequently purported to impose higher charges than those previously agreed. Because the company was unable to find an alternative carrier and was heavily dependent on this contract they reluctantly agreed to the new terms but later refused to pay. On these facts economic duress was upheld and the carriers' claim for additional payment dismissed. Nevertheless, even if duress is found, recovery may not be possible. For example, in *North Ocean Shipping Co. Ltd v. Hyundai Construction Co. Ltd, The Atlantic Baron* (1978) shipbuilders threatened to break a contract to build a tanker unless the buyers increased their remaining four instalment payments by 10 per cent. The buyers were anxious to get delivery of the ship in order to take advantage of a lucrative contract and accordingly agreed. They paid the instalments and later accepted delivery of the ship without protest. Eight months later they brought an action to recover the additional payments. On these facts Mocatta J. found that there had been economic duress but that the buyers, by failing to protest before they did, had affirmed the contract and were therefore unable to recover the payments.

2. Undue Influence

(1) The Basic Doctrine

In *National Westminster Bank v. Morgan* (1985) Lord Scarman asserted that: "Definition is a poor instrument when used to determine whether a transaction is or is not unconscionable: this is a question which depends upon the particular facts of the case." The essence of the plea of undue influence is perhaps that one party, by abusing their influence, has taken unfair advantage of the other. This can take an almost infinite number of forms but the House of Lords has recently laid down clearer guidelines than previously existed in two important leading cases, *Barclay's Bank v. O'Brien* (1993) (*Casebook*, Chap. 8) and *CIBC Mortgages v. Pitt* (1993).

Both cases dealt with the sort of problems concerning undue influence that have often come before the courts in recent years. In *O'Brien* a wife executed a charge over the matrimonial home to guarantee her husband's business overdraft which the bank subsequently sought to enforce. The bank did not explain the effect of the documents and she did not read them. The House of Lords decided that the bank's failure to warn her of the consequences of the charge fixed them with constructive notice of the husband's misrepresentations to her and meant that she was entitled to set aside the charge as between herself and the bank. A creditor could avoid being fixed with notice if they had warned the surety, at a meeting not attended by the principal debtor, of the risks involved and the need for independent advice.

In *Pitt*, where judgment was given on the same day and is clearly meant to be read in conjunction with *O'Brien*, the situation was different. Here a husband and wife applied for a joint loan ostensibly to buy a holiday home secured by both of them executing a charge on the matrimonial home which they owned jointly. She neither read the documents nor received any advice as to their effect. In fact, the husband lost the money in share speculation. The bank subsequently succeeded in enforcing the charge against the wife. Although she had established undue influence by her husband, the court held that there was nothing to put the bank on notice that this was other than a normal joint loan to a husband and wife. It was not like guaranteeing a husband's debts which, on the face of it, was not likely to be a transaction which could benefit a wife and therefore had to be treated with more circumspection.

What the House of Lords has attempted in these decisions is to balance the obvious need of a spouse or cohabitee for protection, in a setting where undue influence can easily come into play, against the need not to deter financial institutions from entering into such a common transaction. In a trio of subsequent cases, *Massey v. Midland Bank, Banco Exterior Internacional v. Mann* and *TSB Bank v. Camfield* (1995) the Court of Appeal has elucidated how the House of Lords guidelines are to be applied. For example, a bank is entitled to rely on a solicitor's certificate that a wife has received independent advice. What is clear from the recent case law is that lending institutions will need to be vigilant to ensure that the potential victims of undue influence have received proper advice. On the other hand, if it appears that matters have been dealt with correctly, they are also likely to be protected.

(2) Fiduciary Relationships

In some cases the courts have taken the view that the possibility of undue influence being exerted is so strong that it may be presumed unless it can be shown to the contrary. In other words, the normal burden of proof is reversed so that it lies upon the person in whom confidence is reposed to show that undue influence has not been exerted. The relationships usually considered in this category include parent and child, solicitor and client, doctor and patient, trustee and beneficiary and religious adviser and disciple although this list is not meant to be comprehensive. It does not include banker and client nor husband and wife. The presumption can be raised upon facts which show, for example, that one party has become dependent for advice or help upon another and enters an improvident transaction which cannot reasonably be accounted for by friendship, charity or other ordinary motives (see, *e.g. Goldsworthy v. Brickell* (1987)).

(3) Rebutting the Presumption

The most obvious way to rebut any claim of undue influence, as stressed in *Barclay's Bank v. O'Brien*, is to show that the transaction had been entered into only after its nature and effect had been fully explained by some independent and qualified person.

(4) Bars to Relief

Since undue influence is an equitable doctrine, relief will be barred in the event of laches (undue delay in asserting a claim), affirmation after the undue influence has ceased, or third parties acquiring for value and without notice an interest in the property.

(5) Undue Influence and Other Remedies

The type of situation where a plea of undue influence arises may also invite the application of other remedies. For example, in *Cornish v. Midland Bank plc* (1985) the plaintiff was unsuccessful in her plea of undue influence because she could not show that the bank had taken unfair advantage of her. Nevertheless, she was able to establish that the bank had been in breach of its duty of care to give proper advice on the effect of signing a second mortgage in favour of the bank, and so establish liability for the tort of negligence. In *Avon Finance Co. Ltd v. Bridger* (1979) on the other hand, a classic case of a son fraudulently inducing elderly parents to sign documents charging their house, the plea of *non est factum* failed but the court applied the doctrine of undue influence to prevent enforcement of the charge.

Chapter 23

Discharge

So far we have been largely concerned with examining the way a contract may be formed. In this and the next chapter we need to consider the way a contract may come to an end and the remedies available to an injured party when things have gone wrong.

A contract may be discharged in any one of four ways, namely: performance, agreement, breach and frustration. We now need to consider these in turn.

1. Performance

If both parties to a contract properly carry out their respective obligations under it, then obviously their agreement will be completely discharged. The problems that arise centre around what precisely constitutes performance and what happens if one party, for a variety of possible reasons, does not carry out his side of the bargain within the precise terms of the contract.

The basic common law rule is that the performance must strictly and entirely match the terms of the contract. This is well illustrated by the case of *Cutter v. Powell* (1795) (*Casebook*, Chap. 9). Cutter agreed to serve as second mate on a ship bound from Kingston, Jamaica to Liverpool for the sum of 30 guineas, "provided he proceeds, continues and does his duty ... from hence to the port of Liverpool." Unfortunately he died at sea before making port and his widow sued for the wages earned before his death on a *quantum meruit* (as much as he has deserved). Her action failed. The agreement constituted one entire contract which, albeit through no fault of his own, the deceased had failed to carry out. In fact, although the decision in the case seems harsh and somewhat unfair, the rate of pay was well above what a seaman could normally have expected to earn and accordingly the deceased was in a sense taking a deliberate gamble (see also, *e.g. Vigers v. Cook* (1919)).

A similarly strict rule is applied in certain sections of the Sale of Goods Act 1979 (which was based upon the previous common law) and is illustrated by *Re Moore & Co. Ltd and Landauer & Co.* (1921). The buyers agreed to take a quantity of canned fruits packed in cases with 30 tins in each. When delivered it was found that although the correct quantity had been dispatched about half the cases contained only 24 tins each. This variation in the packaging made no difference to the market value of the goods. Nevertheless, this was a sale of goods by description under section 13 of (now) the Sale of Goods Act 1979; the goods did not strictly comply with their contract description and the buyers were therefore entitled to reject the whole consignment. If the facts of this case were to recur today the actual result would probably be different because of the new s.15A of the Sale of Goods Act 1979 introduced by the Sale of Goods Act 1994. This important provision prevents a non-consumer buyer from rejecting goods where the breach is so slight that it would be unreasonable to allow a remedy as drastic as rejection. It does not affect the principle that in *Re Moore & Landauer* there would still be a breach of contract; it would simply be treated as a breach of a warranty rather than a condition.

As with so many legal rules, however, it is in practice less important than the large number of exceptions which qualify it. The possible injustice and harshness of the rule is accordingly heavily mitigated.

(1) Exceptions

(a) *Substantial performance*

Where one party has substantially performed his part of the contract then he may be able to enforce it under the doctrine of substantial performance. The difference in approach between the strict doctrine and this approach can be explained on the basis that certain obligations within a contract are in reality *conditions* whereas others are merely *warranties* or even *innominate terms*. If the effect of the mis-performance is not equivalent to the breach of a condition then it is not surprising that the contract should be left intact but with some financial adjustment to compensate the injured party.

The operation of the so-called doctrine is well illustrated by comparing two cases. In *Hoenig v. Isaacs* (1952) (*Casebook,*

Chap. 9) an interior decorator agreed to decorate and furnish a flat for £750. The defendant paid £400 on account but refused to pay the remaining £350 on the basis that the design and workmanship were faulty. It was found that there were indeed defects but the cost of remedying these came to some £56. The defendant's claim that further payment could be resisted on the basis of *Cutter v. Powell* was rejected. There had been substantial performance of the contract which entitled the decorator to the balance of the money less the cost of remedying the defects. In *Bolton v. Mahadeva* (1972) on the other hand, a contractor agreed to install a central heating system for £560. On completion it was found that it emitted fumes, failed to heat the house properly and would cost £174 to put right. The Court of Appeal refused to allow the plaintiff's action for payment of the agreed lump sum as they did not regard the performance as substantial. In the context of the smaller contract price, the cost of remedying the defects was clearly proportionately very much higher than in *Hoenig*. Rather curiously perhaps, if in this case the defendant had already paid over some of the contract price, then although the plaintiff could not obtain any further sums, the defendant could not recover the money she had by then paid. The reason is that there must be a *total* failure of consideration before such a payment can be recovered and in a case such as this the failure is clearly not total.

(b) *Acceptance of part performance*

Sometimes, although one party only partially performs his part of the contract, it may be possible to infer a new contract in place of the old under which the defaulting party is to be paid an appropriate amount for such work as has actually been carried out. This will only apply when the defendant really does have an option to take the benefit of the work done or to reject it. This is well illustrated in *Sumpter v. Hedges* (1898) (*Casebook*, Chap. 9). A builder agreed to erect certain buildings on the defendant's land for £565. After completing £333 worth of work he abandoned the contract and the defendant had to complete the building himself. The builder's claim on a *quantum meruit* failed. The defendant was in possession of what he could not help keeping and had no real choice but to complete the work on what would otherwise be a useless eyesore on his land. What he did have to pay for was the material left on the site which he later incorporated into the building. In this case there was a real option and he chose to use the materials.

(c) *Performance prevented*

If one party prevents the other from carrying out the contract as specified, then the law properly grants the innocent party a remedy. So in *Planché v. Colburn* (1831) the plaintiff agreed to write a book on *Costume and Ancient Armour* for a fee of £100. He wrote part of the book before the defendants decided to abandon the series of which the book was to form a part. Accordingly, the author recovered £50 on a *quantum meruit*. Alternatively, it seems that he could have regarded the publishers' action as an anticipatory breach and, having completed the book, might have sued for the full contract price (see below, p. 602).

A somewhat similar situation is illustrated by those cases where the contract can only be performed in its entirety with the concurrence of the other party. If one party rejects the other's performance, then the mere fact that the latter has offered or, as is usually said in this context, "tendered performance," will be treated as equivalent to performance itself. A leading case on this point is *Startup v. Macdonald* (1843). The plaintiffs agreed to sell a quantity of oil to the defendants and to deliver it by the end of March. At 8.30 p.m. on March 31, the plaintiffs arrived with the oil but the defendants refused to accept the delivery owing to the lateness of the hour (section 29(5) of the Sale of Goods Act 1979 now provides that delivery must be made at a reasonable hour, and that this is a question of fact). In this particular case it was held that the plaintiffs had done all they could to comply with the contract and that consequently their tender of performance entitled them without more to sue the defendants for damages for their failure to take delivery.

The tender of money to pay a debt is treated slightly differently. Although the tenderer is not obliged to repeat the offer, the debt remains and can be sued upon. Payment must also be offered of the exact amount due and in "legal tender" as defined by statute. For example, "copper" coins are not strictly "legal tender" beyond 20 pence (see Coinage Act 1971, s.2). The result is that one cannot legally tender payment of debts using impracticably large quantities of low denomination coinage.

(d) *Severable obligations*

Very often a contract will be construed as being composed of severable obligations rather than requiring complete performance on the principle of *Cutter v. Powell*. A clear example is the type of standard term contract used in the building industry. These will invariably provide for inspection and payment for the work as it progresses rather than in a lump sum payable upon completion. At each stage of the building therefore a contractor could sue for payment properly due at that stage. Such a provision circumvents (for the builder) the difficulties that would otherwise be placed in his way by a case such as *Sumpter v. Hedges (ante)*.

(2) Vicarious Performance

Has a contract been performed if one of the parties gets somebody else to do the work? The answer depends on the type of contract involved. If A contracts with B, a famous artist, to paint A's portrait, then B's sub-contracting of the work to C cannot constitute performance of the agreement. Clearly it is important, or even vital to A, that B himself should carry out the contract. Each contract will depend upon its own facts, but clearly, where there is a strong "personal" element in the agreement vicarious performance will not usually be enough. At the other extreme, if A is owed money by B and B gets C to pay over the money to A, then this will completely discharge the contract. It is presumably of no consequence to A how he is paid as long as he is paid. In between these two extremes, difficult questions may arise as to whether vicarious performance has discharged the contract (see, *e.g. British Waggon Co. v. Lea* (1880)).

However, even if the contract can be performed vicariously it is important to note that the original contractor is still liable for any default on the part of his sub-contractor, although he may of course join the sub-contractor as a third party. For example, if B agrees to carry out work for A which he sub-contracts to C, then, if the latter defaults, B is still liable to A as if he had carried out the faulty work himself. B can in turn, however, sue C for his breach of contract with B. There is the possibility of a tortious claim by A against C but this may be ruled out by the principle that pure economic loss is generally irrecoverable in tort (see further below, p. 657).

(3) Time

What happens if one party is late in carrying out his obligations under the contract? Not surprisingly this depends on what sort of agreement the parties envisage, or as it is usually stated, whether or not time is "of the essence" of the contract. At common law the rule was that time was of the essence unless the parties agreed otherwise whereas in equity it was not. The historical difference is rendered unimportant now by section 41 of the Law of Property Act 1925 which states:

> "Stipulations in a contract, as to time or otherwise, which according to rules of equity are not deemed to be or to have become of the essence of the contract, are also construed and have effect at law in accordance with the same rules."

The result is therefore, as the House of Lords have affirmed in *Raineri v. Miles* (1980), that although late performance does not automatically give rise to a right to terminate the contract, it is nevertheless a breach which may entitle the plaintiff to damages.

There are three occasions when time is of the essence in a contract. In the first place the parties themselves may specify expressly that this shall be so in their agreement. Secondly, the subject-matter of the contract may make it clear that the performance time must be strictly adhered to. For example, if the transaction involves a commodity that fluctuates in value (such as shares) or which is perishable (such as fresh fruit) then performance on time may well be essential. Thirdly, if one party has been guilty of delay and the other then informs him that he will regard the contract as terminated unless it is completed within a reasonable time, this will again have the effect of making time "of the essence" (see, *e.g. Charles Rickards Ltd v. Oppenheim* (1950) *Casebook*, Chap. 9).

2. Agreement

Contracts are made by agreement. Not surprisingly, therefore, a contract can be varied or discharged by agreement. The orthodox distinction made is between bilateral and unilateral discharge which in effect means that in the former there is a mutual benefit to be derived from some variation or discharge in the performance whereas in the latter the modification is for the benefit of one party only. Although this is the normal way of classifying discharge by agreement it is important to realise that the underlying problems in this area are caused by two legal concepts, namely consideration and the requirements of "formality." In the discharge of a contract just as much as in its formation the law looks askance at a promise unsupported by the element of "bargain." As regards formality, particular problems are posed when the law stipulates that a contract must be drawn up in one way, as for example in writing, but the parties purport to discharge it by agreement without complying with the same formalities. Both problems are of course solved if the parties discharge the agreement by deed which, as we saw in Chapter 16, replaces the requirement of consideration.

(1) Bilateral Discharge

In the case of an executory contract where neither party has completely performed his obligations then an agreement to discharge will clearly be effective. Consideration has been supplied by the parties in that both of them have exchanged promises not to enforce all the original obligations.

Complications arise when we consider the case of a transaction that by statute must be evidenced in writing. A common example is a contract for sale or other disposition of land (see Law of Property (Miscellaneous Provisions) Act 1989, s.2). Must any agreement to vary or discharge the contract also conform to this formality? The answer is somewhat involved and depends upon what the agreement was seeking to achieve but there are three possible alternatives, namely: (a) the parties intend to discharge the agreement altogether; (b) the agreement is intended to vary the original contract; and (c) the parties intend to replace the original agreement by a completely new one. Quite what the parties intended will have to be inferred from their agreement or conduct if it is not clearly articulated. In the case of (a) an oral agreement to discharge the contract will be effective even without written evidence. Section 2 is designed to regulate the formation of contracts not their discharge. In the case of (b) on the other hand, their agreement will be completely ineffective. The "new" contract is simply not evidenced in writing and so the original contract continues in being. Where (c) occurs the effect is that the original agreement is completely rescinded but the new agreement fails because it is unenforceable through lack of written evidence. In this last case a difficult question of construction may arise as to whether the parties intended the result in (b) or (c). The crucial difference is that in one case the original agreement continues unaffected whereas in the other it is completely abrogated (the distinction is illustrated by the contrasting cases of *United Dominions Corporation (Jamaica) Ltd v. Shoucair* (1969) and *Morris v. Baron & Co.* (1918)).

A slightly different situation that frequently arises is that one party requests the other not to insist on the strict performance of a contract and the party so requested agrees. A simple illustration might arise in the sale of goods. Delivery has been agreed for April 1, but the supplier obtains an agreement that the goods will not actually be delivered until May 1. What is the effect of such a forbearance or "waiver" as it is usually called? Not unnaturally the judges have reacted against the unfairness of allowing such a waiver to be evaded, especially as it is a common business practice. Nevertheless, the rather unclear result has been an apparent sacrifice of principle to business expediency. At common law there has developed a doctrine of waiver which provides authority for the proposition that both the recipient and the grantor of the waiver are bound by the indulgence. Despite the sensible result the obvious objection to such a doctrine is that it appears to dispense with the essential ingredient of consideration.

Equity provides a more elegant solution. In effect, it is an application of the doctrine of "promissory" or "equitable" estoppel. The approach of equity to waiver is well illustrated by *Charles Rickards Ltd v. Oppenheim* (1950) (*Casebook*, Chap. 9). The defendant ordered a body to be built on a car chassis he had purchased, the work to be completed within "six or seven months." At the end of this time the work was not finished but he agreed to wait a further three months. The work was still by then unfinished so he gave final notice that unless it was completed within another four weeks the order would be cancelled. At the end of this period the body was still not complete and the car was only offered to him three months later when he refused to accept it. The plaintiffs thereupon sued him for his failure to accept the car. The Court of Appeal decided that although originally time had been of the essence the agreement to extend the performance time by three months operated as a waiver. If the car had been delivered within that time the defendant would have been bound to accept it. However, the defendant, by giving reasonable notice that time was once again of the essence, rendered the plaintiffs in breach of contract by their failure to complete the work. Accordingly, their action against the defendant failed. The result is satisfactory and in accordance with the principles enunciated on a case such as *Hughes v. Metropolitan Railway Co.* (above, p. 495).

(2) Unilateral Discharge

As the title suggests, a unilateral discharge occurs when only one party has an obligation left to perform and the other purports to release him from that obligation. For example, A owes B £1,000 for goods delivered. A is in financial difficulties and B agrees to accept £900 in discharge of the contract price. The difficulty with this arrangement is of course that it is a *nudum pactum*; there is no consideration for B's promise (see above, p. 492). There needs to be a further element of bargain, no matter how notional, to make the agreement valid.

Where there is a fresh element of bargain this is known as "accord and satisfaction." "Accord" is the agreement that the contract should be performed in a modified way and "satisfaction" is the consideration to support the promise. If in the above example A paid over £900 and a bag of sweets then this would support the requirements of accord and satisfaction. It is not even necessary that the consideration be executed to make the agreement effective so that, if it is the intention of the parties, even an executory promise may be sufficient "satisfaction." This is illustrated in the case of *British Russian Gazette Ltd v. Associated Newspapers Ltd* (1933). A Mr. Talbot agreed to compromise (*i.e.* to settle) a libel action for a sum of money. His letter stated: "I accept the sum of one thousand guineas ... in full discharge and settlement of my claims ... and I will forthwith instruct my solicitors to end the proceedings now pending." Before he had actually received the money Mr. Talbot disregarded his agreement and continued with the action arguing that until the payment had actually been made there was no effective discharge. The Court of Appeal rejected this view. There was accord and satisfaction; a promise had been exchanged for a promise and Mr. Talbot was bound by the terms of the compromise. He had promised to discontinue the action; the newspaper had promised to pay him the money.

3. Breach

(1) Consequences of Breach

It is something of a misnomer, or at least an over-simplification, to talk of breach as discharging a contract. Nevertheless, it is convenient to consider it in the context of a chapter concerned with how contractual obligations can come to an end. What is said here also needs to be read in the context of what has already been said about terms in a contract in Chapter 18. Every failure to perform satisfactorily any of the obligations in a contract will entitle the innocent party to sue for damages. If it is the breach of a comparatively minor term, a breach of warranty, then damages will be all the innocent party is entitled to and the contract continues. If it is of a serious kind, a breach of condition, then this is a repudiatory breach which entitles the injured party not only to damages but also to regard himself as excused from further performance of the contract. In this area many of the problems have arisen as the result of confusing terminology.

The correct way of describing the situation has been emphasised by Lord Wilberforce in *Johnson v. Agnew* (1980) where he quoted with approval Lord Porter's comment that, "to say that the contract is rescinded or has come to an end or has ceased to exist may in individual cases convey the truth with sufficient accuracy, but the fuller expression that the injured party is thereby absolved from future performance of his obligations under the contract is a more exact description of the position."

Although it is usually clear what is in fact meant, it is therefore strictly quite wrong to say that a contract has come to an end as a result of a repudiatory breach (see, *e.g. Photo Production Ltd v. Securicor* (1980) below, p. 601). In the first place this may be just the sort of occasion when an "agreed damages" clause in the contract will come into operation (on which see below, p. 602). Secondly, the injured party always has an option in the face of a repudiatory breach either to treat the contract as still in force or to accept the repudiation. Even a major repudiatory breach does not therefore operate automatically to end the innocent party's obligations. This is well illustrated by the old case of *Avery v. Bowden* (1855). Bowden effectively repudiated a contract to load Avery's ship in a way that would have doubtless given the latter an opportunity to sue immediately for breach of contract. Instead the ship waited in the hope that the agreement would be fulfilled, but the contract was then frustrated before the time agreed for loading the cargo had expired owing to the outbreak of the Crimean War. The contract therefore remained in existence until the frustrating event preventing Avery from suing for breach (on which see p. 604 below).

(2) Forms of Breach

Breach can take two forms, what one might call actual or anticipatory. Actual breach is the result of any failure by one of the parties to fulfil one or more of the obligations under the contract. This may arise as the result of non-performance, for example failure to deliver goods, or defective performance, if say the goods fall below the contract quality. Alternatively, a promissory statement of fact in the contract may turn out not to be true.

Anticipatory breach arises when one party gives notice of breach before performance has even started. Before considering this, it is necessary to examine what has sometimes been treated as a separate sub-heading, namely fundamental breach.

(a) *Fundamental breach*

One particular form of breach which has been a fruitful source of legal difficulty is so-called fundamental breach. The complications that surrounded this area even after the decision of the House of Lords in the *Suisse Atlantique* case (1967) have hopefully been largely swept away by the decision of their Lordships in *Photo Production Ltd v. Securicor Transport Ltd.* (1980) (*Casebook*, Chap. 9). It must now therefore be open to doubt whether it is strictly necessary to consider fundamental breach under a separate heading at all. This case dispels any remnants of the view that a fundamental breach or a breach of a fundamental term means that the guilty party cannot rely on an exemption clause. The facts of the case vividly illustrate this point. Securicor had been employed to provide a night patrol service to their client's factory. In the course of such a visit one of Securicor's employees decided to light a small fire. The result was £615,000 worth of damage to the factory, although it was found that the employee did not intend to burn down the premises and that Securicor had not been negligent in employing or supervising him. It would be difficult to imagine a more serious breach of contract. Securicor had been employed to protect the premises; in fact they had been responsible for burning them down. Nevertheless a widely drafted exclusion clause stating that: "Under no circumstances shall the company be responsible for any injurious act or default by any employee of the company unless such act or default could have been foreseen and avoided by the exercise of due diligence on the part of the company as his employer" was held appropriate to cover the breach in question and exempt Securicor from liability.

In an appropriate case the victim of a fundamental breach may choose to treat the contract as ended. What constitutes such a breach? Lord Diplock in the *Photo Production* case said that it was a breach such as would effectively deprive the innocent party of substantially the whole benefit that it was intended he should receive under the contract. It must therefore be a very serious breach. Devlin J. in *Smeaton Hanscomb & Co. Ltd v. Sassoon (I) Setty, Son & Co.* (1953) stated that, "It is, I think, something which underlies the whole contract so that, if it is not complied with, the performance becomes something totally different from that which the contract contemplates." An example given by Devlin J. was delivering pine instead of mahogany logs in a contract for the supply of the latter.

The fact that a fundamental breach gives the innocent party the option or election to refuse to perform further his obligations under the contract is perhaps not surprising considering that this is the effect of any breach of a condition. By its very nature breach of a fundamental term or a fundamental breach goes to the root of the contractual nexus. What, however, the *Photo Production* case emphasises is that even in the case of such a fundamental breach the parties are at liberty to provide for its consequences in a suitably drafted provision. Again, there is nothing automatic about even a fundamental breach.

(b) *Anticipatory breach*

An anticipatory breach arises when before the due date for performance of the contract the party at fault gives notice of the fact that he has no intention of fulfilling his obligations. An example is the case of *Avery v. Bowden* already referred to. In the event of such a repudiatory anticipatory breach a plaintiff has a choice. He may either elect to treat the contract as thereby ended and sue immediately for breach or he may wait until the performance date has arrived and then sue for breach when the other party fails to comply with the contract.

The first possibility is illustrated by *Frost v. Knight* (1872) (and see also *Hochster v. de la Tour* (1853)). Mr. Knight agreed to marry a Miss Frost on the death of his father. Before this had occurred he broke off the engagement. Miss Frost successfully sued Mr. Knight for breach of promise of marriage. The case is a strong one because at the time of the action the right was still contingent since either of the parties might have predeceased Mr. Knight's father. Although actions for breach of promise have now been abolished by statute (Law Reform (Miscellaneous Provisions) Act 1970, s.1(1)) the principle of the case still remains perfectly valid.

The second possibility was the basis of *Avery v. Bowden* (above, p. 600). In that case, as we have seen, the election to treat the contract as continuing led to the innocent party being probably worse off owing to the effect of frustration than he would have been had he sued immediately. In many cases there may not be much incentive for the innocent party to treat the contract as continuing because he will be unable to complete his side of the bargain without the co-operation of the contract breaker and hence will be unable to claim the full contract payment as opposed to damages. Sometimes, however, one of the parties may be able to fulfil his obligations without further reference to the other and so produce rather surprising results. In *White and Carter (Councils) Ltd. v. McGregor* (1962) advertising agents supplied litter bins to local authorities which were in effect paid for by the advertisements affixed to them. McGregor signed an agreement advertising his garage for three years but later on the same day purported to countermand the contract. Even though the agents realised that this was not what their client any longer wanted they refused to accept the repudiation, duly carried out the agreement for the three years of the contract, and sued for the price of their services. The House of Lords upheld their claim. Although the case is somewhat unusual on its facts and apparently strange in its result it is defensible in principle. Any other result would undermine the fact that the injured party has an election as to whether or not he will accept the repudiation. Even so, the innocent party in this situation does not have a completely unfettered right to elect whether to accept repudiation or not. In *White v. Carter* Lord Reid observed that a party might be unable to enforce his contractual remedy if "he had no legitimate interest, financial or otherwise, in performing the contract rather than claiming damages." The meaning of this qualification was subsequently explored in *Clea Shipping Corp. v. Bulk Oil International Ltd, The Alaskan Trader* (1984). In this case the charterers of an elderly ship announced they had no further use for it and were thereby clearly guilty of an anticipatory breach. The owners nevertheless spent £800,000 on having the vessel repaired, maintained it at anchor with a full crew for the remaining period of the charterparty and then sold it for scrap. On these rather extreme facts the court was unwilling to disturb the arbitrator's finding that the owners had no legitimate interest in continuing to perform the contract. This case therefore suggests that a court may be willing to intervene when the effect of the innocent party's election is commercially quite futile and simply inflates the damages.

4. Frustration

The early common law took the harsh view, also exemplified in *Cutter v. Powell* (above), that contractual obligations must be strictly adhered to. In *Paradine v. Jane* (1647) a tenant was sued for arrears of rent notwithstanding the fact that for the last three years the King's enemies had prevented him from occupying the property. The court decided he still had to pay. He had voluntarily undertaken an obligation and must therefore go through with it. Had he wished to excuse himself from his liability under certain circumstances he could have made provision for this in the contract.

The rigour of this rule was partially relieved by the case of *Taylor v. Caldwell* (1863) out of which the modern doctrine of frustration was developed. In this case the parties had entered into an agreement for the use of the Surrey Gardens and Music Hall for a series of "grand concerts, and day and night fêtes." Before the day of the first concert the building was accidentally destroyed by fire. The claim against the defendants for breach of contract failed. Blackburn J. commented: "We think ... that the Music Hall having ceased to exist, without fault of either party, both parties are excused, the plaintiffs from taking the gardens and paying the money, the defendants from performing their promise to give the use of the Hall and Gardens. ... "

From this it can be seen that the doctrine of frustration operates to relieve the parties from further obligations when performance of the contract has become impossible. The practical sense behind this approach is obvious although its precise juristic basis is more controversial. The two most important explanations are what one might call the "implied term" and "imposed solution" theories. Both require examination but the latter appears to be the currently preferred approach.

The "implied term" view was adopted by Blackburn J. in *Taylor v. Caldwell*, and is similar to the reasoning in cases such as *The Moorcock* (see p. 517) in that it rests on the supposed intention of the parties. If at the time when the contract was made the parties had contemplated the frustrating event then the assumption is that they would have regarded the contract as terminated upon that event. This may have been an approach attractive to adherents of nineteenth-century laissez-faire individualism but it now rings as somewhat artificial. As Lord Radcliffe said in *Davis v. Fareham U.D.C.* (1956) there is "a logical difficulty in seeing how the parties could even impliedly have provided for something which *ex hypothesi* they neither expected nor foresaw." There is more to be said for the view that the law is intervening to impose a fair solution when events have happened that render the whole situation radically different from that originally envisaged by the parties. As Lord Radcliffe went on to say, "*Non haec in foedera veni.* It was not this that I promised to do."

Whatever the precise theoretical basis, two considerations arise in this area: (1) what events will lead to a contract being in law "frustrated"? and (2) what will be the consequences if it is?

(1) What Amounts to Frustration

The common factor in cases of frustration is that the contract has become impossible or at least pointless. Nevertheless there are various ways in which this situation may come about and certain restrictions on the availability of the doctrine which now need to be considered.

(a) *Contract illegal*

If after the formation of a contract its subsequent performance becomes illegal then the contract is frustrated. A frequent example is the outbreak of war which makes further performance illegal as "trading with the enemy." Another example is provided by *Denny Mott & Dickson Ltd v. James B. Fraser & Co. Ltd* (1944). Here an agreement for the sale of timber was linked with an option to take a long lease or to purchase a timber yard which was to be used in conjunction with the contract. The result of various importation orders was that it became impossible to perform the contract legally. The House of Lords accordingly held that since the main purpose of the contract, trading in timber, had become illegal, the whole contract, including the option, had been frustrated.

(b) *Death*

In a contract where the personality of one of the parties is vital, death is the ultimate frustrating event. Hence a contract of service or, for example, an agreement to paint a picture or write a book, will be frustrated by the death of the employee, painter or author.

(c) *Subject-matter destroyed*

Where all or a vital part of the subject-matter of the contract is destroyed so that performance of the contract is rendered impossible this will lead to frustration. The case of *Taylor v. Caldwell* (above, p. 604) is an example of this.

(d) *Unavailability*

In the case of a contract for personal services death is the most extreme form of "unavailability" but there are other examples. Much will depend on the relationship between the length of time one party is unavailable and the time span contemplated by the contract. For example, in *Morgan v. Manser* (1948) a music-hall artiste known as "Cheerful Charlie Chester" signed a 10-year contract with his manager in 1938 but in 1940 he was called up for military service. The court held that the contract had been frustrated. He was not in fact demobilised until 1946 and in the context of a 10-year contract this absence completely undermined the agreement. Perhaps if he had merely been called up for a short period of "national service" the result might well have been different. Another example of a frustrating event would be illness in an appropriate case (see, *e.g. Robinson v. Davison* (1871)).

Similar principles apply to anything else which through some extraneous cause is rendered unavailable for the purposes of the contract. Hence in *Bank Line Ltd v. Arthur Capel & Co.* (1919) the war-time requisitioning of a ship frustrated the charterparty of which it was the subject.

(e) *Mode of performance impossible*

Where the parties agree that the contract shall be carried out in a particular manner which subsequently becomes impossible then this will lead to the contract being frustrated. It is quite different, however, if the parties merely anticipate that a certain means of carrying out the contract will be adopted, without it being a term of the agreement, and that method subsequently becomes impossible. It is not sufficient to invoke the doctrine of frustration that it has simply become more onerous or expensive to carry out the contract.

This principle is well illustrated by the cases that arose out of the closure of the Suez Canal in 1956. In *Tsakiroglou & Co.*

Ltd. v. Noblee and Thorl GmbH (1962) there was a contract for Sudanese groundnuts to be shipped from Port Sudan to Hamburg. Obviously the usual and quickest route between these two ports was via the Suez Canal. When this was closed to traffic the seller failed to make the shipment and claimed frustration as a defence to the buyer's action for breach of contract. The House of Lords rejected the seller's claim. Even though the journey via the Cape of Good Hope would take four weeks longer and increase the cost of freightage the contract did not have a fixed delivery date and no route had been agreed upon. Consequently it was not a fundamentally different enterprise to take the longer route, merely a more expensive one for the seller. As a result of this many charterparties now contain some stipulation as to the route to be followed or a "Suez Canal clause."

(f) *Performance radically different*

This category represents the furthest limit of the doctrine in that the frustrating event is regarded as sufficient because it in effect renders the whole contract pointless or futile although not strictly impossible. The leading authorities in this area are the so-called "coronation cases" arising out of the postponement of Edward VII's coronation. In *Krell v. Henry* (1903) (*Casebook*, chap. 9) the defendant made a written agreement for the hire of a suite of rooms overlooking the coronation procession. Although the agreement did not expressly mention the procession both parties understood that this was the reason for the hire. When the procession was cancelled the plaintiff nevertheless sued for the balance of the fee. The court upheld the defendant's contention that the contract had been frustrated. Vaughan Williams L.J. extended the notion of *Taylor v. Caldwell*, saying, "English law applies the principle not only to cases where the performance of the contract becomes impossible by the cessation of existence of the thing which is the subject-matter of the contract, but also to cases where the event ... is the cessation or non-existence of an express condition or state of things, going to the root of the contract, and essential to its performance." Although the defendant could have used the rooms on the relevant days it would clearly have been a futile and pointless exercise since the whole object of the contract was undoubtedly to view the coronation procession.

Nevertheless the courts are not quick to invoke this head of frustration as can be seen by contrasting the decision in *Herne Bay Steam Boat Company v. Hutton* (1903). The facts arose out of the same coronation celebrations but the object in this case was to charter a boat in order to view the naval review "and for a day's cruise around the fleet." The review was cancelled but the boat owners still recovered the cost of the hire. The distinction between the cases could be explained on the basis that seeing the naval review was only one of the purposes for hiring the boat. The fleet remained and could still be viewed so that the entire foundation of the contract was not destroyed.

Another more recent case which illustrates the reluctance of the courts to construe *Krell v. Henry* at all generously is *Davis Contractors Ltd v. Fareham U.D.C.* (1956). A building company contracted to build some houses in eight months for £92,425. Owing to shortages the work in fact took 22 months and £17,651 more to complete. The builders claimed that the contract had been frustrated but the House of Lords rejected this view. Lord Radcliffe commented; " ... it is not hardship or inconvenience or material loss itself which calls the principle of frustration into play. There must be as well such a change in the significance of the obligation that the thing undertaken would, if performed, be a different thing from that contracted for."

(2) Self-induced Frustration

It is often said that frustration cannot be self-induced, since its essence is that it comes about without the fault of either party. At first sight this may seem obvious since such an act would normally be a breach of contract in the ordinary way. It need not, however, always be so as is shown by *Maritime National Fish Ltd v. Ocean Trawlers Ltd* (1935). Here the charterers took a ship, the *St. Cuthbert*, for a year from the owners both parties knowing that the ship was of a type that could only be lawfully operated with a licence from the Canadian government. The charterers applied for five licences to cover the ships they were operating but were only granted three and were obliged to elect to which ships the licences granted were to apply. They decided not to include the *St. Cuthbert* and later claimed that the charter had been frustrated by the government's refusal to grant an adequate number of licences. The Privy Council rejected this view explaining that it was the act and election of the charterers themselves that led to the ship being inoperable even though it was not a term of the contract that the charterers would obtain a licence for the ship. This case was purportedly followed by the Court of Appeal in *The Super Servant Two* (1990). The defendants had

contracted to carry drilling machinery from Japan to Rotter-
dam on either of their two vessels. When one of them
unexpectedly sank they found they had insufficient capacity
to carry all the cargos they had contracted for and chose not
to perform the contract for carriage of the drilling machinery.
The court held that their exercise of a choice not to carry that
cargo was fatal to the plea of frustration. A difficulty with this
reasoning is that the *Maritime National Fish* case could surely
be distinguished on the basis that in that case it was perfectly
foreseeable that the Minister would not issue enough licences.
The charterers took a commercial gamble. In *The Super Servant
Two* nobody considered the possibility that the ship would
sink and it seems artificial to say that the carriers had much of
a choice or election in the matter. They were unable to
perform their contract in unforeseen circumstances for which
they may not have been responsible. That is surely just when
frustration should come into play.

Where there is an allegation that the frustration was self-
induced the onus of proving this rests upon the party who
alleges it (see *Joseph Constantine Steamship Line Ltd v. Imperial
Smelting Corpn. Ltd* (1942)).

(3) Foreseeing the Event

If a contract contains a provision which expressly sets out
what is to happen on the occurrence of what would otherwise
be a frustrating event then there is generally no longer any
question of the agreement having been frustrated. The
difficulty will simply be resolved in accordance with the terms
the parties have agreed upon. If the event was not foreseen
then of course this is precisely what the doctrine of frustration
is meant to cover. The difficulty that may arise exists in those
cases which fall between these two extremes. What if the
frustrating event is foreseen, but the scope or seriousness of
the disaster is very much greater than that which the parties
envisaged?

It is clearly a difficult matter of construction whether a term
really does cover the events that have taken place as the
leading case of *Jackson v. Union Marine Insurance Co. Ltd* (1874)
illustrates. A charterparty provided that a ship was to proceed
with all possible dispatch "dangers and accidents of naviga-
tion excepted" from Liverpool to Newport. It had got no
further than Carnarvon Bay before it ran aground and it took
eight months for the ship to be repaired as a result.
Notwithstanding the contract clause mentioned, the court
held that the charter had been frustrated. At first sight the

clause might have been thought apt to cover the delay but the court decided that it was never intended to cover so serious and extensive a delay as actually occurred. A similar problem arose in *Pacific Phosphate Co. Ltd v. Empire Transport Co. Ltd* (1920). An agreement to provide ships contained a clause suspending the agreement in the event of war. This was nevertheless held not sufficient to cover the catastrophic dislocating effects of the First World War which was outside the ambit of anything which the parties had contemplated when they made the agreement. Consequently the contract was frustrated.

(4) Leases

Much controversy used to exist over the problem of whether the doctrine of frustration applied to a lease. The difficulty lay in the fact that a lease is a rather special type of contract in that it bestows an interest in the land itself, (or, as is usually said, *in rem*). The result is that an interest in the land survives even if, for example, a house being leased falls down. There may still be an obligation on the part of the tenant to pay rent and the landlord to repair. Despite this the House of Lords resolved the controversy in *National Carriers Ltd v. Panalpina (Northern) Ltd* (1981) in favour of the view that the doctrine of frustration does apply to leases. They are after all essentially a special form of contract and *Taylor v. Caldwell* itself showed that the doctrine applied to the related concept of a licence to occupy land. Nevertheless the occasions on which frustration will be successfully invoked in the context of a lease are likely to be very rare.

(5) The Consequences of Frustration

When a frustrating event has occurred the contract automatically comes to an end. There is no question of the parties having any choice or election in the matter as there is in the case of a breach of condition. Nevertheless, the contractual obligations are only ended as from the date of frustration. There is no question, as may happen when there has been a fundamental mistake, of the contract being void *ab initio*. In analysing the legal consequences it is still necessary to consider both the common law and statutory provisions separately since it is possible to exclude the operation of the Law Reform (Frustrated Contracts) Act 1943. This approach does, however, have the advantage of showing how the law in this area has been developed and reformed.

(a) *At common law*

The original rule at common law was strict and somewhat arbitrary in its effect. Since the rights and liabilities of the parties become fixed at the moment of the frustrating event, it was said that "the loss lay where it fell." This point is shown by *Chandler v. Webster* (1904), another of the so-called "coronation" cases. The plaintiff hired a room in Pall Mall in order to view the procession for a price of £141 15s payable at once. He paid £100 before the coronation was postponed and after this frustrating event sought to recover his money. Not only did he not succeed in doing so but he was also obliged to pay the balance of £41 15s. The reasoning was that since the frustrating event only terminated the contract from that time, and the money had been payable before this, then he was still liable on what was at that stage a valid contract. By contrast in *Krell v. Henry* (above) the balance of the money due for the hire of the room did not become payable until after the frustrating event. Accordingly the hirer of the room was unable to recover this amount because the contract had already been terminated before this right accrued. Consequently the application of the same principle produced different practical results in the two cases.

The injustice of this state of affairs was to some extent alleviated by the case of *Fibrosa Spolka Akcyjna v. Fairbairn Lawson Combe Barbour Ltd* (1943) (*Casebook*, Chap. 9). Fairbairn agreed to make some machinery for Fibrosa (a Polish company) in July 1939 for a price of £4,800. Of this, £1,600 was payable in advance and £1,000 was indeed paid over by Fibrosa. By September 1940 the place of delivery in Poland was under German occupation and the contract was therefore frustrated. Fibrosa claimed the return of their £1,000 and succeeded. The House of Lords overruled *Chandler v. Webster* because it was inconsistent with the basic proposition that a person who has paid for something and received nothing in return is entitled to recover his money in a claim in quasi-contract. Historically, this is known as a claim "upon a total failure of consideration." Whereas in the context of formation of contract "consideration" may mean the *promise* to perform, in the context of a claim for recovery of advance payment it denotes the *actual* performance.

Although an improvement on the earlier law the case still leaves two areas of possible injustice. The manufacturer might well have expended time and money on the undelivered goods before the contract was frustrated for which he is prevented from being compensated. Secondly, unless the failure of consideration is total the other party cannot recover anything. This is so even if the consideration bestowed is trivial or nominal. Not surprisingly therefore there has been statutory intervention.

(b) *By statute*

The major objection to the *Fibrosa* case was that it produced an "all or nothing" solution, though of a different sort from that produced by *Chandler v. Webster*. Under the Law Reform (Frustrated Contracts) Act 1943 both parties, so far as is possible, can be compensated by the court so that any loss or benefit is fairly distributed between them. The Act does this by instituting two major reforms; (1) money already paid can be recovered, and (2) compensation can be awarded for partial performance. The Act says nothing about what actually constitutes "frustration" which is still entirely governed by common law.

Section 1(2) in effect provides that money already paid can be recovered, regardless of whether the failure of consideration is partial or total, subject to the court allowing deduction of any expenses which the payee has incurred before the time of the frustrating event. Equally if the sum was only payable but not paid before the termination of the contract, the court may allow the recovery of an amount equal to the expenses incurred by the prospective payee. The result therefore is that the common law rule of all or nothing is replaced by a wide discretion in the court to award expenses out of amounts paid or payable before the contract was frustrated.

Section 1(3) allows a claim for partial performance when the contract is frustrated. For example, if A installed machinery in B's factory which operated satisfactorily for several months but before the price became payable was destroyed by fire, then A may claim a sum from B to compensate for the fact that he has received nothing whereas B has received a valuable, albeit short-lived, benefit. Some difficulty, however, arises on the meaning of "a valuable benefit" in section 1(3). Take the facts of *Appleby v. Myers* (1867). The plaintiffs agreed to construct machinery in the defendant's factory and maintain it for two years for a price of £459. When the work was almost completed it was destroyed by fire. The contract was frustrated and as the law then stood the loss lay where it fell since the money was not payable at the moment of frustration. What would be the result of the case if it were decided today? Expenses could not be recovered since no money was paid or payable when the contract was terminated. Is recovery possible under section 1(3)? One view would be that partially completed machinery is of no use and therefore there was no benefit to Myers. Another is that he did have a benefit from the mere fact that work had been carried out on his property even though it had not been completed. Both views are tenable but it seems more sensible on these facts to say that Appleby should recover nothing. The effect of the fire on the "benefit" of the uncompleted machinery was surely to destroy it before it could be of the slightest real benefit to Myers. This is also the view expressed by Goff J. in *B.P. Exploration v. Hunt (No. 2)* (1979) which contains a helpful discussion of the 1943 Act.

The Act is restricted in that it does not apply to most charterparties or contracts for the carriage of goods by sea or policies of insurance. It also effectively excludes contracts for the sale of specific goods where the contract is frustrated by the perishing of those goods. For example, A agrees to sell B all the present contents of his wine cellar but before delivery can take place the wine is destroyed by fire. The Act would not apply to such a frustrating event. Finally, as already noted, the parties may themselves exclude the operation of the Act by the terms of their agreement.

Chapter 24

Remedies

In the course of discussing what can go wrong with the contractual bond certain remedies have already been mentioned in some detail. For example, in the cases of misrepresentation or mistake the remedies of rescission and rectification may be relevant. In other cases where there has been some form of unjust enrichment of one party at the expense of the other we have seen that there may be an action in quasi-contract as in the *Fibrosa* case. What must now be examined are the remedies which the innocent party can obtain against a contract breaker for his breach of contract. These are: damages, specific performance and injunction. Finally it is necessary to consider the circumstances under which the plaintiff's remedy may be extinguished.

1. Damages

An award of damages is the normal remedy in the law of contract. The object of the award is to put the plaintiff, so far as money can, in the same position that he would have been in had the contract been performed properly. In this regard it is different from the law governing tortious liability (on which see below, p. 655) where the object is to put the victim back into the position in which he would have been had the wrongful act never been carried out.

Assessing the level of damages in a case of breach really involves two quite separate considerations. First of all it has to be determined whether or not the damage that has occurred is of a kind for which the law will compensate. Secondly, if it is, it must be decided how the amount is to be calculated. This essentially involves asking: what for? and, how much? It is these two problems which we now need to consider.

(1) Remoteness of Damage

The law could not possibly compensate a plaintiff for every result of a breach of contract. For example, A sells B a faulty vacuum cleaner which B decides to return to A's shop. On his way back to the shop he is run over by a careless motorist and injured. As a result he loses his job and his wife leaves him. In a sense, all of B's difficulties have flowed from A's breach of contract, but as a matter of common sense it would seem strange to link the sale of a domestic appliance to marital desertion. Accordingly, the law draws a line at some consequences which are said to be too remote from the damage to be compensable. Inevitably a general principle designed to do this must be couched in wide and perhaps rather vague terms but an examination of the cases shows the rules a court will apply. At the end of the day it is a question of policy rather than logic where the line is to be drawn.

The case which first laid down the modern rule as to remoteness of damage was *Hadley v. Baxendale* (1854), the facts of which provide a good illustration of the type of problem involved. The plaintiffs owned a mill in Gloucester and asked the defendant carrier to transport a broken mill shaft to Greenwich in order to provide a pattern for a new one. As a result of the defendant's fault the shaft was not delivered on time and work at the plaintiff's mill was held up for longer than it need have been. It was found that all the carrier knew was that he was transporting a broken mill shaft and that the plaintiffs were the millers of that mill. The rule laid down by Alderson B. to assess damages in such a case was that:

> "Where two parties have made a contract which one of them has broken, the damages which the other party ought to receive in respect of such breach of contract should be such as may fairly and reasonably be considered either arising naturally, i.e. according to the usual course of things, from such breach of contract itself, or such as may reasonably be supposed to have been in the contemplation of both parties, at the time they made the contract, as the probable result of the breach of it."

The rule therefore has two elements. A defendant is always liable for the usual consequences of his breach. He is only liable for unusual consequences if he has special knowledge of them at the time when the contract was made.

Applying the rule to the facts of the case the court held that the defendant was not liable for the loss of profit when the mill was closed. In the majority of cases it was found that the absence of a mill shaft would not have caused a stoppage; for example, there might have been a spare. The special circumstance that this mill did not have a spare was not known to the defendant and so they could not be held liable even under the second limb of the rule.

Although the principle in *Hadley v. Baxendale* has frequently been discussed and reformulated the substance of the rule seems to have survived intact. For example, in *Victoria Laundry (Windsor) Ltd v. Newman Industries Ltd* (1949) (*Casebook*, Chap. 10) the plaintiffs, who were launderers and dyers, wanted a large boiler to expand their business. The defendants agreed to install a boiler on June 5, 1946 but owing to their breach of contract it was not delivered until November 8, 1946. The plaintiffs claimed under two heads: (i) £16 a week damages for loss of profits for the extra custom they could have taken on, and (ii) £262 a week which they could have obtained under certain especially lucrative contracts with the Ministry of Supply. It was found that the defendants knew that the plaintiffs were anxious to have the boiler installed as soon as possible but not that they were aware of the lucrative supply contract. Accordingly, they were liable for the loss of profits arising from the failure to enlarge the business and carry out normal contracts but not for the much greater loss of profits obtainable from contracts with the Ministry. By contrast, in *Simpson v. London and North Western Rail Co.* (1876) the defendants knew that the plaintiffs' samples were to be exhibited at an agricultural show in Newcastle. Indeed the goods were labelled, "must be at Newcastle on Monday certain." They failed to arrive on time and the plaintiff claimed for the loss of profits he would have made had the contract been performed properly. The defendants were held liable since they knew of the special circumstances of the case and agreed to contract on that basis.

The rule in *Hadley v. Baxendale* was examined in some detail by the House of Lords in *Koufos v. C. Czarnikow Ltd (The Heron II)* (1969). The result was a series of judgments which appear to generate more heat than light and leave the rule essentially intact. Much of the argument is concerned with what precisely is meant by a person's contemplation of future damage. The view which seems to have commanded the most general support is that it must be such that a reasonable man would regard it as "liable to result" although this does not require that it should be definitely more likely to result than not. There seems much to be said for the observation of Sellers L.J. in the Court of Appeal that, "the phrases and words of *Hadley v. Baxendale* have been hallowed by long user and gain little advantage from the paraphrases or substitutes. The ideas and factors conveyed by the words are clear enough."

Nevertheless the difficulties in applying these principles to specific cases are illustrated by *H. Parsons (Livestock) Ltd v. Uttley Ingham & Co. Ltd* (1978). None of the judgments of the Court of Appeal are entirely free from difficulty in their application of the rule of remoteness to contract damages. What the case does appear to decide is that if the loss is of a *type* that could reasonably have been contemplated, the defendant is liable even if the *extent* of the damage is greater than was reasonably foreseeable.

(2) Quantification

Once it has been decided that the loss is not too remote from the damage to be recoverable, the next question to decide is: how much? It is important to note that the object of damages in contract is compensatory not punitive. If, despite the defendant's breach of contract, the plaintiff suffers no loss, then nothing except nominal damages will be recoverable and he may not even recover the costs of his action. For example, if B wrongfully dismisses A who immediately afterwards gets a similar but much better paid job then A, albeit fortuitously perhaps, has suffered no loss and will not be able to recover any more than nominal damages.

The general principle, as we have seen, is that the plaintiff will receive in damages such an amount as will put him in the same position as if the contract had been performed properly. Quite what this amount will be is entirely dependent on the subject matter of the contract, but there are certain general principles which the courts apply.

(a) *Goods*

There will generally be a market in goods that are bought and sold so that a loss can be quantified by reference to the market. For example, if a seller fails to deliver goods then the buyer's damages will be the difference between the contract price and the greater amount he has to pay for the same goods in the market. If it is the buyer who refuses to accept delivery then similarly the damages will be the difference between what he would have received under the contract and what he actually gets for the goods when he sells them in the market (see ss.50 and 51, Sale of Goods Act 1979).

An example of how the courts proceed when there is no available market price is *W.L. Thompson Ltd v. Robinson Gunmakers Ltd* (1955). Here the buyers in breach of contract refused to accept delivery of a Vanguard car from the sellers who were car dealers. Because of resale price maintenance (see above, p. 561) the car could not be sold at less than the manufacturer's list price. The result was effectively that the market and contract prices were the same. There was at that time no demand for this type of car but the sellers were able to mitigate their loss by persuading their suppliers to take it back. The buyers contended that, although they were in breach, the plaintiffs had in fact suffered no loss. The court disagreed. Section 50 of the Sale of Goods Act only represents a prima facie rule which did not apply in this situation. The sellers were therefore entitled to £61, the profit they would have made on the bargain. The buyer's contention would have succeeded if, as in *Charter v. Sullivan* (1957), the car was of a type which was in such demand that the seller could easily sell it to another buyer.

The distinction between the two cases is clearer if one remembers that in *Charter v. Sullivan* the seller could not obtain a sufficient supply of cars to satisfy the demand. There was therefore no question of being able to make two sales instead of one. In *Thompson v. Robinson* the operation of Resale Price Maintenance prevented sale of the car at less than list price and there was an excess of supply over demand of this type of car. There was no question of being able to sell the car anywhere else.

(b) *Speculative damages*

Where evidence can be given on the quantity of a loss then the plaintiff must give it or risk recovering only nominal damages (see, *e.g.* *Clark v. Kirby-Smith* (1964)). A problem arises, however, when there has been a breach of contract but the precise measure of damages is difficult to calculate. This arose in an acute form in *Chaplin v. Hicks* (1911) (*Casebook*, Chap. 10). The defendant agreed with the plaintiff that if she attended an audition along with 49 other actresses she would have the chance of being one of the 12 chosen for employment. The plaintiff failed to give her a reasonable opportunity to attend according to the agreement but claimed that only nominal damages should be recovered. She only had a one in four chance of obtaining the job and clearly there were many uncertainties involved in her being selected. Nevertheless, the court awarded the plaintiff what was then substantial damages of £100. She had suffered an actionable breach of contract and the mere fact that it might be difficult or impossible precisely to quantify the level of compensation was not a bar to the court making an attempt to do so.

It would be different if it were not just difficult, but quite impossible, to estimate the damages. In *McRae v. Commonwealth Disposals Commission* (1951) (above, p. 544) the plaintiffs failed in their claim for damages based upon loss of bargain. It was impossible to calculate the value of salvaging a non-existent tanker on a non-existent reef. In these circumstances, as in *McRae*, a plaintiff can only recover his *reliance* loss, *i.e.* the expenditure thrown away as a result of the defendant's breach of contract. This is likely to be less valuable than a claim for loss of bargain but at least offers some compensation (see also *Anglia Television v. Reed* (1972)).

The problem of assessing damages has also surfaced in the cases arising out of spoilt holidays. Although compensation will not generally be awarded merely for injured feelings (see, *e.g. Watts v. Morrow* (1991)) the courts have held that where the whole object of the contract is providing pleasure, or at least freedom from distress, a breach of contract in failing to do so may lead to the recovery of substantial damages (see, *e.g. Jackson v. Horizon Holidays Ltd* (1975) (above, p. 557); *Jarvis v. Swans Tours Ltd* (1973); *Heywood v. Wellers (A Firm)* (1976)).

(c) *Tax*

Where damages which are not themselves taxable are recovered as compensation for a loss that is, a question arises as to the amount the defendant should be obliged to pay. For example, A wrongfully dismisses B from his job. Can B recover his total loss of salary or should he be awarded only the net amount he would have received after deduction of tax? In *British Transport Commission v. Gourley* (1956) the House of Lords decided (although it was a tort case the same principle applies in contract) that a plaintiff may only recover the net amount of his loss. Since the principle of contractual damages is compensatory, any other result would in effect have allowed the plaintiff to make a profit. He would always normally receive payment only after tax had been deducted.

The position has been modified by statute in relation to wrongful dismissal awards in excess of £30,000. The effect of sections 148 and 188 of the Income and Corporation Taxes Act 1988 is that the *Gourley* principle applies to the first £30,000 and thereafter, although the damages are paid without deduction of tax, the amount received becomes taxable in the hands of the plaintiff. So-called "golden handshakes" are now therefore subject to tax.

(3) Agreed Damages and Penalties

It is very common, especially in building contracts and charterparties, to have a clause in the agreement which sets out what damages are to be payable in the event of breach. This is known as "liquidated damages"; that is to say, the amount is fixed. Such a precaution is a sensible way to avoid the trouble and expense of the court making the calculation for itself. The effect is that, whether the actual damage suffered is more or less than that envisaged in the agreed damages clause, the plaintiff will only be able to recover the specified amount.

Nevertheless, a party may challenge an agreed damages clause on the grounds that it is in fact a "penalty." It is common in everyday speech to talk of penalty clauses when what people strictly should refer to is a liquidated damages clause. A penalty clause is a term used in effect as a fine or threat against the other party to perform the contract and the courts will not enforce it. If the term is struck out as a penalty the amount of damages will once again be at large and the court will have to do the calculation for itself.

How will a court decide if a term is in reality a penalty? The essential question which the court must ask itself is: does the amount represent a genuine pre-estimate of any loss arising out of breach at the time the contract was made? Although this always remains the central question, Lord Dunedin in *Dunlop Pneumatic Tyre Co. Ltd v. New Garage and Motor Co. Ltd* (1915) (*Casebook*, Chap. 10) laid down a number of useful guidelines to assist a court in determining this issue. They may be summarised as follows:

1. Even though the parties use the words "penalty" or "liquidated damages" this will not be conclusive. The court will look at the substance not just the form of the agreement and decide what the terms really amount to.

2. It is a penalty if the sum stipulated is extravagantly greater than any loss which could conceivably flow from the breach. Clearly such a term, by definition, is not a genuine pre-estimate of loss.

3. It will be a penalty "if the breach consists only in not paying a sum of money, and the sum stipulated is a sum greater than the sum which ought to have been paid." This proposition is of course only a particular application of the previous one.

4. There is a presumption (but no more) that it is a penalty when "a single lump sum is made payable ... on the occurrence of one or more or all of several events, some of which may occasion serious and others but trifling damage."

5. "It is no obstacle to the sum stipulated being a genuine pre-estimate of damage, that the consequences of the breach are such as to make precise pre-estimation almost an impossibility." That is just the situation when the parties would want to employ an agreed damages clause.

It may be a difficult matter of construction to decide whether or not a term operates as a penalty. In the *Dunlop* case itself the clause concerned stipulated a sum of £5 to be paid on each occasion if, amongst other things, a tyre was sold below the list price (such an arrangement would not now be possible, see above, p. 561). The House of Lords decided in this case that the stipulation was reasonable. The potential damage to Dunlop of undercutting their prices was considerable although the quantification of such damage might be almost impossible. It was therefore reasonable to have a fixed but not extravagant level of damages. By contrast, in *Kemble v. Farren* (1829) the manager of the Covent Garden Theatre agreed to employ the defendant as "a principal comedian." One term of the contract was that in the event of a failure to fulfil the agreement "or any part thereof" the party at fault was to pay the other £1,000 as liquidated damages and not as a penalty. The court held, notwithstanding the way it had been described, that the clause was a penalty. A very large sum was payable on the occurrence of what might be a very trivial breach; the clause did not represent a genuine attempt at the pre-estimate of loss. Indeed the case is a good illustration of propositions 1–4 of the *Dunlop* case (see also *Ford Motor Co. v. Armstrong* (1915)).

A related, but quite different, concept to agreed damages is that of an "action for an agreed sum." The most obvious example is an action to recover the price of goods sold. Strictly speaking what is being claimed in such a case is not damages but the recovery of the debt owed by the defendant to the plaintiff. Because of this questions of mitigation (on which see below) and remoteness do not arise (for example see, *White and Carter (Councils) Ltd v. McGregor* (1962), above, p. 603).

(4) Mitigation

The victim of a breach of contract is not entitled merely to sit back and let the damage grow worse if, by taking reasonable steps, he can reduce it. He is under a duty to mitigate his loss although the onus is on the defendant to prove that he has not done so. For example, if A wrongfully refuses to supply goods to B, then B is under a duty to mitigate his loss by immediately going into the market and buying similar goods at the going rate. If he delays and the price rises further he cannot recover his now increased loss.

A fruitful source of mitigation problems has been actions for wrongful dismissal. In the leading case of *Brace v. Calder* (1895) the plaintiff was wrongfully dismissed by a partnership but then offered re-employment on the same terms as before. In the circumstances of this particular case the plaintiff had acted unreasonably in turning down the offer of employment and so recovered only nominal damages. This does not mean that a person in such a position has to accept any job that he is offered. It would only amount to a failure to mitigate if the job was of a kind which it would be appropriate and reasonable for the plaintiff to undertake.

The key-word in this area is "reasonable." If, for example, a plaintiff in reasonably attempting to mitigate his loss actually makes it worse then he will not be penalised for his actions. He will be able to recover his actual loss even though he has himself increased it. In *Pilkington v. Wood* (1953) (*Casebook*, Chap. 10) a solicitor in breach of contract advised that the title to the plaintiff's house was good. The solicitor argued that the plaintiff should have mitigated his loss by bringing an action against the vendor for conveying a defective title. The court, in rejecting this argument, said that it was not reasonable to expect the plaintiff to "embark on a complicated and difficult piece of litigation" in order "to protect his solicitor from the consequences of his own carelessness."

2. Specific Performance

A decree of specific performance is an order by the court to the defendant compelling him to perform his obligations under the contract. The obvious question is perhaps, why is this not the standard remedy in every case? The rather unsatisfactory answer seems to be that it is for reasons of history rather than logic. The basic common law remedy for breach of contract was the award of damages, and the entirely equitable remedy of specific performance was developed by the courts in order to do justice in those cases where an award of monetary compensation would not be an adequate remedy. Various consequences flow from this historical development.

(1) Damages Inadequate

An order for specific performance will not be made unless an award of damages would be inadequate to compensate the plaintiff for his loss. Hence a decree will rarely be issued for a contract to supply goods which are available in the open market since damages will always be an adequate substitute. The only case where an order is likely to be made (provided for by the Sale of Goods Act 1979, s.52) is when similar goods are unobtainable elsewhere. This was illustrated in *Behnke v. Bede Shipping Co.* (1927) where an order for specific performance was granted in relation to the purchase of a ship. In this case there was only one other ship of similar specifications afloat. The occasions on which such an order is made are therefore likely to be very rare.

Rather strangely perhaps, specific performance will always be granted in respect of a sale of land. This proceeds on the assumption that every parcel of land is unique and damages can never be an adequate remedy for its loss. This is so even if the land involved is, for example, merely one out of a street of identical terraced houses. A court will also make an order in respect of an obligation to pay money. This was done in *Beswick v. Beswick* (above, p. 563) where owing to the particular circumstances of that case damages would not have been an adequate remedy.

(2) Mutuality

Although there are certain exceptions, it is generally true that an order of specific performance will not be made against a defendant unless such an order could, if their roles were reversed, have been made against the plaintiff. This is the reason that a minor cannot obtain specific performance; the other party cannot obtain such an order against him (see above, p. 574).

(3) Discretion

Being an equitable remedy, specific performance is discretionary. This does not mean that it can be arbitrarily withheld, but the court might always refuse to grant such an order if it was just and equitable to do so. For example, the plaintiff might have been guilty of unconscionable delay in bringing his action which had in some way prejudiced other parties.

Nevertheless, where a party claims specific performance, a court may always award damages in addition to or instead of making such an order.

(4) Non Specifically Enforceable Contracts

Specific performance will not be granted to enforce a contract of employment, although there may of course be a remedy in damages. Not only would such an order in most cases be impracticable but it would also be an infringement of personal liberty. On the other hand, a greater element of flexibility may be appearing in the grant of specific performance. For example, in *Posner v. Scott-Lewis* (1986) the landlords of a block of flats had breached a term in the lease to provide a resident porter on the premises, and the tenants sought specific performance of this obligation. The landlords relied on an earlier Court of Appeal decision, *Ryan v. Mutual Tontine Westminster Chambers Association* (1893), which rejected such a claim on the grounds that it would involve the court in constant supervision for its proper enforcement. Notwithstaning the fact that this case could only be distinguished on somewhat slender grounds, the court granted specific performance. The relevant considerations for making such an order were said to be: (a) is there a sufficient definition of what has to be done in order to comply with the court order; (b) will enforcing the order involve an unacceptable degree of superintendence by the court; and (c) what is the balance of prejudice or hardships if the order is made or not? A building contract, which might involve a high degree of supervision, would be a clear example of (b) where a court would be unlikely to order specific performance.

3. Injunction

An injunction is an order of the court restraining the defendant from committing a breach of contract. Normally this will simply be what one might call the negative of a decree of specific performance. The defendant is prevented from doing something that he has promised not to do.

Sometimes, however, a so-called mandatory injunction can be obtained to restore the position to that which existed before the defendant's breach of contract. If, for example, the defendant has constructed a building in breach of contract, a mandatory injunction might be obtained to demolish it.

It has already been mentioned that a decree of specific performance cannot be used to compel the performance of a contract of employment. Nevertheless, where there is an express negative stipulation in a contract an injunction has been granted to restrain breach of that undertaking even though the effect of this was to *encourage* the defendant to perform his obligations under the agreement. In *Warner Bros. Pictures Inc. v. Nelson* (1937) the actress Bette Davis entered into an agreement with the plaintiffs in which she agreed "to render her exclusive services" as an artiste and to perform only for them. In breach of this contract she signed an agreement with a third party and the plaintiffs sought an injunction to restrain her from acting elsewhere. They succeeded. The effect of the order was not to compel her to work for the plaintiffs although it might certainly have been a potent encouragement. She could after all have obtained employment in some other unrelated field which would not be within the enforceable terms of any negative stipulation in the contract. This can be contrasted with the decision in *Page One Records Ltd and Another v. Britton* (1968). The defendants, a pop group known as "The Troggs," engaged the first plaintiff as their sole manager and agreed not to employ anyone else in the same capacity. The defendants wished to terminate the agreement and the plaintiffs sought an injunction restraining them from engaging another manager. The injunction was refused. The court held that to grant it would, in effect, be to compel the group to employ the plaintiff as manager or to remain idle.

Of the two cases, it is difficult not to believe that the latter takes a more realistic view of the practicalities of the situation and it seems that the courts are more likely to adopt this approach. In *Warren v. Mendy* (1989) a boxer agreed to employ the plaintiff as his sole manager for three years but the Court of Appeal declined to grant an injunction to enforce the agreement. To do so, they considered, would be indirectly to compel performance of the contract. A realistic approach had to be taken and a court would be less ready to grant an injunction where there was a contract involving the maintenance of a skill or talent and there had been a breakdown in confidence between the parties.

4. Limitation

Based upon the principle *interest rei publicae ut finis sit litium* (it is the concern of the state that there be an end to litigation) a right to a contractual remedy can be extinguished merely by effluxion of time.

In the case of a simple contract debt section 5 of the Limitation Act 1980 states that an action shall not be brought more than six years after the date on which the cause of action accrued. This means the time at which the facts giving rise to the action happened, not necessarily the date when the potential plaintiff discovered that he could bring an action. The result is that it is possible for a plaintiff to be "statute-barred," as it is called, before he even realised that he had any legal redress. Where personal injuries are claimed the limitation period is in general reduced to three years, and where the contract is by deed the period is 12 years (s.11 and s.8(1)). Where there is fraud or mistake section 32 of the 1980 Act stipulates that time does not begin to run until "the plaintiff has discovered the fraud, concealment or mistake ... or could with reasonable diligence have discovered it."

When a person is acting under a disability (in legal terms), for example, a minor, time does not begin to run until the disability has been removed (s.28). In the case of a minor this would therefore be on their eighteenth birthday.

Even though the limitation period has expired, the action may be revived if a debtor either makes a written acknowledgment or part payment of the debt (s.29(5)). If he makes an acknowledgment it must be in writing and signed by the person making it (s.30(1)). The effect is that time begins to run again as from the date of the acknowledgment or part payment.

Although the 1980 Act does not apply to claims for equitable relief such as specific performance or injunction, similar rules are applied "by analogy to the statute" or by the application of the equitable doctrine of "laches" (delay). The result is therefore that if an equitable claim corresponds to a similar common law claim which would be barred by statute then no equitable relief will be granted "by analogy." In any event, courts of equity have always refused to grant relief if the plaintiff has been guilty of unconscionable delay. Accordingly the doctrine of "laches" will be applied if the plaintiff has, for example, acquiesced in the wrong done to him or his dilatoriness in bringing an action has unfairly prejudiced other parties.

Chapter 25

Contracts for Goods and Services

In the remaining chapters in this section more detailed attention will be given to *specific* contracts. While the general principles of the law of contract (concerning such matters as agreement, consideration, capacity and remedies) apply to all contracts and are still largely governed by the common law, Parliament has increasingly intervened to regulate the form and terms of *particular* contracts. Sometimes the aim of Parliament has been merely to codify the case law without effecting significant changes of substance. A good example of such legislation was the Sale of Goods Act 1893, the idea behind which was to reduce a mass of case law to an accessible form without major change. But in this century Parliament has been concerned to intervene in a much more drastic way with the broad view of ensuring that contracts are "fair." We have already touched on this matter (above, p. 464) and now we turn to consideration of some specific contracts the form and terms of which are governed by legislation.

Legislation now closely regulates many kinds of contracts such as those for the sale of goods and hire-purchase, contracts of employment and the letting of houses. Past experience shows that in such contracts one party may take advantage of his superior bargaining power to secure terms which are unduly to his advantage and the purpose of such legislation is to ensure that parity is restored. Such legislation can be extremely detailed, for example, regulating the colouring of paper and the size, colour and density of the type face which must be employed in contracts of hire-purchase and credit sale. Such legislation may therefore severely restrict freedom of contract in the sense that the essential terms of the contract, and its form, may be largely dictated by the relevant statute.

It is not possible here to give a detailed account of this very considerable body of statute law. Succeeding chapters in this section concentrate on that legislation which affects the consumer in relation to everyday transactions concerning the

sale of goods and the provision of services. Even this is a
formidable body of law and we can only highlight certain
features of it.

1. Sale of Goods

The modern law of the sale of goods owes its origins to the
victory of business expediency over the often technical and
cumbersome restrictions placed upon buyers and sellers by
the old common law. The first large scale statutory intervention was the Sale of Goods Act 1893. This largely codified the
existing law although it did undoubtedly make some
modifications. It confirmed the gradual movement away from
a strict application of the maxim *caveat emptor* (let the buyer
beware) in most cases to a position in which certain terms
were always to be implied, subject to the intentions of the
parties, for the protection of the buyer. In particular these
were the implied conditions as to title, description, merchantable quality and fitness for purpose (ss.12–15). Opinions vary
as to its success as a statute but its longevity and importance
are undeniable. Until 1967 it had survived with only very
minor alterations and has been substantially re-enacted in the
Sale of Goods Act 1979.

The amendments to the Act effected by the Misrepresentation Act 1967, Criminal Law Act 1967 and Theft Act 1968 were
of some significance but a more important change was
brought about by the Supply of Goods (Implied Terms) Act
1973. This Act *inter alia* prevented the exclusion of the terms
implied by sections 12–15 in the case of consumer sales. The
Consumer Credit Act 1974 made amendments consequent
upon the new terminology and scope of that Act.

The background to these recent changes was a growing
awareness of the inadequacy of the traditional concepts of
"commercial law" to meet the demands of a consumer
society. The Sale of Goods Act 1893 was adapted to dealings
between businessmen and equals, not to transactions between
large corporations and small scale consumers. The powerful
bargaining position of large organisations made the notion of
"freedom of contract" increasingly unreal. Often the only
choice the consumer had was to take some essential
commodity on the seller's terms or not at all. The widespread
use of so-called "standard form" contracts is an aspect of this
development. In many cases it is of course an acceptable and

sensible way to save time and money. Sometimes however it could (and to some extent still can) mean that unfair terms are foisted upon a reluctant purchaser who has no other real choice. Hence the recognition in the Supply of Goods (Implied Terms) Act 1973, that consumer contracts required special treatment and the provisions in the Unfair Contract Terms Act 1977 for rules relating to terms in standard form contracts. This movement has now been taken a step further with the Unfair Terms in Consumer Contracts Regulations 1994 which came into force on July 1, 1995 and apply to both goods and services.

2. Services

Contracts for the supply *of services* need to be distinguished from the notion of a contract *of service*. The latter is largely regulated by various Acts relating to employment and is concerned with the relationship between employer and employee. The former, with which we are alone concerned, is exemplified in a consumer context by an agreement to mend a leaking pipe or unblock a drain. In marginal cases the distinction is not always easy, but in most consumer contexts it will normally be fairly clear what the relationship is between the parties.

Statutory intervention in the area of supply of services has not been until recently so systematic as in the sale of goods. Nevertheless, the common law applied principles similar to those found in the Sale of Goods Act and the law has recently been codified and reinforced by the Supply of Goods and Services Act 1982 (see below, p. 641). In the field of consumer credit, where the purchase of goods is linked with the provision of financial services, the law has been largely reformulated and strengthened in favour of the consumer by the Consumer Credit Act 1974.

Although much of the law still bears the imprint of its origins in an earlier century with different economic philosophies, the trend, especially in recent years, has been firmly towards consumer protection. The strictness of the approach grounded in laissez-faire individualism has yielded to a concern for the reasonable expectations of consumers in a market that is recognised as being unequal.

Chapter 26

Sales, Services and Implied Terms

The importance of the distinction between a sale of goods and a contract to supply services has been lessened by the Supply of Goods and Services Act 1982. Nevertheless, the distinction is still of significance and it is necessary to decide what type of transaction we are dealing with before we can go on to consider its consequences.

1. The Distinction Between Goods and Services

Section 2(1) of the Sale of Goods Act 1979 contains the basic definition of a sale under the Act and states that:

> "A contract of sale of goods is a contract by which the seller transfers or agrees to transfer the property in goods to the buyer for a money consideration, called the price."

In most consumer transactions the ingredients of this definition are likely to be readily satisfied (although for difficulties that can arise, see *Esso Petroleum Co. Ltd v. Commissioners of Customs and Excise* (1976) (*Casebook*, Chap. 3). It is to be noticed that the reference to "property" means legal ownership of the goods in question. Although the passing of ownership to the buyer is often marked by physical delivery of the chattel this is not necessarily so. It is perfectly possible and normal for the sale of an article to be completed before it leaves the physical possession of the seller. This may be important because if property in the goods has passed to the buyer he will normally find himself responsible for them from that point onwards. In an appropriate case he may, for example, wish to insure the goods against the risk of damage or destruction.

630

A contract to supply services, which may or may not also involve the supply of goods and materials, is clearly outside the scope of section 2(1) of the 1979 Act. In most cases the distinction between goods and services is clear enough. Buying a radio in a shop is clearly a sale of goods, employing a plumber to unblock a pipe is equally clearly a contract for services. But what of a contract to paint a picture or replace the clutch on a car?

In *Robinson v. Graves* (1935) the court held that a contract to paint a portrait was a contract for services. Greer L.J. said that the substance of the contract was the deployment of skill and labour for the production of the article and the fact that some materials might also pass to the buyer was an ancillary consideration.

Applying this test to the facts of individual cases is not entirely easy. For example in *Cammell Laird & Co. Ltd v. Manganese Bronze & Brass Co. Ltd* (1934) it was held that a contract to construct two ships' propellers was a contract of sale. A meal in a restaurant has also been held to be a contract of sale, *Lockett v. A. & M. Charles Ltd.* (1938). On the other hand, repairing a car has been held to be a contract of services, *G.H. Myers & Co. v. Brent Cross Service Co.* (1934), as was a vet's injection of serum, *Dodd and Dodd v. Wilson and McWilliam* (1946). Where there is a contract to install material into a building or to incorporate a new part into a chattel the courts have tended to the view that this is a contract for services. This would cover, for example, an agreement to install central heating or repair some consumer appliance.

2. Implied Terms

(1) Goods

Section 12–15 of the Sale of Goods Act 1979 contain the special implied terms relating to goods. Together they form an important body of protection for the consumer which has been further strengthened by the limits imposed upon their exclusion. The Sale and Supply of Goods Act 1994 has recently made significant amendments to these provisions, in particular replacing the rather outmoded concept of "merchantable quality" with that of "satisfactory quality". Perhaps of even greater practical importance, it limits a non-consumer buyer's right to reject the goods for trivial defects. Although the amended 1979 Act uses the word "term" for the key provisions of sections 12–15 this still means "condition" in England and Wales and for the sake of clarity the Act is quoted as if that is what it states.

(a) Title

Central to the sale of goods is the transfer of ownership or property in the goods to the buyer. Not surprisingly section 12(1) implies a condition that the seller has a right to sell the goods and so will pass a good title to the buyer. Section 12(2) allows for the possibility that the seller may be uncertain as to his title but the buyer may nevertheless wish to take the risk and purchase the goods with whatever title he has.

If there has been a breach of section 12(1), this will amount to a "total failure of consideration." The buyer is then entitled to recover the price of the goods even though he may by then have used the goods for a considerable time (see *Rowland v. Divall* (1923)).

(b) Sale by description

Section 13(1) states that, "Where there is a contract for the sale of goods by description, there is an implied [condition] that the goods will correspond with the description." This section is further clarified by section 13(3) which provides: "A sale of goods is not prevented from being a sale by description by reason only that, being exposed for sale or hire, they are selected by the buyer."

In many cases it may seem rather strange to talk of an implied term as to description. If I buy a pair of all leather shoes which are in fact made of plastic there has been a breach of section 13 but there is also likely to be a breach of an express term of the contract, *i.e.* that the shoes are "all leather." Indeed Professor Goode casts doubt on the utility of retaining section 13 in its present form.

Two related problems arise in evaluating the effect of section 13, namely, (1) what is meant by a sale by description? and (2) what is required to bring about a breach of the section?

A very wide meaning has been given to the term "sale by description." Not only does this include goods of a generic kind, for example a packet of Brand X cigarettes, but also specific goods when they are sold as a thing corresponding to a description. In *Grant v. Australian Knitting Mills* (1936) the sale of woollen underwear was held to be a sale by description "even though the buyer is buying something displayed before him on the counter." Section 13(3) covers the situation which might arise at, say, a supermarket where the shopper himself selects goods from the shelf. If a customer chooses a packet labelled "Ceylon Tea" which in fact turns out to be China Tea this is a breach of section 13. Similarly, if there is an inaccuracy as to the quantity or provenance of the goods this could amount to a breach. It does not matter that the description was not the sole reason for purchasing the goods as long as it was a factor. In *Beale v. Taylor* (1967) the plaintiff saw an advertisement for a "Herald, convertible, white, 1961." He went to inspect the car and also noticed on its rear a disc marked "1200." In fact the car consisted of the rear portion of a 1961 Herald 1200 welded to the front part of an earlier model. The Court of Appeal held that the advertisement and disc together constituted a sale by description to which the vehicle clearly did not conform. There was therefore a breach of section 13. It would be different if the buyer placed absolutely no reliance on the seller's description. In *Harlingdon Ltd v. Hull Fine Art Ltd.* (1990) the buyer was a professional art dealer who knew the seller had no experience or knowledge of the type of painting being sold. There was accordingly no breach of section 13 when the painting turned out to be a forgery. It might well have been different if the buyer had been a consumer with no expertise in the area.

The width of application of section 13 is combined with a strict approach to any deviation from the description. In *Arcos Ltd. v. Ronaasen* (1933) the sellers agreed to sell wooden staves half an inch thick to the buyers. A large proportion of the staves were between half and nine sixteenths of an inch thick although it was found that they were fit for their purpose and merchantable. Nevertheless, the House of Lords decided that there was a breach of section 13. As Lord Buckmaster said:

"If the article they have purchased is not in fact the article that has been delivered, they are entitled to reject it, even though it is the commercial equivalent of that which they have bought."

Similarly in *Re Moore & Co. and Landauer & Co.* (1921) (see above, p. 592) there was a breach of section 13 because the packaging failed to comply with the contract description even though the market value of the goods was not affected by this breach. Both this case and *Arcos v. Ronaasen*, being commercial

cases, might now have a different outcome because of section
15A of the Sale of Goods Act 1979 (see above, p. 592). It
would however, only possibly exclude a right to reject the
goods; a claim for damages would still be possible. In
consumer sales the right to reject for breach of sections 12–15
is unaffected. By contrast, in *Ashington Piggeries v. Hill* (1972)
the contract was for "herring meal." What was delivered
contained a preservative producing a chemical toxic to the
mink for which it was supplied as feed. It was decided that
there was no breach of section 13. Even though the feed
might be unsuitable or useless for mink, the contract
description did accurately identify what had been supplied.
The essence of section 13 was "identification" and the fact
that there may be a failure as to "quality" did not necessarily
involve a breach of the section.

One result of a wide interpretation of section 13 in the area
of consumer sales is that it might be used to circumvent the
requirement in section 14 that goods be sold "in the course of
a business." In effect, if a quality of the goods relating to its
fitness for a purpose can be regarded as part of its contract
description then there may be an action for breach of this
condition even in the case of a private sale. For example,
could a "car" with an engine which had irrevocably seized up
and will not go really be described in any meaningful sense as
a "car?"

(c) *Satisfactory quality*

Section 14(2) states:

"Where the seller sells goods in the course of a business,
there is an implied [condition] that the goods supplied
under the contract are of satisfactory quality.
    This is then qualified section 14(2c) by which states that
section 14(2) does not extend to any matter making the
goods unsatisfactory:

"(a) which is specifically drawn to the buyer's attention
before the contract is made,
(b) where the buyer examines the goods before the
contract is made, which that examination ought to reveal
. . ."

Unlike section 13, section 14(2) only applies to goods sold
"in the course of a business." Although the concept is widely
defined by section 61(1) to include sales by local and public

authorities, and government departments, this requirement excludes private sales. A normal consumer purchase from a shop or retail outlet will of course present no difficulty.

The reference to goods "supplied under the contract" is to make clear that it is the entirety of what is supplied that must be considered. This therefore includes packaging or other material mixed in with the consignment. For example, in the spectacular case of *Wilson v. Rickett Cockerell & Co. Ltd* (1954) the plaintiffs purchased a ton of Coalite. This particular delivery gave new meaning to the slogan "come home to a real fire." Part of the consignment contained an explosive substance which detonated when the Coalite was burnt so damaging the plaintiff's house. The notion that the coal *qua* coal was perfectly merchantable and it was merely the presence of an unrelated foreign body that had caused the damage was rejected. Taking the consignment as a whole the goods supplied were not fit for burning in a domestic grate. Similarly, faulty instructions supplied with the packaging of the goods could render the goods not of satisfactory quality.

The first exception to the provision is clear enough. If the seller points out to the prospective buyer that, say, the clutch in the car being purchased is about to break down then no complaint about lack of satisfactory quality can be made if it does. The second exception relates to when the buyer himself examines the goods before the contract is made. The first point to make is that it only applies if the buyer chooses to inspect the goods. If he fails to do so he is not prevented from complaining about lack of satisfactory quality. Secondly, the use of the formula "that examination" suggests that it is the form of inspection actually adopted by the buyer which matters. If he only inspects the outside of the article and the defect would only have been visible by an internal inspection then again he is not prevented from complaining about the internal defect. On the other hand, if he merely adopts a cursory inspection, whereas a properly conducted examination would have shown up the defect, the exception comes into play (see *Thornett & Fehr v. Beers* (1919)). The result is therefore that no inspection at all may be better than one which is conducted carelessly.

The term "satisfactory quality" is defined in section 14(2A) which states that goods are satisfactory if a reasonable person would regard them as so, "taking account of any description of the goods, the price (if relevant) and all the other relevant circumstances". This is then augmented by a new section 14(2B) which states that relevant factors include fitness for all the purposes for which goods of that kind are commonly supplied, appearance and finish, freedom from minor defects, safety and durability.

A difficulty with the concept of merchantable quality was to give it, particularly in a consumer context, an intelligible meaning. Except perhaps by gleaning clues from the case law, there is no immediately obvious answer to the question: is a new refrigerator which works but has a scratch on the door of "merchantable quality"? It is easier to see that it could now fail the test of the new section 14(2) as not being "satisfactory", particularly when appearance and finish are now expressly articulated as relevant factors. The application of this test to the facts of particular problems may still not be straightforward but at least it should now be easier in a consumer context. For example, many of the cases brought under the former section 14 concerned motor cars. A new car which did not function properly, or did so but was scratched, might not be regarded as satisfactory (see *e.g. Rogers v. Parish (Scarborough) Ltd* (1987) concerning a new Range Rover). Having said that, many of the cases decided under the wording of the old section 14(2) might still be decided in the same way today, and they also serve as illustrations of the sort of problems of quality which have arisen in the past.

The fact that an article is second-hand may still be relevant. Nobody would normally expect a second-hand car to be as reliable or in such good condition as the same car when new. This point was made by Lord Denning M.R. in *Bartlett v. Sidney Marcus* (1965). The plaintiff purchased a second-hand Jaguar car for £950, it being pointed out that the clutch needed repair. After 300 miles it was found that the defect was more serious than the plaintiff had anticipated and it cost £84 to put right. Nevertheless, the Court of Appeal said there was no breach of section 14(2). The car was in usable condition if not perfect; defects are likely to occur in second-hand cars and having regard to the description of the car as having a defective clutch it was merchantable and perhaps now satisfactory. By contrast, in *Crowther v. Shannon Motor Co.* (1975) the buyer bought a Jaguar in which the engine had done 82,165 miles. After another 2,300 miles the engine seized up. It was found that the engine was "clapped out" at the date of sale and that the buyer of a Jaguar car could reasonably expect 100,000 miles from such an engine. The Court of Appeal held in fact that there had been a breach of the implied term as to fitness for purpose under section 14(3) (see below), but it seems likely that a claim under section 14(2) would also have been successful in that the car could not be regarded as satisfactory.

Price is another factor in assessing satisfactory quality. In the Range Rover case (above), Mustill L.J. said that "at more than £14,000 this vehicle was, if not at the top end of the scale, well above the level of the ordinary family saloon. The buyer was entitled to value for his money." Again, in *Shine v. General Guarantee Corp. Ltd* (1988), which concerned a second-hand car, the Court of Appeal stressed that a purchaser's reasonable expectations were to be taken into account. If the buyer thought he was buying an enthusiast's car in good condition at a fair price when in fact he was buying one which no one would have bought without substantial discount then there was, and arguably still would be, a breach of section 14(2). In *Brown & Son Ltd v. Craiks* (1970), Lord Reid commented that if the price for better quality goods was substantially higher than that for the lower quality, a buyer who pays the higher price can reasonably expect to receive the better quality. If he received the inferior quality he would be entitled to regard the goods as "unmerchantable", or now not satisfactory, at that price even though they could be sold at the rate appropriate to the inferior goods. When goods are sold at a discount in a "sale" this is a quite different situation. The retailer is merely claiming to sell his ordinary goods more cheaply and should not be allowed to use this as a cloak for selling inferior or "unsatisfactory" goods. It would be another matter if the goods were sold cheaply and described as "seconds" or "rejects".

A difficult problem arises in the case of latent defects. If the goods sold have at that time a latent defect which is known to be of an injurious kind then there is clearly a breach (see *Bernstein v. Pamson Motors Ltd.* (1987). But what of the situation where goods are sold which are in no way abnormal but which are subsequently discovered to be inherently dangerous? It seems on the face of it unreasonable to make a seller responsible for what he could not at the time have known. On the other hand, liability in contract is strict and it appears on present authority that he would still be liable (see *Henry Kendall & Sons v. William Lillico & Sons Ltd* (1969)).

(d) *Fitness for purpose*

Section 14(3) states:

"Where the seller sells goods in the course of a business and the buyer, expressly or by implication, makes known—

(a)   to the seller, ...
(b)   ... any particular purpose for which the goods are
being bought, there is an implied [condition] that the
goods supplied under the contract are reasonably fit
for that purpose, whether or not that is a purpose
for which such goods are commonly supplied, except
where the circumstances show that the buyer does
not rely, or that it is unreasonable for him to rely, on
the skill or judgment of the seller ... "

Some of the terminology of this subsection has already been
explained in relation to section 14(2), but the similarity goes
further than this. In many cases there will be an overlap
between section 14(2) and (3). When the goods have only a
single purpose then the concept of fitness for purpose will be
an integral part of the requirement for satisfactory quality.
Hence a hot-water bottle that bursts or clothing which causes
a rash when worn will not satisfy the requirements of either
section 14(2) or (3) (see, *e.g. Priest v. Last* (1903); *Grant v.
Australian Knitting Mills Ltd.* (1936)). Similarly the sale of a car
which is defective may well give rise to a breach of both
provisions.

If the buyer requires the goods for a special purpose then
this fact must be expressly or impliedly communicated to the
seller. For example, in *Griffiths v. Peter Conway Ltd* (1939) the
buyer, who had an abnormally sensitive skin, purchased a
Harris tweed coat. It was found that the coat would not have
caused any harm to a normal user but it produced dermatitis
in the buyer. Her action for breach of fitness for purpose
failed. She had not made known her special sensitivity and it
was something no seller could assume to exist. Of course if
the purpose in purchasing the article is obvious, as in the case
of a hot-water bottle, it is not necessary to spell out the
purpose for which the goods are bought. In such a case the
courts will readily imply it (see *Priest v. Last*).

The requirement that the goods be "reasonably fit for that
purpose" reflects the fact that price, age, and the condition of
the goods all have to be taken into account. This point has
already arisen in the discussion of section 14(2), and in the
case of *Bartlett v. Sidney Marcus Ltd* (above, p. 636) the
alternative claim under section 14(3) also failed. The car was
as fit for its purpose as one could reasonably expect a second-
hand car to be. On the different facts of *Crowther v. Shannon*
(above, p. 636), however, the claim under section 14(3) was
upheld. Rather strange as it may seem, the fact that reliance is

placed on the seller's skill and judgment does not mean that he is liable only if there has been some carelessness or lack of judgment in his sale of a defective product. Once there has been reliance on the seller's skill and judgment liability is absolute. It is no defence that if the seller had exercised all possible diligence he still could not possibly have discovered the defect (see, *e.g. Frost v. Aylesbury Dairy Co. Ltd* (1905)).

The condition of fitness for purpose is not implied where the buyer has not relied on the seller's skill or judgment. Nevertheless the courts have readily inferred the existence of reliance and the onus rests on the seller to prove that there was no such reliance. If however the buyer asks for a product by its trade or brand name, in a way that makes it clear he is not relying on the seller's skill and judgment regarding the suitability of the product, the effect would be to exclude section 14(3) (see, *e.g. Baldry v. Marshall* (1925)). If the buyer relies upon the seller's skill in some areas but his own specifications in others it will have to be decided whether the unsuitability arose from the actions of the former or the latter. Only if the defect arose in an area where the seller was expected to use his own skill and judgment will there be liability under section 14(3) (see, *e.g. Cammell Laird v. Manganese Bronze & Brass* (1934); *Ashington Piggeries v. Hill* (1972)).

A further ground for the non-application of section 14(3) is that the reliance is unreasonable. This might arise where, for example, the buyer knows that the seller has no expertise in relation to the goods or where the buyer conducts an examination of the goods which ought to have made it abundantly clear that the goods were unsuitable.

(e) *Correspondence with sample*

Section 15 provides:

> "(1) A contract of sale is a contract for sale by sample where there is an express or implied term to that effect in the contract.
>
> (2) In the case of a contract for sale by sample there is an implied condition—
>
> (a) that the bulk will correspond with the sample in quality;
>
> (b) that the buyer will have a reasonable opportunity of comparing the bulk with the sample;

  (c)   that the goods will be free from any defect, making
         their quality unsatisfactory, which would not be
         apparent on reasonable examination of the sample."

Like section 13 the condition is not limited to business
sales. This reflects the similarity in concept between the two
provisions.

Merely to exhibit a sample in the course of negotiations
does not make it a sale by sample. For example, if I see an
article in a shop window and ask to buy one that is just the
same this will not invoke section 15. What is required is that
the sample be used as the basis for comparison with the
goods which are purchased. The purpose behind a sale by
sample was explained by Lord Macnaghten in *Drummond v.
Van Ingen* (1887) when he said: " ... the office of a sample is
to present to the eye the real meaning and intention of the
parties with regard to the subject-matter of the contract
which, owing to the imperfection of language, it may be
difficult or impossible to express in words."

Even if a buyer is prevented by the operation of section
15(2)(c) from alleging a breach of correspondence with sample,
this will not necessarily prevent reliance under section 14(2) or
(3).

Excluding Sections 12–15

Reflecting the laissez-faire policy of the time, the Sale of
Goods Act 1893 as originally drafted permitted contracting out
of the statutory implied terms. Despite the protection which
had been given to credit buyers under the Hire Purchase Act
1938 it was not until the passing of the Supply of Goods
(Implied Terms) Act 1973 that the cash sale of goods was put
upon a similar footing.

Section 12 of the Sale of Goods Act cannot be excluded in
any contract regardless of whether it is a commercial,
consumer or private sale (Unfair Contract Terms Act 1977,
s.6(1)(a)). In relation to consumer transactions only (on which
see further p. 648), any term which purports to exclude the
provisions of sections 13–15 is void (Unfair Contract Terms
Act 1977, s.6(2)), and even in non-consumer transactions the
terms can only be excluded in so far as they satisfy the 1977
Act's test of "reasonableness" (s.6(3)). In order to prevent
unscrupulous traders from misleading buyers as to their
statutory rights, these provisions have been strengthened by
the Consumer Transactions (Restrictions on Statements) Order
1976 (as amended). This order, made under the authority of

the Fair Trading Act 1973, makes it a criminal offence to purport to introduce a term into a consumer transaction which is void by virtue of section 6 of the Unfair Contract Terms Act 1977.

(2) Services

The law relating to implied terms in contracts for services, received a major overhaul in the Supply of Goods and Services Act 1982. The Act is somewhat less radical than a superficial reading of it might suggest since many of its terms were already part of the pre-existing common law. Nevertheless there are obvious advantages in such a reform. It promotes clarity and certainty, does away with the need to construe the previous common law, and perhaps strengthens the position of the consumer by drawing attention to the obligations placed upon those who supply services. The appropriate implied terms under the Act apply whether or not materials are also provided by the contract.

(a) *Care and skill*

Section 13 provides that: "where the supplier is acting in the course of a business, there is an implied term that the supplier will carry out the service with reasonable care and skill."

This section is essentially a statutory application of the principle illustrated by *The Moorcock* (above, p. 517) which stressed the willingness of courts to give "business efficacy" to the parties' agreement. The limitation both here and in section 14 of the Act to business contracts is a concept that has already been noted in the Sale of Goods Act.

What is "reasonable" will depend entirely on the facts and circumstances of the case. A supplier is expected to be both competent and use his best endeavours to produce the desired result but there is nothing to prevent the contract laying down even stricter terms. If a contract is for the supply of central heating not only must it be installed reasonably but there may also be a stipulation by the purchaser that a certain higher level of temperature or efficiency will be achieved. Liability for such a term would then be strict and it would not be sufficient if the supplier used reasonable care and skill but failed to produce the stipulated result.

It is noteworthy that both sections 13 and 14 speak of an implied "term" not "condition." The gravity of the term must therefore depend upon the circumstances of the breach.

(b) *Time*

Section 14(1) provides that in a business transaction where the time for completion of the services is not fixed, "there is an implied term that the supplier will carry out the service within a reasonable time." What is a reasonable time is a question of fact.

This section is a response to the frequent complaints about delay in the performance of contracts for services, and needs to be considered in conjunction with the observations already made in respect of such cases as *Charles Rickards Ltd v. Oppenheim* (1950).

(c) *Price*

Where the price has not been fixed, section 15(1) states that, "there is an implied term that the party contracting with the supplier will pay a reasonable price." Again, what is a reasonable charge is a question of fact.

The result of this section is that, where there has been no agreement as to price, a customer would not be obliged to pay an extortionate bill for the services. It does not mean that a consumer can challenge the price if it has already been agreed, even though it might in fact have been excessive.

(d) *Property*

Where as part of a contract for services property is also transferred to the customer, sections 2–5 of the 1982 Act imply terms as to title, description, satisfactory quality, fitness for purpose and sample which are substantially the same as those already implied by sections 12–15 of the Sale of Goods Act 1979. Corresponding provisions are made to apply to contracts of hire by sections 6–10.

The result of many of the cases decided before the passing of the 1982 Act would not be different although they would now be decided on the basis of the statute rather than the common law. For example, in *Dodd and Dodd v. Wilson and McWilliam* (1946) a veterinary surgeon innoculated the plaintiff's cattle with a preparation which in fact caused them to become sick. There was no question of negligence and since it was regarded as a contract for services the Sale of Goods Act did not apply. The court decided that there was an implied condition that the serum was fit for its purpose. If the case arose for decision today, the same result would be reached by the application of section 4(5) of the 1982 Act.

Excluding the Statutory Terms

As regards consumer transactions it is perhaps arguable that sections 13–15 of the 1982 Act could never be excluded owing to the effect of section 3 of the Unfair Contract Terms Act 1977 in that both Acts adopt a standard of reasonableness. This is made to apply by virtue of section 16(1) of the 1982 Act.

Section 2 of the 1982 Act cannot be excluded by a term of any contract (Unfair Contract Terms Act 1977, s.7(3A). Sections 3–5 cannot be excluded as against a person dealing as a consumer (Unfair Contract Terms Act 1977, s.7(2)), and in all other cases can only be excluded in so far as they satisfy the 1977 Act's test of "reasonableness."

Chapter 27

Exemption Clauses, Unfair Terms and Unsolicited Goods

The common link in the title to this chapter is that these areas have posed special problems for business people and consumers alike with the result that the law has formulated a number of specific rules to deal with them.

1. Exemption Clauses

An exemption clause is a term in a contract which seeks to exempt one of the parties from liability for what would otherwise be a breach of contract. Closely related is the concept of a limitation clause which is designed to limit rather than extinguish the party's liability in the event of breach. Although "exclusion clause" might be a more accurate description, the term "exemption clause" is commonly used to denote both types of clause. What is said here about such clauses is just as important to the general law of contract as it is to the sale of goods. It is however convenient to deal with them at this point both because of their relationship to the Unfair Contract Terms Act 1977 (see below) and because many of the worst excesses of exemption clauses have arisen in the consumer context. This is to a considerable degree the result of the introduction of standard form contracts and their use in situations of grossly unequal bargaining power.

Before an exemption clause even falls to be construed it must be incorporated into the contract. This area has been examined in Chapter 18 and applies equally to exemption clauses as to any other type of clause. An exemption clause may also be defeated by the device of the collateral contract (see above, p. 518). For example, in the case of *Andrews v. Hopkinson* (1957) the plaintiff wished to purchase a second-hand car and was told by the dealer, "It's a good little bus. I would stake my life on it." Unfortunately perhaps it was not his life that was at stake. The plaintiff took the car on hire-purchase which involved the dealer selling it to a finance company who hired it back to the plaintiff. The plaintiff had signed a delivery note from the finance company stating that he was "satisfied as to its condition" and accordingly would have been in difficulties in bringing an action against the company. Nevertheless, he was able to sue the dealer on the collateral contract. The exemption clause was accordingly successfully circumvented rather than defeated.

Misrepresentation may also have the same effect. In *Curtis v. Chemical Cleaning and Dyeing Co.* (1951) a shop assistant misrepresented the effect of a form which the customer was asked to sign. Accordingly, the rule in *L'Estrange v. Graucob* (above, p. 514) was ousted by the misrepresentation, albeit one that was not fraudulent. If it had been fraudulent then *a fortiori* would the clause have failed.

If after the application of the above considerations the exemption clause still stands there are a number of other factors that may then come into play in order to defeat its effect, and these will be examined in turn. It is important to stress that, as we have already seen (above, p. 601), there is no longer any question of a substantive rule of law preventing exemption clauses from surviving a fundamental breach. This was made quite clear in the *Photo Production* case.

Failure of exemption clauses

(a) *Third parties*

In examining the doctrine of Privity (Chapter 21) we saw that C, for example, cannot normally enforce a contract made between A and B even if it is for C's benefit. Similarly, a third party cannot take the benefit of an exemption clause. The leading case is *Scruttons Ltd v. Midland Silicones Ltd* (1962). Midland Silicones had employed carriers to transport a drum of chemicals under a contract which limited the liability of the carrier to $500 (then £179) per packet. The drum was damaged to the extent of £593 by the negligence of Scruttons, the stevedores whom the carriers had employed to unload the ship. It was decided that the stevedores could not take the benefit of a limitation clause contained in a contract to which they were not parties (see also, *e.g. Adler v. Dickson* (1955)). This remains the general principle despite the fact that, since the result of the *Scruttons* case was found commercially inconvenient, courts are ready to find in the context of such a shipping contract that any reference to the third party brings him within the contract and hence protects him (see *New Zealand Shipping Co. Ltd v. Satterthwaite & Co. Ltd* (1975)).

(b) *Contra proferentem rule*

This is a rule of construction which states that where there is an ambiguity in the meaning of an exemption clause it will be resolved *contra proferentem*, that is, against the person who is putting it forward and relying on it. Where there is an exemption clause which a court regards as unfair, the judges have been quick to find ambiguity in the term and then construe it very strictly.

In *Baldry v. Marshall* (1925) the buyer wished to purchase a car "suitable for touring purposes." The dealers recommended a Bugatti which turned out to be unsuitable and the buyer sought to recover his money. The written contract expressly excluded "any other guarantee or warranty, statutory or otherwise" apart from a year's guarantee against mechanical defects. The Court of Appeal held that the requirement that the car should be for touring purposes was a condition not a warranty and the exemption clause did not therefore apply (see also, *e.g. Andrews v. Singer* (1934)).

The courts have also taken a strict view of attempts to exclude liability for negligence (on which see further Unfair Contract Terms Act 1977, s.2 below, p. 648). In *Hollier v. Rambler Motors (A.M.C.) Ltd* (1972) the plaintiff's car was damaged at the defendant's garage as a result of a fire caused by their negligence. Their usual terms included a condition that "The company is not responsible for damage caused by fire to customer's cars on the premises." The Court of Appeal said that such a clause would not have protected the defendants in the light of what had happened. The court took the view that the clause could be taken to mean that they could not be liable only in the event of a fire caused without negligence. Accordingly, the clause was not sufficiently unambiguous to protect the defendants (for a similarly minded approach see *White v. John Warwick & Co. Ltd* (1953)).

(c) *Legislation*

Various statutes in specific areas have attempted to restrict the efficacy of exemption clauses, for example, section 3 of the Misrepresentation Act 1967. The most important legislation in this area is now however the Unfair Contract Terms Act 1977 and the Unfair Terms in Consumer Contracts Regulations 1994 (considered below).

The whole area of limitation and exemption clauses has been reviewed in two cases which repay examination.

In *Ailsa Craig Fishing Co. Ltd v. Malvern Fishing Co. Ltd* (1983) (*Casebook*, Chap. 9) Securicor agreed to provide security services for certain vessels moored in Aberdeen harbour. As a result of their failure two ships sank. They sought to rely on a limitation clause which restricted their liability "for any loss or damage of whatever nature arising out of the provision of, or purported provision of, or failure in provision of" their services. The House of Lords upheld Securicor's reliance on the limitation clause. In particular it is noteworthy that they rejected the submission that because there had been a total failure on the part of Securicor to carry out the contract the clause could not be held to apply. Construing the clause in the context of the contract as a whole it did indeed cover Securicor's actions. The point was also made that a clause limiting liability was not to be construed as strictly as one exempting it. The former was much more likely to correspond with the intentions of the parties than the latter.

George Mitchell (Chesterhall) Ltd v. Finney Lock Seeds Ltd (1983) (*Casebook*, Chap. 9) was the first case to reach the House of Lords on the issue of reasonableness under the Unfair Contract Terms Act 1977. The defendants had sold seed to the plaintiffs which turned out to be both unmerchantable and not of the agreed variety. The seed merchants relied on an exemption clause which purported to, "exclude all liability for any loss or damage arising from the use of any seeds ... supplied by us and for any consequential damage whatsoever." The House of Lords, in adopting what was essentially Lord Denning's approach in the Court of Appeal, decided that although a limitation clause was to be construed *contra proferentem* and had to be clearly expressed, the recent legislation, "had removed from judges the temptation to resort to the device of ascribing to the words appearing in exemption clauses a tortured meaning so as to avoid giving effect" to them (*per* Lord Diplock). On this basis, the clause was therefore enforceable at common law. The seller's term nevertheless failed the statutory test of reasonableness. An important factor in favour of the finding of unreasonableness was said to be that in the past the sellers had negotiated a settlement of farmers' claims rather than sought strictly to rely on this clause. This suggested that they themselves did not regard the term as reasonable. Quite whether this is an altogether convincing argument must be open to doubt. It may often be commercially expedient to settle disputes without relying on the parties' strict legal rights in order to preserve the goodwill of customers, and it rather appears that the sellers were being penalised for their generous attitude in the past. There seems more to be said for the reasoning that the supply of the defective seed was negligent and that it was a risk against which the sellers could have insured without materially increasing the price of the seeds.

2. Unfair Terms

1. The Unfair Contract Terms Act 1977

The passing of the Unfair Contract Terms Act 1977 was the most important statutory inroad up until then made into the orthodox doctrine of freedom of contract, and very greatly strengthens the hand of the consumer against the imposition upon him of unfair bargains. Some of its provisions, especially sections 6 and 7, have already been considered in the context where they arise but it is now necessary to examine in more detail the overall scope and effect of the Act.

The title of the Act is misleading. It has application to the law of tort as well as contract and does not simply outlaw agreements which a court considers to have been a bad or an unfair bargain (on which see 2. below). Its application is limited to countering the effect of unfair exemption clauses. This effect is achieved in a number of ways by a statute of some complexity in the way its internal elements interact. First of all a basic distinction is made between consumer and other transactions. Secondly, some terms are completely outlawed. Thirdly, certain terms are exposed to a test of "reasonableness" within the meaning of the Act. Nothing in the Act, of course, affects what has already been said about the incorporation of an exemption clause into the contract in the first place.

Dealing as a consumer

Section 12(1) of the Act defines a consumer transaction as one where: (a) the person neither makes the contract in the course of business nor holds himself out as doing so; and (b) the other party does make the contract in the course of business; and (c) the goods supplied are of a type ordinarily supplied for private use or consumption. This last condition only applies to sections 6 and 7 of the Act (see above, pp. 640, 643). "Business liability" is dealt with in section 1(3) and is widely defined to include transactions conducted by a person in the course of a business or from the occupation of business premises.

The distinction is necessary because of the extra protection which is given to consumers. Ordinary high street contracts will therefore fall within the ambit of a consumer transaction but, for example, a sale between two private individuals of a second-hand car will be outside the scope of section 12(1). Auction sales are specifically excluded by virtue of section 12(2). Rather surprisingly, however, a company may deal as a consumer where the purchase is not an integral part of its business, as in *R. & B. Customs Brokers Ltd v. U.D.T. Ltd* (1987) where a freight forwarding company bought a motor car.

Negligence

Section 2(1) makes void any attempt to limit or exclude liability for personal injury or death. This section applies both in contract and in tort and regardless of whether it is a consumer or business contract.

In the case of other negligent loss or damage, section 2(2) states that exclusion or restriction is only permitted in so far as it satisfies the Act's requirement of "reasonableness."

Contracts generally

Section 3 makes general provision for the problem of exemption clauses. This states that where one party deals as consumer *or* on the other's written standard terms of business, the other cannot exclude or restrict his liability for breach of contract or render a contractual performance substantially different from that which was reasonably expected of him or render no performance at all except in so far as the term satisfies the Act's requirement of "reasonableness." The restriction placed upon performing the contract in a "substantially different form" is particularly wide. It does not require that there be a conventional breach of contract, only that in the court's view the different mode of performance was unreasonable. For example, suppose a contract states that accommodation "will be provided" in the Ritz Hotel, "or, if accommodation in the Ritz Hotel is unavailable, in another hotel of comparable quality." Such a clause might fall foul of section 3(2)(a) of the Act. But, even if it is only meant to provide for an alternative mode of performance of the contract, it could still be caught by section

3(2)(b)(i). If a plaintiff could reasonably be expected to be put up only in the Ritz Hotel the clause would be ineffective unless a defendant can show that it satisfies the Act's test of reasonableness. Section 3 is therefore a crucial provision which provides a wide power to strike out unfair exemption clauses in consumer and many other transactions. An illustration of how this part of the Act operates is provided by *George Mitchell (Chesterhall) Ltd v. Finney Lock Seeds Ltd* (1983) (above, p. 647).

Goods and services

These are affected by sections 6 and 7 discussed earlier.

Reasonableness

"Reasonableness" is a key concept in the Act and some guidance on its meaning is provided by section 11 which states that the term must be "a fair and reasonable one ... having regard to the circumstances which were, or ought reasonably to have been, known to or in the contemplation of the parties when the contract was made." The relevant time is therefore when the contract was made, not when it was breached. In determining the issue of fairness and reasonableness regard will be had to the matters set out in Schedule 2 of the Act. These matters include the relative bargaining strengths of the parties; whether the customer had an inducement to enter the contract; whether the customer knew of the nature of the term and also whether the goods had been made to the special order of the customer.

The onus in every case is on the party claiming that the term is reasonable to show that it is (section 11(5)).

Contracts where the Act does not apply

Schedule 1 places some important limits on the scope of the Act. In particular, the Act does not apply to international supply contracts, a contract in relation to land or to any contract of insurance. The latter exclusion means that the Act has no application in an important consumer area.

The meaning of "exemption clause"

The Act makes no attempt at an authoritative definition of an exemption or limitation clause although section 13 suggests a fairly wide interpretation of the concept. This may be because the concept is simply not susceptible to such an approach. How is it possible on a completely logical basis to distinguish between a term that restricts the contractor's liability and one that merely sets out the limits of the contractor's duty? Are they both different ways of looking at the same thing? If so, how will a court decide that it is an unfair exclusion clause and not simply a legitimate means for both parties to set out their respective obligations? Clearly this is an area at the heart of the 1977 Act which seems likely to provide the courts with some difficulty. Although it is a case concerned with tort rather than contract, the speeches of the House of Lords in *Smith v. Eric S. Bush* (1989) at least suggest that the courts are prepared to give the Act a generous interpretation and treat some clauses, which at first sight appear only to define the initial obligations undertaken by a party, as in fact unreasonable disclaimers of liability.

One common provision not to be treated as limiting or excluding liability is an arbitration clause (s.13(2)). Some protection is nevertheless given to consumers by the Consumer Arbitration Agreements Act 1988. This restricts the ability of suppliers to enforce such a clause against a consumer unless either he consents or he has submitted to arbitration in pursuance of the agreement or the court makes an order for arbitration. Such an order can only be made when a court is satisfied that the arbitration would not be detrimental to the interests of the consumer (section 4(2)).

2. The Unfair Terms Regulations 1994

A potentially very important development in the control of unfair terms has been the coming into force of the Unfair Terms in Consumer Contracts Regulations 1994. This is the United Kingdom's response to the European Directive 93/13 which required member states of the European Union to bring in laws complying with the Directive and this has been done by passing a statutory instrument rather than, as one might have expected with so important a piece of legislation, producing a new Act. There is an obvious overlap with the Unfair Contract Terms Act 1977 although the Regulations are in some ways wider and in others more narrowly drawn than the 1977 Act. They are wider in that they apply a test of "good faith" to contract terms, a concept new to English law, and potentially therefore might strike at any sort of term, not simply exemption clauses. They also apply to areas such as insurance which falls outside the ambit of the 1977 Act. They are narrower in that they do not say that some terms will have no legal effect at all as stated, for example, in section 7 of the 1977 Act.

There are several important new provisions. Regulation 5 states, "an unfair term ... shall not be binding on the consumer". An unfair term is defined in regulation 4 as one, "which contrary to the requirement of good faith causes a significant imbalance in the parties' rights and obligations ... to the detriment of the consumer" This is clearly a broad test and some assistance is given in Sched. 2 of the Regulations which is couched in terms similar to that of Sched. 2 of the 1977 Act. Sched. 3 gives further examples of terms which may be regarded as unfair, for example there is a reference to terms "irrevocably binding the consumer to terms with which he had no real opportunity of becoming acquainted before (making) the contract". If, as often happens, a consumer books and pays for a service over the telephone with no discussion as to terms this provision would now seem to assume considerable importance. Regulation 6 states that contracts must be in "plain and intelligible language" and applies the *contra proferentem* rule. This in itself is a provision which should cause all those relying on, for example, their standard form business contracts to look closely to see if their terms are indeed valid.

It is at the moment difficult to assess how significant will be the effect of this legislation although its potential is very considerable. The Office of Fair Trading has now set up an Unfair Contract Terms Unit which envisages publishing bulletins on the work of the unit. Given that in consumer cases where the modest sums of money sometimes involved means that cases often do not reach the level of a law report this should give some insight into the practical working of the Regulations.

3. Unsolicited Goods

There have been occasions when unscrupulous suppliers have delivered goods which have never been ordered and followed this by sending a demand for payment. It has already been seen in the discussion of *Felthouse v. Bindley* (1862) (above, p. 470) that one person cannot impose a contract upon another but it was thought appropriate to embody this principle in a clear statutory form which gave additional protection to the victim of such sales techniques. The result was the Unsolicited Goods and Services Act 1971.

This Act provides that a recipient of unsolicited goods (that is goods sent without his request and with a view to his acquiring them) is entitled to treat them as an unconditional gift if the sender does not reclaim the goods within six months of their receipt (section 1(2)(*a*)). Alternatively, the recipient can give written notice to the sender stating that the goods were unsolicited and giving the address from where they can be collected. If the sender does not come to collect the goods within 30 days of the notice, the property in the goods will pass to the recipient (section 1(2)(*b*)). If the goods are accidently lost or damaged before the expiration of either of the statutory periods the recipient as an "involuntary bailee" of the goods will not generally be liable. It might be different if he deliberately destroyed them.

Section 2 of the Act imposes criminal sanctions on a trader who demands payment for unsolicited goods where he has no reasonable cause to believe that there is a right to payment. It is also a criminal offence in similar circumstances to threaten legal proceedings to enforce such a payment.

Chapter 28

Manufacturers' Liability

Most people (who have not read this book) when buying consumer durables tend to regard the manufacturer as the primary person to whom any complaint about the product should be addressed. This is a view that some retailers do little to dispel, but we have seen that as a matter of law it is entirely unfounded. Unless he buys direct from the manufacturer, the consumer's contract is with the retailer, not the manufacturer, and it is against him that in the first instance a remedy should be sought. The provisions of sections 12–15 of the Sale of Goods Act 1979 will often provide valuable assistance and the retailer may always recoup his loss by in turn bringing an action for breach of contract against his supplier. Similarly if A gives B as a present an article he has bought from a retailer C, then the doctrine of privity ensures that although of course A can bring an action, B cannot sue C if the product turns out to be defective. The only effective way in which B could do this would be for A to transfer to B his rights against C using the machinery of section 136 of the Law of Property Act 1925 (see above, p. 565). This may sometimes be prudent but is a somewhat unusual precaution.

There are however certain circumstances when the manufacturer is directly liable to the consumer. These are: (1) under a manufacturer's guarantee; (2) as a result of negligence; and (3) under the terms of the Consumer Protection Act 1987. These possibilities will now be examined.

1. Manufacturers' Guarantees

Everyone is familiar with the "guarantee" cards which often arrive with consumer goods and in which the manufacturer typically undertakes to repair or replace defective goods within a certain period of time. Rather curiously their precise legal status is somewhat uncertain and the point will presumably only fall for consideration in the unlikely event of a manufacturer refusing to honour a guarantee. The difficulty arises from the requirements of offer, acceptance and consideration. On the face of it the undertaking from the manufacturer appears to be a gratuitous promise from someone with whom the consumer has no direct contractual relationship. One way round this difficulty is to regard the manufacturer's promise as the basis of a collateral contract with the consumer for which the consideration is supplied by purchasing the goods from the retailer. This view could be supported by reference to *Carlill v. Carbolic Smoke Ball Co.* (see above, p. 466). Even though Mrs Carlill had not bought the smoke ball directly from the company it was held that there was a contract between them quite apart from any contract of sale with the retailer (see also *Shanklin Pier Ltd v. Detel Products Ltd* (1951)). Provided the plaintiff knew of the guarantee before purchasing the product *Carlill's* case provides a strong analogy.

In the past some manufacturers included "guarantees" which the customer was invited to sign and return but which in fact had the effect, because of their restrictive terms, of depriving the customer of rights against the manufacturer. In relation to damage or defects caused through the manufacturer's negligence, this practice is now prevented by section 5 of the Unfair Contract Terms Act 1977. Such a clause will be ineffective if the requirements of the section are satisfied. These are: (1) that the goods are of a type ordinarily supplied for private use; (2) they prove defective while in consumer use; and (3) the manufacturer did not sell the goods directly to the consumer. The effect is therefore that as regards defects or damage arising from negligence the manufacturer may provide the consumer with additional rights or remedies, but he cannot take away such rights as the consumer already has.

2. Negligence

If the goods actually cause harm or damage to the ultimate consumer then the manufacturer may be liable in the tort (that is, civil wrong) of negligence. This basis of the modern law was laid down in the classic case of *Donoghue v. Stevenson* (1932). Mrs. Donoghue was bought a bottle of ginger beer by a friend at a café in Paisley. She drank some of the contents, and when her friend refilled her glass, out floated the remains of a decomposing snail. Mrs. Donoghue claimed damages from the manufacturer (she of course had no contractual relationship with the café or the manufacturer) for the resultant nervous shock and gastroenteritis. The House of Lords upheld the claim. Lord Atkin made the now famous comment that " . . . a manufacturer of products which he sells in such a form as to show that he intends them to reach the ultimate consumer in the form in which they left him with no reasonable possibility of intermediate examination, and with the knowledge that the absence of reasonable care in the preparation . . . of the products will result in an injury to the consumer's life or property, owes a duty of care to the consumer to take that reasonable care."

This decision has been generously interpreted over the last 50 years. There is no limit to the type of goods to which it relates and it has been extended to cover the analogous case of those who supply services. It is also possible to make a claim both for breach of contract and negligence in the same proceedings (see, *e.g. Andrews v. Hopkinson* (above, p. 644) where both claims were successful).

There are however considerable hurdles in the way of a consumer who seeks to prove negligence all of which he must successfully surmount.

No intermediate inspection

Only if there was a real possibility of an intermediate inspection before use that would have shown up the fault is the manufacturer exempted from liability. In modern conditions of consumer marketing this is unlikely to present such of a problem.

Goods must be defective

Normally this should not present a difficulty. A bun with a stone in it or a car with a dangerous steering mechanism is clearly defective. Difficulties may however arise in proving that the goods were defective at the time they left the manufacturer (see, *e.g. Evans v. Triplex Safety Glass Co.* (1936)).

There must be negligence

The onus of proving negligence is on the plaintiff and this may be an onerous and expensive task. Sometimes if the negligence is flagrant the plaintiff will be helped by the application of the maxim *res ipsa loquitur* (the thing speaks for itself). If bags fall out of a warehouse onto the plaintiff in the street below (*Scott v. The London Dock Co.* (1865)), or a consumer finds a stone in the middle of a bath bun (*Chaproniere v. Mason* (1905)) then the onus shifts to the defendant to prove that he was not negligent. More often than not the negligence is far from obvious and it is at this point that a plaintiff may well decide that it is unprofitable to pursue the claim.

It is also important to note that the manufacturer need only show *reasonable* care and skill. He is not guaranteeing the goods. Nevertheless in cases where a manufacturer seeks to establish a careful and thorough means of producing or checking goods the courts have sometimes turned this to the plaintiff's advantage. If the system really is so efficient it might be said that the only explanation for a defective product is that someone has been negligent.

The negligence must cause the damage

If the damage to the plaintiff would have occurred in any event the manufacturer will not be liable even though the product happened to be defective. If a car is manufactured with dangerous steering but the accident is caused entirely by another motorist's careless driving the manufacturer will not attract liability for the accident.

Establishing causation can sometimes be a serious problem as cases involving, for example, the effect of drugs have shown.

The kind of damage must be recoverable

There is no doubt that if the plaintiff or his property is physically damaged by the product he may recover damages for his injury or loss. For example, if the central heating boiler explodes a plaintiff can recover for damage to the house and furniture as well as the conventional sum awarded for any personal injury suffered. Beyond this the law as it affects consumers is not entirely clear.

The orthodox view has always been that a plaintiff cannot recover for pure economic loss which does not involve physical damage (*S.C.M. (United Kingdom) Ltd v. Whittal* (1971)). Accordingly, if the consumer suffers financial loss because the product will just not work, it seems that no damages are recoverable on the grounds of negligence. What if the product goes wrong and, so to speak, damages itself? An example would be a component in a car engine which causes the whole thing to seize up. The answer might depend on whether the component had been made by the manufacturer who produced the car or had been supplied by an outside contractor. If it is the latter, damage to the car would arguably be recoverable under the normal principles of *Donoghue v. Stevenson* (above). If all the car's components had been produced and supplied by the manufacturer it seems from the House of Lords decision in *Murphy v. Brentwood District Council* (1990) that no tortious damages would be recoverable. Obviously it seems unsatisfactory for a consumer that the existence of liability should depend upon the accident of manufacture. On the other hand, a car that malfunctions within itself without injuring other persons or property could be regarded as a pure economic loss for which the law of tort provides no remedy.

It might once have been thought that some widening of the concept of recoverable damage in favour of the consumer was to be found in the decision of the House of Lords in *Junior Books v. Veitchi Co. Ltd* (1982). In that case the plaintiffs engaged a building company to construct a factory. The building company sub-contracted the laying of a special floor to another firm which had been nominated by the plaintiff's architects. There was therefore no direct contractual link between the plaintiffs and the sub-contractors. The floor proved to be defective and the plaintiffs brought an action in tort against the sub-contractors for the cost of replacing the floor and the consequential economic loss this would involve. There was no allegation that the floor presented a danger to health or that there was a risk of damage to other property of the plaintiffs. The House of Lords decided that the plaintiffs had a right to recover against the sub-contractors. However, a number of subsequent cases have made it clear that *Junior Books* has a limited application and does not mean that a manufacturer is generally liable for the failure of his products to function. In *Muirhead v. I.T.S. Ltd* (1986) the manufacturers of aeration pumps were liable for the death of the plaintiff's lobsters (property loss) but not for the cost of the useless pumps nor for projects lost while they were inoperative. Those are matters for contract law.

It therefore seems that no wide-ranging principle of recovery for pure economic loss was laid down in *Junior Books*. If there was any doubt this has surely been dispelled by the later decision of the House of Lords in *D. & F. Estates v. Church Commrs.* which rejects any extension of claims for economic loss to the point where *Junior Books* appears to have been effectively repudiated.

3. The Consumer Protection Act 1987

The reforms introduction by Part I of the Consumer Protection Act 1987 have been controversial and long awaited. The passage of this Act is the direct result of the EEC Directive of July 1985 which seeks to harmonise the Law of the member states on liability for defective products. To help ensure that this goal is achieved, section 1(1) provides that the Act is to be construed in accordance with the Directive.

The significant alteration made by the Act is to establish a regime of strict liability. In essence this means that the manufacturer of a defective product will be liable for damage caused by the product unless he can bring himself within one of the defences provided by the Act. It is therefore unnecessary for the plaintiff to establish negligence. Clearly a litigant who can bring himself within the Act will prefer to use this machinery rather than seek to prove negligence at common law.

What follows is only a brief account of a complex piece of legislation written from the perspective of a consumer purchasing a standard manufactured product.

Basic liability

Section 2(1) of the Act is the basic provision which imposes liability for damage caused by a defective product. Much of the rest of the Act goes on to define the key terms used in that section. "Product" is widely defined to mean "any goods or electricity." Only unprocessed agricultural products or game fall outside the scope of the Act. The width of this definition means that the Act may apply to claims made by victims of, for example, sea or ship disasters where it can be shown that a defective product or component was the cause of the injury or damage.

Persons who may be liable

The Act imposes liability on the producer of a product who in most cases will of course be the manufacturer. Section 2(2) of the Act also includes "own-branders" within the definition of producer. If therefore a retailer offers a product bearing his name on the product, as is common for example in supermarkets, the retailer will be regarded as a "producer." It does not matter that the product has in fact been made for him by an unrelated manufacturer.

Defect

Section 3(1) states that there is defect in a product, "if the safety of a product is not such as persons generally are entitled to expect." Clearly this is an issue which will have to be determined in each case, but factors which may be taken into account include the purposes for which the product has been marketed, what might reasonably be expected to be done with it and the time when it was supplied. Section 3(2)(a) also refers to instructions or warnings with respect to the product. No doubt a product which is inherently dangerous will not always be rendered safe merely by supplying a warning. Similarly a product which is otherwise reliable and effective may be rendered defective by inadequate instructions. For example, facts similar to *Warmell v. RHM Agriculture (East) Ltd*, may now give rise to a claim under the 1987 Act.

Damage

"Damage" is defined by section 5(1) of the Act to mean death, personal injury or loss of or damage to property. This wide definition is then qualified in a number of ways. It does not include damage to the product itself (s.5(2)), and in this respect therefore is similar to the position at common law. Nor does it include a claim where the damage is less than £275 (s.5(4)). The object of this limitation is to prevent so-called trivial claims. In these cases the consumer is thrown back upon the pre-existing law.

Defences

A plaintiff may confront a number of defences to a claim under the Act. He may not be able to establish that the product was defective within section 3, or he may have been in any event contributorily negligent. In some cases, for example a claim for a defective drug, establishing causation may be a major difficulty for the plaintiff. The most controversial defence, however, is the so-called "development risks" defence in section 4(1)(e). This provides a defence that at the relevant time the state of scientific and technical knowledge was not such that the producer might have been expected to discover the defect. Strong views were expressed by the Consumers' Association prior to the passing of the 1987 Act that this could lead to the victims of a thalidomide-type disaster being left without compensation. Certainly it considerably dilutes the notion of strict liability. There is nevertheless some protection for the consumer in that the burden of proof to establish this defence rests upon the producer. Further possible defences are the three year limitation period in which to bring a claim and the fact that a right of action under the Act is extinguished ten years after the date upon which the product was put into circulation. Section 7 is emphatic on the point that liability under the Act cannot be limited or excluded by any term or notice.

Other consumer protection under the Act

Part II of the Consumer Protection Act 1987 consolidates and strengthens the law which was previously to be found in the Consumer Safety Act 1978 and the Consumer Safety (Amendment) Act 1986. Section 10 creates a new offence of supplying consumer goods which fail to comply with the general safety requirement of the Act.

In addition the Secretary of State is empowered to make safety regulations regarding such things as the composition, design and labelling of goods. Secondly, he can take action against the marketing of a product after it has been purchased. A "prohibition notice" can be issued to prevent the supply of a specified class of goods. A "notice to warn" can be issued where the goods have already been sold ordering the trader to warn consumers about an unsafe product. The Act also empowers enforcement authorities to serve "suspension notices" prohibiting the supply of specified goods where there has been a contravention of the general safety requirement, safety regulations or a prohibition notice.

Chapter 29

Consumer Credit

Since the turn of this century there has been an enormous growth in the use of hire-purchase to buy consumer durables such as cars, washing machines and almost every kind of electrical appliance. More recently the advent of the credit card has meant that services such as holidays or car hire can also be purchased on credit. The result is that any survey of the consumer field which failed to take account of legislation regulating credit transactions would be substantially incomplete. Having said this, in what follows an attempt is made merely to identify in outline those areas of the law which are of special importance to a consumer involved in everyday transactions.

Two factors require the law's positive intervention in the field of consumer credit. In the first place, the agencies which supply credit facilities such as banks or finance houses are often large and powerful organisations which present a classic case of inequality of bargaining power. Secondly, consumers may be tempted to overreach their resources by the apparently easy expedient of a credit sale, especially if they are the subject of sales pressure.

Recognising these problems the Hire Purchase Act 1938 instituted a degree of protection for the consumer. Subsequent hire-purchase legislation, in a somewhat piecemeal way, reacted to individual abuses and gradually increased the protection offered to the consumer. The culmination of this process is the Consumer Credit Act 1974, a response to the findings of the Crowther Committee. The rationale behind the legislation is to provide regulation of those transactions which in substance if not in legal form are ways in which the consumer receives credit. For example, hire-purchase is not (as we shall see) in its outward legal form a means of supplying credit, but in truth it is in substance just that. The Act therefore embraces a very wide range of transactions. In view, however, of the fact that hire-purchase and credit card sales are probably the two areas most likely to be encountered in the normal run of consumer transactions the emphasis will be on examining these areas.

Before examining what rights and remedies the present legislation gives it is necessary to grasp the legal mechanics of such phenomena as hire-purchase or credit card sales. It was long ago decided that a hire-purchase agreement was not a straightforward contract of sale (*Helby v. Mathews* (1895)). In the typical situation of a car purchase the consumer asks the dealer to arrange the finance. The dealer then makes an offer to a finance company offering to sell them the car. At the same time the prospective purchaser makes an offer to the finance company to take the car on hire-purchase; that is, he will hire the car paying certain regular instalments but have an option to purchase the car outright after all the payments have been made. This right is, of course, invariably exercised. If the finance company accept the offers the arrangement is complete (see fig. 1).

(Fig. 1)

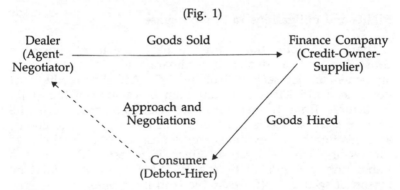

Dealer (Agent-Negotiator) — Goods Sold → Finance Company (Credit-Owner-Supplier)

Approach and Negotiations

Goods Hired

Consumer (Debtor-Hirer)

To use the language of the 1974 Act, the dealer is the agent or negotiator of the finance company (he is the supplier of the goods only in a physical sense); the finance company is the legal owner of the goods until their purchase, and the creditor to whom payments are owed as well as the legal supplier; the consumer is the hirer of the goods and the debtor who owes the payments to the company.

It might be asked, why not simply mortgage the chattel as one mortgages a house in order to purchase it? The reason is that to mortgage a chattel requires that the parties comply with the obscure and technical provisions of the Bills of Sale Acts 1878–82 which has been considered too cumbersome a machinery.

In the case of a credit card sale the machinery is somewhat different (see *Re Charge Card Services Ltd* (1988)). The consumer will normally get immediate ownership of the goods and the dealer will be paid by the credit card company with whom he will have an agreement. The card company will then at a subsequent time seek reimbursement from the consumer (see fig. 2).

(Fig. 2)

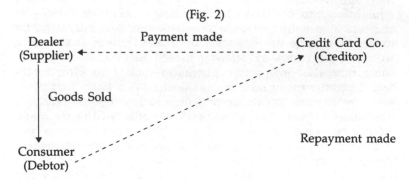

Rights and obligations in hire-purchase

There is no doubt that a hire-purchase agreement between a consumer and a dealer is ordinarily a consumer credit agreement under section 8 of the 1974 Act. The credit must not exceed £15,000 (s.8(2)), although this is one of the major departures from former hire-purchase legislation. It is the level of *credit* which is important, not the price of the goods, and this figure also excludes any deposit and the total charge for credit such as interest. Once it is established that a transaction is regulated by the 1974 Act and not exempt by reason of section 16 (for example land mortgages have special provisions relating to them) the consumer is protected in a number of ways.

Formalities

The formalities regarding a hire-purchase agreement are strict. Not only must the agreement be in writing but even the type of paper and print are controlled. Sections 62 and 63 of the 1974 Act ensure that the debtor or hirer is entitled to at least one copy of the agreement. For something like the hire-purchase of a car, as described above (fig. 1) he will be entitled to two copies. First of all he will receive a copy of the unexecuted agreement. Once his offer has been accepted by the creditor or owner a copy of the executed agreement must be sent to him within seven days of the making of the agreement (s.63(2)). Failure to comply with these formalities may render the agreement unenforceable by the owner or creditor.

Cancellation

Just like any contract the hirer can withdraw from the agreement by revoking his offer at any time before it has been accepted. In addition the consumer has a right to cancel after acceptance in some circumstances (ss.67–73 of the 1974 Act). The obvious purpose here is to allow a consumer who may have been subject to sales pressure a "cooling off" period when he can reconsider the position. The statute provides an exception to the normal rule that a contract once made binds the parties irrevocably.

In order to come within the cancellation provisions it is necessary that oral representations were made to the hirer by the negotiator (the dealer in our example) for the finance company and that the agreement was not signed at the business premises of either the creditor or owner, or the negotiator in any antecedent negotiations, or at the premises of a party to a linked transaction (for example it may be a condition of an agreement that the party take out an insurance policy). The effect is therefore that agreements signed by the consumer in his own home are clearly cancellable. The period of "cooling off time" is five days following the actual receipt of his copy of the final executed agreement (s.68). Cancellation is effected by giving written notice to the creditor or owner, or to his agent. For this purpose a dealer in a normal three party arrangement is deemed to be the creditor's agent (s.56) and the cancellation is effective from the date of posting. Once a cancellation has been made, the agreement and any other transaction linked to it is treated as if it had never been made (s.64(4)). The hirer is entitled to the return of his money and the owner to the return of his goods.

Termination

At any time before the last instalment is due a hirer may terminate a hire-purchase agreement (ss.99–100). Of course it may often be highly disadvantageous to do so if he has already paid a substantial amount in instalments. In order to prevent the owner being left with goods that may have heavily depreciated in value, section 100(1) of the 1974 Act requires the debtor to pay such sum (as when for example the agreement has been terminated early on) as will bring the total payments to one half of the total price. If a court thinks it just it may order the payment of a lesser sum than this as when, for example, the agreement is ended before the goods have depreciated in value to any extent.

Defective goods

In the typical transaction outlined in figure 1 above the goods have been hired from the owner finance company. In such a case the effect of sections 8–11 of the Supply of Goods (Implied Terms) Act 1973 and the Unfair Contract Terms Act 1977 is that there are implied terms on the model of sections 12–15 of the Sale of Goods Act 1979 as against the owner or creditor in respect of defective goods.

In addition the consumer may have an action in negligence (as in *Andrews v. Hopkinson* (above, p. 644)) or on a collateral contract against the dealer. Because such a dealer will be a "credit broker" or "negotiator" within section 56 of the Act, and so in effect an agent of the finance company, any representations made by the dealer are treated as those of the company. Accordingly, any misrepresentation made by the dealer will ground an action against the finance company. The obvious advantage to the consumer of this arrangement is that he can be reasonably sure of having someone solvent to sue.

Enforcement by the owner/creditor

The most obvious obligation placed upon the consumer is to make the regular instalment payments. If he fails to do so then the agreement will invariably contain a term entitling the hirer to terminate the agreement and repossess the goods. Even at this stage however the consumer enjoys a level of protection. By section 87 of the 1974 Act the owner must serve a default notice on the hirer. This effectively sets out the nature of the breach. If the debtor or hirer rectifies the breach it is treated as never having happened (s.89). Alternatively he may apply for a "time order" under section 129 which gives the court power to extend the repayment period.

In the last resort the law will protect the consumer against the owner or creditor "snatching back" the goods. The creditor cannot enter any premises to repossess the goods without a court order (s.92(1)). Often the debtor may already have paid a substantial amount for the goods. Accordingly section 90 states that if he is in breach, has not terminated the agreement and has paid or tendered one-third or more of the total price, then the goods are "protected goods." The creditor cannot then take possession of them without a court order. A potent reason for complying with this provision is provided by section 91. If the creditor does repossess the agreement is terminated, the debtor is released from further liability, and he can recover all sums which have been paid under the agreement.

Credit card sales

As we saw from figure 2 above, in a credit card sale the property is normally transferred directly from the supplier (in both the legal and physical senses) to the consumer. All the terms that are normally implied as part of a sale of goods are therefore implied into this contract.

The Act however goes further than this. Such a transaction is a debtor-creditor-supplier agreement to which sections 56 and 75 of the 1974 Act apply. The thinking behind these provisions is that the credit card company is in business terms closely connected to the supplier and should share his liability. Consequently section 75 states that if the debtor has any claim for misrepresentation or breach of contract against the supplier, he shall have a like claim against the creditor; section 56 treats the supplier as the agent of the creditor for such purposes. This provision is of great potential use to a consumer. If the shop from which the customer bought the goods has ceased trading or become bankrupt there may still be a claim against a fully solvent credit card company.

There are limitations to the application of this provision set out in section 75(3). It will not apply if the cash price of the item is less than £100 or more than £30,000.

Extortionate credit bargains

In the last resort a debtor may use the machinery provided by sections 137–140 of the 1974 Act to claim that the credit agreement is extortionate. These provisions apply to most "credit bargains," even those that might otherwise be exempt under section 16, and has retrospective effect.

A bargain is extortionate under section 138 if it requires the debtor to make payments which are grossly exorbitant or otherwise grossly contravene ordinary principles of fair trading. It is difficult to be sure how generously the courts will interpret their wide power to set aside or alter the agreement between the parties. Factors which can be taken into account include the prevailing interest rates and the age, experience, health and circumstances of the debtor. The matter can be raised either in the county court (s.139(5)) or in other proceedings where consideration of the credit agreement is relevant. An agreement will not be readily upset by the court: for example, an interest rate of 48 per cent a year was upheld in respect of a loan that was made quickly and on little security (*Ketley v. Scott* (1981)).

Licensing provisions

Many individual business activities, such as advertising, are controlled by the Act through criminal sanctions. In addition sections 22–24 and 147–150 set up a centrally administered system of licensing of all those involved in extending credit. This enables the whole industry to be carefully monitored and effectively controlled. Even if there has been no criminal offence committed the Director General of Fair Trading may take into account the business practices of the licensee in deciding whether to grant or refuse a licence. This clearly enables the system to be made sensitive to consumer complaints in the operation of credit facilities.

Index

Attorney-General, 38–39
Auctions,
  advertisements and, 479
  contracts and, 479–480
  offers and, 479–480
Automatism, 186–191
  duress and, 312
  intoxication and, 299–301
  mentally disordered offenders and,
    286, 288, 289
  non-insane, 299

Bail, 119, 139–146
  Crown Prosecution Service and,
    139
  electronic tagging and, 146
  jury trials and, 157
  police, 144–145
  refusal of, 143, 145
  sureties and, 142–143
Barclays Bank v. O'Brien, 588, 589
Barristers,
  education of, 24
  judiciary and, 31
  monopoly of, 32
  recorders as, 32
  role of, 24–25
Battery,
  actus reus and, 371–372
  attempts and, 329
  Caldwell recklessness and, 372
  consent and, 371, 372, 381, 382,
    384
  Cunningham recklessness and, 372
  intention and, 372
  proof and, 372
  reasonableness and, 373
  self-defence and, 372
Bigamy, 74, 229, 231
Bill of Rights, 13, 17
Bills, 71
Blackmail, 449–451
  definition of, 449
  demands with menaces and,
    449–451
  reasonableness and, 451
  threats and, 450
Boxing, 385–386, 571
Breach of contracts, 599–604
  anticipatory, 600–601, 602–604
  consumer credit and, 667
  damages and, 600, 603, 604
  exemption clauses and, 645
  forms of, 600–604
  fundamental, 601–602, 645
  injunctions and, 624, 625

Breach of contracts—*cont.*
  manufacturers' liability and, 654
  repudiation and, 600, 602, 603
  warranties and, 600
Breach of statutory duty, 72–73
Buggery, 228, 272
Burden of proof, 4. *See also* Proof
  actus reus and, 188
  civil proceedings and, 108
  counterclaims and, 108
  criminal proceedings and, 150–151
  defences and, 282
  mentally disordered offenders and,
    284, 286, 289
Burglary, 442–449
  accessories and, 256, 260–261,
    268–270
  aggravated, 448–449
  attempts and, 444
  "buildings" and, 446–448
  consent and, 445, 446
  definition of, 442–443
  "enters" and, 443–445
  intention and, 448
  mens rea and, 448
  mistake and, 445
  recklessness and, 443, 445–446
  sentencing and, 448
  trespass as, 443, 445–446, 448

Caldwell case,
  attempts and, 328, 372
  battery and, 372
  intoxication and, 294, 295
  manslaughter and, 359, 363,
  mens rea and, 217, 218–221
  recklessness and, 217, 218–221,
    294, 295
Capital punishment, 341
Case law, 69–70, 79–84
  law reports and, 83–84
  precedent and, 79–82
Case management, 97
Causation,
  actus reus and, 198–202, 225, 226
  deception and, 421–425
  manufacturers' liability and, 657
  medical treatment and, 200–202
  mens rea and, 225, 226
Certiorari, 44
Champerty, 582
Chancery Division, 42–43
Charterparties, 522–524, 559, 562,
    608–609, 659–661
Cheques,
  cards, 419–420, 423